Wakefield Press

Ochre AND Rust

By the same author

Boomerang: Behind an Australian Icon (1996)

Art and Land: Aboriginal Sculptures of the Lake Eyre Region (1986)
with Peter Sutton

Ochre
AND
Rust

ARTEFACTS AND ENCOUNTERS
ON AUSTRALIAN FRONTIERS

Philip Jones

**Wakefield
Press**

Wakefield Press
1 The Parade West
Kent Town
South Australia 5067
www.wakefieldpress.com.au

First published 2007
Reprinted in this revised edition 2008

Designed by Liz Nicholson, DesignBITE
Typeset by Ryan Paine, Wakefield Press
Printed in China at Everbest Printing Co. Ltd

National Library of Australia
Cataloguing-in-publication entry

Jones, Philip G., 1955–   .
Ochre and rust: artefacts and encounters on Australian frontiers.

Bibliography.
Includes index.
ISBN 978 1 86254 585 4.

1. Aboriginal Australians – Antiquities. 2. Aboriginal Australians – Implements.
3. Frontier and pioneer life – Australia. 4. Australia – Antiquities. 5. Australia –
Race relations – History. I. Title.

994.02.

Government
of South Australia

Arts SA

fox creek
wines

Australia Council
for the Arts

Publication of this book was assisted by the
Commonwealth Government through the
Australia Council, its arts funding and advisory body.

CONTENTS

	ACKNOWLEDGEMENTS	VI
	INTRODUCTION	1
CHAPTER ONE	Master Blackburn's whip	9
CHAPTER TWO	Broken shields	51
CHAPTER THREE	Turning to metal	91
CHAPTER FOUR	Spearing Bennett	131
CHAPTER FIVE	Drilling for fire	187
CHAPTER SIX	Unearthing the toas	225
CHAPTER SEVEN	The magic garb of Daisy Bates	283
CHAPTER EIGHT	Namatjira and the Jesus plaque	305
CHAPTER NINE	That special property	337
	NOTES	379
	LIST OF ILLUSTRATIONS AND MAPS	409
	BIBLIOGRAPHY	417
	LOCALITIES INDEX	428
	GENERAL INDEX	432

ACKNOWLEDGEMENTS

I owe a debt of gratitude to the many Aboriginal people who have shared their perspectives with me on their history and frontier experiences over the years. I am particularly grateful to Frank and Linda Crombie, Ben Murray, John McKenzie and Rufus Wilton.

The staff at Wakefield Press deserve special thanks for their support during this book's long gestation. In particular I would like to thank Michael Bollen for his editorial advice and support and Stephanie Johnston for her encouragement and commitment to the project. I thank Gina Inverarity for her initial editorial assistance. Ryan Paine's attention to detail in copy-editing this large book was outstanding, and thanks are also due to Clinton Ellicott and Kathy Sharrad for lay-out and final copy-editing work. Finally, I greatly appreciate Liz Nicholson's elegant design.

Tim Bonyhady, Helen Jones and Nicolas Rothwell read the complete manuscript at various times and offered valuable comments. Similarly, for their comments on individual chapters, I would like to thank Luise Hercus, Dick Kimber, John Mulvaney, Arnold Reuther, Eric Sims, Michael Shanahan, Bob Reece, Chris Nobbs, Tom Gara, Yasmine Kassari and Peter Sutton.

All photographs of objects were taken by Philip Jones, with the exception of those on page 90 (Michal Kluvanek), page 143 (Scott Bradley) and page 223 (Kylie Gillespie). I am grateful to Angela Makris for her assistance in image processing. I thank Bernard Haseloff at the Map Shop, Adelaide, for his cartographic work.

This book was produced with the assistance of an Australia Council for the Arts grant.

For corrections and additions made in this revised edition, I am especially grateful to Geoffrey and Helen Jones, David Nash and Jane Simpson, Michael Treloar, Rosalie Richards, Margaret Stuart and Howard Speed.

This book is about the lives of frontier objects. It is also about the lives of those who carried these artefacts across Australia's remote frontiers, where Aboriginal and European people first met and were drawn into exchange and conflict. The idea for the book came from a realisation that Aboriginal artefacts not only evoke another culture and another time, but also carry substantial traces of encounters between their original makers or owners and their collectors. As witnesses of those encounters, museum objects have much to tell us about the frontier where they were noticed, desired and collected. The biographies of these objects span that frontier, and are the more fascinating because of it. Having brushed against both cultures they wear a double patina, of ochre and rust.

Frontier encounters in Aboriginal Australia rarely occurred across clear boundaries, between defined groups. Indeed, Aboriginal frontiers themselves have always been liminal zones, interpenetrated by dispersed and fluid populations with flexible allegiances. Individual affiliations usually extended beyond formal linguistic and political boundaries. Polities were formed for particular projects – a hunt, an initiation ceremony, a funeral – and formed anew on each occasion with different leaders, depending on the context. Despite European efforts to identify and confirm Aboriginal chiefs (by bestowing tomahawks or brass kingplates, for example), Aboriginal groups remained less hierarchical and definable than Maori or Native American tribes.

Ceremonial performance or ceremonial conflict provided an exception. In those situations, behaviour and expectations were circumscribed by traditional protocol, a fact which helps us to understand Aboriginal attitudes or demeanour towards Europeans penetrating their territory for the first time. When

Europeans entered Aboriginal territory in tight, numerous groups, especially when armed and in uniform, Aboriginal perceptions narrowed to two possibilities: either the Europeans were going to 'perform', or they were going to attack. European explorers were often aware of this expectation, and many noted the particular, charged atmosphere in which first encounters often occurred.

Engraving, hand-coloured by Felix Danvin, after Louis Auguste de Sainson's *'Premiere entrevue avec les sauvages'* ('first interview with the natives'), apparently documenting the 1826 encounter between J.S.C. Dumont d'Urville's expedition and the Aboriginal people of King George Sound in 1826, but actually based on a drawing by Jacques-Efienne Victor Arago, who portrayed an encounter (with a different background) at Shark Bay on 12 September 1818, as part of Louis-Claude de Freycinet's expedition. Published in D'Urville's *Voyage de la corvette l'Astrolabe, 1826–1829*. Tastu, Paris, 1833.

The local context of an encounter could be critical: whether the Europeans were on foot or horseback, and arrived suddenly, or whether Aboriginal people had the opportunity to engage in their own protocols of welcome or warning. The arrival of a mounted troop of armed Europeans in a rocky gorge where sacred objects were stored could instantly alienate and enrage the Aboriginal custodians, as their very identities were bound up with respect for that place and the traditions it contained. On the other hand, two or three lone Europeans, obviously struggling with the environment and constrained by thirst, posed little threat. They could be indulged with pity, if not kindness. The success and failure of many European exploration parties often hinged on the nature of these particular encounters.

What evidence remains of these encounters today? How were they remembered or recorded by Europeans or Aboriginal people? Europeans kept a range of written records, either official or private, documenting these events. Aboriginal people have preserved oral accounts of first contacts with Europeans, and given the grim history of subsequent relations, such encounters are often regarded today through a dark lens. The oral history of the 1928 Coniston massacre in Central Australia is one outstanding example. Aboriginal people interviewed about this tragic event relate that Europeans were marginal to their own interests at the time, that they were keen to sample the European commodities, but preferred to maintain their independence. Sadly, this was never to be the reality. The frontier often became an entangling, compromising field of barter, in which everything, even sacred objects held to be inalienable, had its price.

One of the earliest encounters between Aborigines and Europeans has left a remarkable trace. Australian historians have tended to concentrate on James Cook's first Pacific voyage, during which he presented beads and cloth to Aboriginal people. At least three fishing spears obtained in exchange at Botany Bay in 1770 are preserved in the Cambridge University Museum of Archaeology and Anthropology.[1] On this voyage Cook's men also distributed a few imitation guineas, depicting King George III. Sir Joseph Banks further developed this idea, prior to Cook's second voyage. He arranged for 2,000 bronze medals to be struck, depicting the king on one face, and Cook's two ships, the *Resolution* and the *Adventure*, on the other. The intention was to distribute these medals to indigenous peoples, as a means of introducing them to the British monarch and to provide those Europeans following in Cook's wake with tangible proof of his intrepid trajectory across the Pacific.

The *Adventure* put in to Bruny Island on 10 March 1773 to replenish supplies of water and wood, and three days later Captain Tobias Furneaux left several of these medals, gunflints and some metal in an Aboriginal shelter, in exchange for artefacts found there. Sufficient of the *Resolution* and *Adventure* medals remained for Cook to take on his third voyage (despite the replacement of the *Adventure* by the *Discovery*). Once again, the Aboriginal people of Bruny Island were recipients, during the expedition's five day sojourn at Adventure Bay. On 29 January 1777, Cook himself presented a medal to an Aboriginal man, in a formal meeting between his men and the Tasmanians, depicted in pen and wash by artist John Webber. This may be the earliest surviving visual record of exchange between Europeans and Aboriginal people, but it is not the only relic of that early encounter. In 1914, 137 years later, the sharp eyes of four-year-old Janet Cadell noticed one of the medals, turned up by her father's horse-drawn plough in a field at Killora, on North Bruny Island. The medal is the only known example with an Australian provenance. As an historical artefact symbolising both the idealism and reality of this country's first frontier encounters, it has no equal.[2]

It is not surprising that a varied picture of these encounters has emerged, given the combination of frankness and obfuscation in written records. Indeed, these nuanced accounts can provide rare insights into the Aboriginal attitudes prevailing at the time. An example in this book is the story of the death of J.W.O. Bennett, the well-meaning surveyor who stepped beyond the artificial boundaries prescribed by the 1869–1870 Goyder expedition. But most European accounts barely skim the surface of the encounter between black and white. The reason for this is clear. Europeans were rarely on the Aboriginal frontier for philanthropic purposes. They often had little interest in the life and culture of these people. Generally they were there to make observations about the

John Webber's pen and wash drawing, *Cook meeting inhabitants of Van Dieman's Land*, 1777 (26 x 38 3/8 in.). Naval Historical Branch, Ministry of Defence, London.

Both faces of the *Resolution* and *Adventure* medal, found in 1914 at Killora, North Bruny Island, by Janet Cadell. The bronze medal has a small hole drilled into the rim, above the King's head, where a suspension ring had been fitted to enable ribbon to be threaded through. Diameter: 42 mm; thickness: 3 mm. Private collection.

country and its potential for pastoral or mineral exploitation, or to establish the commerce or communication networks still expanding into Australia's outback today.

Museums and collections worldwide may hold as as many as 250,000 Aboriginal artefacts dating from the colonial period. Some individual collectors gathered thousands of artefacts, but many contributed no more than two or three. If we accept an average figure of 20–30 objects per collector, then perhaps 10,000 individuals were responsible for this wider, 'distributed' collection, engaging in 10,000 transactions with the objects' primary, Aboriginal owners. Each of these 10,000 frontier encounters, both fair and unfair, brief and prolonged, enlightened and naïve, left its trace in objects, if not in documents, images and memories.

While museum artefacts provide tangible records of those encounters, most were gathered almost incidentally, as souvenirs acquired in the course of dealings with Aboriginal people. Other objects were collected in conscious attempts to document the customs of a people whom Europeans assumed would soon be swept aside by the forces of progress. For many decades these objects served one main function in museums – to mark the culture of the Other. When the anthropologist Evans-Pritchard described material culture as 'the chains along which social ideas run' he was referring to ideas generated within the indigenous cultures of origin.[3] But ethnographic objects also carry information and ideas passing between the cultures of the collectors and the collected.

Until recently museums have not been reflective institutions. They have been better oriented towards measuring the dimensions of other cultures, and towards the natural sciences. Europeans have rarely recognised their own images, or traces of their own past actions, in museum collections. Yet, despite the fact that ethnographic objects document cultures dissimilar to our own, they also carry vestiges of a collector's curiosity.

Most collectors scarcely brushed against the lives of their subjects. But sometimes, in journals and letters, photographs or even museum registers, a particular intensity about those moments of engagement indicates that the object's own story can illuminate that zone of encounter. Comprehending the historical moment of exchange, by which a net bag or boomerang was acquired for a plug of tobacco or metal knife, not only helps to reveal forgotten codes and protocols of remote frontiers, but also confirms that those frontiers were loaded with other possibilities, even with a tentative and provisional interdependence between black and white.

This book explores these frontier moments, through a series of vignettes centred on particular objects originating across Australia and dating from the late eighteenth to the early twentieth centuries. **David Blackburn**'s upended club (the only surviving wooden artefact from the First Fleet) eluded identification as an Aboriginal object for two hundred years. Depending on one's perspective, it still appears alternately as a European or an Aboriginal weapon. It is a most apt metaphorical 'production' of the frontier zone. **J.W.O. Bennett**'s manuscript dictionary represents a store of words and phrases which, despite his care in assembling it, could not cancel the debt of blood which led to his fatal spearing. The manuscript, and the objects associated with it, suggest both the extent of frontier engagement and its limit. **King Peter**'s broken shield, found in a cave long after the frontier had moved across south-eastern Australia, gives a measure of how rapidly history had overtaken the Ngarrindjeri people. On the other hand, **Dick Cubadgee**'s fire-sticks, which he carried from beyond the frontier to Adelaide's Government House, remind us that the frontier could also return to those colonised spaces. Some objects moved the other way, from the European domain into Aboriginal culture, and were subsequently collected by Europeans. The **Calvert** axe, fashioned from the metal frame of a camel saddle abandoned by perishing explorers in the Great Sandy Desert, is an example. It is a relic of a moment when Aboriginal people perceived the European presence as supplementary, possibly assimilable to their own world, rather than heralding its traumatic dislocation. **Johann Reuther**'s mysterious toas also suggest this peculiar confidence, the capacity of Aboriginal people to innovate and remake their history, even as their world began to buckle and fold. The toas provide an example of a collector whose own quest for objects to illustrate his researches perhaps provoked their very existence. At her camp on the Nullarbor Plain, **Daisy Bates** placed herself on the very edge of two cultures, heightening the sense of difference through her anachronistic, Edwardian demeanour, dispensing rags to desert nomads. It was hardly surprising that her most extraordinary ethnographic acquisitions, sculptural forms of the Rainbow Snake, were also arrayed in cast-off, European garb. **Albert Namatjira** too, placed himself between Arrernte and European cultures, understanding that this represented his only opportunity to move ahead on his own terms. His poker-work Jesus plaque marked his transition from the tradition-bound life of his ancestors, and preceding his painting career, symbolised that shift. This ambiguous object also evokes the frontier's capacity to invert and distort, like an image projected through a convex lens, as colonisation gave way to decolonisation. Finally, if Reuther's toas, Bates's serpent and Namatjira's plaque suggest accommodation and innovation, **Patrick Shanahan**'s sample of Flinders Ranges red ochre speaks of allegiance to tradition and a determination to maintain links to the ancient past, despite the dislocations of the colonial period.

With their dual histories – on each side of the frontier and in the frontier zone itself – the objects in *Ochre and Rust* all carry traces which one culture has left on the other. When I began the research behind this book, not all these traces were evident. But working in the museum housing these objects, I was able to regard them from different angles, and to follow the lines of enquiry provoked by this scrutiny. Rather early in that process I understood that the objects of most interest were those which bear the frontier's double patina.

A museum collection contains elements of chance and order. Thrown up by historical coincidence, preserved by luck or a collector's fickle logic, curios and specimens alike are then subjected to principles of classification and interpretation. The French archaeologist Gustaf Sobin coined the phrase 'luminous debris' to describe the result when a curator or a devotee happens upon fragments of a collection and begins the process of reconstruction and interpretation.[4] Once the links are discerned, it is not long before particular objects yield up their stories, interlock with other tales and even, possibly, connect with our own histories. That attempt to connect is the aim of this book.

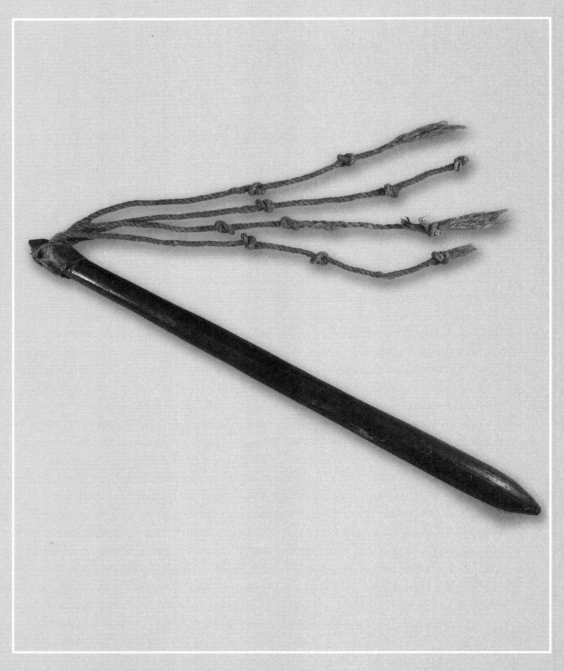

Master Blackburn's whip, comprising an Aboriginal club from the Sydney region and four knotted lashes. A72553, South Australian Museum.

CHAPTER ONE
Master Blackburn's whip

When most of the chapters in this book had already taken shape, I had the task of conceiving and curating an exhibition around a single object. The object is a composite of an Aboriginal club and a European whip, dating from the First Fleet's arrival in Australia. No precedent exists for this artefact. Not surprisingly perhaps, the resulting exhibition hinged largely upon hypothesis and historical circumstance. And yet, as much as any object in this book, Blackburn's whip possesses the tangible quality of evidence. It provides an exemplary case for the proposition that museum objects bear witness to that complex zone of encounter, the European-Aboriginal frontier.

Museums have often drawn their ethnographic artefacts from frontier encounters, in which one strand of history has touched another. Sometimes those strands have entwined briefly, generating hybrid objects with mixed associations. On the Australian frontier, these have included Aboriginal artefacts with a traditional form, but incorporating new materials, such as spearheads of metal, glass or porcelain, metal-bladed adzes and axes, or bags, head-bands and belts interwoven with cloth. Entirely new forms have also arisen – gypsum figurines, carved walking sticks and stockwhip handles, and even the toa sculptures described later in this book.

During the late nineteenth and early twentieth centuries museums tended to overlook or misinterpret such irregular objects. The principal object of enquiry was the uncontaminated 'other', and ethnographic museums preferred to construct that ideal with unambiguously authentic artefacts, free of traces evoking the colonial present. If hybrid artefacts were exhibited at all, it was in order to propose the frontier as a zone of contamination, where miscegenation and cultural degeneration were inescapably linked. As this extract from a 1913 exhibition label suggests, hybrid artefacts carried potent and salutary messages:

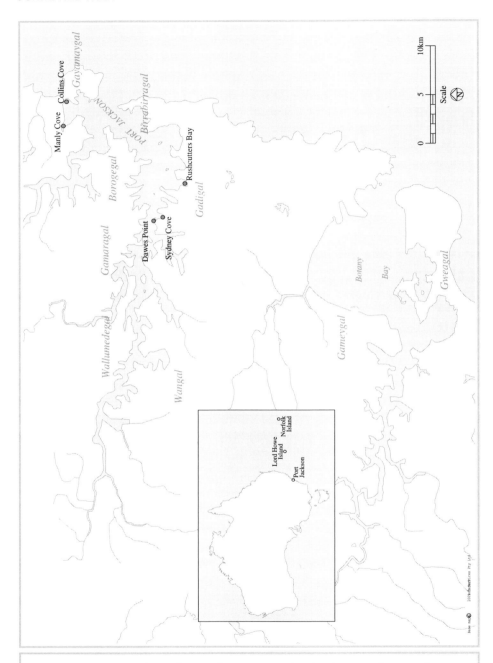

The vicinity of Port Jackson, showing places mentioned in this chapter, and names of Aboriginal language groups.

Articles of Native Workmanship in which
Materials of Civilization have been Wholly or Partly Used

In recent years contact with the white man has led to an increasing tendency for Australian aboriginals to utilise in their handiwork the materials and tools of civilization. This case contains a variety of native-made articles in which such materials have been used, and, as will be seen, the adoption of its methods and materials cause degeneration of native art.[1]

With their European materials and blend of new techniques, hybrid objects in Australian museums unmistakeably betrayed Aboriginal culture's collision with European history, evoking its fall from grace. It was not until the end of the twentieth century that museums began to reinterpret these objects, against a changing political and social background. That development accompanied a re-definition of Aboriginality and a rejection of the nomenclature of assimilationist policy—itself founded upon such terms of exclusion and authenticity as 'full-blood', 'half-caste', 'quadroon' and 'octaroon'.

The vitality of hybrid forms during the twentieth century confirms that Aboriginal people had not 'dropped out of history altogether in order to occupy a twilight zone between nature and culture', nor had they been confined within the ahistorical taxonomies set by nineteenth-century museums.[2] Instead, Aboriginal people were to be encountered on other ground—including ground they had been obliged to explore as a result of European interest in their art and culture. This was the territory of innovation, cultural experimentation and even, using the phrase adopted by Charles Mountford, 'art for art's sake'.[3]

Today, a roving curatorial eye can easily recognise a proliferation of hybrid objects among museum collections. European parcel string has bound spearheads in place, 'Reckitt's Blue' has coloured bark belts and head-bands, red cloth appears among baskets and ornaments, and metal, glass and porcelain provides blades and points for knives, axes and spears. All these objects speak of Aboriginal engagement with European culture during the first years of contact. They suggest opportunism and creativity rather than degeneration and finality. But these are Aboriginal objects. What of the reverse? Did European material culture of the period incorporate Aboriginal elements, indicating an equivalent curiosity and engagement?

Aboriginal baskets and mats found a wide market in south-eastern Australia during the late nineteenth century. Grinding stones were used as door-stops on country properties, spears or clubs sometimes served as fowl perches. There were inadvertent uses of Aboriginal material as well. The cairn on Mount Poole in western New South Wales, which members of Charles Sturt's expedition party toiled to build in 1845 during their enforced stay at Depot Glen, contains silcrete boulders from which Aboriginal stone tools had been fashioned. Stone quarries underlie the ruins of two European stone houses along the Birdsville Track.[4] But examples of direct, intentional appropriation have been rare. The European fascination with the boomerang offers the earliest, most obvious exception, but like the recent interest shown in Aboriginal art, this marked a wholesale detachment rather than hybrid incorporation.[5]

Yet such objects exist, and occasionally find the light. More than two centuries after it was collected and taken to England, a hybrid artefact dating from the First Fleet's sojourn at Port Jackson has been identified. Included among a consignment of naval memorabilia sold by Christie's in London during 1999, the artefact was presented by the auction house as a crude British naval whip. A rough version of a cat-o'-nine-tails, it consists of four knotted strands of rope bound to a wooden stock or handle. The proportions and form of this hardwood handle, lightly fluted by runnels (probably carved with a sharp shell spokeshave set into the haft of a spearthrower) and swelling to a bulbous head, indicate that it was made originally as an Aboriginal club. The weapon is of a type with those large and heavy clubs – part missile, part bludgeon – which Aboriginal men of the Sydney region carried for self-defence.[6]

This is a double object: a tribal weapon upended into a European instrument of correction. As an Aboriginal club and a European whip it represents two systems of law, and something essential in the histories of two cultures is entwined in it. Perhaps more than any other artefact, it also evokes the frontier's closure of the great gap in culture and history which lay between Aboriginal and European societies.

The weapon's twin histories emerge from a mix of clarity and opacity. Its European owner is known, but we have no clear details of the use he made of it. Its Aboriginal owner is unknown, but the context of its use seems clear. Made and used as an Aboriginal object, the club was transformed by its new owner. That person was David Blackburn, Master of His Majesty's Armed Tender, the brig *Supply* – first among the eleven First Fleet ships to sail into Botany Bay on 18 January 1788.

A ship's master could hardly do without a 'starter', to rouse seamen from their hammocks, or to dispense punishment when discipline slipped on pitching decks. The historian Greg Dening has examined the records of fifteen British naval ships sailing in the Central Pacific between 1767 and 1795 (not including the First Fleet), and estimates that 21 per cent of sailors received a flogging during these voyages, but N.A. Rodger's study of the Georgian navy indicates a broad range of disciplinary responses. Punishment varied from ship to ship and officer to officer, but was often regulated 'by public opinion on the lower deck'.[7] Twelve lashes was the upper limit for a peremptory flogging (further discipline required a court martial), but even this required the captain's authorisation.[8] Blackburn's whip seems to have been fashioned for this relatively formal and severe punishment of such infractions as disobedience, insolence, stealing and drunkenness. But it may have been intended more for effect than actual use.

With its heavy knotted lashes and thick handle, Blackburn's whip seems disproportionate to the ordinary business of a ship's master's daily round. For most navy lieutenants and masters of the period a thin stick, a length of rope or even a 'pudding stirrer' was sufficient for punishing trivial offences. These casual weapons could be tucked easily into an officer's belt or pocket. Nor does Blackburn's whip conform to the simple rattans used earlier in the century for 'starting' or herding ignorant or inexperienced landmen and marines about the decks, or for 'chasing up the lazy'.[9] This might suggest that Blackburn, whose profile evokes a mild and sensitive man, shied away from the casual violence of navy discipline, relying on his weapon to intimidate rather than injure. But what are we to make of the fact that his family had also preserved Blackburn's small, lead-weighted cosh? That small but formidable weapon was certainly unacceptable as an instrument of navy discipline on board late eighteenth-century ships. Blackburn might well have relied upon the cosh for personal protection during shore leave, in more dangerous ports than Port Jackson.

David Blackburn made no mention of shipboard discipline in his letters to his family, but it is likely that on embarkation his sea chest contained an instrument of discipline, such as an ordinary rattan or stick. Perhaps during the course of the voyage this had been misplaced or slid overboard. A substitute was needed quickly, and so Blackburn turned an Aboriginal club to advantage, binding and nailing four knotted lashes to the thin handle, and turning the bulbous head into the whip's grip.

Since it emerged at a London auction in 1999, Blackburn's whip has become accepted as the only documented wooden artefact surviving from the First Fleet's encounter with Aboriginal people.[10] It is most ironic that we owe this survival to its 'disappearance' as an Aboriginal artefact. For the object was preserved not as a club with its original associations, but as a somewhat gruesome relic of its new, European owner.

Large numbers of Aboriginal artefacts were collected at Port Jackson by officers and seamen of the First Fleet, and by subsequent British arrivals during the 1790s. Writing later in that decade, following his return from Australia, the Judge-Advocate David Collins confirmed that most officers collected artefacts as mementoes of their adventures. Certain officers had even developed an ethnographic familiarity with the form and function of these objects, sufficient to differentiate styles of manufacture on the basis of tribe and region. Collins wrote:

> It must be observed that the principal tribes have their peculiar weapons. Most of us had made collections of their spears, throwing-sticks &c as opportunities occurred; and on shewing them to our Sydney friends, they have told us that such a one was used by the people who lived to the southward of Botany Bay; that another belonged to the tribe of the Cam-mer-ray ... and they extend this peculiarity even to their dances, their songs and their dialect.[11]

By 1793 the Captain of Marines, Watkin Tench, considered a detailed description of the material culture of Sydney Aborigines unnecessary, as 'very ample collections of all these articles are to be found in many museums in England'.[12] That may have been the case in 1793, but such objects soon vanished from the historical record. Several of these artefacts may have survived in collections, but the documentation confirming their provenance has not. Collected in the days before museums developed registration systems to preserve artefacts' identities, these rare examples of the first exchanges between Aborigines and Europeans sank into anonymity as ethnographic collections expanded. Only a handful of artefacts with a Port Jackson or Botany Bay provenance can be recognised today, and none are unambiguously associated with the First Fleet.[13] Blackburn's whip seems unique.

Blackburn carried the whip on his homeward voyage from Port Jackson to Portsmouth, departing on 26 November 1791 and arriving nearly six months later, on 15 May 1792. His next posting was to the West Indies in October 1793, aboard the *Dictator*. It is not known if he left the whip with his family in Norwich, or took it with him on that final voyage, during which he fell ill and died.

The tragedy of Blackburn's early death imbued his remaining possessions – and especially the whip – with the status of relics. During the next two centuries his family preserved his precious letters, his silhouette portrait, the whip and the cosh. We can only guess how the whip was regarded during those 200 years. Initially perhaps, as a curiosity, with Blackburn's own description of it fresh in the memory of his family: a surviving brother (another had predeceased David), his two sisters and mother, an aunt and his cousin, Peter

Silhouette of 'Lieutenant David Blackburn', retained in Blackburn's family from 1787 until 1999. Mss 6937, Mitchell Library, Sydney.

Martineau, whose brother was a prominent Norwich surgeon.

As the memory of this favourite son faded we might expect the club to have been relegated to a cellar or attic, resurfacing in later years as an unexplained oddity, before its eventual consignment to a jumble sale or a bonfire. Nothing of the sort. The whip seems to have retained its status as an amulet, unlocking the family's memories of Blackburn's antipodean exploits.

During the early 1970s an English book dealer, Derek Neville, was shown a batch of Blackburn's letters and documents relating to his Port Jackson voyage. Tracing their source, Neville encountered the great-great-granddaughter of one of Blackburn's sisters, Elizabeth, and came face to face with the small trove of David Blackburn's relics. Reading through the letters, Neville fastened upon Blackburn's brief mention of a tiny islet in the lee of Lord Howe Island, 600 kilometres off the New South Wales coast. Blackburn's commanding officer had discovered and named the larger island in March 1788, during the *Supply*'s outward voyage from Port Jackson to establish a subsidiary penal settlement at Norfolk Island. Blackburn's navigational skills brought the *Supply* to a safe harbour on Norfolk Island's treacherous coast, and for that his commander named 'Blackbourne's Point', at the harbour's northern edge. After depositing its cargo of convicts and soldiers the *Supply* returned to Lord Howe Island. There, as Blackburn related, Lieutenant Ball 'displayed the English colours on shore and took formal possession of the island in the name of his Brittanic Majesty'.[14] The following day, while Blackburn remained on board the *Supply*, Ball named the island's main features, giving the name of 'Blackborn's Isle' (employing another variant of the surname) to 'a small green island' in the middle of the sweeping western bay.[15]

Neville was disappointed to find that by the mid-twentieth century the name 'Blackborn's Isle' had been supplanted by the more prosaic 'Rabbit Island'.

Determined to marry his historical research to a worthy cause, Neville dedicated himself to restoring the original name. His success was eventually capped when a memorial seat was installed on Lord Howe Island's clifftop, overlooking Blackburn's 'small green island'. In the meantime, Neville was drawn deeper into Blackburn's story.

Hanging in the Norfolk living room of David Blackburn's great-great-grand-niece were the silhouette likenesses of Blackburn's father and mother, his sister Elizabeth, and the mariner himself. More letters and Blackburn's lead-weighted cosh came to light. Almost as an aside, Neville mentions Blackburn's whip itself, leaning in a corner. His description of the object, which uncritically assumed its convict associations, illuminates the mystique it still held for Blackburn's family, and helps to account for its preservation:

> And in a corner of this very room – as a vivid reminder of those harsh days when David Blackburn went with the First Fleet, stood a curious instrument – a long stout handle, stained, weather-beaten and worn smooth with use, and, at one end, the knotted ropes with all their dreadful implications. It was a cat-o'-nine tails. Without much doubt it was used on board H.M. Armed Tender *Supply*.[16]

By now the object had fully metamorphosed from club to whip. Its Aboriginal associations had disappeared, replaced entirely by the 'dreadful implications' of Australia's convict past. Neville assumed the whip to be a part of that history, and this is how the object was described 25 years later, when it finally left Blackburn's family for Christie's auction rooms.

At the auction in September 1999, more than two centuries after his death, Blackburn's remaining papers and his silhouette likeness were knocked down to the Mitchell Library in Sydney. Peter Walker, an Adelaide dealer who purchased the cosh and the whip in a separate lot, was perhaps the only person in the room to recognise the whip's 'long stout handle' as an Aboriginal club from the Sydney region. He brought the two objects back to Australia, and following their resale to another private collector and subsequent exhibition at the South Australian Museum during 2001–2002, both were obtained by that institution.[17]

There is no evidence to suggest that Blackburn ever used his whip against Aboriginal people. It is also unlikely to have been used against convicts; their punishment was meted out with a more precisely regulated instrument – the standard cat-o'-nine-tails used in British and Australian prisons until the early twentieth century. The *Supply* did not carry convicts on the voyage to Australia and consequently Blackburn's role as Master did not merge with the punitive regime on which the voyage was based. In fact, he appreciated Governor Phillip's compassionate treatment of the First Fleet's human cargo. Writing to his sister from Rio de Janeiro, he told her that 'the Health of the Convicts may in good measure be attributed to the Humanity of the Governor who gives them Every Indulgence their situation will admit of'.[18] Blackburn conveyed convicts to Norfolk Island on at least six occasions, but his duties concerned seamanship, navigation and maintaining discipline among his crew. The convicts were under the control of other officers.[19]

As suggested, it was the miscreant sailors of the *Supply* who were most likely to have been on the receiving end of his whip's crudely knotted lashes. These men were probably unaware that the whip's handle was an Aboriginal club. In all likelihood, they didn't care to know. The more interesting question is whether such an opportune, casually made artefact held such a resonance for its owner. The little we know of Blackburn indicates that it may have done.

Blackburn's letters confirm that he was intrigued by the Aborigines of Sydney – initially at a superficial level, but then more deeply. This is evidenced by his abridged transcription of a vocabulary of the Sydney Aboriginal language, made during late 1790 or early 1791. The original, fuller version had been recorded by Blackburn's friend and fellow-officer, Lieutenant William Dawes, at his astronomer's hut on the edge of the Port Jackson settlement, where the southern pylons of the Sydney Harbour Bridge stand today.[20] In a clear indication that he had studied and used Dawes's vocabulary, Blackburn interpolated six new words. Two of these additions – *bardo* (water) and *gwee.ung* (fire) – were terms for the elements; while *tamura* (hand), and *nogo* (nose) were terms for body parts. Blackburn may have checked these terms with an Aboriginal informant. Who might that have been? Might that individual have been the original owner of the club? Perhaps a clue lies in Blackburn's vocabulary, where his additional entry, 'Benelong – The Name of a Man Native', was inserted under the letter 'B'.[21]

During the first months of contact, relations between the British and the Aborigines of Port Jackson swung from moments of tension to farce, and from indifference to intimacy. Against that background the young Eora man, Bennelong, was to emerge as the principal and most influential intermediary. His precocious curiosity, his capacity for independent engagement with British officers (notably Governor Phillip), and his ready enlistment of Aboriginal artefacts and European objects as commodities of cultural exchange, marked

Detail from David Blackburn's annotated transcription of William Dawes's Port Jackson vocabulary, sent to Richard Knight in March 1791. Microfilm CY 1301, Mitchell Library, Sydney.

him singularly as a cultural broker. There could be no original owner for Blackburn's hybrid club more fitting than Bennelong himself.[22]

As one of the principal contributors to the First Fleet's extended vocabulary, Bennelong probably supplied some of its terms for artefacts – such as *Gnallangulla Tarreebirre*, a 'particular club'. We can assume that these names were applied and recorded in reference to actual objects – either in Bennelong's possession or close at hand, perhaps in Dawes's hut. Unfortunately, Blackburn's shortened copy of this list does not contain the word for a thick-ended club, *wudi* or *wuda*. He noted only one additional artefact term, *Gnar.awang*, the word for the wooden paddles which Eora men and women used as they skimmed to and fro on the harbour in their fragile bark canoes, past the *Supply* at anchor.[23]

The small variations Blackburn introduced in his copy of Dawes's vocabulary may seem inconsequential, but they represent an engagement with a people who remained opaque and inscrutable to most of the British. Blackburn's acquisition of the club adds tangible form to that engagement, even if its subsequent transformation from club to whip also suggests something less definable – the harbour frontier as a prism, refracting each culture's image of the other.

BLACKBURN'S VOYAGE

Like much of its human cargo, David Blackburn was not an enthusiastic participant in the First Fleet's voyage. Aged 34 years, he was already an experienced sailor. During the early 1780s he had served on HMS *Victory* with Captain Henry Lidgbird Ball, who was now to be his commanding officer on the *Supply*. In 1785 Blackburn served as Master of the HMS *Flora* in the West Indies, and had been discharged from that posting in early 1787. He was ready for life ashore, or at least an extended period of leave. Apparently unaware of the Botany Bay endeavour, Blackburn considered petitioning the Navy Board to place him on half pay. But with eleven ships of the First Fleet to man, the navy was not about to overlook one of their experienced Masters. Placed quite high on the Navy List, at number 226, he was called in early March 1787 to join the brig *Supply*. The 170-ton brig lay at Spithead, off Portsmouth, and was 'bound with the rest of the Squadron for Botany Bay'. Blackburn would be serving as a 'sixth-rate' officer on a monthly salary of £5, 'which of itself is a Hardship', he complained, as he had previously 'pass'd for a third Rate which is £7 monthly'. The voyage would begin within the month.

The warrant caught Blackburn unawares. Contemplating extended leave, he was now to be propelled to the other side of the world in a 'small and rather uncomfortable vessel', with no opportunity to spend time with his mother and sisters beforehand. On 4 April 1787 he wrote despairingly to his widowed mother:

> I did all in my Power to Decline Accepting of this offer – But I am told that I <u>must</u> go Unless I mean to throw myself Entirely out of the Service … I am a Good Deal Vex'd at this Voyage as I am by no Means Prepared for it, Especially on such short Notice.[24]

Looking for a way out, he approached a well-connected family friend, but was told that 'if I refused to go in her [the *Supply*] I should be Struck off the List & have no Claims to Employment till Every other Master had been Provided for by Rotation & that the Navy Board Considered it a Particular mark of their favour to Employ me so Soon'. Resigned to his fate, Blackburn informed his sister Margaret that it was his 'duty to obey without Murmuring'.[25]

Blackburn had returned from his last voyage quite out of pocket, his seafaring rig worn out. Now, as a ship's master in charge of navigation, he was expected to equip himself for a long voyage and to supply his own instruments and charts of the southern seas. He was obliged to borrow ten pounds from his aunt to purchase the bare essentials. Within a week he had equipped himself with 'a Dozen New Shirts, a Coat, 6 pr Shoes, a Dozen Pr Stockings, some Charts of the E[as]t Indies & South Seas' and hoped to go to sea 'tolerably well hack'd'. By 4 April he had joined his ship.

His fellow-officers spoke of sailing at any time, but Blackburn expected a delay of at least ten days, having heard that the man appointed as Governor for the new colony of Botany Bay was still 'settling his business' in London: 'the Lawyers have not yet finished a Code of Laws for this New Establishment'. The *Supply* and the rest of the First Fleet lay at anchor until Arthur Phillip and the lawyers were satisfied with the terms under which His Majesty's newest colony would be opened for business. Blackburn wrote again to his family, still hoping to see his sister before embarking, and even contemplated paying her fare to Portsmouth. But time had run out.[26]

'His Majesty's Brig *Supply* 1790, off Lord Howe Island'. George Raper, 1792. The Natural History Museum, London.

At last, with only the voyage before him, Blackburn's enthusiasm began to rise. It was not, he confessed to his sister, 'a voyage I should by any means have chose', but at least it was 'a fine climate, and I dare say a healthy one'. Blackburn recalled philosophically, and piously, that the 'Providence which has hitherto protected me in All my Dangers is Still the Same – that the Southern Hemisphere is like this, Equally under his Allseeing Eye'. Perhaps he would even gain from the voyage, having been assured that 'every officer who Returns from this Expedition will Certainly be Provided for by the Admiralty & Navy Boards'. He began to consider the role he might play in surveying the 'New Establishment':

It is to be supposed that we being a Small Vessel are to be employed surveying the Coast of New Holland on that side where we build our fort & land the Convicts – which will take a year at least to make a chart tolerably sufficient for the Part – I have well stock'd myself with Paper, Books & Proper Instruments for the Purpose.[27]

Blackburn knew several officers on the other ships, Lieutenant William Dawes among them. He reacquainted himself with his *Victory* shipmate Lidgbird Ball and found himself on 'good friendly terms' with his new commanding officer:

> It shall not be my fault if we don't continue so; indeed tis his interest to be Civil to me, as I am the next in rank to Himself ... in case of sickness on his side the Command of the Tender must devolve upon me.[28]

There was a firm prospect that Ball's promotion to Captain would clear the way for Blackburn's own rise to Lieutenant from what he considered his own miserable sixth-rate status. As a result of Ball's illness at Port Jackson that double set of promotions never eventuated; but Blackburn's family was sure enough of the prospect to frame the small silhouette depicting David in profile, dressed in his officer's hat, titled 'Lieutenant David Blackburn'.[29]

Finally, at four in the morning on 13 May 1787, the fleet sailed from the 'Home Bank' at Portsmouth, escorted through the English Channel by the frigate *Hyaena*. The journey to Australia took nearly eight months, via Teneriffe, Rio de Janeiro, and the Cape of Good Hope. Blackburn wrote to his sister Margaret from each port. From Rio de Janeiro on 2 September 1787 he informed her that the fleet's human cargo was in good health:

> Having in all from their first Embarkation Buried only 28 Men & two Women & there have been 8 or 10 Births, chiefly females. I cannot Quit this Subject without saying that the Health of the Convicts may in a Great Measure by Attributed to the Humanity of the Governor Who Gives them Every Indulgence their Situation will admit of, none of them are Confin'd in Chains or Even Under the Deck by Day, Except such whose Behaviour Deserves such Punishment & they are Constantly Supply'd with fresh Provisions fruit & vegetables.[30]

The letter gave the first hint of Blackburn's capacity for curiosity, a quality shared by those of his fellow-officers who gathered collections of artefacts and natural history during the voyage. 'I have not', Blackburn wrote to his sister, 'seen any Curious Shells here. But I have got some Skins of Birds of this Country which I think will be worth your Acceptance tho I fear I shall not be Able to Procure Enough to Make a Muff'.[31] At the Cape of Good Hope which they reached on 14 October 1787, the fleet took on sheep, cattle and other livestock. 'Could you see the *Supply*', Blackburn told his sister, 'She would Put you in Mind of Noah's Ark, Except that we have no Woman on Board'.[32]

Blackburn expected to be absent for three years. The *Supply* returned to England in May 1792, five years after it embarked. In that time he had fulfilled all the duties expected of him as ship's master. No doubt aided by his whip, Blackburn had maintained necessary discipline, allaying the need for any court martials or, it seems, more formal floggings. He had prepared charts and readings of harbours and anchorages and ensured that the *Supply* remained seaworthy in spite of the steady deterioration of its timbers. At least three coastal features were named for him: Blackburn Cove inside the North Head of Port Jackson, 'Blackbourne's Point' on Norfolk Island, and tiny 'Blackborn's Isle', which was to provoke the rediscovery of his relics.

Governor Phillip had personally commended Blackburn for his 'very officer-like conduct', particularly for commanding the *Supply* during Lieutenant Ball's long illness in the first months of 1791. This proficiency, Phillip suggested, made it 'a duty incumbent upon me to point him out as an officer deserving of their Lordships' notice'.[33] Unfortunately for Blackburn, Phillip's endorsement did not result in the promotion he obviously deserved. This was probably because illness prevented Ball's own anticipated promotion, blocking Blackburn's advance to the rank of Lieutenant.[34]

THE COMMERCE OF ENCOUNTER

While the precise circumstances of Blackburn's acquisition of the club may never emerge, the record of contact between Aboriginal people and Europeans suggests that he may not have obtained it until at least two years after the fleet's arrival. During that initial period there were few formal exchanges of weapons for European commodities, although these were civilising opportunities which Governor Phillip and his officers earnestly tried to promote. Collecting occurred far more haphazardly, through the pilfering of Aboriginal fishing equipment (spears, spearthrowers and fishing lines), or at moments of chance confrontation, when spears and clubs were thrown at the British. Blackburn's club may have been acquired under such conditions, but it is tempting to consider that it was proffered for exchange in a more considered, intimate manner, perhaps within the same encounters which framed his acquisition of words in the Sydney language.

Blackburn was not a Tench, a Collins, or a Dawes – such avid recorders of detail that they may be termed ethnographers. But he was among the few members of the First Fleet to make personal contact with Sydney Aborigines before their general avoidance of the settlement which lasted from early 1788 until September 1790. His letters show that while superficially dismissive of

Aboriginal culture (remaining 'ignorant of their Particular Manners & Customs if they have any'), he nevertheless wanted to know more.[35] When the time eventually came for the frontier's hard line to soften into a zone of encounter, Blackburn was ready to play a role.

The *Supply* headed the fleet, reaching Captain Cook's old landing place at Botany Bay on 18 January 1788. Realising shortly after leaving the Cape that the small brig was the fleet's speediest vessel, Governor Phillip had transferred to it, together with Lieutenants King and Dawes and a team of builders and carpenters. Phillip's intention was to erect the colony's first buildings at Botany Bay before the rest of the fleet arrived. But the other ships made up lost ground with favourable winds and arrived just two days after the *Supply*. In the meantime Blackburn accompanied Governor Phillip ashore, for the first time.

If the club had been acquired by Blackburn during this first encounter with Aboriginal people on 18 January it is likely that we would know of it, for his papers contain a vivid account. Blackburn described the encounter in a letter to his Norwich friend, Richard Knight:

> At 4 in the afternoon we Anchor'd Safe (& All in Good Health & spirits) in the Long Wish'd for Botany Bay. The Natives as we Sail'd in came Down to the edge of the Cliffs Making a Noise & Lifting up their spears. Immediately after Anchoring the Governor accompany'd by Some Officers went on Shore on the North Side of the Bay & Met some of the Natives on the Beach. He Went towards them singly which as soon as they saw a very old man walk'd from among them to meet him. This Man (Who Probably remembered the Dress of Capn Cook Officers) Did not shew the Least Signs of Fear or Distrust. The Governor put Some Red Cloth About his Neck, Gave him some Beads & other Trifling Presents with which he appeared Well Pleas'd. The Natives However soon Withdrew to the Woods & our Party Return'd on board.[36]

Even before making these personal overtures Phillip had displayed his beads, talismanically, to those Aboriginal men confronting him as he was rowed ashore. He directed his crew to festoon a beached canoe with these baubles. The idea was to begin on a friendly basis with small transactions, just as Cook had done in the Pacific. The broader aim was to cement, amicably, the biggest transaction of all – securing the country itself. But the Dharawal and Dharug people of Botany Bay were only mildly interested in these flimsy objects. Lieutenant Philip Gidley King, who accompanied the party, observed that the principal reaction appeared to be astonishment 'at the figure we cut in being clothed'.[37] Lieutenant William Bradley wrote: 'They all expressed great curiosity as to our sex, having our beards shaved & being clothed they could not tell what to take us for'.[38]

In subsequent encounters at Botany Bay, after overcoming their initial apprehension, Aboriginal men were concerned with establishing the actual humanity and sex of the visitors. They felt and prodded, wondered at the skin beneath the clothing. With no clear evidence that the strangers were men like themselves, they even felt inside the mouths of the officers and men to see whether they, like true men, lacked a front, right tooth (tooth evulsion was practised as an initiatory rite by the Sydney tribes). Extraordinarily, among all the British officers it was Governor Phillip himself who conformed to this ideal. Phillip wrote: 'on my showing them that I wanted a front tooth it occasioned a general clamour and I thought gave me some little merit in their opinion'.[39] George Worgan, surgeon on the *Sirius*, also noted this coincidence:

> Almost all the Men have had one of the Fore-teeth extracted, but from being so universal we are equally at a Loss as to ye Motive of this Custom, they will sometimes thrust their Fingers into your Mouth to see if you have parted with this Tooth. The Governor happens to want this Tooth, at which they appear somewhat pleased & surprized.[40]

Neither Phillip nor his men were comfortable with such intimate and untidy encounters. They had imagined a more formal approach, ideal tableaux in which the meeting between savage and civilised men would be mediated by objects, bestowed with a sense of gravitas. Phillip's aim was to introduce the civilising effect of barter, leading to a kind of regulated intercourse through which the natives might learn the true value of things. Later, Phillip's continued attempts to realise this Enlightenment performance-piece would lead him close to tragedy.

David Blackburn's first Aboriginal encounter followed Phillip's protocol to the letter. It occurred a day after the first landing:

> The Next Day we Landed in Different Parts of the Bay, saw the Natives who Came to us without Fear, Arm'd with Spears, but without any Appearance of Hostile Intentions. They would Receive Anything from us but we could not then get them Either to Eat or Drink with us. I went to an Elderly Man, put a Piece of Blue Cloth Round his Neck & a String of Glass Beads round his Arm, Shook him by the hand wh[ich] he seem'd to take as a Mark of Confidence. I pull'd a Biscuit out of my Pocket, Broke it, Eat Part of it, Gave him the other

Piece. He took it, put it to his Mouth, & Appear'd to be Eating & soon withdrew towards his Companions. I followed him. At a small Distance I saw him throw down the Bread which I took up unseen by him & found that he had not tasted it.[41]

Apparently the club was not obtained then, nor on the following day, when Phillip went ashore once more, and again attempted a friendly exchange.

On that day the air seems to have been thick with uncertainty. David Collins later wrote that the Aborigines of Botany Bay 'by no means seemed to regard them as enemies or invaders of their country and tranquillity' and Tench considered that their meetings 'ended in so friendly a manner that we began to entertain some hopes of bringing about a connection with them', but this confidence is not borne out by other accounts. Several officers were awake to a palpable tension.[42] Aboriginal men took fish assertively from the British nets, and when some officers attempted to follow them into the bush this 'occasioned them to stop & make signs that they did not like to be followed'.[43] The British had brought ashore cloth bags to fill with grass for their livestock. Coveted for their string fibres, these bags soon vanished – the first unmistakeable evidence of an Aboriginal desire for European goods. The Aborigines were, Lieutenant Bradley wrote, 'much inclined to steal any kind of Cloth or covering'.[44] Among this confusion, some willing exchanges took place. Surgeon Bowes Smyth, of the *Lady Penrhyn*, bartered a mirror for a 'heavy bludgeon' – perhaps a club similar to Blackburn's own.[45]

As the British officers returned to the ships, Aboriginal men armed with spears and shields crowded close to the rowboats – as if, the sailor Jacob Nagle wrote, 'they did not approve of our visit'. Blackburn's commander, Lieutenant Ball, was the last to step into the boats, but at that moment the Aboriginal men began 'to be mischievous with him'. As Nagle related, Ball had a sudden inspiration, artlessly demonstrating a new equivalence more convincing than those tentative exchanges Governor Phillip had attempted:

> he took one of their shields and set it up against an old stump of a tree and fired one of his pistols at it, which frightened them when they heard the report, but much more when they saw the ball went through the shield.[46]

Tench described the same encounter, suggesting that the Aborigines' astonishment 'exceeded their alarm' but 'produced a little shyness'.[47] Observing that concern, and 'to dissipate their fears and remove their jealousy, [Ball] whistled the air of "Malbrooke" which they appeared highly charmed with, and imitated him with equal pleasure and readiness'. Later, the French explorer La Perouse informed Watkin Tench that he had whistled this 'little plaintive air' in all his encounters 'with the natives of California and throughout all the islands of the Pacific Ocean'.[48]

Despite Cook's endorsement, Governor Phillip was unimpressed with Botany Bay. Within a few hours of his arrival he decided to examine the coast for an alternative settlement site. Blackburn accompanied this small reconnaissance party to the north on 20 January 1788. Navigating the *Supply* through the Heads at Port Jackson, he was as euphoric as Phillip himself: 'we found it perhaps as fine a Harbour as Any in the World, with Water for any Number of the Largest Ships'.[49] Within a week the fleet had transferred from Botany Bay to Sydney Cove. The British were now among the Port Jackson Aborigines, whose ordinary term for themselves as 'people' has gradually become adopted as their tribal name – the 'Eora'.[50]

Here formal attempts at commerce fell as flat as at Botany Bay. The British hoped for 'a cautious friendship', but even that prospect rapidly diminished as the entire human cargo of the First Fleet came ashore. This combined number of more than 1500 Europeans probably outnumbered the entire Aboriginal population of the Port Jackson area immediately: Bowes Smyth remarked that 'none of them has appeared since we anchored'.[51]

The trees at Sydney Cove were so dense that when the eleven ships dropped anchor the captains were content to tie mooring ropes to the branches. Within a few days this forest was pushed back as the trees were felled for wood and fuel. In Aboriginal Australia an individual's freedom to cut a tree with impunity constituted an acknowledgement of rights to land. Now the harbour forests disappeared before the flashing axes of the Port Jackson convicts, at a speed which disturbed their Aboriginal owners.

The scale of tree-felling matched the tremendous hauls of fish netted by the British from the coves around the settlement. Phillip allocated particular coves as fishing grounds for each ship's crew. Sometimes, as the seaman Jacob Nagle put it, '23 hauls of the seine in one night' would yield no more than a bucketful of fish; on other occasions they could be 'falling in with schools that would be sufficient to fill our sternsheets' in a single haul.[52] These catches drew the attention of Eora who had otherwise studiously ignored the British ships. Blackburn observed this phenomenon in a letter to his sister: 'they seem to have no Curiosity for they will scarce take off their observation from fishing in their Canoes whilst a Ship has Passed close by them in full sail'.[53]

The Port Jackson people did not use large seine nets. They speared individual fish or caught them with shell fish-hooks and line made of two-ply vegetable fibre string, 'fine as silk'.[54] The seeming ease of their actions masked an intense concentration, and they landed only one fish at a time. The sight of newly arrived strangers hauling entire schools of fish from the sea in an instant was disturbing in a fundamental way. None of the European observers, including Blackburn himself, fully understood the Aboriginal reaction to this sight – a mixture of wonder and aggrieved propriety. Surgeon White wrote:

> One evening while the seine was hauling, some of them were present and expressed great surprise at what they saw, giving a shout expressive of astonishment and joy when they perceived the quantity that was caught. No sooner were the fish out of the seine than they began to lay hold of them, as if they had a right to them, or that they were their own.[55]

To the Eora such an extraordinary bounty was an unambiguous signal for a feast. A surplus of this kind should be shared by all, immediately. The British soon realised their obligation to give a portion of the catch to the Aborigines. An officer in charge of one of the fishing crews took this initiative, and Phillip quickly formalised it into a standard protocol. With that the Eora began to understand that they were losing control over their own resources – and to widening sections of their coast. That much seemed clear. What remained to be resolved was the nature of the accommodation.

George Worgan, surgeon of the *Supply*'s sister ship, *Sirius*, wrote of 'a laughable Circumstance' occurring shortly after a group of Aboriginal men challenged convict woodcutters and expressed their anger at the felling of trees:

> A pot was boiling in which there was some Fish for the Workmen's Dinners, One of the Natives (who never had seen or felt hot Water before) very deliberately put his Hand in to take a Fish out, when, feeling a very smart Sensation, he gave an amazing Jump squalling out most Hideously, on which, his Companions seeing us laugh, joined Us very heartily, while the poor Fellow was skipping about & blowing his Fingers.[56]

Phillip persisted in formal attempts at exchange, wanting Aboriginal people to understand his readiness to negotiate over their objects, and his own. Not long after arriving at Sydney Cove two Aboriginal men entered the new settlement. The surgeon George Worgan described the encounter:

Only two of Them have ventured to visit our Settlement to whom the Governor gave many presents, and did every[thing] that he thought might Induce them to stay, or to come again and bring their Companions; the Objects which must have been entirely new to them did not excite their Curiosity or Astonishment so much as one might have expected. They just looked at them, with a kind of vague Indifference. Of all the Things that have been given them the Axes Fishing hooks & Lines, or any spare Instrument or Food seem to please them most. The Drum was beat before them, which terrified them exceedingly, they liked the Fife, which pleased them for 2 or 3 Minutes.[57]

These men did not return, and their visit was not followed by others.

The first accounts of Sydney's settlement make it clear that metal was enthusiastically assimilated within the suite of Aboriginal material culture, as it was elsewhere in the country. That process was hastened from the outset by the British employing it as a trade item. Among its stores the First Fleet arrived with 700 felling axes, 700 hatchets, 700 iron shovels, 700 clasp knives and 747,000 nails.[58] Colonial experience with indigenous peoples in Africa and North America had established metal axes and knives as principal commodities in a universal currency of frontier exchange, and this applied also in Australia. In contrast, the cloth and trinkets valued as objects of barter elsewhere in the Pacific provoked little interest among Aborigines. Their limited appeal seemed confined to the social encounter in which they were presented. Captain Hunter observed that 'we had much reason afterward to believe that such trifles only pleased them, as baubles do children, for a moment: for at other times we frequently found our presents lying dispersed on the beach, although caught at by these people with much apparent avidity at the time they were offered'.[59] Tomahawks and other metal tools had an immediate application though, as well as an accrued trade value. As the historian Inga Clendinnen puts it, the Aborigines 'coveted only those British products which replicated the function of their own tools, like metal hatchets or fishhooks'.[60]

Phillip took trade goods of some kind on all his harbour forays, and rarely missed an opportunity for 'traffic with the natives'. His aim on each occasion was to obtain spears in exchange for European objects, a token disarming of Aboriginal men which was a crucial element of his colonising project. The most telling instance occurred after the spearing of two convict rush-cutters on 30 May 1788. Phillip and a troop of redcoats set out on a reprisal expedition after the perpetrators but were surprised to meet a group of about 200 Aboriginal men, 'the greatest number of the natives we had ever seen together since our coming among them'. Each was armed with spears and spearthrower, a shield, and a stone axe or 'a large club, pointed at one end' – similar to Blackburn's.[61]

One force confronted the other. The alternatives were an exchange of fire or an exchange of objects. Fortunately, as Collins put it, 'a friendly intercourse directly took place, & some spears, etc, were exchanged for hatchets'.[62] Even Phillip's armed reprisal force was prepared for conciliation, carrying a supply of metal axes. If the murderers of the rush-cutters were among the Aboriginal party they were not identified, even through this means. As Phillip soon realised, the rush-cutters' illicit acquisition of Aboriginal objects had provoked their murders. They had 'taken away and detained' an Aboriginal canoe, and for that 'act of violence and injustice they had paid with their lives'.[63]

'The hunted rush-cutter', probably painted by George Raper, ca 1790.
The Natural History Museum, London.

Even after ten months, at the end of 1788, only two Aboriginal men had entered the township itself. Encounters had taken place around the harbour but these had been fleeting, and for the most part, superficial. According to Lieutenant William Bradley, none of these meetings had involved relations between the sexes:

> To speak of the virtue of the Ladies of this Country I believe noone in the Colony can boast of having received favours; whether they are bound by any Tie or their connexions made by promiscuous intercourse is hard for us to determine;

it has been generally observed that they are very jealous of the women being among us when we happen to fall in where they are & that the women are kept at a distance when we do not come unawares upon them.[64]

That was also Tench's view, but chance encounters between white men and Aboriginal women (and perhaps also between convict women and Aboriginal men) certainly occurred. They took place beyond the official scrutiny of the British officers at the settlement's margins, on the shoreline or in the 'woods'.

These were beguiling interactions, and from them an odd, ragged economy emerged, with its own currency or set of equivalences. Each party attempted to draw the other in, to manufacture an advantage for themselves in this unprecedented milieu, devising informal and inventive forms of colonisation. For some of the convicts, opportunities arose from fleeting moments of leisure such as a chance meeting between a party of convict women and a group of Aboriginal men deep in the bush, or even more formal meetings in a particular 'adjoining cove' where an Aboriginal group was based. Collins described these visits – casual but momentous first attempts by Europeans and Aboriginal people to confront each other on their own terms:

> [The Aborigines] were visited by large parties of the convicts of both sexes on those days in which they were not wanted for labour. Here they danced and sang with apparent good humour, and received such presents as the convicts could afford to make them; but none of the natives would venture back with their visitors.[65]

Within the confines of a penal settlement the ground for such encounters was restricted indeed. And while some semblance of an equal exchange might have emerged on these occasions, an opportunistic, acquisitive attitude to the other's possessions was more typical. From the first encounters the Sydney Aborigines understood that European materials such as cloth and metal held value not as exotic novelties in themselves, but as elements to enhance the effectiveness of their own technology. Much of the 'pilfering' which provoked further clashes with the British was purposeful, and directed towards such objectives.

Thefts of European goods also occurred in retaliation for the convicts' own pilfering of Aboriginal artefacts. There was a strong incentive for convicts to steal these items, and to collect valuable natural history specimens. As convict rations were cut during the settlement's worst privations during the winter of 1788, sheer hunger drove this impulse to thieve Aboriginal objects. Convicts used Aboriginal fishing lines and hooks in an effort to obtain enough food to survive. But the officers' demand for curios also encouraged the convicts' thefts. An illegal trade in Aboriginal artefacts and natural history specimens sprang up between convicts and officers. As Daniel Southwell, mate of the *Sirius*, termed it, this traffic amounted to a 'rage for curiosity' and caused a great deal of friction between Aborigines and Europeans.[66] Collins described the process and its outcome:

> the convicts were everywhere straggling about, collecting animals and gum to sell to the people of the transports, who at the same time were procuring spears, shields, swords, fishing-lines and other articles from the natives, to carry to Europe; the loss of which must have been attended with many inconveniences to the owners, as it was soon evident that they were the only means whereby they obtained or could procure their daily subsistence, and although some of these people were punished for purchasing articles of the convicts, the practice was carried on secretly, and attended with all the bad effects that were to be expected from it.[67]

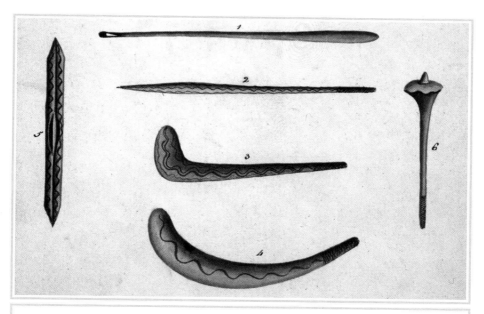

'Implements of Port Jackson'. George Raper's 1792 painting of artefacts obtained from Sydney Aborigines. A club similar to Blackburn's is shown, beneath a spearthrower. The Natural History Museum, London.

The temptation to obtain curious artefacts and zoological or botanical specimens often resulted in misunderstandings with the Aboriginal owners. As Tench so eloquently put it, before formal trade began in September 1790, it was 'a painful consideration that every previous addition to the cabinet of the virtuosi from this country had wrung a tear from the plundered Indian'.[68] Tears were followed by reprisals soon enough, as in the case of the two murdered convict rush-cutters.

In these early weeks and months, any blood spilt tended to be that of the exposed and unarmed convicts paying the price for their clandestine commerce. The sympathy of officers like Phillip, Collins and Tench, schooled in the ethics of the Enlightenment, lay not with the convicts, but with the Aborigines who had become victims of the 'rage for curiosity'. Commands were issued that Aboriginal thefts of tools, equipment and clothing were not to be punished. Aboriginal assaults on convicts were generally overlooked. For Tench, the reason for this lenience was clear:

> the unprovoked outrages committed upon [them] by unprincipled individuals among us caused the evils we had experienced. To prevent them from being plundered of their fishing-tackle and weapons of war, a proclamation was issued forbidding their sale among us, but it was not attended with the good effect which was hoped for from it.[69]

Collins expressed the same sentiment:

> Every precaution was taken to guard against a breach of this friendly and desirable intercourse, by strictly prohibiting every person from depriving them of their spears, fizgigs [fish harpoons], gum, or other articles, which it was soon perceived they were accustomed to leave under the rocks, or loose and scattered about upon the beaches.[70]

The young *Sirius* midshipman Henry Waterhouse referred to this prohibition in a letter to his father. 'While the transports are here', he wrote, 'we are under such restrictions concerning the Natives that I have not been able to collect any of their Weapons or anything else'.[71] The ban was finally lifted in July 1788, with the departure of the six convict transports for England. In the meantime, opportunists like Bowes Smyth, who was offered a stone axe while accompanying a coastal excursion during February 1788, took their chances. These were isolated events. From the time the Eora retreated from contact with the British shortly after the landing at Sydney Cove, until the 'reconciliation' which followed Governor Phillip's spearing in September 1790, there were few opportunities to collect artefacts.

'THE NATIVES ARE BLACK'

When the *Supply* was in port, Blackburn remained on board as the responsible officer but the little brig spent much time away, sailing to Lord Howe Island for supplies of turtle, or to Norfolk Island to deliver supplies and convicts. Following the disastrous wreck of the *Sirius* there in March 1790, Blackburn sailed as far as Batavia to obtain more provisions for the struggling mother-colony. For a navigator of his experience it is not surprising that Blackburn seemed more impressed with Port Jackson's climate and its harbour than with the land or its people. The country and its hinterland mystified him and left him cold. The dour summary, sent to his sister in July 1788, conveys this disillusion succinctly: 'We really know so little of New South Wales that it is Useless to Attempt to Describe it'.[72] Writing a few months later, in November 1788, Blackburn had little more to add:

> we know at present very little more of this country than we did then. The country as far as it has been penetrated affords but a Bad Prospect to the New Colony. It is a Continued track [sic] of swamps & rocky hills covered with a thin loose soil. A mixture of sand and black mould.[73]

Blackburn's verdict remained severe. He shared a 'general opinion' that the new colony 'would never Answer the Ends of Government on the Contrary [it] will be a constant & heavy Burthen on the Mother Country'. The lack of good soil and resultant incapacity of the settlement to meet its own agricultural needs was the main reason. In March 1791 he wrote:

> Our knowledge of this country is still confined to the Extent of about 70 miles along the Coast & nearly as much of the Interior Country. A few small spots of tolerable good ground are to be found but in general the country is either Immense Barren Rocks tumbled together in Large Ridges which are Almost Inacceptable to Goats or a Dry Sandy soil & a General want of Water.[74]

Blackburn displayed little of Henry Waterhouse's ebullient curiosity. That midshipman's letters home brimmed with incisive descriptions of the country and his appreciation of the uses Aborigines made of its plants and animals.

Blackburn's most memorable experience in the bush, in contrast, had been odd and unsettling. On 22 June 1791 he was with the *Supply*'s surgeon 'in the woods … about a mile and a half from camp [when] at 20 Minutes after 4 o'Clock in the afternoon a shock of an Earthquake was felt on Board the ships & throughout Camp'. At the time, Blackburn was 'standing still and silent and examining some Gum running from a large Tree'.[75] He elaborated no further on this phenomenon, and it was Waterhouse who supplied a fuller account of the tree. He had perhaps directed Blackburn to it, describing it as one of the most significant species of the colony: 'the Tree called Sanguinis Draconis from its emiting [sic] a quantity of red liquid gum seems to me to be the predominant both from its size and number, one of which I measured 27 feet in circumference'.[76] Earlier, this gum had been an object of exchange between Aborigines, convicts and officers.

Blackburn's insights into Aboriginal culture and customs began in a similar, disaffected vein. His first observations were made in July 1788, when the natives seemed as baffling as the land itself:

> The Natives are Black. They are Quite Naked & Very Dirty & are to All Appearance most Miserable Wretches. They live in Caves & Hollow Places in the Rocks & so far as we know have no other food but fish & fern Root. They almost always go armed with spears, very long & Barbed at the End with a fish Bone. We have Never been able to Persuade them to come in to the Camp or on board the Ships tho they frequently Pass & once three Canoes came alongside the Supply but would not come in. Nor will they Eat or Drink with us, nor taste any of our food. They seem to be a Harmless Inoffensive People but like all Savage Nations are Cuning & will always sooner or later Revenge an Injury.[77]

Six months later, Blackburn's ethnographic knowledge, and that of his colleagues, had barely increased. This became a source of frustration. 'We have been here now', Blackburn wrote in November 1788, 'above nine months without being able to persuade any of the Natives to live or associate amongst us, or without being able to learn a sentence of their Language'.[78] This inability to comprehend Aboriginal language seemed linked to a growing sense of frustration about the country and its barren soil, which caused crops to fail one after the other. The British were never more aware of their tenuous grip on the new land.

We cannot easily measure the trajectory of Blackburn's curiosity, his expanding capacity to understand the strange country and its alien culture. In March 1791 he sent a package to his sister, containing 'some Drawings of Birds,

Plants, & Fishes of this Country, which you make what use of you please'.[79] And by that date he had taken the trouble to copy out and annotate his abridged version of Dawes's vocabulary of the Sydney language, sending it to his Norwich friend, Richard Knight.

Blackburn's direct interest in the Aborigines was more than matched by Henry Waterhouse, William Bradley and Watkin Tench, all keen diarists. In his first letter home in July 1788, Waterhouse gave this account of Aboriginal material culture, based on his own careful observation:

> They have different kinds of spears, one with four prongs, pointed with bone or fish teeth the use of this seems to be chiefly for striking fish which they are very dexterous at which seems to be their only food the others are of one prong barbed for a foot up with fish teeth & as sharp as a needle which renders it impossible if once enter'd to get out without cutting the flesh this & the club is the only war weapon we have seen them have unless you call their stone axes so, with these & a small net in which they carry their fishing lines which seems to be made of the stringy part of the inside of the Cabbage Palm Tree & is equal to our fishing lines & a small vesel [sic] in the shape of a Canoe in which they carry their water seems to be the whole of their household furniture.[80]

Waterhouse followed this with descriptions of canoe-making, hut-building and the production of resin for use as a fixative. Founded in his natural curiosity, these detailed observations were partly sustained by Waterhouse's acquisitive interest and undoubtedly also by an awareness of ethnography's new relevance.

During August 1788 both Waterhouse and his commanding officer, Lieutenant William Bradley, observed a pitched battle from boats on the harbour. The crews rowed close enough to discern individual warriors and a range of weapons, including clubs similar to Blackburn's:

> They approach'd one another in regular well form'd bodies drawn up in squares, when at the distance of about 20 yards they began to discharge their lances which the opposite party very dexterously fend off with their shields when they were either all expended or broke they advance with their clubs which they seem'd likewise to fend off very dexterously ... we at last perceived a confusion & in the party that ran saw a spear sticking in a man's side but could not perceive any left on the field of battle owing to the intervening bushes & the midshipman that commanded the boat did not think it prudent to go to examine for fear of an ambuscade as he had only one musket in the boat.[81]

Waterhouse's reference to 'fending off' clubs suggests that they might either be thrown or thrust forward, and Bradley's observations confirm this. Writing generally about these weapons, he noted 'the Club is 3 or 4 feet long, of very hard & heavy wood of difft shapes, some are pointed so that it may be used to make a charge with as well as to give a very violent blow'.[82] Bradley's account complements Waterhouse's description, as the first carefully observed European record of Aboriginal conflict:

> the men formed into two parties & fought sometime with spears & using oval Shields, some fought with Club & sticks; when they began the Women & children screamed & ran about screaming much frightened & some of them came close down upon the beach off which the boats lay, some spears were thrown at our boats & fell so near them as to be picked up. One of the officers was of the opinion that this was a sham fight, from their holding frequent parlies & only one seen to fall.[83]

It would take European observers several decades before the difference between a 'sham fight' and regulated conflict (providing a public and ceremonial forum for the resolution of disputes) was recognised. Blackburn's whip was, without doubt, once embedded in that system of Aboriginal law.

As curious and ethnographically aware as Waterhouse and Tench, Bradley was also careful to record those brief, untidy encounters which caught and snagged at the edges of the two cultures during the settlement's first months. In February 1788 Bradley mentioned one of the first thefts from the settlement, of two shovels and a pickaxe. A few days later he documented another of Phillip's attempts to gain a moral advantage:

> the Governor here exchanged a Straw hat for a spear, which when he was taking to our Boat, another of them took hold of it, on which the man who had the Hat ran to him & explained that it had been exchanged; he let it go & seem'd pleased.[84]

Bradley and Waterhouse may have been together exploring in the bush on an occasion described by Tench, leading to some of the most extraordinary encounters of the First Fleet's sojourn at Port Jackson:

> Some young gentlemen belonging to the Sirius one day met a native, an old man, in the woods. He had a beard of considerable length, which his new

acquaintance gave him to understand, by signals, they would rid him of, if he pleased. Stroking their chins and showing him the smoothness of them at the same time, at length the old Indian consented, and one of the youngsters, taking a penknife from his pocket and making one of the best substitute for lather he could find, performed the operation with great success and, as it proved, much to the liking of the old man, who, in a few days after, reposed a confidence in us of which we had hitherto known no example, by paddling alongside the Sirius in his canoe and pointing to his beard. Various arts were ineffectually tried to induce him to enter the ship, but as he continued to decline the invitation a barber was sent down into the boat alongside the canoe ... to his infinite satisfaction.[85]

Before long other Aboriginal men were paddling their canoes alongside the *Sirius* and the *Supply* for these assignations, willingly submitting themselves to the razor, but always refusing to step aboard. These were tantalising encounters for the British officers, and especially for Phillip. For by now Aboriginal people's knowledge of their landscape had become of crucial interest. An inability to engage directly with the people, to learn their language and to comprehend their country in order to exploit its full potential as a colony, was hampering the Governor's project.

'TAKEN BY SURPRISE'

Writing to his sister in August 1790, Blackburn conveyed this sense of an impasse, and described Governor Phillip's decision to abandon his genteel attempts at engagement with the Eora: 'They will not come among us though every Method has been used to Invite them – we have had some taken by surprise'.[86]

Phillip had reached this conclusion in late 1788. On the last day of that year he had ordered Blackburn's commander to take the *Supply* 'down the harbour with directions ... to seize and carry off some of the natives'. It is likely that Blackburn navigated the ship during this operation, even if he was not one of the actual kidnap party. Their sole captive on this occasion was Arabanoo, a man of about 30 years, whom Blackburn described as 'of a meek Disposition'. He was brought to the Governor's residence and was washed, shaved, clothed and fed. 'Every blandishment was used to soothe him', wrote Tench, but when Arabanoo found himself constrained by an iron handcuff, which he had first regarded with some pride as a *ben-gad-ee* or bracelet, 'his delight changed to rage and hatred'.[87] After one unsuccessful escape attempt Arabanoo apparently became reconciled to his situation. According to Blackburn, he was 'very fond' of the Governor and seemed 'very contented', but 'for want of understanding him little was learn'd from him'.[88] Tench had a high regard for Arabanoo, describing him as 'perhaps, the only native who was ever attached to us from choice, and who did not prefer a precarious subsistence among wilds and precipices to the comforts of a civilised system'.[89] That choice was possibly fatal, as Arabanoo was still living at Port Jackson during April 1789 when a smallpox epidemic ravaged the Aboriginal population of Port Jackson.

Arabanoo perished in that epidemic, after witnessing the death of several of his people. He would be remembered as the first Aborigine of the Sydney region whose personality impressed itself upon the British. More than that, Arabanoo might also be regarded as the first Aboriginal person to provoke self-doubt among the new arrivals, concerning the application of British justice to their own people. During March 1789 Arabanoo witnessed the severe flogging of a group of convicts who had provoked a battle with Aborigines by attempting to steal their fishing gear. The intention was to reassure Arabanoo that British justice would protect his people's interests, but 'he displayed on the occasion symptoms of disgust and terror only'.[90] Once again, the frontier prism projected an inverted image.

The 1789 smallpox epidemic also resulted in a small artefact collection, so far untraced. Two survivors of the epidemic, a boy and a girl of about fourteen years, were found and brought into the settlement. The boy died soon after but the girl, Boorong, lived for the next fifteen months with the colony's chaplain, Rev. Richard Johnson and his wife, Mary. Johnson sent several objects back to England, including a girl's fur tassel apron and fishing lines and hooks, presumably belonging to Boorong herself.[91]

As historical figures, Arabanoo and Boorong pale in comparison to the 'mercurial' Bennelong, whose presence and influence among the British decisively swung the course of frontier relations towards accommodation.[92] Following Arabanoo's death Phillip issued more orders, resulting in the dramatic kidnap of Bennelong and Colebee on 25 November 1789 at Manly Cove. Blackburn was with the *Supply* at Norfolk Island at that time, but subsequently came to know Bennelong during his captivity and sojourn at Port Jackson. Colebee had escaped days after his capture, but in a letter written in the first months of 1790, Blackburn informed his sister that Bennelong 'is a Merry fellow & does not Seem inclin'd to go away'.[93]

But the presence of Bennelong as Phillip's hostage did little to break the deadlock. Aboriginal people continued to avoid the settlement. They were, as Tench put it, 'a people who would condescend to enter into no intercourse with us. The same suspicious dread of our approach, and the same scenes of vengeance acted on unfortunate stragglers, continued to prevail'.[94] The impasse continued beyond the separate escapes of Colebee and Bennelong and ended only in September 1790 with an encounter between an Aboriginal group and a British reconnaissance party under Captain Nepean. Laden with coincidence, this unfolding encounter has the character of a set piece in a frontier drama.[95]

The scene was Collins Cove, next to Manly Cove. It was the very beach from which Bennelong and Colebee had been kidnapped a year earlier. Now about two hundred Aborigines were congregated in the cove at a whale stranding. This was the same whale which had destroyed a British boat in the harbour a few days earlier, drowning its crew. On sighting Nepean's party the Aboriginal men immediately asked for metal hatchets, a request undoubtedly linked to the task facing them on the beach. Bennelong was their spokesman:

> He was greatly emaciated, and so far disfigured by a long beard, that our people not without difficulty recognized their old acquaintance. His answering in broken English, and inquiring for the governor, however, soon corrected their doubts.[96]

Expressing pleasure at hearing of Governor Phillip's presence in the harbour nearby, Bennelong told Nepean that he would send the Governor some whale meat in exchange for some metal axes. Alerted to his former captive's presence, Phillip himself hurried to Collins Cove, unable to resist the opportunity to convince Bennelong to return to Sydney. But the Governor came ill-prepared for barter, with only 'a knife, some food and other articles', and his crew was poorly armed, with only one working musket.

Meeting him on the shore, Phillip at first failed to recognise his former house guest. At Government House a few months earlier, Bennelong had been shaven and clothed, handling his cutlery with aplomb. Now Phillip was unsure of this wild-looking character, armed with spear and spearthrower. Using his rudimentary knowledge of the Sydney language, the Governor asked 'where was Benallon?' The man before him 'answered immediately that he was there; he told him that he was the Governor, his Father, which name Benallon had desired to call him by while living with him'.[97] Phillip advanced up the beach toward the larger group of Aboriginal men, 'with his hands & arms open, [but] they did not seem much inclined to come down'. Phillip was, after all, armed with a dirk and a pistol. He stepped into the woods after them, almost disappearing from sight and musket range of his boat crew.

Bennelong repeatedly called him 'Governor' and 'Father' and the two shook hands, but Phillip remained unconvinced. He called back to the boat for 'wine, beef & some presents', to remind Bennelong of the hospitality he might expect through his capitulation. Now Bennelong proved his identity, by drinking a toast to the King. He used the pidgin term, *da-king* ('The King').[98] This rendering of the English toast had already entered the Sydney Aboriginal language as the term for alcohol.

The encounter unfolded. Bennelong again demanded metal tomahawks from the Governor. Phillip agreed to supply them in two days' time, together with the clothes Bennelong had worn at Port Jackson. Having stated this though, Phillip could not resist his usual gambit. He coveted Bennelong's barbed spear, a most impressive specimen, four metres in length: 'Benallon either could not or would not understand him but took the spear & laid it down in the grass, during all which time perfect Harmony subsisted'.[99] Bennelong returned from this position and gave Phillip his spearthrower instead.

By now Phillip had been joined by two other officers from the boat, including Henry Waterhouse. These men noticed that twenty or so armed Aboriginal men now encircled them, barring the Governor's path back to the boat. Realising this, Phillip began a courteous attempt at disengagement. He proposed 'retiring to the boat by degrees', but this was countered by Bennelong's extraordinary deployment of etiquette. Collins' description suggests that Bennelong was now cannily directing events. He began introducing Phillip to more of the Aboriginal men, and in particular presented him to Wileemarin, whom Collins described as an Aboriginal 'doctor'. 'Thinking to take particular notice' of this man, Phillip stepped forward to meet him, holding out both his hands. With this action, the dynamic of this peculiarly charged encounter, weighted with ambiguity until now, suddenly inverted. Phillip's naïve gesture of friendship had been used once before, in this exact place, months earlier, when Bennelong and Colebee had been captured in this cove, lured closer by the same proffered handshake. Wileemarin became terrified. Observing this, Phillip tried to allay his fear, thinking quickly. He unbuckled his dirk and threw it to the ground. But this disarming gesture had the opposite effect, as Collins described:

> The savage not understanding this civility, and perhaps thinking that he was going to seize him as a prisoner, lifted a spear from the grass with his foot, and, fixing it on his throwing-stick, in an instant darted it at the Governor. The spear entered a little above the collar-bone, and had been discharged with such force that the barb of it came through on the other side.[100]

Chaos ensued. At first the Governor's companions believed he had been killed. They ran to the boat, then realised that Phillip was calling for the spear to be removed from his shoulder. One of the crew jumped ashore and fired the only working musket. More spears were hurled as the stricken Governor attempted to run to the boat. 'A situation more distressing than that of the governor', wrote Tench, 'cannot readily be conceived: the pole of the spear, not less than ten feet in length, sticking out before him and impeding his flight, the butt frequently striking the ground and lacerating the wound'.[101] Henry Waterhouse ran to the Governor and struggled to remove the spear, but realised that it was barbed and could not be drawn back through the wound. He desperately broke off the long shaft and Phillip now stumbled down the beach to the boat, firing his pistol, still pierced through the shoulder and believing himself to be mortally wounded.

The crew rowed frantically, as Phillip was given the last rites. He remained conscious – alert enough, in fact, to prepare his will. Within two hours they were back in Sydney Cove, where the broken spear-shaft and the barbed wooden spearhead (which had passed through his upper shoulder, well away from his lung) was removed by a surgeon. The Governor's life was out of danger.

Bennelong's exact role in the choreography of this extraordinary debacle remains unclear. It was Bennelong's own spear which had wounded the governor, and which Bennelong had placed within Wileemarin's reach. Phillip

'The Governor making the best of his way to the Boat after being wounded with the spear sticking in his shoulder'. Unknown artist. Natural History Museum, London.

was convinced that Wileemarin's action proceeded from a 'momentary impulse of fear', and both Tench and Collins supported that view: 'No other motive could be assigned for this conduct in the savage than the supposed apprehension that he was about to be seized by the Governor'.[102] Understandably, historians have been tempted by the notion that Bennelong was responsible not only for orchestrating the actual spearing, but the preceding events in which the Governor was lured to Collins Cove. The historian Keith Smith has interpreted the spearing as 'a ritual punishment against Governor Arthur Phillip, instigated and organised by Bennelong as a payback for his abduction and capture in 1789'.[103] Inga Clendinnen mounts a similar argument for a ritual spearing, 'swiftly organised over a couple of hours and with representatives from the local tribes already fortuitously gathered, where Phillip would face a single spear-throw in penance for his and his people's many offences'.[104] She rejects the 'panic/accident' hypothesis on the grounds that it bolsters the stereotype of the 'irrational savage'. But the explanations offered by Phillip and Collins suggest that on this occasion at least, they did not resort to this stereotype. Instead, they understood the situation as an unprecedented, knife-edge drama in which the very uncertainty of the characters involved (white and black), and the ill-defined protocols which were being observed and infringed, tipped events one way or the other. Tench, for example, located the crucial moment in Willemarin's alarm at hearing the unfamiliar sound of metal on stone – the 'rattle of the dirk' as it hit the rocky ground – 'and probably misconstruing the action, instantly fixed his lance in his throwing-stick'.[105]

Smith and Clendinnen propose that Phillip's symbolic prominence as a colonising figure exposed him to inevitable and formal punishment. But perhaps this proposition too neatly fits a resistance model of history rather than reflecting those 'interactive, improvisational dimensions of colonial encounters' which the multiple accounts of Phillip's spearing all suggest.[106] Instead of confirming safe paradigms of conquest, domination and resistance, the episode at Collins Cove reminds us that these uncertain frontier moments (turning on a sideways glance or a glint of metal), may offer a less determined, more contingent, explanation of historical events. In particular, the objects featuring in those encounters – such as Blackburn's whip or Bennelong's spear – emerge as more than mute witnesses. They are charged with the agency of their bearers, black and white. It is worth reflecting on how differently the Collins Cove encounter might have unfolded if Phillip had brought the metal tomahawks Bennelong had been anticipating.

Phillip now recognised Bennelong's power as a cultural broker, more than ever. Both men understood that the ground had shifted. Ten days after his spearing, Phillip had recovered sufficiently to meet with Bennelong in a genuine, if tenuous, reconciliation. Like the events which preceded it, this historic meeting on the harbour opposite Sydney Cove was captured by the Port Jackson Painter in a watercolour painting, *Ban nel lang meeting the Governor by Appointment*.

Just an hour or so before that meeting, Phillip had encountered Maugoran, another of the harbour's key Aboriginal brokers. Maugoran was the father of the girl, Boorong, who lived with Chaplain Johnson. Phillip gave Maugoran some fish and received in exchange a short spear pointed with a metal knife, 'which the natives now used when they could procure one, in preference to the shell'.[107] Perhaps it was this spearhead which was sold at auction by Christie's in London during late 1998, together with Henry Waterhouse's original account of Governor Phillip's spearing. The spearhead has the form of a European bone-handled dinner-knife blade, with a narrow tang providing an ideal means of hafting into a wooden spear-shaft. The auction catalogue described it as the actual spearhead which Waterhouse drew from Phillip's shoulder on 7 September 1790, but this could not have been the case. The contemporary accounts agree that the spear which Wileemarin threw at Phillip was barbed and wooden.[108]

'**Ban nel lang meeting the Governor by appointment after he was wounded by Wal le maring in September 1790**'. Unknown artist. Natural History Museum, London.

Portrait of Bennelong a native of New Holland who after experiencing for two years the Luxuries of England, returned to his own Country and resumed all his former Habits.

Vignette portrait of Bennelong, as dressed during his voyage to England, embellished with Aboriginal artefacts. Engraving, ca 1798. U4073, Rex Nan Kivell Collection, National Library of Australia.

A week after their reconciliation, Phillip delivered the promised metal tomahawks to Bennelong, and regained his own dirk. From this moment contact between Aboriginal people and Europeans, 'though partially interrupted, was never broken off'.[109] Bennelong came to live again in Government House, taking tea in the afternoon with Phillip, before the Governor built a small brick house for him at Bennelong Point, where the Sydney Opera House now stands. The nature of the exchanges widened to include Aboriginal labour, the sexual services of women, and a range of European goods including tobacco and, disastrously, alcohol. Aboriginal people were now commonly seen within the town boundaries, either in groups or alone. Unattended items of European property became fair game. Bennelong himself robbed a wheelwright of a tomahawk during December 1790, justifying the theft as recompense for the fatal shooting of another Aboriginal man, Bangai. Even so, when Bennelong made the first of his sea voyages to Norfolk Island during October 1791 (preceding his remarkable voyage to England with Phillip), he brought with him a traditional kit of material culture – 'his spears and fish gig, stone hatchet, bones for pointing his spears and his basket'.[110] Given Bennelong's pioneering role in brokering radical change to his own people, this was a poignant conservatism.

OVERLAP AND EXCHANGE

Aboriginal and European people stepped through the mirror of contact into each other's worlds. Blackburn's whip is a relic of that transition. Indeed, its inversion from club into whip helped to ensure its preservation for two centuries as the only identifiable wooden artefact remaining from the time of the First

Fleet. Had Blackburn retained it as an Aboriginal curiosity rather than converting it for his own personal use, the artefact is unlikely to have survived.

As a memento of a hybrid frontier, Blackburn's whip seems unique. But the historical record reveals an analogous object which was conveyed across the frontier in the other direction – from the European to the Aboriginal domain. This extraordinary, syncretic object, deriving directly from Bennelong's assertion of equivalence with Governor Phillip, was a tin-plated leather shield.

Observing the Governor's speedy recovery from his wound, Bennelong may have imagined that, as Phillip's 'brother', he could expect a similar inviolability. At their reconciliation Phillip promised him the shield in return for Bennelong's own spear – the very spear that Bennelong had laid aside and which had almost taken the Governor's life. Phillip had the shield made according to Bennelong's specifications. Composed of 'sole leather and covered with tin ... likely to resist the force of their spears', it was presented to Bennelong in mid-October 1790.[111] Bennelong was 'highly delighted' and used it in ritual conflict at Botany Bay a few days later. Perhaps he believed that it carried some of the newcomers' own magic, and would protect him from bullets as well as from spears. After all, he was now twice exposed, between two cultures. But Bennelong's status among his people as the Governor's 'double' could not last. According to Collins, the shield was taken from Bennelong 'by the people of the north shore district and destroyed; it being deemed unfair to cover himself with such a guard'.[112]

Phillip had always considered that if Aboriginal people could become accustomed to bartering goods with the British, his goals of pacification and reconciliation might be achieved. It was a unifying Enlightenment strategy, perfectly congruent with the advice formulated by the French philosopher Joseph-Marie Dégerando, whose *Observation of Savage Peoples* (1800) included the admonition to:

> influence them in our favour by kind deeds and presents ... these contacts will perhaps serve to inspire in the Savage some new desires which will bring him still closer to us ... he will perhaps attach himself to us from gratitude or interest, will call us among his people to teach them how to reach our own condition.[113]

Neither Dégerando, nor the French *anthropologues* who attempted to apply his principles during Nicolas Baudin's Australian voyage from 1801 to 1804, appreciated that a similar expectation lay beneath Aboriginal participation in the 'skilful game of exchange'. The phrase is that of the French anthropologist, Claude Levi-Strauss, who understood that the deployment of objects and favours by indigenous peoples in contact situations could also be regarded from their perspective as a civilising act – one of enlightening Europeans and taming their apparent barbarity.[114]

If Phillip's constant efforts to barter for spears were founded in the logic expressed by Dégerando, they were directed only towards the single end of disarming Aboriginal men and making them amenable to British authority. Despite his obvious goodwill, Phillip's indulgence of Bennelong did not extend to the level of appreciation of Eora language and culture demonstrated by William Dawes, whose word list Blackburn copied. The dialogues and evidence of mutual curiosity recorded in William Dawes's notebooks suggest that, among the British officers, he was most likely to have understood the risks associated with Bennelong's role as a cultural broker.

Dawes's notebooks also remind us that by late 1790 encounters between Aboriginal people and Europeans had moved from the fringes of settlement, the woods and the beaches, to the interiors of the Europeans' own homes. Dawes recorded his informal, even intimate, conversations with a number of Aboriginal people, not only with the young woman Patyegerang, but also with Aboriginal men such as Bennelong himself. Already well acquainted with Dawes, and sharing an interest in the Sydney language, David Blackburn was certainly present during some of these encounters. When Aboriginal men entered Dawes's small hut at Observatory Hill they brought their weapons, and Dawes recorded their language terms for these artefacts together with terms for his own European objects. Thus the colonists' vocabulary included the following equivalences, evidence of the way in which two cultures and their objects were beginning to overlap:

No-roo-gal Ca-my	holes made in a shield by a spear
Gnan-gnyella	a glass to look through a telescope
Tallangeele	window glass
Gnallangulla Tarreebirre	a particular club
Gna-mo-roo	A Compass (so called by the Natives, Gna – to see)
Dje-ra-bar	the name given to the Musquet – the natives frequently called us by the name they give to the Musquet.
Boo-mer-ut	the Scimitar
Ka-mai	a Spear
Wo-ma-ra a	Throwing Stick
Ar-ra-gong	a Shield made of Wood

The surgeon, Mr White, visiting Colebee at Botany Bay after he was wounded in a tribal fight. Watling Collection, Natural History Museum, London.

E-le-moong	shield made of Bark
Bill-lar-ra	a Spear with a Barb
Njunmal	they call a palisade fence by this name.[115]

It was Bennelong, more than any other Aboriginal or European individual, who enabled this cultural interpenetration. William Dawes's notes record at least one occasion on which Bennelong visited the *Supply*. During early 1791 Blackburn noted that 'when I wrote last the Natives were Very Shy, but many of them are Since come Among us … they often Come on board our ship, which they call an Island & are very troublesome for Bread, which they are Extremely fond of'.[116] By this time Blackburn's captain, Henry Lidgbird Ball, occupied a cottage next to Dawes's own meteorological observatory, which became the scene of many informal meetings between the British and the Eora. Ball was drawn into those encounters during his convalescence on shore during early 1791, while Blackburn assumed command of the *Supply*.

Following Aboriginal practice, the *Supply*'s captain exchanged names with the Cameragal clansman, Carradah, who became known as 'Mr Ball', afterwards 'corrupted into Midjer Bool'.[117] The precedent for this practice had been set by Bennelong, who had given one of his names, Wolarawaree, to Governor Phillip. Blackburn was aware of name exchange and probably experienced it himself, while drinking tea with Ball, Dawes and their Aboriginal visitors at Observatory Hill. Copying Dawes's vocabulary entry, '*Taamooly* ... to change names', Blackburn added his own comment: 'which they are very fond of doing'. Among the range of possible circumstances for Blackburn's acquisition of the club which became a whip, perhaps this setting is the most fitting.

TO WISH THE JOURNEY AT AN END

During August 1790 Blackburn had confided to his sister Margaret that he was ready to 'wish the voyage at an end & once more visit my Native Country and be happy Among the Small but Social Circle of our Acquaintance ... I shall probably feel more pleasure when I see the White Cliffs of Albion than Ever I did'.[118] Another year passed before the *Supply* finally sailed for England, sorely in need of repair. On board was an Aboriginal youth from Port Jackson, unnamed in the historical record, but possibly a young boy named Bondel, who had already travelled with Blackburn to Norfolk Island.[119]

Blackburn carried the whip with him, finally disembarking at Portsmouth in mid-May 1793. Within four months he had another posting, to the West Indies aboard the *Dictator*. In contrast to the weeks before his Australian voyage, nothing survives in Blackburn's correspondence to illuminate his hopes or fears regarding this new assignment. He fell mysteriously silent during this West Indies voyage, failing to write any of his accustomed affectionate letters to his sister Margaret or his mother. Their subsequent grief-stricken enquiries, contained in a packet of Blackburn's letters sold at auction with the club in late 1998, revealed some of that mystery. Blackburn had also fallen ill and silent on one occasion during his Australian voyage, sufficient to cause concern to his family. The cause had been a 'rheumatic complaint'.[120] This time it was more serious, a fatal consumption (tuberculosis) which gradually overwhelmed him. As a family friend put it later, 'very anxious was I on his acct, when I found that he was gone to breath the pestilential Air of the West Indies'.[121]

Blackburn had been 'extremely ill' when the *Dictator* arrived at the West Indies at the end of 1793, and 'from that period kept gradually growing worn so much so that on his arrival at Portsmouth he cd scarce walk the Deck'. The *Dictator* docked at Portsmouth in early December 1794, but out of a sense of duty Blackburn did not take to his bed until the month's end. His shipmates finally 'deemed it prudent' to remove him to the naval hospital at Haslar, close to Portsmouth, on 9 January 1795. This was where Blackburn died on the following day, aged 42 years.[122]

Blackburn had stopped writing to his family months earlier, apparently fearing that if he set pen to paper he would reveal his illness and cause his family to worry. It was a misplaced solicitude. The anguished letters which Blackburn's mother and sisters wrote to his shipmates show that his silence had driven them to distraction. In one letter, Margaret Blackburn wrote:

> I call upon you sir to give us every particular circumstance that relates to his last illness … where he was seized, what was his complaint, what the state of his mind, and intelects [sic]; whether he thought or talked much of his dear Mother and family whom soon he was going to leave forever, was he comfortably nursed and attended, where did he die and where was he buried.[123]

It was several weeks before his family learnt the truth from his shipmates and took delivery of the trunk containing his few possessions. Among these, we can assume, was Blackburn's whip.

Unlike his brother John, who was to die of shocking gunshot wounds during the Napoleonic Wars at a hospital in Leghorn (Livorno, Italy) two years later, David Blackburn had been spared the tumult of battle. As a family friend put it in a letter to his mother, soon after news of his death had reached her, Blackburn was not well disposed towards the conflicts which distinguished his times:

> I have frequently heard you speak of several remarkable interferences of provi- dence in his behalf, indeed his life has been a scene of trials, and there is no reason to think that the eye which watched over the events of his life slumbered at his death. … I have several times thought it a happy thing that he had been preserved from engaging actively in a war, to which his military engagements bound him contrary to his principles & his judgement.[124]

It is Blackburn's whip, with its grim associations and uncertain context, which unsettles this benign image of its owner, as much as it provokes a reassessment of Australia's first colonial frontier.

Bark shield found in a cave at Point Malcolm, South Australia, by the lighthouse-keeper
G.F. Edmunds. A2210, South Australian Museum.

CHAPTER TWO

Broken shields

This warped and fractured object looks like an ancient carapace. It is bowed and slightly convex, roughly oval, two centimetres thick, the size of a road-side stop-sign. Across the bark's surface four sets of opposed arcs curve to the ragged edges; russet ochre against a chalky, dusty white. The pigments have bonded to the bark like aged rock art. The shield's asymmetry gives the best clue to its original shape; the upper and lower tips have been broken off long ago. Remains of a once-pliant withy handle are still threaded through two of three sets of small holes at the shield's centre. The third set is empty. There are other scars and one pronounced hole, perhaps from a spear, near the shield's centre.

In this brittle state the shield has survived nearly 120 museum years, sharing shelf space with more burnished and brightly ochred artefacts. It was exhibited just once, soon after its acquisition in 1887. Since then it has spent most of the decades in comparative anonymity, unconnected in the minds of its curators or the public with its original owner or the circumstances of its collection. In the museum register it is described simply as 'A2210, shield, Point Malcolm, donated G.F. Edmunds'. The registration system began only in 1911 and by then the original letter (dated 29 June 1887) in which Edmunds explained the shield's background, had been separately filed. Finding this letter (bound into an old donations book in the museum strongroom), and understanding that it related to the twisted old relic, set me on this story's path. It is a tale of broken shields, and collisions between histories.

KING PETER'S SHIELD

In the faded ink of a confident longhand, Edmunds' letter explains why this object seems more ancient, more forgotten than most. He wrote:

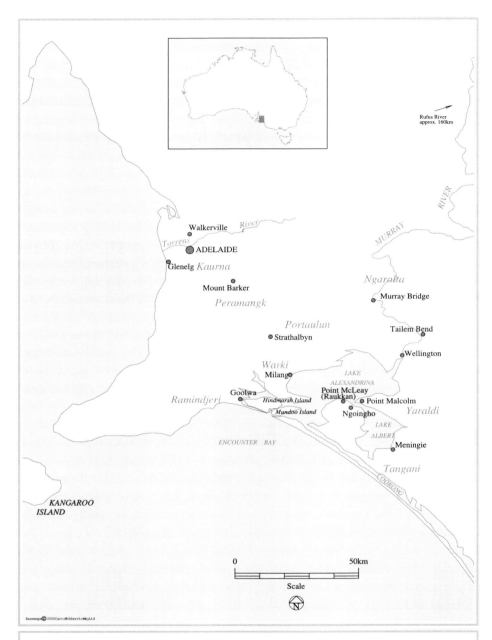

The Lower Murray and Adelaide Plains, showing places mentioned in this chapter, and names of Aboriginal language groups.

I beg leave to forward a shield found in a cave nearly buried in the crumbling debris of sandstone. The shield is broken on the lower side, has some spear holes in it, but is otherwise in a fair state for a very old shield. The old chief 'Peter' here claims it, as one belonging to his tribe, and claims it was used in a regular fight 'long long time ago'.[1]

The 'here' in the letter was the Aboriginal mission of Point McLeay on Lake Alexandrina, barely five miles from Point Malcolm. Point McLeay was G.F. Edmunds' postal address; his own residence was the Point Malcolm light-house. More than a century later it still stands on the small cliff overlooking the channel between Lakes Alexandrina and Albert, which together comprise the debouchment of Australia's greatest river, close to its mouth. Edmunds had kept the Point Malcolm light since 1880, primarily for the commercial ship-ping which passed down the Murray to the river ports of Milang and Goolwa. The river-trade was still booming, but in his seven years at the lighthouse Edmunds had time enough to explore the district and to become familiar with the Aboriginal people of the Point McLeay mission, known to Europeans as the Narrinyeri tribe.

The Narrinyeri (today's Ngarrindjeri) comprised people from at least three language groups who had congregated at the mission since its foundation in 1859. For these people, particularly the clans of the Yaraldi of the Lower Murray, the grey and green shades and soft contours of lakes and inlets, reed-beds and midden-mounds, formed an ancient mosaic, their religious landscape. Its shape-changing heroes dwelt there still, with sorcerers and devils, beguiling spirits, and a panoply of ancestors.

In mid-1887, when Edmunds decided to donate the old shield to the museum in Adelaide, he may have been aware that a group of Ngarrindjeri men, women and children were preparing to travel from the mission to visit and perform at the Adelaide Jubilee Exhibition. Perhaps it was that impending event which reminded him of the old shield, and prompted him to send it to Adelaide.

In 1887 there was more than one Peter at Point McLeay, but only one who could be described as an 'old chief'. Peter's Yaraldi name was Pullami, of the Karatindjeri clan. His traditional country was Point Malcolm itself, where the shield had lain mouldering in its cave. The Karatindjeri clan derived its name from the language term for Point Malcolm itself, Katang, and held the black swan and teal as their totemic birds.[2] Those birds are still numerous on the grey-green lake which laps the reed-swathed headland.

When Edmunds discovered the shield, Pullami was an impressive patriarch

The Point Malcolm lighthouse, ca 1885. Photographer: Samuel Sweet. B9803, State Library of South Australia.

of 80 years. He had fought his fiercest battles before Europeans settled permanently in his country, half a century earlier. According to his own account, as a young man of twenty years or so, he had met Captain Sturt in 1830. This was probably as the explorer's longboat crossed Lake Alexandrina on the way to and from the Murray Mouth. A dozen years later, following bloody Aboriginal clashes with overlanders droving cattle to Adelaide along the explorer's route, Pullami may have been drawn north to the river settlement at Moorunde, near Blanchetown, where Edward Eyre and E.B. Scott dispensed rations and blankets, together with the *pax Britannica*. Despite those inducements he may have been party to rhetorical, if not actual, moves to oust Europeans from Yaraldi country. No doubt he had heard the tales of the massacre of European survivors of the *Maria* shipwreck on the Coorong during 1840, and learnt of the massacre of Aboriginal people by mounted police at Rufus River in the following year.[3] Even so, it is difficult to imagine that, having observed Europeans in this first decade of contact, Pullami could have resisted the urge to visit Adelaide. Perhaps he was among those 'Murray River blacks' who visited

Adelaide during the early 1840s, joining ceremonial battles with Aborigines of the Adelaide Plains, Mount Barker and Encounter Bay.

Although, like others of his people who came to live at George Taplin's mission, Pullami had adopted an English Christian name, he had not embraced the missionary's faith. Despite ensuring that his children received a Christian education, he remained outside the ambit of the mission regime until his death. When Taplin wanted to speak with Pullami, as he often did, the missionary was obliged to visit him in his camp on the high ground at the mission's periphery. The mission benefactor, C.B. Young, described that camp in 1887, the year in which the shield was sent to Adelaide:

> At a short distance from the permanent buildings there were 13 large wurleys, constructed with bent pine frames, covered with sacking, in which the more casual natives were located. These huts seemed pretty comfortable, and were larger and better than the ordinary native wurley. In these were living remnants of the Coorong, Milang, Goolwa, Lake Albert and Wellington tribes. The average number of persons to each hut was about six. Many of them were of great age, some being, as far as could be guessed, between 70 and 80 years of age and two or three were supposed to be even older; these latter were quite childish. Three of these old people had been chiefs of various tribes, and there was one chieftainess with a white beard.[4]

If by 1887 Pullami had become known as a stalwart of the traditional religion, he had also been one of his people's first leaders to recognise the necessity of accommodation with Europeans. An alliance with Taplin had been an essential element of the new political and social order which Pullami had helped to broker.

Arriving at Point McLeay in 1859 as a missionary for the newly formed Aborigines' Friends' Association, Taplin's task was to form an amenable congregation from the disparate clans of the lakes and river and from further south, along the Coorong lagoon. Taplin was among the first ethnographers to record those distinct clan territories, appreciating the nuances of dialect and site affiliation which set one apart from another. He was also the first to blur these distinctions, subsuming the clans' identities not only under the larger language groups, such as those of the Yaraldi and Tangani, but under a still broader social category which may never have existed as a tangible entity – the 'Ngarrindjeri nation'.[5] Taplin's 'Ngarrindjeri language' was a mission argot probably based mainly in Yaraldi, with contributions from Tangani and

Camp of King Peter, Pullami (seated at left) at Point McLeay mission, ca 1885.
Photographer: Samuel Sweet. South Australian Museum Archives.

Ramindjeri. As early as 1860 though, Taplin noted that 'the different tribes whose languages are different now communicate in English', maintaining that these groups 'used not to communicate at all before English was introduced'.[6] The missionary's achievement in first learning Yaraldi, then preaching and writing in it, was founded upon assistance given by senior Yaraldi men such as James Unaipon of the Piltindjeri clan, and Pullami of the Karatindjeri clan.

While Taplin was unable to win Pullami over to Christianity, the Yaraldi elder recognised Taplin as an ally, someone to be relied upon to consider the interests of his people as their lands were swallowed up by pastoralists on every side.[7] There were many forms of engagement, many ways of dealing with the European presence. Some of the older men and women, including Pullami himself, kept their distance. They remained outside the bounds of the mission village and camped on the high ground overlooking the lake, rather than entering the mission economy and its regime. This decision did not prevent these influential men and women – including Pullami himself – sending their children or grandchildren to the mission school, or obtaining rations and the most desirable European commodities from Taplin. In the course of a generation this frank reciprocity had slipped into a more familiar pattern of complex but unavoidable dependence, as seen elsewhere in colonial Australia. Within the mission ambit though, Taplin did not have it all his own way. His Aboriginal converts regarded his religion through the lens of their culture, and the particular image they discerned often baffled and angered him. Most turned Christianity to their own advantage, weaving it together with those 'heathen' beliefs Taplin intended to replace.

For a year or two James Unaipon was Taplin's brightest hope. This Yaraldi man had been the mission's first convert, taking his Christian name from James Reid, the Scottish Free Church missionary who had preceded Taplin in the area. After Reid drowned in the lake in July 1863, Unaipon came to Point McLeay, offering his services as an itinerant evangelist but on particular terms –

a boat of his own and his freedom to come and go. Taplin measured the depth of his faith and was not reassured. Despite Unaipon's assistance with his linguistic efforts the missionary quickly understood that it would be the following generation, rather than these canny elders, which offered the only convincing possibility of conversion. Some elders, like Unaipon, maintained a degree of Christian faith. Others, like 'King Peter', reached for Christianity just long enough to fill the missionary with fervent hope. For Pullami this new religion was a necessary encumbrance, integral to this strange new life in a lakeside township run by serious-minded, if fickle, Englishmen.

During the first months and years of the mission at Point McLeay, Taplin could make little progress

The missionary George Taplin during the early 1860s, with a son of Pullami (probably David Laelinyeri, who died in 1865). Photographer unknown.
M. Angas Collection, South Australian Museum Archives.

without the support or acquiescence of Pullami and men like him. Pullami became a pivotal figure in the hybrid society being formed at the mission. According to the anthropologist Ronald Berndt, who worked closely with his great-nephew Albert Karloan, Pullami was the last of the Ngarrindjeri leaders to wield the particular form of concentrated, inherited power which made this group distinctive in Aboriginal Australia. Most notably, for the purposes of this story, Pullami was the leader of the Karatindjeri, the clan centred upon Point Malcolm itself, close to Taplin's mission. The 'Point Malcolm tribe', became Taplin's crucial ally during the first months of the mission. The relationship was reciprocal. Pullami enlisted Taplin's support just a month after his arrival in 1859, to arrest a 'white fellow' who had stolen fish from a pound, where Pullami was keeping them alive to sell to Europeans.

During that episode, in which the thief was ambushed and handed over to the police, another unfolded which provides a possible context for the shield in the cave. As Taplin and his 'Point Malcolm tribe' allies were taking the Englishman into custody, a group of 'Mundoo Blacks' (referring probably to the conjoined Hindmarsh and Mundoo Islands, at the Murray Mouth) attempted to steal a woman already promised to a Point Malcolm man. Taplin described the ensuing fight as the woman was taken back: 'spears were thrown, and there was a tremendous row ... the Point Malcolm blacks showed great forbearance, but the Mundoos were very bouncible'.[8]

Taplin's journal is punctuated by similar events in which direct conflict provided a resolution for traditional tensions and imbalances, now often exacerbated by the European presence. Writing in May 1861, Taplin recorded that almost the entire population of the mission, 'except for a few old woman and children' – and notably, Pullami himself – had gone to Mundoo Island for a tribal fight, and 'afterwards are going to Adelaide'.[9] The town of Adelaide, two days' walk to the north, had become a magnet for adjacent Aboriginal groups during the previous twenty-five years. For the first ten years of that interaction (as discussed in the second part of this chapter), tribal fighting with spears and shields had been a necessary accompaniment to those encounters.

Towards the end of his twenty-year mission among the Ngarrindjeri, Taplin recorded that this form of combat had 'passed away before the influence of Christianity and civilization. The old warriors died; a party grew up and became strong which was opposed to it, and at last it ceased'.[10] In the meantime though, the bulwark of custom and belief which Peter and other senior men and women personified loomed as the main obstacle to Taplin's missionary goals and (following his death in 1879) those of his son, Frederick. Even by 1887, despite healthy attendances at the mission church, a rigorous dormitory system ensuring Christian education for Ngarrindjeri children, and a Young Men's Christian Association (with its own temperance arm, the Band of Light), that conservative element remained. In George Taplin's time its most visible form was a formal council of elders known as the *yanarumi*, with powers to impose punishment, solve disputes, undertake inquests and organise major rituals. Pullami had been a key figure in that system of social control, apparently unique to the Ngarrindjeri people. Shortly before Taplin's arrival Pullami had inherited the title of *mungkumbuli*, head of the *yanarumi*, from his father, Ngakun.

Taplin had no direct knowledge of the *yanarumi* and its functions until the mid-1870s, and so it is not surprising that during the 1860s he considered Pullami's chieftainship lacking in real power. That much is clear from his diary entry of 13 August 1861, following a conversation with Pullami at his wurley:

> Peter's father was the last chief who exercised full authority in this tribe. He used to share out all which was taken in hunting and had six or seven wives, who dwelt in one wurley while he lived in a separate one. At his death his sons could not agree to give his authority to any one of their number because the paramount authority of the whites made their chief powerless. So at last they settled it that Peter was to be chief in battle but in all other respects the chieftainship ceased.[11]

In fact Pullami took little part in tribal fighting, even by Taplin's time. He deferred to his tribal 'brother' Tooreetparne, the Point Malcolm man known to Europeans as 'Captain Jack'. Tooreetparne and Pullami were probably close kin. Taplin recorded that on at least one occasion they left the mission to camp on their own tribal ground at Point Malcolm. Tooreetparne had led the Point Malcolm men against the Mundoo men in retrieving the kidnapped bride during November 1859, and Taplin wrote of him: 'although he is not officially chief yet he has a great deal more influence than anybody else, principally on account of his known intrepidity'.[12] Perhaps it was Tooreetparne's shield, rather than Pullami's, which was placed in the Point Malcolm cave following his death in November 1864.

Taplin perceived Tooreetparne as the chief obstacle to his mission, and his death marked the end of Taplin's first phase in his Christian campaign at Point McLeay. The missionary's description of Tooreetparne's death recalled that of an ancient Greek warrior:

[in] his delirium there was something in character with the intrepidity of the man ... He sat up and looked with a smile of defiance around him ... he started up and called for a spear and shield. His little son Andy took up his spear to carry to him, but of course was prevented from doing so, and the father sank back exhausted ... Last night Captain Jack died. In him his tribe loses its most intrepid and skilful warrior. The man with more like military genius than anyone I ever saw among the natives. But he was feared and hated by many as a great sorcerer. ... Alas he died a heathen and I feel that really he is an obstacle removed from my path in my efforts to save this people by preaching Jesus. His influence was against us. But I am indeed distressed at his fate, for he was a superior man intellectually. I never knew him afraid.[13]

It was consistent with traditional practice for Tooreetparne's shield to be taken back to his tribal ground at Point Malcolm, either to be placed on his plat-form burial after his body had been smoke-dried, or to be secreted in a safe place nearby, such as the cave where the lighthouse-keeper was to discover it, twenty years later.

With Tooreetparne's death, the mantle passed unmistakeably to Pullami, already the nominal leader of his people. But Pullami had no intention of playing Tooreetparne's 'intrepid' role, particularly in relation to the mission. Pullami had defined a new role for himself, recognising the mission as his power-base. He forged a relationship with the missionary, and cleared the path for his son's succession, based on Christian authority rather than the traditions of authority which Pullami had inherited from his own father. It was plain enough that those structures had become fragile and archaic within a single generation.

Taplin observed that Pullami was generally left behind at the mission when more able-bodied men set off for fights, or even on hunting, fishing or ceremonial expeditions. The missionary concluded that Pullami was too old for such expeditions, although he cannot have been aged more than 55 years. But despite his tractable demeanour, Pullami retained formidable physical strength, as circumstances would reveal, following the Duke of Edinburgh's visit of 1867. The explanation for Pullami remaining at the mission might lie in the fact that both he and his Yaraldi kin enjoyed Taplin's protection there. Under the altered conditions brought about by European presence throughout the region the risks of forsaking that protection were high. We can read that explanation into Taplin's account of the Yaraldi's reluctance to allow Pullami to leave the mission as a witness in the case against the fish thief, during late 1859:

This morning police trooper Rickaby came for Peter to go to the Goolwa as a witness against the fish stealer ... I had to assure the natives that no harm would befall him before they would willingly let him go into the territory of a hostile tribe.[14]

Taplin took advantage of Pullami's long periods of residence at the mission. During March 1860 he set him to work making a fishing net, noting that he was 'very industrious for a blackfellow'. The missionary began to have 'interesting talks' with Pullami at his wurley, realising that 'old King Peter' might assist his developing skills as a linguist. In December 1859 Taplin had written that 'words cannot express the anxiety I feel to master the native language'. Pullami helped Taplin to acquire that skill and while Taplin became confident that he had 'conveyed some ideas of religion to his mind', the missionary also became struck by Pullami's own qualities, and the strength of his character.[15] He related one incident which reflected the old man's continued standing as a traditional leader. It probably occurred during 1862:

One night Peter, the chief of the Point Malcolm tribe, was sleeping in a native hut, with a lot of other people. As he lay dozing he felt a large snake crawl up his naked body under his opossum rug. Now, he knew that if he jumped up he would most likely get bitten; so he carefully put his hand down and seized the reptile by the back of the neck and held him at arm's length. And now he felt that it would not do to throw the venomous creature from him, lest it should fall on some of the surrounding sleepers and bite them; and yet he felt that it would soon writhe itself from his grasp, so he brought the snake's head down to his mouth and gave it a crunch with his teeth, and then shouted to his friends, and they jumped up and cast it from him.[16]

There is some doubt as to whether the *yanarumi*, which Pullami headed, was entirely a traditional institution. Its formal character, recorded directly by Taplin and indirectly by the twentieth-century ethnographers Ronald and Catherine Berndt, may have evolved as a reaction to Taplin's establishment of a church council of elders during the 1860s.[17] In any event, with the erosion and collapse of traditional institutions which accompanied colonisation, the *yanarumi*'s persistence and its overlap with the church council meant that the Ngarrindjeri were better equipped to deal with those imposed political forms now weighing heavily on Aboriginal society and personal lives. By the time G.F. Edmunds gathered the shield from its cave in 1887, Ngarrindjeri literacy at Point McLeay was as high as in surrounding European farm districts.[18] Pullami was as much an agent of this new order as a defender of the old ways. He encouraged his children to attend the mission school, and clearly understood the importance of literacy. During 1862 Taplin recorded that Pullami had become worried about his eldest son, Nipper, who had gone to the Aboriginal camp at Lake Albert:

> After he was gone the old chief, his father, got anxious about him and with some pride asked me to write him a letter telling him to come back. I did so and Nipper came back. I hear that the Lake Albert people at Baker's Station were very much surprised to see a black boy read a letter. May the Lord grant that this may become common and not only this but blackfellows reading the scriptures and praying.[19]

It is not surprising to find letters of the alphabet, individually and in combination, inscribed upon wooden artefacts such as spearthrowers dating from this period. Taplin enlisted these perceptions of literacy as a potent force in his struggle to overcome 'savage customs', such as tribal fighting. In December 1863 for example, hearing that a fight was brewing close to the mission, he set out to stop it:

> So I took my glass and a piece of paper and pencil and sat down in full view of the contending parties and deliberately, by the help of the telescope, took down the names of the ring-leaders. They were Lazy Billy (Menatowe), Old Katyirene and Bailpulare Solomon. I shall send and enquire what can be done with these peace-breakers. My appearance, armed with a telescope and pencil and paper, stopped the scrimmage. Spears were lowered, warriors put down their shields and slunk off afraid of the revelations of my glass and the results of getting their names put down.[20]

During the 1860s and 1870s Pullami and the *yanarumi* elders fought a losing battle to maintain continuity in three traditional spheres: funerary rites, marriage and male initiation. Each of these rites was supported by a taut web of relationships and mutual obligation, always at risk of rupture in traditional times. Those ruptures were expressed in physical conflict – man against man and group against group – which also provided their resolution. These were set battle-pieces and individual trials by combat in which spearthrowers, light dart-like spears and bark shields were essential elements. Albert Karloan's description of a trial by combat refers to his boyhood during the 1870s when Pullami, his great-uncle, was still a man to be feared:

> People assembled in a clear place some little distance from the main camp, with the man's younger and elder brothers and father about fifteen to twenty yards behind him ... ready to stand by him if necessary or, if he were injured or killed, to carry him away. The sole defender was the man himself: he held a small wokali (bark shield) and wore on his head a thumi (hair cord) smeared with dead person's fat and of course held his spears and thrower. Before him were aligned about thirty to forty warriors who had been invited from different camps ... With them was an elder or leader who had called them together, as well as the man who had been insulted. Their intention was to kill or injure the single warrior who stood by himself.
>
> That man was defiant. Around his waist was his kanderi to which had been attached a bunch of emu feathers, red-ochred and smeared with dead person's fat ... When he dodged the spears that were thrown at him, they were deflected from his body and passed through the feathers – the feathers waved up and down as he moved.
>
> The warriors gathered before him threw their spears as the elder told them to begin the fight. The spears come thickly towards him, 'smothering him'. However, he dodged them by jumping. The power of the kunali (emu feathers) and thumi (hair cord) enabled him to jump higher, above the flight of the spears. The spears thrown by the others fell to the ground with the sound 'thump'. The one warrior waved his shield in derision calling out, 'Arr!'
>
> The others made ready to throw their spears again. He was looking for the one spear among them that was smeared with dead person's fat; this would usually find its way to its quarry because of its magical quality. He held his shield away from his ribs, his chest and the side of his body: he appeared to be unprotected. The others were waiting in readiness to throw. Then he saw that power-laden spear coming straight towards him. He deflected (yogi-an) the others with his shield. Then the fat-smeared spear hit his shield, missing his body. His power was stronger than the spear and he called out, 'Arr!'[21]

Such open, if measured, aggression was a direct threat to Taplin's ideal community of docile converts. In fact, each Ngarrindjeri rite of passage carried elements offending Christian principle, and the particular sense of moral decorum imbuing Taplin's mission. His journal records numerous forceful attempts to transform and domesticate the 'barbarous' and 'disgusting' aspects of rituals which had sustained traditional Ngarrindjeri society. At the same time, like other missionaries who understood that it was necessary to 'enter the mental world of the heathen' in order to effect conversions, Taplin sought to know the full details of Ngarrindjeri traditional life and belief. His key informant, James Unaipon, was married to Pullami's daughter Nymbulda, and in his visits to the 'wurleys' to obtain ethnographic and linguistic information Taplin also relied heavily upon Pullami himself.

Taplin knew of the pressures his evangelising efforts exerted upon men such as Pullami, who carried heavy obligations to transmit cultural knowledge and power. 'It is very evident', Taplin confided to his diary, 'that if the tyranical power of the old blacks is not checked our mission is useless'.[22] His efforts to convert Pullami's son Nipper heightened these tensions. On one occasion during October 1864, angered when Pullami failed to save him enough flour from Taplin's ration distribution, Nipper set a match to his father's large wurley with near-disastrous results:

> His mother and two infant children were within at the time and the poor things barely escaped the flames as a high wind was blowing. Some dozen dried bodies and a lot of spears and also a large quantity of clothes and blankets were burned.[23]

Taplin's passing description of Pullami's hut confirms its status as a repository for the smoke-dried bodies of significant Yaraldi people. Taplin was determined to eradicate that particular funerary practice and it is unlikely that he sympathised with this loss. He was astonished when Pullami took his son's side after this event. When Taplin refused to 'take Nipper into favour again' following the fire, Pullami ordered Taplin's Aboriginal female assistants to stop assisting the missionary at the school, and dissuaded most of the Aboriginal churchgoers from attending his services.[24] A fortnight later Taplin considered that he might have the last word, when police-troopers arrived to take Nipper away to face charges for the arson. Pullami's wife, Minkulutty, was then called as a witness, and the old man himself accompanied her to the Strathalbyn courthouse. The boy was eventually sentenced to three months imprisonment with hard labour.[25]

Released from prison, Nipper returned to the mission and was at last converted to Christianity. Now baptised as John Laelinyeri, his marriage to Witurindjina (Charlotte Jackson) defied traditional kinship rules. Taplin encouraged this transgression and celebrated the union as the mission's first Christian marriage. When the young wife's traditionally intended spouse, an older man named Fisherman Jack, later 'decoyed her away' to an island in the Coorong,

Pullami advised his son to forget about the Christian marriage. John Laelinyeri would not let it pass, and Taplin saw his chance:

> It is however necessary to show the natives that when a young man & a woman have been legally married there is a power which will protect the blacks from arbitrarily separating them. In fact it is monstrous that all the efforts of Government and Christian people should be overridden by a few old blacks.[26]

Accompanied by Pullami, John Laelinyeri, and three others, Taplin confronted Fisherman Jack on Tauwitchere Island:

> I jumped into the dingey [sic] with Nambalare and made him put me ashore. At this time the Wellington blacks & some others were all standing in a row at their camp looking very glowering & angry & with their fishing spears all stuck in a row in front of them. I could see they meant to overawe me. But it would not answer I directly walked up to the wurley where I saw Charlotte & told her to go & get into the dingey & to go off to my boat. She obeyed with an alacrity which shewed how glad she was that I had come. Then old Fisherman Jack who had been her captor when he saw she was going off to my boat seized his fishing spear and began swearing & abusing white people generally & me in particular & calling on the other blacks to rescue Charlotte from me. He shook his spear at us & did all he could to persuade them to attack us. But it was no use, the Lord would not let them. He withheld them & made them fear us.[27]

Once again, Pullami encouraged a retaliatory boycott of Taplin's church services, but now the missionary was confident that traditional custom was weakening under his pressure. 'I will', he wrote, 'steadily & with good temper set my face like a flint against their debauchery and beastliness and may the Lord be with us & help us'.[28]

PULLAMI AND THE DUKE

Taplin's journal makes it clear that Pullami's status as a tribal leader was unquestioned during the early 1860s. What are we to make then, of the fact that when the time came in 1867 for him to meet Queen Victoria's son (the Duke of Edinburgh) during his tour of Australia, he panicked and ran? On the eve of the meeting he hid in the lakeside rushes at Ngoingho in his own clan territory, across the strait from the Point Malcolm lighthouse and the cave. The ceremonies planned for the Duke's visit went ahead, with Pullami's kin and related groups performing fire-lit dances on the Lake Albert shore, in picturesque scenes reproduced in the Adelaide newspapers. A chartered steamer brought as many as 400 Aboriginal people to Point McLeay for the event, from Milang, Goolwa and other river ports.

According to his great-nephew nearly 80 years later, Pullami believed that the Duke was leading a punitive expedition to exterminate the Yaraldi and had tried vainly to warn the younger men.[30] A month earlier, Taplin had noted rumours spread at Meningie (possibly by whites), suggesting that if Aboriginal people came to Point McLeay 'when the Prince comes they will be captured and taken to an island where there are nothing but snakes'.[31] Taplin's diary entry for 13 November 1867, on the day a full-scale 'corroboree' was due to be performed for the Duke, involving the assembled tribes, confirms this apprehension:

> Old Peter took fright last night & under the impression from a remark he heard that the white people were going to carry him off to Kangaroo Island he went & hid himself in the reeds, sleeping there in the swamp all night.[32]

To the Yaraldi, Kangaroo Island was known as *Karta*, the distant spirit-land of the dead. More pertinently, in recent history the island was associated with the kidnapping of their women by sealers, particularly in the period immediately preceding South Australia's official settlement. Taplin had previously noted that several of these kidnappings had occurred at Point Malcolm itself. Perhaps Pullami witnessed these events as a boy.[33] The trigger for Pullami's flight may have been the formidable sight of the Duke and his party armed and mounted on horseback, in full fox-hunting regalia. The last force armed and mounted in that manner had been Major O'Halloran's expedition sent against the murderers of the *Maria* shipwreck survivors on the Coorong, 27 years earlier.

Pullami returned to Point McLeay the following day, apparently recovered, but three days later he succumbed to 'a fit of apoplexy' and 'inflammation of the brain ... brought on by fright'. He went to stay with his daughter who was living at a nearby station on the Lake, but as the weeks passed it became clear that he had become unhinged by this episode. Finally, on 14 February 1868, his mind snapped. Taplin wrote:

> ... Today at noon while at MacBeath's he seized a tomahawk and attacked Kitty Boord and chopped her frightfully. He inflicted nine wounds, some of them dangerous, before he was pulled off. It then took six men to hold him. He tried

to attack others and to injure himself but was prevented. Kitty's husband brought her down here and I sent her off at once in the boat to Milang to the Doctor and also sent information to the Police. This poor old madman has been going about insane for many weeks and it cannot be endured longer that he should be at liberty.

Taplin arranged for Pullami to be taken to Adelaide, to the Lunatic Asylum on North Terrace. Just before his departure on 17 February the missionary wrote:

The old man seems strong but has a very strange look … It a great relief to all of us that Peter is taken. The blacks altho' sorry are yet evidently glad he is in custody as it is dangerous to be near him. And it would have been trouble to have him roaming about the country in his insane condition.[34]

Two days later, Pullami was admitted to the Lunatic Asylum, classified as suffering from 'homicidal mania'.[35]

Pullami was not the only Aboriginal person incarcerated in the Asylum. A Mount Barker man named 'Tom Oakley', alias Paukaringara, was admitted during 1869, and another man from Point McLeay, 'Laughing Jack', was admitted for a second time during 1872.[36] The fracture of reason which made Pullami a danger to his own people was not uncommon, an unanticipated outcome of the pressure exerted as colonialism closed in on individuals, particularly those who carried traditional responsibilities of leadership. The definition of Aboriginal 'lunatics' allowed doctors to apply this judgement, occasionally avoiding the death penalty. During the mid-nineteenth century most Aboriginal 'lunatics' incarcerated among strangers, far from their kin, could hardly expect to regain their sanity, in European terms, let alone find their way back home. Luckily, Pullami was an exception.

George Taplin did not forget his old rival and adviser. Two years passed and then, on 18 March 1870, he sent John Laelinyeri to Adelaide to visit his father, 'to see if he is sufficiently recovered to leave the Lunatic Asylum'.[37] The doctors judged the old man to be cured and a fortnight later the *mung-kumbuli* returned to Point McLeay. Taplin was surprised to find that the old man looked 'very well indeed and has got quite stout'.[38]

Pullami resumed his former role at the head of the *yanarumi*, with no apparent loss to his traditional authority. His reputation may even have been enhanced by his experience of incarceration with Adelaide's most hardened lunatics. Barely a month after Pullami's return he refused Taplin's attempts to give a Christian burial to his daughter Tina. Taplin wrote frustratedly:

> I cannot get her father to bury her body. He wants to take it away and of course I cannot enter upon a conversation with him on the subject.[39]

The old men continued to store the smoke-dried bodies and Taplin found it almost impossible to visit the wurleys for that reason: 'I really think they put more bodies into the wurleys than ever. I wish this bad practice could be stopped'.[40] In fact, the tide was turning.

Pullami in about 1870, perhaps at the time of his incarceration in the Adelaide Lunatic Asylum. Photographer unknown. M. Angas Collection, South Australian Museum Archives.

By the early 1870s numbers of the old men had also begun attending Taplin's Sunday church services. Younger men held prayer meetings in their own cottages, following the example set by Taplin's native evangelists, James Unaipon and Pullami's son, John Laelinyeri. A new form of Ngarrindjeri Christianity was evolving, influenced by millenarianism, of which Taplin made cryptic mention:

> The movement amongst the old men continues. Several were at Chapel today – James says they think that Jesus will soon come and feel they are not ready. Several are anxious to give up ngadjungi [a form of 'bone pointing'] and become Christians. I have set James to talk with and instruct them.[41]

Pullami's son-in-law, James Unaipon, became the key broker. He not only transmitted Christian principles to the elders but also advised Taplin on the ethnographic details of Ngarrindjeri custom and belief for his forthcoming book on that subject. During November 1873 James told Taplin of the significance of the Ngarrindjeri creation hero, Ngurunderi, 'a great chief who led a tribe down the Darling to this country round the Lakes'. Seven months later, in July 1874, James told Taplin of 'the Judgement Council of the elders of the tribe', the *yanarumi* or *tendi*, and the qualities required of its leader:

[a man] chosen for his ready speech, temper and capacity for authority. Peter was Chief of the Tandé of the Point Malcolm Tribe. The office was not heredi-tary but elective in the lakalinyeri or tribe, the brother or son of the chief being preferred.[42]

Taplin still considered that this institution was obsolete, operating only when 'the natives were in their primitive state'. In January 1875 he finally became aware that the council continued to operate, with Pullami in the 'Tandé lewurmi or the judgement seat'. Tribal groups totalling more than 200 people had gath-ered at the mission from the Coorong, the Murray River and Mundoo Island. The *tendi* itself, held apart from the mission, comprised 46 men. These were mainly drawn from Pullami's Point Malcolm group and from the 'Coorong tribe'. Taplin's account, brief and unsatisfactory as it is, represents the only eye-witness account of this unique institution:

> At the tendi the men were arranged in two parties. On the one side was our Tribe with King Peter sitting in a very dignified manner at their head as presi-dent and on the other side was the Coorong tribe and old Minora seemed to preside over them. Several Murray and Mundoo natives sat at the side between the two parties and joined in the discussion apparently as amici curiae. There was a great talk, sometimes one speaking, at others several talking altogether. I could not learn the outcome or drift of the discussion as the talk was so confusing. If it had been English it would have been puzzling but in native it was worse. The number all talking together were often quite incomprehensible.[43]

Taplin soon discerned that the hearing concerned the attribution of responsibility (if not an actual trial) for the suspected murder of Benjamin Tippo, recently exposed by his wife's relatives as an adulterer. The missionary immediately contacted the Sub-Protector of Aborigines to investigate this apparent homicide. In taking that step, Taplin may have been struck by the fact that almost twenty years after his own arrival at the mission, and 40 years after colonisation, an Aboriginal legal system was still governing important matters. Pullami remained its respected and potent leader.

Taplin was now engaged on the final chapters of his revised ethnography of the Ngarrindjeri, to be published in the year of his death. But rather than investigating the structure and operation of the *tendi*, Taplin grasped at the single aspect which suggested a link between this institution and his own, over-riding missionary project. This was the concept of the 'Tandé lewurmi or the judgement seat'. James Unaipon (by now as keen as Taplin on creating analogies between Ngarrindjeri and Christian religion) related an anecdote concerning his old uncle, who had died many years earlier, 'before ever the gospel was preached to the natives':

> James sat by the wurley and the dying man was being held in the arms of his friends who expected him to die every minute. As he lay there he pointed upwards to heaven and James heard him say 'My tandé is up there'* My judgement is up there. It was a remarkable recognition of the judgement to come. And James says that it was no uncommon thing to hear the idea expressed amongst the old men that there was a tandé for the departed, in the heavens.[44]

The asterisk in Taplin's entry marked his later initiative to obtain translations of the phrase 'My tandé is up there', both in James Unaipon's Portaulin dialect, and Pullami's Point Malcolm dialect. Taplin incorporated these entries on the same page:

> * In the Potauwallin dialect 'Tand in amb Kiathangk waiithamb'. In the Point Malcolm dialect 'Tand in amb Keran waiirrangk-or waiiramb-'

Taplin's likely purpose in obtaining the phrase in the Point Malcolm dialect was to deploy it in his discussions with Pullami himself, hoping to sway the old man, finally, to Taplin's path of righteousness. The ploy did not work, although Pullami was an occasional visitor to church services, both before and after Taplin's death. In 1885 for example, a church official attending the funeral service of James Unaipon's daughter noticed Pullami among the congregation:

> Amongst those present was old Chief Peter, the grandfather of the deceased girl, who is upwards 70 years of age, but still hale and hearty. Peter, though not a practising Christian, has a respect for religion, and is an upright and honest man.[45]

The unofficial account of Taplin's death in 1879, following a heart attack apparently precipitated by conflict with elders over a 'moral issue' involving his son and successor, Frederick, confirms that these tensions remained close to the surface.[29] A rare surviving photograph of Pullami shows him standing with other Ngarrindjeri elders by Taplin's grave, contemplating the passing of their friend, mentor, and – often enough – their implacable moral adversary. By

Pullami with other Ngarrindjeri elders at Taplin's graveside, 2 November 1880.
Photographer: Samuel Sweet. M. Angas Collection, South Australian Museum Archives.

Detail of Samuel Sweet's photograph of Taplin's grave, showing Pullami, aged in his early 70s. South Australian Museum Archives.

then, if Pullami gave thought at all to the old shield lying in the cave at Point Malcolm, perhaps he would have linked it nostalgically with those days before the mission, when his own authority had been challenged only in combat, by others of his people.

In 1882 Pullami presided over the initiation of his great-nephew Albert Karloan, the last public affirmation of Yaraldi tradition of its kind. That Karloan was also baptised in May of the same year suggests something more than mere syncretism, that these Ngarrindjeri and Christian initiations were balancing – or countering – each other. According to the anthropologists Ronald and Catherine Berndt, no more full initiations of Ngarrindjeri youth took place in the Lower Murray.[46] That closure may have had much to do with Pullami's passing, just five years later.

So we come to 1887, the year in which Edmunds the lighthouse-keeper asked Pullami about the shield in the cave, before sending it to the museum in Adelaide. During that year Pullami and his people also received a visit from Charles Burney Young, a senior official of the Aborigines' Friends' Association which administered the mission. Young's philanthropy was practical. He liked the way the mission was run, and he saw especial promise in the Ngarrindjeri children. He approved of the way they were being taught, but considered that his own resources might work even greater changes:

> I brought away with me ... a living proof of the excellent training of the children. I only wish the majority of white boys were as bright, intelligent, well-instructed and well-mannered, as the little fellow I am now taking charge of. He is the son of our old friend, James Unaipon.[47]

This was Pullami's fifteen-year-old grandson, David Unaipon, who spent most of the following year under Young's tutelage before developing his diverse interests in physics, perpetual motion, literature and his people's political and social future.[48] Unaipon's drive to achieve success in European terms can surely be traced to the pivotal roles his father and maternal grandfather played at Point McLeay.

1887 was also the year of Adelaide's International Jubilee Exhibition, held to commemorate the 50th year of Queen Victoria's reign. Coincidentally, the Point Malcolm shield arrived at the South Australian Museum during the week in which the exhibition opened. A fortnight later the shield featured in 'Notes upon Additions to the Museum', published in the *Observer*. The sight of the shield provoked a stream of reminiscence from the anonymous journalist who had witnessed such weapons in use, either on the Murray or on the Adelaide Plains, many years earlier. He wrote:

> The old bark shield from Point Malcolm, Lake Alexandrina, is considered a most interesting donation by Mr Zietz [Assistant Director]. Looking at it one would not feel that it was safe to stand behind it with a powerful enemy in front armed with spear and wommerah ... But these implements were not used in any case to stop the spears or to ward a blow. The native depended upon the quickness of his eyes and the agility of his body. The shield would be used to divert a

Adelaide Plains man warding off spears. Original watercolour painted by William Cawthorne, ca 1843. Mitchell Library, Sydney.

spear in its flight, throwing it upward or downward as it passed its intended victim. In their mock battles, where blunt spears were used, I have seen a black-fellow jump 3 or 4 feet in the air to dodge a spear or to strike it out of its course ...[49]

Few of the newspaper's younger readers could have imagined such a sight. By the 1880s Aboriginal people were rarely seen in Adelaide. 'A solitary black-fellow and his lubra come within the city boundaries once in a while', wrote another journalist a few weeks later, 'but they are generally regarded as intruders'. This was about to change, with the decision by the Jubilee Exhibition organisers to incorporate an Aboriginal performance (including a mock battle) within the opening ceremonies.

As a consequence, a total of 77 Aboriginal men, women and children were brought from the Point Pearce and Point McLeay missions for this royal commemoration. They included relatives of Pullami himself, whose last journey to Adelaide had taken him to the asylum. The elaborate programme unfolded in the Exhibition Hall, specially prepared:

A wurley was erected of evergreens and shrubs in front of the organ, and the platform was covered with carpet. Rush mats and bags, made by the natives, and spears, boomerangs, waddies, swords, shields, and other weapons were distributed over the platform, to make the scene as natural as possible.

After demonstrations of fire-making, basket- and mat-making, consecutive tableaux of 'Savage Life' (with traditional song) and 'Civilized Life' ('Jesus loves me', sung by the children) were performed against this setting, followed by recitals of verse and choral singing. Then came the main event – a sham battle choreographed to reveal the extent of historical change affecting Pullami's people since the shield had been placed in the cave at Point Malcolm, decades before:

The people stood around the esplanade and crowded the balconies. About 9 o'clock several natives with spears and shields rushed into the enclosure from the western part of the crowd, and treated the spectators to a sham fight – such as it was. The rattling of shields and the tossing and tumbling of the aboriginal soldiers caused considerable merriment ... Presently the ranks were strengthened, but for a long time it was difficult to tell whether the attacking or defending force had the best of the contest. The wooden spears flew about in every direction, and there was a regular quarrel, and at last a man on each side was carried off the field, supposed to have been killed. The aboriginals finished their entertainment by singing 'God Save the Queen'. Throughout the utmost good humour prevailed, and nothing objectionable or obscene occurred ... The people of Adelaide could see for themselves on Tuesday evening the great alterations made in the manners and customs of the aboriginals, and if the blacks can thus be brought to comparative civilisation, it seems desirable that every effort should be made to extend mission work amongst them.[50]

With the contrast between the 'savage' and the 'civilised' evoked so clearly by this performance, Edmunds' shield might be said to have emerged from the darkness of its Point Malcolm cave only to enter the ethnographic cavern of the museum, where the 'uncontaminated savage' was prized above all. Certainly, the nostalgic associations the shield had conjured up for the *Observer* journalist had little to do with the historical pageant of the Jubilee Exhibition and its mock battles. Those memories harked back to the very beginning of Queen Victoria's reign, 50 years earlier, when warriors armed with spears and shields faced each other on the Adelaide Plains, in full view of alarmed colonists.

WILLIAM CAWTHORNE'S SHIELDS

The shield had been used a 'long long time ago', Pullami had told the light-house-keeper in 1887. He may have meant the 1860s, when he had assumed the role of *mungkumbuli* following his father's death, or as far back as the 1830s. At that time Europeans were not yet as thick as ants in Yaraldi country, and Pullami had yet to prove himself as his father's successor. The lighthouse-keeper's letter mentioned a 'regular fight'. This was likely to have been a full-scale battle, a field full of red-ochred warriors armed with barbed spears and *wokali* shields, chants and abuse filling the air before the spears flew as thickly as swooping flocks of waterbirds. European observers found these massed battles intimidating and confusing; the predictable antagonism of one side against the other splintered into individual conflicts, rarely corresponding to the initial pattern. It was apparent anarchy until some small signal, undetected by onlookers, brought a halt to the event, with no clear indication of victory for either side. European observers did not understand that the main conflict had somehow preceded the battle. For the battlefield was not so much a theatre of dispute, but of resolution. Once that resolution had been confirmed – when a certain spear had either found or slipped past its mark – the battle had run its course.

These battles were not events for European spectators and nor, for the most part, were ceremonies. These were even more difficult to follow, with their ragged, indeterminate beginnings and unresolved conclusions – a sense of rehearsal always restraining the drama. Literal accounts of these events rarely capture their true flavour. In Adelaide during the early 1840s, the best descriptions came from the pen of the anguished, ambivalent young William Cawthorne.

Aged just 20 in 1842, Cawthorne seemed old before his time, self-conscious about his presence in this infant colony, oddly lodged on the frontier between gentility and savagery. The son of a sea captain, he lived with his mother in a leaky house on the corner of Morphett and Hindley streets in Adelaide's west end. He earned a pittance as a schoolteacher and was ashamed of his poverty. He came to wish himself an Aborigine one day and to despise them on the next. Their camp was just 'a furlong away' across the River Torrens; he would cross it in the morning to be among them or bathe in it in warmer weather, sometimes catching the eye of a pretty Aboriginal girl and feeling himself sink into romantic shame. Once he saw a beautiful black swan alight on the water. His heart jumped when Aboriginal people descended upon it with clubs and spears to kill it for food. They would have done so, 'had it not been for a stupid Englishman who happened to be at the place where the bird was and threw something at it which drove the swan away just as the natives reached the banks. I was so mad with the fellow because I should so liked to have seen the Aborigines kill it'. A few days later Cawthorne knocked a hawk from a tree, 'sent it tumbling down' with a well-aimed rock, and gave it to them. He was, he admitted, 'rude and barbarous in all feelings'.[51]

If he had been anchored more securely in Adelaide society, Cawthorne's alignment with the Aborigines might have raised eyebrows. But he was an unprepossessing character, one of perhaps a dozen individuals who were attempting to learn the Adelaide Plains language and record Aboriginal customs. These men were either pursuing the hobby of ethnography or were missionaries, intent on saving the Aborigines from themselves. Few would have appreciated the nature of Cawthorne's peculiar anguish. His savage yearnings confronted the bourgeois pieties on which his betterment depended.

In the evening the sound of Aboriginal chanting reached his mother's shabby parlour and his tiny study where he sat at his desk, working on his 'native manners and customs'. Before him on the table were the objects he had obtained from his Aboriginal friends for illustration – a club, a spear, a feather plume, a bark shield. He set himself the task of drawing and describing them to produce a small book which might win him recognition, a place in Adelaide society. But it was difficult to make progress; there were always distractions. The words flowed more freely into his chaotic daily journal, peppered with sketches and confessions. He called it his 'Diarium':

> But hark! The natives are singing and dancing their wild corroboree. There is something ever soothing in that unnerving and ferocious song. Ah! oh! oh! etc. Wail on natives, louder, louder, shriller, deeper, lower. Thou art blessed above us, no care, no mental misery to afflict thee. Thy house is the earth and thy home a few branches, thy clothing the opossum's skin and thy only sorrow a hungry belly occasionally. Little does the savage of Australia [know] the many many causes of trouble and pain that the white man suffers and the 100,000 petty grievances he has to endure, of the difficulties he is often placed in by that unknown thing to thee, money. Wail on natives. Your day will come, the next generation of black men will be the servants of the next generation of white man ...[52]

Cawthorne was tormented by guilt for his people's dispossession of the Adelaide Plains Aborigines. Wary of romanticising the 'natives', Cawthorne nevertheless fell headlong into sentiment until reminded of the frontier's disturbing reality, and especially the brutality of spirit it seemed to provoke. Then he anguished for the Aborigines who had every opportunity to know the worst of his culture, and little chance of seeing its best. In early 1840s' Adelaide it was not possible to escape the raw frontier and its effects. It was there in the main street. Weary of the toll it took on his own idealism, Cawthorne still grasped at any opportunity to participate in adventure. He dreamt of expeditions, imagined shooting wild animals, even Aboriginal people themselves. He was 'wild and barbarous' in all his feelings, but the Aboriginal people of Adelaide became his 'special friends'.

The Aboriginal leaders King John Mullawirraburka, Captain Jack Kadlit-pinna and Willawilla were his frequent visitors, and Cawthorne sought their opinions on his work. Willawilla visited him during late September 1844 to ask the young white man to witness a ceremony at Cowandilla, between Adelaide and the coast. A few months later Cawthorne sketched Willawilla lying fast asleep on his kitchen floor, his spearthrower grasped to him, his club as a pillow. Later, Cawthorne was to give two of his own children Aboriginal names. At times his own attitude towards Aborigines caused him to doubt his own sanity: 'I prefer the dance of the barbarous savage to that of the polite European, and why is this? What causes me to like that which most people put down as terrifying and indelicate, which most people dislike and shun?'[53]

Cawthorne moved easily through the Aboriginal encampments, making his observations. He watched the men stripping bark from the city's trees for making the broad *wokali* shields and observed how these and other weapons were kept close at hand in the camps, ready to be snatched up in

Adelaide Plains warrior decorated for battle, late 1843. Original watercolour painted by William Cawthorne. Mitchell Library, Sydney.

a moment. Every day brought new combinations of circumstances, different simmering tensions: 'I saw two men throw, at once, both their spears at one man, who received it on his shield and the other he allowed to pass through his legs. Had a European been in his place and had the spears been real ones, he would have been transfixed, pierced through and through'.[54]

Cawthorne was protected by his pen and his power of making images. It gave him the authority to create a scene, to conjure up its characters. In July 1843 he painted a warrior, Goorongnabeer, decorating himself for a fight, arming himself with spears and a shield:

> His body was fully ornamented to his satisfaction and he gave a glance at the bystanders expressive of vanity. But now he was to accoutre himself. He soon picked up his 'Woculta' (shield) which was also painted with circular lines of red on a white ground, then the 'Uwinda' (large spear) was also put into his left hand, besides a wirri or two, which is a stick of about 2 feet long, with a knob at the end, to fight with in close combat. But now he took his 'Midlah' and 'Cootpee', the throwing spear of about 4 or 5 feet long, which is propelled by the Midlah, a handle, and placed them in his right hand. Lastly the 'Tento Yantanddanaloo' was grasped exultingly – this is a stick of about 2 feet and more long, very hard and no knob, and used entirely in single combat by striking alternately on the shoulders and held till one of them is dead or stunned. Now 'Goorongnabeer' (the native's name) gave a glance at all present, at the same time rattling his shield and flourishing his spear, cutting a warlike caper or two, and uttering a yell to be heard ever so far off to the envy of all near. The young girls thought he looked exquisite as he strode with gigantic steps towards the field of battle. The young men envied him exceedingly, the old men turned their heads away at the thought of bygone days.[55]

Cawthorne's Diarium became a rehearsal for his own grand entrance as a writer. He cast and recast his words, writing different versions of these events, all grounded in his daily experiences.

SHIELDS IN THE STREETS

During the first days and weeks of the Province of South Australia, in the high summer of 1836, the small band of settlers had looked anxiously toward the hills as they blazed with bushfires. These were lit by lightning or by the Aborigines themselves. Among the huts and tents clustered by the waterholes of the Torrens, colonists discussed what they might do if those savages came down onto the plain and besieged their settlement, fired their dwellings, murdered them in their beds. A stockade was contemplated.[56]

The weeks passed, then something unlocked the impasse. Contact was made, the Aboriginal people of the plains came into the heart of the small town, camped by the river. They began carting and chopping firewood for the settlers in exchange for tobacco, flour and even small amounts of money. Now, seven years later, Colonel Light's grid of streets and squares had become the locus for commerce and order. Disreputable and miscreant in the eyes of respectable citizens, the Aboriginal population was subject to by-laws restricting their access to waterholes, their freedom to strip bark from the trees, their nakedness, their ceremonies on the Sabbath and of course, their ritual conflict.

By the time Cawthorne arrived during 1840 the Adelaide Aborigines were receiving occasional visits from their neighbours – the 'Mt Barker tribe', the people of Encounter Bay, and even from the Murray. Adelaide Aborigines hosted these groups uneasily. Cawthorne noticed these tensions. A few days before Christmas of 1842 he heard of the arrival of an armed party of Mount Barker men and 'as a matter of course, went to see what it was all about'. He interpreted what followed as a precursor to a battle in which the *wokali* played a prominent part, adding details to his Diarium, more colour for his kaleidoscopic account:

> I saw about a 100 or more blacks ... when I came amongst them most of them were standing together & talking vehemently – after a little while an irregular line was formed by them & talking angrily as if an Enemy were before them & going through all the motions as if they were already fighting. But all at once they began running towards the place where the Adelaide tribe was sitting calm spectators – with their spears elevated – their shields clattering – & their mouths yelling & neighing – jumping, crouching, in a word making the wildest antics they possibly could – & halted a few yards before the opposite tribe at the same time forming themselves into a sort of a phalanx. On a sudden their spears were elevated & as one man they clattered their shields for a space of a minute or so & immediately & all in the same movement they covered their heads with the same forming a sort of a roof – accompanied with a noise very similar like a small explosion – this movement was performed twice & the effect exceedingly pretty – & at the last explosion* (* This noise is neither a shout nor a yell but the escaping of their breath) they all dispersed. ....[57]

In fact, Cawthorne was witnessing a ceremonial encounter preceding the participation of both groups in initiation ceremonies for the Mount Barker boys. The encounter may have had a particular historic resonance. By initiating their boys in Adelaide, the Mount Barker people may have been acquiring rights of access to the new European resources of the Adelaide Plains. Cawthorne observed that the Mount Barker people camped in Adelaide from then on, and fought with the Adelaide men against men of the Murray River.

Many years later, another English observer, Edward Stephens, recalled one of these fights. He witnessed a conflict arising from an argument over a marriage of a Murray River girl to an Adelaide man. The matter could only be resolved by battle and so 'as the sap was up in the trees as high as the blood in their bodies, they prepared for the contest by stripping the bark from the white and blue gums, in pieces of about three feet by two feet six inches, out of which they cut their shields'. Stephens followed the combatants to their position, 'a clear space of a few acres a few hundred yards to the east of Mr Gwynn's residence'. There the young man sought the refuge and vantage point of a tree, and watched the battle unfold:

> On reaching the ground, each side formed itself in single file, facing each other, separated only by a space of not 100 yards; the women and children of each tribe occupying the rear of each side respectively. Then followed more palaver ... Each side did its best to 'rile' the other ... The signal for battle was given, and out shot from both sides a volley of spears – the sharp-pointed ones used in hunting large game. These were neatly caught on the shields. The descent of the spears, as they reflected the light of a brilliant sun – both sides being moved by one impulse – and each shield catching its respective spear at the same instant the whole scene, for a moment, had the appearance of a magic temple from fairy-land, whose aerial roof was made tangible by the lines of moving spears, and supported by telamonic columns of living men ... Presently their passion became more inflamed, and then began as lively a bit of fighting as the most inveterate fire-eater could have desired, and called into play all the attention that the quick-eyed men could command. Some spears flew in graceful but deadly curves through the air, while others hissed along, like so many flying serpents, about a foot or so from the ground. The shields were now up, now down, as instant emergency required. The lines drawing closer, one of the Murray tribe had a barbed spear through the calf of his leg; the spear had to be broken to get it out of the wound. Things at this moment began to look critical, when a posse of mounted police, which had been sent for and hurriedly despatched from Adelaide, galloped forward and stopped further bloodshed.[58]

As Stephens protested in his reminiscence, he was 'not writing a romance, but ... recording what actually took place, and what I saw myself'. Cawthorne's experiences bear him out. We have the impression of two cultures operating side by side, each tolerant and even curious of the other, until the sensibilities of Europeans became so offended that a line was drawn. Then the frontier became palpable and outsiders like Cawthorne and Stephens were left straddling it.

Whether from Mount Barker, the Murray or the Adelaide Plains itself, Aboriginal people were becoming an inconvenient nuisance in colonial Adelaide, increasingly intent on its own betterment. In high summer, with its diminishing supply of fresh water, the River Torrens became a contested site. Living a stone's throw from the river, Cawthorne followed the unfolding events with fascination and dismay:

> The other night they being encamped above the bridge, a policeman came with orders to burn all their wurlies, or huts, which was done, and the whole tribe had to decamp and it was a rather a curious sight to [see] them all go, some angry, some laughing, some sullen, some jeering the police, as for instance – the Policeman looked back to see if any blacks still remained at the old encampment, two or three blacks observing it, exclaimed in a very ironical manner 'Oh yes, plenty blackfellow there, you go see', and they turned away apparently disgusted ... a black was ordered to burn some parts of the break which were not burnt. 'Oh yes <u>me</u> burn him', and immediately thrust a brand amongst them angrily. The reason for them burning them out was because they swam and made the water so dirty above the hole where the whole town was supplied from. Still I thought it was hard, that the real possessors of the land could not make a fire where they liked.[59]

Cawthorne worked on his 'manners and customs' during 1843, producing a set of sketches of artefacts and decorations with descriptions of their uses. By August he had moderated his ambitious plans for a full-scale ethnography. He was partly constrained by his own sense of inadequacy, but also by the news that two other ethnographic publications were being contemplated – by Governor George Grey, and by George French Angas, son of the Chairman of the South Australia Company.[60] Cawthorne could not hope to compete on that level. George Grey had already published on the Aborigines of Western Australia and on his explorations in that colony. George French Angas may have been as young as Cawthorne, but he was a trained artist and his father was the colony's principal financial backer. Neither man could be crossed.

Instead, Cawthorne's 'first literary child' would be 'a little book with about 20 plates entitled 'The Implements of the Adelaide Natives' … I have only the afternoon[s] to work in it and then only about an hour and a half … but if it is possible I will finish it before this year is over … The painting of the implements takes me some time for they must be done accurately and neatly'.[61] He refined his accompanying descriptions, reworking them to conform to a more objective standard, and muting his own, tremulous voice:

> Plates V, VI and VII, represent the 'Mulubakka' and 'Wocaltee' Shields which are unique and warlike in appearance more than any other implement they possess. The first signifies a Shield made of Wood as Nos. 1 and 2 of Plate V, which is a <u>side</u> and a <u>front</u> view. The wood is the first layer next to the bark of the Gum tree. The second (Wocaltee) is made of bark. This distinction is great in the thing itself; the Shield is painted with a mixture of grease and red ochre or chalk (as seen in the plates) and frequently carved like as No. 1, Plate V and No. 1, Plate VII. No. 2 of Plate VI is not painted but blackened over the fire, and the cross grooves filled with paint. The Woccaltee is made and lasts but for a fight; for the bark soon loses its moisture, the sun warping it, and so rendering it unfit for use. Some Tribes prefer the Mulubakka to the Wocaltee, and others the latter sort, because it is not so apt to break on receiving a 'Wirri' (Plate VIII). A Spear striking the Wocaltee generally penetrates and sticks in it.
>
> … The Shield is the only defensive weapon they possess, it forms rather a pretty part of their accoutrements, and the manner of handling it is peculiarly striking. In shaking their Spears, clattering their Shields and quivering their limbs, the effect is wild and indescribable, and these actions they accompany with loud shouting. The Shield is grasped in the left hand, the Spear in the right. In the attitude of defence it is held slantingly across the breast, ready to move in any direction required. Add to this a fierce grim looking face, bone thro' the nose, feather on the head, a naked body ornamented with white and red dots or stripes, and the beau ideal of a savage is pictur'd to the minds eye.[62]

Cawthorne was now confident of success, but knew he could achieve little without support and backing. He turned to the pious Anthony Forster, who had taken a missionary interest in Adelaide Aborigines, founding a Sunday school for Aboriginal children at the nearby village of Walkerville during 1844. Forster was also a financial agent for George Fife Angas.

Cawthorne also approached Matthew Moorhouse, the colony's Protector of Aborigines who had already prepared an extensive vocabulary of the Murray

River Aborigines.[63] He visited Moorhouse, hoping to learn more about the native implements he was sketching and describing, but the Protector told him no more than he already knew. Moorhouse admired Cawthorne's naïve sketches ('said they were very natural') but now revealed more of Governor Grey's plans for a large illustrated work on the Aborigines. Cawthorne came to earth with a thud:

> he is employing hands in all quarters to sketch their habits and implements . . . making a book that embraces the manners, customs, habits etc. of the Aborigines of South Australia with first rate illustrations which alone, Mr Moorhouse supposed, would cost £100 in publishing . . . he told me that the Governor did not intend bringing this said work out in this colony but when he went home to England.[64]

Cawthorne clung to that last snippet of news, believing that he might still have an opportunity to publish his own work. Then he learnt from Forster of the detail of George French Angas's proposed folio volume, to be titled *South Australia Illustrated*. In Cawthorne's words this would comprise:

> views of the Harbours, Bays, Coasts, Lakes, Rivers, Lagoons, with Mountains and agricultural scenery, and lord knows what. Natural history, birds, beasts and fishes. The history etc. etc. of the natives and etc. etc. and all illustrated. That he would be about 20 months about it. Begged for support (the idea of the thing. What aid does he need. His father rich as Job).[65]

Angas arrived in Adelaide at the very end of 1843, in high summer. For a brief time he was to become Cawthorne's closest, most-loved and most-resented friend. Three days before their first meeting on 2 February 1844, Cawthorne's *Diarium* listed thirty-five 'things that the Adelaide natives use'. This inventory probably represented the content of the young artist's ethnographic collection and is the fullest surviving statement of an Adelaide Plains 'repertoire' of material culture. Cawthorne's notes suggest that his three Adelaide Plains friends, Captain Jack, King John and Willawilla, were important contributors to this collection. According to Cawthorne, these men, who were 'the best critics in these matters', all agreed that his plates were 'naturally executed'.

Elsewhere in Adelaide, bourgeois society was forming itself into polite circles, with soirées and morning teas. Cawthorne and his mother entertained the Aborigines:

The natives often come into our house and I allow them to smoke and do what they like. One particular one always plays a dance to me, singing at the same time and going through all their evolutions. Oh it is a fine play. I like it much, although mother does not. I dress the beggar up in all the finery of the natives (which I have by me) and he becomes so excited and performs beautifully.[66]

Captain Jack was Cawthorne's 'favourite' and his main source of information: 'very kind-hearted and intelligent. I am greatly indebted to him for most of my information about his tribe'.[67] Cawthorne was to regret not acknowledging him formally when his small booklet was eventually published. During early 1844 Cawthorne taught English to Captain Jack, as payment for ethnographic data. The Aboriginal man was an irregular pupil, but felt at home with the Cawthornes. After each visit Captain Jack and his wife took their leave in the same manner, bidding them 'Good bye, Wilyamse ... good bye Wilyame's mother'.[68]

Cawthorne's first encounter with George French Angas arose from the latter's request to borrow some of his collection for the purposes of illustration. Cawthorne's description of that first meeting set the tone for a one-sided ethnographic partnership in which Angas built a corpus of finely executed watercolours based upon the younger artist's efforts:

At 5 Mother and me had tea and who, in the name of fortune, should come upon us in this precious plight but Mr G.F. Angas!!! ... I managed to bundle him into my study ... He began by saying ... that he had been given to understand that I possessed a good deal of knowledge upon the natives and their implements ... and that he would be very much obliged if I would just name a few of them. I did so. And if I would be so ... kind as to let him have a few of the implements, he now saw before him, at his house to draw from. Most decidedly, I answered, and if I would just give him all the names. Certainly. And if I would be so kind to come up to his house in the evening. Of Course. And if I would bring this, that, and the other with me. Oh, he would be so <u>very</u>, <u>very</u> much obliged to me, etc. etc. To all these 'ifs' and 'ands' I readily acceded and after each he gave a beseeching smile that would have captivated a 'hyena', let alone me.[69]

Angas took with him a small collection of objects, including the shields which Cawthorne had already painstakingly illustrated for his 'small book'. Later that evening Cawthorne visited Angas and found him working on this material:

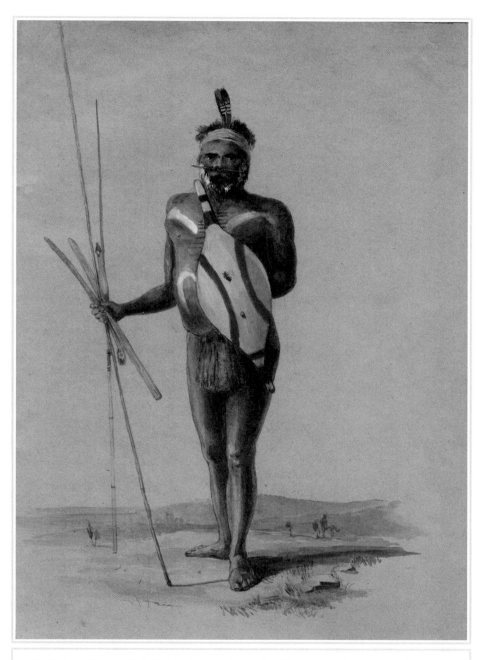

Kadlitpinna, Captain Jack. Original watercolour painted by George French Angas in Adelaide, 5 February 1844. South Australian Museum Archives.

> Before Mr Angas was a beautiful picture, with all the paraphernalia of an artist, representing 4 shields, 2 curious implements and two large bunches of emu feathers (kariwoppa) exquisitely done, with an outline of a native drawn in the centre, in the attitude of throwing a spear. He showed me many other things, equally honourable to his talent ... After tea, set to and told him the aboriginal names of all their implements and described them besides.[70]

During ensuing weeks Cawthorne fell under the spell of Angas's talent, becoming disgusted in the process with his own 'futile, puerile attempts'. Cawthorne's detailed knowledge of artefacts and their uses was crucial to Angas's project. Angas had ready access to Cawthorne's artefact collection and, through his agency, to Aboriginal people. On 3 February 1844, Cawthorne wrote: 'I am going to take Capt. Jack ... up to Mr Angas, full dressed as a <u>warrior</u> oiled, painted, decorated etc, precisely as they dress themselves when a fight takes place'. Two days later, Cawthorne recorded that he had 'marched up with <u>my</u> native dressed as a warrior to Mr Angas at 10 am'. The resultant watercolour painting of a confident, virile tribesman armed with clubs and *wokali* shield blazoned with its opposing arcs, served to define the image of Adelaide Plains Aborigines for the ensuing century and a half.[71]

Angas left for an exploring expedition with the Governor a few days after painting Captain Jack. Cawthorne returned to his journal and his own ashamed attempts at emulating Angas. The history of colonial encounter in Adelaide continued to unfold. In mid-April Cawthorne noted the arrival of Encounter Bay Aborigines, friendly to the Adelaide people. In a rare instance of 'tribal' solidarity the two groups began preparing for a battle with the Aborigines of the Murray River, aiming to repel them once and for all from the Adelaide Plains. The Encounter Bay men began 'making shields for the interesting occasion. All are in high expectancy, parading up and down the streets in small parties with their spears and cuttas, wirris and shields'.[72] Cawthorne anticipated that the battle would take place on a Sunday, but it was postponed for three days. The locality was just south of Adelaide, between the city and the original settlement of Glenelg. Cawthorne went to watch the event at about two in the afternoon with a Mr Foulkes, who was later to accompany Charles Sturt's epic 1844–1845 exploration expedition:

> At 2 pm I went down to the battlefield to see this said fight with Mr Fooks. From Adelaide I could see about 2 miles away, on the Plains, a moving body of blacks, with a great many stragglers, making towards a belt of trees. This was

Confiscated shields lying on the field of battle, south of Adelaide, 22 April 1844.
Original watercolour by William Cawthorne. Mitchell Library, Sydney.

one part of the Dramatis Personae, the other lay in the trees, quite ready to take the field. But, unluckily, the horse police got scent of the fight and three armed up to the teeth soon galloped past us to stop proceedings, which they accordingly did, without any opposition being offered, by having every spear and shield laid on the ground – and afterwards broke up. Some of the heads of spears I preserved as trophies and have them now hanging up in my study! There were a good many jagged spears and glass pointed spears, a lot of shields, besides all the etceteras. Poor fellows they were very much cut up. I pitied their hard case. Oh! it was cruel of the police.[73]

In its matter-of-fact naïveté, Cawthorne's watercolour vignette of this event is one of the most telling images of the colonial encounter. The brightly ochred shields, each with their design of opposing red arcs against a white ground, lie confiscated on the ground, ready to be smashed and trampled by the hooves of the mounted police. The clattering percussion of a hundred-shield phalanx, itself a mesmerising patterning of pulsating red arcs on a white ground, is about to be replaced by an uglier, splintered drumming. Cawthorne didn't note the fact, but the police were led by Major O'Halloran, the leader of reprisal parties on the Coorong and the Murray River during 1840 and 1841. It is likely that all the Aboriginal men present knew his identity. On this occasion no overt violence had been committed by his troops, but there could be no plainer proof of the transformation and subversion of Aboriginal destiny. While it was not the first time that Europeans had intervened against the capacity of Aboriginal people to make their own adjustments with each other, it had rarely occurred in such a dramatic and devastating manner.

The intervention was bitterly and immediately resented. No longer possessing the innocence of a bystander, Cawthorne was called upon by those Aboriginal men who had provided him with his ethnographic data, the basis of his understanding. He was visited by King John Mullawirrabirka and urged to explain the 'black man's' case to the citizens of Adelaide. The result was Cawthorne's letter to the *Register* newspaper, published on 24 April 1844, a study in shared indignation:

On Monday last, a fight was to have taken place between the Moorundee, Encounter Bay, and Adelaide natives. Great preparations were accordingly made. The young men were all in high glee – tattooed [probably a mis-transcription of 'karkoed' or red-ochred], oiled, and all ready for the coming amusement, but unfortunately they were disappointed for, as they were marching to meet each other on the old Bay road, three horse-police very unceremoniously stopped them, and had every spear and shield laid on the ground, and broken up. The astonishment that this act produced, was truly remarkable – some looked quite aghast, others were confounded, and many for the moment, I dare say, doubted their senses, whether such a collection of beautiful uwindas and shields, kylahs and midlahs, were absolutely to be destroyed. After this summary manner of settling old differences, whether right or wrong, the cry was 'What for policemen do this? When white man fight in Adelaide, black fellow say nothing. When blackfellow fight, policeman come break spears, break shields, break all no good. What for you no stop in England?' 'But what for you fight', I asked. 'What for? Me tell you', replied King John, 'but no good tell you. You write in the paper and tell white man what for we fight. Before white man come, Murray black fellow never come here. Now white man come, Murray black fellow come too. Encounter Bay and Adelaide black fellow no like him. Me want them to go away. Let him sit down at the Murray, not here. This is not his country. What he do here? You tell Captain Grey to make Murray black fellow go away, no more fight then. Adelaide and Encounter Bay black fellow no want to fight but Murray black too much saucy. Let him stop in his own country'. At the conclusion of his speech, all responded 'very good'. It seemed to be the sentiments of all, and it was the cause of their intended battle and I think that either the Murray blacks ought to be sent away to their own country, or that a proper understanding be effected between the belligerent parties. Unless this is done, there will sure to be fights and affrays ... although trivial and unimportant as they appear to us, still in the eye of the natives, they are of first importance, so much so, that force of arms can only settle the matter. And it would be more in accordance with their notions of right and wrong, were such a measure adopted, than the off-handed manner in which the police decide their differences galloping up – peremptorily demanding and breaking their 'all in all', and then threatening them into the bargain with the jail and manacles. This is not the way to raise our character in the estimation of the Aborigines – the reverse is the consequence – contempt and disgust.[74]

Cawthorne gathered up some of the broken spearheads as sad trophies. No doubt the trampled shields were too shattered to serve as souvenirs. They had taken only a day or so to make, but Cawthorne gave no indication that they were replaced by others. Too much anticipation, too much 'high expectancy', had been invested in them.

The anonymous journalist who wrote of Edmunds' shield in 1887, and of the prowess of the men who used such shields in combat, described himself simply as 'The Naturalist'. There is reason to conclude that this individual was Cawthorne himself, not simply because of the specialised knowledge of Aboriginal customs which the article revealed, but because since the 1840s Cawthorne had continued to practise as a journalist. In that intervening period he had published several small books and articles, developed a detailed knowledge of conchology, and had served on the board of the South Australian Museum. The raw sensitivities and over-mounting enthusiasms of his early prose had calmed to a sober level. But even so, when the anonymous journalist wrote that long ago he had 'seen a blackfellow jump 3 or 4 feet in the air to dodge a spear or to strike it out of its course', we might easily imagine Cawthorne's own watercolour sketch of this very scene, and see Pullami himself as the young man captured in that extraordinary moment.[75]

Hafted axe fashioned from metal abandoned by doomed members of the Calvert Exploring Expedition, 1896. A31043, South Australian Museum.

CHAPTER THREE

Turning to metal

An Aboriginal axe, small and light enough for a child, barely 35 cm long, weighing 230 grams. Its head is wrapped around by a thin withy handle of split wood, precariously cemented in place with desiccated fragments of plant resin. Probably once restrained by a loop of hair-string, the handle's ends have sprung apart: the axe is just one light blow away from disintegration. Its most durable element is the head, not stone but metal – old iron, ground to a shiny cutting edge.

The disparate Aboriginal and European elements of this decrepit object barely cohere. It takes an effort to realise that when the resin was fresh and its handle was green and pliant, it might have easily sliced a boomerang from a tree or hollowed out a precious water container. It was that imperative, to create the most efficient tools in the face of scant resources and harsh conditions, which accounted for this hybrid object appearing during the late 1890s in the heart of one of Australia's most forbidding deserts. But behind this example of efficient incorporation of European materials by Aboriginal desert-dwellers lies the story of how those materials arrived in the desert at that time, and how the failure of Europeans to come to terms with those desert conditions made its construction possible.

On entering museums, anthropological artefacts usually cease to function as souvenirs of the historical moments which projected them into the zone of contact. Instead, they become specimens of a timeless ethnography. That is what happened to this small metal axe, which joined a museum series illustrating the broad effects of cultural contact. Its particular history of transformation and shifting ownership on a remote frontier slipped from view, and its role as a poignant relic of an engrossing tragedy was almost forgotten.

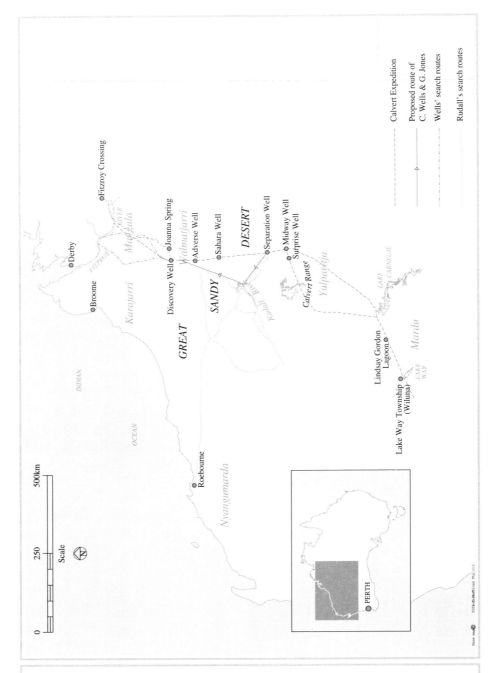

The Calvert expedition's route of 1896–1897 across the Great Sandy Desert, showing places mentioned in this chapter and Aboriginal language groups.

The general circumstances of the axe's collection are known, well enough, evoking one of those absorbing tragedies of Australian exploration in which vigorous white men came to grief with a remorseless inevitability, trapped by their own decisions in the desert sand as surely as Scott was gripped by polar ice. Unaware of the network of desert waters around them, and unable to connect with the Aboriginal people for whom the forbidding, parched desert was home, the victims lay themselves down to perish, prayer-books and last letters clutched close to their breasts, guns at their side.

According to the museum register this axe was collected on the Fitzroy River, in north Western Australia. The Fitzroy became the northern base of the surviving members of the Calvert Scientific Exploration Expedition as they mounted a series of searches for their lost comrades from November 1896 to May 1897. But this provenance was a poor assumption on the part of museum staff, who were surely aware that the expedition's own scientific collections had been abandoned in the desert to the south. In fact, this axe and other hafted metal tools were obtained much closer to the scene of the lost explorers' final demise. The metal axe, in particular, was one of the clues which finally led the last of six search parties to that 'scene of awful desolation'. It was labelled as a police exhibit before it was catalogued as an ethnographic object.

An elegy of the doomed explorer, defeated by the harsh land or by its fickle Aboriginal inhabitants, has resonated through Australian colonial history. The refrain began before the Burke and Wills expedition of 1860–1861, although that fiasco established its verse and cadence through a combination of key images, objects and imagined moments (the missed rendezvous, the Dig Tree, the lock of hair, the vial of nardoo seeds). Before the Calvert axe sank into anonymity in a museum cupboard it also held that resonance, as a memento mori, evoking a chain of tragic circumstances not dissimilar to those of the Burke and Wills expedition. In the words of Reverend James Jefferis at the memorial service, the 'sad calamity' of the Calvert expedition, 'for which all Australia mourns, is the old, old story of the advance guard of the race, toiling with bleeding feet in the desert ways, and toiling often to death in order that the millions might safely follow'.[1]

But the Calvert axe is more than a relic of an emerging pioneer mythology, which Jefferis was ready to enlist in his impassioned advocacy of a federated Australia.[2] The object also evokes a less familiar theme. It recalls a time when Europeans travelling beyond frontiers of settlement reached desperately for Aboriginal technologies and solutions to aid their own survival, and a time when a scant supply of European commodities exerted a remarkable and compelling attraction for Aboriginal people as they relinquished the stone tools of past generations, and turned to metal.

THE LAST BLANK SPACES

According to Albert Calvert, its sponsor, the Calvert Scientific Exploring Expedition had the objective of filling in the 'last blank spaces on the map of Australia'. During the early 1890s a map of these spaces was produced by the South Australian branch of the Royal Geographical Society. By traversing and mapping Western Australia's Great Sandy Desert between the upper Murchison and Fitzroy Rivers, the Calvert expedition was to traverse the largest of those blanks. The Society proposed three main justifications to Calvert for selecting this desert:

> Geographically, because of the existence of a string of salt lakes trending away to the north-west of Lake Macdonald; because, too, possibly high ranges of hills may be found in the north-easterly part of its area. You yourself have traversed its north-west area, and, therefore, know what exists there.
>
> Historically, because Baron Sir F. Von Mueller is of opinion that possibly traces of the long-lost Leichardt may be found there; and should your expedition unravel the mystery of his fate, it would be a good deed.
>
> Commercially, because, through the eastern part of space C will probably be found a stock route, if there is to be one, opening communication between our Northern Territory and North-west of Queensland with the goldfields to the south-west of Western Australia.[3]

It is extraordinary that such a weighty project should be entirely funded by a 24-year-old adventurer, but by late 1895 Albert F. Calvert had already undertaken three expeditions into north-western Australia and had gained a fortune from the Western Australian goldfields. Among his fifteen publications were books on the Western Australian Aborigines and the European discovery of Australia. His decision to fund a major exploring expedition (estimated to cost £5000) arose from his most recent enthusiasm, a book on Australian exploration. For his own name to be inscribed alongside Leichhardt, Sturt, Eyre, Burke and Wills, it simply required Calvert's expeditioners to complete their part.[4]

Calvert was not the only philanthropist to have scented immortality in these western deserts. A year older than Calvert, David Carnegie was another young Englishman who had made his fortune in the goldfields. He had learnt enough bushcraft to equip his own expedition. His party of five men and nine

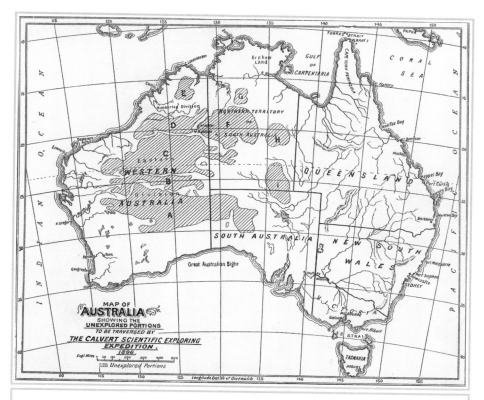

The last blank spaces – the Royal Geographical Society's map of the 'unexplored portions of Australia, prepared as a justification for the Calvert expedition, ca 1895 (Hill 1905).

camels set out from Coolgardie on 9 July 1896, just a week before the Calvert expedition, and also aimed to forge a stock route from south to north. Remarkably, the two expeditions took little account of one another until the Calvert expedition foundered. Despite the loss of one man through a shooting accident, Carnegie's expedition could be judged a success. It covered more country, mapped more features and produced much of ethnographic interest, but as a private expedition without official backing it attracted little attention. Predictably, Carnegie did not feature in Calvert's own history of exploration.[5]

With an eye on posterity, Calvert engaged the South Australian Branch of the Royal Geographical Society to equip and organise the expedition carrying his name. He specified that its instructions should be 'on precisely the same lines as those issued by the Elder Scientific Exploring Expedition' of 1891–1892, which the Branch had also organised.[6] The Society's secretary, the Adelaide 'armchair ethnographer' A.T. Magarey, became Calvert's agent and organised the multitude of detail required to send the expedition into the field. For Magarey and his colleagues, Calvert's venture was an opportunity to redeem the Society's reputation, which the mismanaged Elder expedition had severely tarnished.[7] Magarey assured the young sponsor of his place in Australian history:

> the Calvert Exploring Expedition would fill up the Map of Australia, & finish for ever the roll of territorial expeditions. Noone can follow after for nothing remains to be done.[8]

Calvert himself was not tempted to accompany the expedition and remained in London. He accepted Magarey's recommendation of the experienced surveyor Larry Wells as the expedition leader, commanding a party of six men and twenty-four camels. This party was large enough to be divided into two groups on occasion, a strategy Wells had adopted when he had taken over leadership of the Elder expedition, to enable more of the 'blanks' to be filled. Other members included the leader's cousin and deputy Charles Wells, the cook James Trainor and two Afghan cameleers, Bejah Dervish and Said Ameer. The expedition's scientific brief was addressed by the naturalist George Keartland (who had accompanied the Horn Scientific Expedition of 1894), and the young Adelaide School of Mines student, George Lindsay Jones. He was engaged as 'Scientist representing Anthropology, Mineralogy & Photography'. As his middle name suggested, Jones had other qualifications for joining the expedition, even as an inexperienced eighteen-year-old. His mother was a sister to David Lindsay, the explorer (see chapter five). His father, James W. Jones, an eminent surveyor, had explored the Nullarbor Plain and was a founding member of the Royal Geographical Society's South Australian Branch. During 1887 (when George was aged just nine years), James Jones had proposed the motion that all the society's branches 'unite in securing the due exploration of the present unknown portions of the interior of Australia'. At the time of the Calvert expedition, during which his son would die of thirst, Jones was the colony's Conservator of Water.[9]

An official photograph taken before the expedition left Adelaide (including Magarey, but without Said Ameer and James Trainor, who would join them later) shows a composed, confident group, ready to confront the wilderness. 'Everything conceivable has been done', wrote Magarey. 'We may claim, I believe, that a more perfectly selected and equipped expedition to do Australian exploration, has never been sent away'.[10] After a farewell service in

Members of the Calvert expedition photographed in Adelaide in early 1896.
Seated: C.F. Wells, L.A. Wells, G.A. Keartland. Standing: G.L. Jones, Bejah Dervish,
A.T. Magarey (expedition organiser, did not accompany the expedition).
Not included: Said Ameer, James Trainor. B9758, State Library of South Australia.

North Adelaide's Congregational church (in which memorial windows to the expedition would be dedicated 40 years later), the party sailed by coastal steamer to Geraldton, 400 kilometres north of Perth. They obtained their camels from Afghan traders at Mullewa, 100 kilometres inland, and officially began their journey at Cue, 250 kilometres further north-east, on 19 June 1896. A cable announcing this fact was sent to Albert Calvert's telegraphic address, 'Spinifex, London', just as he was about to deliver the second volume of his Australian exploration history to his publisher. Calvert completed his book with these words:

> My deep interest in the exploration of our great Australian Continent, and my gratification at being connected, even – if I may so term it – as a non-combatant

in this warfare against the hostility of the wilderness, is my apology for referring at some length to the newly-started expedition.[11]

After reaching the gold prospecting camp at Lake Way, a further 120 kilometres to the north-east, the camel train finally wound into the desert on 16 July. The cooler months had almost passed, and Wells knew that he had lost valuable time. Despite that, he divided his party almost immediately, and conducted a wide survey of country already partly traversed by the Elder expedition, and by Ernest Giles and John Forrest during the 1870s. With the searing summer heat and the tallest desert dunes still ahead, Wells was squandering his best chance of crossing the Great Sandy Desert.

Wells was unable to engage an Aboriginal guide who knew the desert and its cryptic signs, or could act as an intermediary with its inhabitants, the Mangala and Martu peoples. An Aboriginal boy agreed to join the expedition at Lake Way, but left a fortnight after, soon after they entered the desert. From that point the explorers were obliged to rely on their own crude deductive powers. Tellingly, Wells did not adopt a single Aboriginal name for the desert's features until he felt obliged to capture Aboriginal guides, once disaster struck.[12]

Despite publishing a small book on Western Australian Aborigines four years earlier, Calvert had not outlined any specific ethnographic project for the expedition.[13] This was formed largely through chance encounters and discoveries, and suggestions from A.T. Magarey, who had published scientific papers on Aboriginal tracking and water sources. He had a particular interest in smoke-signals and message-sticks, and encouraged George Jones to investigate these subjects.[14] Magarey also placed photography firmly on the expedition's agenda, noting that Calvert had specified that one of the expedition members should be 'a competent photographer'.[15] Photography had been considered 'a very weak point' in the Elder expedition, and in fact no Australian exploration had used photography to good effect, in spite of David Lindsay's fine intentions (discussed in chapter five). Magarey made this suggestion to Calvert:

> 2 or 3 Kodaks should be taken with sufficient supply of film for the journey. Natural features – trees – natives – weapons – specimens of native paintings etc etc could be secured in picture form at least: so adding immeasurably to the value & interest of journals (& publications thereof).[16]

George Jones responded to these challenges. On the eve of the expedition's departure from Lake Way he visited the Aboriginal camp and 'measured and photographed some of the natives', no doubt observing the procedures suggested in the Elder expedition's handbook of instructions.[17] These glass-plate negatives did not survive the expedition. Nor did his sketches and photographs of 'native rock drawings' in the gorges of the Calvert Range, which half of the party visited during the 800-kilometre 'flying trip' during August and September. These were among the first photographic records to be made of desert rock paintings, and certainly the first of this remarkable site.[18] At an old Aboriginal camp nearby, Jones and Larry Wells happened upon an isolated skeleton. Wells described the subsequent acquisition:

> We were surprised to find here the skeleton of a human being, in a hollow scraped out in the sand, with old dry boughs pushed into the ground, presumably to form a shade. The bones and skull were bleached, the latter being perfect except for one missing tooth, which we found afterwards. I suppose this to be the skeleton of an aboriginal, but it is the first instance in which I have known natives to leave their dead without burial of some kind. It is possible that, the water failing, the natives may have been compelled to go away, leaving an invalid behind. Mr Jones took possession of the skull for scientific purposes.[19]

The smoke-signals which expedition members noticed at this point indicate that they were being shadowed by small, mobile bands of Aboriginal people, who were probably attempting to decipher the explorers' movements and motives, and who must have taken account of the metal and other new and useful materials carried by the expedition. The party's removal of a skull, together with the unprecedented consumption of water by men and camels at particular wells and the toll taken on local wildlife by the naturalist's firearms, might have been expected to polarise relations. When the reunited party returned to the main depot after the 30-day 'flying trip', finding evidence that an Aboriginal ceremony had occurred there, Wells interpreted the evidence of blood-letting and the trodden ground as 'perhaps a little witchcraft foreboding us ill luck for our having taken possession of their water & slaughtered their wildfowl etc'. But when they encountered three Aboriginal men seen here a month earlier, these men gave no indication of ill-will. They were as friendly as before, and Jones succeeded in bartering some handkerchiefs for their 'only articles of dress, waistband and headgear'.[20]

These were rare meetings, and Jones obtained few other artefacts through direct contact. Most of the references which he and Wells made to Aboriginal people during the weeks which followed were to more cryptic traces – tracks, smoke-signals, fragments of artefacts lying in old camps, and scarred trees. The trees at isolated soakages often bore evidence of removal of bark for wooden containers and scoops used for digging out the wells. On one occasion the muffled passage of the camels brought the explorers within a stone's throw of an Aboriginal man and a woman seated together, absorbed in the task of carving out one of these essential artefacts. They 'bolted into the mulga scrub', leaving their tools and weapons behind. Wells 'deemed it best to leave them undisturbed'.[21]

In early October the discovery of an Aboriginal well sufficient to water the camels and fill the party's kegs gave Wells the confidence to suggest that the expedition split in two again. The parties would reunite about 300 kilometres to the north, in the vicinity of Joanna Spring, which had only ever been tentatively mapped by its discoverer P.E. Warburton. The leader's cousin, Charles Wells, and George Jones would firstly head north-west from Separation Well for about 130 kilometres, before turning north-east towards this vague rendezvous. If either party failed to locate the other, or Joanna Spring, they were to continue north to the Fitzroy River.

In the days of relative ease before the expedition divided, Charles Wells and George Jones experimented with water-collecting methods, referring to A.T. Magarey's publication on the subject.[22] The expedition leader summarised the pair's investigation wrily, with no presentiment of its relevance:

> My cousin and Mr Jones spent some hours extracting water from the roots of the bloodwoods ... in order to find out whether sufficient could be obtained to save a man's life, if he were lost, and without a drink ... they found it hard work. They were not very successful, only procuring altogether about half a wineglassful of fluid, whilst they drank a much greater quantity from the kegs to enable them to continue work. On the return of Mr Keartland and myself from a ramble after birds, my cousin said he thought that in reading 'The Aborigines Water Quest', they had probably missed some important injunction, and that perhaps the tap root should be manipulated.[23]

Jones's own, unpublished account confirmed that the method might, in fact, save lives:

> With first lot of roots we were not very successful but starting on another tree I ran a root out for about 8 feet, and breaking it into several pieces succeeded in obtaining about half a wine-glass of clear water. It tasted very sweet and fresh.[24]

Two days later he tried again, cutting the lateral roots of three mallee trees, but with no success.

On 11 October the two parties bade each other farewell at Separation Well. Charles Wells and George Jones set off on their fateful traverse. The pair took the best three camels, light equipment, provisions for a month and 60 gallons of water in two pairs of kegs and their water-bags. This supply of water was considered generous, more than enough for the journey to the Fitzroy River. But the two men were soon in trouble, struggling against soaring temperatures and the burning sand. During the first two days they passed numerous

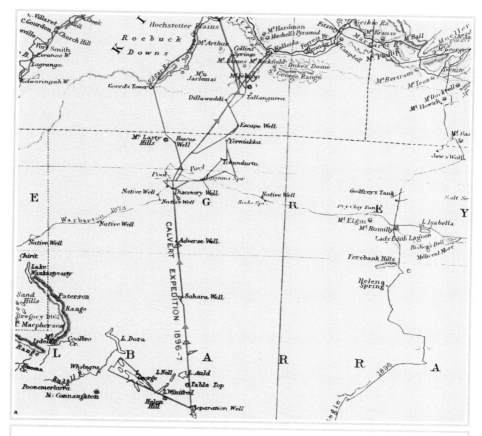

Detail of the northern route of the Calvert expedition across the Great Sandy Desert, showing Jones and C. Wells' western traverse from Separation Well, the routes of rescue parties south from the Fitzroy River to the vicinity of Joanna Spring, together with portions of Warburton's 1873 route and Carnegie's 1896 route (Wells 1902).

Aboriginal campsites, then entered more saline country with no suitable camel feed. The three animals rapidly lost condition. Facing a long salt lake with a 'shining surface of spotless white' blocking their north-eastern traverse, the two men retreated to Separation Well, arriving near dawn on 20 October. Both were ill, perhaps as a result of over-eating 'water bush' (the desert succulent, parakylia). They rested at the well for five days, before making the decision to follow the main party on 25 October.[25]

Meanwhile, by 17 October the position of Larry Wells and his men had also 'become most serious owing to the intense heat, the sand-ridges, and need of both food and water'.[26] Struggling over the 'glaring red sandridges' which lay at right angles across their path, they saw freshly burnt patches of spinifex, marked with a confusion of tracks which Aboriginal hunters had made while pursuing small mammals and reptiles. Small bands of Mangala people were leading their normal lives as the heavily laden explorers lost further momentum. Signal smokes could be seen in several directions. On 19 October Lawrence Wells sighted the elusive Aborigines who seemed to be shadowing him. He used 'all his powers of persuasion', but this extended-family group of a dozen men, women and children vanished over the sand-ridges. In their haste the men took only their spears. The next morning, before enlarging the soakage at which the Aboriginal people were camped (and dubbing it 'Sahara Well'), Wells took the opportunity to inspect the objects they had left behind:

> I noticed amongst their implements a piece of sharpened steel or iron fixed up as an axe, a large quantity of different varieties of acacia seeds, and a preparation of these made into a paste and ready for cooking. There was also a dish of berries resembling small melons, with hairy rind; these, I notice, grow on small bushes around here.[27]

Despite the remote locality and the minimal European contact experienced by these desert people, the axe was not the first metal implement to be noticed here. During his 1873 expedition through this region P.E. Warburton had recorded that a group of six Aboriginal men visited one of his camps and, despite being watched 'with the utmost care and closeness, as we thought ... they were too much for us ... [and] stole an axe'. In an Aboriginal camp to the west Warburton had noticed an old iron tomahawk and later 'a small bit of hoop iron sharpened at one end, like a chisel'. He considered that the hoop iron might have derived from the water kegs which the explorer Augustus Gregory had abandoned on the eastern fringe of the Great Sandy Desert in 1856.[28] Metal was considered rare enough in this huge desert to be traceable to particular historic moments and personalities. This held true for another generation, until the Carnegie and Calvert expeditions. It is possible that the hafted axe which Wells noticed at Sahara Well was constructed with metal circulating among the desert people many years after its initial acquisition from an explorer.

A few weeks earlier, and just 250 kilometres to the south-east in the same sandy desert, David Carnegie had also noticed metal crafted into Aboriginal objects. On 29 September he bartered with Aboriginal people for two hafted metal axes, one made from 'the half of a horseshoe, one point of which was ground to a pretty sharp edge'.[29] This axe, and another acquired at the same locality, were subsequently figured in Carnegie's published account. Two weeks earlier he had obtained 'an old iron tent-peg, the lid of a tin matchbox, and a part of the ironwork of a saddle on which the stirrup-leathers hang'.[30] Carnegie's opinion was that 'trade from tribe to tribe sufficiently accounts for the presence of such articles as tent-pegs and pieces of iron'. Subsequently the Victorian police magistrate to whom he sent these iron relics advised him unequivocally 'that the tent-peg was the property of Dr Leichhardt', the legendary explorer whose inland expedition had vanished in 1848.[31]

Leichhardt's fate was one of the Calvert expedition's stated objects of enquiry, but the discovery of anomalous metal objects did not arouse Lawrence Wells' curiosity, and he did not entertain the possibility that Leichhardt had ever entered this desert region. Indeed, in contrast to Carnegie's account, Wells' expedition journal rarely strayed from the task at hand. Wells' published account was leavened only with strangely apt verses from 'Australia's poet', Adam Lindsay Gordon, after whom Wells named a waterhole on 23 July. On the basis of his prosaic nomenclature of desert waters – 'Surprise', 'Midway', 'Separation', 'Sahara', 'Adverse', and 'Discovery' for example – it would be easy to dismiss Wells as an archetypal, anglophile explorer whose insensitivity to the landscape's Aboriginal dimension brought on disaster. But he was a better bushman than that, and Wells' own attempt at poetry confirms an appreciation of the desert landscape more complex and sympathetic than those names suggest. His rueful ode to the spinifex or 'porcupine grass' which tormented his party was written just four days after the parties separated. It was not included in his published account. The poem and its introduction, describing spinifex as an irksome but integral element of the Australian landscape, are worth quoting in full, if only for the reminder that it was spinifex resin which enabled the desert people to successfully haft their stone and metal axes:

We camped at a few desert gum trees, after clearing the porcupines, which we frequently have to do. One cannot move without coming into contact with this aggravating grass, predominating and flourishing alike on ridge, of stone or sand, or flat. One may wonder why such an enormous area should be covered with such useless growth. But on reflection it can be seen that this vast and dreary wilderness would in reality be a most barren desert, but for the porcupine. For it impedes the drift of sands and afford the only shelter for the game or vermin, which are the source of supply for the heathens who inhabit this inhospitable region, and but for which they could not possibly subsist.

At nightfall the solitude of the surroundings is broken by the chirping of myriads of crickets which find shelter, under these wiry bunches, from an over-powering sun.

'Triodia irritans'
All Nature – clad with porcupine
Bristling points so superfine
Finding repose in clothes or skin
Adding to mortals' suffering

But uses has this wiry weed,
Which Cattle serves 'ere shedding seed
The dusky savage a gum extracts,
For fixing woomera, spear or axe

Shy wallabies, rats and bandicoots
In search of lair precisely suits,
Refuge from eagle or cannibal band,
Throughout this dreary desert land.

The cricket's shield from cruel Sun,
'Ere myriad chirps when night's begun.
Does impede the drift of burning sands
Our Creator's 'Triodia irritans'.[32]

Two days after he and Charles Wells returned to Separation Well, George Jones pencilled a brief note in his journal. He seemed to have partially recovered from the ordeal of the 'flying trip' and was taking an interest in his role as an expedition member once more: 'Made a bough shade and got things snug around camp, found piece of native boomerang amid old camp fires'.[33] It was to be his last journal entry. Three days later, on 25 October, the pair set off to the north, trailing the main party. They must have realised very quickly that this trek would be even more taxing than their earlier traverse to the west, which had generally followed the sandhill valleys. Now they were crossing sand-ridges up to 30 metres high, as many as five to a kilometre. The heat was rising above 40° Celsius by mid-morning.[34]

It is remarkable that the pair managed to reach the agreed destination, the vicinity of Joanna Spring. By that time, perhaps a week later, they were on foot and rapidly failing. The scribbled note later found next to Jones's body told the sorry tale:

after severe trials one of the camels died so we have had to walk we are both very weak and ill. The other two camels are gone and neither of us have the strength to go after them. I managed to struggle half a mile the day before yesterday but returned utterly exhausted. There is no sign of water near here and we have nearly finished our small supply have about two quarts left so we cannot last long. Somehow or other I do not fear death itself. I trust in the almighty God. We have been hoping for relief from the main party but I am afraid they will be too late.[35]

It was not unreasonable for the pair to hold out some hope of being rescued. Although they had lost several days by doubling back to Separation Well and resting there, Jones and Wells were less burdened by equipment and were probably making up lost ground, perhaps even doubling the main party's average daily mileage. The main party had also been delayed, twice taking 36 hours to bale out more than 50 buckets of water for their camels, using a single pannikin in narrow wells. Their travelling time was restricted to the cooler hours, at night. Lawrence Wells was forced to abandon the great bulk of his equipment on 26 October at Adverse Well, named not only for the hostile reception he received there from a band of eleven armed men, but as a reference to one of Gordon's poems. On the following day, close to the stated rendezvous, the leader abandoned the balance of the equipment, and all the expedition's natural history collections. Wells' decision merited a regretful diary entry:

Mr Keartland, who has displayed so much energy in attending to his duties must also feel it hard to part with all his treasures, but Lindsay Gordon says:

> With adverse fate we best can cope
> When all we prize has fled;
> And when there's little left to hope,
> There's little left to dread.[36]

Among the abandoned collections were the ethnographic objects and mineral specimens gathered by George Jones.[37]

Lawrence Wells considered that having reached the vicinity of Joanna Spring (not actually located until a later search expedition) with no trace of the 'flying party', it was reasonable to push on to the Fitzroy River, 200 kilometres to the north. His hope and expectation was that the missing pair had already arrived there. Wells' own party was perilously short of water and the decision could not be delayed. Even so, he and his men did not leave the vicinity of Joanna Spring until the evening of 31 October. By that time it is quite possible that George Jones and Charles Wells were only half a day's march away, and that their smoke-signals were among those which the main party noticed to their south-west.[38]

George Jones and Charles Wells died just 25 kilometres west-south-west of the permanent waters of Joanna Spring, on the saddle of a prominent ridge. Other soakages were close by, part of a network of desert waters used by small, interconnected bands of Mangala people. The pair would lie on that ridge for seven months, until the last of four search expeditions led by Lawrence Wells reached the scene from the Fitzroy River. Two other expeditions were mounted from the west by a Western Australian surveyor, William Rudall. Extraordinarily, Rudall's interrogation of Aboriginal people led him to the bodies of two murdered white men at the eastern end of the Opthalmia Ranges, but these were unknown prospectors, rather than Jones and Wells.[39]

It was only when Larry Wells decided to adopt the technique routinely used by Carnegie throughout his expedition – of capturing Aboriginal individuals and forcing them to reveal water sources – that his northern search parties yielded results, months later. During the third search party, Wells was finally led to Pikarrangu, Joanna Spring, by a man named 'Lirmi'. It was, he wrote on 10 April 1897, a 'beautiful water', with 'shelving limestone sides and a pool in the centre'. One of the Aboriginal men camped there wore 'a girdle of native string over which hung a piece of tweed'. Wells recognised it instantly as 'the exact pattern of a pair of trousers my cousin had taken with him when he left me'. Suddenly, after almost six months of frustration, the puzzle of his companions' disappearance seemed about to be solved:

Without asking questions, I took hold of the tweed, when 'Lirmi' said 'Purrunng white fellow', pointing in a Westerly direction. The other natives repeated this, laughing, in which I joined, so that they should not be suspicious. I asked if there was one white man dead ('Untu white fellow purrunng') when they all replied 'Kutharra purrunng', holding up two fingers. Pointing to the sun they said 'Parra white fellow purrunng', thus informing me that the sun had killed them.[40]

Wells arranged for Lirmi to lead his party to the scene on the following morning, but found that their guide and his fellows 'had all decamped'. 'I almost wish now', Wells wrote, 'that I had broken my promise and chained one of these fellows up to make sure of a guide'.[41]

Wells was now in a desperate mood. Two days later, when he came upon Aboriginal people camped south-west of Joanna Spring, he was tempted to use violence to obtain a guide. What caused him to show restraint was the most important discovery so far – a geological map which he had given to his cousin six months earlier, a complete array of metal objects belonging to the pair, and several pieces of metal adapted for use as Aboriginal tools. Among these, it seems, was the hafted metal axe illustrated on page 90. Wells collected all these objects, and named the site 'Discovery Well'. But without a willing guide he could make no more progress. Unwittingly passing within 400 metres of the bodies, his small party returned to Joanna Spring.

Two months later, Wells undertook the final search expedition with Sub-Inspector Ord and Trooper Nicholson from the Fitzroy River police station, three native trackers, and the Afghan cameleer Bejah Dervish, who would live to tell tales of the Calvert expedition more than 40 years later. On this occasion there were to be no half measures. En route to Joanna Spring they captured two Aboriginal men, a 'wizard or doctor rejoicing in the name of "Yallamerri"' and a 'bold-looking customer' named 'Pallarri'. Several pieces of iron were found in Yallamerri's camp, 'including a large piece of a part of the bow of a camel riding saddle . . . sharpened at one end, evidently for use as an axe'. The pair were handcuffed together and were forced to keep pace with the horses and camels as the party moved towards Joanna Spring. Reaching it, Sub-Inspector Ord made sure that they would not escape. Wells wrote:

The natives are fastened to the tree by means of chains padlocked round their necks, and their legs are fastened with handcuffs. They have a break of bushes and some firewood, the nights being cold now.[42]

Sergeant Ord's photograph of Yallameri and Pallari, chained to a tree at Joanna
Spring on 26 June 1897, one day before leading the party to the explorers' remains.
B61249, State Library of South Australia.

Ord's hazy photographs show the two Aboriginal men, manacled and bemused,
awaiting the next unpredictable moves of their captors. It was 24 June, Queen
Victoria's birthday. Wells and the troopers drank her health in whiskey.

Wells reflected upon the unwillingness of any of the Aboriginal people,
including their captives Yallamerri and Pallarri, to direct him to the bodies of the
missing men. Although he suspected that this reluctance may have resulted
from 'foul play' in which his companions lost their lives, he recognised that
the more likely cause was cultural, or spiritual: 'No doubt they are afraid and
naturally think we are in quest of the equipment our friends had, and cannot
understand our coming after the bodies or bones of dead men'.[43]

At last, on 27 June, a day after leaving Joanna Spring, the two 'guides' led
the party to the high point of a sand-ridge, with a low saddle on which the
bodies lay:

Ord's photograph at the scene of Wells' and Jones' demise, 27 June 1897, showing Said Ameer packing the camels. The camel at left is bearing the body of one of the dead explorers. B61225, State Library of South Australia.

The natives, now at the foot of the ridge, exclaimed in one awed breath 'Wah! Wah!' I could then see my cousin's iron-grey beard, and we were at last at the scene of their terrible death, with its horrible surroundings.[44]

Sub-Inspector Ord's photographs convey the desolation of the scene and its random disorder. For Lawrence Wells this was a long-imagined tableau, laden with meaning and imbued with symbolism. He regarded his cousin's body and shed a tear. 'Looking at my cousin as he lay on the sand, with features perfect and outstretched open hand, I recalled the time we last parted when I felt his hard, strong grip'.[45]

Charles Wells had apparently left no note, although his prayer book lay nearby. Lawrence Wells filled the gap. His journal entry for this occasion contained two verses from 'Gone', the famous poem penned by Adam Lindsay

Gordon on the unveiling of the Burke and Wills statue in Collins Street, Melbourne:

> With the pistol clenched in his failing hand,
> With the death mist spread o'er his fading eyes,
> He saw the sun go down on the sand,
> And he slept, and never saw it rise.
>
> God grant that whenever, soon or late,
> Our course is run and our goal is reach'd,
> We may meet our fate as steady and straight
> As he whose bones on yon desert bleached.[46]

Forty years later this last verse would be inscribed on a memorial window in Adelaide's Brougham Place Congregational Church, where the expedition had received its blessing in 1896.

George Jones had been the first to die. His body lay a few metres away, in a shallow grave apparently dug by his friend. The young man had produced his own epitaph. It was written on the piece of paper addressed to his parents, which also contained the rough account of the pair's last days. Jones had revealingly misquoted the famous verse uttered by 'brave Horatius' in Lord Macaulay's 'Lays of Ancient Rome', a poem which rang in the ears of British Empire schoolboys. He had written:

> How can a man die better
> Than facing fearful odds
> For the ashes of his fathers
> And the country of his God.

The final line of Macaulay's verse should read 'And the temples of his God'.[47] It is tempting to read significance into George Jones's error. In a letter to the eighteen-year-old at the beginning of the adventure, A.T. Magarey had assured him that 'God is with you in the desert as with us in the City', but perhaps the young man had found it to be god-forsaken after all.[48]

The bodies were sewn up in canvas for the final journey home and the elaborate funeral awaiting them in Adelaide, with all its echoes of the Burke and Wills finale. Lawrence Wells and his party picked over the site during the afternoon, searching for any more clues. They noted that Charles Wells' journal and plans, sextant, compass, artificial horizon and star charts were all missing. The expedition leader wrote:

> The natives have rifled the spot of everything that would be of any service to them. They have by some means cut up and removed the whole of the iron from the riding saddle, and taken all the hoops from both pairs of water-kegs, fire-arms etc.[49]

Leaving the site, Wells and Ord kept Yallamerri and Pallarri with them for another four days as they searched for nearby waters to add belatedly to the expedition's record of discovery. Finally, on 31 May 1897, the pair were set free:

> Presenting the natives with knives, handkerchiefs, some food and water, we liberated them, telling them they could go back again to 'Djillill'; they stood on the first sandridge and watched us out of sight.[50]

As Tim Bonyhady has described, the mythology of Burke and Wills continued to evolve during the late nineteenth century. In December 1862, when the remains of those two explorers had passed in procession through Adelaide en route to Melbourne, thousands of people lined the streets.[51] Now, 35 years later, two of Adelaide's own sons were returning. The funeral was a testament to the potency of the exploration myth, a unifying force at this critical period in Australian history. More than 5000 people attended the service in the Exhibition Building on North Terrace and heard the stirring, patriotic sermon delivered by Rev. James Jefferis, one of the principal advocates of a federated Australia. The funeral procession itself was a mile in length. According to the *Observer*, its 65 carriages and vehicles took 27 minutes to pass a given point. The crowd was 20–30 deep along its route and numbered at least 50,000 people. The cortège not only contained anyone of significance and power in Adelaide society, from the heads of the public service to the military; it also included a veritable who's who of Australian exploration. Representatives of every major Australian exploration, including Sturt's 1844–1845 party, Goyder's 1869 Northern Territory Survey team, Lindsay's Elder expedition party and, of course, the Calvert expedition survivors, all marched together to the final resting place at the North Road Cemetery.[52] There the remains of Charles Wells and George Jones were lowered into the same grave.

A small committee was established to devise a suitable memorial for the two explorers. Here the parallels with Burke and Wills end, for despite initial public enthusiasm, the committee failed to agree on a recommendation. The austere marble monument erected over the grave suggests a restrained compromise. Perhaps the imminence of a new century, and the newly federated identity of Australia helped to place the exploration myth firmly in the past. For the Royal Geographical Society in Adelaide, the expedition was unambiguously the last of its kind, as its society's President, Simpson Newland, underlined just months after the funeral:

> The Chapter of Australian Exploration closes as it began, with deeds of splendid endurance and courage, with deeds of awful suffering, and with the loss of heroic lives. I say 'closes', for it cannot be supposed that any other expedition will ever be fitted out, for there is nothing more to discover. The blanks still to be traversed may wisely be left to the squatter, the prospector, and other hardy adventurers to fill up when good seasons and opportunity occur.[53]

Forty years later, the death of Lawrence Wells during the mid-1930s may have revived the idea of an additional monument, and it was finally agreed to install memorial windows in North Adelaide's Congregational Church. The stained-glass design, depicting the expedition's camel train winding across a desert expanse, together with names of George Jones and Charles Wells, and an inscription incorporating the final verse of Adam Lindsay Gordon's ode to Burke, was dedicated in 1937. The sole survivor of the expedition, Bejah Dervish, was brought south from Marree for that event.

In the meantime, the metal axe collected during Wells' third search expedition, the metal objects confiscated from Yallamerri, and a selection of other artefacts, including two examples of bark sandals worn by the desert people as protection against the burning sand, found their places in museum cupboards and display cabinets.[54]

ENCOUNTERING METAL

A metal axe hafted in Aboriginal fashion encapsulates the frontier more than most hybrid objects. To its Aboriginal maker, undoubtedly skilled in hafting and using stone axes, the metal blade represented a quantum leap in efficiency for all its intended tasks. Those included chopping and shaping the hard wood required for making boomerangs, spearthrowers or wooden containers, stripping bark, or chopping out tree trunks for possums or for sweet 'sugarbag' (honeycomb). The last might seem almost a frivolous use for an object as sombre and weighty as a stone axe, but among the multiple congruences observed by the

Detail of one of the memorial windows dedicated to Charles Wells and George Jones in the Brougham Place Uniting Church, North Adelaide, showing the expedition camel team traversing the desert. Photographer: P. Jones.

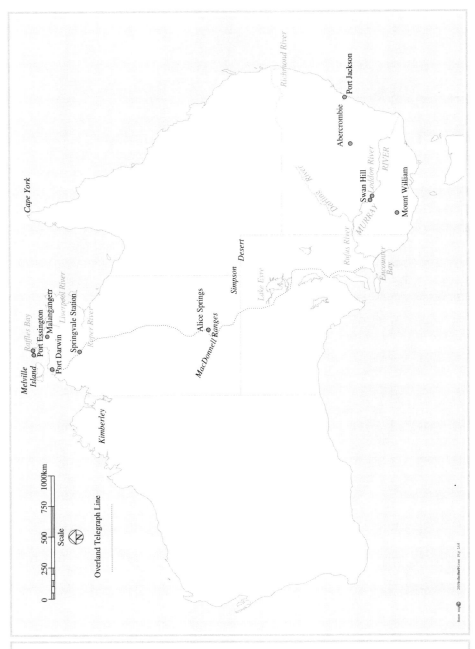

Localities mentioned in chapter three.

anthropologist Norman Tindale was this remarkable fact: the occurrence of edge-ground axes in northern Australia neatly matches the distribution of the stingless Trigona bees, which store their honey in hollow eucalypts and other trees.[55]

Axes are among the most evocative artefacts. In all their associations they suggest the frontier. It is thought that man did not venture out of Africa until an adequate hand-axe had been developed. Stone axes enabled those first human colonisations, just as the ringing of metal axes against virgin forest signalled the opening of New World frontiers, millennia later. In 1992, at Malangangerr in the Northern Territory, archaeologists excavated an edge-ground stone axe-head dated to 24,000 years ago. Some time before this, ancestors of Australian Aborigines brought edge-ground axes (probably mounted in handles) with them from south-east Asia. But axes brought by the earliest arrivals, about 50–60,000 years ago, were without handles. At the time of first European contact neither Tasmanians, who are thought to have been descended from those pioneers, nor Aboriginal people of south-western Australia, used edge-ground axe technology. A map of Aboriginal axe distribution suggests Cape York in north-eastern Queensland as an entry point for edge-ground axes, with bands of distribution radiating south and west to a boundary running diagonally from the Kimberley to Port Augusta.

Hafted in wooden handles or hand-held, chipped or edge-ground stone axes were fundamental elements in the material culture of northern and Central Australia for at least 20,000 years. Stone axes are more ponderous and much less efficient in the short term than iron equivalents, but constant use against wood does not blunten a stone axe; it actually sharpens it. The effectiveness of a stone axe derives as much from the mass behind it as from its edge. Of course this sharpness never approaches that of an iron blade, but a stone axe-blade has the advantage of durability. Against that advantage was the fact that stone axes were laboriously won from their original matrix. Suitable stone (usually diorite) had to be quarried and roughly shaped in particular, remote localities. Then it was transported, worked and shaped from an obdurate lump into a form which could be hafted into a wooden handle. Only after hours of grinding – stone against stone – did its cutting edge reach an acceptable minimum. Iron, in contrast, was ready to use and, relatively speaking, sharp in an instant.

Metal was known and used in Central Australia by Aboriginal people from the mid-nineteenth century. It had travelled ahead of explorers, being exchanged and circulated along trade routes together with other valued objects. In northern

Australia, contact with earlier European expeditions and the annual visits of Macassan trepang fishermen accustomed Aboriginal people to an array of new commodities including metal, cloth, glass and tobacco, but in sufficient quantity to stimulate a pervasive protocol of barter. Elsewhere in Australia, metal circulated only in the smallest quantities, ahead of the European frontier. Until the Overland Telegraph Line and its infrastructure arrived in Central Australia during 1871, sources of supply were inseparable from white men themselves. It was not possible to obtain metal except by engaging with white men, face to face, object to object, in direct exchange – or to steal it. Even twenty years after the Telegraph, metal axes still represented a durable unit of value in Central Australia, controlled by Europeans.

During the 1890s Francis Gillen, telegraph station manager, magistrate and anthropologist, became known to Aboriginal people in the Alice Springs region as a likely dispenser of prized metal tomahawks in exchange for ethnographic data. Writing in March 1896 to anthropologist Baldwin Spencer, Gillen related that a 'very old and celebrated Railtchawa from the northern side of the West'n McDonnells [sic] – about 80 or 90 miles distance – is here on a visit to me in quest of tomahawks etc'.[56] Gillen observed the direct effect of his interventions as a cultural broker on traditional patterns of production and exchange. His fieldwork with Spencer highlighted a special irony: the European commodities most intensely desired by Aborigines seem to have facilitated the pair's elicitation of the Aboriginal traditions and ceremonies most coveted by Europeans. During the 1901–1902 expedition Spencer and Gillen set up a 'trading table' as soon as they reached a new Aboriginal camp, as a necessary precursor to making records of ceremonial rites. Gillen wrote:

> In a very few years the stone weapons of these central tribes will be a thing of the past and I am afraid we shall contribute very largely to their extinction by distributing iron tomahawks & knives. With the present generation of middle aged men the art of making the implements will pass away, there will soon no longer be any necessity for their manufacture as the white man's tools are so vastly superior & they are gradually coming into general use owing to the annual distributions made at the various Aborigines depots at the Telegraph Stations throughout the continent.[57]

As the history of the Calvert axe suggests, metal was desired at the very instant of contact. For many Aboriginal people the mystery of the white man's appearance and the reason for his presence may have been of less concern than this remarkable material which he brought to the frontier and placed tantalisingly within reach. If the precise origin of iron was a mystery for Aboriginal people it required no solution; it was simply brought by white men.

The lure of metal drove Aboriginal people to discount the risks in obtaining it as well as the subsequent impact on their own, internal, social relations. In southern Australia, this can be observed from the early encounters between Aborigines of Sydney and the First Fleet, as the first chapter has shown. Writing of the subsequent period of contact in the Richmond River area, north of Sydney, a settler observed:

> It must have been a very weary business, cutting an opossum out of a hardwood tree, with a stone axe, and so the blacks thought; and when the whites first came the blacks would kill a white man, or run the risk of getting shot themselves to get possession of the axes and tomahawks they saw were so very superior to their own.
>
> Most of the early settlers on this river were cedar getters, and they found that the blacks were constantly watching them from the surrounding scrub and would rush and seize their axes even a few yards from them, taking the chance of a shot from the exasperated owner of the disappearing tool.[58]

A wealth of anecdotal evidence in the exploration record suggests that the prospect of obtaining metal might entirely reorient frontier encounters, by defusing hostile situations, or charging friendly meetings with danger or risk. Metal instantly became the highest stake in barter, with an unprecedented capacity to influence the protocols of exchange. Joseph Hawdon's 1838 journal of his overland expedition from Melbourne to Adelaide provides an example, documenting an encounter with Aboriginal men near the Loddon River:

> One of their party was very anxious to get a tomahawk, and offered me in exchange one of his spears, his boomerang, or his old opossum-cloak, or the whole of them together; but finding these insufficient, he at last offered to go and bring his wife, and make her over to me in exchange for the desired implement![59]

Hawdon's party established the route for overlanding stock from the eastern colonies to Adelaide, along the Murray River. Three years later, the Rufus River massacre was precipitated by concerted Aboriginal attacks on the heavily laden expeditions now traversing this route. Norman Tindale observed that the Aborigines of the Rufus 'knew the Europeans had tomahawks, blankets and food, and they were determined to take them, let the consequences be what they might'.[60] Joseph Hawdon noted two instances of the effect which the acquisition of a metal axe might produce on an individual. In the first instance, he bartered a tomahawk with a Swan Hill man, for two nets:

> I gave him in return an iron tomahawk, in which he was perfectly enraptured, leaping in the air with delight, and scarcely able to believe his senses that he was the master of such a treasure. (A European receiving such an unexpected fortune could not have been more completely overjoyed.) With the tomahawk he would be enabled to cut out the opossums and other animals living in hollow trees, which constitute a great portion of their food. This work they frequently perform with an instrument made of stone, but it is only certain kinds of trees that they can thus cut into.[61]

In the second example, not far from the Darling's junction with the Murray, Hawdon made a gift of a tomahawk to the leader of a group of forty men. The man expressed delight:

> Taking my hand, he placed it on his breast, and pointing to a little boy, his son, and gradually raising his hand above the boy's head to the height of a man's stature, he by these signs gave me to understand that he would keep this toma-hawk for him and give it to him when grown up, to hunt opossums with, at the same time imitating the manner in which these animals were taken and killed.[62]

Here we have an indication that metal axes, like the stone axes they supplanted, were not regarded as common, or readily alienable, property. While they were certainly traded across wide distances, particular axes were associated with individuals during their lifetimes, and might lie with them on their death. Aboriginal burials often incorporated the deceased's treasured objects. The value of such offerings is most obvious in localities where stone tools were regarded as exotic items, such as at a central Simpson Desert site visited by this author, many kilometres from any source of stone, where unblemished edge-ground axe-heads mark three separate burials. Undoubtedly, metal axes also entered this sacred domain. The South Australian Museum holds two iron tomahawk-heads which had been placed with other metal objects on the mid-nineteenth century grave of Miranda, 'King of Burra Burra', near Abercrombie south-west of Sydney. In south-eastern Australia stone axes hovered on the edge of sacrality, invested with their owners' qualities as well as reflecting the objects' rarity and the skill required to mine and shape them. For the Ramindjeri of Encounter Bay in South Australia, the *mokani* diorite axes traded from the distant axe quarry at Mt William in south-western Victoria, were objects of enchantment.

Metal and stone axes formed part of a category of Aboriginal artefacts less readily exchanged than most secular tools and weapons, but outside the inalienable class of sacred objects. Unlike Aboriginal objects and substances, such as particular woods, shell, ochre and stone, there was no totemic relationship to metal, no essential affinity. The anthropologist Lauriston Sharp noticed this for the Yir Yoront of Cape York: the metal axe 'has no distinctive origin myth, nor are mythical ancestors associated with it. Can anyone, sitting in the shade of a ti tree one afternoon, create a myth to resolve this confusion?'[63]

On the one hand, under certain conditions, metal objects joined the great pool of tradeable artefacts in Aboriginal Australia, passing along chains of connection and obligation linking Aboriginal individuals to others, even beyond their social horizons. The metal tomahawk-heads and cutlery found at Miranda's grave were probably relics of a fluid colonial traffic which extended across the early nineteenth-century frontier. On the other hand, metal in Aboriginal society seems to have become an instantly efficacious, but disturbing element. We can observe the great craving which Aboriginal people like Bennelong possessed for metal, and how this craving skewed and transformed encounters with Europeans, but the Aboriginal relationship to this new substance is poorly understood.

One thing is clear. A commodity as desirable as a metal axe did not take its place within the Aboriginal material culture repertoire without disrupting the social order. In fact, in anthropological texts, the introduction of metal axes within Aboriginal Australia has come to represent an archetype of the unanticipated effect of innovation upon tradition-oriented societies. In his 1940s fieldwork, anthropologist Lauriston Sharp observed the results when well-meaning missionaries introduced metal axes among the Yir Yoront, in order to save labour and effort. Previously, the use and distribution of stone axes had been tightly controlled by senior Aboriginal men. This reflected a regulated and complex system of authority which was expressed in other social and ceremonial behaviour. Stone axes were not just inefficient tools, to be readily abandoned in favour of metal; they were key social markers, which helped to articulate the mechanism of Yir Yoront society. Only men could own stone axes, having obtained them through particular trading relationships with other groups closer to the actual quarry sources. Access to stone axes was carefully controlled, reflecting the structures of kinship and authority. Traditionally, those axes remained in the man's camp:

> A woman would expect to use her husband's axe unless he himself was using it; if unmarried, or if her husband was absent, a woman would go first to her older brother or to her father. Only in extraordinary circumstances would she seek a stone axe from other male kin.[64]

A sudden surfeit of metal axes during the 1940s, equally available to all members of Yir Yiront society, represented a direct assault on this tense and delicate order: women and uninitiated boys now had ready access to a tool which had previously been carefully regulated. But Sharp's analysis suggests that even if the Yir Yoront realised the corrosive social effect of this new commodity, the metal's efficacy made it irresistible.

Such a compulsion, or magnetism perhaps, can be traced across every frontier which separated indigenous users of stone tools from European users of metal during the exploration era. During his first voyage, James Cook was obliged to modify his relations with the Tahitians so that their demand for metal as a trade item did not debase its currency value. 'No sort of Iron, or anything that is made of Iron', he decreed, was 'to be given in Exchange, for anything but Provisions'.[65] Encountering the Indians of Nootka Sound, Cook had attempted to seduce them with trade beads and cloth, but soon found that 'nothing would go down with them but metal and brass was now become their favourate [sic], so that before we left the place, hardly a bit of brass was left in the Ship, except what was in the necessary instruments'.[66] Cook's experience on the Canadian frontier in 1778 might have served as a reliable indication of the expectations which the sight of a sailing ship provoked among Arnhem Land Aborigines, who had come to associate metal with the Macassan visitors to their shores since at least the early eighteenth century.

British explorers along that northern coast were intrigued to find that a familiarity with metal had preceded their own arrival. During his brief 1818 encounter with the Tiwi people of Melville Island for example, the coastal explorer Philip Parker King observed that they 'repeatedly asked for axes by imitating the action of chopping'.[67] The British distributed tomahawks at their meetings with Aboriginal leaders at the Arnhem Land settlements of Raffles Bay and Port Essington during the 1820s and 1830s, understanding these to be the premier objects of exchange. After the 1839 cyclone at Port Essington the beached wreck of the *Pelorus* provided the Iwaidja people there

Iron axe-head collected at the Adelaide River, Northern Territory, by Belgrave Ninnis, surgeon aboard the South Australian survey vessel, *Beatrice*, 1865. A31044, South Australian Museum.

with an El Dorado of metal. A British officer wrote to his commander, 'complaining that the master blacksmith had been making spearheads for some of the natives from iron which had been picked up under Minto Head'.[68]

South Australia's assumption of the Northern Territory during 1863 resulted in a fresh wave of encounters between Aboriginal people and Europeans, and new observations on material culture. The Royal Navy surgeon, Belgrave Ninnis, accompanied the South Australian survey vessel *Beatrice* to the short-lived settlement at Adam Bay (see the following chapter), and collected a hafted iron axe which had been in use among the Djerimanga people of the Adelaide River (see Fig. 30).[69]

During Francis Cadell's 1867 exploration of the Arnhem Land coast he found one of his own crew, an Aboriginal man from Cape York, making spearheads out of iron at the expedition's forge, presumably on demand for the local Liverpool River men.[70] Along the Arnhem Land coast metal axes not only took the place of stone axes within traditional material culture; they were also applied to entirely new activities. Since at least the eighteenth century, intermittent contact with Macassan fishermen enabled Aboriginal people to acquire limited supplies of metal axes and presented new models for their use. More seaworthy than bark canoes, the Macassan dugout became the preferred mode of transport, and it could only be made successfully with metal axes. Moreover, the occasional Macassan death and burial on these fishing voyages probably offered a model for the increasingly elaborate burial poles carved by the Tiwi of Bathurst and Melville Islands. The Aboriginal people who accompanied Macassans back to the islands of the Malay archipelago must have noticed the finely carved burial poles there. Aboriginal people in Arnhem Land and the adjacent islands may have had more direct experience of these carvings, as Macassans presumably erected similar, if simpler poles for those who died during the course of Australian trepang expeditions. By European arrival an indigenous tradition of sculpture in the round, largely unknown on the Australian mainland, was evolving on Melville and Bathurst Islands. Simple hardwood poles could certainly be hewn, charred and then painstakingly shaped with stone axes, but the carved spikes and 'windows' which characterised poles collected in the early twentieth century could only be fashioned effectively with metal tools.

The Tiwi people of Melville and Bathurst Islands were completely dependent upon external supplies of metal axes. They were isolated from mainland patterns of trade which had enabled Macassan tomahawks to circulate through Arnhem Land before British arrival. During 1935 the anthropologist Donald

Thomson discovered a 'drawing of an iron axe of the special type called *lunga linya*, brought in former times by the Macassan people', painted on a rock shelter wall 'far inland'.[71] His research suggested that although highly prized by coastal people for making dugout canoes, the vitality and dynamism of the ceremonial exchange system pushed metal objects inland.

Of course, Arnhem Land rock paintings bristle with secular images of material culture – spears and spearthrowers, bags and tassels, even boomerangs – and the inclusion of a metal axe does not necessarily suggest that these objects had acquired sacred status. Much depends upon the context. But we do know that the stone axe occupies an important place in Arnhem Land mythology and that this is reflected in the region's ancient rock art. Paintings of the Lightning Brothers invariably depict these Beings with stone axes dangling from their elbows and knees – a reference to the thunder and lightning unleashed when they hurl the weapons crashing and sparking to the ground.

METAL ON INLAND FRONTIERS

Metal axes and knives quickly rendered their stone equivalents redundant across Australia. The rapidity with which the new material was incorporated surprised European observers. Thomas Mitchell's exploration journals are peppered with references to his bartering of metal tomahawks among Aboriginal groups along the Murrray, Darling and Murrumbidgee rivers. More than any explorer, he established these objects as the expected standard of exchange, the price of unimpeded progress through Aboriginal territory.[72] John Harris Browne, a member of Sturt's party, wrote:

> Several of the natives had old Iron Tomahawks which they had got from Mitchell's stores which he buried when he turned back to decrease his loads. Some of them had pieces of a Cart's [metal] tire fastened to a handle with string for a Tomahawk.[73]

Sturt dispensed tomahawks liberally during his inland expedition of 1844–1845. He had begun that practice during his Murray River expedition of 1830, when even Aboriginal people ahead of the expedition seemed to know of his cargo of trade tomahawks. At times his progress along the river resembled that of an itinerant ironmonger. Sturt's preferred protocol on meeting a new group was to take his deputy McLeay, and sit apart from his men, nearer to the Aborigines:

that being the usual way among the natives of the interior, to invite for an interview. When they saw us act thus, they approached, and sat down by us, but without looking up, from a kind of diffidence peculiar to them ... As they gained confidence however, they shewed an excessive curiosity, and stared at us in the most earnest manner. We now led them to the camp, and I gave, as was my custom, the first who had approached, a tomahawk; and to the others, some pieces of iron hoop.[74]

Sturt's epic journey to the Murray Mouth and back during the first weeks of 1830 seems to have been facilitated by this awareness of Aboriginal protocol. Gifts of objects helped to secure territorial access. On his return voyage, as his men rowed grimly against the current, Sturt's attempts to circumvent these obligations almost resulted in tragedy. He did not perceive the precise role gifts of metal axes played in mediating relations with key Aboriginal figures who held the power to ruin his venture. He was aware of the relative value attached to metal, but his descriptions of transactions generally reflected an unattuned colonial rhetoric: 'We occasionally exchanged pieces of iron-hoop ... with the natives, and the eagerness with which they met our advances to barter, is a strong proof of their natural step towards this first step in civilization'.[75] Sturt's old rival Thomas Mitchell better understood the reality of these encounters. In 1838 he wrote: 'I have more than once seen a river chief, on receiving a tomahawk, point to the stream, and signify that we were then at liberty to take water from it, so strongly were they possessed with the notion that the water was their own'.[76]

After Sturt, the exploration literature of Central Australia is peppered with references to explorers who encountered Aboriginal people already familiar with metal. This was especially the case after the erection of the Overland Telegraph Line. John Lewis's 1874 exploration north of Lake Eyre provides an example. His naturalist, F.W. Andrews, observed Aboriginal people who were:

diligently intent on what they called 'tealing'. It was evident by the cut timber about the creeks that they had axes or tomahawks; and on enquiry 'where blackfellow get um tomahawk', the answer received was 'him 'teal' um along a whitefellow'. There is no doubt they had stolen several during the construction of the Overland Telegraph. They, however, always kept these tomahawks out of our sight. Knives, tomahawks etc, are their principal weaknesses.[77]

The weight of evidence relating to the spread of metal ahead of the inland frontier comes from these exploration journals. Occasionally Aboriginal people provided direct testimony. Tindale's 1953 interviews with Walmadjeri men in north-western Australia (close to the Calvert expedition's route) confirmed that traded metal came to them before they had set eyes on white men. At Anna Plains Station, Tindale's principal informant was a Nyangamarta man:

> Old Charlie ... whose father had for many years roamed along the seashore as had his father's father. His father had been born at Malumbur on the coast before white men had settled here. Charlie had first seen a white man, Mr Zumfelde, a German (about 1900) when the last-named had opened Anna Plains Station. His father had possessed a metal axe before that, having obtained it by trade from DeGrey River blackfellows.[78]

There were two ways of obtaining metal on these remote frontiers: barter or theft. Direct engagement with Europeans in barter could yield the best results – iron tomahawks already strongly hafted and made especially for working with wood. But these face-to-face encounters could also lead to complications and misunderstanding, often ending in conflict. At various times Europeans and Aboriginal people concluded that the disadvantages of engagement outweighed the advantages, and that it was best, after all, to keep a distance. This was as true of the Eora at Port Jackson during the two years following 1788, as of the Mangala people shadowing the Calvert expedition. Europeans also had reason enough to maintain this distance, as the experience of the Overland Telegraph parties showed.

THE LIGHTNING LINE

A policy of non-fraternisation with Aboriginal people was applied during the Overland Telegraph Line's construction, on the recommendation of South Australia's Surveyor-General, George Goyder. His assessment was formed during the 1869–1871 South Australian Survey Expedition to the Northern Territory when it became obvious that Aboriginal people had mixed motives for developing a familiarity with Europeans. The events surrounding the spearing of J.W.O. Bennett during 1869 (see the following chapter) hardened Goyder's resolve. He issued several directives to his men that they cease bartering for artefacts with the Larrakia people of Port Darwin. Even prior to Bennett's spearing, Goyder had ordered a stockade constructed around the settlement. Port Darwin had become Fort Darwin, and Aboriginal people were no longer permitted within its confines. Another stockade was constructed around the Telegraph base camp at Roper River, and the Line parties were forbidden to fraternise with Aboriginal people. Despite breaking his own rule (he marked several encounters with gifts of tomahawks), Goyder's ban generally held. Aboriginal people of the northern coast had been long aware of the qualities of metal axes. Now they were denied access to this intensely desired material, but from the hill overlooking Fort Darwin, outside the stockade, they could still see it flash and hear it clang.

Further south along the Telegraph Line the result was predictable enough. The 1870s Telegraph construction parties were observed at a distance by Aboriginal people prepared to wait for their opportunities. Smaller groups of workers leaving the base parties were often followed and sometimes pursued. Aboriginal men chose the moment to attack according to the circumstances, terrain and vegetation. But the best opportunities came when Europeans left supplies of metal unattended. The pioneer drover and pastoralist Alfred Giles recorded an instance in which Aboriginal men dismantled and destroyed two of his drays which had been left unloaded and unattended for a few days. Europeans perceived this as wanton destruction by treacherous blacks, but these were systematic operations. A few days after this event members of a Line party came across a number of characteristic boat-shaped, wooden carrying vessels, hidden 'in a tree, with a lot of iron off Giles' drays in them'.[79]

The Telegraph Line was constructed under the supervision of Charles Todd during two years of intensive work from 1870 to 1872. Construction parties pushed north from Port Augusta and south from Roper River. The southern parties used wooden poles (subsequently to be replaced by metal), but large numbers of iron poles were used by the northern parties from the outset, because of likely damage by termites. The Line was targeted by Aboriginal people not just for metal, but for the porcelain insulators sitting atop the poles. Dislodged with a well-aimed stone these insulators provided a light, sharp and consistent material for spearheads. The porcelain was easy to work and as effective as another new substance brought by the Europeans – glass. Supplies of broken bottles were placed along the Telegraph Line in Central Australia and north-western Australia to deter Aboriginal people from smashing the insulators for spearheads.

Sir Charles Todd, as Superintendent of the Telegraph, owned at least two axes which had been fashioned from his own telegraph poles. A label on one of those axes read:

A hafted axe made from the iron footplate of a telegraph pole, once owned by Sir Charles Todd. A3941, South Australian Museum.

> Tomahawk made by the natives at Newcastle Waters on the Northern Line, from the footplate of an iron telegraph pole. The natives dug up the pole, broke the footplate and formed it into several tomahawks like this one. They sharpened it. Given me by C. Todd, C.M.G., S.A. 1884.[80]

Todd's axes were made from the iron footplates used to anchor the Overland Telegraph poles firmly in the soft soil of the Line's northern section. In Todd's words, these footplates had been 'dug up, broken, and made with much ingenuity, into tomahawks, of which I possess some very creditable specimens'.[81] Perhaps he considered that the 'ingenuity' of these hybrid objects reflected nicely upon his own remarkable achievement. The axes might represent tentative but admirable first steps by Aboriginal engineers along the long path towards the feat of civilisation which his own Overland Telegraph Line embodied. It is tempting to think of these mementoes securing piles of telegrams on Todd's desk, paperweights with tales of their own.

As custodians of that single strand of wire binding the colonial capitals to London, the metropolis of empire, the telegraph station managers were largely unaware that it bisected a seething complex of Aboriginal lines of mythology and communication. Bound to office routine in the limitless space of desert and bush, Francis Gillen and his pragmatic colleagues nevertheless had some appreciation of the surreal dimension of their role, sparking telegrams from one horizon to another. They called each other 'lightning squirters' – a playful if deprecating reference to the ounce of current they sent coursing along the Line, from the northern coast to Adelaide and back again. Perhaps behind that evocative term lay an oblique, playful reference to the power of those ancient European gods, Vulcan, Thor and Zeus, who arced thunder and power across the universe. The European peasant belief, that prehistoric stone axes found in ploughed fields were thunderbolts hurled from the sky, was not far removed from the mythological frame in which Aboriginal stone axes are located, and in which Dreaming Ancestors dispense lightning and thunder at their whim.[82]

Gillen's letters remind us that irony was appreciated on the Australian frontier. During 1890 the South Australian Museum's director wrote to telegraph station managers, police and remote pastoralists, soliciting Aboriginal artefacts for the collection. Drawing attention to the 'rapid disappearance of the Aborigines of Australia', Edward Stirling's letter asked for 'all articles made and used'. The letter drew a quick response from Alfred Giles, the pastoralist whose own drays had once been dismantled by Aboriginal people for the metal they contained. Giles gathered a collection of more than 100 artefacts from Aboriginal people camped near his Springvale Station, west of Katherine. In his accompanying letter to Stirling, he wrote:

> With regard to your request to be furnished with native weapons etc you are quite right as to the increasing difficulty of procuring these articles, especially with regard to articles of the 'Stone Age'. Iron dray tires, horseshoes and shear blades are now sharpened on sandstone rocks by the natives themselves. Does it not seem remarkable that at the moment when they rejoice at the dawn (to them) of the iron age (not through their own efforts) but by the wonderful advance of our own race we should now be anxious to exchange our iron and even silver & gold (by barter) for their discarded stone![83]

Hafted in traditional Aboriginal fashion, metal axes immediately eased and simplified the task of making those wooden items of material culture sustaining life in northern Central Australia. But almost as quickly, these hybrid objects were obsolete, replaced by European tomahawks, as nomadic hunters and gatherers adopted a modified suite of material culture improvised from the detritus of European colonial activity – tins, bottle glass, metal fragments, cloth and leather. The range of useful wooden objects eventually contracted to saleable tourist souvenirs, which have progressively borne less and less resemblance to the elegant tools and weapons of a self-sufficient desert culture.

In fact, almost as soon as the Calvert axe was made – a small masterwork of improvisation in its desert setting – it had become a relic of a marginalised economy and culture. The very objects for which it was required – small wooden scoops carved from desert trees, for digging out and maintaining remote wells – were being abandoned as superfluous elements in a fringe-dwelling culture of dependence. This historical reality, or succession of events, seemed to vindicate the sentiments expressed by Alfred Giles. It also suited the emerging discourse of nineteenth-century museums, founded on evolutionist principles. The German ethnographer, Adolf Bastian, stated the underlying principle:

> For us, primitive societies (Naturvolker) are ephemeral ... inasmuch as they exist for us all. At the very instant they become known to us they are doomed.[84]

The portentous certainty of that conclusion has long vanished. The remaining kernel of truth relates not to the question of cultural survival, but to the difficulty which evolutionists had in rationalising the collision between two cultures. For them the 'ahistory' of colonised peoples and the 'history' of the colonisers seemed quite incompatible. But the history of the Calvert axe and other metal artefacts suggests a different conclusion, that the frontier could also draw the two cultures together, and briefly entangle them. For these objects can remind us that for a period at least, Europeans on the frontier represented a tangible resource, as much as a threat.

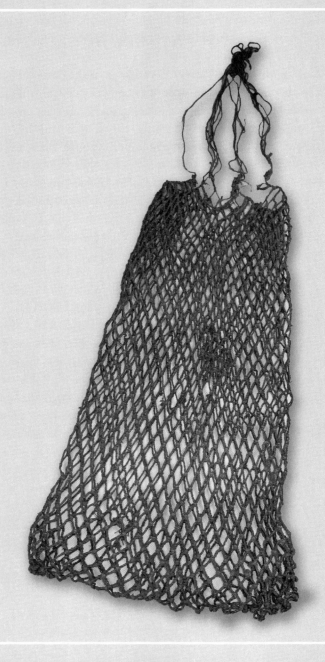

Knotted string bag collected by W.W. Hoare at Port Darwin, 1869.
A68380, South Australian Museum.

CHAPTER FOUR

Spearing Bennett

A museum's cobwebs can snare a rich haul of unrelated objects. Decades may pass until a nondescript piece catches the light, casts a shadow. A scrap of paper lies in the bottom of an ochred, finely-knotted string bag, ignored for a century. Unfolded, the carefully inked inscription reads:

Native String Bags
From Port Darwin
North Australia
W.W. Hoare[1]

That name struck a chord. William Webster Hoare was the surgeon's assistant and artist who accompanied George Goyder's North Australian Surveying Expedition of 1869–1870. A particular, eccentric man, his surviving scrapbooks describe his life within the fragile outpost of Fort Darwin as Goyder's men traced their survey lines across the lands of the Larrakia and Woolna on behalf of the South Australian government. Hoare's scrapbook is peppered with his vignette sketches of insects, birds and Aboriginal artefacts.

Another object: an unsigned manuscript, compressed for sixty years among a stack of correspondence in ethnologist Norman B. Tindale's 'in-tray'. The manuscript was sent to Tindale in his absence, during the Second World War. On his return there were letters and papers to deal with, galleries to reorganise and collections to retrieve from wartime safe-keeping. The manuscript, titled 'Vocabulary of the Woolner District dialect, Adelaide River, N.T.', sank through layers of papers. Neatly handwritten in ink on heavy foolscap paper, it is annotated for publication, with red diacritics over the Aboriginal vowels.

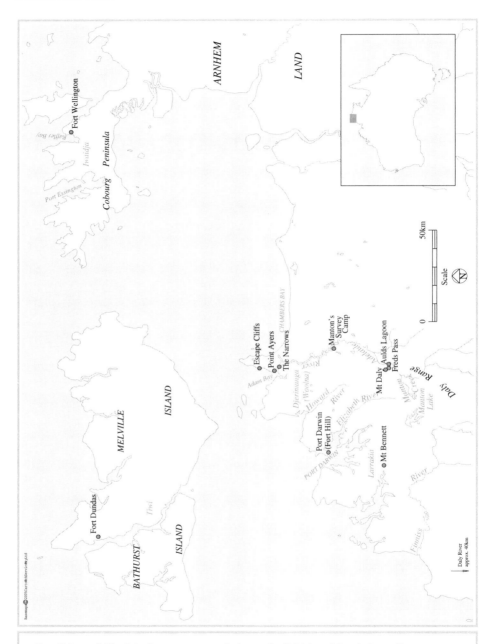

Localities and Aboriginal group names relating to the British and South Australian settlements in northern Australia, 1820s to 1870.

Tindale may have realised that the annotated manuscript conformed almost exactly with a vocabulary published in 1879 under the name of J.W.O. Bennett, as the final chapter of the edited volume *Native Tribes of South Australia*.[2] But Tindale believed that he had already located the original manuscript of that vocabulary, in a small notebook preserved in the papers of the South Australian Surveyor-General, George W. Goyder.[3] Tindale attributed Goyder as its author, not realising that the notebook was, in fact, Bennett's original. The annotated manuscript in Tindale's 'in-tray' was a copy.

A few months later I located yet another copy, in the same hand, catalogued among the papers of William Patrick Auld in Adelaide's State library. This second copy, clearly based on the first, was more hastily made, with a few errors of transcription and some additional information.

W.W. Hoare's copy of J.W.O. Bennett's 1869 vocabulary of the 'Woolner District' (Djerimanga) language, marked for publication.
South Australian Museum Archives.

The scribe of both copies can now be identified as the collector of the string bag – William Webster Hoare.[4] He was also Bennett's close friend. The woven bag, the original notebook and Hoare's copies all belong to the same story, which pivots on the death by spearing of the young draftsman and linguist, John William Ogilvie Bennett.

Bennett accompanied two expeditions which left Adelaide for the tropical north during the 1860s: the Finniss expedition to Escape Cliffs of 1864–1866 (during which Bennett began the vocabulary) and Goyder's expedition of 1869–1870 (during which Bennett lost his life). William Webster Hoare accompanied that second expedition as the surgeon's assistant. Like several other members of Goyder's party, Hoare kept a journal which detailed Bennett's peculiar fate. Hoare's journal also contains illustrations of artefacts obtained through barter with Aboriginal men and women, including one resembling the

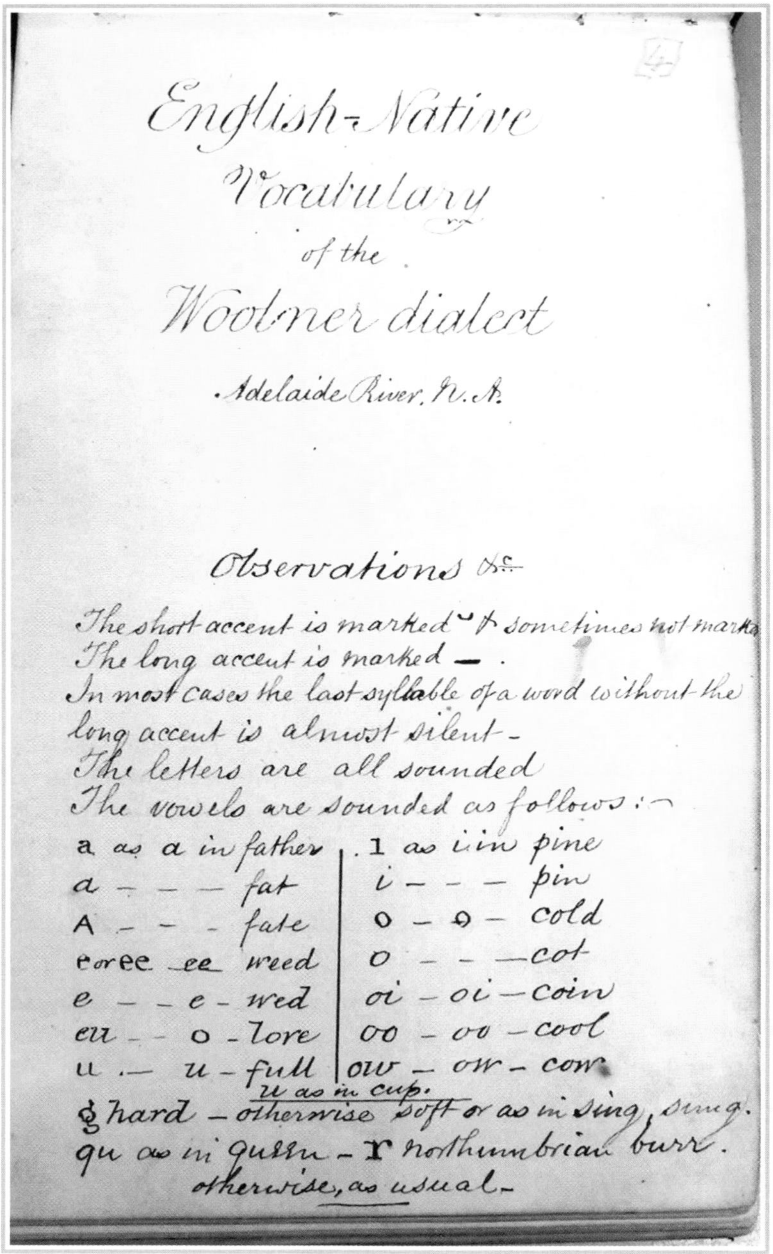

English = Native

Vocabulary

of the

Woolner dialect

Adelaide River. N.A.

Observations &c.

The short accent is marked ˘ & sometimes not marked
The long accent is marked — .
In most cases the last syllable of a word without the
long accent is almost silent —
The letters are all sounded
The vowels are sounded as follows :—

a	as a in father	1	as i in pine
a	— — — fat	i	— — — pin
A	— — — fate	o	— o — cold
e or ee	ee weed	o	— — — cot
e	— — e — wed	oi	— oi — coin
eu	— — o — lore	oo	— oo — cool
u	— — u — full	ow	— ow — cow

u as in cup.

g hard — otherwise soft or as in sing, sing.
qu as in queen — r northumbrian burr.
otherwise, as usual —

J.W.O. Bennett's original manuscript of the 'Woolner Dialect, Adelaide
River'. Goyder Papers, GRG 35/256/11, State Records, Adelaide.

Portraits of W.W. Hoare (left) and J.W.O. Bennett (right), before George Goyder's survey party sailed from Adelaide, late 1868. Photographers: H. Anson and W. Francis, Adelaide. W.W. Hoare album, PRG 294/1, State Library of South Australia.

small netted bag. That object accompanied Hoare to England and, passing through the hands of an unknown 'Mr Page of Wimbledon', was eventually acquired by the South Australian Museum.

Hoare's handwritten copies of Bennett's vocabulary speak most eloquently of the link between the two friends, and of the efforts both made to understand something of the Aboriginal world in which they had found themselves. Somewhere behind the original manuscript and the copies lies the significance of the words and phrases they contain, a series of encounters defining the relationship of Aboriginal and European people on the northern Australian frontier of the 1860s.

THE LIMINAL FRONTIER

When Goyder's men had stepped ashore at Port Darwin on 6 February 1869, their expectation of what awaited them along the Arnhem Land coast was already coloured by the experience of those who had served on B.T. Finniss's 1864–1866 expedition to Escape Cliffs a few miles to the east. Dining at table with Goyder and his senior officers, John Bennett conveyed his enthusiasm for the country, and for his particular project, begun during the Finniss expedition. This was his dictionary of the language of the Djerimanga people, known to the South Australians as the 'Woolna'. The Woolna were centred on the Adelaide River to the east of Port Darwin. Unlike the Larrakia people, whose country included the actual site of the new settlement, the Woolna had considerable prior experience with Europeans. In particular, as related below, they had borne the brunt of Finniss's clumsy diplomacy just four years earlier. This frontier was no longer a clean slate.

The Aboriginal response to Goyder's party was conditioned not only by the Finniss expedition, but by generations of encounters with outsiders. The annual expeditions to the shallow waters of the north Australian coast by Macassan fishermen from southern Sulawesi, seeking the trepang delicacy for the China trade, are now considered to have begun during the 1720s. Contact with Europeans commenced a century later, following Matthew Flinders' voyage. The three British settlements of Fort Dundas on Melville Island (1824–1828), Raffles Bay (1827–1831) and Port Essington (1838–1849) then provided the focus of contact.

The mainland settlements at Raffles Bay and Port Essington were largely peaceable intrusions. With no intention of colonising the interior, the British did not directly threaten the territory of the Iwaidja or Djerimanga people, or the bases of their existence. These encounters resulted in new social formations between black and white, and creative protocols of accommodation. The British outposts provided the Aboriginal people of the north coast with a fresh and diverting suite of experience, a contrast to their encounters with the Macassan visitors. Navy ships arrived in Raffles Bay with uniformed troops in stripes and unimagined shades of red and blue, drilling and marching to compelling rhythms. The angular architecture of raw-edged stone buildings rose up above the jungle at Fort Wellington. Strange plants and exotic fruits appeared in the garden. Metal flashed alluringly in every corner of this new landscape. Bell chimes and the aroma of tobacco hung in the tropical air. As soon as they were unloaded from the ships, the first buffalo broke through their fences and lurched into the bush, offering a dangerous bounty. Metal spearheads bartered or skilfully inveigled from the Europeans were the only effective Aboriginal weapons against these thick-skinned beasts.

The soldiers marched around and sang. That seemed to be the reason for their presence. They didn't venture inland, didn't seem interested in leaving the settlement, just built their barracks and store-buildings, dug ditches, worked in the garden, waited for the next ship.

On the Cobourg Peninsula the Iwaidja people watched the activity and came to know some of the white men. At Raffles Bay they lay in the bush outside Fort Wellington, listening while the men drilled inside the stockade. The Commandant, Collet Barker, met them a few at a time, in chance encounters on the beach and at the fort itself. Barker met Meriak and then Yacana, both Iwaidja elders. These men were already known to the British, who had named them Wellington and Waterloo.

Casual exchanges of objects marked these meetings, light touches laden with meaning in this new colonial space. Spears, spearthrowers, baskets, stone axes, vegetable-fibre string and tortoise-shell for buttons, handkerchiefs, knives, fish-hooks, tomahawks, flour, sugar and tobacco. On the first occasion, meeting Meriak in early December 1828, Barker watched the Iwaidja move back into the bushes, leaving an unfilled blank. It took an object to fill that blank, linking black to white for a moment and diverting attention from the real collision. Barker offered his red handkerchief to Meriak and received in return 'a spear unheaded, & the stick for throwing it. He had perhaps taken off the head'.[5]

The colonial dance began, a dance of objects proffered and accepted, discarded and pilfered. Small exchanges masked the main event, trivial thefts countered the loss of a land. That Barker noted each transaction suggests that he saw these as indicators of progression or regression in that larger project – the permanent inscription of colonial presence. Soon each encounter entailed a play for objects, initiated by one or the other. Barker understood that information and intelligence about this inscrutable country could always be obtained for a price; his objective was to establish the currency of exchange and to negotiate for parity. This process of translation inevitably involved language. An exchange of words was facilitated through the barter of desirable objects. On 8 December 1828, Barker began to collect an Iwaidja vocabulary. He managed to record several words before 'Wellington seeing me writing down the words begged the pencil case from me, which I gave him & he stuck it under the bracelets on his arm'.[6]

Exchange was an endless cycle. Like other Europeans on the frontier, Barker was hoping for a final accommodation, a squaring of the ledger. In Aboriginal eyes that prospect could never occur. Barker was disturbed to find satisfying equivalences undermined by 'pilfering'.

The stores were raided on 4 March 1829. There was no sign of the Aborigines for six weeks, then Wellington and Luga appeared, 'exceedingly anxious to make friends with us, offering ... as presents everything they had with them, being three or four spears, a basket etc'.[7] On 4 June the doctor's boat was stolen from the beach near the settlement. Barker's men retrieved it immediately and a few days later Barker surprised the four culprits on the beach: Waterloo, Luga, Nagary and Maigena. They were 'disposed to make off', but on seeing Barker they approached slowly: 'Luga [the suspected thief] came in front of the others & gave me two spears & a wamara [spearthrower], for which I presented him with a towel I had with me. Waterloo gave me a basket in return for my handkerchief'.[8]

The British abandoned Fort Wellington in 1831 and the bush swallowed up the ruins. Seven years later they made another attempt to establish a northern Australian beachhead for their navy, at Port Essington to the west. Functioning for eleven years until 1849, the settlement of Victoria became the most substantial European outpost in the region. This was not colonisation though; the British were entirely focused upon the coast and the seas beyond and their presence held few threats for the Iwaidja. The benefits of this new settlement probably outweighed the inconvenience of its intrusion. Victoria became a fascinating hub of diversion and entertainment, attracting not only Iwaidja people of the Cobourg Peninsula, but also Woolna and Larrakia from the west. The more curious and precocious of these individuals became sufficiently familiar with the ways of the British to retain knowledge of their marching songs when the South Australians arrived during the 1860s.

The first South Australian expedition, following the province's acquisition of the Northern Territory in 1863, was led by Colonel Boyle Travers Finniss. His 1864–1866 expedition to Escape Cliffs was accompanied by the Royal Navy survey schooner *Beatrice*, whose captain, Frederick Howard, was preparing detailed surveys of the northern coasts. Howard was surprised to meet Aboriginal men and women who spoke good English and seemed familiar with European customs. One encounter, which occurred in January 1865 near the Cobourg Peninsula, was described in detail by Alfred Webling, engaged as 'tide-watcher'. Webling was astonished when a bark canoe approached the ship and hailed it 'in English asking if we came from Sydney'. The fragile craft came alongside and four Aboriginal men and a woman climbed aboard without hesitation:

> The Chief . . . introduced himself as Mr Robert or Bob White and could speak English very fluently, from him we learnt that there were a number of Malay Prows on the coast. They wanted Bacca and pipes and Bob asked the Captain for a bottle of Grog. They were onboard about two hours talking and smoking. They told us there are plenty of Buffaloes and Horses running wild on the

mainland which were left by the settlers at Port Essington. The Lubra said her name was Flash Poll, she was very much marked with small pox.[9]

Flash Poll had once been a servant of Lieutenant Lambrick, second-in-command at the settlement. She further amazed the *Beatrice*'s crew with renditions of 'My old Kentucky Home' and other songs learnt from the British at Port Essington.

Music was to play a further part in establishing contact. During June 1864 the *Beatrice* sailed up the Adelaide River for a distance of nearly 50 kilometres. It was, as Webling wrote, the first European vessel 'to disturb the waters' of that river. Aboriginal people (probably Woolna) followed the ship's progress from the banks with great interest, but with little experience of Europeans they were reluctant to come on board. The *Beatrice*'s crew were keen to make closer contact though, and on 4 June, 'with nothing particular to do' the men assembled an improvised orchestra on deck, hoping to lure the Woolna. The ploy worked:

> we tried what effect music would have in enticing them on board which made them skip about in the mud like a duskie. On hearing the music a lot more came forward and among them were three females and some Dogs the[y] all appeared quite delighted with our band which consisted of a Violin tin Whistle Concertina and Drums. By this time the tide had left the bank and we could see they were quite naked.[10]

Two men and a boy came aboard. One of the men, Webling considered, held higher status: he wore a bark belt around his waist and a kangaroo-tooth head-band. His hair was coated in red ochre, like his fellows. This man 'shouted' from the moment he came into view until he arrived on board, perhaps indicating that his status also entailed a responsibility to placate ancestors, the spirits of the place, or at least the forces propelling this apparition into the Woolna's world.

Everything the men saw, wrote Webling, 'they looked at with wonder and surprise'. It may have been the first time they had stood on a vessel's deck, but in other respects their shipboard encounter conformed to the earlier visitation from Bob White and Flash Poll. The European ship had sailed into Aboriginal waters, and so the boarding involved a doubled intrusion, or a doubled invitation. If each was the other's guest, each was also an interloper, exercising a peculiar diplomacy in this overlapping, liminal space. The liberties taken with each other could not have occurred on land. Webling described the scene:

After they had feasted their eyes they shouted to their companions on shore and the rest of them came off but we had to pick them up with the dingy. We had two Pigs on board which attracted the greater part of their attention especially when we made them squeak. We gave them numerous articles of wearing apparel, there were some curious looking objects among them when they were dressed. We had to put the clothes on them for they had no idea of doing it themselves. There's one with only a Vest another with a white shirt such a contrast to their black skin, there's one tall fellow with only a pair of White Kid Gloves on. We could only pursuad [sic] one Boy to come on board and him we clothed from head to foot the three Females and two boys remained on shore. One of the [men] had a European knife but nothing would induce him to part with it. I noticed the boys had a reed through the cartilage of their nose and when we landed them, the dogs went howling into the bush ... We proceeded up the River. After we had left that reach we saw them again on a plain away back they took off the clothing we gave them and we saw they had lots of spears with them and a great many more of them than we thought following us until they were stopped by a Creek.[11]

During its 1865 voyage the *Beatrice* ventured further up the Adelaide River and there were more encounters with the Woolna, close to the scene of Bennett's spearing four years later. Despite the remoteness of these encounters, Webling was surprised to find that the Woolna were familiar with metal objects and even knew some English, shouting the words 'Very Good!' as they approached. Visiting Adelaide before this second voyage began, the *Beatrice*'s captain, Frederick Howard, had been cautioned against familiarity. He issued this warning to his men:

he advised us not to encourage the natives in any way whatever such as giving them Clothing or Knives for he said he believed by giving them things and treating them with kindness led them to think that they had a perfect right to [them], and to check this afterwards ended in bloodshed. Alfred Horn asked the Captn how we should act if they gave us any thing wether [sic] we should take it and give them something in return or not take it from them. He said in a case of that sort, the best way would be to deal with them quietly and form a sort of bargain.[12]

Despite Howard's directive, the Aboriginal people obviously expected exchange. Soon there were several 'sorts of bargains'. On 17 May two Aboriginal men swam out to the *Beatrice*, and met the crew on the deck. Recognising one of them from the 1864 voyage, Webling recorded three Woolna language terms: 'as well as we could understand the native name for Snake is *Mulla Mullagee* and Alligator *Comumbera* and Water *Quiro*'. The Aborigines promised to bring some weapons for exchange at sunset on the following day and, true to their word, they attached two spearthrowers and a net bag to a line thrown from the ship. They received a sheepskin and an old knife in return.[13]

Among the *Beatrice*'s crew was Lieutenant M.S. Guy, one of the first photographers to visit the Northern Territory. He took views of the landscape and the new settlements. A week after the encounter just described, his images also joined the series of transactions:

> [At] 9 am five Natives came down to the ship on the opposite side to which we saw the last but shouting out the same 'very good'. Gov. Finnis said he thought they were of a different Tribe yet it is very clear they have heard of us before by their 'very good'. They had spears and womerahs with them, one of them swam off alongside climbed on board and seated himself on the Taffrail in which posture Mr Guy took his portrait and shewed it to him but he did not seem to make it out. We took his measure he stood 5 ft 11 in and seemed to be Chief of the party the others were young men. We gave them a few presents and landed them in the dingy in return they gave us three spears and womerahs and made signs they were going to their Camp.[14]

These passing encounters carried little of the weight of full cultural contact, in which the land, its resources and future control were at stake. As the South Australian survey parties under Finniss and Goyder began to entrench themselves, new forms of accommodation were required. At Escape Cliffs during 1864, Colonel Finniss's nondescript party of surveyors and volunteers (including the nineteen-year-old John Bennett), had a more confronting task than the British garrisons at Raffles Bay and Port Essington. Now they faced the inland, intending to map it and, by extending their grid of survey lines across it, to possess it.

John Bennett, it seems, drew the straightest and most reliable of those lines. His maps of the Adelaide River and Adam Bay, overlain with the pencilled town sections, streets and parkland envisaged for them, are proficiently drafted, convincing in their detail. He had first shown an interest in drawing and surveying while a student at the prosaically named Adelaide Educational Institution, where his father was a master. Young Bennett's name was 'very frequently to be found in the half-yearly prize list' and on leaving school he 'found occupation congenial to his tastes' in the Government Survey Department. There his closest friend, with whom he shared a love of philosophy's 'pleasant teachings', had been William Finniss, one of the sons of his new master.[15]

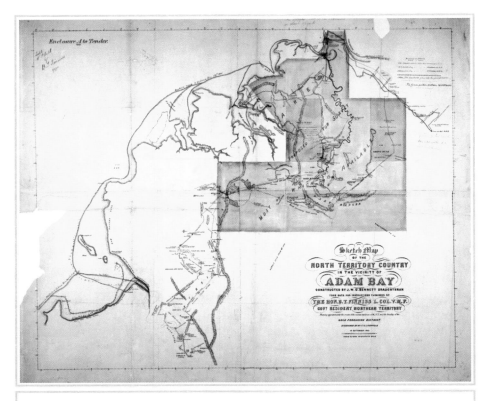

J.W.O. Bennett's September 1865 map of proposed survey regions to the south of Adam Bay (original map 82.5 x 97 cm). C25/2, State Library of South Australia.

ESCAPE CLIFFS: TWO FORMS OF ENCOUNTER

Colonel B.T. Finniss began his survey expedition at Escape Cliffs with good intentions towards the Woolna people. During July 1864 those encounters had opened with an exchange of presents. Woolna men danced for the new-comers. Finniss's fragmentary journal contains a partial Woolna vocabulary, the names of individuals and some pencil sketches of them.[16] The most tangible product of these exchanges was a delicate sewn-bark canoe which Finniss acquired at Escape Cliffs. Now in the South Australian Museum, it is the earliest surviving example of Aboriginal watercraft from northern Australia.

Four-metre long sewn-bark canoe obtained by Boyle Travers Finnis in 1864–1865 at Escape Cliffs. A6446, South Australian Museum.

Finniss's first task as Government Resident was to select a capital for the new province, the Northern Territory of South Australia. Then he was to open up the country to the south by measurement and division, advancing from his clifftop camp by theodolite and chain. But his choice of Adam Bay, with the main settlement at Escape Cliffs to be named Palmerston North, and the port known as the 'Narrows' (at the mouth of the Adelaide River to the south-west) to be named Palmerston South, was roundly condemned. Both settlements were surrounded by mosquito-ridden mangrove swamps, and the Narrows was prone to flooding. Finniss refused to reconsider, despite protests from his senior officers who were aware of the superior anchorage at Port Darwin to the west. Finniss relied upon tractable, junior officers like Bennett, and the labourers Frederick Litchfield and Patrick Auld, whose promotion to the status of surveyors caused further discontent. Work proceeded nevertheless. Bennett charted Auld's and Litchfield's explorations along the courses of the Adelaide, Finniss and Daly rivers, and documented several town surveys, including Palmerston North and South.

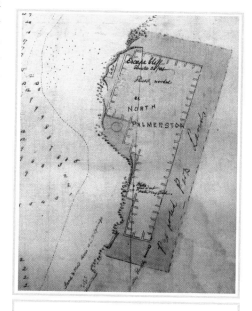

Bennett's plan of the proposed settlement of 'Palmerston North' at Escape Cliffs, 1865. Detail from larger map. C20, State Library of South Australia.

As Bennett's meticulously drawn maps show, each of these ideal townships was to consist of wide streets laid on a grid, surrounded by parklands like Adelaide itself. With these detailed inscriptions of a civic presence onto the blank wilderness, the young draftsman gave Finniss some purchase against his critics.

In contrast to the orderly progress of the surveyors and draftsmen, the Finniss expedition soon degenerated to a shambles. Finniss's authority was openly challenged. Later, several of his officers took to the sea in an open boat rather than remain under his command.[17] In the meantime the Government Resident sat in an armchair on the cliff, overlooking the unloading of stores. He regaled visitors in his tent with wallaby and porter while the men scraped by on meagre rations. Bennett was caught in the middle. He dined with the officers who poisoned the camp against Finniss, yet became his most trusted confidant, bringing him news of the 'court circular' which was read out as a diatribe each day in the officers' mess. At a subsequent enquiry Bennett was recalled as a 'nice, gentlemanly person', but yes, he did 'carry tales' to Finniss and for this he became known as 'the government pimp'.[18] The surveyor Robert Edmunds described him as one of Finniss's 'toadies who will say anything they think will please him'.[19] Of the 'court circular', Bennett wrote to his father:

> You may be sure I enjoyed my meals very much when listening to such insinuations as 'the bloated lump of carrion', The B**y T*m F**l [Bloody Tom Fool, corresponding to Finniss's initials, B.T.F.], and many others, [such] as Prince Chaw Bacon, accompanied His Majesty in his yacht to Chambers Bay, when having visited some stations there, and partaken too freely of a repast of wallaby, found himself so far indisposed as to prevent his sailing any farther'. This last is a sentence or announcement that appeared in a manuscript document entitled the 'Court Circular' and [was] placed under Mr Ward's plate every morning for some time, in the handwriting of Mr Pearson (disguised), and this was read by Ward always to the mess. Some of them had allusion to myself – '"The Chief Pimp", dined with His Majesty and Prince Chaw Bacon yesterday afternoon'.
>
> This was all done at the time we were so badly off for food, just about the time the *South Australian* came in. This shows the selfish, envious, feelings of men; and those men say they know of no one so selfish as the Government Resident (or, as they say 'Finniss').[20]

Finniss also trusted Bennett with the task of taking meteorological readings.[21] As the subsequent enquiry into Finniss's management found, Bennett 'had to undergo a tremendous amount of persecution in the officers' mess, on account of being a good deal employed writing for our Governor'.[22] Additionally, one of Bennett's closest Adelaide friends was William Finniss, one of the Colonel's sons, and Bennett's correspondence with him made it plain that his loyalty would not waver: 'I should never think of such a thing as rebelling against the Governor of a place under any circumstance, while I knew & believed that he was the man to obey & respect … & therefore I <u>will not</u> coincide in my opinion <u>with the other officers</u>'.[23] Bennett went so far as to characterise the dissension as a fundamental political division between Tories like himself and the expedition members who shared 'radical' Whig tendencies which Bennett considered to be infecting South Australia. In supporting his leader, he would resist these tendencies to the last.

Immersing himself in Walter Scott's Waverley novels, Bennett's loyalty for Finniss became his own defining *cause celebre*. Of the attempted uprising against Finniss, he wrote to William:

> The late <u>rebelling or Conspiracy</u> as I may justly call it, strongly reminds or tends to remind me of the Civil War Rebellion in Reign of our (I think I may <u>safely</u> say, 'our') Martyrd King Charles I (Jany 30th). My dear friend I act now as I should undoubtedly have acted then – I am as you must know, a staunch Loyalist & otherwise cannot act than by upholding the King's authority – & further being a High Churchman – I have to support & obey the King and <u>all</u> who are put in authority under him … I have only one wish – that I had lived during the Triumphant time of the Tories of England – their name & character <u>may I ever bear</u>.[24]

Despite Bennett's determination to adopt a deeply conservative stance, his fellow-officers soon accused him of the most radical liberalism – exposed by his efforts to learn the Woolna language. Finniss had approved this initiative, but as relations between black and white soured, Bennett complained to a friend that his colleagues were 'sadly cutting him to pieces respecting the black niggers up here'. The officers want to make out, he wrote,

> that these miserably degraded (animals more than) men are my brothers and sisters. God grant that I may never live to acknowledge such a thing. I was taught by my father to follow his opinion & may I never leave it. I know your opinion is similar. The idea of calling a half-cannibal a brother, one that would spear you at his first opportunity, this is the philosophy of the present age! How long will it last?[25]

But Bennett was protesting too much. In the light of his deepening interest in the Woolna language and the particular fate awaiting him, these vehement denials suggest that the officers' criticism had found its mark.

At the end of each day's watch the sentries at Escape Cliffs fired 'practice' volleys into the mangroves, precisely where the Woolna crossed from one part of the coast to another. Finniss set the example for this style of aggression, warning the Aborigines away from the camp with flares, rather than attempting those forms of complex engagement successfully pursued by Collet Barker more than 30 years earlier. The Government Resident's treatment of the Woolna was 'very absurd', wrote surveyor Robert Edmunds: 'Auld or any of the stockmen have only to report that they saw fresh tracks, when an armed party is formed to drive them away. Fortunately they never see any on these expeditions'.[26]

Bennett tried to distance himself from this belligerence, but as the Government Resident's favourite, he was compromised by association. Shortly after arriving at Escape Cliffs he had accompanied Finniss on a hunting expedition. The expedition leader 'shot 3 pheasants, 3 cockatoos and 2 quail, Bennett had little luck'. Bennett fared better during the Christmas Day sports organised by Finniss at Escape Cliffs, winning first prize in the carbine competition over 200 and 400 yards.[27] As apprehension of an Aboriginal attack grew, Finniss chose Bennett as a member of his guard.

The first flashpoint came just two months after the Finniss expedition's

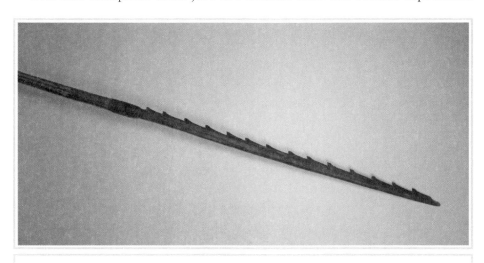

Detail of a barbed spear removed from the leg of a horse at Escape Cliffs, 1864. A4699, South Australian Museum.

arrival, shortly after the settlement had been reprovisioned. Winching the stores up the six-metre cliffs was a slow process. Most of the goods remained on the beach, within sight of the Woolna concealed in the mangroves nearby. Finniss's surveillance was lax and quantities of the stores soon disappeared, including an entire sail for one of the boats.

A similar chain of events occurred at J.T. Manton's survey camp on the Adelaide River, close to the *Beatrice*'s furthest anchorage. Sentries left their post at the store depot for a meal, and on their return found Aboriginal men cutting and emptying the flour and sugar bags, valuing the burlap above the contents. Manton ordered out a party of four men on horseback, armed with revolvers and carbines, to recover the stolen property. They were met with a volley of spears. The party's leader, Edward Pearson (author of the 'court circular'), was thrown from his horse and received seven spear wounds, none fatal. One barbed spear, extracted from the leg of his horse, survives as a relic of that fracas.

Back at the camp the men heard the commotion and set off to assist:

> foremost among them was a man named [Alaric] Ward ... After discharging his Rifle he made through the bush when he saw a Native not more than 15 yards off with a spear pointed ready to throw in an instant. Ward was behind a tree, snap went the revolver but misfired, [the] second went off but missed the object, third shot fatal, entering the native's forehead and he fell instantly. The others seeing this made off like smoke.[28]

Alfred Webling observed that the dead man had been one of those invited on board the *Beatrice* a few weeks earlier. Alaric Ward had previously expressed his intention to kill Aborigines. An inquest led by the medical officer and official Protector of Aborigines, Dr Goldsmith, pointed the blame at Finniss for siting the camp dangerously close to the mangroves and for leaving stores within tempting reach of the Aborigines.[29]

The pattern was soon repeated. Unguarded supplies disappeared (not all taken by Aborigines, according to the surveyor Robert Edmunds) and a flag was removed from a pole at Point Ayers. During early September two horses returned to the Escape Cliffs camp with spear wounds. Colonel Finniss, whom the writer Ernestine Hill later described as 'allergic to blacks', was determined to teach the Woolna a lesson. They were, he wrote to Henry Ayers in Adelaide, 'most determined thieves, regular wreckers'.[30] On 8 September 1864 Finniss armed a group of cavalry and foot soldiers, including Alaric Ward, Frederick

Litchfield (who had also been wounded in the Adelaide River affray) and Patrick Auld. Ignoring the surgeon Goldsmith, despite his official designation as 'Protector of Aborigines', Finniss placed the force under the inexperienced command of his son Frederick. The party's official objective was to recover stolen property.

Near Chambers Bay the party came upon a group of Woolna, mainly composed of women and children collecting yams. An 'elderly man' in that group, holding a digging stick and with a small basket containing roots or tubers suspended around his neck, was chased by the horsemen into scrub near the beach. He was wounded in the knee at a distance, then Patrick Auld shot him in the chest at close range. Mortally wounded, this individual was shot in the back of the head by one of the party, Dugall, 'out of pity as he was staggering away'.[31] The party recovered a few items of stolen property, mainly comprising knives and forks and an 'electroplated ladle'. In turn they looted the camp of artefacts, including nets, baskets and weapons. Then they put it to the torch and returned to Escape Cliffs, to be offered a congratulatory sherry by Finniss.

A commission of enquiry and a Royal Commission in Adelaide later confirmed that Frederick Finniss had given orders to 'shoot the bloody natives', and that these orders had issued from his father. The Commission concluded that this 'retaliation against the aborigines was not in the spirit of the instructions received by him [Finniss] for his dealings with the native race'.[32]

John Bennett had taken no part in the Chambers Bay expedition and made strenuous efforts to distance himself from it, angrily charging Frederick Finniss not to shoot any Aboriginal person 'within fifty yards of his camp'.[33] Unfortunately, Bennett's own lengthy account of the episode, contained in a letter to his father, has been crossed through in heavy ink.[34]

Fifty yards was still within range of spear and carbine, hardly a sufficient distance to absolve Bennett of his connection with these events. Later, that naïve confidence in his own boundaries was to contribute to Bennett's own demise. For now, he took care to note the sites of these collisions, marking them on his map. The beach at Chambers Bay, *Me-tar-ler*, became number five on the list of place-names accompanying his vocabulary. The site on the Adelaide River where Pearson was wounded and where the first Woolna man was killed, was number eleven, *Mul-wy-la*. Almost a year to the day after the Adelaide River killing, Alaric Ward was speared to death and his body mutilated, apparently in direct payback. This occurred barely 100 metres from the camp at Escape Cliffs, within sight of the four-metre stockade which Finniss ordered his men to construct during July 1865. From this date Finniss strengthened the defences, forbidding contact with the Woolna. He directed that they 'must be mistrusted whatever their professions, and on no acccount permitted to enter the camp, or to approach near enough to examine the situation of things, or ascertain the number within'.[35]

But there were alternative ways of interacting with the Woolna. Surveyor Robert Edmunds joined the expedition in late 1864 with the task of surveying a port at the Narrows, near the mouth of the Adelaide River. His first duty was to convene an enquiry into the Chambers Bay affair, reporting directly to the South Australian government, Edmunds concluded that Finniss had effectively sanctioned murder. Edmunds' attitude to Finniss was not improved by the fact that the Narrows site, like Escape Cliffs itself, was patently unsuitable; it was mostly under water during the wet season.

Edmunds considered that 'with ordinary precautions the blacks will do no harm'. Finniss criticised this 'foolish policy with the natives', and strongly advised Edmunds 'not to allow natives near ... and not to go unprepared, for he finds them still unsubdued'. Defiantly, Edmunds encouraged interaction with the Woolna, and even tolerated occasional pilfering: 'all they wanted was iron or iron hoops and bagging or things of that nature'. Alaric Ward's murder did not provoke Edmunds' sympathy with this mood for reprisal. He informed the more belligerent of his men that each 'could use his own discretion, but if I could find that he or his party had fired upon any unoffending natives within fifty miles of this camp so help me God if I could get a rope around his or his parties necks I would do so'. Edmunds knew that Finniss already faced a further official enquiry into his actions and had little to lose with further bloodshed. 'It appears to me', Edmunds wrote in his journal, 'that Mr Finniss is anxious to see a few natives shot, that the Chambers Bay affair may appear less glaring'. But, Edmunds reiterated, 'if a native dies through me it shall be in fair fight and he shall be the aggressor'.[36]

Edmunds' 'foolish policy' soon brought results. While Finniss's party at Escape Cliffs cowered behind their stockade and attempted to frighten the Aborigines away with flares and fireworks, Edmunds ran an open camp. A crucial meeting occurred just three weeks after Ward's death, in late August 1865:

This morning about 10 am a lot of natives appeared on a rise about 3/4 mile west of the camp and shouted, at the same time throwing up their arms, showing they were unarmed. After some time and much confab amongst themselves 14 of them ventured to the camp and eventually others followed and gave us a short corroboree.[37]

Edmunds dressed a spear wound on a man's foot.

A few days later more visitors arrived, among them the man who had speared Pearson a year earlier. Objects began to pass between the Woolna and the Europeans. Edmunds gave an old shirt and other 'trifles'. He demonstrated the use of a gun, shooting five kites out of the sky. The Woolna men 'were greatly astonished to see the birds fall without seeing anything hit them'. One man promised some spears, and brought them to the camp some days later. He had been fighting and Edmunds dressed his spear wounds. Within a few short weeks the surveyor had established a formidable reputation as a doctor. 'Now', Edmunds wrote, 'if anything is the matter with any of them I am sought after, and when any of them come to the camp and they don't see me, they want to know where I am'.[38]

Was trust established so easily? Perhaps not. Edmunds' conciliatory optimism overlooked the Woolna's basic assumptions: that the Europeans were temporary invaders who might yet be driven away, and that an unadjusted debt of blood remained. In that light, Finniss's narrow and fatalistic policy of 'subduing the natives' accorded more with the reality of colonial encounter. Finniss expressed it clearly enough in his defence before the Royal Commission later held into his management of the expedition: 'The government had sent the party to occupy their [the Woolna's] territory without regard to their wishes, and if we were to remain there we were to overcome their hostility, and this, as we had proved, could not be done by means of conciliation and forbearance'.[39]

Finniss might have predicted the outcome of the fraternisation at Edmunds' camp: a gradual lessening of vigilance allowing the Woolna to deliver a devastating blow against the Europeans. The day arrived on 20 September, just three weeks after Edmunds opened his camp to the Woolna. The crisis was reached when Edmunds returned to the camp in the afternoon, after working on the surveys. He found the camp 'swarming with natives all armed'. More disturbingly, most of his men were surrounded among a group of '74 as fine savages as you could wish to see, all armed to the teeth, with some young fellows, reserves, a short distance off, with bundles of spears'. Two of his officers held carbines, but these might easily have been wrested from them: 'had a fight started our men would have been knocked on the head at once'.

In a moment the frontier, manageably distant a few hours earlier, had contracted to this fragile encampment. Edmunds kept his head. He quietly told the men accompanying him to make for the arms tent, unobtrusively. In the meantime he walked to his own tent and checked that his gun was loaded.

He left it there and approached the large group of armed Woolna. Facing one of them, he spoke loudly and rapidly in clear English (still largely unintelligible to the Woolna), but actually addressing his own men. He told them 'to quietly make for the arms tent, to light their pipes or do anything so as to show no fear or hurry'. No one was to fire a shot unless commanded. Edmunds continued talking at a volume, making a spectacle of himself for the Woolna:

> Having got the men clear one by one and [seeing] that should anything now happen we were ready for them, I pointed the blacks to the place they usually were allowed to be and pushed the leaders towards it. They resisted at first but when they saw I was determined they went. They evidently saw the move that was made. If they had acted promptly everything would have been their own, but it was now too late, eventually they went away.[40]

The frontier settled back into place, a balance of sorts.

A few days later, when the Woolna visited the camp, once more on friendly terms, Edmunds now learnt how close his camp had come to annihilation: 'one of my patients tried to show me that when the mob came to the camp on the 20th they intended to kill our party and appropriate our belongings'.[41] His had been a knife-edge feat of diplomacy. One of its effects was to convince the Woolna that the just targets of their retribution remained the jittery defenders of Finniss's stockade, a few miles away. Bennett, despite sharing Edmunds' sympathies, was in the wrong camp.

During September 1865 the South Australian government recalled Finniss to face the parliamentary enquiry which would firmly condemn his management of the expedition. His proposed site for settlement had also been comprehensively discredited in favour of Port Darwin, to the west. Bennett remained at Escape Cliffs until late 1866 with the main party, under Manton's command. By then, his fellow-officers' enthusiasm for South Australia's tropical colony (and for each other) had steadily soured. Once again, Bennett was an exception, proudly informing his father of the expedition doctor's opinion:

> Dr Ninnis only the other day told me how well I was looking & said he did think I intended going back by [the] Bengal with the rest judging from my looks & appearance of health, the country evidently agreed with me. I assure you, although I now do feel the heat & can appreciate cool weather & cold too, that the country will be very comfortable to live in, providing a person has a few luxuries – I mean such as plenty of water . . . verandahs, fowls or geese, milk and butter, ale

& beer & light colonial clarets might be added. With these I fancy a European might live here comfortably.[42]

By 1865 the Northern Territory Company's chief shareholder, Henry Ayers, was already ridding himself of his investment, but Bennett had no such qualms. He applied for two land orders, using his own and his father's money.[43] His 'great idea' was to establish a commercial garden on the Adelaide or Howard Rivers, after the style of the successful Highercombe fruit and vegetable garden in Adelaide, and a cotton plantation on the coast, run with imported 'coolie' labour. Bennett laid out this vision for his father:

> I picture to myself a fine Garden – 160 acres – tilled by Coolies – Residence of 'My dear Father' & family – with coolie servants. If we go-a-head in Commerce soon we <u>may</u> see <u>this</u>. If so I should be most happy. I know my dear Papa & Mama would enjoy themselves here.[44]

He imagined himself living on the Howard River in a wooden house similar to that built twenty years earlier by the 'White Rajah', James Brooke of Labuhan, in Sarawak. There would be a cool and 'lofty' sitting room, built of logs:

> with canvas lining to drop or roll up, as required. The logs not close but just put alongside one another, they must leave an opening between each – with a well-watered floor, which treads down very hard is most excellently cool here – seldom or never above 86 [deg. fahrenheit] inside – With a nice couch or mat my papa could either sit or lie & smoke & enjoy spreading the Times or <u>St James Chronicle or Standard</u>!!!![45]

It may not be a coincidence that Bennett wore his hair and sideburns in the style of 'Rajah Brooke' who ruled over his Sarawak principality during the 1840s and 1850s. This extraordinary figure combined a 'Boys' Own Annual' adventurism with the ideals of an enlightened despot, a convincing role-model for young men of the British Empire.[46] As for Bennett's ideas about 'coolie labour', these may have been inspired by George Samuel Windsor Earl, whose publications provided the main source of intelligence on the Aboriginal people in the region prior to South Australian colonisation. Earl had recommended against the suitability of Aboriginal people as a source of labour.[47]

Returning to the survey office in Adelaide during late 1866, Bennett had two years to revise his utopian notions, before setting off for the northern coast once more. None of his letters survive from that second expedition, and so it is not possible to chart the progress of his scheme to settle there. What is clear though, is that his interest in recording the language of the Woolna deepened. Within a short time of his arrival the idea of regarding these people as his 'brothers and sisters' might not have provoked such a sense of outrage in Bennett.

BENNETT RETURNS

The South Australian colonists set foot on the northern coast once again during early 1869. This time they were more dedicated pioneers, competently led by Surveyor-General George Goyder. The first project was to map the country, connect it to the south by surveyed tracks and townships, and clear a straight path for the telegraph line now being proposed to connect Adelaide with the heart of empire, London itself.

Goyder's expedition provided Bennett with an opportunity to expunge the slurs levelled at him during his association with Finniss. Goyder was a master surveyor, able to reward those achievements in draftsmanship and cartography of which Bennett was capable. Goyder also appreciated Bennett's talent for language. In contrast to Finniss, who had explained to Henry Ayers that until 'a settlement is actually formed, no steps can be taken to conciliate them, or to learn the language, the ignorance of which, constitutes our great difficulty', Goyder was prepared to encourage Bennett's linguistic work in the field, beyond the pale of settlement.[48]

The new settlement of Port Darwin was sited in the territory of the Larrakia, but these people were soon joined by the Adelaide River

Portrait of George Goyder, Surveyor-General, before his expedition's departure in late 1868. Photographers: H. Anson and W. Francis, Adelaide. W.W. Hoare album, PRG 294/1, State Library of South Australia.

Woolna, from the east, who knew Bennett well. In fact, when the expedition's schooner, the *Moonta*, anchored at Port Darwin, and Goyder and a small party stepped ashore on 6 February 1869, it was probably Woolna men who met them on the beach. William Webster Hoare noted in his journal that as they landed: 'two Blackfellows came to see us and spoke to Bennett & other old N.T. hands ... they seemed pleased to see us'.[49] But the apparent pleasure the Woolna showed in renewing their former acquaintance masked a deeper obligation. Bennett was probably the only one in the party with sufficient knowledge of the Woolna language to have understood the import of the exchange. It was Goyder who wrote later that: 'we were informed on arrival of the *Moonta* by the blacks here that those on the Adelaide or near that locality intended to kill two of our party'.[50]

This was not a random blood debt, to be exacted on any Europeans. We know that partly because of the way events unfolded from this point, during the first months of 1869. As well, the Woolna had encountered another South Australian party in the meantime, and had not acted against them. This meeting was with Captain Francis Cadell's 1867 expedition, charged with locating a new site for the capital. When Cadell anchored at Escape Cliffs on 31 October and visited the old settlement, he expected to find it ransacked after its abandonment a year earlier. Instead, his men were greeted by the old Woolna 'chief', Mira, who raised the settlement flag as they approached, then escorted the South Australians around the buildings. Nothing had been touched since Finniss's party had sailed away. In view of the great interest shown in European metal and cloth elsewhere on the frontier, this forbearance is difficult to explain, except in terms of a taboo resulting from the Woolna's rationalisation of the Finniss party's departure:

> Looking up to the town we saw the flag hoisted on the staff of what used to be the superintendent's house, from which we knew that Myra, the old chief, was at home; but he had hoisted the Union Jack half-mast and upside down, which would have been rather ominous if we had thought that he knew the usages of civilization; as it was, we took it as a token of rejoicing at our arrival. As we neared the beach twenty to thirty natives came rushing into the water to meet us, with old Myra at their head, with a large felt hat on, and carrying a red flag. We proceeded in a body to the town at the top of the cliffs ... On the beach the horse boat or ferry punt was lying perfectly sound. It had cost about 800 pounds in Adelaide. There were also iron water tanks, wooden casks and vats, never moved nor a hoop taken off. We were surprised at such self-denial on the

part of the blacks, but on getting into the town our astonishment was greater. We found everything as it had been left – not a window broken, nor table nor chair moved; not a bottle or paper disturbed. There they were as they had been left, the remains of books, papers, memoranda (many of these the owners would rather they had not been so carefully preserved), bottles without number, inkstands, a fine plough, never used, wagons, harness, etc etc. The very gardens had been left untouched; the vegetables and fruit had been left to wither and rot on the trees, rather than that anything should be injured. We plucked some fine bunches of bananas and three or four pineapples. Several cocoanut trees were thriving well, also cassava trees and cotton plants. The 'Julia' cutter was lying sunk in the creek where she had been left, and perfectly sound, with all her gear about her. The captain and I went a little way into the bush, accompanied by two or three of the young natives, when to our surprise they struck up in excellent time and tune 'John Brown' and several other airs of similar stamp.[51]

Cadell presented Mira with a shirt, a pair of trousers, a sword and belt, and sailed on, having determined that Port Darwin, to the east, would be the new capital. This was where Bennett's story recommences, in early 1869.

At Port Darwin the dance of objects began again. Thirty years earlier the colony of South Australia had directed its first collections of natural history and ethnography to the British Museum. Now Adelaide had its own museum with cupboards to fill, ledgers to complete, new species to describe. Friedrich Schultze was the expedition's naturalist. Assisted by his son Alfred, Schultze was an assiduous collector; within a month of the Goyder expedition's arrival the pair had consigned twelve crates of dried plants and animal specimens to the Adelaide Botanic Gardens and the museum. Among the preserved bird-skins, crustaceae, shells, insects, fish, reptiles, and corals was a solitary Aboriginal weapon and some emu feathers 'used by the Natives as Ornament'.[52]

More Aboriginal material followed in later months. The Woolna asserted their right to enter the European camp, often in opposition to the Larrakia. A collection of 'native weapons and manufactures', including 'spears, basket-work, amulets etc' was among Schultze's June consignment of natural history specimens. Among 35 boxes of animals, birds, fish, reptiles, corals, insects and plants sent south by ship in January 1870, Schultze included examples of Aboriginal head-dress – perhaps worn in ceremonies to mark the arrival of these new, single-minded colonists. In total, Schultze and his son collected more than 8000 natural history specimens.[53]

William Webster Hoare, the surgeon's assistant, assumed the role of scientific

155

William Hoare's watercolour painting of a crab collected by the expedition naturalist,
Friedrich Schultze. PRG 294/4, State Library of South Australia.

illustrator, drawing and painting 'perishable specimens of natural history' with his
box of government-supplied watercolours. He bartered with Aboriginal men and
women for specimens and ethnographic objects, illustrated them and passed
them to Schultze for consignment to Adelaide. On 4 May 1869 he collected a
reed necklace from Biliamuk, a young Larrakia man. Two days later he 'obtained
a few things from the natives viz. yam bag, necklace, Emue feather ornament,
a headdress with bills of the Spoonbill attached, bracelets of reed and Native
string'. On 14 May it was 'a bunch of Sea Bird feathers', followed by 'two large
fishing spears and a basket' (19 May), 'another Native Basket only better than
that got yesterday' (20 May), and 'spears in exchange for food etc' (23 May).[54]
That last exchange occurred a day before the holiday declared for Queen
Victoria's 50th birthday on 24 May 1869, the day Bennett was to meet his fate.

Unlike Schultze, whose interest in the Aborigines extended only to their
abilities as natural history collectors, Hoare was diverted by their habits and
appearance. He made the most of chance meetings on those occasions when
Woolna and Larrakia men (and sometimes women) entered the camp, mostly
during Goyder's absences. His curiosity extended to details of their appearance:

William Hoare's watercolour painting of a blue-spotted fantail ray (*Taeniura lymma*) collected by the expedition naturalist, Friedrich Schultze. PRG 294/4, State Library of South Australia.

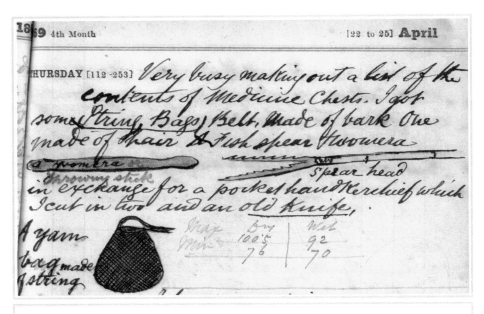

Detail of a page from William Hoare's scrapbook, recording his acquisition of artefacts including a string bag, in exchange for a knife and a pocket handkerchief, April 1869. W.W. Hoare album, PRG 294/1, State Library of South Australia.

The Natives paint themselves with Red, Yellow, White in different styles. It is curious to see the scars on the body of the Natives. They are raised folds of flesh very much in relief nearly half an inch above their skins and half an inch wide'.[55]

Each had something for the other. For some of the Europeans, mere exoticism was enough. Men like Schultze and Hoare wove this contact into their daily routine, exchanging food, tobacco and cast-off items for animal and plant specimens or artefacts. For the Aboriginal people, who were used to obtaining tobacco and metal through occasional contact with Malay fishermen, the desirable commodities were sweet and processed foods – particularly flour, sugar, tea and tobacco – and iron objects which could be incorporated into traditional weapons.

Other miscellaneous objects caught the eye, on both sides. An Aboriginal woman came to Hoare's tent, curious to see his drawing of an insect. Hoare showed her, then gave her a looking glass: 'she was highly delighted ... looked at herself with such a contorting countenance as to cause convulsed laughter'. More than anyone in the camp, Hoare came closest to stepping into the ambiguous zone in which Bennett already found himself. The pair were friends, after all. After Goyder assigned Bennett to his old Escape Cliffs duty of taking meteorological readings, Hoare accompanied him as an assistant each evening, beyond the stockade.

Bennett and Hoare both shared Goyder's table in the officers' mess. This time there was no 'court circular', no facetious gossip. The camp ran smoothly. An accomplished surveyor who appreciated the rigours of the task, Goyder enjoyed the unwavering respect of his men: his nickname was 'Little Energy'. Within six months he had completed the survey of Palmerston, a number of outlying townships, section blocks and the roads between, comprising a total of 600,000 acres claimed from the wilderness. Goyder was the son of David George Goyder, the notable Swedenborgian and phrenologist (1796–1878). The father traced lines on human skulls; the son traced lines across the Australian landscape, probing for its latent tendencies. Goyder's Line in South Australia's mid-north is still accepted as the boundary, often ambiguous, between areas of reliable and unreliable rainfall. But here, in the remotest bush, Goyder was intent on keeping boundaries sharp, unblurred.[56]

The Port Darwin camp in 1869, from the top of Fort Hill, before the stockade was erected. The tent on the opposite slope was probably used by the naturalist, Friedrich Schultze. Photographer: Joseph Brooks. W.W. Hoare album, PRG 294/1, State Library of South Australia.

Before the expedition set out, Goyder had proposed a scheme of relations with the Aboriginal people. Its prudent wording suggested that he had studied the evidence of the Finniss enquiry:

> ... care would require to be taken to prove to the natives that though, except under strong provocation, they would never be harmed or interfered with, yet that, persistent aggression on their part, would be followed by effective measures to prevent interference on ours, and to ensure the peaceful prosecution of the survey. In doing this, all cause of annoyance or interference would be strictly avoided, and familiarity rarely, if ever, indulged in: and the parties would be so arranged as to be able to concentrate their forces, and support and protect each other, and upon all occasions, to avoid any appearance of isolation or weakness, which too frequently induces the aborigines to indulge in the promptings of their savage instincts, causing reprisals, which, though they may secure the object sought, only does so at a great sacrifice, and one that cannot be too much regretted.[57]

On 6 March 1869 Goyder issued a memo advising his men against fraternisation of any sort and then, following Finniss's example, ordered a stockade constructed around the camp.

'Fraternisation' was an ill-defined term, but it seems to have been the last thing in the minds of most expedition members. Men in the line-clearing parties strapped on Colt revolvers before their forays into the bush. Schultze and his 'great fellow' of a son roamed around outside the stockade with nets and jars, intriguing Aboriginal people with their desire for specimens, but keeping to themselves. The bush was swarming with life, a rich haul of rare and new species. Almost all could be captured, collected and brought back to Schultze's tent – 'not a very savoury place to be near'. For that reason it was pitched well away, half-way up the hill behind the settlement.[58] Inevitably, Schultze overstepped the mark. Goyder recorded that on 29 April the young Larrakia man, Biliamuk, had saved the German naturalist from being speared by another, Nalunga, who had demanded food. Biliamuk then dissuaded Schultze from getting his revolver, saying 'no good, no good'.[59] Schultze moved his tent within the stockade and had no further trouble.

The closer the lens descends on these moments of contact, the more clearly individuals are exposed as agents, swinging events one way or the other. Despite his policy, even Goyder became enmeshed in the reciprocities which continually defined and redefined relations between his men and the two Aboriginal groups, whose approaches to his camp remained inconsistent, unpredictable. In this context bartered objects took on additional significance. On the day of Biliamuk's intervention on Schultze's behalf, Goyder gave an Aboriginal man a 'tomahawk and a little food' in exchange for a canoe and paddles, observing that the man 'would have sold all he had save only some dry human bones which the doctor coveted, but which he was not allowed even to look at'.[60]

As the earlier failures of British settlement made clear, little certainty attached to the isolated efforts of Europeans in this region. The success of the colonial venture hinged on the cooperation of local Aboriginal groups. Just as in Barker's time, particular Aboriginal individuals assumed prominence as brokers between their people and Europeans. Besides acting as guides, interpreters and advisers on water sources and landing places, Aborigines were crucial to those natural history and ethnographic projects interleaved with the colonial mission. Goyder, Schultze, Bennett and Hoare relied on three Aboriginal men: the Woolna elder Mira, and two young Larrakia men, Biliamuk and Umballa. The British anglicised the last two names as 'Billy Muck' and 'Tom Powell'.

Studio photograph of 'Lillawer, Billimuck [centre] and Lungaba', after their arrival in Adelaide, late 1870. From W.W. Hoare album, PRG 294/1, State Library of South Australia.

Biliamuk seems to have become the most adept in this new game of slipping in and out of situations, camps, stockades. A year later, in the wake of Bennett's spearing, Biliamuk, Umballa and another Larrakia man, Lirawa, were taken south by ship to Adelaide for a visit 'in order to impress them with the number and power of the white races' and thus convince the local Aboriginal people to desist from hostilities.[61] On Biliamuk's return he worked as a police tracker in Darwin, but soon found himself in gaol for stealing government property. His pencil drawings of animals were included with other drawings made by Aboriginal prisoners, in the first public exhibition of Aboriginal art. A year later Biliamuk worked as a gardener in the grounds

Biliamuk Gapal, aged about 38 years, at Palmerston in 1890. Photographer: Paul Foelsche. Foelsche Collection, South Australian Museum Archives.

surrounding the prison, before spending more time inside. He was photographed at least three times by the police superintendent-cum-ethnographer, Paul Foelsche. These photographs were part of a series sent by Foelsche to International Exhibitions and museums. Together with the 1870 photograph of Biliamuk in Adelaide, the images convey the breadth of this individual's engagement with frontier society, from protégé, to inmate, to ethnographic type.[62]

In the meantime the Woolna elder Mira played a key role in mediating relations. No photograph of him survives unfortunately, but he is prominent in the written record of encounters between his people and the South Australians. In April 1869 he intervened to prevent his own people spearing two Malay trepang-fishers who had survived the wreck of their boat. Mira brought the two survivors to Fort Point (as Port Darwin was known) and the surveyor ordered him 'a ration for his humanity'.[63] The Malays were welcome strangers for Bennett, who had been surveying on the Adelaide River, to the south. Visiting Port Darwin on that day, he took away one of the 'Timor natives' (as Hoare described the shipwrecked sailors) to his camp, 'to learn their language'.[64] Three weeks later Mira became 'an object of annoyance', when he or his fellows stole some bread from the Darwin settlement. Goyder's men became 'flurried' and Mira was turned away from the settlement the next day. Quiet returned, but Goyder felt it necessary to send a note to the nearest survey camp, warning the men to be on their guard.[65] Later, at least one of Goyder's men considered that the eviction of this senior Woolna man provided the trigger for Bennett's death.

Mira's presence at Fort Point was barely tolerated by the Larrakia of the Darwin region and Goyder's men were obliged to come to his defence more than once. As Goyder put it: 'Even the Chief Mira had to be protected from the natives here by the men of the expedition, as spears were raised against him in the camp at Fort Point, because his policy was friendly to us'.[66] But Mira's 'policy' may not have been so friendly. As Hoare noted, Mira was a 'chief from Escape Cliffs'.[67] He had been the main intermediary between the Woolna and Finniss's party at Escape Cliffs, and the killings of two Woolna men there had set events in train which were still to be played out. The two men shot by Finniss's men were, at the least, Mira's classificatory kin, if not his blood relatives. The score was his to settle. It may well have been Mira who approached Bennett when he stepped ashore on that first day, to inform him this debt would inevitably be paid.

Mira was conciliatory enough to remove himself from direct suspicion. Neither Goyder nor Bennett appreciated that he may have been laying groundwork for events about to unfold. The fact that Mira was also a visitor at Fort

Point, reliant upon the Larrakia people's hospitality but not always tolerated by them, brought him more easily within the European sphere. Goyder had an additional reason for indulging Mira, for he could see his worth as a language informant, to Bennett in particular. The Surveyor-General understood, just as Finniss had done, that facility in Aboriginal languages was the key to winning the land. 'Until the object and motives of the whites can be clearly explained in their own language, and the natives be satisfactorily convinced of the futility and impolicy of opposition', Goyder wrote, 'the prevailing state of fragile uncertainty and constant danger' would continue.[68]

Bennett's language project was more than his own passing hobby. Like Hoare's natural history illustrations and Schultze's specimens, his words and phrases were essential to the colonial programme, a means of gaining a footing in the trackless bush and civilising its inhabitants. By early April Goyder and his deputy, surgeon Robert Peel, had taken an official interest in Bennett's vocabulary. Hoare was requested to make a copy for Peel. It was this copy, with its several errors of transcription, which was eventually published in 1879, ten years after Bennett's death and which surfaced among N.B. Tindale's papers, decades later.

Some of these errors are slight. They mostly relate to the placement of hyphens within Woolna words, or small errors of transcription by Hoare which were directly reproduced in the published version. Identifying those errors (and additional errors and omissions) in Hoare's second copy, and in the published version of Bennett's vocabulary, helped me to place the different manuscripts in sequence, and to better understand Hoare's role in Bennett's project.

Hoare tended to misread Bennett's letter 'l' as 't', particularly when that letter was followed by an emphasis over a following vowel. Hoare read Bennett's entry for 'bracelets: reed, grass', as 'bracelets: reed, glass'. A slip of the same order, reproduced in Hoare's second copy and in the published version, is more glaring. Bennett gave Woolna terms for two forms of a spearthrower – 'womera, heavy and light'. Hoare misread this as 'woman, heavy and light', posing a challenge for future linguists not knowing of Bennett's original notebook.[69]

The notebook also makes sense of the fifteen apparently miscellaneous Woolna place-names listed in the 1879 Bennett publication and in Hoare's copy. In Bennett's notebook that original list of sites is numbered and keyed to a small accompanying map (reproduced here, on p. 167) which represents Bennett's knowledge of the Aboriginal landscape. Most of those sites figured in the following events.

FRED'S PASS

As the wet season floods abated during late April 1869, Bennett prepared to join a small party under John Knuckey. Their task was to survey country 30 miles to the south-east of Fort Point, where a pass through the Daly Range led to open country. Finniss had named this pass after his son Fred, and had compared it to 'some of the romantic pretty scenes' in the Scottish Highlands. According to Bennett, Finniss had been most impressed by the locality, even dreaming of 'the chance of building a Castle in character with the scenery – rocks almost perpindicular & running stream beneath with fallen rock on opposite side – 300 ft high'.[70]

Goyder visited Fred's Pass on 15 May and decided that it should be surveyed as a 'small township', to be named 'Daly'. There would be ten streets, sloping south from Mount Daly almost to the shores of the extensive lagoon named for Patrick Auld (of the Chambers Bay shooting). It would be surrounded by parklands and there would be a cemetery. Bennett set to work with his set square and compass, delineating this vision. Perhaps he imagined his own residence there, overlooking the lagoon. Like other townships south of Darwin envisaged by Goyder, 'Daly' would never take physical form.[71]

Away from the regimented life of Fort Darwin, neither Knuckey nor Bennett had need of a stockade. A rope laid on the ground was enough to mark off the small camp from the surrounding bush, where the Woolna came and went. They arrived at the rope each morning, out of curiosity and expectation. But Bennett had already blurred the line. In a moment, a new word or phrase could draw him across it, into the Aboriginal landscape beyond. By the middle of May, Bennett seemed to consider that his English–Woolna vocabulary was complete, a couple of hundred equivalences – each a small expression of the tension drawing these two cultures together, and holding them apart. The following selection from his vocabulary illuminates that liminal edge of contact as a zone of fascination. This suite of objects and actions is marked with the imprint of Bennett's own traverse:

Be off	*ber.ro.que*
Boat, box, case, ship	*mo.erty*
Bring here	*line.ter*
Bullet, stone, pebble	*lung.a*
Come with me	*min.ee*
Dancing	*ya.wer*
Don't touch	*nal.yer*

Dream	*we.ye.ler.met.ping.er*
Frightened	*ngin.mar*
Give me	*ker.nan.mer*
Headache	*mud.lo.qua*
Knife, scissors, razor	*merry.merry*
Laugh	*wal.er*
Likeness, image, reflection, portrait	*ler.mur.lee.che*
Masts (ship)	*wur.nung.er*
Name	*mer.wal*
Pin, needle	*na.a.nin*
Silence! Hold your tongue!	*cup! nim.ee*
Singing, song	*men.in.yer*
Sit down	*loorl*
Sores, smallpox	*purrer.purrer*
Speak out!	*peb! nimee*
Sugar	*wag.kee*
Swim	*mo.il.wer*
Talk with us	*lil–ye*
Well, good health, safe	*ngeud.lo*
You, yours	*ne.lan.gee*

The term recurring most in Bennett's vocabulary is *ler.mur.lee.che*, defined variously as an 'image', a 'portrait', a 'likeness', and a 'reflection'. It was as though Bennett encountered this term anew each time, not readily accepting that something as clear to him as a portrait might be confused with an image reflected in the lagoon, just a spear's throw from his tent.

Bennett enjoyed swimming in the lagoon. During the Escape Cliffs expedition he had swum in the sea until December 1865, when Finniss recorded that the young surveyor was 'stung by a jelly fish on the leg and wrist'.[72] Bennett also swam in Auld's Lagoon, and the Woolna told him its name – *Qua-kee*. This term was appended to his vocabulary, with a list of other place-names keyed to his small sketch map.[73] The map contained several of the places he had come to know during the Escape Cliffs expedition, particularly during the surveying voyage of the *Beatrice* which followed the Adelaide River as far south as Auld's Lagoon, to the west of Fred's Pass. Escape Cliffs, *Patter Purrer*, was marked, as well as the Narrows, *Loeil.wil*. Finniss's first survey camp on the Adelaide River, *Mul.wi.ya*, had been the site of 'Pearson's fight' in 1865. This place, and the 'Sandy Beach' at Chambers Bay, *Met.arler*, were the sites of the two killings of Woolna men.

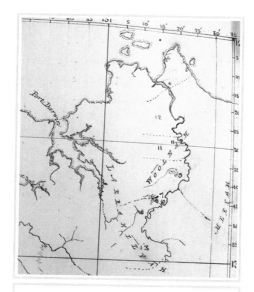

Detail of Bennett's map, showing numbered sites along the Adelaide River, 1864, local boundaries and three tribal names. J.W.O. Bennett notebook, Goyder Papers, GRG 35/256/11, State Records, Adelaide.

Bennett's little map has greater significance. It was the first of its kind since the Catholic missionary-priest Angelo Confalonieri had mapped seven Aboriginal groups of the Cobourg Peninsula from his base near Port Essington during the late 1840s. Bennett placed four tribal names across his map – the 'Warnunger' well to the west of Port Darwin (Tindale's Kungarakan), the 'Larrakia' of Port Darwin, the 'Woolnah', centred on the Adelaide River, and the 'Meerah', perhaps corresponding to Tindale's Erei or Beriguruk.[74]

More than that, Bennett's map contains several dotted lines bisecting the region of the Adelaide River, where most of his place-names are situated. Interpreted in conjunction with his identification of three 'chiefs' associated with particular named localities, it is reasonable to interpret these lines as Bennett's attempt to define, cartographically, the territories of local groups of the Woolna and Larrakia. His vocabulary term for 'country, district' – *te-eng-er* – confirms that this notion had attracted his interest.[75] Mira's name does not appear on Bennett's list, perhaps because his association with Escape Cliffs (*Patter Purrer*) was so well known. The three 'chiefs' identified by Bennett may all have had a role in the events about to unfold at Fred's Pass and *Qua-kee*, Auld's Lagoon. It might be expected, for example, that *Neur.lung.er*, the 'chief' of *Mul.wi.ya*, would play some part in determining the revenge to be exacted for the murder there of his countryman or relative four years earlier. Bennett recorded that '*Timowry*' was the chief of the *Ler-mar-wehl* district, just upstream from the Narrows, close to the second murder at Chambers Bay. *Neur.lunger* and *Timowry* were undoubtedly local Woolna headmen. Bennett also recorded 'Chief *Deringee.aboom*' of the *Win.din.din* district, just south of Auld's Lagoon and Fred's Pass. He may have been a Larrakia elder, for Auld's Lagoon itself was at the south-western edge of Woolna country, bordering Larrakia country.

At Fred's Pass, Bennett was permitted to attend Aboriginal ritual performances which went beyond those public 'corroborees' presented to the main camp at Fort Point. According to witnesses, the Woolna painted his face and body for these ceremonies. Bennett had become more than an onlooker, but it is unlikely that he comprehended the reciprocal obligations entailed by this privilege.

Now the most nondescript objects, previously exchanged freely at the surface of contact, were embedded in meaning, strung with attachments and expectations. The Woolna brought natural history specimens to Bennett, who sent them on to William Hoare at Fort Point. Bennett noted down the Woolna terms, expanding his vocabulary. On 8 May he sent a skinned specimen of 'a pink or rose-breasted Grey Cockatoo' (recording its Woolna name, '*Galah*'), for Hoare to sketch. In the accompanying note Bennett wrote that he had just obtained a 'fair specimen of native pheasant ("*Lee-a-wer*" (native name)) and am very glad to send it for your acceptance'. Hoare fixed his friend's note into his scrapbook journal.[76]

Detail of a photograph of one of Goyder's survey camps, south of Palmerston, 1869, taken by an unknown photographer. Goyder is the bearded figure seated at centre. The tents and drafting tables were probably very similar to those used by Bennett. State Library of South Australia.

INSIDE THE CIRCLE – 24 MAY 1869

Following Goyder's visit to Fred's Pass on 15 May, four separate survey parties converged on the locality for a week, in order to complete the survey of the township. A small village of tents was erected close to the small lagoon – round, conical tents for the men, square tents to accommodate the stores and the drafting tables. With all these surveyors, draftsmen and chainmen the task was largely completed by Friday 21 May. Two of the parties left for other duties, basing themselves at Manton Lake, *Mum.mer.me.a.ker*, to the north-east. Then Surveyor Mitchell's party departed on the morning of Sunday 23 May, leaving just Knuckey's party of five men, including Bennett, to finish the survey. Before the departure of these parties the camp had been visited on most mornings by two or three Woolna men. After Mitchell and his men set off, fifteen Aboriginal men made their appearance and approached the camp, 'but did not attempt to go beyond a certain point which Mr Bennett had told them not to cross'.[77] This 'certain point' was the rope circle laid on the ground around the camp's perimeter. The Woolna generally approached this boundary each morning 'some hours after sunrise', but remained outside it, unless invited inside.

On that Sunday morning Bennett went out shooting with the Woolna, and took the spoils to their camp. There they cooked a bush turkey he had shot, and he remained with them for a midday meal. Afterwards, they 'painted him after their native fashion'. Perhaps there was some dancing, or some singing.

By now Bennett's appearance must have borne little resemblance to the foppish, manicured photo-portrait taken in Adelaide. When he returned to the camp, still bearing evidence of body paint, his fellow-surveyors may have drawn comfort from this obvious intimacy with the natives. Bennett seemed to have achieved a balance of trust with the Woolna, based reassuringly on the reciprocity of small exchanges. In any event, the party was well enough armed with rifles and revolvers; any risk of attack seemed adequately countered by a shadow of retribution. Bennett and his fellows were unaware that his compromising excursions had caused their rope circle to be regarded as a target, rather than a boundary.

Bennett had been warned. The fifteen Woolna who came to the survey camp on Sunday afternoon did 'all in their power to induce the men in camp to bathe in the waterhole', but 'Mr Bennett was the only one who did so'. Bennett later admitted that 'he had done so in order to show them that he had every faith and confidence in them'. Emerging from the lagoon he had heard the men speaking in their own language. They asked him if he understood them; he told them that he did, but that 'it was no good for them to attack the whites'.[78]

Returning to the camp after his swim he took the precaution of loading the firearms. Even so, as the later account in the *Observer* had it, he did not seem 'to have seriously entertained the idea that the blacks would be guilty of such heartless treachery' and he did not mention his misgivings to the other men.[79] Bennett may have considered that each word and phrase of his vocabulary, gathered in his joint project with the Woolna, would cancel the Finniss expedition's unadjusted debt, and that the rope boundary and his body paint offered more protection than a stockade and a Colt revolver.

During these days Goyder continued his extended tour of the survey camps. By 23 May he was camped to the west, near the Finniss River. Ironically enough, his base was at the foot of Mount Bennett, named for the draftsman during the Escape Cliffs expedition. Goyder had now been absent from Fort Darwin for more than a month, leaving the camp in charge of Peel, the surgeon. Peel's assistant, William Hoare, detected the rising tension. On 24 April he wrote that 'the natives required our attention'. A few days later, at Easter, he noted 'it was absolutely necessary to establish nightly guards for the security of our Camp in case of the savages coming on us or our animals'. But even during this period when the natives were 'troublesome', Hoare was still sketching and bartering for their artefacts. On 22 April, he obtained 'some String Bags, belt, made of bark one made of hair, a Fish Spear & woomera in exchange for a pocket handkerchief I cut in two and an old knife'. He sketched the artefacts.[80]

These infiltrations continued, an exchange of laughter, words and specimens, partial understandings, misunderstandings. On 4 May Hoare made a box for Surgeon Peel to pack his specimens for Adelaide. He painted a flower for a butterfly picture and bartered for a reed necklace with Biliamuk. He observed 'some natives with bamboo thrust into a perforation in the nose and with girdles of twisted human hair'. At least two photographs of Biliamuk show that he wore such a nose-peg. Hoare's diary entry includes his sketch of an Aboriginal nose, with a bamboo peg through the septum. Two days later he painted a bee on a flower and a small frilled lizard, and bartered for some more artefacts. Beyond the camp, at night, Hoare noticed that Aboriginal campfires surrounded the settlement on both sides of the wider harbour, 'like the beacons of old'.

On 7 May, one of the workers returning to camp in the evening fired at an Aboriginal man and warned Aboriginal visitors in the camp that he would fire again if anyone 'molested him'. A body of armed men were sent out to see 'what was up'. Hoare observed that 'the blacks strange to say have kept out of our sight all day', but the following day, Hoare marked a decisive shift, heading his journal entry:

> <u>200 Natives on the War Path</u> ... A number of armed blacks came and wanted to fight us. Old Mira tried to stop them, all the camp took up firearms ... In consequence of the blacks behaving badly Dr Peel organised an extra guard viz of 4 men and is leader to them. I have to be on from 4 to 6 am Sunday. The Magnesium Light was burning this evening.[81]

On 10 May, Hoare received the skin of the pheasant '*Lee-a-wer*' which Bennett had collected for him. The danger seemed to have passed, and Woolna and Larrakia people began visiting the camp once more. On 14 May a group of Aboriginal women arrived. By now Hoare had an official direction to illustrate natural history specimens for the government and during the following week or so he traded for a wide range of objects: 'a curious fish ... belonging to the Rays also a few Cowries and other shells ... two large fishing spears and a basket ... another Native basket only better than that got yesterday'. On Sunday 23 May, the day before the Queen's Birthday, Dr Peel read the service at 10.30 am and then some Aboriginal men visited the camp, 'with spears in exchange for food'.

These Aboriginal visitors observed extraordinary preparations afoot in Goyder's camp, momentous and perhaps alarming. In such a remote and fragile outpost of empire the Queen's Birthday was an event like no other, particularly on this Golden Jubilee. The camp was being festooned in bunting, men were practising theatrical routines, clearing courses for running races, cooking food, cleaning guns. Hoare described the events at Fort Darwin:

> A day of great rejoicing. Racing, jumping in sacks, 3 legged race, diving, swimming, throwing 14lbs weight, high & low jumping, Rifle & Revolver shooting. Everyone enjoyed themselves in Head Camp. I subscribed 10/ by an I.O.U. A large bonfire was lighted at night amidst much cheering etc. etc. Dr Peel did everything to make the men jolly and Messrs Hood, McCallum assisted greatly in the sports. Amongst the successful was North Smith, for racing, McCallum for throwing the weight, Hayes diving, N. Smith Rifle, Robinson revolver, Hood carbine, & Miller swimming.[82]

No Aboriginal spectators were mentioned. Perhaps knowing what may have been about to occur, a day's walk to the south, they had moved closer to Fred's Pass.

If Knuckey and his small party had intended to celebrate the Queen's Birthday at Fred's Pass, an evening toast was their most likely concession to the occasion, or perhaps a meal prepared by the labourer William Guy, who doubled as camp cook. Work would continue. On the mornings of 23 and 24 May, Knuckey and two men set off at seven o'clock to complete the town survey and were soon out of earshot.

Near dawn on 24 May, in contrast to the small groups of two or three who had appeared on previous mornings, a dozen Aboriginal men arrived at the rope boundary. Knuckey had set off to work nevertheless, with labourers Kelly and Ryan. He instructed Guy to guard the camp. With only Bennett and Guy remaining, this camp was suddenly more exposed than any, since the Goyder expedition's arrival, four months earlier.

Bennett had plans to draft, but was soon distracted by the Aboriginal men, who seemed determined on his company. He took his fowling-piece and accompanied them down to the lagoon, intending to bag some ducks for the evening meal. He returned a little later but then went out with them once more, this time unarmed. Perhaps this expression of trust in his Aboriginal hosts, together with their own obligations of hospitality, protected him when he stepped outside the circle. Once again, he returned to the tent and sat at his desk.

The Aboriginal men remained on the other side of the rope, but at about eleven o'clock two of them crossed the boundary line and 'walked towards the square tent calling out "Bennettie come on" and "Guy come on"'. Guy noticed the two men squatting down outside the tent and went to investigate. They walked off towards the lagoon. Guy found four spears and two spearthrowers placed on the ground at the edge of Bennett's tent, just outside the mosquito curtain. He called to Bennett to ask the Aboriginal men why they had done this. Bennett interrogated them, using his Woolna language. His reply to Guy was hardly convincing: 'they say they saw a wallaby in the rock and were waiting till it came out again'.[83]

Bennett took up the spears and spearthrowers and handed them back to the Aboriginal men, telling them to go away. Perhaps he used the Woolna term in his vocabulary: '*Ber.ro.que*, Be off'. He returned to his tent, but did not remark to Guy about any perceived danger. For his part, despite Bennett's instructions, Guy neglected to arm himself.[84] Both ends of Bennett's square tent were open. He sat at his desk, writing. He may have been working on the township plans; he may also have been adding new words or phrases to his vocabulary. Guy stood near the curtain of his own tent, looking out. It was after midday.

Suddenly Guy heard Bennett calling: 'Guy look out!' He found the young draftsman lying on his side outside the square tent, blood flowing freely from his wounds. He had been struck by four spears, 'two entering his lungs, one grazing the upper lip, and another slightly wounding his neck'. Under cover of the long grass fringing the lagoon, at least three Aboriginal men had appeared at the door of Bennett's tent and 'without any warning commenced throwing spears at him'. Guy ran for a revolver which Bennett had tucked away behind Ryan's mosquito curtain, but at that instant he saw an 'elderly black about 40 or 50 years of age with grey hair and long beard come round the corner of the tent'. The Aboriginal man fitted a spear into his woomera. Guy fumbled to retrieve the revolver but as he stooped to do so, he 'received the spear in the lower part of the back'. In agony, Guy broke off the spear and threw it down, but the barb remained in the wound. Guy struggled to extract the revolver from its case. His assailant advanced further, shouting to another man standing by the lagoon's edge. Bennett told Guy later that 'he had called out for more spears and the other refused to bring them'.

Before Guy could cock the revolver Bennett himself fired off a shot, then called out to Guy to come to him. Guy replied that he could not. Bennett asked him if he was afraid. Guy said yes, he was afraid, but despite his own injury he managed to reach Bennett. Incredibly, he found the draftsman 'walking outside the tent with his fowling piece on his shoulder'. Bennett fired once more; their attackers dived into the lagoon and disappeared.

The two critically wounded men began a long wait, not expecting to see Knuckey until sundown. They sat at either end of the tent, sustaining themselves with shots of rum. Bennett told Guy: 'the wretches think they have done for me but I am not done for yet, I think I am injured in the left lung'. He sat on a camp stool with his fowling piece across his knee, facing Fred's Pass. Guy took a rifle and revolver and sat on the other side of the tent, keeping up a continuous fire through the long grass at edge of the lagoon, 'to prevent the natives showing themselves again'.

More than an hour passed. Later, Guy commented that Bennett 'made no remark as to the cause of the attack' during this agonising wait, 'nor did he mention any of the names of the Blacks concerned in it'. Fortunately Knuckey and his men returned before two pm.[85] They found 'Mr Bennett and Guy in a state of great exhaustion, with the blood streaming down them from their wounds'. Knuckey went for help from the main camp at Manton Creek, about

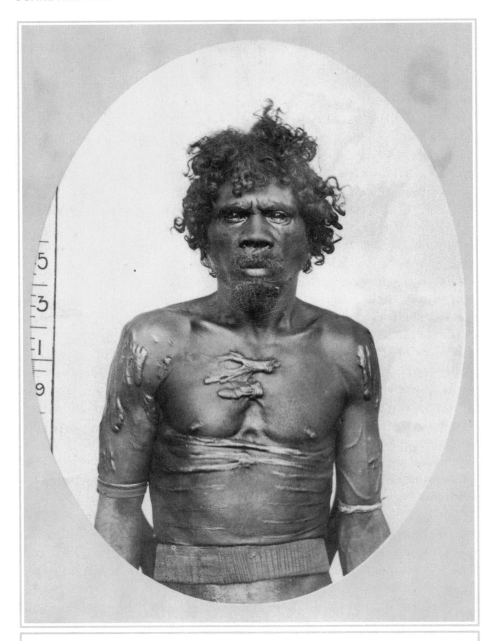

The Woolna (Djerimanga) man Lialoon-me, aged 40 in May 1879, ten years after Bennett's spearing. Photographer: Paul Foelsche. Foelsche Collection, South Australian Museum Archives.

five miles away. At 8 pm a messenger was sent to fetch Dr Peel, reaching Fort Point at 7.15 am on the morning of 25 May. The surgeon arrived at Fred's Pass at 3 am on the following morning, almost 36 hours after the spearings.

Peel's initial diagnosis was that Bennett had 'two spear wounds in the back, apparently only flesh wounds'. He considered then that these wounds 'were not of much extent – the largest being about an inch and a half long, both were closed, and as I fancied there was little, if any spear in them, I did not deem it advisable to reopen them until I got him to Fort Point'. The surgeon extracted the spear from Guy's wound under chloroform, noting that this spear had probably 'been previously thrown, & then picked up again, as the point was gone'. Peel had both men placed in a spring dray for the overland stage to the Elizabeth River, from where they embarked by boat for Fort Darwin. The wounded men arrived there at noon on Thursday 27 May, three days after the spearings.[86]

During the journey to Fort Darwin, Bennett finally confided in Guy, and gave an account of the attack which Guy later included in his official report to Goyder. Bennett also revealed the names of the principal assailants: Mundab, Lialoon-me, Adulma and Me-nin-dab. The man who stood near the waterhole while Guy was speared was 'very often about camp'. Guy did not remember his name but considered that he would recognise that man and the old man who speared him. Guy considered that the actual assailants were 'strangers to the camp', while those who acted as lookouts were local men who had all been 'peaceable' and were 'treated with kindness' by the surveying party up to the morning of the attack.[87] Of the assailants identified by Bennett, only Lialoon-me has surfaced elsewhere in the historical record. He was photographed ten years later by the police-inspector, Paul Foelsche, who was unaware of his association with the episode.

Guy could not explain the attack. He considered that the 'officers and men at all times were friendly towards the natives and treated them with kindness, especially Mr Bennett who seemed to take a great interest in them'. This paradox suggested the explanation most often employed in European rationalisations of frontier violence, a savage propensity to 'treachery'. This explanation reduced the Woolna to the caricature which Bennett himself had employed during his first term at Escape Cliffs, when he had ridiculed 'the idea of calling a half cannibal a brother, one that would spear you at his first opportunity'. Bennett had clearly ceased to hold that view though; his growing familiarity with the Woolna, their language and customs, and his apparent acceptance by them had engendered confidence among all the expedition members, even Goyder. The 'poor fellow', wrote one journalist, 'considered himself perfectly safe among them, and others of his party supposed him a source of protection against attack'. But now they knew better: his spearing 'proved how little they understood the treacherous nature of those with whom they had to deal'.[88] It would take Goyder himself to question this simplistic account of the tragedy.

THE GRAVE ON FORT HILL

At Fort Darwin, Peel remained optimistic about Bennett's recovery until he discovered that the larger 'flesh wound' concealed a fragment of spear barb. With Bennett under chloroform, he probed the smaller wound and found an entire barbed spearhead lodged in the cavity of Bennett's chest. It was nine inches long. He extracted it, administered a draught of morphia and pronounced the case hopeless.

Hoare had been among the shocked reception party as the wounded men were brought in to Fort Darwin. He wrote:

> At 7.40 pm poor Bennett had a piece of spear about six inches taken out of his back under chloroform by Dr Peel with three barbs and part of a fourth in a splintered condition when removed. I fear it is a case with him.

Bennett lingered on for ten more hours. Surgeon Peel wrote:

> Bennett has been delirious ever since operation, alert at intervals during the night, expressed himself quite well ... talking very loudly & asking to have the bandages removed, as they were not wanted now. At 9.30 am Bennett asked for some hot tea and told me he was going to read himself to sleep.[89]

Half an hour later Bennett was dead.

On the following day, Hoare inked a black border around his journal entry:

> At 10.45 am I heard poor Bennett was dead which has made the whole of us very sad as he was such a <u>favourite</u>. I painted the coffin Plate on Zinc with black block type. I saw him laid therein, he had a smile on his face. I put some everlastings and a <u>white</u> waterlily in his coffin. I shook hands with him in the morning and he said he was hungry and much better. I gave him water he then fell into my arms ...[90]

William Hoare's black-bordered journal entry describing Bennett's demise on 28 May 1869.
PRG 294/1, State Library of South Australia.

Bennett was buried a day later in a grave atop Fort Hill, overlooking the settlement and the harbour, a few steps from the flagstaff. It was, as a friend later put it, 'a solemn and affecting sight to witness the burial of an old schoolfellow, far away from his relations, in a place hundreds of miles from civilisation, to see the ensign flying half mast, and hear the impressive burial service'.[91] Later, Goyder himself would design the tomb, 'a heavy pedestal, surmounted with a cross', standing three feet high.

In the meantime Hoare devoted himself to inscribing Bennett's temporary epitaph, and carefully copied it into his journal. In ensuing weeks he climbed the Hill each day, making sketches of the tomb for men in the camp to send home in their mail. Bennett's epitaph was simple enough, inscribed within a heart-shaped copper plate fixed to the headstone:

J.W.O. Bennett
Aged 23 years

Died
May 28th 1869
From spear wounds inflicted by the Natives
Of Fred's Pass,
May 24th 1869 [92]

Goyder was still away from the camp. He did not hear of Bennett's spearing until 1 June, and news of his subsequent death did not reach him until five days after that. In Goyder's absence there was no immediate move to close commerce with the Larrakia or the Woolna, and when the old 'chief' Mira returned to Fort Darwin two days after Bennett's death, the camp was opened to him. Hoare observed that Mira arrived with several other Escape Cliffs men, and that the party hid their spears before descending the hill to the stockade: 'When Dr Peel was dressing Guy's wound Old Mira cried bitterly, and he had the spear heads shown to him'. Hoare traded with Mira's party, obtaining 'a bunch of feathers from the natives also a sword of wood, in other words a club about 4 ft 7 inches long'.[93] On the next day, 1 June, Hoare made a note that the Aboriginal visitors to the camp 'require careful watching. They have been grinding hoop iron for knives to make spears with them'.[94]

Displaying an unprecedented degree of restraint, Goyder took no steps to mount a reprisal expedition. He remained out on his survey for three weeks following Bennett's death and Peel, holding the fort at Darwin, also advised caution. Returning to Fort Darwin on 12 June, Goyder's small party was ambushed by Aboriginal attackers who lit the long grass so that the wind swept fire and smoke around the party. Hoare wrote: 'the Natives wanted to surround them with fires so that they could spear them when almost blinded with smoke'. But Goyder again held back. 'We could easily have shot one or two of them', he wrote, 'as three were visible at one time within twenty yards of me, but in the position of Protector of Aborigines as well as that of Surveyor-General, I knew that these miserable specimens of humanity were only following their savage instincts in doing what they did . . .' According to Goyder, the Woolna kept firing the grass 'near and in advance of us for a distance of 18 miles', but he and his men reached Fort Point safely, and without bloodshed. There he found 'the old native hangers-on at the camp about as usual, though they knew of all that had transpired'. Goyder ordered them away. Later that night, Hoare wrote:

the whole camp [was] alarmed by some Natives going into the mangroves. Schultze heard them talking and the guard also heard a noise. Mr Goyder with a number of men armed, stood ready to fire on them by aid of the Magnesium Light.[95]

Again, Goyder's response was relatively conservative and precautionary. He expelled Aboriginal visitors from the Darwin camp and forbade all commerce with them, consolidating security, reorganising his parties and issuing Colt revolvers to his men. William Guy was recovering, but remained 'very nervous ... afraid of his own shadow'. The 'blacks', wrote Goyder on 20 June, were 'crawling about in bushes round [the] camp'.[96] When a party of Aboriginal men arrived on the beach in five canoes, on 22 June, they were turned back to sea. They camped nearby and were later seen 'prowling round the camp at night'. But Goyder took care not to allow this volatile situation to ignite. When he found that two of his men had destroyed Aboriginal canoes on a nearby beach, and had set others adrift, he roundly chastised the culprits and anticipated the consequences:

> I was grieved and annoyed at this act of malicious folly, and pointed out the probable consequences, in strong language to them, as well as the injustice of the act, stating that we had now given cause of aggression on their parts, and this would probably follow. Our boats might be cut away, wells filled in, and all possible damage done by them – and that I could no longer blame them. Set a watch to look out for the two canoes adrift, with orders to have them taken back, if they could be discovered. Whatever aggression results from this act, it is due to the want of proper feeling, and great lack of judgement of Mr Hardy and Cadet Greene.[97]

Goyder could justify his modest response to Bennett's death on more than one ground. There was little to gain and much to lose from a reprisal expedition. He was well aware of the way in which Finniss's command at Escape Cliffs had unravelled four years earlier, after two reprisal expeditions. And he understood those excessive reprisals to be a direct cause of the Fred's Pass tragedy. Goyder later wrote that he 'considered the attack upon Bennett and Guy the result of feelings of revenge on the part of those who had probably lost relatives in some previous contest with the whites, the more so as we were informed ... by the blacks here that those on the Adelaide or near that locality intended to kill two of our party'.[98]

Goyder had no doubt that had he given the order for retaliation, 'the punishment of the natives would have been a simple matter for the party so armed', as both officers and men were 'naturally indignant at Bennett's murder'. But to allow that to occur would be to 'secure to our successors less able to

179

defend themselves a debt of lives to be paid for our act of reprisal, unless we had annihilated the tribe, which was not to be thought of'. Goyder went further in his rationalisation, suggesting that his status as Protector of Aborigines was more than a token appointment:

> I had also to bear in mind that we were in what to them appeared unauthorised and unwarrantable occupation of their country, and where territorial rights are so strictly observed by the natives that even a chief of one tribe will neither hunt upon nor remove anything from the territory of another without first obtaining permission, it is scarcely to be wondered at if, when opportunity is allowed them, they should resent such acts by violence upon its perpetrators.[99]

Goyder had also considered the possibility of applying milder forms of British justice to Bennett's attackers:

> We might have surrounded and captured the murderers of Bennett and sent them to justice, when from the evidence of witnesses, and the declarations made, convictions and executions might have followed. But they could not have understood our language, nor could they have made themselves intelligible to us. The expense and trouble therefore would probably have been incurred in vain, and their subsequent experience detailed to their tribes might have given rise to other murders to ensure similar experiences.[100]

The contrast between Goyder's approach and that of B.T. Finniss could not have been starker. Goyder understood that Bennett's death was not a random act of savagery at all, but an act of retribution. Bennett was the least deserving of that fate, but his association with Finniss's expedition made it inevitable. The young draftsman might even, it could be said, have offered himself up.

This was not Hoare's view of the matter, nor of other expedition members, who regarded Bennett's death as an uncomplicated consequence of reprehensible Aboriginal treachery. In early September, Hoare designed another inscription for Bennett's grave, to underline this point:

> Sacred to the Memory of Mr J.W.O. Bennett who died on the 28th May 1869 aged 23 years from spear wounds inflicted by the Natives at Freds Pass on the 24th day of the same month. Mr B. placed implicit confidence in the Blacks and treated them with familiar kindness. They requited his kindness and confidence by treacherously spearing him when off his guard.[101]

In Adelaide the news of Bennett's death attracted an outpouring of grief from his former schoolmates, colleagues, and friends of his bereaved parents, who were 'known to half the residents of Adelaide'. The Northern Territory surveys, wrote one journalist, 'are dearly purchased by the heart's blood of one of her best citizens'.[102] It was suggested that the memorial at Fort Hill might be matched by a cenotaph in Adelaide, erected by subscription.[103]

Marble memorial tablet commemorating J.W.O. Bennett, sculpted by Samuel Peters. Erected by subscription in St Paul's Anglican church, Pulteney Street, Adelaide, 1869. Photograph: Anglican Diocesan Archives, Adelaide.

Most accounts of the tragedy assumed its inevitability. Bennett and Guy had been exposed to the raw edge of savagery in the wrong place, at the wrong time. As at Fort Darwin, 'treachery' was the most commonly employed epithet in these accounts. The neutral term 'natives' was recast as 'niggers' or 'savages':

> Bennett was treacherously murdered by the niggers ... the cowardly wretches attacked the camp, and mortally wounded him ... The niggers ... are the most cowardly treacherous lot of savages imaginable.[104]

But an extract from a 'private letter', also reproduced in the *Observer*, offered the hint of an alternative and more complex account to readers whose assumptions had been reshaped by the events at Escape Cliffs. 'There are many reports', wrote the anonymous correspondent, 'as to why the natives attacked him, but of course they are only surmises. Poor fellow, he stated shortly before he died that he knew several of them who threw spears at him, and recognised them as having been about Escape Cliffs'.[105] Another correspondent went further, sheeting the blame home to just one 'treacherous black' rather than an entire tribe. Bennett, he wrote,

Appeared to be well liked by the natives, who were always treated by him with the greatest kindness, and in whom he placed the utmost trust and confidence. One would have thought that he would have been the very last in the whole expedition to have incurred the anger or subjected himself to the treacherous vengeance of the natives. Mr Bennett appears to have known only one of the attacking party, an oldish man, who during the former expedition had proved himself very troublesome, and Bennett in consequence had him turned out of the camp. This is the only assignable cause that can be given for this unprovoked attack.[106]

The 'troublesome' older man was Bennett's chief language informant, the Woolna elder, Mira.

EPILOGUE

At Fort Darwin, Goyder now forbade any exchange or commerce. The edict spelt the end for Hoare's small acquisitions, and for the apparently easy interactions which had continued up to that point, even as the deeper currents of antagonism swung back and forth. The Woolna and Larrakia were prevented

Photograph of Bennett's grave on Fort Hill, sent to W.W. Hoare in 1905 by his old friend, Paul Foelsche. W.W. Hoare album, PRG 294/1, State Library of South Australia.

from entering the camp. On 6 July, Hoare recorded that 'the natives came to the top of the Hill but were driven back by firearms'. Soon the Aboriginal camp outside the stockade was abandoned; there was no reason for them to remain. Hoare was reduced to drawing flowers and insects and Fort Darwin became a prison of boredom.

Bennett's grave continued to exert an attraction. Goyder's design was admired and the tomb became a landmark in its own right: 'being at a considerable height above the water it presents a conspicuous appearance for a long distance over the harbour'. Hoare's new inscription, tinged with bitterness for a betrayal which seemed to echo around the camp, was placed upon 'a sunk panel' on a marbled plate. The grave itself 'was neatly fenced in with chamfered and rounded posts and chains'.[107]

Hoare worked on his drawings of the grave over the following weeks, finishing one, beginning another. On 8 October he almost joined Bennett in the cemetery:

> W. Stanborough was cleaning a carbine and it went off accidentally and the bullet went through the Armory & my Surgery whilst I was drawing a crab and whistled by my head. It came through the Galvanised Iron House used as an Armoury and into my Iron House and curled up the Portion nearest to my head and finally fell from the inside of the roof.

A few days later he was back at the gravesite. He 'painted some Clouds and two Fern Palms in the Picture of Bennetts grave', and began yet another picture of it. Christmas Day came and went with 'geese and plum pudding ... and each man had half a bottle of Bass ... so we spent our Xmas day in the N.T. and thought of Friends and <u>Home</u>'. Again, perhaps attracted by these celebrations, Aborigines 'tried hard to visit the Camp'. Goyder ordered them away, 'much to their disgust'. Only 'old Mira' could approach: 'many went to speak with him', but he also was not allowed to enter.[108]

On 30 December, at the end of this eventful year, Hoare wrote: 'I had nothing to paint and felt very uncomfortable all day, in fact homesick. No news and the everyday sameness makes us dull'. He and his fellows scanned the horizon for the steamer, now overdue, which would return them to Adelaide, away from Fort Hill and its lonely grave, away from a frontier tilted out of balance.

After a varied career, much of it spent as a dispensing chemist in Adelaide and New Zealand, Hoare eventually returned to England in 1892. He occupied his later years by dressing in pantomime at charity fêtes and expositions, stepping into costumes and roles which were always of another time and place, evoking the other side. Hoare's scrapbook contains a 1904 photograph of him at the St Alban's fête, dressed as an 'Assouan Arab', seated on a donkey. For four months during the 1911 Festival of Empire at London's Crystal Palace he appeared as an ancient Briton dressed in animal skins. He also impersonated a Viking and a Good Samaritan.

Hoare kept in touch with a few old friends such as the Northern Territory police-inspector and photographer Paul Foelsche, a fellow-Freemason. The pair may already have been acquainted in Adelaide, before the Goyder expedition. Hoare's scrapbook contains two letters from Foelsche, interleaved among newspaper cuttings, sketches of artefacts and animals, and his accounts of Fort Darwin. Foelsche wrote to Hoare during 1904:

> You are a wonderful man. I would have liked to have seen you dressed as an Algerian Arab going in the procession at the Demonstration in aid of St Alban's Hospital Fund; you always seem to be employed in some good work.[109]

William Hoare (left) dressed as an 'Assouan Arab' on a donkey at the St Alban's fête, 1904. W.W. Hoare album, PRG 294/1, State Library of South Australia.

Foelsche had arrived at Port Darwin in early 1870, travelling by the ship which would carry Hoare back to Adelaide. His police contingent was assembled partly in response to Bennett's death, but it appears that Foelsche was given no particular brief to investigate the murder. His later series of Aboriginal portraits contain several individuals who had figured in the events preceding and surrounding Bennett's death. Of these, the Woolna man Lialoon-me had been specifically identified by the dying Bennett as one of his attackers. If Foelsche was aware of Lialoon-me's role in those events he took no action. The old 'chief' Mira died of snake-bite before Foelsche commenced his portrait series in 1877.

By the time of Foelsche's arrival in the Territory the grave on Fort Hill (which Bennett shared with another, later casualty of the Goyder expedition) had become a salutary reminder as well as a personal shrine. Even three decades later it had the capacity to stir powerful memories. In 1905, when Foelsche and Hoare were approaching old age, the police-inspector sent a photograph of the tomb to Hoare: 'I found that some amateur Photographer took a snap-shot of poor Bennetts & Hazards grave on top of Fort Hill ... it will show you that the Grave is looked after and in good order'.[110] In fact, the site remained intact for only another 60 years. In 1965 Fort Hill was entirely removed to make way for iron ore export facilities. Bennett's and Hazard's remains, together with the memorial plaque, were transferred to the MacMillan's Road cemetery.

The records do not tell us whether Hoare's pantomime appearances included an impersonation of an Aboriginal warrior, old Mira for instance. Hoare may have retained sufficient of his ethnographic collection to sustain such a performance. This collection included one of the intricately knotted 'yam bags' pictured in his Port Darwin journal. That little bag was apparently given by Hoare to a friend in Wimbledon, England, before it entered the final chain of circumstance which returned it to its country of origin and linked it, eventually, with Hoare's handwritten copy of Bennett's vocabulary.

Dick Cubadgee's fire-sticks, donated to the South Australian Museum in 1924 by David Lindsay's widow. A12919, South Australian Museum.

CHAPTER FIVE

Drilling for fire

The museum case displays a series of Aboriginal fire-sticks, ranked set by set. Aboriginal fire-makers across the country used variations on these simple rotary drills and their matching hearths. In the right hands the drills could generate hot blackened powder ready to ignite into flame, inside a minute. Here in the museum they seem nondescript objects, enlivened only by their subtle ochred surfaces. Cool light plays upon them as a video monitor nearby reveals the fire-making process to the visitor.

Among these drills and hearths, one set seems slightly out of place. The length of hearth wood, with a row of eight drill-holes along it, is an irregular stick of the Central Australian bean tree (*Erythrina vespertilio*), a softwood tree associated with Aboriginal fire mythology. But the accompanying fire-drill is less typical. Its smooth shaft is made of two different wood types spliced together in a neat, diagonal join, similar to those used in billiard cues. It is an amalgam of materials and technique, Aboriginal and European.[1]

Filed away in the archives is the letter which accompanied the fire-sticks' donation in 1924. This was

Detail of Dick Cubadgee's fire-sticks, showing spliced, 'billiard cue' mend in the fire-drill.

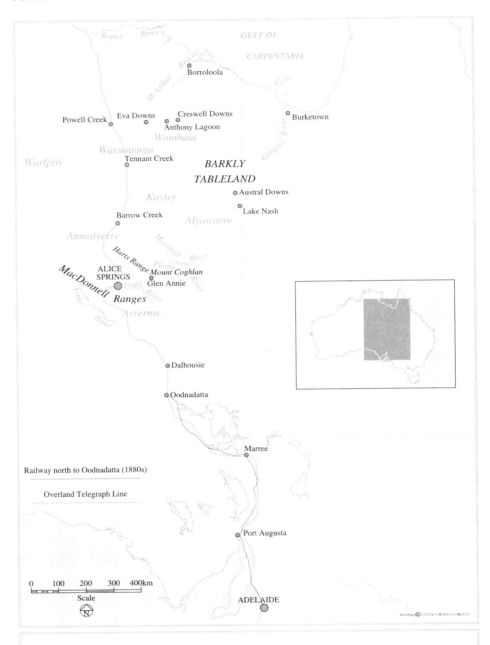

Localities mentioned in chapter five, with relevant Aboriginal group names.

written by the son of Mrs Annie Lindsay, widow of the Central Australian explorer, David Lindsay. The letter reads:

> ... included in this box is a set of Fire Sticks, used by 'Dick Cubidgee' ... when demonstrating, to guests at Government House, the method used by the Aborigine in making fire. Such a demonstration, by Dick, is described in one of Lady Brassey's Books ... It is my Mother's desire to present these Fire Sticks to the South Australian Museum.[2]

With that letter in mind, the fire-sticks on display no longer fit neatly within the museum series drawn from the remote frontier, where Aboriginal fire-makers bent to their task, apparently unmindful of the changes sweeping towards them. Dick Cubadgee's fire-sticks were partly fashioned on that side of that frontier, but partly also on this side. They twirled and smoked in the heart of Adelaide. And while the Lindsay letter points to the destiny of these objects, what of their origin, their original owner and his fate?

There are enough photographs of Cubadgee scattered through archive collections to suggest that a tale lies behind his striking appearance. One glossy sepia photograph on thick card, with the society photographer's name embossed in gold at the base, shows a tall, fine-featured young Aboriginal man, standing against a backdrop of artefacts. It seems to be a photograph of trophies from the frontier, trophies which include the young man himself.

The photographer positioned his subject against a display of spears and spearthrowers, boomerangs, armlets and other artefacts. The youth steadies himself with a long club, more than half his height. He is naked, apart from an apron of fibre string suspended from a European leather belt. His chest is decorated with long, horizontal keloid scars, or cicatrices, suggesting that he has undergone initiation as a man. The long spears propped beside him reach out of the frame, and the youth's height is accentuated by these vertical forms. He has one leg slightly raised; an impressively large foot rests on a wooden log. The curve reveals the leg's musculature and echoes the shape of the hooked boomerang hanging beside him on the canvas backdrop, a photographer's ploy. Despite this artifice the youth has an easy, rangy look. Not quite captured by the frame he seems, nevertheless, a fine museum specimen.

Among the artefacts attached to the photographic backdrop are two fire-sticks, placed cross-wise. One is the drill, not much thicker than a finger, perhaps half a metre long. The other stick is the same length but broader. Five or six shallow circular holes are visible along it, each the diameter of the drill. The

Dick Cubadgee at the Adelaide Jubilee Exhibition in 1887, posed in front of artefacts collected by David Lindsay. Cubadgee's fire-sticks are displayed cross-wise, at his left shoulder. AA108, South Australian Museum Archives.

knobbed, irregular character of the 'hearth' stick and the slight curve of the drill match the fire-sticks donated by Lindsay's widow, now on display.

'A CERTAIN AMOUNT OF BLACK POWDER'

A companion photograph shows the same young man, sitting cross-legged and bent over the two fire-sticks which have been taken down from the display behind him. He is rotating the drill between the palms of his hands, onto the other stick – the wooden 'hearth'. If we could see the detail in the image perhaps we could make out a stream of blackened, trit-urated powder spilling out along a channel cut in the side of the hearth-stick, onto a wooden tray. When enough super-heated powder built up on this tray the young man would lay the sticks down, take the powder, tip it onto some tinder and fan the embers into life.

Aboriginal fire-drills are flimsy objects. You could snap them into pieces. It is remarkable that so many survive in museum collections, from

Dick Cubadgee making fire at the Adelaide Jubilee Exhibition of 1887. PXE 724/26, Mitchell Library, Sydney.

across Australia. The fire-drill technique was practised from Cape York to Encounter Bay, only missing the most arid of the central western deserts where an alternative friction method was used. This involved sawing a hardwood edge of a spearthrower across a split in a log, or across the surface of a softwood shield. In southern Australia the rotary fire-drill could be made from a single plant, the grass-tree or yacca (*Xanthorrhea*). An Aboriginal legend of Encounter Bay links the grass-tree and Kondole the Whale. Like other legends of fire's origin, this story hints that the friction technique evolved from an earlier method based on creating sparks by striking flint.

Kondole the Whale was one of the legendary animals invited to a dancing ceremony at Encounter Bay. He was, needless to say, the most impressive performer. The other participants wondered at the sparks flying from his huge body as he danced. Nobody had fire then in this damp, cold country, and two Bird Ancestors plotted Kondole's demise in order to steal it from him. As Kondole danced closer the Skylark fitted a spear to his spearthrower and flung it so that the spear sank into the whale's neck. His life-blood gushed out as fire, setting alight to the country, and it fell to the ground as flints. Maddened with pain, Kondole fled from the fire and dived into the sea with the other sea creatures. When he surfaced, the steam continued to shoot from his wound. In the meantime Skylark had stolen the fire, placing it in the grass-tree where it could be released by using the fire-drill made from its wood.[3]

In Aboriginal Australia fire was a constant companion, an indispensable tool, but it was also dangerous and elusive, a scarcely tameable essence. Stories of its capture and of the origins of techniques which brought it safely within the human domain are elevated within Aboriginal mythology, just as in ancient European folklore. The prominence given to these accounts must reflect the remarkable culture-defining achievement which fire-making represents. Now taken for granted in western culture as the easy gesture of 'striking a match', Aboriginal fire-making was never a casual matter. In Aboriginal societies the fire-drill and the fire-saw methods had the concentrated intensity of a small ceremony, a tiny miracle.

Aboriginal men (usually, if not invariably the fire-makers) would sing a fire-chant as they twirled the fire-drill or rubbed the fire-saw across a softwood shield, until the tinder caught and flared. Such a chant, sung by Arrernte men of the MacDonnell Ranges, was transcribed by the anthropologist Francis Gillen during the 1890s. It was believed to be that sung by Algurawartna, a man who became the first Fire-Maker in the Altjuringa, or Dreaming. Tantalised by the sight of a giant Euro's (kangaroo) campfire appearing in the distance each night, Algurawartna managed to reach it one evening, at last. He cooked his meat by its fading coals, but despite his best efforts was unable to kindle his own fire. Finally, after a long chase, he managed to catch and kill the Euro, and he dis-membered it, searching for the fire essence. Eventually he found it – a red-hot flame in the Euro's penis. Algurawartna used this fire to cook his food but eventually it too went out. Once more he tried to kindle his own fire. Now at last his *urpmala* or fire-making worked, for the very first time. From then on Algurawartna and all Arrernte men chanted the same verses as they worked the fire-saw, to ensure success:

Urpmalara kaita
Alkna munga
Ilpau wita wita[4]

Perhaps a similar verse was on the lips of the young Aboriginal man in the photograph as he twirled the fire-drill. Knowing his identity, it is possible to speculate on that. The photograph was taken during Adelaide's 1887 International Jubilee Exhibition, an event celebrating the 50th anniversaries of Queen Victoria's reign and of South Australia's foundation as a colony. Just before the Exhibition began, an English travel writer named Lady Anne Brassey visited Adelaide, sampling the cultural features of that self-conscious outpost of empire. The Art Gallery, Botanic Gardens, University, School of Art and Museum were all on her list, strung like pearls along tree-lined North Terrace. Her visit to Government House, further along the boulevard, was memorable in an unexpected way:

> At half-past eleven Mr D. Lindsay, the Australian explorer, came with his aboriginal servant, Cubadjee, whom he had brought from some place in the interior. This youth, it seems, is considered the short member of his family; but, although only seventeen years old, he is six feet five inches in height, while his elder brother, they declare, is seven feet six inches, and the rest of the family are equally tall. Cubadjee made fire for us with two pieces of wood (a process of which I had often heard), by rubbing a piece of wood with holes bored in it against another piece, quickly producing sparks, which easily ignited a piece of paper, and left a certain amount of black powder.[5]

Lady Brassey's appreciation of Cubadgee's demonstration, as a piece of appealing magic, overshadowed her understanding of the fire-making process. But her account of Cubadgee and his physical presence conveys the effect which the young Warumungu man exerted on Adelaide society during his tragically brief southern sojourn. Half a century after the invention of the safety match (with the tinder-box a distant memory), Cubadgee's fire-making was an impressive sight. A near-naked young giant of a man, as handsome an Aborigine as could be imagined, Cubadgee worked elemental magic in mixed company. It was a graphic reminder of how the frontier could intrude, a colonial frisson. As the wisps of smoke rose from his concentrated effort, Cubadgee's fire-stick performance delivered an experience of powerful intimacy to these colonial gentlemen and women, satisfying proof of primal forces tamed.

Setting the hardwood drill into one of the blackened holes of the softwood base, then rubbing his hands back and forth at great speed to spin the drill, Cubadgee soon generated a flow of smoking wood powder which spilled into a groove cut next to the drill-hole. 'The smell and smoke grew stronger, until at last a red spark appeared, spread to the powder in the groove, and the instant that happened the operator would tip the glowing spark onto a handful of teased grass or bark, blow gently, and with a faint "pop" a flame would appear'. During one of Cubadgee's performances South Australia's Chief Justice, Samuel Way (who befriended Cubadgee), timed the young man with a stop watch, 'to find that it could be done in a few seconds over a minute'.[6] For Cubadgee himself, each ignition achieved among such luminous company might have brought a complementary sense of satisfaction, a brief colonising moment on his own account. For until his death it seems he retained the confidence that somehow he might derive the best from both of his worlds.

Cubadgee was claimed as the discovery and protégé of one of Australia's most vigorous explorers and self-promoters, David Lindsay, best known for his leadership of the 1891–1892 Elder Scientific Exploring Expedition.[7] In fact, the Aboriginal youth was more closely linked to the explorer's brother-in-law

'David Lindsay, Explorer, FRGS', photographed in 1894 astride his camel 'Devil' in Coolgardie, Western Australia. PXE 724/41, Mitchell Library, Sydney.

George Lindsay (who shared the same surname). Cubadgee accompanied the pair on their Central Australian expeditions and southern enterprises between 1886 and 1889. These brought the young man from the frontier of contact to the colonial capitals of Melbourne and Adelaide. And it was in Adelaide, a thousand miles from his people, that Cubadgee died in September 1889, aged just nineteen.

ENCOUNTERING CUBADGEE

Cubadgee joined an exclusive band of Aboriginal men and youths who received widespread recognition for their roles as trackers and guides for famous Australian explorers of the nineteenth century. Thomas Mitchell's Piper and Yuranigh, Edward Kennedy's Jacky-Jacky and Edward Eyre's Wylie provide examples from earlier in the century. But Cubadgee also qualified for membership of another, tragically constituted group – those Aboriginal men and women whose physical and cultural identities made them into coveted scientific specimens.

David Lindsay and his young brother-in-law met Cubadgee at the very end of their 1885–1886 expedition from Hergott Springs (Marree) in South Australia to the Barkly Tableland, bordering Queensland and South Australia. The object of this expedition was to fix the boundaries of recently leased cattle stations on the Tableland, and to confirm adequate water supplies for them. An influx of pastoralists had begun arriving in the region following Charles Winnecke's 1877–1881 survey of the Northern Territory–Queensland border. As cattle and sheep stations became established on the Tableland during the following decade, this extent of grassland and permanent waters was progressively alienated from its original owners, whose response varied from implacable resistance to varied forms of accommodation.

Lindsay's expedition consisted of a survey team of five men as well as a 'supposed German scientist' and an Afghan cameleer, Joorak, who attended the eleven camels which gave the expedition greater mobility across the dry interior than horses could provide. Dalhousie Station, in the far-north of South Australia, provided a reconnaissance base before the party set out for the main destination at Lake Nash on the Barkly Tableland, about 500 miles (800 kilometres) to the north-east in a direct line. From Dalhousie, Lindsay firstly 'satisfactorily settled the much disputed question as to the debouchment of the Finke River', and investigated a rumoured site of the demise of the famed explorer, Ludwig Leichhardt, who had vanished 40 years earlier. Then, guided by a Wangkangurru man identified only as 'Paddy of Murraburt', Lindsay and the pastoralist Charles Bagot made a reconnaissance by camel-back eastward from Dalhousie, 'over a perfect sea of sandhills' (later to be named the Simpson Desert). The small party visited and sampled the waters of nine obscure Aboriginal *mikari* wells, before turning back at the Queensland border.[8]

In early February 1886 the full expedition set off from Dalhousie, initially attempting to strike north across the desert dunes to reach the Todd River. Defeated by lack of water and ailing camels, Lindsay turned back after 55 miles. From that point his expedition pursued a more conventional route. They followed up the Finke River to the MacDonnell Ranges and Harts Range, before setting a course for Lake Nash.

Lindsay relied upon Charles Winnecke's recent exploration maps and made few additions to knowledge of the Australian map's remaining blanks. In contrast to his pioneering explorations in eastern Arnhem Land during 1883, Lindsay was the first to admit that this expedition scarcely merited inclusion in the annals of Australian exploration. Despite that, he did discover a new gorge in the Harts Range, which he named Glen Annie in his wife's honour, as well as Mount Coghlan, standing at its entrance. More significantly, strewn through the gorge's sandy bed Lindsay found camel-loads of 'red stones of great brilliancy, which, after careful examination, [he] believed to be rubies'.[9] On his return to Adelaide these stones (actually garnets) were convincing enough to provoke a 'ruby rush', bringing dozens of miners to the Centre and provoking a new phase in Central Australian colonisation.[10] Lindsay's conviction that this country contained potential for gem and gold mining led to the region's first influx of Europeans, and with it, the first serious rent in the social fabric of Central Australia's Aboriginal population.

Despite the expedition's limited geographical objectives, Lindsay did intend it to contribute to science and to his own reputation. He employed Lieutenant Hermann Dittrich as the expedition's naturalist, charging him with specimen collecting as well as photography. Dittrich had been recommended by the esteemed botanist, Baron von Mueller, and had worked as a naturalist in other countries. A camel expedition in the Sahara had been mentioned. At Dalhousie Dittrich showed initial promise as an ethnographer, collecting 'a Vocabulary of the Charlotte Waters, Dalhousie, Stevenson & Macumba tribes', together with four song transcriptions and descriptions of customs. This four-page manuscript was sent south from Dalhousie in December 1885, together with a consignment of plants and seeds, some photographs and a 'box of native weapons'.[11]

But Dittrich fell far short of Lindsay's expectations. His plant collecting was desultory at best; his specimens were not well prepared, and a number 'were allowed to become worthless through mould'.[12] After Dalhousie, Lindsay became progressively disillusioned with Dittrich's work, and by the time the party reached the Plenty River, he was complaining loudly:

> I am very disappointed with him for he rarely, if ever, goes plant collecting, all he gets are what he chances to see as he rides behind the caravan or what we give him. His attention is often called to a plant, but being too indolent to get off his camel, says 'never mind we will see more bye & bye'.13

Dittrich was also the expedition photographer, and Lindsay had held high hopes for this branch of the naturalist's work. Writing to von Mueller before the expedition, Lindsay expressed his ambition to photograph 'the natives all through Australia' – certainly an unprecedented project.14 A box of Dittrich's photographs was sent south from Dalhousie, but these and subsequent efforts were either 'over-exposed, under-exposed or fogged with double exposures'.15 Lindsay considered that 'all the photographs taken save two were worthless … Mr Dittrich had all material and assistance he required … [but] he obstinately refused to accept any suggestions I might make about photographing'.16 No other Australian exploration expedition had so far incorporated photography as a key element of its programme, and Lindsay was justifiably frustrated when Dittrich's photographic skills seemed to match his inabilities as a naturalist. Six years later, Lindsay's leadership of the Elder expedition was to yield better results, with a series of landscape and anthropological photographs competently taken at his direction by the medical officer, Dr Frederick Elliot.17

Lindsay's enlistment of Cubadgee as an Aboriginal guide and assistant had its precedent during earlier phases of the expedition, when he was obliged to turn to the local inhabitants for assistance in finding water. As he entered territory to the north-east of the MacDonnell Ranges, Winnecke's map references to native waters proved unreliable. The country was in the grip of drought, and Lindsay made at least four separate and increasingly desperate attempts to engage Aboriginal guides. On the first occasion in late February, shortly after reaching the dry bed of the Todd, Lindsay was assisted by two Aboriginal men, who undertook to guide the party 'to certain waters' and onward through the MacDonnell Ranges. Further north-east at the Plenty River ('what a misnomer', as his journal reads) Lindsay was again obliged to rely upon local knowledge. He succeeded only in capturing two young girls aged about six and nine, who clung to each other in fear as they regarded the unimagined combination of Lindsay's camel and its rider. Lindsay hoped that these children would lead him to their relatives, who had obviously fled. He took them to his camp and tied up one girl, giving the other some flour and tobacco and instructing her to join her family. She refused to leave her companion though, and Lindsay placed both under guard for the night. According to Lindsay, the pair awoke 'at day light … their faces all beaming with smiles having slept peacefully the whole night'. During the day they led the expedition to water:

> by this time the poor creatures were not at all afraid, and walked along with us quite happily. Understanding that the water was some distance to the south, started the caravan off easterly, while I with the two Queis [young girls] in front of me went away south for 'Quatha ninta' [good water]. After passing about 9 miles of good country grassy & bushes with low hills dotted here and there, we came to a native well 6 feet deep in a sandy gum creek. The sand had, as is always the case, fallen in and no water was visible. The smallest girl jumped down and in a very few minutes digging with her hands revealed the existence of the precious fluid. What the supply was I could not ascertain, gave Lukkool [Lindsay's camel] a gallon in my satchel. Leaving the two Queis sitting beneath a gum tree with their arms around one another, I went to overtake the packs. When going the Queis waved their hands and called out 'Larram Larrama'.[18]

A traumatic kidnapping, which might easily have led to bloody reprisal, instead seemed to unfold into a mutually friendly encounter. Lindsay's matter-of-fact account suggests that even framed by the harsh facts of colonialism, outcomes on the Central Australian frontier were not always predetermined.

Five days after parting with their juvenile guides, Lindsay had another chance encounter at the Marshall River. Sighting an Aboriginal man at a waterhole, Lindsay called out and the man stopped:

> I held up my hands, when he dropped his spears, held up his hands and came towards us. He appeared not at all afraid, but embraced us each in turn by placing both his hands on our shoulders. He could speak no English. Turning around towards a low hill he called out, when three lubras (two old & one young girl about 16 years of age) came to us, we had to submit to an embrace from each of these. Although their language is similar to that of the natives of the Macumba and Finke our limited knowledge of that was but of little use to us.[19]

Lindsay's expedition camped at this waterhole for a few days before setting off again to the north-east. They soon required guidance. The region had been subject to a long drought and none of the waters marked on Winnecke's maps satisfied the thirst of their eleven camels. Luckily, while bringing in the camels Joorak encountered Aboriginal men, and four later visited Lindsay's camp:

> I understood from them that there are three or four waters on our intended route and one of them will go with us as a guide, they also promised to bring in a Wei (small boy) for me next day, in exchange for our dog, 'Toby'.[20]

On the following morning this boy arrived with his father, who turned out to be the man whom Lindsay had met at the Marshall River. Lindsay 'considered the little fellow too young and not over intelligent looking, so did not take him'. He was happier with another candidate for native guide:

> A young man was given me to act as a guide to certain waters, a smart active looking fellow to whom I took a fancy and resolved to keep if possible. Cut off his hair close, gave him a red cap and a good breakfast then took him down to the waterhole for a wash. When returning to camp he asked permission to go somewhere. I was to go on and he would overtake me. Thinking if he wished to run away better he should do it here than after we had started, let him go and he was out of sight in an instant. I waited some time but he returned not.[21]

Lindsay eventually travelled on with another guide, a young man who stayed with the party until a few days before they reached Lake Nash and the Queensland border, on 3 April 1886.

Lindsay's intensive survey of the newly established stations in the region began almost immediately and took the party across a huge tract of country, spanning the tribal territories of the Warumungu, Wambaya, Wakaya and Bularnu. It was in Wambaya country on Eva Downs Station, between Anthony Lagoon and Powell's Creek, that the Lindsays first encountered the sixteen-year-old Cubadgee and his older half-brother. Fifty years later, George Lindsay related an account of that meeting:

> One morning I saw two young natives sitting under a tree near the camp, and I walked over to have a talk with them. As I drew near they rose to their feet, and I was surprised to see that they were both at least 5 in. more than 6 ft. in height. Perfectly proportioned, their bodies had thin, graceful and sinewy strength, while their faces were frank, honest and intelligent.[22]

George Lindsay had little difficulty conversing with the boys in English. He found that they had the same father but different mothers, and had been born a year or two before the Overland Telegraph survey began in 1871. As a consequence they had picked up a fair knowledge of English at the Tennant Creek telegraph station, sited in Warumungu country. The younger step-brother, Cubadgee, who gave his English name as Dick, wanted to accompany the expedition and was engaged immediately. Presumably David Lindsay saw to it that like his erstwhile predecessor on the Marshall River, Cubadgee was given a wash and a haircut, a set of clothes and a cap. According to George Lindsay, the young Warumungu man proved to be 'the most intelligent, honest and likeable aborigine I had met. He soon became a good man with camels, and an excellent rifle shot, while as a tracker I never saw his equal'.[23]

Aged nineteen years in 1885, George Lindsay was just two or three years older than Cubadgee and the pair soon formed a special bond. 'Our liking for each other', wrote George Lindsay, 'was mutual, and he soon suggested that I let the Old Men of his tribe make us blood brothers'. George Lindsay's descendants have retained a memory of that friendship between the two young men, based largely upon the record left by George's son, the journalist Harold Lindsay. He described the event which not only cemented the pair's special friendship, but which may have also provided the origin of the 'Cubadgee' name:

> One Sunday he asked my father to come to where a clan of the tribe was camped. They rode across and there a korobori ceremony was staged, at which Dick and my father were the central figures. Riding back, Dick stated that they had been made blood-brothers according to tribal law. From now on he would call my father Pubadti ('older brother') and he was to be called Cubadgee ('younger brother').[24]

George Lindsay's new fraternal relationship with Cubadgee entailed obligations. In the first instance, he fitted out Cubadgee with a stockman's kit, including 'a Snider carbine and 100 cartridges, with strict instructions that the rifle was to be used only for his own protection if the [neighbouring] Wombiahs ever molested him'. This gift in particular must have reinforced Cubadgee's self-perception as an influential actor on the new frontier, for few Aboriginal men possessed such weapons. The rising tension between newly arrived pastoralists and the Warumungu, Wambaya and other Aboriginal groups affected by their presence meant that misunderstandings and minor grievances often escalated rapidly. The historian Tony Roberts has documented the extent of frontier violence accompanying the spread of pastoralism along 'Hedley's Track', running west to Anthony Lagoon, which was used to stock Brunette, Corella, Cresswell and Eva Downs stations during the early 1880s. Local Aboriginal groups suffered significant loss of life in reprisals for the spearing of stock or of white pastoralists themselves, as on Corella Downs in 1886 or Cresswell Downs during 1892 and 1896.[25] As Lindsay put it, 'driven from their tribal hunting grounds and water supplies, often into the territory of their hereditary enemies, their young women stolen, and the men shot if they protested; no redress from the white man's law possible – the lot of the aborigine was a terrible one'.[26] Eva Downs itself was something of a refuge during these turbulent years. Its first managers were the brothers Frank and Tom Traine, who treated the local Wambaya and Warumungu people with unusual respect, despite losing numbers of cattle on their arrival at the station during late 1884. Tom Traine's 1920 reminiscence helps to explain Cubadgee's initial confidence in approaching the Lindsays:

> The natives of the Barkly Tableland were very fine specimens. Many of the men stood over six feet, and measured forty-two inches round the chest. They showed no hostility to the white men, unlike coastal natives, and this friendliness was an incentive for us to devise some plan of treating them fairly. We agreed not to interfere with them and they were encouraged to roam about where they liked, but not to hang about the white man's camp … After a while natives began to come in fives and sixes, and the only English they could speak, learned from our boys, was 'Want him white fellow name.' I would call them something and they would go away quite pleased, repeating the name over and over.[27]

Despite such evidence of reconciliation, there is little doubt that Aboriginal people continued to regard the European presence as temporary, believing that the white pastoralists and their herds could be driven away eventually. Cubadgee himself was to express that sentiment. Two or three years after Cubadgee's departure, Traine was informed by an elderly Aboriginal woman at Eva Downs that 'When big fellow rain come, black fellow kill him all about white fellow'.[28]

It was against this background of dispossession, exploitation and occasional resistance that George Lindsay took the step of arming Cubadgee. 'Many white men told me that I was a fool to arm him like this', he wrote, 'but I had formed the opinion that he was to be trusted, implicitly, and I never had any reason to alter this judgement'.[29] In this way Cubadgee began his transition to another world, from savage to stockman. Before this metamorphosis was completed, David Lindsay took the trouble to record the bare details of Cubadgee's tribal background. The expedition ethnographer was apparently absent at this stage. By the time of the expedition's arrival at Lake Nash, Hermann Dittrich had reached the point of utter incompatibility with David Lindsay, if not the rest of the party. Soon after, probably before the encounter with Cubadgee, the German botanist set off on a 'solitary scientific trip on a riding camel to the Gulf of Carpentaria'. This solo expedition followed the Gregory River to Burketown and was not without risk. Dittrich later observed that the Aborigines were 'getting bold and recently killed a white man and his boy on the open road on the Gregory'.[30] His report on this expedition has not been traced, but it apparently included a 'Vocabulary of the Albert River, Nicholson and Gregory River tribes, with some additional information about certain customs and habits, as correct and exact as I could gather them'. It is likely that the report was forwarded to the ethnographer Edward Curr for inclusion in his published survey of Aboriginal languages and customs, but arrived too late for publication.[31] Lindsay later interrogated the Secretary of the Royal Geographical Society in Adelaide on this point: 'Did Lieutenant Dittrich have your permission to forward to Mr Curr of Melbourne a copy of all information gained by him concerning the natives?'[32] Assuming that this untraced report refers only to Aboriginal groups well to the east of the Warumungu, the earliest written record of the language spoken by Cubadgee's people remains that obtained during the later 1890s by the Alice Springs telegraph operator and pioneer anthropologist, Francis Gillen.[33]

According to David Lindsay, Cubadgee had come into Tennant Creek with his family 'when a very little boy' and subsequently 'had been more or less about the telegraph stations'. Since it began operation during 1872 the Tennant Creek Station attracted numbers of Warumungu people, curious about the new commodities of metal, tobacco, flour, sugar and tea – and the people who brought them. Cubadgee's family was among these early arrivals. As a result, Cubadgee had learnt a little English and had probably picked up some skills as a stockman.

Among the tantalisingly brief details recorded by David Lindsay was the fact that Cubadgee was the second son of '"Tapanunga" [the Warumungu subsection Japanangka], king or chief of the "Warramunga" whose country [was] called Djungrooarrgoor'.[34] Lindsay defined this country as lying 'about Tennant's Creek and in the unexplored region to the westward, say between latitude 19° & 21°, longitude 131° & 135°'. This is a rough approximation of the country accepted today as traditional Warumungu territory.

The name 'Cubadgee', as Lindsay spelt it, is identifiable as one of eight 'subsection' terms, to which each individual in Warumungu and related societies belongs. Lindsay mistakenly identified 'ten families or divisions regulating the intersexual relations', rather than eight.[35] Today Warumungu people use subsection terminology adapted from the Warlpiri people to their west, and no longer use the term 'Cubadgee (or 'Kapiji', to use Warumungu orthography). Here an important link is provided by the 1890s' research of the Alice Springs telegraph station manager Francis Gillen. He not only recorded the term 'Kabidji' as one of the eight Warumungu subsection terms, but confirmed its correspondence to the Warlpiri term 'Japaljarri', which Warumungu use today for that subsection.[36] In fact, in 1994 this correspondence helped Warumungu people to place Dick Cubadgee as one of their own, more than a century after he had left their country.

Similarly, Lindsay's term 'Djungrooarrgoor' can be recognised as *Jurn-kurakurr*, a sacred Carpet Snake waterhole in Tennant Creek. This is still an important place for Warumungu people, who agree that Jurnkurakurr is a key site for the Wurlurru patrimoiety, or 'clan', to which they consider Cubadgee must have belonged. Through that affiliation he shared responsibility with other members of his patrimoiety to perform ceremonies for the Jurnkurakurr site, to sing its ancient verses, and to apply its sacred Carpet Snake designs in body decorations and ground paintings. As his totem, the actual snake would have been taboo for the young man. Tellingly, George Lindsay observed this fact, that the 'great native delicacy, the Wamby snake' (carpet python), was forbidden to Cubadgee.[37]

Cubadgee's pronounced chest cicatrices confirm his status as an initiate. The fact that the Lindsays encountered him at the north-eastern extremity of Warumungu country (or in neighbouring Wambaya country, according to Norman Tindale's tribal map) suggests that he had already participated in an initiatory 'grand tour' of his country, perhaps accompanied by his step-brother. Neither David nor George Lindsay made any record of Cubadgee's tribal lore, although George later wrote that 'around the campfires at night he told me all the tribal legends, and explained all the beliefs and ceremonies of his people'.[38]

Cubadgee's father or step-father, the source of much of this knowledge, had apparently died by the time of Lindsay's expedition. David Lindsay wrote that this Warumungu man, renowned as a 'king', was 'reported to have been almost a giant, being broad enough for two children to sit upon each shoulder and very tall'.[39] Lindsay recorded his name as 'Tapanunga', but this name was also a subsection term, and under standard Warumungu marriage laws this man's son would have been a Jappangarti, but not uncommonly a Jappaljarri, the equivalent of 'Kapidgi' (Cubadgee). But it is worth remembering that Cubadgee and his brother were, in fact, step-brothers. Cubadgee's actual father may have been another individual, of another subsection.

This question raises the issue of Cubadgee's name, and whether it was a Warumungu subsection term, or whether, as George Lindsay maintained, it was a term for 'younger brother'. Gillen recorded the Warumungu term *Papirti* for 'elder brother', which corresponds to George Lindsay's term, 'Pubadti'. But Gillen's term for younger brother is *Kukatcha*, which also resembles 'Cubadgee'.[40] George Lindsay may simply have confused the term 'Kukatcha' with the subsection name, 'Cubadgee'. In any event, 'Cubadgee' is the name which came to be applied by the Lindsays, and which Dick accepted.

According to David Lindsay, Cubadgee's elder step-brother was even taller than him: '6 feet, 8 inches high and ... about 17 1/2 stone'. During late 1888, when Cubadgee was accompanying the Lindsays on a gold and gem prospecting expedition in the MacDonnell Ranges, he learnt that his step-brother had been speared to death by Wambaya men when on a hunting expedition outside Warumungu territory. By now accustomed to the Snider rifle which George Lindsay had given him, Cubadgee had to be restrained from leaving the camp to take revenge.

As a result of his brother's death, Cubadgee undoubtedly assumed additional ritual responsibilities among his Warumungu kin. But well before that event, David Lindsay had interpreted Cubadgee's status to a southern audience as 'King of the Warramungas', in a royal line passing through his father. The notion of Aboriginal 'kings' or paramount chiefs is rejected by anthropologists today, in favour of a complex series of domains of responsibility and obligation in which individuals may combine their inherited rights with authority accrued during their own lifetime, but must always defer to the intersecting rights and authority of other individuals, and other Dreaming Ancestors. David Lindsay's own 1886 notes suggest that he had considered this issue, but he was able to communicate only in pidgin English, and without a deeper understanding of Aboriginal systems of authority and cultural transmission, the white explorer could only reach a simplistic conclusion. Lindsay wrote: 'Lake Nash ... The kings are hereditary – if king dies and his eldest son is a boy then an old man, brother to the dead king, takes charge of the youthful king until he comes of age'.[41] In Adelaide and Melbourne Cubadgee did nothing to dispel the image created for him by Lindsay as the 'King of the Warramungas'. His height, bearing and fine physical features seemed to confirm him in the role.

By late 1886 Lindsay's survey of pastoral properties was complete. With Cubadgee's assistance, his men had surveyed more than 800 kilometres of new station boundaries. Cubadgee accompanied the full party north to the McArthur River on the Gulf of Carpentaria.[42] David Lindsay and three expedition members, including Dittrich who had rejoined the party, embarked for Port Darwin and then to Adelaide by steamer. Lindsay took second-class tickets in an attempt to humiliate Dittrich, 'because of his insulting and generally disagreeable behaviour throughout the trip and while in Pt. Darwin'.[43]

The plan was for George Lindsay to remain as a stockman at Anthony Lagoon for some months, and for the camel-driver Joorak to take the remaining camels and horses overland to Hergott Springs. Here was a dilemma for the young Warumungu man. He could either return to his people, with the likely prospect of working for the newly arrived pastoralists as a disenfranchised 'station black', or to penetrate further into the world of Europeans, on his own terms. Deciding to accompany Joorak south, and on to Adelaide, Cubadgee chose the second alternative.

Neither George nor David Lindsay commented on this decision or mentioned any incentive which might have influenced Cubadgee. After all, the young man was 'very intelligent and good tempered, remarkably apt at learning the manners of the whites'. In fact, David Lindsay gave only the briefest account of their meeting and of Cubadgee's subsequent arrival in Adelaide: 'I picked him up on a newly formed cattle station and he accompanied Joorak (my camel-driver) on the journey from the McArthur River to Hergott Springs whilst I and the rest of my party returned to Adelaide by water'.[44] Yet it is possible that Cubadgee's decision to make this journey was the first step in a project taking shape in his mind which only his 'elder brother' George Lindsay would comprehend, and then much later.

The Warumungu youth and his Afghan companion accomplished the 1350 mile (2000 kilometre) journey from Borroloola (on the McArthur River) to Hergott Springs in twelve weeks, without losing any camels or horses. It was an achievement likely to have attracted widespread acclaim had David Lindsay accompanied the pair.[45] Cubadgee was under no compulsion to make this journey, and he might easily have abandoned it after venturing south beyond Warumungu and Kaytej country, out of touch with his own language affiliations. But by now of course, he had a new language, the English learnt around the telegraph stations and polished during his time with the Lindsay expedition.

Hearing that Joorak and Cubadgee had arrived safely at Hergott Springs with the camels and horses, David Lindsay travelled there by train from Adelaide and returned to the city with Cubadgee during mid-January, 1887. A few days later Cubadgee's presence was announced in a short article in the *Observer* which, in recording the pair's achievement, could not avoid drawing the public's attention to Cubadgee's outstanding physique: 'Joorak was accompanied only by a black "boy", who, though reputedly merely a youngster of 17 years old, is 6ft, 5 1/2 in. high'.[46]

This emphasis on Cubadgee's physical form would never abate, and would eventually govern his fate. That said, Cubadgee seems never to have resented such attention. He understood the impact of his presence in the streets and drawing rooms of the southern cities of Adelaide and Melbourne, far from the remote frontier. Half a century after Adelaide had tamed and put aside its own frontier, Cubadgee provided a tangible reminder of its existence. Using the unanticipated charm of his assumed nobility, and through the patronage of the Lindsays, he became one of only a handful of Central Australian Aborigines able to modify prevailing nineteenth-century European views about his people.

CUBADGEE IN ADELAIDE

In Adelaide, Cubadgee lodged with David Lindsay's father-in-law, Arthur Lindsay, who was Chairman of the Destitute Asylum Board. After George Lindsay returned to Adelaide early in 1888, Cubadgee may also have shared accommodation with him.[47] Cubadgee sat at table with the Lindsays. He is remembered even today as a family member, although perhaps a more accurate comparison could be the school friend brought home for the holidays – who might also pay his way. Arthur Lindsay employed Cubadgee at the asylum and paid him a small allowance for odd jobs there. Cubadgee also served as the Lindsays' coachman, driving the family around the city and accompanying them to church on Sundays.

During early 1887 a professional photographer photographed Cubadgee in front of Lindsay's coach-house. The camera fixed his status anew, but dressed in his coachman's outfit, top-hatted and cane in hand, Cubadgee seems as loose-limbed and relaxed as in those portraits depicting him as a naked warrior.[48]

The Lindsays took Cubadgee to performances at the Theatre Royal and introduced him to leading figures in Adelaide society, including members of the Royal Geographical Society, Sir Edward Stirling at the South Australian Museum and the Chief Justice, Sir Samuel Way. As Lindsay family tradition has

Cubadgee in his coachman's attire, Adelaide, 1887. Photographer: Unknown. PXE 724/29, Mitchell Library, Sydney.

it, Cubadgee's acceptance by a wide social circle might well indicate that many Adelaide people (at least among the bourgeoisie) were 'receptive to clever and communicative Aborigines'.[49] Samuel Way became a particular mentor, and Cubadgee was a frequent visitor to his Montefiore Hill mansion, with its rooms full of oriental antiquities and fine furniture. Aboriginal artefacts adorned the walls of its billiard room, in the style of many grand houses, but Way's interest in Australian ethnography went deeper. A decade earlier the judge had hosted his own young Aboriginal house-guest. This was Nanyena, a son of 'Jack Davis', the Iwaidja man who had been a key intermediary with the British settlers at Port Essington during the 1840s. Jack Davis had learnt English and had sailed aboard trading vessels in the Pacific, as far as Hong Kong. He readily gave permission for Nanyena to accompany Way's friend, John Lewis, to Adelaide in 1873, attaching only one condition – that the boy should never give up his Aboriginal name, as Davis himself had done. According to Lewis, Davis said:

'If you take him to Adelaide always call him "Nanyena", never call him any other name, because when I went away my name was – [Lewis could not recall it], and when I came back I had forgotten a great deal of my native language, and went by the name of Jack Davis; and my people did not believe that I was the king or heir to the throne'.[50]

Given that Cubadgee was to become known to Adelaide society as the 'King of the Warramungas', the parallel with Jack Davis is worth noting. Among

Europeans, both Aboriginal men may have gained notions of their indigenous status reflecting British concepts of royalty rather than their own people's social structures. Although he retained 'Cubadgee' as an Aboriginal name, this was a Warumungu kinship term, rather than a personal name. A century later, that particular term was to provide the key to his eventual 'homecoming' and acceptance by Warumungu people of the Tennant Creek region. But it seems that, like Davis, Cubadgee's own personal name has slipped from memory.

Strangely, the attention lavished upon Cubadgee in Adelaide did not result in any focused ethnographic investigation of the young Warumungu man, unless shallow curiosity about his physique can be regarded in that light. According to George Lindsay, 'anatomists and anthropologists examined him; dentists came to see an absolutely flawless set of human teeth, so powerful that they could bite through copper wire'.[51] He was introduced to the Royal Geographical Society as 'a living specimen', one of the finest of his race, and was apparently unfazed by this status. Perhaps he accepted this attention as the deference due to the 'King of the Warramungas'.

In any event, this anthropological curiosity seems balanced by Cubadgee's own self-confidence, and by the degree of acceptance he met in his encounters with strangers in Adelaide. Years later, George Lindsay related several anecdotes about 'Cubadgee at large':

> He was fond of a joke. One day he and I were walking down Gawler Place together when he stopped, put his head inside the door of a chemist's shop and said 'Hoo!' The startled chemist, who had been reading, took one horrified glance at the huge black figure with gleaming teeth and eyes, and then dived under the counter, sending bottles flying in every direction as he did so. Cubagee walked on roaring with laughter at the fright he had given the unfortunate dispenser of drugs.[52]

Cubadgee's long rambles through the Adelaide Hills became a talking point. On his return to his quarters at Arthur Lindsay's home or George Lindsay's lodgings, he would recount the places he had visited during a day's walk and it was realised that he covered up to 50 kilometres on these outings. The length of his stride was measured on Glenelg beach and 'found to average forty-two inches – even tall Europeans seldom have a stride exceeding three feet'.[53]

It was a pity that Cubadgee was known mainly for such characteristics, for these were banalities in comparison to the riches of his people's lore which he carried. The scars across the young man's chest confirm the transmission of that store of knowledge and tradition. Yet no indication exists that Cubadgee was ever interviewed with serious intent about his cultural knowledge, or even about the languages he spoke (undoubtedly extending beyond Warumungu). In the meantime, Cubadgee drew 'sand pictures' for A.T. Magarey, a Royal Geographical Society member interested in Aboriginal tracking techniques. A 'perfect adept', Cubadgee made 'representations of lizards, snakes, wallaby and emu footprints, of the human footprints, and of camel pad[s] … drawn with marvellous rapidity and accuracy'.[54]

TWO VISIONS

In the light of his subsequent fate, it is easy to regard Cubadgee as an historical victim, a casualty of colonialism. There is no doubt that he was enlisted in David Lindsay's own grand vision, a complex project of multiple opportunities involving international exhibitions and exploration, mining and commerce. Yet even as he collaborated in these schemes, and perhaps became compromised by them, Cubadgee was forming his own clear ideas about an alternative future for himself and his people, which he might control.

The clearest indication of Cubadgee's attitudes underlining his role as an actor rather than an historical victim comes from George Lindsay's reminiscences. During their prospecting expedition of 1889 and shortly before his final illness, Cubadgee had time enough to discuss his hope and dreams with his 'Pubadti' or elder white brother:

> Cubadgee revealed his great plan. The white people had no right to take away the tribal lands of his people. They should pay for them in cattle, leave the tribe with sufficient land for a cattle station of their own. Surely men like the Chief Justice [Sir Samuel Way] or my grandfather [Arthur Lindsay] would see that it was done? He, himself, having learned how the white people managed these things, would boss the venture.[55]

If Cubadgee considered he was taking charge of his own destiny by coming to Adelaide, it is worth remembering that David Lindsay had his own motives for becoming a mentor for the Warumungu youth. During 1887 and 1888 Lindsay presented Cubadgee at Adelaide's Government House, to the Royal Geographical Societies of Melbourne and Adelaide, and at the International Exhibitions in those two cities. As with Lindsay's own exploring expeditions, these endeavours could be regarded as worthy attempts to add to scientific knowledge in a new age of discovery. But there was an additional factor. Lindsay's own commercial projects and entrepeneurial schemes were closely entwined with the nobler, patriotic endeavour of exploration. Cubadgee's elegant and arresting performances on Lindsay's behalf contributed, at least indirectly, to his people's own dispossession by the very pastoral and mining interests so vigorously promoted by the explorer.

The soirée held by the Royal Geographical Society in Adelaide in the Town Hall Banqueting Room on 29 June 1887 provides a case in point. As an event associated with the Adelaide Jubilee Exhibition, the evening's scientific agenda was coloured with a rosy, patriotic tinge. The room itself 'was nicely draped with flags and photographs of the Northern Territory and native weapons which had been lent by various gentlemen'. On his arrival, Lindsay and Cubadgee were greeted with cheers by the assembled company, which included the Northern Territory's Government Resident, J.L. Parsons. Lindsay's introduction to his paper described his recent Central Australian trip in detail, encapsulating the esoteric, scientific and pragmatic objectives of late nineteenth-century exploration. Directing his audience to a large map of Central Australia, Lindsay suggested that:

> it needs no mind reader ... to anticipate the questions you would ask an explorer who has examined it. If you are a geographer with a knowledge of the history of early Australian exploration, the first question on your lips will be – what of the brave but unfortunate Leichhardt? Can you tell us how and where he died, or is there the faintest hope that any of the members of his party still survive? Then you will ask about the aboriginal people, if any prehistoric records exist; and you will want a description of the striking geographical features of the country. If moved by an enterprising spirit for pioneer settlement, your questions will be – what of the lands, its waters, its woods, its grasses?[56]

Those lands, waters, woods and grasses were, of course, Cubadgee's own, and were still regarded as inalienable by his Warumungu kin. But it is unlikely that the presence of the 'King of the Warrumungas', in a picturesque validation of Lindsay's endeavour, provoked more than a frisson of irony at this soirée. When the cue was given, Cubadgee took the floor himself, fire-sticks in hand:

> Mr Lindsay's blackboy Cubadgee, who is 6 feet 6 inches high, although only 17 years old, demonstrated the method adopted by the aborigines for starting a fire. One stick was laid horizontally on the table and the end of another, placed in a small hole made in the first, was rapidly turned around in his hand. The boy did not cause a flame to burst forth, but created smoke. Mr Lindsay explained that he had not known the boy to fail previously.[57]

If Cubadgee felt disappointed by this performance, his mood is unlikely to have lifted after hearing the Government Resident's response to Lindsay's glowing account of his country's pastoral potential. As Parsons put it:

> To practical South Australians the question immediately resolved itself into, What is the Northern Territory worth? Can the Northern Territory be made a field into which capital can be invested and a profit be made? ... Mr Isaac Little, one of the proprietors of the Austral Downs Station, close to the Queensland border, had written to him that he calculated that the country south of the Herbert River could carry from 5,000,000 to 6,000,000 sheep, and an intelligent man told him that the central plateau would carry from 30,000,000 to 50,000,000 sheep when the country was opened up by a railway ...[58]

Within the year Lindsay was rewarded for his contribution to the exploration of the Australian continent with a fellowship of the Royal Geographical Society in London. He had already sent the Society a set of 'photographs of an Aboriginal boy whom I brought from the interior of the Continent some months ago'.[59] As in his Adelaide soirée, Lindsay was ready to combine the various strands of his enterprise, employing Cubadgee as the personification of his achievements.

Cubadgee's athletic physique suitably complemented the persona of a vigorous and resourceful Australian explorer at the height of his abilities. During May 1887 Lindsay sent another set of Cubadgee's photographs to the Victorian branch of the Geographical Society, who forwarded them to the leading Australian pictorial newspaper, the *Australasian Sketcher*. An artist's rendition of Cubadgee standing against the backdrop of artefacts at the Adelaide Jubilee Exhibition was published in the June issue as 'a more than ordinarily fine specimen of the aborigines of Central Australia'.[60] Cubadgee himself was less than impressed with this rendering. 'I am afraid', Lindsay recorded, 'the artist who was responsible for the reproduction of Cubadgee's would not have felt flattered if he had heard Cubadgee's remarks theron'.[61]

In an individual of Cubadgee's qualities and physical attributes it was probably inevitable that the diverse fields of anthropological science, frontier adventure and fairground curiosity would intersect. By mid-1887 David Lindsay had seen enough of Cubadgee's impressive demonstrations of traditional skills in tracking, fire-making, boomerang and spear-throwing, and his confident demeanour with strangers, to conceive of a bold new project. This was to be based upon Cubadgee's role at the International Exhibitions, but would also include his fellow Warumungu, in an unprecedented exposition of the 'full life of the Aboriginal'. David Lindsay's intention was to display an entire tribe of 40 Aborigines, Cubadgee's own kin, before an international audience.

Lindsay's contact with the Royal Geographical Society and with other scientific journals had made him aware of similar projects being undertaken in Britain and Europe during the 1880s. The kidnapping of a group of north Queensland Aboriginal people by the entrepreneur Robert A. Cunningham (an agent for the Barnum and Bailey circus), and the subsequent display of these people in European circuses and sideshows may not have been widely known in Australia, but the subsequent tests and scrutiny applied to these people had been noted in anthropological journals available in Adelaide. Lindsay may have developed his scheme after seeing these accounts. But even if he had not, his voyage to North Queensland and to Darwin during late 1887 (while Cubadgee remained at the Adelaide Exhibition) took the explorer to ports visited by Cunningham. At one of those ports, Darwin, Lindsay was well-acquainted with Paul Foelsche, the police inspector who had advised local Aboriginal people to seek shelter in the bush or 'they would never return', when Cunningham attempted to obtain 'five fine specimens' there during 1883.[62]

It was en route to Darwin via Cooktown during August 1887 that David Lindsay formulated his scheme. He included it in a letter to a potential partner, a Mr Renault, whom Lindsay had recently met in Adelaide. It is likely that Renault had encountered Cubadgee there, the integral figure in Lindsay's grand project – not only for his fire-lighting and boomerang-throwing skills, but probably also for his abilities as a 'buck-jumper'. Lindsay's letter is worth reproducing in full:

S.S. Taujaun, 29 August 1887

Dear Sir,

Referring to our conversation in Adelaide a fortnight ago, re taking a troupe of aboriginals to England for show purposes, I now beg to append my thoughts on the subject.

I have, for some time past, thought that a well organised band of Australian natives taken to London would prove attractive to the public and therefore remunerative to the promoters.

I think that the number should be 40 including women and children.

That they should not be taken from the semi colonized tribes, but from those tribes who are living in their natural state.

Special attention would be paid to:

1st Adepts on throwing the boomerang and spear.

2nd Good specimens of humanity – for instance my boy, who stands 6/2 feet weighs 13 stone and is only 16 or 17 years old, and his brother whose weight is 171/2 stone and his height 6 feet 81/2 inches.

All necessary material for forming a camp would be taken. Native dogs (dingo) and any other native animals.

Fire sticks to illustrate the method of producing fire. Natives skilled in making their stone implements and other manufactures (spears, boomerang, stone implements, rope, baskets, mats etc etc would be made).

The various corroborees could be represented. In fact, the full life of the Australian aboriginal would be shown. All the implements of war and chase, the dresses and ornaments.

	Pounds
Estimated cost as under	
To get the 40 people and their implements and camp gear together . . . in Adelaide, say	500
Clothing – for they must be well provided with warm clothes	400
Passages to England	500
2 attendants and myself wages and expenses to England say . . .	300
Total to land the troupe in England	1700
Return expenses about the same	1700
I suppose the expenses of myself and attendants and troupe while in London would be per day	20

This estimate is necessarily approximate but I think I have not estimated it at less than it would cost, but perhaps it may not cost as much.

For myself I have only calculated bare expenses and a salary of 1 pound per day, therefore I would require, as you suggested, a fair share of the profits to repay me for the special knowledge in selecting and managing these peculiar people.

Hoping that you will be able to put this before your people in a favourable light and that they will consider the venture a sound one.

I am, yours faithfully, David Lindsay FRGS

ps. How would it do to take home a couple of Australian buck jumping horses for one of the black boys to ride. DL.

It would take me about 2 months to collect the troupe.

It would be necessary to pay me the estimated cost of taking the natives to England before I could commence to get them together. Then an agreement undertaking to pay the return expenses and setting for the share in the profits to be paid to me would have to be set out.[63]

In Adelaide, nothing like Lindsay's scheme had been proposed since the mid-1840s, when the watercolour artist George French Angas had planned to present a troupe of South Australian Aborigines and their artefacts at the Egyptian Hall in Piccadilly, as a 'savage tableau' promoting his own paintings. Angas had come to South Australia in 1844 wanting to emulate the 'Indian Gallery' of the North American artist George Catlin, who had gathered hundreds of artefacts to complement his own paintings, and subsequently incorporated live performances by Ojibwa and Iowa Indians during the early 1840s. But Lindsay's scheme may also have been influenced by an event during the Adelaide Jubilee Exhibition, in which 77 Aboriginal people from the Point McLeay and Point Pearce missions participated. The event involved acting out juxtaposed tableaux of 'Savage Life' and 'Civilized Life', centred on an Aboriginal wurley with recitations and songs, followed by a 'sham fight' with shields and spears. The object of this choreographed performance (described in chapter two) was to remind the engrossed audience of the worthy transformation which mission Christianity had wrought on savage society:

> Having been brought under the influence of civilisation they feel that it is degrading to resort to their old bush life, and on the mission stations corroborees are entirely discouraged on account of the immoral tendencies. A little dancing was introduced by the natives in their excitement, but nothing to speak of.[64]

Cubadgee and David Lindsay may have been among the audience. If so, we can assume that Lindsay, at least, had in mind a more robust event, less constrained by conventional morality. A more likely model was Barnum, Bailey and Hutchinson's 'Greatest Show on Earth', which toured North America during the mid-1880s and included the Aboriginal people kidnapped by Cunningham. Lindsay may have seen Cunningham's own promotional pamphlet published in 1884, titled *A History of R.A. Cunningham's Australian Aborigines, Tatooed* [sic] *Cannibals, Black Trackers and Boomerang Throwers*. But it may be too easy to cast David Lindsay into Cunningham's role as exploitative entrepeneur. Cubadgee might even have approved of the scheme and recommended his people's involvement. With his own recent experiences as an indication, he may have relished the idea of an international tour with his extended family, demonstrating both their ancient and newly acquired skills to an appreciative audience, perhaps conceiving this as another step in his greater scheme of an independent future.

Whatever the nature of their personal relationship, neither Lindsay nor

Cubadgee could avoid the realities of colonialism which shaped their respective roles. Cubadgee's indigenous qualities were enlisted in the surveyor-explorer's colonial projects, from ethnography and exploration to geology and land sales. In Adelaide during late 1887, the youth's role was largely, if not entirely, picturesque. Sending copies of Cubadgee's photographs to Melbourne, Lindsay had written: 'If I do not require the boy he will be engaged about the South Australian court in the Adelaide Exhibition where also my collection of native weapons, curios and other interesting articles will be on view'.[65] Those 'interesting articles' included the supposed rubies Lindsay had discovered in Glen Annie during early 1886. The list of articles in Lindsay's exhibit follows below. Most of these objects had been collected during his 1883 and 1885–1886 expeditions. Notably absent from the list are Cubadgee's fire-sticks. Perhaps Lindsay recognised these as Cubadgee's own property:

> 1 bundle containing 7 stone spears
> 56 barbed spears
> 2 plain spears
> 1 wire spear
> 9 reed spears
> . . . and 3 clubs
> 1 bundle containing 8 womeras [spearthrowers]
> 1 bundle containing 4 boomerangs
> 1 bundle containing 1 Cooliman (water vessel)
>> 1 Haliman (shield)
>> 2 waddies
> 1 box containing 2 coolimans
>> 2 flint adzes & chisels
>> 2 stone tomahawks
>> 1 piece native rope from Macarthur River
> 1 Headdress
> £50
> 1 Map Australian Ruby Fields, mounted on cloth & roller   10/6
>>   £50/10/6 [66]

At the Adelaide Exhibition Cubadgee represented his people as the 'King of the Warramungas', against a backdrop of a pastoral and mining map of the Northern Territory and a display of Lindsay's 'rubies'. He demonstrated the use of these artefacts, chatted to visitors, and performed his fire-making. He also

Cubadgee as 'King of the Warramunga tribe', photographed at the Adelaide Jubilee Exhibition in 1887. South Australian Museum Archives.

gave demonstrations of boomerang and spear-throwing at the Adelaide Oval. Returning boomerangs were rarely made or used by Warumungu people, and it is likely that Cubadgee picked up this skill from Murray River Aboriginal men. His particular feat was 'to make a returning boomerang circle three times around him in wide sweeps, then flutter gently to the grass at his feet'. Another trick involved skimming a boomerang 'breast-high across the Oval until almost invisible, then [it] would soar so high into the sky as to resemble a small, twinkling speck, and descend in a slow and graceful spiral to within a few feet of him'.[67]

David Lindsay was also at ease in the colonial capital: the tall urbane bushman, successful prospector and heroic explorer (full-bearded after the fashion of John McDouall Stuart), whose intimate knowledge of the frontier's potential made him welcome at the city's better addresses. Lindsay had taken up employment as a stock and land broker in Adelaide with the aim of advancing land sales on the Northern Territory's Roper River, country which he had surveyed during the early 1880s. Investment interest in this region was founded partly in perceptions of the region's pastoral promise, but substantially also in its mining potential. Lindsay's 'ruby' find at Glen Annie in Central Australia underlined that potential, a tantalising hint of the wealth lying in those frontier expanses which Lindsay proposed to unlock for investors. Conveniently for Lindsay, the identification of these stones as mere garnets was still to be resolved by tests in London.

Cubadgee's own impressive appearance lent authenticity to the exhibit and to Lindsay's enterprise, as genuine as the artefacts on display. Witnessing the young Warumungu 'king' make fire within a matter of seconds, visitors would hardly have been concerned to notice that Cubadgee's fire-drill had been repaired in European fashion, its two halves finely spliced together like a billiard cue. Perhaps this was another of Cubadgee's new skills, acquired through observation in the Chief Justice's billiard room.

IN THE DOCTORS' HANDS

Soon after his appearance in the Melbourne Exhibition during August 1888, Cubadgee left with the Lindsays for their prospecting expedition to the MacDonnell Ranges. David Lindsay was still convinced that rubies existed there and had formed the 'Glen Annie' company to extract them. He also believed in the existence of goldfields, having seen reefs of quartz in Harts Range during 1886. It was during this expedition, several months later, that Cubadgee became ill, complaining of a lump on his neck and stiffness. By early April 1889 George Lindsay considered this serious enough to warrant taking the young man south to Adelaide for medical attention. The pair travelled by camel to Oodnadatta and caught the train south to Adelaide. There Arthur Lindsay organised Cubadgee's admission to the Adelaide Hospital, on 27 April 1889. Cubadgee now found himself in the hands of those Adelaide medical men, inclined towards physical anthropology, who had come to regard him as 'a more than ordinarily fine specimen'.

The precise nature of Cubadgee's illness is unclear, but at least one operation was performed to remove a large tumour on his neck. Arthur Lindsay had arranged for the notable surgeon and foundation professor of the Adelaide Medical School, Archibald Watson, to treat Cubadgee and to operate on him. Watson was no ordinary surgeon. He had been trained in Europe by the pioneer in physical anthropology and craniometry, Paul Broca, and was a medical school colleague of Edward Stirling, appointed in 1888 as Honorary Director of the Adelaide Museum.[68] Not surprisingly, Watson had become an enthusiastic participant in the late nineteenth-century international traffic in indigenous people's skeletal material and body parts, centred in British and Continental museums.

Watson's operation on Cubadgee was judged a success and the young man began a slow convalescence at the hospital. He befriended the members of the Women's Auxiliary who came regularly to visit him. According to George Lindsay, the young man remained astonished at the number of single, elderly women in Adelaide, an impression formed perhaps through his earlier employment at the Destitute Asylum. He was keen to talk about his country and his people with his visitors. Once again, he spoke of the fact that the whites were intruders in Warumungu country and that they should leave his people alone, or at least supply them with the cattle and equipment to make a living under the new, changed conditions. He left his visitors in no doubt that if anyone possessed the capacity to undertake that initiative, almost a century before the first Aboriginal-owned cattle stations became a reality in the Northern Territory, it would be himself.[69]

Cubadgee's convalescence lasted the length of the Adelaide winter. He seemed to have recovered from the operation, but with his lowered resistance he was vulnerable to forms of cross-infection, almost inevitable in hospitals of the period. After developing 'tubercular meningitis' Dick Cubadgee died on Sunday 15 September 1889.

Mystery still surrounds the fate of Cubadgee's remains following his death. According to records, three other Aboriginal people died in the Royal Adelaide Hospital on 15 September 1889 and death certificates were issued for these individuals. Apparently no death certificate was issued for Cubadgee. Perhaps plans had already been made to transfer his skeleton to the Museum. Notwithstanding that, a funeral service was held for Cubadgee in Adelaide's Holy Trinity Church on 18 September and a burial took place. A plot number in his name is recorded at the West Terrace Cemetery.[70]

The death of this young man, a dynamic and articulate spokesman for his people, who entered Adelaide society with ease and grace, shocked his patrons and friends. For those beginning to grapple with the 'Aboriginal problem' (itself caused by the European displacement of Aboriginal people), Cubadgee was a key broker; he had left his country voluntarily and had seemed to thrive in white society. But now he had died, far too young and out of context. The flame he conjured up had been snuffed out, but his qualities were too enduring for him to be forgotten easily. David Lindsay's newspaper obituary notice, despite its inevitable tone of paternalism, nevertheless evoked a genuine sense of loss among the circle who had known Dick Cubadgee:

Two studio portraits of Dick Cubadgee, Adelaide, ca 1888. Photographers: W. Lingwood Smith and Tuttle & Co. South Australian Museum Archives.

Death of an Aboriginal King

The King of the Warramunga tribe of aborigines, who inhabit the country near Tennant's Creek, died in the Adelaide Hospital on Sunday, 15th September, 1889. Deceased, who was better known as ... the explorer's black boy Dick, was about nineteen years of age, and was 6ft 6in. in height. He had been with Mr Lindsay in all his journeys since 1886, and had proved a very faithful and trustworthy attendant. He was a perfect gentleman in his behaviour, never misconducted himself in any way, and when he became King of the Warramungas, through the shooting of his brother last year, his aspirations for a higher form of life than he could get by going back to his tribe prevented his assuming his royal rank. He seemed to have a very fair idea of a future state, and frequently asked the nurses to read the Bible to him. About four months since he went in to the Adelaide Hospital suffering from tumours on the chest, and, despite every attention, succumbed to tuberculosis. Dick was a good representative of a large tribe and was introduced to more representatives of the English nobility than perhaps any other Australian aborigine. During the building of the Jubilee Exhibition many visitors sought his acquaintance, and all found him intelligent and pleasing in his manner. Mr Lindsay, who was very much attached to Dick, feels his death very keenly and says he was the best specimen of an Australian black he has ever met.[71]

By the 1880s there were already numbers of Aboriginal people, mostly men, who had entered the frontier zone or even stepped beyond it into towns and cities, and then returned to their own societies. Cubadgee was one of these individuals, but was no longer content with a mute role as 'Lindsay's boy'. He had not intended to remain within the ethnographic frame in which, conforming to the image of an impressive and noble savage, he had performed his fire-making. Encouraged by well-meaning Adelaideans curious to know more about his people, Cubadgee had begun to suggest ways in which his people might gain some agency on the frontier. He had direct access to powerful individuals within Adelaide society, including pastoralists and officials whose decisions had already transformed conditions of life in Warumungu country. This made his role more significant, his future more interesting, his idealism less utopian. His death removed those possibilities and they were quickly forgotten. Cubadgee's persona retracted once more to that ethnographic frame.

Both Archibald Watson and the South Australian Museum director, Edward Stirling, had become Cubadgee's friends, but both also regarded him as an important exemplar of a racial type, 'the finest specimen of an Australian black'.

Portrait study of Cubadgee, from the collection of Nora Lindsay, daughter of David Lindsay. South Australian Museum Archives.

Both men were co-founders of the Adelaide Medical School and were pioneer physical anthropologists. Their first action, which may be interpreted as a gesture of respect, was to arrange for a death mask to be taken. Cubadgee's last, and most compelling portrait shows him bearded.[72] The pair then persuaded Cubadgee's guardians, the Lindsays, to allow them to preserve his skeleton for science. According to family tradition Arthur Lindsay gave his permission most reluctantly. By 1890 the articulated skeleton formed part of a comparative display at the Museum, and was later incorporated into an exhibit devoted to primate evolution. It remained on public display until the 1960s.

Cubadgee's transition from an agent of change to an object of science was not smooth. His death created a dilemma for those who knew him and held power over his memory. Evidence of a struggle for ownership over his remains lies in the lack of a death certificate, a partly empty coffin in the West Terrace cemetery and even the suggestion that despite undertakings to keep the skeleton in the South Australian Museum, its director had planned to consign it to the University of Cambridge Anthropology and Archaeology Museum. Forty years later, George Lindsay maintained that he had intervened through the Royal Geographical Society to prevent this, and that 'the skeleton was returned post haste'.[73] The strength of George Lindsay's attachment to the memory of his former companion emerged through his reminiscences of their time together, later published in the *Bulletin* under his *nom de plume*, 'Larrapinta'. During the 1890s George joined David Lindsay in the Western Australian goldfields and engaged an Aboriginal boy of Israelite Bay, named Ivo, as his assistant. Ivo accompanied George Lindsay to Adelaide and was photographed in precisely the same pose as Cubadgee several years earlier – in profile, with one foot resting on a log of wood. But Ivo's life in Adelaide was even shorter than Cubadgee's. According to George Lindsay's descendants, the boy became involved in an argument with 'a Chinaman in Hindley Street' and was knifed to death.[74]

EPILOGUE

More than a century after his death, Cubadgee still possessed the power to disturb. During 1990 a delegation of Warlpiri and Warumungu men viewed his articulated skeleton in Adelaide and made the decision that Cubadgee should be laid to rest in his country, at Jurnkurakurr. His memory had lingered in the oral record and Warumungu people agreed that Cubadgee belonged there. It had been his intention to return. Cubadgee was remembered as of the Japaljarri subsection or 'skin', and his Dreaming was recognised as the Carpet Snake, residing eternally in Jurnkurakurr waterhole.

During May 1991 eight senior Warumungu and Warlpiri men drove to Adelaide to carry out the first ceremonies in preparation for the return of Cubadgee's skeleton. A few weeks later the museum's director, Lester Russell, flew to Tennant Creek with the casket containing the bones. The casket was placed in a grave at Jurnkurakurr on 4 June, but only after Warumungu men, women and children from the area had paid their respects to 'the old man' in the traditional way. Each knelt before the casket and rubbed their chests against it, the same ritual as carried out earlier at the museum. It is a gesture symbolising the 'touching of spirits'.[75]

It had been 105 years since Cubadgee had stepped into the white man's world, sending a plume of smoke curling through the Governor's drawing room, with a twirl of his billiard-cue fire-drill.

Glass goblet with engraved inscription, 'Dick Cubagee 1887'; height 13 cm. It was probably presented to Cubadgee at the time of the Adelaide Jubilee Exhibition. Owned by Margaret Stuart, great-granddaughter of David Lindsay. Photographed by Lindsay's great-great-granddaughter, Kylie Gillespie, 2008.

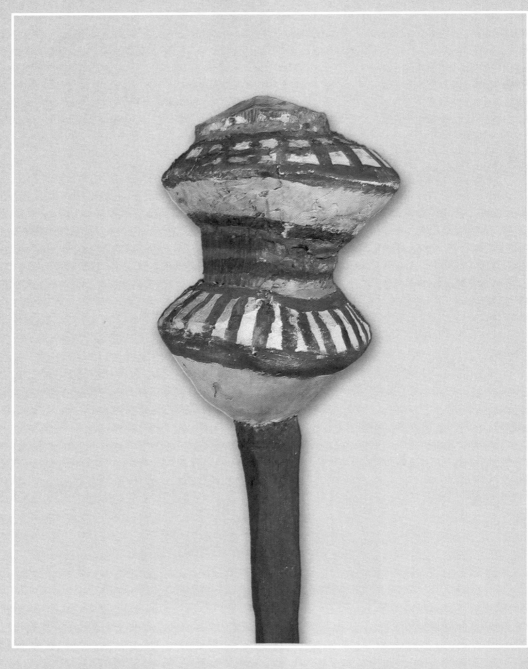

One of Reuther's toas, directing travellers to the place where the mythological ancestors Mitjimanamana and Likimadlentji saw the spirits of the dead arriving from all around and climbing upwards to the stars. A6168, South Australian Museum.

CHAPTER SIX

Unearthing the toas

In May 1906 the Lutheran missionary Johann Reuther retired from the remote Killalpaninna mission on Cooper Creek, east of Lake Eyre. Since his arrival in the desert from the Neuendettelsau seminary in Germany in 1888, Reuther had worked without cease among the Diyari and related peoples. It was, he later wrote, 'a stony field of work, full of human bones. I have stood at about 200 heathen graves and preached to the living'.[1]

On his retirement Reuther sold his ethnographic collection of more than 1300 pieces to the South Australian Museum for £400, the largest sum paid for such a collection in Australia until that time. The jewel in the collection, which the museum's director assured Reuther 'it would be clearly stated you were the discoverer of', was a series of 385 small painted objects sculpted from wood and gypsum, known as *toas*. According to Reuther, each toa was a signpost erected by people leaving a camp. Its painted or sculpted form depicted their chosen destination. No such objects had previously been documented or collected from Australian Aborigines. Reuther supplied an accompanying description of the toas and their function, but his thirteen-volume, 5,000-page manuscript describing the objects, beliefs and customs of the Diyari and related tribes was not acquired until after his death in 1914.[2]

On a first reading of Reuther's manuscript, the description of toas and their function accords with the version received by the South Australian Museum, subsequently endorsed through its public exhibition and publication of the collection. But a closer reading suggests that the toas were not only hybrid artefacts of a particular frontier encounter, but that within Reuther's own manuscript and collection they were anomalous objects. Rather than being 'discovered' by their collector, the toas came to light through the very process of his ethnographic enquiry.

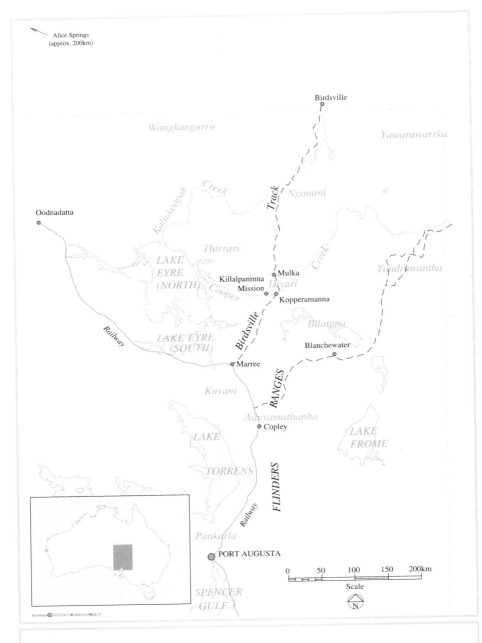

Alice Springs
(approx. 200km)

Birdsville

Wangkangurru

Yawarawarrka

Creek

Track

Ngamini

Oodnadatta

Kallakoopah

Thirrari

Creek

LAKE
EYRE
(NORTH)

Yandruwantha

Killalpaninna
Mission

Mulka

Diyari

Cooper

Kopperamanna

Birdsville

Bilatapa

Railway

LAKE EYRE
(SOUTH)

Blanchewater

Marree

Kuyani

RANGES

Adnyamathanha

Copley

LAKE

LAKE
FROME

TORRENS

FLINDERS

Railway

Pankarla

PORT AUGUSTA

0   50   100   150   200km
Scale

N

*SPENCER
GULF*

Basemaps © 2009 Cartographic Services Pty Ltd

The eastern Lake Eyre region, with relevant Aboriginal group names.

At the time of their acquisition at the turn of the twentieth century, innovative forms of Aboriginal art had not achieved any currency among collectors and ethnographic museums. It was quite reasonable for the toas to be regarded as artefacts with an ethnographic, rather than artistic, function. Their collector had proposed this definition, and the South Australian Museum saw no reason to modify it. But the toas do not rest easily within that ethnographic frame. They are perplexing objects. When I first encountered the toas eighty years after their manufacture, no Aboriginal person remembered them in their original context, at the Killalpaninna mission. If their enigmatic origins were to be traced, it would be through the archives, the paper trails left by their collectors. That is why, even if the jigsaw fragments of this story cohere, the picture lacks the full contour of its human figures. Those Aboriginal and European people responsible for the toas remain as shadows in this frontier mystery.

REUTHER'S TOAS

According to Reuther's initial account, toas were made as 'signposts', 'way-markers' and 'location finders'. Members of a departing group placed a toa in their camp (sticking it into the ground in the shelter of a wurley), symbolising their precise destination to those following. In their shape and decoration, toas alluded to particular episodes of the Dreaming. These mythological events were so grounded in the landscape of eastern Lake Eyre that a single toa could only represent one place, and no other. So, rather than indicating a general direction from which a locality might be deduced through the ordinary clues left by departing groups, each toa suggested an actual place. Like all significant places visited in the ethnographic present, that place was also on the itinerary of a Dreaming Ancestor.

In a few cases the toas evoked these sites directly, through a visual resemblance of shape or form – a particular curve suggesting the sweep of a waterhole or the shape of a plain, for example. In most cases though, the analogy was more cryptic. It required the viewer to interpret a toa's painted or sculpted symbolism, whether figurative or more abstract, and to understand that this symbolism referred to a particular, site-based episode in one of several dozen Dreaming stories. Only by matching the visual clues against the relevant mythology could an allusion to a particular event emerge, and the destination become evident.

Here is Johann Reuther's description of these objects, translated from his manuscript volume dealing with the toas, which he prepared following their manufacture:

To the Aborigine, toas are way-markers and location finders. Each toa indicates a particular locality according to its topographical character, and by its shape bears reference to the name of the place in question.

From the colours the Aborigine recognises the present whereabouts of his friends' camp as concerning its geographic formation, while head-pieces on some of the toas help through their symbolism to determine the place-names more accurately. An Aborigine deciphers the relevant place-name from the toa. For this reason one can probably say with justification that the toas are an Aboriginal 'sign language'.

When Aborigines travel from one campsite to another, but expect friends or acquaintances to visit them within the next few days, a toa is made relevant to the present camp, informing the visitors that they have moved for one reason or another to this or that place, and may be found at [such and such] a place. They are traced to the spot, accordingly.

Since the Aborigine has an expert knowledge of the local terrain, and since he knows the place-names which emanate from the legend of the Muramuras, he has no difficulty in finding the place where his friends or acquaintances are presently encamped.

That efforts are made to let one's friends or acquaintances know one's present whereabouts, and to describe these accurately, is quite obvious. One could be attacked by enemies and be in need of help, a relative could be ill or have died, requiring one's unconditional presence, and so on.

A toa is stuck by its nether point [into the ground] in one of the unoccupied wurleys of the camp, in order to protect it against wind and weather. Signs are engraved in the sand in front of the wurley, so that any visitor [will] know that he [can] obtain information from within.[3]

Reuther's explanation conveys the essence of the toas' significance, as Edward Stirling understood it when his Board purchased Reuther's ethnographic collection in 1907. With its internal inconsistencies (for example, the notion that Aboriginal people might pause to fashion objects as complex as toas in the process, or even expectation, of being 'attacked by enemies' or being 'in need of help') and mistaken assumptions as to the way self-contained groups of Aboriginal people 'visited' one another, the description became the basis of the authorised museum version of the toas for most of the twentieth century.

By the time major Australian museums installed their permanent exhibitions of Aboriginal culture between 1900 and 1920, it was assumed that the full range of types and styles of Aboriginal 'productions' had been located and described.

The new permanent exhibitions sometimes incorporated small displays showing Aboriginal adaptations of Western materials, like that in the South Australian Museum titled 'Articles of Native Workmanship in which Materials of Civilization have been Wholly or Partly Used' (see chapter one). These displays operated as salutary warnings, marking the boundaries of authenticity. They supported dominant perceptions of Aboriginal culture as unchanging until its disastrous collision with the West. That this collision might result in hybrid cultural expressions worthy in their own right, was tantamount to a suggestion that the 'half-caste problem' was not a problem at all, but indicated an emerging, vigorous Australian identity. Such a notion was not comprehended. Instead, the head-dresses fashioned from European string and coloured wool, hafted metal axes, glass spearheads or poker-work decorations were presented as degraded forms, unfortunate consequences of cultural miscegenation.

It was not until the 1980s that cultural regeneration was recognised as an essential element in contemporary Aboriginal art. Again, this shift accompanied an awareness that the Western Desert painting movement had acquired its own momentum, and was not merely reproducing conventional Dreaming images in new media. Subsequently, that dynamic aspect of Aboriginal art has flashed and evolved with a verve and style overshadowing most metropolitan forms of modernism. For historians and scholars aware of the radical shift in Aboriginal art represented by this change, the challenge was to validate the new dynamism by locating its analogue in the classical Aboriginal past. Rock art research provided one means. It revealed great stylistic shifts occurring throughout prehistory, but these changes had occurred over thousands of years, infinitely slower than the rate of change fuelling the contemporary Aboriginal art market. Certainly an impression of dynamism could be gained in survey exhibitions of the classical oeuvre, juxtaposing traditional artefacts from across Aboriginal Australia. But this impression was often countered by the careful conservatism of the Aboriginal works themselves, with their intense but limited elaborations of particular regional motifs.

During the 1980s and 1990s vitality and dynamism were identified within the recently rediscovered body of paintings and drawings made by Aboriginal artists working with European media during the nineteenth and twentieth centuries, such as William Barak or Albert Namatjira. This work arose manifestly from the zone of contact.[4] Like the post-1970s Western Desert art movement, it confirmed a creative response by Aboriginal people to cultural tensions and trauma, an opening of new visual codes and ways of seeing the world. Large survey exhibitions of the 1980s and 1990s gave notice of the frontier's capacity to disturb and reshape the deep traditions of Aboriginal art. Art historians turned their attention from the repetitious conservatism characterising museum collections, and came instead to seek and value dynamism as an ideal in itself.

With their whimsical sculptural forms evoking Brancusi or Miro, their deep cadences of the Dreaming and a storm of discourse relating to their status as art or artefact already brewing, the toas of Killalpaninna seemed made to order. They confirmed the new ideals of dynamism and innovation in Aboriginal art. Speaking of the distant, classical past, they nevertheless signalled across the frontier, to European culture and iconography. The closer one looked at these apparent survivors of an ancient past, the more modern they appeared.[5]

The toas are powerful objects. During the past 30 years a single collection, obtained at one place by one individual on a single occasion, has exerted remarkable influence over Aboriginal art and its interpretation. The toas have lent authority to a new paradigm of innovation and dynamism, replacing one based on notions of an unvarying, classical past. It is a shock to recall that a century ago when the toas first came to light at the remote Killalpaninna mission, these objects were interpreted as a newly discovered form of traditional culture, expressing a most conservative world-view. For at that time, if Aboriginal art was spoken of at all, it was regarded only as a primitive, relict indicator of what other world cultures had already achieved during the previous centuries.[6]

Two factors have operated to place these objects at the centre of discussion about Aboriginal art, together with bark paintings, acrylic paintings, carved wooden objects and even sacred stone and wooden *tjurunga*. Firstly, toas share with bark paintings, acrylic paintings and tjurunga a manifest linkage between place and Dreaming. Secondly, the aesthetic code of the toas is not self-evident. Toas may be public, non-secret objects, but they require interpretation. As cryptic objects, they share this crucial characteristic with secret-sacred tjurunga, for which museum curators, art historians and anthropologists are privileged gatekeepers.

The toas have been 'discovered' twice by the West during the past century – once as artefact and once as art. But they have rarely been scrutinised in their own right or measured against the historical events and personalities surrounding them. Now, as the toas enter their second century, it is worth re-examining their origins and their relationship to the frontier which spawned them. That scrutiny suggests that, rather than conforming either to ancient tradition or to modern dynamism in Aboriginal art, the toas of Killalpaninna represent an intriguing episode in the history of commodification and colonial encounter.

Group of 15 toas from Reuther's collection, showing the main forms and designs.
South Australian Museum Archives.

FUNCTION AND FORM

It is useful to think of toa symbolism in the same terms as the iconography
of bark paintings or Western Desert dot paintings. Each toa-place is a mythological site, transformed through a Dreaming event and named by a Dreaming
Ancestor. The visual symbolism of each toa represents some aspect of that
event, sometimes pivotal, but often oblique or apparently inconsequential.
The figure above includes a sample of some of the most graphically rich toas
and their stories from Reuther's collection. Reading from left to right, these
are his ascribed meanings, extracted from his manuscript:

Mambudirkani: to the plain where Wittimarkani gathered seed in her
Pirra (wooden bowl). As it was time to return to the camp, she placed it on
her hip to carry it, but made the wrong movement and it fell to the
ground. Toa = plain on Cooper Creek with cracked earth (red stripes).
Dots = bushes or holes (two versions given).

Wirkaripudlani: to the Wirkaripudla Plain where the two creeks join. Discovered by Godagodana. Red dots = small stones on upper part of plain (white). Yellow = soil on plain. Black = two creeks.

Kutirani: to a very crooked part of Cooper Creek which Patjalina noticed on his travels. Toa = bed of Cooper Creek. Dots = gum trees standing in creek bed.

Manataulawuluni: to the plain where Kirlawuluni (Kirlawilina) saw the two wild ducks opening their beaks to quack. White = shape of plain and head of duck. Projections = beak of a duck quacking.

Manawilparamarani: to the plain where Wadlulana died with his mouth open, like a yawning man. Top = tree with a broken trunk. White knob = plain, overgrown with bushes (red dots).

Pirrapirrani: to the flat, ringed by a sandhill, where the two Muramuras, Putantara, camped.

Tampangaraterkanani: to the lake where Mandramankana saw many pelicans standing. Top = head of pelican. White = lake.

Ngurluwarilani: to the plain on Cooper Creek, which Darana named after Ngurluwarila, one of his dogs. Stripes = cracks on plain in dry season. White band = plain.

Ngantiburanani: to where Karuwontirina saw two emus sleeping behind a bush. Toa = shape of emu. Yellow dots = ribs.

Panjiworduni: to the plain overgrown with Palpuru bushes, where Mardalbuluna camped. There he found people who used finely pointed emu bones to dig out prickles from their feet. Top = bone. White = plain. Red dots = Palpuru bushes.

Womamokuni: to the creek which Billipilpana noticed was shaped like a snake's skeleton which he found on the plain nearby. The smaller creeks which joined the main creek resembled the snake's ribs. Toa = backbone and ribs of snake. Red dots = trees on lower part of plain, where water lies after rain.

Ngatjinani: to the hill where Kirliwilina implored his uncle to let him chase after the girls who lived there. Toa = hill which resembles a human head. Red = red soil. White = chalky soil. Eyes, mouth and nostrils = caves in which the girls hid from Kirliwilina.

Witjikurawinpani: to the sandhill on Cooper Creek where Patjalina came while hunting. A whirlwind had obliterated animal tracks and swept debris together. White knob = sandhill. Red dots = bushes. Black lateral stripe = Cooper Creek. Black vertical stripe = deep waterhole at base of sandhill. Yellow = sand. Dots = gums.

Idiburinani: Reuther's volumes 12 and 13 have differing explanations: to the plain where Kirrapajirka, in the form of a bird, lost his tail feathers; and to the plain where the Darana and his men plucked out the hairs of their beards. White = plain. Top = tail feathers or hair.

Paruwalpani: to Lake Kirlawilpa (Killalpaninna itself, the site of the mission where the toas were made), where Pitikipana once found many fish dying as the water had become brackish. He gathered them up and dried them on the shore for later consumption. Toa = fish.[7]

Approximately a fifth of the Reuther toas are fashioned from a single piece of wood, often thinly coated in gypsum or painted with ochre, but otherwise quite simple in construction. Another fifth conform to a single type; a flattened wooden shaft with its top wrapped around with string (most often European parcel string). This string binding forms an armature for the gypsum 'head', originally applied as a viscous paste. This type of toa carries the collection's most conservative, repetitious iconography (usually evoking reference to bushes or stones and sandhills or waterholes), through the use of white or yellow dots and vertical bands of black on red. These designs are painted on one face only. Several toas of this design bear almost identical imagery, but represent widely varying localities.

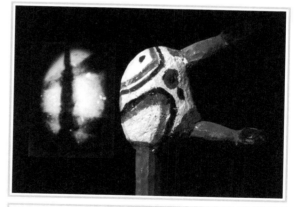

Head of a toa depicting two peninsulas jutting into Lake Gregory, where the two female Ancestors, Watapijiri and Nardutjelpani, gathered swan eggs. The x-ray image confirms that the gypsum head conceals a 'mortice and tenon' carpentry construction, unknown in the region's Aboriginal material culture; the wooden prongs are neatly pegged into the central shaft. A6169, South Australian Museum.

About three-fifths of the toas are more complex in their construction. These construction techniques depart radically from what we know of the traditional material culture of arid Australia. Many of these 'composite' toas consist of separate elements pegged together in a form of 'mortice and tenon' carpentry, bound in place by string. The string binding is also the usual means of securing separate elements such as pieces of stone, feathers or vegetation. These details of construction are concealed in every case by a thick coating of pipeclay which constitutes the head of the toa.[8]

The carpentry construction is a reminder that, by the turn of the twentieth century, the Lutheran mission at Killalpaninna had been supplying its own furniture and repairing its own European artefacts for at least three decades. The wood for many of these composite toas is a softwood, perhaps deriving from packing cases or other wood brought to the mission. It was easily worked for the purposes required. Most toas bear the marks of metal tools on their carved shafts.

In their form and design the toas are beguiling objects. Reuther's broader ethnographic collection contained a full range of material culture for the eastern Lake Eyre region. He had little difficulty in finding a buyer for it, for the unique visual characteristics of the toas made this collection irresistible to its eventual purchaser. And it is those characteristics, rather than the obvious European influences in their construction, which provoke doubts about the collection.

In the first place, the toas are undoubtedly all freshly made and show no signs of being collected from the particular context of use described by Reuther. This raises no especial doubts, for at least two-thirds of Reuther's larger ethnographic collection (comprising fishing nets, spears, clubs, shields, belts, head-dresses and so on) also appears new, made to order. The idea of an 'industry' in ethnographic artefacts at this time, even on a frontier as remote as this desert mission, does not in itself suggest that those artefacts were spurious. At exactly the same time for example, Aboriginal people on the Anglican Karpalgo mission on the South Alligator River in Arnhem Land were producing standardised 'sets' of ethnographic artefacts for collectors.[9] Although several artefacts in Reuther's ethnographic collection are clearly exaggerated forms (very large waist-belts and head-rings, oversize net-bags and boomerangs with embellished carvings, for example), these types conform to those recorded and collected by visitors to the region since Sturt's expedition of 1844–1845. But the toas do not.

The iconography of the toas is particular and specific, aligning discrete mythological events with particular localities. Apparently public and secular, these objects nevertheless allow for only a restricted interpretation. For that reason alone (aside from the question of who, and under what circumstances, might

Photograph included as fig. 48 in A.W. Howitt's *Native Tribes of South-Eastern Australia*, showing an unconvincing 'obal' hovering in mid-air, within a museum diorama of an Aboriginal camp-site (Howitt 1904).

'read' them), toas should not be conflated with those casually made 'way-markers', indicating general direction or stating the obvious, which are known from across Aboriginal Australia. Such informal objects have been noted occasionally in the ethnographic record but were rarely, if ever, collected. Even Alfred Howitt, who showed keener interest in Aboriginal communication than any colonial ethnographer, resorted to publishing a contrived photograph of such a marker, which he described as an *obal*, 'a guide to a following party', used by the Kurnai people of Victoria. This object consisted of a stick with some bark tied to one end, placed in the ground at an angle indicating the direction of the departing group.[10]

Norman Tindale's 1963 photograph of a Nakako man, Charlie Witjawarakuru, standing next to a stick used as a direction marker in the Great Victoria Desert, is more convincing. Tindale's documentation nicely illustrates the improvised nature of most direction indicators, supplementing and confirming existing information, rather than replacing it. Tindale noted that when he met him, Witjawarakuru had been hunting kangaroos and was on his way back to a small

Charlie Witjawarakuru interpreting a direction marker in the Great Victoria Desert, 1963.
Photograph: N.B. Tindale. AA338, South Australian Museum.

granite rockhole where his party had been camped. He came across the marker on his track back to the rockhole. The marker, which consisted of 'a stick with a line drawn with the foot extending from it and some footprints beside it', told him that the party had left the rockhole and moved north, to a destination he could easily deduce.[11]

Agreed or obvious symbols were used for direction markers, minimising possible confusion. Among the Dyirbal rainforest people of northern Queensland, the linguist Robert Dixon recorded way-markers known as *jilan*. A jilan made by breaking a twig of ginger leaf, for example, would indicate that one had gone for fish; a broken twig of the *muruga* tree would tell people that one had gone looking for grubs.[12] Deaths or funerals provided a common reason for abandoning a camp, and two documented examples of direction indicators relate to this. According to a teacher at the Cummeragunja mission on the Murray River in 1898, 'a long pole with a big lump of mud on one end [probably gypsum, an indicator of mourning], supported by a forked upright, was left for the information of visiting tribes'.[13] Working among the Adnyamathanha of the Flinders Ranges during the 1930s, Charles Mountford recorded their practice of laying down a branch of a particular bush associated with funerals (emu bush, *Eremophila longifolia*) in a vacated camp, to indicate the destination of its occupants.[14] Mountford recorded a number of 'bush signs' used by the Adnyamathanha and related groups, mostly simple configurations of sticks and stones arranged or piled on each other to indicate a destination. The basic form of these signs – such as a stick placed between two stones to indicate a gorge and its rocky walls, or a crescent of soil raked up to symbolise the hills encircling a spring – undoubtedly made sense within the local context. These symbols could indicate precise destinations, just as agreed codes were used for smoke-signals or on message-sticks to convey particular messages. And if they also incorporated references to mythology, such as an Adnyamathanha sign indicating the Akurra Snakes in the form of two hills at Copley, this reminds us of the force of the Dreaming landscape as present reality, rather than a separate construct.[15] But these allusions were all evoked by simple combinations of the materials to hand – a bent branch or leaves, sticks or stones. Such objects could be arranged to indicate any deviation from the main track, as the ethnographer Walter Roth observed of western Queensland Aborigines (culturally adjacent to the Diyari) during the 1890s: 'a finger post, in the shape of any small stick, tussock of grass, etc, is stuck into a small mound of sand, earth, etc, two or three inches high, erected on the roadway'. In the ordinary course, not even these indicators were required. 'The most definitive forms of track signal', wrote Roth, were 'the actual footprints of the party preceding'.[16] Throughout Aboriginal Australia, from early childhood, people could read footprints belonging to their wider group and could identify members of travelling parties.

The elaborate, composite constructions of the toas are in stark contrast to this well-documented ethnographic reality. Sculpted, drilled, bound and painted, evoking their localities through secondary allusions founded on art and mythology, the toas do not match the ordinary experience of nomadic life, the daily round for which they were proposed. In fact, the level of preparation and complexity behind their manufacture was generally associated with the sacred, ceremonial sphere.

The toas' individual and quirky forms contrast with most Aboriginal material culture objects, which vary only slightly within broadly similar types. At one level there is a discernible uniformity among the 385 toas – in their general dimensions, repetition of horizontal bands or stripes and dominant motifs of heavy dotting. Those elements are also identifiable in historic photographs of ceremonial body decoration used by the Diyari and other groups of eastern Lake Eyre. But these conservative visual elements are almost overwhelmed by the toas' vigour of form, and by figurative designs, quite unlike the region's traditionally 'abstract' Aboriginal art.

The toas display other unusual characteristics. More than three-quarters of the small wooden posts are topped by moulded heads of white gypsum or pipeclay. These provide either a canvas for a toa's principal design or, in the case of more than half the toas, a means of fixing crests of vegetation, bone, shell, wood, stone, feathers, claws or human hair to the toa. The gypsum heads also serve to conceal the main construction elements of the toas.

Among eastern Lake Eyre groups white was, in Reuther's own words, the colour 'of sorrow', associated most often with mourning. The source of this colour was a hard-won substance. Gypsum was mined from particular outcrops, heated over fire, crushed to powder, and mixed with water to form a sticky, plaster-like paste. Such a process was undertaken most often on ritual occasions, to produce the thick plaster or lime caps worn by mourning widows during their period of isolation, or to distinguish young initiates who were similarly set apart from the group. This gypsum coating was also used as a decorative surface in head-bands and head-dresses and was used for ceremonial body painting. Other than the toas, and another anomalous example of moulded spinning tops (probably copies of European toys), gypsum was not applied to wooden artefacts in the region, either for decoration or as a fixative. Plant resin was preferred for that purpose. A small store of resin, easily heated for

Killalpaninna mission buildings, ca 1890. A pile of mud bricks, made by Aboriginal people at the mission, is visible at right. Tom Reuther Collection, South Australian Museum Archives.

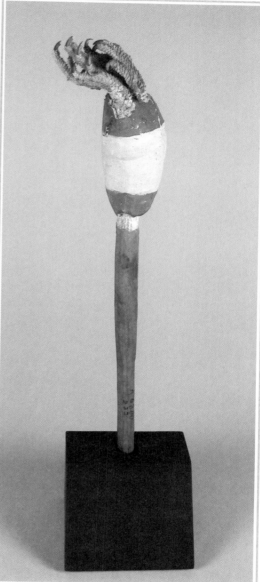

Toa referring to the mythological site where the children of the ancestor Narimalpari split mussel shells open. A mussel shell is embedded in the toa's gypsum head. A6269, South Australian Museum.

Toa referring to the mythological site where the ancestor Pitipikapana watched a lizard climb to the top of a sandhill. Three lizard claws are fixed to the toa. A6300, South Australian Museum.

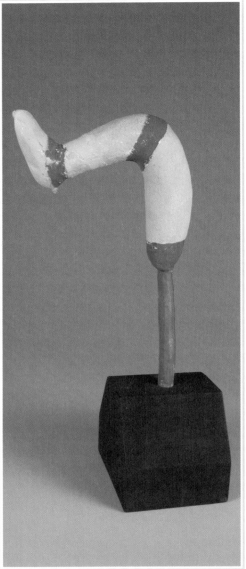

Toa referring to the two sandhills where
the ancestor Karuwontirina saw two
animals crouching behind a bush.
A6225, South Australian Museum.

Toa referring to the part of Cooper Creek
where Jelkabalubaluna was asked by another
ancestor if he was tired. He replied that
he was not, shaking his leg as proof.
A6229, South Australian Museum.

use in a campfire, was integral to every man's personal kit and was used for fixing stone blades to adzes, repairing holes in wooden containers and so on. Resin was easily obtained from the roots of bushes, the trunks of several tree species and from 'spinifex' grass in the sandhill country. But there is no trace of plant resin on any of Reuther's toas.

In its raw form, gypsum was available only in certain localities throughout the wider region, which is characterised by expanses of sandy dunefields and stony plains. Gypsum mines, or *tudnapiti*, were rare enough to be distinctively named sites with mythological associations; one of these, to the east of the mission, was still being used as a source of gypsum in Reuther's time.[17] It is inconceivable that people would burden themselves with quantities of this heavy substance while travelling, simply in order to make toas. On the other hand, the Lutheran mission itself became a centre for the production of gypsum, or lime, particularly during the main period of building construction during the 1890s. Wagon-loads of gypsum were carted to the mission, where a kiln generated sufficient quantities to plaster the walls of the mud-brick buildings, and to whitewash them occasionally. This surfeit of fine-quality gypsum may help to explain Killalpaninna toas.

Miscellaneous items were bound to the heads of toas, and fixed in place with wet gypsum, forming head-pieces or crests. Reuther was at pains to point out that these materials – particularly twigs or grass stems, stone tools, shell or animal bone – were specific indicators of the destinations to which toas directed travellers. He did not explain how these distinctive materials came to be fixed to toas before their makers had set out for those destinations. There are four possible explanations for this apparent lapse in the collector's logic, of which the first two are equally unlikely.

The first explanation is that the toa-makers travelled to the destination, obtained the necessary plant or animal species, stone or shell, then returned to fix these samples to their toas. The second is that people travelled with a full selection of materials, catering for all potential destinations. It is as difficult to envisage the corollary of this, that Aboriginal people felt constrained to visit only those destinations for which they had relevant toa-indicators. A third possibility is that Reuther's toas were only representative examples, being made to order on the mission. That may well be the case, but it begs the question of what might constitute a 'real toa'. For the idea of attaching materials deriving from the indicated destination, rather than from the locality where the toa is made, remains logically inadmissible.

The fourth explanation is the most intriguing. This is that toas do not conform to the ethnographic reality of the pre-European past, but instead emerged as unique artefacts of encounter on a complex colonial frontier. That frontier was a crucible combining elements of evolving material culture, forces of acculturation and a growing market for Aboriginal artefacts. This explanation seems to me to be the most compelling, for the reasons advanced in this chapter.

The missionary Johann Reuther revealed the existence of the toas for the first time during early 1904, at a time of intense speculation within international anthropological and linguistic circles as to the origins of language and writing. His first announcement of the toas as examples of 'pictographic writing' might be interpreted, most charitably, as a bold contribution to this debate. Less generously, Reuther's action was later regarded by the ethnographer George Aiston as part of what he described as the 'great toa hoax'.[18] If Aiston was correct, Reuther's initiative was a canny attempt to exploit an emerging market for Aboriginal artefacts by playing upon the enduring fiction of a frontier where, even after two generations of pervasive European contact, it might still be considered reasonable to discover an entirely new category of authentic, traditional artefact.

In the century since their manufacture, the weight of anthropological opinion has endorsed the authenticity of the Killalpaninna toas, despite the absence of analagous examples elsewhere in Australia. The case of the toas seems to provide an example of a tendency to interpret cultural data according to prevailing assumptions about authenticity and tradition, rather than any considered interrogation of historical circumstances surrounding the appearance of these objects. That interrogation might produce an explanation for toas more likely than the role concocted for them as signposts, but falling short of the transparent fabrication suggested by Aiston. This chapter suggests such an explanation: that Reuther's concerted elicitation of place-names with their accompanying mythology, combined with his encouragement of artefact manufacture at the mission, prompted Aboriginal people to produce a series of hybrid objects which encoded those place-names and their mythology.

FRONTIER MESSAGES

Shortly after Reuther announced the toas' existence in early 1904, the acknowledged expert on the ethnography of eastern Central Australia, Alfred Howitt, published his major work, *Native Tribes of South-East Australia*. One chapter contained a reworking of his 1889 paper on message-sticks and communication. In it, Howitt wrote the following:

There has been much misunderstanding, not to say misstatement, as to the
real character of . . . message sticks and the conventional value of the markings
on them. It has been said that they can be read and understood by the person
to whom they are sent without the marks on them being explained by the
bearer. I have even heard it said that persons, other than the one to whom a
stick is sent, can read the marks with as much ease as educated people can read
the words inscribed on one of our letters[19]

Howitt died in Melbourne in 1908. By then he was probably aware that the
South Australian Museum had purchased 385 toas with precisely such 'message-
stick' characteristics. In May 1904 he had received a letter from Reuther in
which the missionary announced the discovery of 'pictographic writing', and
Howitt's own notes contain a transcribed description of a toa, similar to that published in a 1906 Adelaide newspaper interview with Reuther.[20] Howitt may
have been intrigued to discover that these objects had emerged from the very
mission which, through the medium of Reuther's ethnographic rival Pastor
Otto Siebert, had already supplied him with so much detailed anthropological data.

As director of the South Australian Museum, Edward Stirling did not
share Howitt's scepticism about the 'message stick fad'. In that respect perhaps
Reuther had luck on his side. For Stirling played a crucial role in placing the
toas within a credible ethnographic context, making them a centrepiece of
the museum's new Aboriginal gallery which opened in 1914, and publishing an
authoritative account of the objects in 1919.[21] By then the source of the toas,
Killalpaninna mission, had closed. The rapid population decline which Reuther
had struggled to halt, caused mainly by European disease and a plummeting
birth rate, had continued unabated. The old men who provided his ethnographic data, and who presumably played a key role in the production of the toas,
had died. The mission population fragmented. Soon the most authoritative
statement on the culture of the Diyari and their beliefs rested not in their own
community, but in Reuther's ethnographic collection and its accompanying
manuscript. For seven decades the toas stood in their museum cases, in convincing ranks, each with its translated text.

As museum objects the toas seemed to speak eloquently for themselves,
but they remained relatively unknown. They were not included in any of the
first large exhibitions of Aboriginal art during the mid-twentieth century,
nor were they mentioned in the comprehensive survey of Aboriginal material
culture published by museum ethnographer Frederick McCarthy in 1957.[22]
Perhaps we can detect the first hint of professional scepticism.

The decades passed until the 1970s and 1980s, when the toas were rediscovered within new contexts. Howard Morphy's 1977 study, 'Schematisation, meaning and communication in toas' (based on an M.A. thesis), took Reuther's and Stirling's characterisation of the toas, as traditional artefacts revealing a coherent sign system, at face value. He undertook a detailed semiotic analysis of their designs in relation to their ascribed mythological categories.[23] But it was the Western Desert painting movement, emerging during the 1970s, which provoked the most far-reaching re-evaluation of the toas as art objects. Through this second 'discovery', the toas gained a momentum which made them integral to discussions about Aboriginal iconography and about Aboriginal art's relationship to the mythological landscape.

The South Australian Museum's 1986 *Art and Land* exhibition and accompanying catalogue exposed the toas' uncertain origins, but concentrated on their artistic qualities. The exhibition featured the entire collection of toas, dramatically lit against black backgrounds, as a central element of the 1986 Adelaide Festival of Arts. The toas' artistic quality was further stressed through their inclusion in the influential 'Dreamings' exhibition which opened at New York's Asia Society gallery in 1988, followed by the 'Aratjara' exhibition which toured Europe in 1991.[24] This modish artistic context has suited these objects far better than their problematic ethnographic role.

In his subsequent syntheses of art history and anthropological analysis of Aboriginal art practice, Morphy has confirmed the toas' shift from their stated role as utilitarian 'way-markers' or 'direction posts', towards the realm of Aboriginal art which now embraces even more vigorous and unconventional forms.[25] But the closer the toas fit with this new paradigm, the less they conform to their original, stated function, to provide useful direction to those 'following behind'. Additionally, as Morphy's own analysis shows, if the symbolism conveyed by the toas conforms to Reuther's proposition of a 'pictographic language', only a limited number of travellers might 'read' these messages accurately.

Like other examples of Aboriginal art emerging since the mid-twentieth century, such as bark paintings or Western Desert dot paintings, the toas come from the frontier of contact. That phrase seems to evoke a defined, unambiguous line. Objects, ideas and things might pass across it; here a word list, there a plant specimen, a shield or a clutch of spears. Assembled taxonomically into collections, listed and catalogued, their characteristics appear self-evident. A shield is for defence, spears are for attack. Naturally, they have other, secondary meanings: a particular shield may have been decorated with symbols locating it within a ceremonial context, or the spears may be tipped with glass or metal, indicating not only a particular period in Aboriginal and European frontier relations but perhaps also the context in which they were collected. These associations lead out of the museum and into the fields of history and social anthropology.

As the primary, evident meanings of artefacts ceased to hold their interest during the mid-twentieth century, social anthropologists turned away from museums and their collections. But ethnographic collections have become appealing once again, precisely because of these secondary associations. The role of ethnographic objects within indigenous culture, and in the spaces between indigenous culture and the culture of the collectors, meshes with the research interests of social anthropologists in ways rarely appreciated a century ago.[26] Nevertheless if ethnographic objects from the space between cultures are now considered in a new light, their basic definition remains the same: a shield is still a shield, a net a net, a boomerang a boomerang. The toas provide an exception, as objects whose uncertain ethnographic identity evokes the fluidity of a frontier in which Aboriginal and European interests not only clashed, but also merged and overlapped.

For the frontier is not a hard line separating cultures but a zone, which may unify and can also create new forms of engagement, new forms of exploitation. In constructing a 'resistance' model of Aboriginal history, many historians of the colonial frontier have not been so interested in documenting what historian Robert Reece termed 'that other major characteristic of Aboriginal–European interaction: accommodation'.[27] This is not to imply that the frontier was an even ground. Writing of the colonial period in North America, one historian has observed that while a model of ruthless conquest by Europeans could usefully be replaced by a more complex account, the result is nevertheless 'a society dominated by transplanted Europeans but modified by a persistent Indian subculture'.[28] Extending the analysis to the Australian context, the historian of religion Tony Swain has written that 'Aboriginal people in early south-east Australia ... used symbols of European power and culture *not* in attempts to eradicate Whites or even merely to overthrow their hegemony, but rather to establish moral relationships within an increasingly immoral world'.[29]

Creative processes of mutual acculturation did occur in frontier Australia, despite unequal power relations between coloniser and colonised. But notwithstanding examples of innovation in Aboriginal art, religion or language, resistance to the idea of mutual acculturation has been strong in most fields of

Aboriginal studies, ranging from archaeology, linguistics and religion to material culture analyses. Indeed, despite its doctrine of cultural relativism, the discipline of social anthropology continues to rely upon notions of the 'primitive', persistently locating Aboriginal culture within another, implicitly prior, frame.[30] The anthropologist Jeremy Beckett suggests that notions of antiquity have pervaded 'constructions of Aboriginality, whether popular or official'.[31] The identification of Aboriginal culture with past, primitive forms has been most readily achieved within museums, where the 'aura' of objects (as Walter Benjamin termed it) often masks the intentions, meanings and skills of their makers, as well as the actions and motives of their collectors.[32] It would be ironic then, for museum collections to play a key role in countering, or even dispersing, the aura surrounding their objects.

Artefacts have played a crucial role on the frontier, as a medium along which important ideas passed, from colonised to coloniser and back again. Artefacts have been silent witnesses to many diverse transactions and events unfolding in that space. Many of these transactions were banal; new forms of contempt and hatred as well as curiosity and tolerance, expressed and unexpressed desires and covetousness. Communication across this zone was often inarticulate or misunderstood, as one culture tried to see into, or past, the other. But for all the misattribution of motives and actions on the frontier, there has been a countering, positive impulse towards genuine communication and exchange. For the tangible residue of those interactions we might look not only to museum collections of objects, but also to libraries and archives, which often contain the first considerations and conclusions of Europeans involved in those exchanges.

Aboriginal attempts at communicating with Europeans on the various Australian frontiers are not easily assessed. One measure might be the concerted European investigations of Aboriginal communication, expressed in collections of vocabularies and grammars, and papers dealing with message-sticks, smoke-signals and gesture language. These investigations began to proliferate as anthropology emerged as a social science after the 1870s. Alfred Howitt, later to become a respected ethnographer of the Diyari, had first noticed sign language used by Aboriginal people of the region during his Burke and Wills Relief Expedition in 1861. In 1879 the police-trooper Samuel Gason published on the subject, describing Diyari gesture language as 'a copious one … all animals, native man or woman, the heavens, earth, walking, riding, jumping, flying, swimming, eating, drinking and hundreds of other objects or actions, have each their particular sign, so that a conversation may be sustained without the utterance of a single word'.[33] The idea that a

Johann and Pauline Reuther in Reuther's study at Killalpaninna, ca 1905. Lutheran Archives, Adelaide.

chaos of images and actions could be reduced and codified into a system was compelling.

Discussions of message-sticks, smoke-signals, hand-signals, tracking, designs on artefacts and word lists all became fashionable anthropological subjects during the late nineteenth century. These topics proliferated during the 1890s, just as ancient scripts were being analysed and decoded by classical archaeologists. A striking example was the discovery in 1900 by the English scholar and archaeologist Arthur Evans of inscribed clay tablets in the ancient Cretan palace of Knossos. Evans' identification of the 'Linear B' script as an antecedent of ancient Greek fuelled enormous interest in the origins of writing and language. These revelations were discussed by the anthropological community in Australia, providing a fillip to the development of Australian anthropology, while exposing deeper tensions within this emerging intellectual community. The subject was reported by the popular anthropological journal, *Science of Man*, which also published a series of papers concerning an emerging controversy over Aboriginal message-sticks. On one side were those who believed that message-sticks showed that 'Australian Aborigines developed a means of communicating with one another at a distance by means of marked sticks or symbols'. Their opponents, led by Howitt himself, considered that 'the message-stick is only a sort of reminder to the messenger who has to deliver the message verbally, and that it is also to prove his (the messenger's) bona fides'.[34] Howitt's key findings were published in 1889, and during the 1890s the 'message-stick controversy' developed new momentum. The decade prior to the toas' appearance saw the publication of more than twenty papers dealing with Aboriginal message-sticks and related topics of Aboriginal communication.

The division between adherents to the theory that message-sticks constituted an ideographic form of writing, and those considering them purely as mnemonic devices, roughly corresponded to a division between an emerging professional anthropology and amateur observers. On Killalpaninna mission at the turn of the twentieth century, the two Lutheran missionaries ostensibly toiling together to claim the souls of heathen Aborigines were in fact aligned towards these two diverging forms of anthropology. Johann Reuther was self-taught as an anthropologist and a linguist and had a limited educational background. Prior to joining the Lutheran seminary at Neuendettelsau in Germany he had been a postal messenger – a sufficient irony perhaps, for one who became so absorbed by Aboriginal 'finger-posts'. His fellow-missionary and ethnographic rival, Otto Siebert, was a scholar with great facility for language. Siebert worked closely with people in the bush camps outside the mission settlement at Killalpaninna. For most of his time at the mission, from 1894 to 1902, Siebert was in close correspondence with Alfred Howitt and sent him at least 56 letters detailing the culture and beliefs of the Diyari and related groups.[35] Siebert supported the views of Samuel Gason and of Howitt himself, that the Diyari used messengers, rather than message-sticks, to convey information.

Siebert immersed himself even more deeply in the 'mental world of the heathen' than Reuther, spending considerably more time with Aborigines in bush camps around the mission. His correspondence with Howitt reveals a clarity of thought and an understanding of the broader anthropological project which can be contrasted with Reuther's more haphazard, less focused approach. On the matter of visual symbolism, Siebert undertook basic analysis of carved motifs used on boomerangs of the region, and contributed data gained from this research to a German publication. He collected a boomerang-shaped wooden object engraved with such symbols, later described in a Frankfurt museum catalogue as 'wood with picture-writing (*bilderschrift*) used by an Aboriginal to explain different legends to the European missionary . . . out of the collection of Dieri customary designs'. But, in contrast to Reuther, who strove to interpret such motifs and symbols as precursors of a written language understood across the region, Siebert's analysis followed ethnographic convention, observing the primacy of function and context.[36]

To a small but expanding group of ethnographers, the carvings or marks on the small sticks carried by inter-group messengers were cryptic, yet concrete enough to admit interpretation as an encoded form of language. Encountering the hand-signs used for forms of discrete communication by desert Aborigines, explorers such as Sturt, Stuart, Giles and Gregory were convinced that they were observing masonic signs, remnants perhaps of ancient influence from Egypt.[37] Fanciful as it seems, this idea meshed with the powerful theme of 'degenerationism' in Victorian social theory – the notion that 'primitive peoples' had regressed from a former state of culture. Living among the Diyari for five years from 1866 to 1871, Samuel Gason shared this view. While confirming to Howitt that these people did not use message-sticks, and only communicated information across distances by using messengers (or smoke-signals, to indicate 'the whereabouts of their respective camps'), he nevertheless maintained a 'firm opinion that they at one time could write, but have lost the art'. The Diyari had, he considered, 'without doubt degenerated from a greater Race'.[38]

Ironically, when explorers and others noticed cryptic hand-signs and smoke-signals, or saw message-sticks being used as passports or aids to memory, they were observing external manifestations of wide-ranging networks of Aboriginal communication. All these elements joined a web of signs and interpretations, by which Aboriginal people constructed their own mental maps of the landscape. But the central referent for that encompassing grid was the Dreaming, rather than Cartesian reality – emanating from the landscape rather than laid over it. The difference is clearly understood by anthropologists today, but a century ago it was barely perceived. At that time, elementary systems of communication were being sought in Aboriginal culture, primarily to illuminate European cultural origins. For early anthropologists inclined towards evolutionary theory, such discoveries might also provide a reassuring sign that 'primitive peoples' were, despite contrary appearances, on the right track to civilisation.

Here we can identify a broad division between those ethnographers and missionaries excited by the possibility of Aboriginal society possessing its own, intrinsic and self-sustaining systems of belief and social action, and those regarding Aboriginal society as a primitive, nascent precursor to late nineteenth-century European civilisation. A minority of missionaries understood that Aboriginal people possessed their own religious system, an alternative to Christianity. More numerous were those (like Reuther and the Hermannsburg missionary Carl Strehlow, who began his career at Killalpaninna) who considered that Aboriginal people believed in High Gods. Among these, the highest God, a Paramount Being, could be rationalised as the missionaries' Christian God. Confident of that analogy during the 1890s, Strehlow and Reuther translated the New Testament into Diyari at Killalpaninna. Otto Siebert arrived at Killalpaninna shortly before Strehlow left for Hermannsburg in 1895. He was at least Reuther's equal in scholarship and ethnographic ability, but he shared the opposing view of anthropologists Alfred Howitt, Baldwin Spencer and Francis Gillen, rejecting the notion of a Supreme Being in the Aboriginal cosmos. Siebert returned to Germany two years before the toas appeared.

Siebert, Howitt and Gillen were also united in their dismissal of the theory that either smoke-signals or message-sticks suggested the existence of an encoded system of communication, a primitive form of written language. Spencer was less convinced, but accepted Gillen's arguments relating to the Arrernte. It was Spencer's museum rival, Edward Stirling, director of the South Australian Museum, who eventually purchased the toas from Reuther. And Stirling was, in Gillen's words, 'a believer in the message stick theory'.[39] Moreover, Stirling's acceptance of the toas also implied acceptance of Reuther's claim of a Supreme Being, the Mura. These alignments in the history of Australian anthropology are crucial for understanding the theoretical positioning taking place in the years before the toas appeared.

Reuther's proposition behind the toas appeared quite simple. A toa was like a European finger-post, only instead of indicating a direction, it depicted the actual destination (or its name). The 1906 newspaper account of the toas, based on an interview with Reuther at Killalpaninna, where the toas lined the passage of his house, reads:

> These symbols correspond to European finger posts, and through their agency the blacks indicate to each other the place to which they have gone – for instance, assuming a place is called Fishpond, a fish would be shaped out of limestone, fastened to a stick and stuck in the ground.[40]

Behind this simplistic journalistic account lies an assumption that Aboriginal travellers required that kind of direction across an empty landscape. It is a Eurocentric notion, that Aboriginal people travelled in disconnected groups across a *terra nullius*, like busloads of tourists arriving at a destination, having read the brochure.

The reality was far different. During the 1840s and 1880s respectively, the explorers Charles Sturt and David Lindsay led expeditions through the country represented by the toas. Their journals provide a direct insight into the way in which Aboriginal groups constantly fragmented, reformed and interlocked, with smaller groups, messengers or intermediaries constantly setting off to pursue subsidiary aims. Groups were rarely out of touch with each other. Viewed over time, a constantly shifting pattern of fluid and tenuous connection and reconnection would best characterise the physical appearance of the social dynamic, not dissimilar to that described by anthropologist Fred Myers for the Pintupi of the Western Desert; 'there was no band of unvarying individuals traveling constantly between points'.[41] General and particular itineraries of one's colleagues and kin were either well-known or deducible, and this knowledge was supplemented or confirmed by reading the tracks left behind as people moved camp.

The use of messengers between Lake Eyre groups is well documented in Reuther's own manuscript, but significantly, it is these intermediaries which the toa model displaces. That model, advanced by Reuther, Edward Stirling and more recently by others, assumes that Aboriginal groups remained intact as they moved about the landscape, unaware of other groups' movements until they happened upon toas left by them. In this sense, toas might be regarded as message-sticks *in situ* – message-sticks read without reference to their bearers.

If toas functioned as Reuther maintained, then the 'message-stick theory', discredited by Howitt, was alive and well. For if a group of strangers knowing the codes of the wider group could interpret a toa independently, without its maker, this is hardly different from a carved or painted message-stick being understood independently of its bearer. Reuther well understood the implication of his claim that a form of 'pictographic writing' existed among the Diyari and related groups. This was the discovery for which he claimed credit.

CLUES IN THE MANUSCRIPT

Comprising more than 1300 objects, Reuther's ethnographic collection represents a *catalogue raisonné* of eastern Central Australian Aboriginal material culture. We know from other ethnographic accounts, notably by Gason, Howitt and Siebert, that the region's material culture included objects carried by intergroup messengers. These writers all agreed that these objects did not include the notched or painted message-sticks used among other Australian groups, and unsurprisingly, none of those objects are to be found in Reuther's collection.

If we wanted to locate a possible prototype for the toas, it would be in the form of small sticks or pegs placed in the ground. Are such objects evident in the ethnographic record? The answer is 'yes'. The Reuther manuscript contains several references to 'marker pegs', fashioned at a moment's notice to convey information of a particular kind. Like the peg used by the Nakako man in 1963, and photographed by Tindale, these were made of any piece of wood which came to hand, sharpened to a point if necessary.

The Diyari placed marker-pegs in the ground to stake claim to an area of plant tubers, a patch of ripening grass, a cache of seed or a nesting-ground where swans had laid their eggs. In the latter case, Reuther noted that a bundle of feathers might be attached to a nearby tree. Stakes also indicated where a man had died, or marked limits of ceremonial ground. In some cases, these pegs also carried attachments, adding specificity to the message. For example, Reuther wrote:

> **paua malka** = 'seed sign'. If somebody finds a flat where he intends to gather seed, he erects a peg in the middle of it and attaches a small bunch of grass to it. Nobody will gather seed here. Whoever does so is regarded as a thief.[42]

The Diyari and related groups also used pegs as magic charms in a range of contexts; stuck in the bank of a flooding creek to prevent the inundation of a camp, or at the edge of a camp to prevent disease spreading or encroaching.[43]

In the earlier parts of his dictionary, written before the toas appeared in early 1904, Reuther defined these pegs with the Diyari term *malka* ('sign' or 'mark'). Expanding this definition to cover the concept of marking a route, or indicating the correct path, he used two terms: the phrase *wandrani-malka* – 'signs that indicate direction', and the noun *milki-wondrani* ('eye-direction'), a 'distinctive sign or mark; signpost; traveller's guide'.[44] According to Reuther, this latter term could be applied to 'any tree or finger-post, by which one may recognize locality or direction'. Neither of these terms, appearing in the earlier volumes of Reuther's dictionary (before he had reached the letter 't'), were cross-referenced to 'toa' or to anything similar. This is in contrast to Reuther's other dictionary entries, where explanations refer to other relevant entries.

By late 1903 Reuther had filled half of the 4180 entries in his four-volume dictionary and had completed other volumes relating to cultural concepts, ancestors and beliefs. But volumes 12 and 13 of his manuscript (devoted to the toas and other artefacts), volume 7 devoted to place-names, and the last section of his dictionary, which included the entry for 'toa', remained incomplete.

Put another way, although Reuther had been working on his dictionary and other manuscript volumes since the mid to late 1890s, neither the word *toa*, nor the apparent function of these objects in Diyari culture, were mentioned until after the objects themselves materialised, during late 1903 or early 1904.

Reuther's manuscript is a vast and complex document. It is unindexed, and on almost every page it departs on several tangents. But because of this, it constantly reinforces and amends its own meanings, and is richer for it. Artefact types and their accompanying cultural actions are embedded and cross-referenced throughout the manuscript. Few isolated references to artefacts or their associations occur without a supporting context. Reuther's standard method was to provide multiple examples of phrases and words (whether in everyday or sacred use), so that concepts, objects and actions continually resurface in his dictionary, his descriptions of cultural practices, and particularly in his accounts of the mythological ancestors. This constant cross-referencing probably resulted from Reuther's ethnographic technique, in which he elicited data from a 'panel' of elders on subjects forming the basis of his manuscript volumes – place-names, totemic ancestors, dictionary terms, and so on. Although Reuther gave minimal indications of his working methods, evidence suggests that these interviews occurred at Killalpaninna over a period of years, beginning during the mid-1890s.[45] If terms such as 'toa' (or even the cultural actions framing their function and manufacture), do not occur and recur in Reuther's manuscripts, it is reasonable to conclude that the subject did not arise during these interviews.

There are more dead-ends and cul-de-sacs. In 1904 Reuther commissioned the mission schoolteacher, Henry Hillier, to draw a map of more than 2700 sites in the eastern Lake Eyre region. Reuther's accompanying gazetteer volume describes these places in the same manner as the toa-sites. Given this, it is reasonable to expect that the toa-sites would appear on the map and in the gazetteer. But only 50 of the 385 toa-sites appear in the gazetteer, although perhaps a total of 80–90 may be found on the map, which contains more names than the gazetteer.[46] Of the 50 toa-sites described in the gazetteer, barely a dozen contain a matching mythological account.

At a broader level, although Reuther's toa descriptions make constant reference to place-names, and to Ancestors who first applied those names, neither his place-name volume nor his volumes dealing with mythology mention the existence of toas. The mythological origin of every significant artefact of the Diyari and related groups is discussed somewhere in the manuscript (whether in the dictionary itself or in other volumes), except toas. In contrast to every other Diyari artefact, the toas lack a mythological precedent.

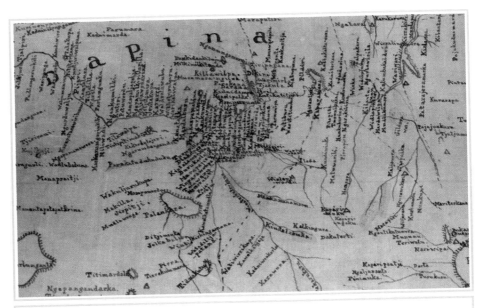

Detail of H.J. Hillier's 1904 map of place-names, showing the concentration of names around Killalpaninna mission, on the Cooper Creek. South Australian Museum Archives.

For reasons which remain mysterious, it seems that Reuther missed the most obvious opportunity to validate and document his own collection. Not only is the very function of a toa unsupported by his own manuscript, more than three-quarters of the toa collection refers to sites which are not otherwise documented. More disturbingly, many of the 86 named Ancestors ascribed to the toas are unmentioned elsewhere in Reuther's manuscript.

READING THE TOAS

Reuther's dictionary entry for 'toas' was written in late 1905. This was almost two years after their manufacture, and just as they were being marketed to museums.[47] The entry differs from most of those in his dictionary, in that it consists of a single, self-contained, descriptive paragraph. It corresponds to an abridged version of the description already quoted, from his first volume of toa descriptions, completed by late 1904. In contrast to other dictionary entries, the toa paragraph contains no reference to the word's etymology. The usual illustrative examples, by which he explained words in their linguistic context, are missing. Reuther ordinarily supplied half a dozen (and often as many as twenty) of these examples for each of his nouns and verbs.

This is his dictionary entry for 'toa':

3348. *toa* (n, m) 'guide; finger-post.'
See the names of the various *toas* on the pictorial illustrations.

These *toas* are a type of sign-language. After they are made, they are placed inside camp wurleys, so that they are not discoloured ('washed out') by rain that may chance to fall.

The 'native' visitor perceives from the various colours, from the toa's shape, or from the things that are pasted on the top, whither the people have moved.

The feathers, bones, or different plants, etc. correspond to the place-name, the colours and shapes indicate the nature of the terrain.

For an explanation of the various place-names and of the toas, see in another book.[48]

Reuther went to greater lengths to ensure the toas' linguistic validity. He did this by applying a suffix, *-ni*, to each toa, explaining it in these terms:

The -ni ... denotes the correlative (i.e. demonstrative) pronominal adverb: 'to [some] distant [place] yonder; in that direction' (Lat: eo, illic). For example, the place-name associated with Toa 1 is called Dakarawitjari, but in the designation of the toa it is called Dakarawitjarini, i.e. 'to Dakarawitjari', or 'in the direction of Dakarawitjari'.[49]

Here it seems that Reuther, who despite his labours was not as linguistically proficient as he appeared, made a fundamental error. As the author of the definitive Diyari grammar, linguist Peter Austin, has demonstrated, the place-name suffix *-ni* (rendered as 'nhi' in modern orthography) is a locative, not an allative. It denotes 'at a place' or 'of a place', not 'to' or 'in the direction of'. The Diyari allative suffix is *-ya*.[50] It is ironic that by appending *-ni* to the toas, Reuther was providing a more accurate description of a toa – as a representation *of* a site, rather than a direction-post *to* it.

Reuther also went to lengths to make sure that the toas could not be regarded as elaborate, mission-grounded representations of places. While this would render them as 'art' in today's terms, in 1904 the category of saleable Aboriginal art (as opposed to craft items) did not exist, and Reuther was not ready to pioneer it. When the first toas materialised in response to his concerted elicitation of mythology, place-names and an ethnographic collection, he described them as artefacts, ascribing utility. At the time, this description was convincing enough, although it is now apparent that the toas simply do not mesh with the rest of his manuscript. Perhaps to deflect attention from the possibility that the toas had emerged as artistic elaborations of place-names, and to reinforce their role as 'authentic' artefacts, Reuther separated the two bodies of information which describe the same sites. His toa volume contains no reference to his place-name volume, and vice versa.

But this does not take us much closer to the actual origin of the word, *toa*. Reuther's fascination for the language, and his labyrinthine manuscript devoted to these linguistic origins, hold the key to that mystery, finally casting light on the first appearance of the toas at Killalpaninna during early 1904.

Like his dictionary, Reuther's place-name volume probably existed in an earlier draft form, but Reuther finalised and neatly transcribed it into a leather-bound ledger between early March and late May 1905, more than a year after the toas appeared as artefacts. The volume contains only two place-names which incorporate the word *toa*. Taken together, these place-name entries supply a fascinating insight into the way in which Reuther may have enlisted an obscure language term for a new purpose, matching it with a new object.

According to Reuther's practice of identifying the relevant language group, both of these place-names were from Bilatapa country, to the south of the mission and the Diyari themselves. These are Reuther's entries:

1890 Toa Pill. [Bilatapa] = 'sign, way-marker, indicator, sign-post; sign-language.'
Meaning: 'a way-marker, indicator'.

    Here Pillatapana buried his millstone, and made himself a marker by which he could locate the spot again. He therefore named the place accordingly. (For more on toas, see the dictionary.)[51]

1974 Toari Pill. [Bilatapa]
Meaning: 'to bury.'

    When Ngutirini brought her dead son Kakalbuna to her brother Kukurukana, she said to him: 'He will come back to life again in three days.' But he replied: 'He will not revive again, for he is putrefying already. Just bury him!' This last gave rise to the place-name.[52]

Both places are concerned unambiguously with the action of burying. In the 'Toa' place-name entry it is this particular action, recalling the place's mytho-logical background, which is distinctive, and it is an action associated with one of the *malka* or marker-pegs, previously noted. This is despite Reuther's confusing suggestion that his own dictionary meaning of the word *toa* should be consulted. In making that suggestion, and in supplying the introductory definitions, was he shifting the word's meaning? And did he then commission a collection of objects to match and confirm this new term?

The evidence suggests that he was doing just that. For while Reuther defined a toa as something which reveals or signifies, the word *toa* seems to be linked inextricably with the action of burying or covering up. Despite his introductory definitions for the two place-names, the actual descriptions suggest that there was a Bilatapa verb, *toa* or *toari* (linguistically, the suffix *-ri* is not intrinsic to the root, *toa*), associated with the act of burying. More accurately, the term recognised by linguists today would be *thuwa*, meaning 'to bury'.

Recent linguistic research has confirmed that a similar term existed in neighbouring languages.[53] In Wangkangurru, to the north-west, the word *thuwa* was used in a restricted sense of the term 'to bury'. For example, it might indicate the action of inserting down-feathers into a string ornament – along the lines of the imperative: 'push it in' or 'insert'. A similar term was found in the Yarluyandi language to the north, employed almost as an uncouth expression: 'stick it in!' In fact, the Yarluyandi used the term *thuwa* even more explicitly, associating it with a thrusting action, as in 'to bury a stick into the ground'. Such expressions might be used in the imperative voice in conversation, as we can imagine the Ancestor Kikurukana using in Reuther's 'Toari' example, quoted above.

In these languages, Bilatapa, Yarluyandi and Wangkangurru, the term *thuwa* was not the only, or even the principal, verb for the action 'to bury'. It was a relatively obscure colloquial term, probably used only in certain contexts. It took a concerted effort by the linguist Luise Hercus, working with the last speakers of these languages and with audio tapes recorded three decades earlier, to identify it. We can assume that the term also existed in the neighbouring Diyari language, describing a similarly abrupt action of 'shoving' a stick into the ground. In fact, Reuther's listing of the verb *todina* may be the cognate Diyari term used for the action of 'burying'.

Reuther's failure to record *thuwa* (or *toa*) as a verb in his extensive Diyari dictionary may not have been an oversight. It may signify his enlistment of that term for a novel purpose, as a noun describing an entirely new artefact. Reuther may even have mistakenly assumed that a term used for shoving a peg or stake into the ground applied to such objects, and then extended the definition. He may then have applied the term *thuwa* or *toa* to a range of objects bearing little resemblance to those pegs, stakes, marker-pegs or even 'direction markers' (the *wandrani-malkas*) which he had already documented. Reuther's explanation of the place-names 'Toa' and 'Toari' are good indications that he had liberated the term *toa* from its original, restrictive meaning, and was redefining it for a new purpose. These place-names may hold the key to understanding the emergence of the 'toa concept'.

Reuther's description of the 'Toa' place-name contained a necessary ambiguity. This allowed him to reapply the word in a new context, suiting the extraordinary role toas were to fill. His description contains two actions – the Ancestor's burial of his millstone, and his fashioning of a simple peg to mark that spot. It appears that Reuther took the little-known verb *thuwa*, 'to bury', and applied it to pegs of another kind – redefining these as signposts indicating specific, distant localities.[54]

At some point in this process, we must imagine that Aboriginal people played an active role, projecting their own artistic creations into the ambiguous zone created by Reuther's concerted elicitation of myth, place and object. For example, it is easy to imagine a decorated head-piece, bearing symbols of a place-centred Dreaming, being proffered as a contribution to Reuther's collection, and immediately interpreted by him as a direction *to* that place, rather than an illustration *of* it. Whether or not the toa series stemmed from Reuther's original error or his canny opportunism, the result was a spectacular and unprecedented collection. Reuther reinforced the new meaning of these objects by adding a cross-reference to his dictionary definition, more than a year after the toas first appeared. It was this revised meaning which clearly defined the word *toa*, for the first time, as a signpost.

But Reuther had even greater ambitions for the toas. He was prepared to extend the definition of their function well beyond that of a simple collection of indicative symbols. Unprecedented as it was, that extension of meaning was signalled by the introductory reference in his 'Toa' place-name entry, to 'sign language', and was complemented by the new dictionary entry in which Reuther defined the toas as 'a kind of sign language'.

As we know, Reuther completed the latter part of the dictionary after the toas had appeared. In that final section one more reference to the toas can be found, confirming Reuther's ultimate attempt to connect the objects to the concept of a written language. Discussing the etymology of the word *ngujamana*, 'to know', Reuther used the phrase *toa ngujamana*, translating this as 'to know the written characters'. Here Reuther was inserting the noun *toa* in place of the term *malka* or 'mark', which had previously served to define letters of the German alphabet from which he and his mission predecessors had already generated a substantial Diyari literature of religious tracts.[55]

By late 1904, the definition of a toa in Reuther's completed manuscript spanned a range of cryptic meanings, from simple marker-pegs to way-markers indicating general direction and elaborately sculpted and painted direction-posts indicating specific localities, and from elements of an ideographic sign system to pictographic script and, finally, to written characters. When the time came for Reuther to sell his collection during 1905, he was obliged to select and apply the most convincing, and most saleable, of these definitions. At it happened, during the years immediately preceding the announcement of the toas' existence in early 1904, he had several opportunities to gauge an emerging ethnographic market, within Australia and beyond.

VISITORS TO THE DEAD HEART

In 1902 Reuther was relieved from onerous mission duties with the appointment of a stock station manager, Johannes Bogner, a fellow-missionary who was later to purchase the mission outright as a pastoral property. Otto Siebert also departed in that year, and Reuther redoubled his ethnographic investigations. By early 1904 he was on the brink of completing his most important ethnographic work, his four-volume dictionary of the Diyari and related languages. His joint publication with Carl Strehlow of the Diyari New Testament had given him the confidence to continue this work and it was endorsed by the mission committee, headed by Pastor Kaibel. But Reuther's evangelical zeal had already waned. He had begun conceiving of himself as an ethnographer, rather than a missionary. A close analysis of his correspondence and reports confirms this shift.[56] Reuther's new ambitions were partly related to the poor state of his personal finances, and the imperative of providing his children with an adequate education. There was another important factor. As an outpost of civilisation on the edge of the desert, Killalpaninna had suddenly become a focus for scientific and ethnographic interest. If nothing else, a series of new visitors to Reuther's mission opened his eyes to the commercial potential of an ethnographic collection.

The first of these visits was by the German ethnographer Erhard Eylmann. He spent a fortnight at the mission during July 1900, gathering data and assembling a large ethnographic collection. Eylmann relied upon both Siebert and Reuther for information on the Diyari and published this in his ethnographic survey of Aboriginal groups encountered during his journeys across the continent. Eylmann investigated message-sticks and sign language and was particularly interested in the visual symbols painted or carved onto artefacts. He devoted a chapter to the question of 'the beginnings of pictorial art' (*die anfänge der*

View of Killalpaninna mission from the north side of Lake Killalpaninna, full of water after a Cooper Creek flood, early 1890s. South Australian Museum Archives.

bildenden kunst), paying particular attention to any form of material culture incorporating designs or motifs, as well as examples of sculptural forms. He singled out the Diyari's boldly painted wooden shields as the principal expression of their pictorial art. Eylmann did not confine his discussion to traditional forms. In fact, his 500-page book stands out as one of the few monographs of the period to discuss European influence on Aboriginal cultural practices. There can be no doubt that, if the toas existed at this time, Eylmann would have collected examples, and incorporated references to them into his book or his detailed journal.[57]

The second visit was by Scottish geologist J.W. Gregory, whose desert investigations at the close of the great drought of 1895–1902 also included the region's ethnography. During December 1901 he spent several days at Killalpaninna and made specific observations on the material culture of the Diyari. He noted that they showed 'the usual Australian skill in the utilisation of every available natural product'.[58] By this time, possibly in response to Eylmann's interest, Reuther had assembled a private museum in his house. It accommodated an expanding collection of artefacts, plant specimens, jars of seeds and fossils. Aboriginal artefact-makers at the mission were responding to greater interest in their creations, and Reuther was now adopting a proprietorial attitude to his collection. As he indicated in a letter to his mission superior Pastor Kaibel, if Gregory wanted to obtain any of his artefacts, they would not be cheap:

> Don't imagine, dear sir, that I will give up my collection easily. It would have to be a good price, since it has already cost me a fair amount from my own pocket. The Blacks do not hurry in giving things away, they ask for Kalala [recompense]: many of their things are already very rare, even for themselves, so that they ask for incredible prices.[59]

While Reuther still considered that his mission toil was undertaken in 'stony ground', he could now see it bearing fruit.

In mid-1903 a further opportunity presented itself, with the visit of Professor Aleksandr Yashchenko, a Russian zoologist. Yashchenko had an active interest in ethnography as well as natural history, and spent a fortnight at the mission. He relied upon Reuther who was now, following Siebert's departure a few months earlier, the undisputed ethnographic authority. On the day of his arrival Reuther showed Yashchenko his 'collection of rare native utensils and weapons' and allowed the Russian to inspect his manuscripts: 'several books in ledger format containing well-organized data and information on the blacks' way of life, their beliefs, legends, language and nomenclature as well as material on their perceptions of the animal world'.[60] Yashchenko impressed upon Reuther the importance of publishing his material. That encouragement may have awoken Reuther to his collection's potential value in the world outside the mission, in commercial as well as ethnographic terms. Yashchenko photographed the ethnographic collection two days later and obtained several artefacts as gifts from Reuther and the mission teamster, Jack Ruediger, who also collected natural history specimens. These objects (and presumably also the photographs) joined the larger collection assembled by Yashchenko during his Australian visit. Most of this collection survives today in the St Petersburg Museum of Anthropology and Ethnography. It does not include toas, nor are they mentioned in Yashchenko's detailed account of his visit.[61]

These visits to Killalpaninna, coupled with Reuther's clear interest in ethnographic publication, amounted to considerable pressure on him to produce a saleable ethnographic collection. The missionary began to consider a new relationship with Aboriginal people, mediated more by ethnography and the production of artefacts than by Christianity and the salvation of souls.[62]

By mid-1905 Reuther was negotiating with museums in London, Berlin and Adelaide for the sale of his ethnographic collection, at a value of £400. The decision to do this can only have been encouraged by the presence at Killalpaninna of Henry J. (Harry) Hillier, an English schoolteacher and trained artist who had returned several times to his native England around the turn of the century, taking ethnographic objects from Killalpaninna with him. Hillier had been at the mission during late 1903, just before Reuther announced the toas' existence. We can assume that he was present at their birth, if not their conception. None of Hillier's collections, now in the Horniman Museum, British Museum, Cambridge's University Museum and the Royal Scottish Museum in Edinburgh, include toas. A trained artist, Hillier produced two sets of finely-painted watercolour illustrations of Reuther's collection, including the toas. At Reuther's direction he also produced the remarkably detailed map of the eastern Lake Eyre region, inscribed with more than 2700 names.[63]

Reuther's preparation and elaborate marketing of his ethnographic collection coincided with his own impending retirement from Killalpaninna. His approach contrasts with the usual model of missionary collecting, in which artefacts gathered haphazardly during the course of a missionary's career were offered to museums for barely more than the cost of packing and transport. In Reuther's case there were powerful incentives to behave differently. Despite having spent eighteen years at Killalpaninna he was still only in his early forties, and had a young family to support and educate. He was progressively entering into conflict with his superiors, and by 1905 a contrived scandal, involving the pregnancy of a mission girl to a nearby station owner, was to precipitate his resignation.[64]

H.J. (Harry) Hillier, school teacher and artist, ca 1940. Lutheran Archives, Adelaide.

Before this storm broke, Reuther was already disillusioned with his

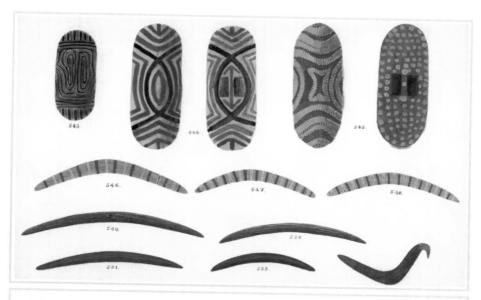

Hillier's watercolour minatures of shields and boomerangs in Reuther's ethnographic collection, ca 1904. South Australian Museum Archives.

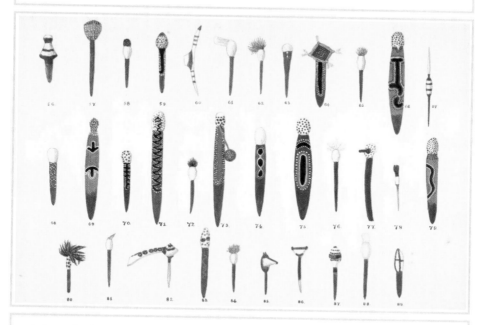

A sheet of Hillier's watercolour minatures of Reuther's toas, ca 1904. South Australian Museum Archives.

Johann Reuther with his wife Pauline, seven children and Aboriginal maid at Killalpaninna, ca 1900. South Australian Museum Archives.

work as a missionary. Siebert's departure in 1902 opened the field for his own future as an ethnographer, particularly in terms of supplying European museums with commissioned collections. This approach was later to be developed to a sophisticated level by Carl Strehlow, his brother-missionary at the Hermannsburg Lutheran Mission in the MacDonnell Ranges. Probably inspired by Reuther's example, Strehlow sold as many as nine collections (averaging 175 objects) of Arrernte artefacts to German and Swiss museums between 1906 and 1922.[65]

In contrast to Reuther's collection, Strehlow's Arrernte collections were conventional in their composition. They contained object types well-documented in the material culture descriptions for the Arrernte region. The point is important, as Strehlow was more than Reuther's equal as an ethnographer. Like Siebert, he worked closely with an academic mentor – the Frankfurt-based ethnographer Baron Moritz von Leonhardi, who acted as an agent for his collections and supervised the publication of his multi-volume work on the Arrernte and Loritja peoples.[66] Having worked with Reuther at Killalpaninna from 1892 until 1895, Strehlow had a detailed awareness of variations throughout the broader Central Australian ethnographic region. Of the knowledgeable visitors to Killalpaninna prior to the appearance of the toas in early 1904, Strehlow was the last, and in some ways, the most significant. He and his wife stayed with the Reuthers during July and August of 1903, overlapping with Yashchenko's visit. Had the toas existed at that time, Strehlow would surely have mentioned them to von Leonhardi. We can assume then, that these objects were made during the months after his departure in late August but prior to March 1904, when Reuther announced their existence. During that period of six months Reuther was master of his remote domain, uninterrupted by visitors.

Reuther's first announcement of the toas was made not to a fellow ethnographer, but to his superior Pastor Kaibel, in charge of the mission committee at Light Pass, north of Adelaide:

> What do you think for instance when I tell you that the natives know a 'picture script' drawn in colour onto wooden sticks, and that I have about 300 of these in my hands? Has anybody ever found anything like that in connection with the Australian natives? The religion of the natives is much the same as this 'picture script'.[67]

Here is an important and revealing indication that the toas did not materialise gradually as single objects, which Reuther noticed and then prevailed upon their makers to produce in numbers. Rather, the sudden appearance of an entire group of 300 toas, where none had existed in previous months and years, raises the likelihood of their fabrication *en masse*.

Kaibel's immediate response is not known, but he certainly disapproved of his missionary's enthusiasm at a time when mission finances at Killalpaninna were beginning to crumble. Two years later he was directly attacking Reuther for his fixation with ethnography:

you are not leaving your cell and don't know what is going on at the station ...
In your extensive work that you wish to bring to print ... you have not been
driven to further God's word, but to a large extent by your ambition.[68]

Reuther had been vocal in denouncing Siebert for pursuing ethnography to
the detriment of mission work. He was now exposing himself to the same
criticism.[69] Reuther's March 1904 letter to Kaibel may have represented a
considered attempt to retrieve the deteriorating situation by announcing a
momentous discovery; a tantalising connection between language and religion
he alone could illuminate. The question is whether Reuther himself believed
in his discovery.

Reuther's announcement to Kaibel was quickly followed by a similar revela-
tion to his anthropological mentors. Perhaps considering that he had brought
to light something as ethnographically compelling as the myths, legends and
data which his brother-missionary Otto Siebert had supplied to Alfred Howitt
during the 1890s, Reuther sent news of his discovery to the elderly Victorian
anthropologist in May 1904. Among other ethnographic observations relating
to a particular plant species, he made this announcement, almost as an aside:

> I have discovered a form of pictographic writing (Bilderschrift), which has
> never been heard of. My Museum so far carries the number 865.[70]

Reuther may not have been aware of the strength of Howitt's views against
the existence of independently interpreted message-sticks or 'pictographic
writing'. Howitt's comprehensive study, *The Native Tribes of South-East Australia*,
was about to be published, including large extracts of Siebert's Diyari data.
This book, together with Spencer and Gillen's *Native Tribes of Central Australia*
of 1899 and Walter Roth's *Ethnological Studies* of 1897, provided clear rebuttal
of the notion that coded systems of communication might underly message-
sticks or smoke-signals. That said, we have no record of Howitt's response to
Reuther's claims for 'pictographic writing'. Nor do we know Howitt's views
on the following description of a toa, which he transcribed by hand from
an unknown source, probably at this time. It corresponds to Reuther's description of toas in his newspaper interview of 1906, quoted above. It also contains
the same, extraordinary proposition that a substance from the toa's destination could be incorporated in the object before its makers set out for that
destination:

Memo

Not to my knowledge have the niggers messagesticks [sic].

    The only case where they use sticks is to denote to traveling blacks where they have shifted a camp, viz. a camp of blacks remove their quarters to a place the name of Napa-tunkina – at the old camp they leave a stick bent in the direction of Napa-tunkina (stinking water) & on the top place a puddled clay cup containing stinking water – so traveling blacks have no difficulty in finding [the] main camp.[71]

The source of the information in this memorandum remains a mystery, although a claim by art historian Mary Eagle that it was written in 1882, by the policeman-ethnographer Samuel Gason, can be readily dismissed. Gason had, in any event, already responded to Howitt's 1882 circular letter soliciting information on message-sticks and communication, to the effect that the Diyari did not use these objects or any similar method of conveying non-verbal messages. He had written: 'No message sticks are used, only distinguishing Marks on Breast, arms or face with paint, but [they] have no means of carrying messages by sticks or otherwise'. Gason's 1894 publication on the Diyari and related groups reiterated that 'all messages are sent verbally'.[72] There were several possible sources for the memo, including Henry Hillier, whose own later version of toas was very similar to that expressed for the Napatunka example – that is, referring to a topographic (rather than mythological) feature, and incorporating some physical element (in this case, the particular water from the destination waterhole). Likelier candidates were the Neaylon brothers, lease-holders of Appatoonganie (Napatunka) Station, situated twenty kilometres to the north-east of Killalpaninna mission.

THE RECEPTION OF THE TOAS

When the time came to offer his collection for sale, Reuther turned first to his home country, approaching Berlin's Museum für Völkerkunde. He sent the museum a catalogue of the collection, together with one set of Hillier's water-colour sketches. The precise chain of events is unclear, but it seems that the Berlin authorities contacted the principal German authority on Australian ethnography, Baron von Leonhardi, for his opinion. The Baron was most intrigued, not by the toas, but by a set of seven small dingo models, sculpted out of resin, in Reuther's collection.[73] Even more than particular toas, these objects suggested the existence of unprecedented figurative sculpture among Aborigines of Central Australia. Von Leonhardi wrote to his principal Australian

267

Two dogs modelled in spinifex resin, painted with pipeclay and red ochre, representing
Pajamiljakirina ('bird-like', 'small-eater') and Dundukurananani ('big-eater'), a female dog
belonging to the ancestor Darana (at front). A68461, A68458, South Australian Museum.

correspondent, Pastor Carl Strehlow at Hermannsburg mission, asking him
for corroboration of Reuther's discovery of sculptural forms among the Diyari.
Strehlow had obviously seen nothing of the kind during his time at Killalpaninna from 1892 to 1895 or presumably, during his 1903 visit. Without pro-
nouncing upon the Diyari situation, he indicated only that sculptural figures
did not exist in the suite of traditional Arrernte material culture. Von Leonhardi
drew a similar blank from Otto Siebert, by now retired and living in Germany.[74]

Baron von Leonhardi had the power and influence to anoint Reuther as an ethnographer and as a reliable source of authentic Aboriginal artefacts for German museums. He withheld that endorsement, and the Museum für Völkerkunde did not proceed with the acquisition of Reuther's collection. It was Carl Strehlow, Reuther's former colleague, who became the foremost supplier to German museums during the following decade. The Baron's disillusionment with Reuther was to increase further. Reuther had assured von Leonhardi of the validity of the Diyari belief in a supreme being, personified in the Mura, or Dreaming. Criticised for supporting the idea, von Leonhardi turned to Reuther for further corroboration, but was disappointed again. The German scholar wrote in 1909:

> The only thing that matters is whether Reuther can come up with proof for his assumption ... He brings forward yet another piece of evidence which at first glance seems remarkable ... Reuther ... has no satisfactory response ... so it seems to me that his proof of the existence of the Dieri's belief in God has completely failed.[75]

Von Leonhardi's reference to another 'remarkable piece of evidence' suggests that he was also aware of Reuther's proposition of the toas as 'pictographic' symbols.

During early 1905 Reuther turned his attention to the South Australian Museum, visiting and then corresponding with its director, Edward Stirling. In these communications he restrained himself from making any claims for the toas as a 'pictographic script'. The toas were described as 'way markers', and Stirling had no qualms about claiming this new ethnographic discovery for his museum. He had reasons for scoring ethnographic points against his interstate rivals, and this may well have affected his objective assessment of the toas. In his argument to his Board for the purchase of the collection Stirling stressed its novelty and significance, and in his letters to Reuther he gave a clear assurance:

> It would be made clear that you are the discoverer of these items ... which are new to science. The object ... is to make known a class of articles which are new to this museum and unknown I believe elsewhere.[76]

At the zenith of his influence as director, Stirling's recommendation for purchase was accepted. A sample dozen of the toas, illustrated in colour and supplemented with data supplied by Reuther, was published in the museum's 1906 Annual Report.[77]

Surprisingly perhaps, in light of their impact in later decades, the acquisition of the toas created very little controversy or excitement in Adelaide. This is partly because they were not placed on display until Stirling's new ethnographic gallery was opened during 1914. By this time Reuther, Howitt and Gillen were dead, the Killalpaninna mission itself was on the verge of closure, and the First World War was about to push ethnographic controversy well into the background. The toas were installed in a central position in the new gallery and five years later, shortly after Stirling's death in 1919, his own 40-page monograph on the objects was completed by his successor and published.[78] In 1920 a summary of this appeared in the journal *Nature*. The linguist Sydney Ray observed in restrained terms that the 'whole collection and its elucidation form a most interesting contribution to the study of Australian symbolism'.[79]

In the original message-stick debate, Baldwin Spencer was the only ethnographic specialist left who might have responded to the proposition in Stirling's paper that toas effectively operated as a sign system, similar to that proposed for message-sticks. Spencer had harboured doubts about Gillen's confident dismissal of the message-stick theory, but there is no record of his opinion of the toas. He took progressively less interest in museum matters after 1920 and died in 1927.[80]

In the meantime though, two individuals with direct knowledge of Aboriginal art and of Lake Eyre Aboriginal people commented on the toas. George Aiston, principal author of the main ethnographic publication on the region, had lived in the area since 1912. Several of his informants were elderly men who had lived at the Killalpaninna mission. Two of these men – Peter Pinnaru and Sam Dintibana – are mentioned in Reuther's diary or his manuscript. These men, if no others, could have been expected to remember the toas and some details of their use or manufacture. Aiston's main published work contains a single, gently facetious reference to these objects:

> The shaped sticks stuck into the ground on departure and spoken of as *toas* were not known by the old men of the Wonkonguru. These would have been most useful, as they described the destination sought.[81]

Aiston's private correspondence with his friend, Sydney stone tool collector W.H. Gill, is more forthright. In May 1930 he wrote to Gill:

George Aiston, policeman, ethnographer and later, bush store-keeper, relaxing at Mungeranie Police Station, ca 1915. Aiston Collection, South Australian Museum Archives.

Our blacks did not carve idols in wood, although the German Missionaries collected a lot of what they called toas, these were images and figures representing various waterholes and the Mooras who looked after them. But the blacks who made them for the missionaries told me that the missionaries supplied the designs and got the blacks to make them, neither I nor any of my black friends had ever heard of them until they were made for the Missionaries.[82]

Aiston's next pronouncement on the toas was even more damning. It came a few months before the outbreak of the Second World War and perhaps contains a tinge of xenophobia. Writing to Gill about Hermannsburg, the sister-mission to Killalpaninna, he observed:

I know some of the German teachers there and they are as cunning as rats. The great Toa hoax was got up by one of the teachers who is now at Hermannsburg – he suggested the designs and supervised the making of those toas – a thing totally unknown to any of the tribesmen in this country.[83]

271

The content of Aiston's own extensive ethnographic collections makes it plain that he actively filtered out objects he considered tainted by modern influences. In this he conformed to the norms of the period. He told the Aboriginal men offering their artefacts to him that he would only accept those made in the traditional way, according to particular standards. In September 1926 he wrote to Gill from Mulka, a few kilometres north of the former mission site at Killalpaninna:

> I am gathering in any weapons belonging to the blacks that I can get hold of – in a very short time now there will be no one with the knowledge of how to make them left – I have one splendid old weapon maker here – he has made me some beautiful things – not with stone tools of course, although they were smoothed off with stone flakes.[84]

Aiston was also aware that the most nondescript-looking objects could convey deep meaning, evocative of the 'Moora' Dreamings of the region. These objects and their associated mythology were being entrusted to him at this time and he cannot therefore be accused of suggesting that traditional knowledge had vanished, or become irrelevant. What disturbed him about the toas was not their external appearance – nor perhaps, their individual meanings – but the proposition that they served as a system of communication.

The Melbourne ethnographer and stone tool collector A.S. Kenyon was active during the period from 1900 until 1930. He had become aware of the minor industry in Aboriginal artefacts emerging in north-eastern South Australia at the close of the mission period. In a tantalisingly brief reference to toas he wrote to Edgar Waite, Stirling's successor as museum director, in May 1920:

> I should be specially pleased to get the 'Record' containing the Toa's [sic] article as their use as given in the annual report for 07/8 conflicted with the accounts given me by men who had lived among those tribes.[85]

One month later, in another brief letter, Kenyon wrote:

> I shall be glad if you would forward me the one with the article on Toas ... I trust you have noted my doubt about the genuineness of those implements. In Melbourne there is a continued supply of spurious implements from the same locality.[86]

Aiston and Kenyon aside, the toas were barely mentioned in surveys of Aboriginal ethnography and art during the mid-twentieth century. The main categories of academic discussion relating to those subjects did not intersect with these anomalous objects. Nor did any mention of them occur in the large body of ethnographic and linguistic work undertaken during the mid and late twentieth century with elderly men and women of the Lake Eyre region, by scholars such as T.G.H. Strehlow, Ronald Berndt, Peter Austin, Gavan Breen or particularly, Luise Hercus, whose research bears directly on the mythology associated with the toas.[87] And yet the toas had surfaced once more, most mysteriously, on the other side of the world.

OSKAR LIEBLER'S TOAS

Baron von Leonhardi may have swayed Berlin's Museum für Völkerkunde from acquiring Reuther's collection, but this did not prevent toas from reaching German museums. During the period 1910 to 1913 Carl Strehlow was relieved

Oskar Liebler and his wife leaving Hermannsburg for Germany, 1913.
Lutheran Archives, Adelaide.

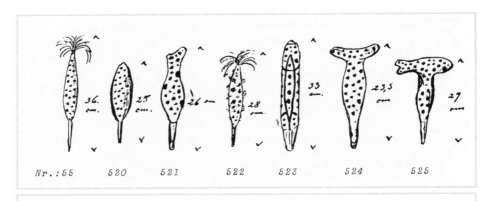

The seven Oskar Liebler toas in the Linden Museum, Stuttgart, sketched by Theo Koch-Grünberg in 1921, eight years after their acquisition (Schlatter 1985, p. 150).

as missionary among the Arrernte people at Hermannsburg in Central Australia by Pastor Oskar Liebler, who soon became an avid ethnographic collector. In the space of four years he accumulated and sold more than 1500 well-documented Arrernte secular and sacred artefacts. Though he did not visit Hermannsburg's sister-mission at Killalpaninna during this time, he managed to obtain a total of nineteen toas. Two of these were among the collection sold to the South Australian Museum. He sold a further two to the Hamburg Museum für Völkerkunde, eight to the Munich Museum für Völkerkunde, and seven to the Stuttgart Museum für Völkerkunde.[88]

Taken together, this small collection is intriguing in more ways than one. Most of the nineteen Liebler toas conform to the same design and at least ten of them are virtually indistinguishable, despite representing entirely different localities and Dreamings.[89] The nineteen sites described by the Liebler toas are all Diyari sites, mostly found within a twenty-kilometre radius of Killalpaninna mission. In contrast to the Reuther toas, all of those sites are marked on Hillier's map. The ten similar toas consist of simple wooden shafts covered with elongated bulbous heads of gypsum, decorated with vertical rows of red and black dots. Three others are topped with plumes of emu feathers and one with pieces of bone, one has an outline of a lizard drawn against the dotted background, and the remaining four are shaped to resemble a fish, a dingo's head and two waterholes. A comparison of these toas with the Reuther series suggests that the Liebler toas are cruder and simpler, and that they may have been made by a single person.

How might these toas have appeared at Hermannsburg mission, hundreds of kilometres from Killalpaninna, and nearly a decade after Reuther's toas were made? There are perhaps two possibilities, bearing in mind that Liebler himself did not visit Killalpaninna. One is that the toas were brought to Hermannsburg by Harry Hillier, who spent the years 1906 to 1910 there (just overlapping with Liebler). This seems unlikely, although Hillier may well have shown Liebler the set of watercolour drawings he had retained. Hillier had not included toas in any of the ethnographic collections he sent to England. Moreover, the Liebler toas are more roughly made than Reuther's toas, which Hillier had observed at Killalpaninna. The second possibility is that a Killalpaninna man, who remembered the toas, arrived at Hermannsburg and was prevailed upon to make examples relating to sites familiar to him. Knowing of Killalpaninna as the source of the toas, it makes sense for Liebler to have commissioned the toas when a Diyari man arrived at Hermannsburg from that mission. This interpretation is strengthened by a note accompanying one of his toas, which Liebler wrote at Hermannsburg. After describing the toa, it reads: 'Rev Reuther has written about this subject in the S.A. Museum; we have one of his blacks here'.[90]

The chronicle of daily events at Hermannsburg mission records the arrival of at least one Killalpaninna man during the critical period in which these toas appeared. This was the Diyari man Petrus, who arrived at Hermannsburg on 5 June 1910, and accompanied a consignment of mission cattle back to Killalpaninna six weeks later. He then returned to Hermannsburg and following his marriage to an Arrernte woman in October of that year, remained there. As 'one of Reuther's blacks', Petrus may well have been Liebler's toa-maker.[91]

A further note suggests that the Liebler toas were not only made at the Hermannsburg mission, but that at least one of these innovative objects was being adapted to the Arrernte situation. One of the Hamburg toas (conforming to the most conventional type) is accompanied by the following documentation:

Platz-zeichen für den Corroboree Platz [Place-marker for a corroboree ground]. (Murra = Dieri ancestor. 'Tjurunga' = sacred stone or board of the Arrente (Aranda) people living in the region of the Hermannsburg Mission.)[92]

With its conjunction of Arrernte and Diyari terminology this particular toa may even have reflected the situation of its maker, Petrus, who was about to marry a Western Arrernte woman. Such an alliance was beyond the traditional bounds of the two groups' marriage relationships, but had become possible through the commerce between the two missions.

Without an outlet for their creativity, and with the major European sponsors (if not collaborators) now absent from Killalpaninna, the Aboriginal toa-makers there had no reason to sustain the efflorescence of creativity represented by the toas. But a decade after Reuther's departure, the sketchy information accompanying the Liebler toas indicates that these objects had not been completely forgotten.

WHAT TOAS MIGHT MEAN

When the toas finally emerged as subjects of interest in their own right, it was through the art-history analysis undertaken by Howard Morphy, who completed an M.A. thesis based on photographs of toas during 1972. His careful semiotic analyses, the major survey exhibition at the South Australian Museum, and associated publications since, have ensured the toas' continued prominence in discussion about Aboriginal art.[93] Several decades of intense European exposure to Aboriginal art have disclosed many of its elements and have helped to make its underlying principles apparent. But, for one important reason, Aboriginal art remains largely opaque, requiring interpretation. This is because, region by region, its visual vocabulary is composed of a relatively small but highly flexible set of motifs. Even in the formalised domains of sacred representation, Aboriginal art arises from subjective manipulations of these limited sets of motifs. Despite the repetitive character of sacred verse, dance and design, these motifs never cohere predictably in the same way. A bird track can represent many different species, but a particular context dictates that only one is relevant and 'true'. The concentric circles symbolising a honey-ant nest in one ceremony might, rendered in just the same way, be a possum's home in another ceremony. The multiple meanings of Central Australian tjurunga preclude the possibility of a standard catalogue of symbols. Just as the message-stick requires its bearer, the art-object requires its maker or, failing that, its interpreter.

As artefacts of ordinary or even sacred life, Reuther's toas were *too objective* to be of use to Aboriginal people. In his terms, they were designed to admit of a single meaning, and to proclaim that single meaning in any space, independently of their makers. But if the toas existed as Reuther explained them, all our ideas about Aboriginal art are wrongly founded – there would be, in fact, a predictable suite of relatively fixed meanings, open to all those who happened upon them.

If a kind of stasis or freezing of meaning did occur, this happened only at one place and at one time, under very particular circumstances – at Killalpaninna mission during the summer of 1903 to 1904. The urge to undertake it was probably more European than Aboriginal. The result had more to do with creating saleable museum artefacts than capturing the ethnographic moment. The more figurative and demonstrative of the toas, with their flamboyant attachments and allusive forms, betray the self-consciousness of this ethnographic alchemy.

Even so, a number of the least figurative toas retain an enigmatic quality. In their conservative iconography, perhaps 50 of the 385 toas seem directly opposed to the playful individualism of the majority. These toas suggest that it may not always have been the missionaries who, in Aiston's words, 'supplied the designs and got the blacks to make them'. Among this group of toas the combinations and recombinations of strips of black surrounded by dotting, on a red or white field, and topped with feathers, evoke most immediately the traditional ceremonial body-painting designs and ceremonial head-gear documented for the region.[94] These toas suggest that if an ethnographic hoax was perpetrated at Killalpaninna, not all its collaborators shared the same motives. For in contrast to the majority of toas, whose individuality matches their specificity of meaning, these 'generic' toas are more fluid and elusive in their associations. Even more than their quirkier fellows, these toas seem to demand their makers' presence.

Notwithstanding the great variations within it, Reuther's total collection of toas is bound together by its texts, each an elaboration of the named places which the toas were manufactured to represent. The texts retain a uniformity which the toas do not, and in this sense the word holds precedence over the object. This order was the reverse of the logic Reuther wished Kaibel, Howitt, von Leonhardi and Stirling to accept – that his discovery of the toas as objects had led to knowledge of their function. But Reuther had long understood that archaic or obsolete terms might provide a foothold for his linguistic research. An object might not only provide access to previously unencountered words, but words themselves might lead to undiscovered objects. In a 1900 article for a mission newspaper, Reuther had written that it was possible to 'find names of decorations ['schmuck'] and weapons, and because they have names these should still be used, but they only exist in the memory'.[95] The toas may well have arisen at just that moment, when Reuther's imperfect insight into an obscure item of material culture such as a simple marker peg, his readiness to barter for ethnographic objects and his enthusiasm for eliciting the mythological background to place-names, met the creativity of mission Aborigines suddenly encouraged to combine their artefact-making skills with their intimate knowledge of sites and Dreamings. As the remarkable expression of their response, the toas embody both this knowledge and the missionary's own desires, converging in an unprecedented form.

If, as it appears, Reuther's enthusiasm for words not only preceded, but also provoked his collection of toas, then we come closer to understanding the genesis of these remarkable objects. Toas were visual explications of Reuther's insights into the Aboriginal landscape surrounding him. Even more, they can be regarded as distortions or amplifications of those insights, through a frontier lens. Reuther had come to understand something of the symbolic weight carried by every named place, but his imperfect knowledge resulted in a jumble of information, which remains unsorted a century later. That confusion, and Reuther's apparent reluctance to document the actual processes of artefact manufacture still obscures the origins of the toas. These were unprecedented objects, but so is much Aboriginal art of the present, which nevertheless expresses ancient links between myth and place. It is tempting to simply redefine the toas as one of the first authentic expressions of what we now regard as modern Aboriginal art. And yet doubts remain as to the authenticity of a large number of the toa stories, which refer to otherwise undocumented places and Ancestors, and as to the role of Europeans (Reuther among others) on the mission, in fashioning artefacts which depart so markedly from the norms of Aboriginal material culture documented for the region.

Aboriginal camp within five kilometres of Killalpaninna, photographed in about 1895. South Australian Museum Archives.

Pastor Johann Reuther (at right) with his Aboriginal congregation at the Killalpaninna mission church, ca 1895. South Australian Museum Archives.

The precise role of Aboriginal people themselves in the toa phenomenon remains indistinct. Reuther rarely mentioned his informants, and his manuscript does not refer directly either to the manufacture of artefacts or the formation of his collection. His sole reference to the makers of the toas comes in this observation, made in reference to the final three toas in his collection:

> I was no longer able to ascertain the historical background to the last three toas. The owners of the legends (derived from the Muramuras), with which the meanings of the toas are connected, religiously, had meanwhile died, vanished from the face of the earth.[96]

Reuther's regretful note tends to undermine his own proposition that these objects constituted a 'pictographic script', understood by a wide sample of knowledgeable men and women. His note implies that rather than being understood independently, toas did, after all, require their makers.

Newly located mission records, including Otto Siebert's detailed ethnographic diary, may offer new insights into the identity of Aboriginal men who played a role in producing the toas, men such as Petrus or Peter Pinnaru, Emil Kintalakadi, Elias Palkalinna, Elisha Tjerkalina, Andreas Dibana and Johannes Pingilina. These are known to have supplied both Siebert and Reuther with information and undoubtedly also made artefacts.[97] During the 1930s Ted Vogelsang (who grew up on the mission) worked briefly at the South Australian Museum as an attendant, and added this note to the first attempted translation of the Reuther manuscript:

> The following Natives were the principle informators [sic] of who Mr Reuther obtained his information.
>   Johannes Pingilina (Diari)
>   Mose[s] (Tirari)
>   Joseph Ngantjalina (Diari Lake Hope)
>   Titus (Diari)
>   Isaac (Diari)
>   Elias (Diari) is also mentioned in Prof. Horns & Aiston Book.
>   Elis[h]a (Diari)[98]

Reuther was content to leave an impression that his collection had arisen almost unbidden from an untainted ethnographic reality, preserved behind the façade of mission buildings and elicited by his own acuity. We know this not to be the case. We know that the mission church and buildings were constructed with Aboriginal labour, that many Aboriginal people on the mission were familiar with spoken and written German and English, with Christian iconography, music and art. Several had acquired particular European skills such as sheep-shearing and carpentry – the latter perhaps learnt from Reuther himself, who made all his own furniture on the mission. We know that gypsum, or lime, a principal ingredient of the toas, was manufactured there in quantity for building purposes. Under these circumstances, with the stimulus offered by Reuther's rapidly expanding ethnographic project and a new imperative – to provide artefacts to illustrate his manuscript and the ideas which it contained – it might have been more extraordinary to find that something like the toas did not materialise.

It is possible then, to propose a more complex account of the toas than Aiston's and Kenyon's propositions of outright fraud suggest. That explanation might lie in the syncretism imbuing the spiritual and social life of Aborigines and Europeans on frontier missions, finding expression at Killalpaninna in a remarkable efflorescence of material culture. Reuther's fantasy of a picture-script with its unique signifiers had fused both with the flexible Aboriginal motif-set of the Dreaming and the nondescript wooden stakes or pegs used to mark resources or activities. It is in that combination, heated in the particular crucible of this frontier, that we can glimpse the origins of these enigmatic objects.

Gaberdine suit purchased by Daisy Bates in about 1904 and worn by her until her death in 1951. South Australian Museum Archives.

CHAPTER SEVEN

The magic garb of Daisy Bates

All of the existing photographs of Daisy Bates present her as an anachronism. Her trim Victorian jackets and skirts, the selection of hats and veils, parasol, white gloves and button boots make a light and ethereal assemblage. The image is at apparent odds with the context of her life and work, and with the earthen shades and ochred forms of the Aboriginal landscapes and desert people, the absorbing focus of her energies. It is a contrast stark enough to provoke the question of how it was that the desert Aborigines and Daisy Bates could live with each other and tolerate the difference. What were their points of connection?

Nobody has been able to pin Mrs Bates down. She was, as Ernestine Hill put it best, 'a surprise in the primeval scene, a question mark'.[1] As journalist and linguist, social activist and monarchist, Victorian lady and confidante of tribal initiates, Bates remains elusive enough to evade most modern (and post-modern) attempts at classification. The reason has much to do with the fact that more than almost any other European figure of the frontier, she sharpened the very edge between cultures – heightening a sense of dissonance – and then self-consciously dwelt there. Tinted eyeglasses and a dustcoat were her only concessions to the climate and conditions. She materialised among 'her natives' in her Victorian garb, arriving with her parasol and a carpet-bag full of manuscripts and gentle admonitions, a frontier Mary Poppins with a lilting Tipperary brogue.

Bates was as aware as anyone of the displacement in time and space conveyed by her old-world garb. In fact, the unforgettable image of 'the little Dresden figure' was painstakingly constructed by her, each morning of her life:

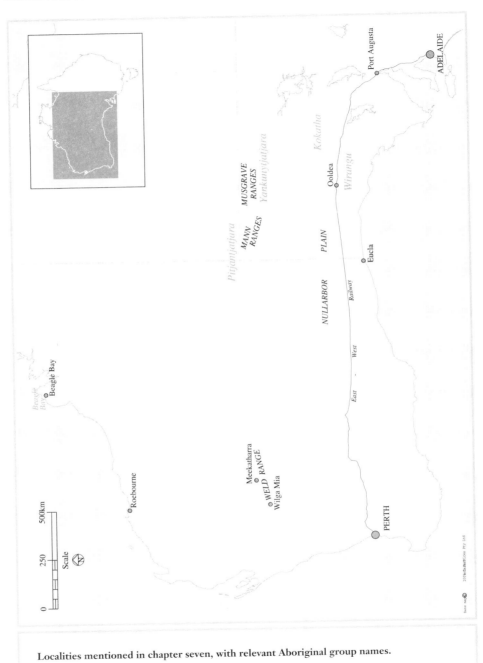

Localities mentioned in chapter seven, with relevant Aboriginal group names.

It was a fastidious toilet, for throughout my life I have adhered to the simple but exact dictates of fashion as I left it, when Victoria was queen – a neat white blouse, stiff collar and ribbon tie, a dark skirt and coat, stout and serviceable, trim shoes and neat black stockings, a sailor hat and a fly-veil, and, for my excursions to the camps, always a dust-coat and a sunshade. Not until I was in meticulous order would I emerge from my tent, dressed for the day.[2]

Daisy Bates among Aboriginal men at Ooldea, South Australia, ca 1922. Photographer: A.G. Bolam. South Australian Museum Archives.

By the time of her arrival at Eucla on the Nullarbor Plain in 1912, Bates knew that the forms of Aboriginal society which most interested her were becoming as anachronistic as her clothing. Her self-conscious adherence to outmoded codes suggests this dogged allegiance to lost causes, but is it sufficient explanation?

Daisy Bates could not have created a persona more dissimilar from the subjects of her study. It was as if, comprehending the depth of the gulf separating cultures, she decided against the fiction of bridging it. During the 1920s missionaries across Aboriginal Australia were attempting that task. Bates was a firm Christian and had spent several months with the Trappist missionaries at Beagle Bay in north-western Australia during 1899–1900.[3] Despite her later antagonism toward the social effects of missions, she had great admiration for certain missionaries. She had even tried to translate the Lord's Prayer into Aboriginal dialects of the desert, but could not succeed beyond '*Mama ngalia*' – 'Our Father'. Her veneration for the Prayer was, she said, 'too great ... to reduce it to pidgin English'.[4] Instead, she undertook a secular task, providing a buffer between the desert people and European society, giving them a grasp of the white man's laws and customs, a few shillings and a change of clothes. To succeed in this she needed to be unambiguously distinct from both Aboriginal and European societies, to float between. Her carefully constructed appearance as a kind of fairy godmother, 'Kabbarli', enabled her to create that persona.

As Bates constructed this role for herself during the 1920s and 1930s, actual relationships between black and white people in the desert settlements of Eucla and Ooldea on the Nullarbor Plain were reaching a balance. Frontier history was unfolding. The European economy snaked out along the East–West railway line after 1917 and soon every Aboriginal community came to understand the value of money and the new price of subsistence. Pragmatism gradually overtook mutual incomprehension and distrust. The primacy of the esoteric and sacred religious rites was becoming displaced by new codes of behaviour and a remorseless, lop-sided economic dependency on Europeans for rations and essential goods. It was a system of values in which European trifles and commodities dominated.

Daisy Bates in Adelaide in 1950, attired in her clothing of 50 years earlier.
People magazine, 19 July 1950.

Across the dunes though, out of sight of the railway line but within earshot of Daisy Bates's tent, old ceremonies were still being performed. Ancient kinship obligations flattened and reshaped the new social distinctions embedded in European transactions. Metal, glass, wool, cloth and hessian became grafted and woven into Aboriginal material culture, secular and sacred. Debris shimmered in the firelight.

Daisy Bates fed this syncretic stream. Her daily work among the Aborigines of Ooldea made that inevitable. Out of those banal transactions and exchanges she sifted and retrieved her version of a traditional past unpolluted by European contact. It was that store of esoteric knowledge and associated objects, maintained by Aboriginal people in the face of traumatic pressures from within and outside their society, which Daisy Bates continued to investigate and mine. Her tent at the desert ceremonial centre of Ooldea became part infirmary, part welfare agency and part museum and office. Her mix of practical philanthropy, solicitude, ritual knowledge and unabashed enquiry helps to explain her hold on the Mirning, Wirangu, Kokatha and Pitjantjatjara people living there during this period. Her confidence was unquestioned. That 'her natives' regarded her in a more complex, problematical light seemed not to occur to her. She wrote this of the groups arriving at Ooldea during the late 1920s, forced from the desert by the great drought:

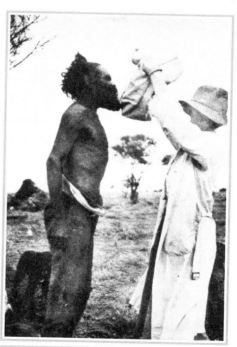

> Each mob was more reckless and difficult to control than the preceding ones. My duty, after the first friendly overtures of tea and damper, was to set them at ease, clothe them, and simply to explain the white man's ways and the white man's laws.[5]

Bates's belief in her ability to define these new realities to Aboriginal groups who had travelled long distances to Ooldea from north and west did not stop there. Despite her antagonism towards missions, she took credit for imposing a moral code to replace their own. This code was expressed most graphically in her

'Clothing a native for his entry into civilization' – this photograph was included in Daisy Bates's *Passing of the Aborigines* (1941).
Photographer: probably A.G. Bolam, 1930, South Australan Museum Archives.

act of 'clothing the natives', and in her own, rigidly maintained wardrobe. As she put it:

> ... I have always shown them by my own example amongst them that there are two kinds of white women and so I must always let them see me as I should like our King and Queen to see me!! The fringes of civilization carry such 'flotsam and jetsam' and it is this that the wild native first sees![6]

Dressing new, naked arrivals in the cast-off clothing sent to her from well-wishers in Adelaide and Perth, Daisy Bates prepared them for their first full confrontation with European culture – the weekly passenger train which stopped at the Ooldea siding:

> Just as I was buttoning the men into their first trousers, a thunder came from the Plain. All rose in terror to watch, wild-eyed, the monster of Nullarbor, the ganba (snake) coming to devour them. I needed all my tact and wisdom to prevent their flight.[7]

This was not an isolated event. Since 1917, when the transcontinental line was completed at Ooldea (near the centre of the world's longest extent of straight railway), successive groups of Aboriginal travellers arriving there were

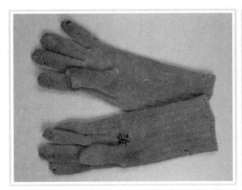

Pair of carefully darned woollen gloves worn by Daisy Bates during her work with the Aboriginal people of Ooldea, preserved among her effects.
South Australian Museum Archives.

Repair kit used by Daisy Bates for maintaining her wardrobe during her time with Aboriginal people on the Nullarbor Plain. South Australian Museum Archives.

similarly affected by the sight of the train. As late as July 1932, Daisy Bates observed that one of these new arrivals, a man named Junburr, 'came into Ooldea Water but fled when he heard & saw the ganba (local term for jeedarra) creeping over the plain & snorting & whistling: – the train'.[8]

With their cargo of curious white people anxious for some exotic contact, these trains became the focal point of Bates's 'mission' – concentrating her hopes and her fears. Without their regular appearance, and the stimulus they provided in the otherwise isolated desert, Bates's constant attention to her own and 'her natives'' appearance might gradually have diminished, relaxed. As it was, the remorseless timetable of the iron *Ganba* thundering and steaming past Ooldea kept her vigilant. Her combative attitude towards the polluting influence of the white railway workers helped her forge critical alliances with Aboriginal elders seeking to maintain their control of the complex social protocols of marriage, kinship and conflict resolution. But as those elders died and the desert camps aligned themselves further towards the dominating economy and the social exchanges of the railway line (the trade with Europeans which it brought, as well as the opportunity it offered for an unprecedented mobility), her authority began to wane.

Daisy Bates's awareness of her anachronistic image as 'Kabbarli' passed beyond self-parody to a kind of defiance. The pathetic remnants of the contents of her last suitcase, preserved at the South Australian Museum, suggest this: a shoe-cleaning kit in a lace bag – Kiwi boot-polish set rock-hard in its tin together with a 'canned heat' apparatus for melting it – a collection of her gloves with intricate darns to the finger-tips, worn away with solicitude, and a roll of starched collars (which she regularly sent away across the Nullarbor to Port Augusta to be renewed). With their darns and discolouration her clothes were beginning to resemble those cast-off garments she dispensed so assiduously to the Aborigines of Ooldea. In fact, her last act at Ooldea was to pass some of her own work clothes to her tribal relatives, a final blurring of the boundary which had set her apart:

My grandsons squatted on the slope above me, and I proceeded to shed my working clothes, pushing the garments piecemeal beneath the closed tent flap for eager black hands to grasp. When I emerged it was to find Yalli-yalla glorious in my white dust-coat and Gindigi resplendent in a mackintosh. Being my oldest grandsons, they had confiscated the most dashing raiment, and proudly they strutted in Kabbarli's magic garb. The others divided the shirts and skirts to give to their women.[9]

'Farewell to my natives' – Daisy Bates bidding adieu to Aboriginal men at Ooldea siding, 1934. South Australian Museum Archives.

The last photograph of Bates at Ooldea, waving to Aboriginal people from the carriage as the train pulled away, is an image of a grandmother departing for home after a visit in the country. But this visit had lasted for half a century, and the life which matched her anachronistic costume no longer existed. Her allegiances lay with an Aboriginal world also slipping from view. In that world, analogy had often been the best form of description. Metaphor replaced observation, and with one notable exception – a misunderstanding over 'cannibalism' – Bates had observed the nice distinction between the actual and the analogical. She insisted that the Aborigines of Ooldea regarded her 'as one of their own kind, reincarnated', but her elevation of cannibalism as a pervasive and entrenched cultural trait ensured that she would preserve the essential distinction between her moral self and the 'savage'.[10]

The references to cannibalism which suffused her journalism and correspondence rested almost entirely upon anecdotes related to her by Aboriginal informants. They must have become familiar with her appetite for such tales. Bates failed to identify or analyse the kernel of truth in these anecdotes – metaphorical references to 'eating one's totem' or the documented practice among desert people of limited infanticide under conditions where a mother could not support an infant born within a year or two of another. Her assiduity in filtering the degrees of difference in kinship systems or material culture deserted her in favour of a bland acceptance of cannibalism based almost entirely upon anecdotes elicited through her own leading questions directed at desert people newly arrived at Ooldea.

Once again, to account for this apparent blind spot in Bates's anthropological practice, we might turn to her role, as she defined it. Her vigilance over the cultural boundary she patrolled matched her solicitude for those crossing it. Bates wrote:

> My first work, when these new natives came to see me, was to obtain their names, waters, relationships, the number & sex of the killed & eaten on their way to and from their far off waters etc, & also to study the character of each man in the new group. In this way I had them well under control, thus giving them as much as I knew they could fully understand of our laws regarding murder either of their own kind or white men, I kept all the groups law abiding.[11]

This peculiar and unwavering certainty, a refusal to regard the frontier as a liminal place, prevented Bates from recognising the distinctions between Aboriginal rhetoric, allusion and actual cultural practice. It is ultimately what gives her insubstantial form a leaden weight.

Daisy Bates was not a tolerant person. She wore her intransigence as an emblem and carried it with her to the streets of Adelaide where, frail as tin foil in her eighties, she was pointed out to small children by mothers who might have read her confident journalistic accounts of *Ganba* the Rainbow Serpent, of desert ceremonies or of networks of soaks, ancient tracks and the trade routes arcing through Ooldea. Bates's unwavering commitment to an Aboriginal past meant that she had little interest in untangling the influences reshaping contemporary Aboriginal society. Instead, like some other anthropologists of the time, notably T.G.H. Strehlow, she subscribed to notions of finality and closure. In the process her own data became similarly imbued with the value of a crucial and unique record. Like Strehlow, she witnessed Aboriginal ceremonies weaving the past into the present. She had similar opportunities to obtain syncretic objects evoking the transformation of tradition. But to recognise the worth of these cultural expressions, to collect and therefore validate them, might have entailed a further admission of her own marginality. Bates believed herself to be crucially sited, holding a mirror between the ancient and the modern, between authentic and debased culture. If she lost that confidence, Bates might then have been obliged to turn the mirror on herself, and to regard her own threadbare state.

BATES THE COLLECTOR

Most Europeans placing themselves at or beyond the frontier of contact during the nineteenth and early twentieth centuries did so for economic reasons or to administer the communities established through these initiatives. But missionaries, anthropologists and more rarely, writers and journalists, were drawn to that extremity by Aborigines themselves. Daisy Bates combined attributes of each of these professions and achieved maverick status as a result. Her investigations among Aborigines began in earnest during her 1900 reconnoitring tour of north-western Australia, in search of a suitable property for her second husband, Jack Bates. She had wed Bates bigamously following her first marriage to Breaker Morant, some fourteen years earlier, during her first Australian sojourn. It was during that period, as a young woman in her late twenties, that she experienced her first Aboriginal encounter. It occurred most dramatically, as an apparition prefiguring her own apocryphal vision of a dying race:

> In the eighties, travelling through the various States, I do not remember seeing one blackfellow, or even thinking there were any in Australia, but once, when we were riding to a station 30 miles or so from Crookwell, N.S.W., a thunderstorm suddenly broke on the slope before us, and the lightning struck a large dead tree trunk. The tree trunk seemed to divide in half, and there appeared for an instant the upright skeleton of a man with a spear and another weapon that

I now know to have been the spearthrower. Even while we gazed, thunderstruck, indeed, the skeleton tumbled into a heap. The bones and weapons were later collected by the Branson family, but no history of the skeleton could be obtained. Even in the eighties the blacks of this region had disappeared.[12]

Before her 1900 trip in north-western Australia, Bates received anthropological guidance from a colleague of Bishop Gibney (one of the founders of the Beagle Bay Trappist Mission) and from the Western Australian Premier and explorer, Sir John Forrest.[13] By the time she met Bates in Cossack and reached nearby Roebourne she had begun the anthropological record which was to occupy her life for the next half-century. Accompanying this data collection was an incidental interest in objects. She wrote:

> The natives of Roebourne number about 200 ... some of them fine looking men; the women are very inferior looking. They make several articles from spinifex grass which grows so abundantly about here. Netted bags ... which they manipulate with a small kangaroo bone, beads, rope and a splendid glue, which they use to fasten their glass spear heads on the end of their wooden spears.[14]

Unaligned with any institution or academy, Bates remained an anthropological outsider throughout her life. This status was not assisted by her gender, her eventual inability to produce a monograph, or her eclectic approach to her subject. Her newspaper and journal articles covered topics as diverse as kinship, infanticide, trade, material culture, ceremony and mythology as well as natural history. In this respect her reputation invites comparison with the Queensland anthropologist Ursula McConnel, who undertook fieldwork on Cape York Peninsula during the 1920s and 1930s. Unlike McConnel, whose surviving ethnographic collection totals more than 500 artefacts, Bates was not, according to one of her biographers, Ernestine Hill, 'a curio collector'. Hill wrote:

> Their sacred tribal objects – churinga, wanningi, totem boards, initiation knives, rain and fertility stones, phallic symbols and man-making regalia, ceremonial spears, stone tools, letter-sticks, music-sticks, utensils and charms, in her time authentic and of unique interest, she never claimed.[15]

But Hill's assertion is difficult to reconcile with her own text, in which she described the contents of three tin trunks kept by Bates in her Ooldea tent. The third trunk, containing death bones, medicine stones, quartz knives, carved snakes and kurdaitcha shoes, was 'her chamber of horrors'.[16] From a comparison with Bates's artefacts later acquired by the South Australian Museum and through other collectors, it seems that this particular assemblage, with a few additions and supplemented by the sacred objects discussed below, represented a large part of her complete ethnographic collection.

Bates's 1903–1904 commission for the *Western Mail* to report on the mines of the Weld Range, Murchison River, Meekatharra and Nannine districts presented an opportunity to investigate Aboriginal life from an anthropological point of view. This fieldwork also yielded a small ethnographic collection. It included an adze, fire-making sticks, ochres from the famed Wilga Mia mines, a wooden container, a boomerang, a spearthrower and a shield, a bone awl, 'string made from sheeps wool found on bushes', a bull-roarer and a pointing stick. Bates presented this small collection to a friend, Dr Lillian Cooper, who subsequently passed it to the South Australian Museum in 1909, on condition that Bates not be revealed as the source. During 1914 Bates had sent items from the same localities directly to the Museum. During the 1920s she sent many artefacts to the editor of the *Australasian* newspaper, for which she wrote.[17] Other artefacts collected by Bates were passed in turn to a range of collectors, including medical anthropologists R.H. Pulleine and J.B. Cleland. Her direct relationship with Adelaide scientists may be traced back at least as far as 1905, when she sent Aboriginal hair samples to Cleland (then Government Pathologist in Perth) for analysis: 'his report the hair was elliptical meant that the western Aborigines, like the Europeans, were Caucasian and not negroid, by origin'.[18] Bates also corresponded with Edward Stirling, Herbert Hale and Norman Tindale at the South Australian Museum, sending collection items to each. Writing to Edward Stirling in January 1919, Bates offered her own frank view on collecting Aboriginal ethnographica:

> The only way to make a thorough collection in the areas north of the line is to follow the precedent of Dr Clements [British collector, Emile Clement] in the Roebourne area and Dr Mjoberg [Swedish ethnographer] in the Kimberleys. When I met Dr Clements in Roebourne in 1900–1 he had even then the most comprehensive collection of native articles, which I was told he disposed of for £1,600. The members of Dr Mjoberg's party whom I met told me that their systematic research with this object only in view gave them such substantial results that the disposal of their surplus supply covered their expenses.
>
> I have never done any systematic collecting principally because I rather

desired to give my means to the natives than to make any money out of them. Just a personal 'fad'. This has been with me throughout my work.[19]

From the outset, Bates's scientific interest in Aborigines was combined with her solicitude for their welfare. That sentiment was sharpened by her 1900 journey with Bishop Gibney to the Beagle Bay mission north of Broome and her subsequent report on its activities. Bates spent later decades applying the welfare principles characteristically practised on missions, wrote some 270 newspaper articles concerning Aborigines, and gathered volumes of anthropological data, intended for her magnum opus. This was eventually published long after her death, as *The Native Tribes of Western Australia* (Bates 1985). Her observations on Aboriginal artefacts formed a distinct section of this manuscript, dealing with 'weapons, arts and crafts'.[20] From her official appointment by the Western Australian government during 1904 as compiler of 'a native vocabulary', and through her participation in the Cambridge Research Expedition led by A.R. Radcliffe Brown during 1910–1911, Bates adopted a participant-observation technique which was years ahead of its time. She followed advice from Australian ethnologist R.H. Mathews and British anthropologist Andrew Lang to concentrate upon facts rather than theory, and acted on the latter's exhortation to 'get out among the blacks herself'.[21]

The inclusion of ceremonial men's objects among Bates's early collection from north-western Australia signalled a trend that was to continue during her later work on the Nullarbor Plain. Bates's capacity to deal with the sacred aspects of Aboriginal men's tradition hinged upon her acceptance as, in Ernestine Hill's words, 'the sexless stranger at these secret phallic rites'.[22] At the end of the 1930s, aware that her status as a white woman among initiated men required clarification, Bates proposed that 'right through my 35 years of journeying, and including the twenty years in Central Australia, I was believed to be not so much a woman as an age-old spirit of Yamminga, the dreamtime, and keeper of all the totems'.[23] Writing of her presence at a Western Desert ceremony involving sacred objects sent to the South Australian Museum, she observed:

When I go to these night dances I go as Kabbarli ('spirit' 'magic' grandmother) so that I shall still, in the natives' minds, keep my apartness from them, and I find that they all felt this apartness.[24]

Bates attributed her ceremonial status to two pivotal events at the end of her intensive period of field investigations with Western Desert Aborigines in the

Meekatharra region. Here she had pioneered the method of obtaining Aboriginal renderings of their sites and country by supplying them with brown paper and pencils, allowing them to map 'an early history of their home waters and wanderings'.[25] This level of engagement signalled a commitment to Aboriginal beliefs and cosmology – undoubtedly a factor in the Aborigines' subsequent decisions to transfer sacred objects to her. One object in particular was cited by Bates as 'the magic *bamburu* which has been my passport among all the central circumcised tribes throughout the years'.[26] The second incident involved her induction by a man of the red ochre totem into the 'mysteries' of Wilga Mia in the Weld Range, the principal ochre mine in Western Australia. Wearing a 'cream holland coat and skirt', Bates became, like her companion, progressively coated in red ochre, a potent symbol of rebirth and initiation:

> I came out a Woman in Red. There was not an inch of me that had not been ochred all over, even my face and hands were smeared with the greasy stuff.[27]

The decision of Aboriginal elders to extend initiated status to Bates during ceremonies held at Eucla during 1913 may be traced partly to her willingness to stand so close to their cultural life, on Aboriginal terms. In this way she became the recipient of objects which would otherwise have been destroyed at the conclusion of those ceremonies. It may also be that in supplying flour, tea and sugar to sustain the performers she was paying for the privilege of receiving knowledge and objects, just as Francis Gillen had done at Alice Springs during the 1890s. Certainly she had become accustomed to the idea that 'to accept the gift of information in the way of vocabularies and legends, she must reward the donor, perhaps with a tin of fruit, perhaps with a new shirt'.[28] According to her own account, Bates always paid for objects or information with rations rather than money. Whatever the reason, sacred objects , such as engraved wooden boards, gradually accumulated in her possession at the various camps maintained during her Nullarbor sojourns, together with the responsibility 'to grease and freshen these boards occasionally, and to hide the place of their storage from white men'.[29]

Bates showed no great enthusiasm for collecting secular objects, partly because she was unwilling to sell them on to collectors or museums. In a 1932 letter to Herbert Hale, the South Australian Museum director, she stated that she 'had never before disposed of native objects for remuneration of any kind'.[30] Knowing this from the early 1920s, museum staff had supplied her with clothing and rations to facilitate exchanges, and a small collection of sacred

Daisy Bates and a group of women and childern who had recently arrived at Ooldea from the north, early 1920s. They are wearing clothing supplied by her. Photographer: A.G. Bolam. South Australian Museum Archives.

and secular objects gradually passed to Adelaide as a result. During the last two years of her Ooldea sojourn Bates devoted considerable effort to gathering and documenting sacred and secular objects for Hale and his colleague Norman Tindale, on the same terms. The documentation of the sacred boards made for her by Western Desert men was notable for its detail, later transcribed by Tindale into the museum registers.

In 1932, realising that her time at Ooldea was drawing to a close and that she should find a more secure home for the sacred objects which had been passed to her, Bates finally broke her own rule against selling to museums. She would, she wrote, 'prefer Adelaide to purchase and possess all these special things'.[31] In her efforts to explain the weight of this decision, she gave one of the few extant accounts of the transfer of sacred boards or *larra*, notable for its careful description. The making of these boards, wrote Bates, 'takes some time':

> The wood must be picked from root or stem, then chipped and chipped to the desired thinness. Then rounded and pointed and trimmed along the sides (the point is the face and the broad end the head of the totem) and the grooving of the totem symbol (or symbols) will be done by two or three whose totems are associated with each other. There is always a little ceremony connected with the presentation. They bring the larra [sacred board], get some green small branches usually of mallee if it is near, and place the larra face downward (grooving downward) on its green bed. Then more green branches are placed

on top, each man holds a green branch in his hand. Then one comes and with a sort of 'st' (hist) draws my attention, and when I go out, he rubs his nose with one or two fingers. I follow him to the place where the larra is lying, picking a green branch off a tree as I go. The others are sitting down round the larra, I go to it and squat down ... 'flicking' my branch along it for a little. At this they 'shiver' a little because the spirit of the totem symbols is either going into my heart with the other totem spirits, or is going out of my heart into the larra as mine. I presently catch hold of it and turn it over. Then we talk of the totem groovings and each man shows me his work on it and names the symbols. There is always this little ceremony, and when they come with these things, when I hear the 'st', whatever work I am doing, I drop and go at once to them. These little observances mean a great deal to these poor fellows. There must be no hurry or the spirit of the totem within the larra might be angry (bee'-gain'yi angry). I carry it gently in my boughshed, and give them the promised payment, no matter how many may come and all go away quite satisfied.[32]

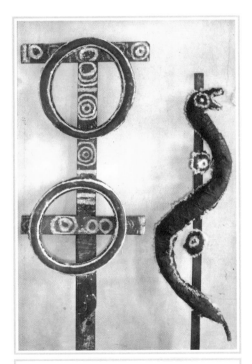

The male and female Snake effigies presented to Daisy Bates at Ooldea, 1930. Photographed on arrival in Adelaide, 1931. A17228, A17229, South Australan Museum.

Bates had also made significant acquisitions during 1930, when a group of 26 Anangu men, women and children arrived at Ooldea siding. They had walked 600 kilometres south across the Nullarbor Plain to escape drought conditions in the Mann and Musgrave Ranges. Bates sent a collection of artefacts obtained from this group, including kurdaitcha shoes, spear-throwers, fur and hair-string decorations and wooden dishes, to Herbert Hale. Two years later she sent a *waninga* or hair-string cross made by Guinmarda, one of the Pitjantjatjara men, for which she had given 'shirt and trousers and blanket and a dress for his woman ... although I supplied the hair (for string) and for one (or two) of the *larra*.[33]

Members of the Mann Ranges group were also responsible for making two remarkable sacred objects, male and female representations of the ancestral Ganba or Jeedarra Snake, fashioned with a mixture of traditional and European materials. The male Snake, 'of most wonderful interest', was brought to Daisy Bates during January 1932. It was, she wrote,

> the totem representation of the Jeedarra ceremony (Jeedarra is the great magic snake of C.A. & the Kimberley term for the same magic snake is 'tchooroo' ...). The object is a long pole about 10 feet ... on this pole was the jeedarra made of canvas, grass (covered with ochre, birds down etc.[34]

Bates was no longer strong enough to walk from her camp to Ooldea Water to attend the ceremony in which the male Ganba or Jeedarra was used. Instead, the performers carried it four kilometres to her camp and re-enacted the latter part of the ceremony for her benefit. She wrote:

> they also performed the final stage of the ceremony by slowly erecting the object, setting it in a hole in the sand and then bowing or standing most reverently

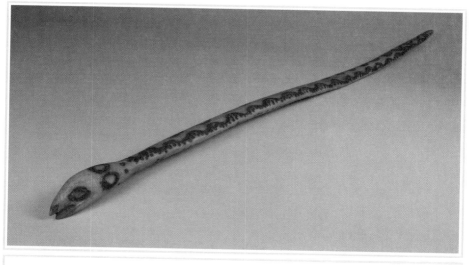

The 'ganba' Snake, carved by Mujamujana, one of the 1930s arrivals, and decorated by women with hot wire for the railway tourist trade. A17131, South Australian Museum.

before the erect image. At once Moses lifting up the serpent in the wilderness came to my mind and just the same way Kimberley men erected their tchooroo on a carved pole and stood in reverence around it. As Mr Tindale will know the magic snake was known and feared in every group in Australia.[35]

Bates's excitement at receiving this object had less to do with its hybrid form and construction than with its role as evidence for one of her own theories relating to the origin and dissemination of Aboriginal traditions. 'The significance of this object is great', she wrote, 'because, taken with other customs etc – names of 'larra' etc, it confirms my statement that the circumcised hordes landed in the Kimberley area & travelled S.E.E. & S.E. & Central South in the ages of their existence here'.[36]

Five months later, Bates was invited to witness the female version of the Jeedarra ceremony. Men and women participated in this ceremony and presented her with the female Snake effigy at its close. This was composed of two halves of an old Dunlop motor tyre, nailed one above the other onto a wooden plank which was embellished with concentric circles, and decorated with bird down and ochre. In its circularity the dominant motif, a disconnected figure-eight, suggests the endless winding of the giant ancestral Snake. Thirty years earlier Bates had witnessed a similar Snake ceremony in the Kimberley. In her mind this had been elegant in comparison, constrained by rigorous ancient protocols and uncontaminated by hybrid influences. But now, writing to Herbert Hale at the South Australian Museum in early June 1932, she found it difficult to contain her feelings:

> I find the jeedarra inma as presented here is altogether phallic, & I have the female 'inma' – made of a split motor wheel [tyre], fastened to a long flat planed board, part of a hut I think. What I thought were the 'eggs' of the jeedarra (serpent) are the women's wombs – all concentric rings are women's wombs. I went to see the dance by request. It is a travesty of the old Kimberley tchooroo (snake) dance. It is altogether libidinous.[37]

Bates downplayed the syncretic, hybrid nature of these objects. She probably understood that without a strong ceremonial association of the kind she documented for the museum, such objects would be regarded, museologically, as degenerate. Even if she considered it apt that a motor-car tyre, with its sinuous tracks, ability to cross deserts and an endless circularity, had been incorporated into a representation of the sacred Water Snake of the desert, she

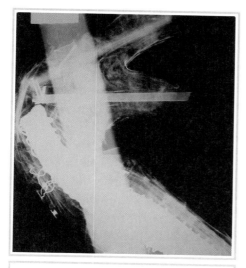

X-ray image of the male snake, showing the wooden 'jaw' held in place with nails, and the snake's spine, consisting of a flexible rubber hose, reinforced with metal casing. Artlab Australia.

kept this insight to herself. What is most remarkable about these two shabby objects is their evocation of the zone of encounter shared by Bates and 'her natives'.

Fashioned from cast-offs like the very rags Bates dispensed to her natives, these effigies embodied the Ganba, the sacred Snakes of the sandy deserts beyond Ooldea. In former times Ganba effigies had been made of desert grass tightly bound with human hair-string, decorated with bird down, ochres and blood. Following their deployment in traditional ceremonies these were normally abandoned in the desert, left to moulder to nothing. Now, doubly cast-off perhaps, they were passed to Daisy Bates herself.

Acquiring her own objects with such nostalgic care, Bates was understandably dismissive of the transactions undertaken by Aborigines with 'the new and rather vulgar travelling public' at the Ooldea siding. She played a slight role in the emergence of an Aboriginal souvenir trade along the East–West line, but saw this as one more indication of the railway's pernicious influence. This artefact production was encouraged more actively by her successor at Ooldea, missionary Annie Lock. Even so, Bates documented some crucial developments in this field. She noted, for example, that one of the 1930 arrivals, a left-handed man named Moondoor, had carved a wooden model of a *milbarli* or 'long-tailed iguana', an example of 'new art' learnt by the group from examples made by the Aborigines of Fowlers Bay nearby for sale to tourists. Bates was also the first to observe the emergence of women's creativity in this field, noting how they began to burn poker-work designs onto these carvings with hot wire. Women added the burnt designs to the *ganba* snake illustrated here, carved by another of the 1930 men, Mujamujana. She recognised that Aborigines obtained a limited amount of economic autonomy through these transactions, but her attitude to the effect of the railway remained uncompromising:

Biscuits and cake were thrown to them from the train windows, while their boomerangs and native weapons, and their importance in the landscape as subjects for photography, brought many a shilling and sixpence for them to spend, which they promptly did, without any knowledge of its value, and sometimes were wickedly imposed upon. The train was their undoing.[38]

In 1931 Bates observed that those men who had arrived at Ooldea a year earlier from the north were making short journeys to collect wood 'for <u>very poor</u> boomerangs & other objects which the ordinary train passengers buy'. Bates was apparently unaware that Aborigines of the Mann Ranges did not make boomerangs traditionally, and that she was witnessing a considerable adjustment to an altered cultural reality. She did note though, that 'the "bacca" & tinned foods & other luxuries bought with these monies from the fettlers' wives, with the rabbits that swarm round the siding & camp & are caught by women or dogs – suffice for them'.[39]

Bates had begun her encounters among Aborigines as a journalist, a passing stranger. Her point of view in those early days was similar to that of other frontier adventurers and travellers who exchanged money or commodities for artefacts with Aborigines. For many of those travellers, the objects collected in those brief encounters symbolised the imagined reality of Aboriginal life behind the exchange. By the time Bates left Ooldea as an elderly woman, casual exchanges of artefacts served more than ever to mark the ground between tourists and Aborigines. These collections compensated the railway passengers for their lack of dialogue with Aborigines themselves. That much is clear from the journalist A.G. Bolam's 1927 advice to travellers passing through Ooldea:

> When you are buying a boomerang from a black at Ooldea, remember that you are not necessarily getting a man-killing instrument, but rather a 'black-fellow's plaything'. You will, however, be buying a genuine boomerang, made by the blacks with infinite labour, and well worth the 'bob' or two that the native asks for it. Treat these blacks then, a little generously, and their happy smiles will be something given in with the unique boomerang, which you should be proud to possess.[40]

Newly made, unthrown boomerangs became souvenirs of unshared, fictional experiences. Bates's self-conscious disavowal of collecting may have been partly rooted in her awareness of the role spurious artefacts played on the East–West railway frontier. Part of it may have rested in her discomfort at the symmetry of her own exchanges, of worn-out European commodities for supplanted artefacts.

As with T.G.H. Strehlow in Central Australia or the policeman-ethnographer George Aiston of the Birdsville Track, an element of Bates's solicitude for her natives lay in the fact that as each year passed she lost more of her old Aboriginal friends and confidants. This steady toll and her own age, as much as the obvious changes being wrought throughout the outback landscape by mechanisation and European expansion, helps account for her concern. Bates knew that the same Aboriginal men who solemnly passed sacred objects to her were also 'jumping the rattler' to visit stations along the East–West line where ceremonial life was being actively pursued. Her role was not to engage in or document such activity but to preserve the objects and lore entrusted to her. This task had become increasingly hazardous during the late 1920s and 1930s, when even the railway staff ('those spoon-fed railway men') posed a threat to Bates's carefully guarded cache and her discreet efforts to forward objects to the museum. Later, when she came to leave Ooldea at last, she wrote that until the date of her departure, she had 'managed for sixteen years to secrete from keen native eyes the totem boards of [her] own initiation and the sacred *eenma* of the dead groups that [she] had been entrusted to keep "alive"'.[41]

Bates's opposition to the railway and its culture masked her utter dependence upon it. Each week it brought the news of the outside world she craved. Often those newspapers contained her own journalism – a kind of affirmation that despite her desert exile she maintained a relevant presence in metropolitan Australia. The parcels of used clothing and blankets freighted to her became the medium of exchange with her Aboriginal informants and dependants. Her own carefully wrapped parcels of artefacts and letters sent back along the railway to Cleland or Hale became the currency with the academic world which she still dreamed of influencing through her publications.

Among the last consignments which Daisy Bates sent from Ooldea were those male and female snakes, unwieldy objects weighing more than a slight woman in her seventies could easily manage. Perhaps the impulse to parcel up these shabby, cruciform relics was driven by the simple need to clear her tent of their bulk, just as she rid herself of her old dustcoat. Perhaps their syncretic qualities, as flimsy objects constructed of European detritus but speaking of a deep Aboriginal past, reminded her too much of her own incongruity.

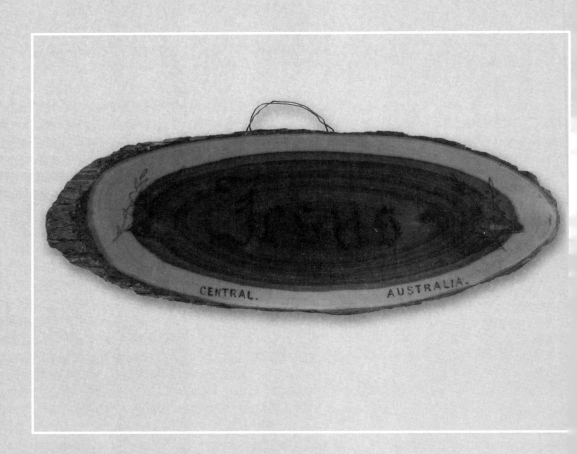

Engraved mulga plaque made by Albert Namatjira, early 1930s.
A72418, South Australian Museum.

CHAPTER EIGHT

Namatjira and the Jesus plaque

Almost half a century after his death, Albert Namatjira (1902–1959) remains the best-known Aboriginal artist. Although few Australians know the tragic details of his life, and his paintings no longer hang as reproductions in Australian living rooms as they did during the 1950s and 1960s, his work still provides the most identifiable, reassuring representation of the Central Australian landscape. Reassuring, because now that landscape is problematic, politically uncertain, no longer a pristine territory. Bus tours still drive west from Alice Springs to visit Palm Valley and Namatjira's birthplace and home at the historic Lutheran mission of Hermannsburg, but the 'natives' are no longer on display, as they were in Namatjira's time. The Western Desert painting movement which arose during the 1970s and 1980s has made it clear that the landscape's full meaning is not available for casual viewing.[1]

Namatjira's art once seemed as apolitical as a summer's day in the

Albert Namatjira painting in the MacDonnell Ranges during the mid-1950s.
Photograph: *Herald Sun* newspapers.

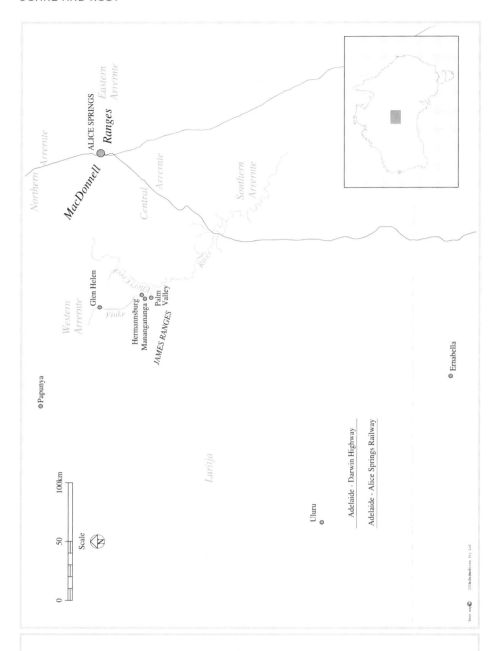

Localities mentioned in chapter eight, with relevant Aboriginal group names.

'Amulda, James Range', painted by Albert Namatjira in 1941, and acquired by the
South Australian Museum in that year. A41747, South Australian Museum.

James Range. Today his red rock outcrops, grey-blue mountains and mottled
white gums remain beguilingly true to life, but now we recognise that his actions
as an Arrernte artist had a deeper resonance. By mastering the art of landscape
painting Namatjira was the first Arrernte man to take an element of European
culture and, in a subversive sense, make it his own. Against this single appropriation stands a litany of examples in which the cultural productions of
Aboriginal people, as well as the natural history of Central Australia, have been
collected and classified.

Namatjira began to paint in watercolour in 1936 under the tutelage of the
Melbourne artist Rex Battarbee at Hermannsburg. There was a remarkable
prologue to that assertive act. Four years earlier, Namatjira began producing
a series of mulga-wood plaques bearing images of animals, bush scenes and
biblical phrases, seared onto the burnished surfaces with hot wire. Even more
than his watercolour paintings of sacred landscapes, these tourist plaques belie
their ordinary appearance. They speak of an inventive, resourceful adjustment

Undated watercolour painting attributed to Richard Moketarinja, a pupil of Namatjira. Sacred objects hover above a Centralian landscape. This image is a reminder of the thin veil separating Arrernte landscape painting from the art of their ancestors. Moketarinja died in 1983, and if this was one of his late works, it reveals the influence of the rising Western Desert painting movement in its depiction of sacred motifs. A65295, South Australian Museum.

to the colonial frontier, suggesting that if most of its forms were supplanting and oppressive, an innovative response was also possible.

Pyrography was not unknown in the traditional arts of Central Australia. It was expressed particularly with men's hairpins and nosepegs, on which dots and spirals were branded with tiny live coals. A transition to hot metal 'poker-work' occurred during the early twentieth century, with ready access to metal wire and a growing European demand for tourist artefacts. With almost exclusive control of stone tool technology, Aboriginal men had previously been responsible for carving and embellishing wooden artefacts. To an extent unprecedented in traditional artefact manufacture, Aboriginal women now played an increasingly prominent role in making these new objects, as the use and distribution of metal tools were not subject to traditional regulation.[2] Nor, apparently, were the forms and shapes metal tools could produce: figurative designs of animals began to proliferate, where traditional art had involved only representations of their tracks or other cryptic references.

Poker-work carving emerged at two key portals to the Western Desert – Ooldea on the East–West railway line, and along the Stuart Highway in the vicinity of Alice Springs. The production of carved wooden animals and modified artefacts with poker-work designs became a new staple for those Aboriginal people attempting to gain a foothold in the European economy. The growth of these crafts during the 1930s and 1940s paralleled the first attempts of Arnhem Land missions to promote the commercial production of bark paintings and carved figurines. For the missionaries this artwork constituted 'useful toil'. For their Aboriginal makers who even under transformed conditions of mission life bore continued responsibility to depict and honour creation ancestors and their sites, these images and figures also carried essential religious significance.

Namatjira's plaques seem far removed from such affirmations of traditional continuity. Their subject matter is prosaic and self-evident – plants, animals, bush scenes, Christian imagery and texts. They suggest triviality, light gestures which might erase a depth of ancient symbolism as easily as tourist art seems to degrade its origins. If it were not for the fact that the plaques were made by an artist later renowned for his masterly command of light, shade and colour, they might not detain us. It is because they are Namatjira's that they illuminate the blurred boundaries between art and craft, the sublime and the kitsch.

One plaque in particular, bearing the gothic-lettered 'Jesus', seared onto its burnished mulga surface, evokes a further, even hazier distinction, between the secular and the sacred. It is this aspect of the plaques, their uneasy positioning at the conjunction of Arrernte religious life and Lutheran evangelism, and their suggestion of the way art, kitsch and the frontier have overlapped, which infuses them with a talismanic quality.

Namatjira's mulga plaques are often overlooked in accounts of his rise to fame. Their bland appearance and unaffected imagery partly accounts for this, together with the fact that the artist soon relinquished poker-work for a subtle palette of watercolour. Placed alongside his rich evocations of the Central Australian landscape, with their depth of perspective and their precise and delicate shades of colour which he was the first to define, the plaques seem justly forgotten. Rarely objects of attention in their own right, these unassuming objects have rarely been represented in museum collections. Yet, as Namatjira began to colonise the space between Arrernte and European cultures, these objects played a crucial role in his creative development.[3]

APPARITIONS IN A HOLY LAND

The Hermannsburg missionary F.W. Albrecht documented the early phase of Namatjira's artistic development in the context of his efforts to create viable mission industries and crafts. Albrecht confirmed the link between the mulga plaques and the homily-plaques of his own German homeland:

> In Germany, some mission auxiliary of which we had been members, presented us with a plaque cut from a birch tree on which a Scripture text had been etched with poker-work. It looked attractive, and was being sold in quite large quantities in practically every Christian bookshop. There were no birch trees in Hermannsburg, but we had mulga trees, and when we explained the matter to our people, some of them thought they would give it a try ... only one persevered and continued for more than a year: Albert Namatjira. Before long, he produced some beautiful work; examples of such plaques can still be found in various Lutheran homes in Australia ... This period of working with mulga was a definite stepping-stone to his phenomenal success as an artist.[4]

On Hermannsburg mission during the early 1930s the space between Arrernte and European societies was only partly secular. Of the 50 or so mulga plaques which Namatjira produced, most bore secular images, but a significant minority were engraved with psalm verses or Christian symbols. As Albrecht inferred, it was the European religious plaque, carrying sacred texts or revelatory scenes, which provided the original inspiration, the template for Namatjira's innovation. But it is not only the inscriptions carried by their plaques, but something about their form, which made them an enduring medium for Namatjira's transmission of cultural and religious messages.

As Albrecht made plain, the mulga plaques have their analogy in European folk culture. Often no more than thin slices of wood, revealing the heart of a tree and the span of its life, their inscribed psalms and homilies reminded their owners of evident, reassuring truths. They hung in poorly lit corners or, in poorer homes, over a kitchen mantlepiece. Their other role has been commemorative, serving as souvenirs or marking particular events. In the era of mass tourism this association has enabled the form to regenerate and thrive.

During 2001 I found such a plaque in a Brussels flea-market. Its face combines two images: a tinted photograph of a street scene in the southern Belgian town of Beauraing, and a painting of the holy apparition which brought that town to the attention of Europe in 1932 (the year in which Namatjira began making his plaques). Like one of Namatjira's own ghost gums, a white-barked

Painted wooden plaque depicting the 1932 apparition of the Virgin Mary at Beauraing, Belgium. Photographer: P. Jones.

birch tree divides the secular street scene from the sacred event – the Virgin Mary's appearance before three small children. The apparent repetition of this apparition subsequently attracted thousands of pious sightseers to the town.[5]

The Beauraing plaque reminds us that an apparently banal form can carry powerful associations. It also indicates deeper cultural and historical origins for this overlooked element of Aboriginal tourist art. When Namatjira first experimented with the mulga plaques he was a committed and practising Christian. During 1931 he had travelled 'out west' as one of the native evangelists accompanying an itinerant missionary, Ernest Kramer. The leading native evangelist on this trip was Albert's uncle, Titus. Albrecht later recalled the episode:

> It may not be generally known that Albert, prior to starting his career as an artist, had offered to go out as an Evangelist to the tribes living West of Hermannsburg. Since it was impossible under prevailing conditions to support him out there he was even prepared to live off bushfood like any of the other tribesmen. After he had lost a considerable amount in weight, he returned admitting he could not do it, as he had been brought up on white man's food. But it clearly shows what made his concentration possible: that consecrated mind.[6]

Ernest Kramer's own photographs of his late 1920s and 1930s evangelical expeditions to remote country west and north of Hermannsburg, which

Namatjira briefly accompanied, show formal gatherings of seated men facing the camera. In one photograph of Warlpiri people near Central Mount Stuart in 1927, an old man displays his oval shield bearing a painted image of a lizard, as though marking his totemic identity and that of his group for Kramer's benefit.

Kramer understood that his challenge was to supplant these heathen images with his own Christian imagery, packed in his camel boxes. In another photograph

Group of Warlpiri men and boys at Central Mount Stuart, 1927.
Photographer: Ernest Kramer. South Australian Museum Archives.

A native evangelist among a desert group, north of Hermannsburg, ca 1930.
Photographer: Ernest Kramer. South Australian Museum Archives.

Kramer's own native evangelist sits next to the senior men, holding an illustrated biblical poster depicting the Holy Land. The poster depicts Jesus in beard and flowing robes in Palestine's desert landscape. The shades of purple, light blue and orange are not dissimilar to those Namatjira later selected for his own landscape paintings. In front of the group rests a gramophone, an accordion and a bible.

Albrecht considered Namatjira to be a pious man who had accepted the substitution of Christian imagery and belief for the Dreaming. The 'Jesus' plaque seems to confirm that transition. But Albrecht must also have been aware that, in its shape and dimensions, the mulga plaque resembled the very object which Albrecht's evangelism was intended to supplant – the Arrernte *tjurunga*, the most sacred object in Central Australian religious life. Is it a coincidence that in their size and proportion the birchwood plaques of European folk culture, introduced to Hermannsburg by Albrecht, most closely resemble the tjurunga, stone and wooden tablets graven with totemic designs of creation ancestors, ritual objects which in Aboriginal tradition were handled and regarded only with the utmost reverence?

In considering that Namatjira did not have the 'stomach' for evangelism, Albrecht might not have

JOHN TELLS THE PEOPLE TO GET READY FOR JESUS

Mark 1:1-11

MEMORY VERSE—
"Be thou faithful."

Evangelical poster used by Hermannsburg missionaries, 1930s. Burns-Albrecht Collection, South Australian Museum Archives.

appreciated the challenge it offered to an individual already testing the limits of his culture. With their tjurunga-like form and Christian messages, his mulga plaques suggest that until he mastered the innocuous art of watercolour painting, Namatjira was using this form of tourist art to accommodate the incongruities facing his 'consecrated mind'. Perhaps the plaques offer a glimpse of the tension later resolved in his landscape masterpieces.

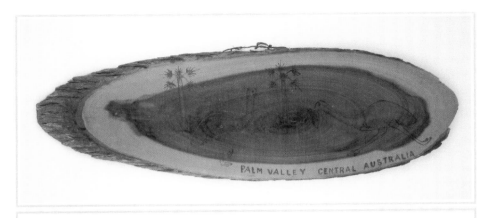

Mulga plaque depicting two emus and palms at Palm Valley, near Hermannsburg, ca 1932. A68997, South Australian Museum.

A dozen or so of Namatjira's mulga plaques of the 1930s have now come to light. Of these, several reinforce the correspondence between the European folk icon and Arrernte tjurunga. One is a souvenir of Palm Valley, close to Hermannsburg. By the late 1930s improved accessibility and the vogue for photography had combined to make this valley, with its ancient vegetation and spectacular rock walls, one of the first 'Centralian' tourist destinations. The plaque is decorated with poker-work designs of palm trees, set off against the inscription, 'Palm Valley, C.A.'[7] Namatjira placed the tallest palm trunk at the

'Other refuge have I none'. Mulga plaque made by Albert Namatjira, ca 1930–1934. Flinders University Art Museum.

centre of the concentric rings which occur naturally in the mulga wood. This alignment was unlikely to have been coincidental; a feathered and bedecked ceremonial wooden pole rising from concentric painted rings is a characteristic element of traditional Arrernte ceremony. Namatjira later used a similar design on two of his exhibition catalogue covers.[8] The face of another plaque, in which a Christian crucifix rises from the centre of concentric rings, strengthens the impression that, for Namatjira at least, these had become charged surfaces.[9]

The correlation becomes explicit on a fourth plaque, which not only resembles a tjurunga in shape and form, but has an actual tjurunga design burnt onto the face. The accompanying documentation identifies the design as a 'sacred honeybee totem'.[10] This was not a totem associated with Namatjira. It is the first indication that the eclectic choice of landscape subject characterising his later career may have been prefigured in this early phase of his work, when he seemed unrestrained in his choice of sacred designs.[11] In choosing the Honey Dreaming as a design for this plaque Namatjira may have been inspired by designs on actual tjurunga. By the early 1930s Albrecht was embarked whole-heartedly on desanctification of these objects, and had begun to acquire them in some quantity.

A cross-section of mulga wood, resembling at once a sacred tjurunga, a Christian homily plaque, and a tourist souvenir might carry all three associations. From the 1930s to his death in 1959 Namatjira carried the weight of these three influences – his sacral heritage, Christian dogma and a corrosive secularism. Each was graphically expressed in his plaques, but when Namatjira stands before us in early 1930s photographs holding mulga-wood blanks or the finished product, we have little certainty of whether he considered these to be icons laden with cultural meaning or mere handicrafts.

Albrecht's annual mission report of 1934 confirms that the first mulga pieces offered for sale contained tjurunga designs. The 'honey-bee' plaque provides one example. Another appears in a list Albrecht compiled of 'tjurunga stories' recorded from those Arrernte and Luritja elders who brought their sacred objects to the mission for sale.[12] Most of these stories documented stone and wooden tjurunga, but one, titled 'Description of Mulga piece, with Tjurunga design', described the Dog Dreaming at 'Parurultja', north of Glen Helen Station. The matching mulga plaque was probably one of those sold by Namatjira.

Albrecht went to considerable trouble to document these stories. He immersed himself in the story-tellers' own logic, the Dreaming:

> He sat with old Loritja men to write down the stories connected with the tjurungas they sometimes brought to the store to sell, noticing the eagerness

in their eyes and voices as they explained the stones and their engravings. Sometimes they became so unconscious of their surroundings that, in the midst of speaking Aranda, they would lapse into Loritja without realising it. As he gently reminded them to tell him the story in Aranda, he asked himself if they would ever be so gripped by Christianity as to speak of it with such zeal.[13]

In June 1928, when Albrecht asked his congregation to express their gratitude for the printing and delivery of Carl Strehlow's Aranda translation of the New Testament, he was astonished by the numbers of artefacts brought to him: 'spears, boomerangs, shields, stone axes, stone knives, strings of human hair, red bean necklaces and some sacred artefacts were brought in as the days passed and many expressed their happiness in being able to bring such an offering to God'.[14] Those making this offering could not have been unaware that Albrecht gathered them for sale. Their tangible value helped to ensure the viability of the mission during the worst drought in memory. As the drought tightened its grip Arrernte and Loritja elders came to recognise the commercial value of these 'offerings'. Such transactions for basic food items had become critical to their own survival. It was the sacred tjurunga, particularly with their stories attached, which accrued the greatest value, eventually realising between three and seven shillings on resale.

Albrecht sold the objects with a 50 per cent mark-up to anthropologists such as N.B. Tindale or Géza Roheim, and to artists such as R.H. Croll, Una Teague or Rex Battarbee himself. The latter were among the first westerners to be drawn to Hermannsburg for aesthetic and cultural, rather than religious, economic or scientific reasons. Not surprisingly, the mulga plaques with tjurunga designs had less appeal to these visitors than the authentic originals, the ancient relics of ochred stone and wood which may have lain in keeping places for decades, if not centuries. 'The first pieces', Albrecht wrote, 'where we used old engravings of tjurungas as a design, did not sell'.[15]

Namatjira was the first to gauge the new market. He had demonstrated his adeptness in the cultural space between Arrernte tradition and modernity, but he also understood that collectors and Hermannsburg visitors were largely uninterested in that ambivalence. They wanted either primitive, authentic relics of the past or unmistakeable souvenirs of the present. Mulga plaques with tjurunga designs provided a confusing trace, not only of the culture which tourists to Hermannsburg were now exploring for the first time, but of a tourist's own intentions. After his initial experiments with mulga plaques during 1932 and 1933, and before his first forays into the field of watercolour landscapes,

Namatjira turned away from the tjurunga designs to a more reassuring repertoire: 'free-hand drawings of local animals, palms etc, which appealed and sold
well' and engraved psalm verses, which remained a dependable standby with
Lutheran visitors.[16]

One of Namatjira's best customers was the Central Australian policeman
Constable W. McKinnon. In 1932 he ordered a dozen of Namatjira's plaques
depicting his camel team's traverse across desert country south-west of
Hermannsburg, and paid 'a handsome 5/ each'. Each plaque represented
McKinnon's desert patrol in slightly different country, evoked by distinctive
vegetation. One surviving plaque depicts McKinnon preceded by his string of
camels, with a Palm Valley palm in the background. Another showed:

> the constable on the first camel, followed by a spare mount, two pack camels,
> another spare mount, and his black tracker bringing up the rear on a sixth
> camel. The sparse trees and clumps of spinifex in the background captured
> faithfully the aspect of the country. Each plaque was inscribed 'Greetings from
> the S.W. Patrol'.[17]

Namatjira's biographer, Joyce Batty, considered this individual commission a
crucial step in the artist's progress. It enabled him to understand that the market
was composed of individual connoisseurs, each appreciating the work for their
own reasons. McKinnon's commission was quickly followed by more diverse
artistic influences – the visits to Hermannsburg by the artists Violet and Una
Teague, Arthur Murch and, most importantly, by the two friends John Gardner
and Rex Battarbee. Namatjira still made plaques occasionally, but by Gardner
and Battarbee's second visit in 1934 he had become committed to their medium –
pencil, ink, and ultimately watercolour paint, on paper.

TRANSITION AND TRANSGRESSION

Batty once asked Namatjira whether he would be prepared to incorporate his
totem, '*rennina*' the carpet snake, within a landscape painting. He refused to
do so, making it clear that 'this was something which his followers did but
which he would never do'.[18] It is uncertain whether Namatjira meant that
symbols of his totem were too sacred to be depicted in a public painting (under-
standable in the decades before the Papunya artists placed such depictions in
the public domain) or whether his evolving approach to the conventions of
landscape painting prohibited the incorporation of overtly symbolic material.
The latter is perhaps the most likely interpretation, although several of his

early watercolours had contained human figures and even ceremonial subjects. Namatjira had no qualms about depicting the totemic design of the Yelka Dreaming of Palm Valley for the anthropologist Charles Mountford, even while working on a landscape painting. This was something, Mountford wrote,

> I never expected to see, even in my most fantastic visions. It was surely an experience without parallel to watch a man depicting, in the most primitive of all arts, beliefs that stretched back to the dawn of his creation, while lying beside him, the product of the same hand, were beautiful water-colours in the art of today. It scarcely seemed possible that any man could have bridged that immense gap in artistic expression.[19]

Albert Namatjira sketching his totemic motifs of the Carpet Snake for Charles Mountford, ca 1940 (Mountford 1944, p. xxii).

Syncretism of this kind has become more familiar since Namatjira's death, as Aboriginal people's lives began to span even greater incompatibilities and dissonance than he had experienced. Had Namatjira lived until his seventies there is little doubt that he would have embraced the Western Desert painting movement's liberal expression of sacred motifs.

Namatjira was informed, but not confined, by his traditions. He felt able to depict tjurunga designs which were not his own, and to paint ceremonial events traditionally forbidden to him. The question may be posed whether these 'inappropriate' choices reflect the confusion of an historical victim beset by unprecedented pressures and temptations, or a confidence born of a new sense of power as an historical actor. Whatever the interpretation, this course of action casts doubt on the orthodoxy that Namatjira slavishly depicted his main Dreaming sites throughout his twenty-year career as a watercolourist.[20] The evidence suggests that while he spent more time painting certain sites in preference to others, these choices were driven by artistic considerations rather than traditional, religious affiliations.

Namatjira and other Hermannsburg painters chose their landscapes primarily according to their potential as watercolour subjects. Topographic composition, the effect of light, or whether the scene was 'new', were all factors outweighing traditional criteria of significance. Namatjira and other Arrernte artists often ventured into entirely foreign country in search of pictorial subjects. As Albrecht observed: 'they would go out to the areas covered by our Evangelists; it was by now quite safe for them to go where before they would have thought twice before starting'.[21] The Mobil Company's presentation of a motor vehicle to Namatjira in 1956 enabled him to select painting locales far beyond limits prescribed by tradition. On one occasion he drove to Uluru (Ayers Rock) for a painting session, to be told by Pitjantjatjara and Yankantjatjara men (whose permission he had not sought) to leave immediately.[22]

In Arrernte culture the strictures against revealing another's totemic designs were as severe as if one had revealed one's own. By decorating mulga wood plaques with tjurunga designs Namatjira was straining these taboos in a way punishable by death a generation earlier. But his transgressions were not restricted to the construction of imitation tjurunga. In 1941 the South Australian Museum purchased a watercolour painting of Namatjira's titled 'Malu (wallaby) Corroboree', depicting a Pitjantjatjara men's ceremony. It was apparently painted during his 1939 camel trip with Rex Battarbee to Ellery Creek, and forms a companion piece to Namatjira's 'Achilpa (wild cat) Corroboree', painted on the same trip.[23] Namatjira used an ink drawing of the Arrernte Achilpa ceremony to illustrate the cover of his catalogue for his Melbourne exhibition, held in 1938. Battarbee had also photographed and painted scenes incorporating performers in the Achilpa ceremony. Several of those paintings were purchased by T.G.H. Strehlow, son of the former missionary who had banned such ceremonies at Hermannsburg. It is a reminder that T.G.H. Strehlow and Namatjira were each operating at the edges of their cultures.

Influenced by Strehlow's anthropological concerns, Battarbee painted ceremonial subjects not only for aesthetic reasons, but in order to preserve a permanent record of them in colour (before colour film became a proven medium). But his motives for encouraging Namatjira to portray those subjects were of a different order. The 1938 catalogue cover projected Namatjira to his Australian public as an authentic 'savage' with a remarkable talent for European art. Without this primitive/modern juxtaposition, Namatjira's work might have had considerably less impact. This ploy was used many times to market Namatjira's paintings and continues to be a favoured strategy in promoting Aboriginal art.[24]

Catalogue cover drawn by Namatjira for his 1938 Melbourne exhibition
(Hardy, Megaw & Megaw (eds) 1992, fig. 8.5).

Battarbee's encouragement prompted the Arrernte artist to experiment with depictions of ceremonies other than those he was traditionally entitled to portray.[25] It is unlikely that Namatjira painted the Malu ceremony from life, although Battarbee recorded that the Arrernte artist consulted an elderly

Pitjantjatjara man regarding details of colour for the work.[26] This choice of a restricted ceremony of a different tribal group was adventurous in the extreme. In fact, both the Arrernte Achilpa ceremony and the Pitjantjatjara Malu ceremony were beyond traditional bounds for Namatjira as legitimate subjects. Both ceremonies involved the final acts in the second stage of men's initiatory rites, a level which Namatjira himself had not reached.[27]

In his artistic allusions to restricted subjects Namatjira was on safe ground within the regulated confines of Hermannsburg mission itself. This was so at least until after the Second World War, when the mission became less isolated from other Central Australian communities.[28] Led by Namatjira, Arrernte artists developed a painting style in which even human and animal figures, let alone events, ceremonies or sacred objects, became superfluous. Just as in the formative years of the Papunya Tula painting movement though, this style did not emerge without exceptions and anomalies. These continued to recur, particularly in paintings made for white Lutherans associated with Hermannsburg. Examples include Oscar Namatjira's painting of the crucifixion of Jesus, complete with Roman legionaries, Reuben Pareroultja's watercolour of Jesus speaking with Nicodemus at a Central Australian campfire, or Richard Moketarinja's remarkable image of three sacred objects suspended in a landscape like massive Zeppelins.[29] Such images confront viewers with an incongruity between discrete subjects (apparently grounded in history) and the timeless landscapes which frame them. But to the Arrernte artists of the 1930s and 1940s this incongruity was not apparent.

Located within a timeless Arrernte reality, the crucifixion, ceremonial tableaux, and sacred objects have existed like the Dreaming itself, the 'power-filled' dimension of present reality, for ever. They are not discrete events, easily separable from the landscape and the Dreaming which frames that landscape. It is a further irony that the watercolourists have appeared to re-render Arrernte landscape as European, constructing it from a Western perspective and its constituent Western elements of space and time. What appear to be precise events occurring in timeless landscapes can also be seen in inverted terms, as finite scenes which frame transcending events.

As the Arrernte watercolour movement began during the mid-1930s it was Namatjira who engaged most intensely with these ambiguities. His transition from highly sanctioned depictions of Arrernte sacred art to the precise techniques of European landscape painting did not occur without compromise. But by the time he came to teach his sons and other younger artists, a path had been cleared. Exceptions certainly remained; the power of particular subjects

Pintubi men absorbed in an exhibition of paintings by Namatjira's art mentor
Rex Battarbee, at Haast Bluff, west of the MacDonnell Ranges, during the early 1940s.
Photographer: Rex Battarbee. South Australian Museum Archives.

demanded that they be incorporated within new renderings of the Arrernte landscape, as in the crucifixion scene later painted by Oscar Namatjira or the sacred objects hanging in space, by Richard Mokaterinja. Despite those anomalies, Namatjira successfully established the conditions and a code of conventions by which other Arrernte artists could operate. The rigour of his own painting technique and the uncompromising way in which he selected his subjects, without necessary reference to their place within the Arrernte cosmography, reflect this historic shift.

Namatjira's mulga plaques, referring to Arrernte religion in their form, and to Christian religion or secular events in their texts and designs, convey the dilemma confronting him during the early 1930s, at the very beginning of this process of accommodation. Perhaps the plaques' allusions to the restricted sacred art of his ancestors helped him resolve a key question – how to disengage from that art and its enveloping obligations by re-rendering it as secular, unthreatening. Namatjira embarked on this critical phase at a time when traditional Arrernte art and religion were under attack both from within and outside his society. The plaques served their purpose for Namatjira. They represented the transition between two cultures as well as the space which separated them.

AN 'EXPONENT OF THESE NEW DESIRES'

Historians have formed a new view of Albert Namatjira's life and work. Purchased during his lifetime as naturalistic and apparently entirely secular depictions of Central Australian landscapes, his paintings are now reinterpreted against the phenomenon of Western Desert acrylic painting. The dynamism of this cultural revival and its roots in 'traditional' Aboriginal societies of Central Australia are obvious. A view has emerged that the sacred traditions of Central Australia expressed in Western Desert painting were also incorporated within the paintings of the Arrernte watercolourists, and especially in Namatjira's art. Seen in this light, Namatjira's art issues directly from the people's contemporary social and political identity and aspirations, as well as their ancient totemic landscape. Such a seamless interpretation of Arrernte cultural history tends to downplay Namatjira's individuality and his role in rupturing and reforming Arrernte traditions.

The historical evidence points instead to tremendous strains and dislocations within Arrernte society during Namatjira's formative years as an artist. Rather than illustrating the continuity of Arrernte traditions, Namatjira's paintings are perhaps better understood as the work of an artist working at the limits of his cultural milieu, a fringe-dweller of a particular kind.

Anthropologists and historians have recently begun to recognise the capacity for individual autonomy among a people previously regarded as forming their identity only within the group.[30] In fact, it can be argued that a model for Namatjira's singular decision to begin painting in watercolour was already present within his culture at the time, and was encouraged by the Hermannsburg missionary, Pastor F.W. Albrecht. His decision to supply Namatjira with expensive painting materials during a period of extreme privation at Hermannsburg was made against the advice of other significant Lutheran officials.

Albrecht himself was specific enough about this, admitting that the breakdown of the old patriarchal social system among the Arrernte provoked an appetite among the younger men in particular for 'more freedom, and more compensation for their labour'. Namatjira became 'the exponent of these new desires'.[31] Albrecht experimented with several industries to cater for this trend. Brush-making, boot-making and a tannery were launched, with varying degrees of success, but it was the mulga-plaque business which attracted Namatjira's attention. Albrecht wrote:

> After working for a while at these slabs we bought him a poker machine with a platinum needle, which was heated in a methylated spirit flame. This was of great assistance in carrying on the work, and as a result he did fairly well out of it.[32]

Pragmatism and an eye to profit were key factors in Namatjira's decision to persevere with the mulga plaques. But the craft was also a stepping-stone to a new Arrernte aesthetic. In refining the 'pyrographic' art, he was already moving beyond the workshop crafts of his fellow Arrernte, widening his creative scope. The results gave him an early taste of the excitement his later mastery of the art of watercolour would bring. Namatjira's biographer Joyce Batty explained the initiative:

> The blank plaques were made by sawing diagonal sections of the mulga ... with its fine grain, reddish brown heartwood and pale amber halo of sapwood, [it] permitted fine carving which could be polished into a fine patina. [The plaques] were evidence of his rapidly developing skill in capturing in form the world – the only world – that he knew.[33]

Namatjira's decision to experiment in this way was driven partly by the fact that the traditional sacred art of the Arrernte no longer represented the inevitable course, for him or for others of his generation. Even more directly, his was the adventurous and opportunistic decision of a gifted, ambitious individual. It was spurred by his expectation of earning a sufficient living to rise above the crushing poverty characterising the Hermannsburg mission during the early 1930s. The fact that in later years the Hermannsburg school of water-colourists, inspired by Namatjira's success, came to represent the Arrernte cultural establishment, should not obscure these aspects. Namatjira was not one painter among several, nor was he simply a more articulate spokesman for his people. He was a pioneer. The other Arrernte painters quickly developed their distinctive styles, each centred upon a different view of landscape, but the freedom to create those idiosyncratic depictions had been won by Namatjira himself.

Albert Namatjira with mulga wood plaques, early 1930s, Hermannsburg Lutheran Mission. South Australian Museum Archives.

At Hermannsburg today, and in surrounding outstations, the Finke River Mission Board enacts a policy of religious 'parallelism', rather than 'syncretism'. The Lutherans acknowledge, as they have formally done since Hermannsburg became an autonomous Aboriginal community in 1976, that aspects of traditional Arrernte religion have survived, and can survive, alongside Christianity.[34] There is no perceived conflict today between an Arrernte elder's status as an active and respected Christian and his status as a ceremonial leader, just as there is no apparent disjunction between Arrernte watercolours and Arrernte acrylic painting.[35] Evidence suggests that for Aboriginal people themselves, both at Hermannsburg and elsewhere in Aboriginal Australia, the option of syncretic or 'parallel' religious practice was always open, since Christians first arrived in their midst. But for most of Hermannsburg's mission history since its foundation in 1877, Aboriginal people were actively dissuaded from pursuing these options. Mission policy at Hermannsburg during the 1930s differed markedly from that of the Presbyterian mission at Ernabella in northern South Australia, where it was assumed from its foundation in 1936 that 'there should be no compulsion in religion; that Christian living should be exemplified

325

by the white missionaries in their daily life and that it be left to the aborigines to make the change if they judged our way better than theirs'.[36]

This approach was emphatically rejected at Hermannsburg. According to the policy which Albrecht inherited from his predecessor, Carl Strehlow, Aboriginal people were forbidden from taking part in ceremonies if and when they became Christians.[37] While there were occasions between 1928 and 1934 when Albrecht allowed brief expressions of Arrernte traditional religion at Hermannsburg, these were strictly associated with external stimuli and pro- voked strong protests from Aboriginal Christians. These events reinforced Albrecht's determination to continue his ban on these activities.[38] Namatjira and others of his generation at Hermannsburg did not have the freedom to follow two ways, two parallel religious paths. Namatjira was further disad- vantaged in Arrernte religion through having made a 'wrong marriage' (according to kinship rules) to Rubina, daughter of Wapiti, one of Carl Strehlow's chief Kukatja informants. Following his initiation Namatjira did not receive full access to ceremonial knowledge. These circumstances, themselves a conse- quence of the pressures brought to bear on Arrernte society through the colonial period, helped to place Namatjira in the space 'between two worlds'.

At least two major campaigns against Arrernte religious traditions were waged at Hermannsburg, following the arrival of the missionary Carl Strehlow in 1895 and after Friedrich Albrecht's arrival a generation later, in 1926. Namatjira's rise as an artist occurred at the height of the second of these campaigns, in which Arrernte native evangelists played a leading part, and it can be interpreted against these events. In aligning himself with his uncle Titus, one of the most active evangelists, Namatjira was assisting that campaign.

Despite its resilience throughout the 60 years since European contact, Arrernte society could not withstand this strain without effect. Ceremonial life did persist in localities outside the mission, and certain individuals retained their ceremonial status, but the pressure to adopt the 'New Way' was irresistible for many young Arrernte men. Once they had taken that path or walked on it for a time, alternatives to the ancient traditions seemed even easier. Namatjira's own experiment with evangelism undoubtedly smoothed his transition to western art.

In any event, by the time the Hermannsburg school of watercolourists finally emerged during the late 1940s, Aboriginal art in Central Australia had under- gone a fundamental, paradigmatic shift, unprecedented since European contact. The extent of this change is obscured today by Namatjira's conformity to an art style often characterised as bland, 'chocolate box' art. We can better appreciate the extent of Namatjira's transition as an artist by observing the way in which he distanced himself from Arrernte art traditions. A crucial step in Namatjira's development as a landscape painter appears to have been his part in 'desanctifying' and rendering harmless the potent decorative art of his ancestors.

Namatjira was not alone among his people in contributing to this process, which had begun with the first European incursions into Arrernte country during the 1860s and 1870s. But while the questioning or abandonment of ceremonial life and its trappings during the first decades of this century may be regarded as a way of adjusting to the social trauma associated with European contact, the process was certainly hastened by the attention which European collectors, artists and designers paid to sacred objects.

SEPARATING THE SACRED

Ethnographic collectors played a crucial role in separating tjurunga and other ceremonial paraphernalia from their original sacred contexts, making them available for radically different uses. During the 1930s, 1940s and 1950s the concentric circle motif of the Arrernte tjurunga found its way onto a multitude of secular European objects, from book covers and ceramics to caravan curtains. Perhaps the most public incorporation of Aboriginal sacred motifs within European design forms occurred with the commissioning of bas-relief sculpture panels on the upper walls of Sydney's Central Station saloon bar.

During the 1920s and 1930s the Aboriginal population of Australia began to recover demographically from the shock of European contact, more than matching an appalling death rate with an increasing birth rate. Ironically, the public perception that Aborigines were a dying race also strengthened during this period, bolstered by population statistics gathered years earlier. Against this background, the incorporation of Aboriginal symbols within European art and design had an added poignancy. This was reflected most strongly in the work of the Victorian artist and sculptor William Ricketts. He visited Hermannsburg during the early 1940s, spending time with the linguist T.G.H. Strehlow, from whom he learnt first-hand of the disruption to Arrernte ceremonial life. The Dandenongs 'sanctuary' built by Ricketts still reflects this perception of a doomed race, noble in defeat. Among the numerous clay sculptures of Arrernte men, women, children and native animals are entwined tjurunga motifs, serving both as markers of authenticity and as epitaphs. In one remarkable, forceful sculpture an Arrernte Jesus hangs crucified on a cross made of engraved tjurunga.

Despite their best efforts, when Ricketts, Margaret Preston and other artists and museum curators incorporated sacred objects within their exhibitions, they assisted in a remorseless process, one which has accompanied the colonial experience throughout history. The appropriation, desanctification, and subsequent incorporation of Arrernte tjurunga and their motifs within European contexts were key stages in it. As the art historian George Kubler wrote:

> The triumph of one culture over another is usually marked by the virtual cessation of the art of the vanquished, and its replacement by the art of the conqueror. When the offending objects and monuments finally cease to correspond to any living behaviour, they become symbolically inert. They then are 'safe' to play with in recombinations emptied of previous vital meanings, as in tourist souvenirs, antiquarian reconstructions, or archaizing revivals.[39]

This analysis applies to the Arrernte situation. Ceremonial life *did* greatly diminish in the region, particularly after the 1930s. More than that, young men such as Namatjira actively participated in the process of making tjurunga symbolically inert, by manufacturing souvenir replicas, or by calling for the surrender of these objects to the missionaries and collectors.

As the youngest son of the pioneer missionary Carl Strehlow, and an avid scholar of his father's work, the linguist T.G.H. Strehlow became deeply committed to the Arrernte's classical past. In the decades following his return to Central Australia in 1932 he worked harder and harder to elicit ceremonial performances. His opinion of Arrernte art was that it could not function adequately as a visual form without the support and context of ritual song-poetry to enliven it and supply 'its full emotional appeal'. Because of this, Strehlow considered that 'the pictorial art of Central Australia will probably always rank, at least in the eyes of alien observers, lower than the anthropomorphic and x-ray designs of northern and western coastal Australia'.[40] Strehlow lived long enough to observe the first creative surge of the Western Desert painting movement at Papunya during the early 1970s and may have been prepared to modify his views. The anthropologist A.P. Elkin, on the other hand, considered that the enthusiasm with which Arrernte artists embraced watercolour painting was a measure of their own art's poor development:

> This poverty of local pictorial art in Central Australia in particular, provides a justification for the lines taken by the Aranda 'school' of water-colour artists. They have deserted nothing, for there was almost nothing in their own art tradition that could be developed.[41]

Today Arrernte artists range back and forth between the art traditions of Europe and the Western Desert. This creative mobility is possible partly because the sacred art of the tjurunga was rendered safe enough to be recombined by Aboriginal artists in forms suitable for public display and wide consumption. That process gathered pace after Namatjira's death, particularly during the early years of the Western Desert acrylic painting movement. During his lifetime this middle way, a compromising syncretism, was not the easy option it later became. If conditions for the emergence of the Western Desert painting movement had existed during the 1930s Namatjira may have excelled in that field, rather than as a watercolourist. But neither he nor others of his generation had such a choice. A career in art was not possible until Namatjira made it so, and then in a European art form. This is the nature of the quandary facing the indigenous artist in a colonial situation – a dilemma with barely any middle ground.

In abandoning the sacred art of the tjurunga and adopting European water-colour technique Namatjira was acknowledging the nature of cultural change overtaking his people and the incompatibility between the two forms of art. Considering the introduction of the conventions of European landscape painting to nineteenth-century Turkish painting, art historian John Berger has written:

> The traditional pictorial language was one of signs and embellishment: its space was spiritual not physical. Light was not something which crossed emptiness but was, rather, an emanation.[42]

We might apply this analysis to the first engagement between European and Arrernte artistic traditions. A concept of 'emanation' is particularly applicable to traditional, or 'classical' Aboriginal art. As a key Arrernte symbol the con-centric circle motif is above all an emblem of emanating power. The rings of these circles contain and radiate sacred essence, the locus of 'country' and home. The circles multiply and reiterate that essence, just as the repetition of song verse and dance step makes the Dreaming true, and true again, eternally.

With their differential perspective and complex horizons, Namatjira's paintings represent a disengaged view of Arrernte country. And while these paintings may have recently acquired a referential sacred force similar to that of acrylic dot paintings, their potency during the 1930s and 1940s was minimal when considered against Arrernte tjurunga. As objects recently made with European materials, Namatjira's watercolours lacked any overt reference to historical time, and referred only obliquely to mythic time. Arrernte tjurunga in contrast, evoke both of these dimensions, summoning at once the ancestral past and the Dreaming present. It is that very dissonance between past and present, Dreaming and History, which make tjurunga 'sacred'.[43] This is not to say that Namatjira abandoned an understanding of the Arrernte landscape as the vital forum for the Dreaming's founding drama. Rex Battarbee's diaries often refer to Namatjira's explanations of the mythological significance of various sites which he and the white artist visited together.

Two of the most potent elements of Arrernte cultural life have been the sacred tjurunga and the landscape embodying these objects. Since European contact the tjurunga have undergone a remorseless process of separation from their integral place within Arrernte society and religion. These objects had variously become the currency of European science through museum collecting and the activities of anthropologists; of European art through the attention of artists; and of European religion, through missionaries and evangelists. Of these influences the most direct and pervasive has been that of Christian religion. The Arrernte response has been complex and is not fully understood, although one aspect is plain enough. That is the way in which Arrernte native evangelists made Christianity their own, powerful base. Particularly striking during the Strehlow and Albrecht eras was the commitment which traditional ceremonial leaders made to Christianity, a decision involving disavowal of Arrernte religion and of tjurunga in particular.

The land itself has continued to dominate Western Arrernte life. This is despite the isolation of the Hermannsburg mission within a sea of pastoral leases and national parks. Like Aboriginal people elsewhere in Australia, the Arrernte did not consider that this legal alienation of their land obliterated their own complex links to it – relationships made explicit through their depiction on engraved tjurunga for each Arrernte man, woman and child. Given the power of symbolic depictions of landscape and implicit social relationships contained within it, Rex Battarbee's and John Gardner's first exhibition of watercolour paintings held at Hermannsburg in 1934 may have been a more confronting experience for the Arrernte than the knowledge that yet another pastoralist was commencing operations in their country.

During his lifetime Namatjira's accomplished watercolour landscapes represented a remarkable feat of assimilation. Today perhaps, these paintings might be regarded as an expansive gesture of reconciliation. Either way, perhaps they mask a more sophisticated and subversive response. Namatjira's assertion to Battarbee, his teacher, that 'I can do the same', expressed his independence and a determination to engage with European culture. It might also be interpreted as a counter-claim to Battarbee's visual appropriation of the Arrernte landscape. Namatjira's short-lived and little-known experiments with photography during Battarbee's 1938 painting trip perhaps contained a similar motivation, a desire to regain control of the way in which his people's landscape was being depicted.[44]

GRAVEN IMAGES

The late 1920s and early 1930s saw an accelerated erosion of the influence of traditional religion at Hermannsburg. Anthropological interest in the Arrernte also increased during those years. During 1929 the Hungarian psychoanalyst Géza Roheim and the eight-member Adelaide-based Board for Anthropological Research visited the mission. The psychologist Stanley Porteus visited in the following year. T.G.H. Strehlow arrived at the mission in early 1932 as a linguistic student, on his first return to Central Australia since his father's death. Missionary Albrecht tolerated and even actively assisted the work of these, and other, scientists. He was confident that their elicitation and encouragement of traditional song, ceremony and belief would not jeopardise the Arrernte's ultimate destiny as Christian converts. Perhaps he was justified in this view, for while the anthropologists encouraged the production of sacred objects and performances of songs and ceremonies (Harold Davies paid one shilling per song), the longer-term result of this interest was a further objectification and disintegration of traditional religion.

Another basis for his confidence was the Arrernte's own evangelism. The Lutheran pastor J.J. Stolz had observed this phenomenon a decade earlier, following the death of Carl Strehlow. Stolz considered that the Arrernte had, in his terms:

> broken with their heathenism, handed over their witchcraft and corroboree utensils and declared their sacred places free; they speak about the Word of God amongst themselves, and in meetings they bear witness of the Word to their heathen kinsmen. They compose hymns of their own.[45]

The impetus behind this social movement built during the 1920s. It enabled Albrecht to engineer an extraordinary public repudiation of Arrernte traditional religion soon after his arrival at Hermannsburg. The Manangananga Cave episode of early 1928 symbolised the sweeping changes affecting Arrernte society.

This cave, about four kilometres south-west of Hermannsburg, had been a traditional storehouse for tjurunga. Even Carl Strehlow at his most repressive had respected its sanctity, and the fact that it was forbidden to women and children. Albrecht saw the symbolic value in breaking this taboo. After consulting his evangelists and other elders, he arranged for the entire population of Hermannsburg to hold a Sunday service and picnic at the site. The tjurunga were taken from the cave and placed before the congregation, a fire was made under a large copper brought from the mission, the people drank tea and sang hymns. The Aboriginal evangelist Blind Moses delivered an impassioned sermon titled 'Churinga or Christ?' in which he exhorted his people to give up their sacred objects.[46] This initiative was reported in the *Observer* as a 'shrewd blow' aimed at 'the whole framework of magic which supports native law and custom'.[47] Many years later, an Aranda woman recalled the event:

> Everybody was watching, man and woman and young girls and young boys everybody watching for the cave, little bit frightened. Before service, took stones out and put them on the ground. Everybody sat in big circle, and stones were put in the middle … First time we bin see that stone … Old man [Albrecht] start those opening words. In the name of the Father, the Son and the Holy Ghost, then everybody relax, we start to sing hymn. Then he preached about Moses and Aaron and the golden calf. Tjurungas were like the golden calf. Old man preach and everybody look up, yes, that's really true … We bin think about God make us free. Yes, stones very frightening for Aboriginal people, that's why Pastor Albrecht go there.[48]

The Manangananga Cave episode undoubtedly succeeded as a highly charged and cathartic event intended to reinforce the missionaries' power to liberate the Arrernte from the apparent tyranny of their own religion. Five years later, when T.G.H. Strehlow accompanied the Hermannsburg population on another pilgrimage to the site, he observed:

> No visible trace of timidity had remained even amongst the oldest people there present. This is only the second visit of the congregation hither since the knaribatas [ceremonial leaders] permitted this bulwark to fall. They have also decided, just a short while ago, to abandon the marriage-class system, so as not to prevent people from marrying who have no class-husband or wife available.[49]

Albrecht's subsequent efforts to collect and sell tjurunga and to encourage a series of new crafts at Hermannsburg should be seen in this context.

By 1932 Arrernte men were manufacturing tjurunga for sale to tourists in Alice Springs, a trend which continued for the following four decades. Strehlow later wrote of the 'feeling of hopelessness which accounted for failure of men who were still in their twenties and thirties in the 1930s to take any care in preserving even the tjurunga that had been entrusted to their care by their anxious elders, when failing in health'.[50] But this passing of tjurunga to missionaries or to tourists, together with other forms of religious accommodation, was not only a reaction to social change; it could also be a means of provoking it. During a 1932 expedition, T.G.H. Strehlow's Arrernte cameleer Tom Ljonga reported to him that:

> the men everywhere wanted to sell their tjurunga to the whites, and to settle down like white men: the only reason for their walkabout was their duty to protect the sacred caves. Now they would sell not newly manufactured tjurunga but the really old treasures made by the erilknabata [ceremonial leaders], so that they could change their old ways of living.[51]

In the context of the times these men were making agonising decisions, drawing a line under traditions which had seemed everlasting. The young anthropologist T.G.H. Strehlow found himself witnessing a process which had begun well before his father's attempts to stifle Arrernte ceremonial life:

> [With the] shocking depopulation of the Aranda area since the coming of the whites, all Aranda men in the 1920s – and certainly after the coming of the railway line to Alice Springs in 1929 – must have asked themselves, was there any use in learning verses, or performing acts, when not only the old religion but the whole of the Aranda population seemed destined to perish within another thirty years or so. Disasters such as the Spanish Influenza epidemic in 1919 and the scurvy epidemic at Hermannsburg in 1928/29 shook everyone's faith in survival itself. ...[52]

Strehlow believed that he could do little more than acquiesce in this, undertaking to preserve the objects brought to him by Arrernte men, and recording the frustration and sadness of those involved. Strehlow spoke of a 'terrible silence' descending upon Central Australia as he watched particular Arrernte ceremonies performed in their entirety for the last time. This lowering perception of finality was a characteristic of Strehlow's anthropology and social commentary. During the early 1930s it matched Albrecht's own rhetoric, but while the closure of Arrernte ceremonial life gave the missionary grounds for optimism, it fed Strehlow's increasing bitterness:

> the Tjilpa man had given Tom [Ljonga] a slightly different version of the Jiramba tradition this morning; and Tom was thoroughly disgusted: 'Many countries, many stories, many lies', he exclaimed. In fact, what was the use of tjurunga in the caves? He was disillusioned, and strangely moved, like a white man who has felt everything that he relied on giving way under his feet. 'Sell the tjurunga, I say, sell them, get rid of them. They won't make manna while they are lying in the caves; sell them to the whites and get some manna that way.'[53]

Strehlow was well aware that his own acquisition of tjurunga occurred under different circumstances, and that such objects could be acquired by Europeans within the frame of traditional practice. Unfortunately, given the later controversy over his ethnographic collection, he failed to articulate this distinction clearly enough. It was left to others such as Géza Roheim to explain that even in traditional Aboriginal society there were few utterly inalienable objects. Most had their price:

> The old men taught the ceremonies to the young men in exchange for food. The idea of selling tjurunga, or (what amounted to the same thing) performing ceremonies for the white man in exchange for supplies, was entirely in accord with their social system. When I asked to see some ceremonies, the old men told me that I was doing the same thing as the young men of the tribe did when they offered food in exchange for learning the rituals.[54]

Albrecht and the Hermannsburg schoolteacher, H.A. Heinrich, were responsible for gathering, documenting and selling dozens of tjurunga during the late 1920s and early 1930s. In 1933 sixteen tjurunga, objects ordinarily forbidden to women, passed easily into the hands of the Melbourne artist Una Teague, on her visit to Hermannsburg.[55] A few months later the founder of Ernabella mission, Charles Duguid, visited Hermannsburg and purchased the following items at the store: 'a snake skin for 5s [shillings], two stone knives at 2s each, a message stick for 6d, and two ceremonial beaters for 2s 3d ... some of the women's fancywork for 19s 6d and three stone *tjurungas* for 15s, together with their stories which Albrecht wrote out for him'.[56]

Albrecht did not package and send collections of Arrernte artefacts abroad as his predecessors Carl Strehlow and Oskar Liebler had done. If these objects subsequently found their way as far afield as Basel and Budapest it was through the agency of collectors such as Géza Roheim, who later deposited his collection in the Neprajzi Museum in Budapest. Neither that collection, nor the South Australian Museum's collection of Albrecht–Heinrich objects, include mulga plaques. To museum collectors, the gap between the categories of traditional artefact and recently made souvenirs seemed clear enough. But by the early 1930s the tensions in Arrernte society at Hermannsburg had generated a series of anomalous transactions between Aborigines and Europeans. Sacred objects became commodities for tourists, and tourist art assumed some of the characteristics of sacred objects. The intimate possessions of Arrernte individuals had become public, operating as generic indicators of an entire culture. It was at this time, that Albert Namatjira began experimenting with his poker-work. Into the stream of objects passing from Arrernte to European hands he inserted his own graven images, innocuous tourist plaques still bearing more messages than we can easily read.

Cake of red ochre collected by Dr Patrick Shanahan, 1904, 18 cm in diameter.
A1863, South Australian Museum.

CHAPTER NINE

That special property

Red ochre is the most ubiquitous substance in Aboriginal Australia. Mined directly from the earth at a myriad of sites from Tasmania to the Top End, it has also been the most trafficked item, both in the recent past and in remote antiquity. It passed along chains of connection, from close to distant kin, across the horizon. Linked through exchange, even relative strangers were within the social universe, and the use they made of this substance fitted the expectations of their trading partners. And beyond those trading networks, red ochre's symbolic significance as the sacred blood of Dreaming Ancestors extended throughout Aboriginal Australia. That particular analogy is one of its great cultural markers. As Europeans began to understand this, towards the end of the nineteenth century, the concept of the Dreaming itself became comprehensible.

An association between blood and ochre is implicit in religious beliefs of many cultural groups worldwide. In Aboriginal Australia, this link was held as an essential and intimate value, not readily shared with outsiders. Although a variety of Aboriginal artefacts were offered in exchange for European commodities during the contact period, helping to define the complex, shared space of the colonial frontier, red ochre was rarely traded with white people. It continued to be locked within the Aboriginal sphere and, for the most part, remained an item of internal currency.

For European colonists in Australia, red ochre was at once too esoteric and too mundane a substance to attract much attention. Popular literature of the frontier described it simply as 'ruddle' – an unprocessed, elementary form of paint, another marker of primitivism. Red ochre had little appeal as an independent collectable item; ochred spears, shields and boomerangs evoked the

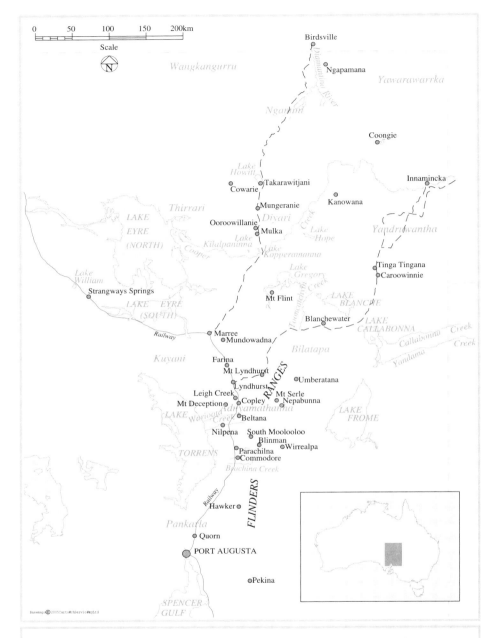

Localities in the Flinders Ranges and eastern Lake Eyre, with relevant Aboriginal group names.

culture convincingly enough. This chapter is the story of an exception – a cake of red ochre collected in 1904 by Patrick Shanahan, a country doctor in northern South Australia.

Like many natural colours formed from the landscape itself, the colour of this particular ochre is beyond simple description. Dark pinkish with a tinge of silver – a metallic hue which becomes apparent only when rubbed across the skin – it is not accommodated within the familiar palette. Shanahan's ochre is in the form of a cake or a large lozenge, twenty centimetres in diameter and six centimetres thick. For a century this nondescript object has spent most of its life on display at the South Australian Museum, resting comfortably on an old glass saucer. Its register entry reads simply: 'Pigment, ochre, red. Prepared for use. Source – Parachilna. Donated by P. Shanahan, 1904'.[1]

Among a sheaf of correspondence received by Edward Stirling, the museum director of that period, is an eight-page letter written in Shanahan's confident, flowing hand, dated 26 December 1904.[2] It describes the acquisition of the sample sent to the Museum, but also goes much further. The letter is a primary document in the history of European understanding of Aboriginal culture, for Shanahan provides one of the first eyewitness accounts of red ochre's symbolic significance as a religious, transformative substance.

Dr Shanahan's letter recounted the final stages of an Aboriginal expedition to the source of the ochre, a series of mine workings near the western entrance to Brachina Gorge in the Flinders Ranges. The doctor accompanied four Europeans and their guide, a Kuyani elder known as 'King Hal' or Harry Bailes. It was this man's initiative to approach Shanahan and R.J. Matheson of Nilpena station, following the agreement of elders from Aboriginal groups north of the Flinders Ranges, whose ancient rights to the mine were now threatened by white prospectors. The other Europeans in the party included two sympathetic pastoralists from nearby stations, J.W. Lindo of South Moolooloo and R.J. Matheson, as well as two government officials, the geologist F.R. George and the Protector of Aborigines, Percy Stone.[3]

The party's destination was the flank of a high outer range, overlooking a steep gully running down to the western plains which stretch to the distant, salt-hazy shores of Lake Torrens. The view from that vantage cannot have altered much in the past century. It is a vast and silent, engulfing vista; you have the sensation of gazing directly into the continent itself. The sun glints off an isolated metal tank and might catch the distant roof of Commodore station, almost twenty kilometres away. The township of Parachilna, 25 kilometres to the north-west, is hidden from view by a higher, adjacent ridge. Nothing can

The first page of Patrick Shanahan's letter to Dr Edward Stirling at the South Australian Museum, December 1904. South Australian Museum Archives.

be seen of the highway, or of the Leigh Creek coalfields railway line which replaced the old Ghan line, once linking Port Augusta with Marree and the stations to the north, terminating at Oodnadatta and, after 1929, Alice Springs.

To reach the remote mine today requires careful navigation in an off-road vehicle along disused and rough tracks, then a stiff walk which becomes a steep climb. We can imagine that Shanahan and his party set out on horseback or buggy from the railway siding at Commodore or Parachilna, until they reached the gully itself. His letter suggests that he may have commenced the journey with an ochre party on foot, but the description of that initial part of the journey south from Parachilna was supplied by Harry Bailes. As it was, Shanahan noted that his own short trek to the mine suggested 'the necessity of a course of further training'.

The doctor's readiness to undertake this expedition and to document it in such detail cannot be explained simply by the tangible object of his enquiry – the cake of ochre itself, resting securely in its museum case a century later. His understanding of something more abstract, fundamental to Aboriginal beliefs surrounding the mine, also impelled the journey. If he hadn't grasped it beforehand, Shanahan understood by the expedition's end that the mine was a crucial element in a sacred landscape, and that the Aboriginal participants in the ochre expeditions entered that landscape's time and space. In this

sense Shanahan came as close as any contemporary European to an understanding of the Dreaming. He documented his insight in a matter-of-fact manner, leavened by an irony preserving his own critical distance. It is an engaging description, rich in metaphor.

The ochre mine had been a source of fascination for Europeans in northern South Australia since the 1880s. The doctor had probably heard it mentioned in several contexts. But the proximate reason for his visit during that hot December of 1904 had little to do with curiosity or sightseeing. He and the two pastoralists, J.W. Lindo and R.J. Matheson, had been enlisted by Harry Bailes on behalf of his people to accomplish something beyond the power of other

Dr Patrick Shanahan, ca 1903. Photograph courtesy of Dr Michael Shanahan.

Europeans in the district – the preservation of Aboriginal access to a resource embedded at the heart of their religion. Shanahan's letter confirms that his response to this request was based on a sense of justice rather than sentiment. He understood the gravity of his role. His intervention, and particularly the letter reproduced below, contributed to the mine's protection from European mining, as a gazetted reserve. It appears to have been the first instance of such protection in Australian history.

The history of the frontier is scattered with examples of particular Europeans who became enlisted as advocates by Aboriginal people or found themselves in sympathy with their point of view at critical times. Four of these men are discussed in other chapters of this book. Lieutenant William Dawes, First Fleet meteorologist and self-made linguist, produced a grammar and vocabulary of the Sydney language reflecting his own intimate relationship with the Port Jackson woman, Patyegerang. His refusal to join a reprisal expedition organised by Governor Phillip may represent the first documented European act of conscience in defence of Aboriginal interests. William Cawthorne, a young and poverty-stricken Adelaide school-master at the margin of his own society, was another 'dissenter'. His researches into the manners and customs of Adelaide Aborigines were tinged with his anguish over their predicament, and he advocated their interests in his newspaper articles. John Bennett, the young draftsman and cartographer engaged on the 1869 Goyder expedition to assist the division and alienation of Larrakia and Djerimanga lands near Darwin, placed himself close enough to his subjects for his own life to become the price of the linguistic knowledge which he gained. The Alice Springs telegraph station manager and magistrate, Frank Gillen, had few misgivings about his place in the tough milieu of the 1890s Central Australian frontier. A sense of justice, rather than sympathy, led him to charge the powerful Northern Territory police-trooper W.H. Willshire with murdering suspected Aboriginal cattle thieves in 1891. Gillen's remorseless curiosity about Arrernte religious belief and practice was also largely unsentimental. But he understood that an engrossing puzzle with international implications – 'the secret of the totem' – could only be solved by entering the mental world of Arrernte elders.

At the turn of the twentieth century, when Patrick Shanahan put the case to Stirling for the ochre mine's preservation, Australian anthropology had neither a professional base nor a defined ethical position. Frank Gillen defended the right of Arrernte and Loritja people to a fair trial for spearing pastoralists' cattle on their lands, but was complicit in the theft of their sacred objects. Daisy

Bates built a reputation as an anthropologist and linguist, yet morally distanced herself from her subjects by raising the spectre of cannibalism, and by constructing Aborigines through her journalism as helpless victims and welfare recipients. The Queensland Protector of Aboriginals, Walter Roth, distilled Aboriginal traditions and customs into his *Ethnographic Bulletins* even as he enacted policies rendering those practices obsolete and marginal. During the late nineteenth and early twentieth centuries anthropology rarely afforded political outcomes aligned towards Aboriginal objectives. A commitment to anthropological enquiry might arise through engagement with Aboriginal people but it rarely entailed sharing their point of view. The story of Shanahan's ochre provides a powerful exception.

The Aboriginal man who approached Shanahan about the risk to the ochre mine had no means of knowing that his advocacy would be effective. As a sympathetic doctor bound by the Hippocratic oath, Shanahan was probably contacted because Aboriginal people trusted him and were aware of his status among the European community. Fortunately, Shanahan's connections extended beyond the country town of Hawker, to Adelaide society, and ultimately to the South Australian government itself. For Shanahan's correspondent in Adelaide was his old Medical School lecturer, Professor Edward Stirling, former Member of the House of Assembly, influential member of the Adelaide Club, and director of the South Australian Museum.[4] Shanahan's letter is reproduced below:

Hawker, 26.12.04

My dear Professor,

I must apologise in the first place for my apparent neglect in delaying an answer to your letter but as I knew little then concerning the ochre deposit and its legends and even that little was only hearsay I deemed it advisable to visit the place, see for myself and learn on the spot from the King himself all that I could.

Before I go further I must thank you very sincerely for the immediate and deep interest you manifest in the endeavour to secure a reserve for the natives of the particular spot which they consider not only sacred, but their richest inheritance.

When we consider that the ochre from this one particular area is distributed up as far as the Northern and North-Eastern boundaries of Australia, locally East and West as far as I know, South as far as our tribes survive, that the ochre is used in nearly all of their ceremonies and is essential in the performance of the majority of their rites, we can easily understand the attitude of the aboriginals and the justice of their demands.

King Harry informed me that the King of the Yerkinna (Parachilna) tribe is responsible to all other tribes for its supply – no other tribe can take it without his permission, and in his presence, unless he appoints a deputy who then acts as a regent.[5] Should he not be able to secure the ochre on account of its being leased by white men (who would not allow him access to the sacred spot) his speedy death would follow and also [those of] his successors. Reprisals would follow also on the whites if not in localities near at hand at least on many living outback – the area claimed would not require to be more than twenty acres. There are thousands of tons of this ore in sight that the blacks do not want. The lode being 30 to 40 feet wide and running across ranges for miles. It is a clayey ironstone, the colouring matter being red oxide of iron, it is known to contain a small percentage of mercury[6]. It is embedded in a crystalline limestone and cambrian fossils are plentiful in the vicinity.

Our party of six included Mr R.J. Matheson of Nilpena Station, the prime mover in seeking to obtain from the Government a reserve for the Aboriginals and Mr F.R. George, Assistant Government Geologist. The latter will send a report of the nature of the deposit to the Mines Department, he was also successful in defining the exact locality of the spot which has not hitherto been done. Mr George with a small Kodak was enabled to photograph the excavations.[7] Possibly the geological features you would like to possess can be obtained from the Mines Department.

The Legend

Two dogs (= Kintalawoola[8]) named respectively Kilowilinna and Perilinguninna chased an emu (= Kuringii) starting from near Innamincka, down the Cooper passing through Tinga-Tingina, Caraweena, Monte Collina, Mt Freeling (here the emu had a drink and left in the solid rock the imprint of its foot) the emu then skirted the western slope of the Flinders Ranges to Mt Alick (this mountain the blacks maintain is the emu petrified), here it turned and ran through the Lake Torrens Plain, dodged once more and made for the Flinders travelling due East, the first check (hill) it met was a man who had a pack of dogs one named Thorijurra, a savage brute. The bird raced up the staircase (I will define the staircase later on) but the dogs caught it on top of the hill. The man assisted in the bird's despatch with a yam stick and was instantly turned into a hill (note the parallel with the unfortunate saline disaster which Biblical teaching tells us befell Mrs Lot). The blood from the emu (Emu's blood = Kuringie Warragurta) now forms the ochre (Murragurta) deposit at the sacred cave (Yerkinna).[9]

Opposite the Yerkinna cave, due west on the next steep hill and situated about a quarter of a mile from it is another cave into which the dogs went for a rest and there died, the dogs which perished there after death rolled down the hill and are now symbolised by huge dolomite limestone boulders rounded off by the influence of rain.

The original dogs of the chase – Kilowilinna and Perilinguninna – are represented by two high mountains, one St Mary's Peak the other I think unnamed in the Flinders Ranges.

The Murragurta rite

The blacks (male only) assembled at the Yerkinna Creek (Parachilna Creek) and stripping naked, corroboree all night, no sleep being allowed, under a big penalty. They must not collect any water or food en route, except such as they can carry in wallaby skins. The varying corroborees pertain to different phases of the chase only. The journey 1st stage is done at a jog trot, it is about eight miles distant. Iguanas are caught en route and killed and roasted to provide grease at the 1st stopping place where they make the sacred fire (at the time of my visit there were many skeletons strewn around).[10] At the sacred fire they may take their last drink but no food until their return, a mile from here at the same trot, in single file with bodies all greased with iguana's fat. They meet the stone representing the first dog Kilowilinna. Each native hurls stones at him with vim and vengeance. Further on more dogs, some sluts with puppies (all limestone boulders) are encountered and treated with similar ceremony. The scores on the rocks and the cairns at their bases signify a rather hot fusil-lade. Next comes the staircase, it is about a mile in length and ascends very nearly at an angle of 45° about three yards wide & composed of huge boulders, some 3 feet others 10 feet high. It is a succession of steps and flats the flat being about the same length as the height to be climbed (the journey accomplished at my leisure suggested to me the necessity of a further course of training).[11] Arriving within about 40 feet of the cave we met a flat area where all the younger blacks are left while the initiated proceed to the cave and chanting the Emu dirge proceed to gather his blood, the Murragurta. The dust alone may be collected, not the pieces – a Peeche [wooden container] three times full (a vessel shaped like a coolamon and about the size of a soft felt hat) is handed to each man, he is warned neither to waste nor to spill a drop. The initiated then proceed to where the boys are and paint the bodies of the whole of those present with ochre which adheres readily to their bodies anointed with iguana grease. The King then running makes a detour & all the young fellows chase him – he eventually pulls up at the Yerkinna cave & initiates them into the Murragurta rite. After their descent they remain at the sacred fire and feast off the iguana's remains and may drink water which they brought with them. There is a spring close by but they dare not touch it. One native in a fainting condition begged on one occasion for a drink but was told by the King it was poisoned (which was untrue). At the ochre cave the natives divest themselves of every hair on their body save their heads and scatter it about to represent emu feathers.[12] No-one but the King or his deputy can visit the cave where the dogs died.

a) No lubras are allowed within miles of this place, if discovered to have visited the vicinity they are speared, if found within sacred area they are thrown down a precipice and never touched afterwards for burial.
b) No bird, animal or reptile is allowed to be killed from the sacred fire to the ochre cave the penalty being death.
c) It is the oldest mine in Australia.
d) The devastation of hair on the body of the natives is now done by a stone knife or a pocket knife. Formerly it was burnt off with a glowing fire-stick.[13]
e) About 30 years ago [i.e. about 1874] whilst natives were at the Murragurta site, 30 natives were entombed in the excavations, one only escaped and he belonged to the Dearii-quiainie tribe [Diyari-Kuyani] (Killalpaninna).
f) Natives coming from a distance to the ochre follow the track taken by the emu in the chase. If the whole of the track is covered by them the chase occupies from one month to six weeks.

Dear Professor if this somewhat hurriedly written account be of any service to you, you are at liberty to make what use you like of it. My desire is simply to obtain the fullest possible particulars which ethnologically may be of value, of a race which will before long be as dead as the dodo. The only credit I claim is to certify as to its authenticity.

I might relate a stunning rejoinder given by King Harry to one in my presence who ventured the remark that 'he (King Harry) knew that ochre was not emu's blood, it was only a religion that he had been taught and handed down by his ancestors'. 'Oh', said King Hal, 'Just the same as your Christ, you have never seen Him'.

Wishing you the Season's Compliments and every good wish,
Yours sincerely,

P.F. Shanahan

Under separate cover I am forwarding addressed to you at the Museum a cake of ochre with head gear as made up and carried by the blacks hundreds and hundreds of miles and exchanged as barter for pitchuri, beads etc. If you are having the notes typewritten I will ask you to have a copy made out for me – cannot obtain same here. P.F.S.

OCHRE AS ESSENCE

Across the Australian continent the range of Aboriginal material culture varied a great deal, from the minimal necessities used by desert nomads to the complex fishing technology of coastal groups. But the single element common to all Aboriginal groups and which, according to the archaeological record, has persisted since the earliest occupation, is red ochre. Red stains of pigment coated a skeleton interred 40,000 years ago at Lake Mungo in western New South Wales. Ground haematite and pellets of red and yellow ochre were found in the lowest levels at the Malakunanja II rockshelter on the Arnhem Land escarpment, dated to at least 45,000 years ago.[14] These finds, confirming red ochre's use for both religious and aesthetic purposes, exemplify its crucial role within Aboriginal culture in the distant past. That role continues, uninterrupted in some parts of Australia, into the present.

Red ochre's significance is founded in its symbolic status within Aboriginal religious belief. The basis of that belief, the Aboriginal concept of the Dreaming, has tangible expression in the landforms and visible features believed to have been created or shaped by Dreaming Ancestors across the continent. Red ochre deposits symbolise the blood of those Ancestors spilled directly onto the earth. Applying ochre to the body, sacred or secular objects or on rock walls, Aboriginal people derive some of the original, transforming power of those events to which they are linked totemically or through classificatory kin networks.

Red ochre's perceived equivalence to sacred blood, with its sustaining and regenerative associations, has probably persisted in Aboriginal belief for many thousands of years. This accounts for the use of red ochre in mortuary practice, rock-painting, body and artefact decoration, and even as a healing substance. Similar uses for red ochre have been documented in other hunter-gatherer societies and also in prehistoric sites in Europe, the Middle East, Africa and China. The recent discovery of red ochre associated with mortuary practice occurring 100,000 years ago in the cave of Qafzeh near Nazareth, confirms the role of this substance as a marker for the emergence of 'symbolic reasoning'.[15] Red ochre has undoubtedly played a fundamental role in humanity's philosophical development, and as the archaeologist Ernst Wreschner put it, a 'red thread' runs through 'more than 500,000 years of human history'.[16]

While the identification of red ochre with the sacred blood of ancestral beings holds true across Aboriginal Australia, not all ochre deposits were equally valued. This is dramatically illustrated by the documented pilgrimages for Flinders Ranges ochre undertaken by eastern Central Australian Aboriginal groups. These journeys covered several hundred kilometres, passing directly by other known sources of red ochre such as those at Mungeranie Gap near Cooper Creek, or Lyndhurst at the northern extremity of the Flinders Ranges. This single-mindedness had much to do with the mythological associations of the mine, but the superior quality of the ochre there, with its dark pink hue and silvery sheen, was evidently also a powerful attraction. It is worth noting that the two other ochre mines focusing Aboriginal attention from wide regions of central and western Australia – Karrku near Yuendumu and Wilga Mia in the Pilbara – yield ochre with a strikingly similar pinkish hue and silvery sheen. It is as though these qualities in particular have appealed to an Aboriginal aesthetic, combining to produce a sacred colour of particular potency.

In the Flinders Ranges and the Lake Eyre Basin, as in the rest of Aboriginal Australia, red ochre was not reserved solely for ceremonial use. It was applied to children's toys, men's and women's utensils and weapons as well as on ritual objects. The thirteen-volume manuscript of Pastor J.G. Reuther, the Lutheran missionary at Killalpaninna on the Cooper Creek from 1888 until 1906, provides us with the clearest picture of red ochre's use throughout this region.[17] The numerous ochre references in Reuther's manuscript fall into several categories.

Firstly, red ochre was used medically, in the form of an ointment applied to wounds, bruises and swellings. Reuther's transcription reads: '*karkujeli ngato nina dapa dijana warai, nauja wolja tepirila nganai* = in having spread red ochre over the wound I have checked it, so that it will soon be healed'.[18] Red ochre was used as a magic charm: mixed with water and blown from the mouth, it could abate the heat of the sun or the force of the wind.[19] Red ochre was also an essential part of a rainmaker's equipment. It was a symbol of spiritual renewal and of ritual cleansing. Red ochre purified those associated with the dead; widows were released from their prescribed mourning period by an application of red ochre and women were anointed with it after the completion of menses.[20] Youths entering the phase between boyhood and initiation as men were coated in the substance as a symbol of this transition, their symbolic rebirth.[21] The practice continues in parts of central and northern Australia today. In those regions also, red ochre was used to coat secular objects such as wooden bowls, shields and boomerangs. But even here, the rationale for using ochre as a protective layer derives from its sacred properties.

In all of these examples red ochre is a medium or agent of transcendence, from sickness to health, death to renewal, ritual uncleanness to cleanness, the secular to the sacred, the present reality to the Dreaming. The point is underlined by Reuther's description of red ochre as a substance of 'life' and 'joy', and by his translation of the phrase *ngani kalumarai marukutuni* as 'I am craving for red ochre'.[22]

CONVERGING STORIES

The Aboriginal man who entrusted Shanahan with the story of the mine was known to him as 'King Hal'. Genealogical research suggests that this individual was a Kuyani 'doctor man' named Harry Bailes, aged about 45 years, who worked as a boundary rider on Nilpena station, in his tribal country. In previous decades Bailes had been a police tracker, based at the Adelaide police barracks, and was credited with tracking the escaped Aboriginal 'outlaw', Logic.[23] Bailes had also worked as a coachman for the wealthy pastoralist Peter Waite, owner of the 'Urrbrae' estate and, as in the case of Dick Cubadgee (see chapter five), a familiarity with Adelaide society and its workings undoubtedly contributed to Bailes's confidence in approaching Nilpena's lessee, R.J. Matheson, for assistance in protecting the ochre mine against desecration.[24]

While Shanahan described Matheson as the 'prime mover' in attempts to protect the ochre mine, Harry Bailes' own role was fundamental. During late 1904 Matheson hosted a small group of Adelaide visitors engaged on an official tour of inspection, and used the opportunity to introduce the topic. The group included W.H. Matthews (Inspector of Mines), G. Degenhardt (an Adelaide solicitor) and the Mayor of Port Augusta, T. Hewitson. Having raised the possibility of government protection for the mine, Matheson invited Harry Bailes to address the group. Speaking 'fluent English', this 'upstanding native' proceeded to give the visitors an account of the mine's mythology and signficance which mirrors Shanahan's account in the main particulars, with several interesting variations. These details were recorded and passed on to the *Register* newspaper by Degenhardt. For example, Bailes noted that it was his obligation, as chief of the Beltana tribe who held the mine as their 'exclusive property', to accompany any visitors to the mine 'to supervise the removal of ochre'. If he was unable to do this, 'one of the members of his tribe' would be deputed for the purpose. Bailes also gave additional details regarding the preparation of the ochre for transport by northern groups:

> On returning to the camp with a full bag the aborigines dress again and each one damps some ochre, kneads it to the consistency of dough, and makes a cake of it. This when moulded is placed on the ground, and each native stands his head on it to make a cavity so that the cake may subsequently be carried with ease. The ochre having dried it is borne away on the head, and where the supply of hair is limited grass tufts or leaves are inserted to afford protection.[25]

It seems to have been this particular newspaper article, together with the visitors' official representations in Adelaide, which prompted the subsequent visit to the mine which Shanahan accompanied a few days later. Despite its condescending irony, the final paragraph of the article is a reminder of the historic nature of this collaboration between Harry Bailes as a spokesman for his people and these visitors to Nilpena, whose concern and influence extended from the frontier to the cabinet room:

> The Beltana natives fear the intrusion of white men under the mining laws, and Mr Matthews promised to bring the matter under the notice of his Minister in the hope that the wishes of the blacks would be respected. King Harry has a consort, Mary Ann, and a son named Andy, who in due course will succeed his royal father. In the event of Harry's death before Andy attains manhood (he is now about eight years old), the mother will appoint some other native of the tribe to act in his stead in the meantime. Harry assumed the regal office on the death of his brother. The dusky king evidently feels it is his duty to uphold the dignity of his position, for on a recent occasion when some of the tribe came down for a supply of the coveted ochre he exercised his royal bounty by purchasing a bag each of flour and sugar and giving it to his subjects.[26]

The Kuyani people's heartland lay out on the plains west of the Flinders Ranges, extending north as far as Lake Eyre. To Harry Bailes the red ochre at the mine was *Kuringie Warragurta*, the sacred blood of the ancestral Emu, run to ground at the *Yerkinna* cave by giant Dingoes. This Emu Dreaming was held in common by other northern groups, notably the Diyari, Yandruwantha and Yawarrawarrka peoples of Cooper Creek, the Ngameni of the Warburton River, and the Wangkangurru of the Simpson Desert. For those people also, the mine itself was probably known as *Yerkinna*, though in colonial times it was more often referred to by reference to the nearest settlement, Parachilna.

But if Shanahan had explored the matter further, and enquired about the mine's mythology from other Aboriginal peoples of the Ranges such as the Wailpi or the Parnkarla (groups usually associated today with the Adnyamathanha people), he would have learnt of other Dreamings converging upon the site, and other names for it.[27] For the mine and its surrounds offer a remarkable example of a mythological landscape perceived quite differently, simultaneously, by various Aboriginal groups. In the surviving oral and written record there are as many as five differing Dreaming explanations for the red ochre mine. This variation is probably unique in Aboriginal Australia and reflects the different resonances this site held for the spectrum of Aboriginal groups relying upon it during the course of centuries.

Three of these Dreamings are mentioned infrequently in the ethnographic literature and seem not to have survived in the oral record. An Arabana Dreaming recorded by the anthropologist A.P. Elkin during the 1930s is similar to Shanahan's Emu story, but involved the tracking and killing of Dingoes by a human hunter travelling south-east from the Oodnadatta vicinity.[28] Secondly, the missionary J.G. Reuther recorded a Diyari belief that the Flinders Ranges ochre was formed as the Red Ochre *mura* or ancestor, Timpiwalakana, emerged from the earth. One of the toa sculptures in Reuther's ethnographic collection in the South Australian Museum represents Timpiwalakana's route to the ochre mine.[29] Thirdly, the ethnographer Charles Mountford recorded an explanation for the ochre mine relating to the travels and exploits of the Adnyamathanha ancestor Witana, the central figure in mythology underlying the second stage of initiation among the Flinders Ranges people.[30]

These three accounts aside, the weight of oral and ethnographic evidence confirms that the main Dreamings relating to the mine were held in common by two principal groups or clusters of Aboriginal peoples. For the Aboriginal groups visiting the mine from north-eastern South Australia and south-west Queensland, the red ochre represented the Ancestral Emu's sacred blood. For

Aboriginal groups of the Ranges itself and the adjacent plains to the south, the ochre represented sacred Dingo blood, the subject of an entirely different Dreaming, and to them the mine's name was *Pukardu*, a language term meaning 'heart'.

During 1937 the anthropologist Norman Tindale recorded an ochre myth from a Ngadjuri man, south-west of the Flinders Ranges. In this story the ochre was formed from the blood of a red Dingo, Marindi, one of a vicious pack belonging to a Cannibal Woman who had terrorised Aborigines in the Flinders Ranges area. The Woman was halted by two Lizards who devised a wily scheme for tricking her, disposing of her Dogs one by one. The Jew Lizard finally overcame the Red Dog, last of the Woman's guardians, spilling his blood to create the ochre mine.[31] Charles Mountford recorded a similar version from Wailpi people in the Flinders Ranges during 1937, and confirmed the site's name as *Vukartu*, a variant of *Pukardu*.[32] This story is retained in the oral record today by Adnyamathanha and Parnkarla people of the Ranges and adjacent plains, and it seems clear that these southern groups held the 'dog's blood' version in common. The most recently recorded account, carefully documented in 2002 by the northern Parnkarla men, Leroy and Randolph Richards, reiterates this story. The site's name, *Pukardu*, is explained as the term for the heart's blood of the fierce dog-like animals which was spilt at the site.[33] Pukardu (sometimes anglicised as Bookartoo) has now become widely accepted as the site's name, and will be used in this chapter.

The Emu Dreaming provided a binding rationale for ochre parties' expeditions to the Pukardu mine from hundreds of kilometres to the north. The perception by these northern visitors that the mine was an elusive and dangerous, almost unattainable goal, makes more sense when we realise that the local, southern custodians of the ochre regarded the mine's mythological origins quite differently. The northern people were journeying beyond the limits of their world in every sense.

The anthroplogists Alfred Howitt, A.P. Elkin and Kenneth Fry, the policeman-ethnographers Samuel Gason and George Aiston and the missionaries Otto Siebert and Johann Reuther all recorded detailed accounts of the Emu mythology.[34] They also documented the routes followed by ochre expeditions and described the ceremonial activity which followed the parties' return. The *mindari* was the most important of these ceremonies in the eastern Lake Eyre region and took place upon the ochre parties' return to their home countries. It celebrated the ancestral Emu and was performed to ensure the increase of the species. The participation of several hundred men and women from related groups amounted to a key socialising event for the entire region.[35] Significantly, the mindari ceremonies were held at localities close to the starting points of the ochre mythologies – for example at Lake Howitt, at Kanowana on Cooper Creek and at Ngapamana, near Birdsville. It would not be misleading to regard the ochre which returning initiates presented to the mindari performers as sacramental in form – the Emu's retrieved body.

EXPEDITIONS FOR OCHRE

In his letter Shanahan asserted an Australia-wide distribution for pukardu ochre. That may have been the perception of his informants, but it was not the case. Trade in pukardu ochre consisted of an inner and an outer range. The inner range comprised groups for whom the Pukardu mine had a primary mythic significance. For groups in the outer range this significance was interpreted anew or overlain by local mythologies. Ochre was transported beyond the inner range through an extended series of short distance transactions rather than by expeditions and large scale movements. A similar pattern of distribution seems to have applied to trade in axe-heads throughout south-eastern Australia.[36] The exception was provided by the ochre expeditions mounted by Wangkangurru, Yarluyandi and related groups who travelled up to 600 kilometres to collect pukardu ochre. They transported it a similar distance northwards on their return, beyond the present site of Birdsville and along the Diamantina and Georgina Rivers. There they traded parcels of ochre for bags of *pituri*, the psychoactive drug obtained from the plant *Duboisia hopwoodii*.[37] A secondary trade in pukardu ochre extended several hundred kilometres further, as far as Cloncurry, as far north-east and east as Charleville in Queensland, Tibooburra and the River Darling in New South Wales.[38] Individuals or small groups from these regions may also have joined larger parties or even mounted their own expeditions to the Pukardu mine. In conversations with the linguist Luise Hercus during the 1960s, Wangkumara men George Dutton and Cecil Ebsworth recalled such expeditions from north-western New South Wales, following the Yandama and Callabonna Creeks to the eastern slopes of the Ranges.[39]

Westward, expeditions are recorded from the Oodnadatta region and beyond, from Southern Arrernte territory on the western side of the Simpson Desert.[40] From the south both Parnkarla and Ngadjuri peoples travelled to the mine. The southern neighbours of these groups – the Nauo of Eyre Peninsula and the Kaurna of the Adelaide Plains – may also have visited it. Linguistic evidence also suggests a connection with the Adelaide Plains. A Kaurna term for red ochre is *karko*, very similar to the Diyari term *karku* recorded by Reuther. According to the missionaries Teichelmann and Schürmann the Kaurna word *jernbana* meant 'a species of red ochre, brought from the Far North' and used for decorating the face and body. The term is equivalent to the Arabana and Wangkangurru term for ochre, *yarnparnu*.[41]

The accounts of Alfred Howitt and Samuel Gason are the most quoted descriptions of red ochre expeditions.[42] Both agreed that parties of Diyari men set out for the mine in July or August of each year. According to Howitt some 'seventy to eighty picked fighting men of the tribe' travelled as far as 450 kilometres to the Flinders Ranges, often fighting their way to and from the mine. Each man collected up to 35 kilograms of red ochre. This version has been accepted by later commentators, but requires modification.

Firstly, it is clear that ochre expeditions did not set out solely from Diyari country but from a range of other places as well. The northern groups may have held the Emu myth and its sacred destination in common, but there was no unanimity among them as to its point of origin or its route. There were at least two main routes and multiple points of origin, each regarded by local groups as the beginning of the mythological chase. On the Birdsville Track side the myth originated in Ngameni country at Cowarie, Takarawitjani (near Lake Howitt) or Ooroowilanie. On the Strzelecki side the starting points included an undefined locality in Yandruwantha country just north of Inna-mincka, or at the Cutrabelbo or Wadriwalani waterholes near Kanowana. The Shanahan letter describes this second route. It is corroborated by accounts of sightings of Aboriginal parties after 1860 and roughly corresponds with the old Strzelecki Track. Both the Birdsville and Strzelecki Track routes, reliably punctuated by waterholes in most seasons, were adapted as stock routes by early pastoralists before becoming the main outback highways of the region today.

Another northern route, originating at Lake Hope in Diyari country, is referred to in police correspondence of the 1860s. Expedition parties skirted the eastern edge of Lake Gregory, passing Tooncatchyn Creek and Mount Flint before joining the lower Birdsville Track near Mundowdna. A route from Arabana country originated at Lake Kalpuruka or Lake William. A local Flinders Ranges reference even has the myth originating much closer to the Pukardu mine, at Windy Creek, south of Copley.

Howitt and Gason each asserted that ochre parties set out in July or August, and this is generally supported by the observations of pastoralists and police after 1860. The expeditions set off during the cooler months when waterholes were full and game was more plentiful. Reuther translated a sentence in his Diyari dictionary as: 'the sun (winter sun) is moderate (weak) at present; we ought to be going for red ochre'.[43] In his official correspondence during 1864, the police corporal James Wauhop observed that 'the Natives have come down for several seasons in the month of June'. In 1863 he had reported that 'mobs of these natives come down every three months and are getting worse every time they come'.[44] This increased frequency can perhaps be explained by the extraordinary events of that year, culminating in the shooting, during November, of several members of a northern expedition at Beltana. Shanahan's trip to the mine during the December heat of 1904 was also atypical, prompted by Harry Bailes' initiative.

The police-trooper and ethnographer Samuel Gason gave the fullest account of the departure of an ochre expedition. The men set off from Lake Hope, where Gason was stationed during the 1860s, 300 kilometres to the north of the mine. He described the foreboding and grief of the womenfolk about to be left alone and conveyed the intense drama of the separation. This drama was heightened by the mothers' realisation that this parting marked their sons' inevitable departure from the maternal, hearth-based domain to the male sphere. The boys would return as men. The expedition members took up their weapons and set off, 'singing a rather mournful ditty, encouraging the young lads to keep up their spirits'. Indeed, Gason wrote, 'some of them require encourage-ment, knowing that besides having to travel over three hundred miles through strange country, many a hungry belly they will have before reaching their destination, independent of the load of ochre they will have to carry back'.[45] Reuther spoke of the 'secret reservations' of one participant and his wife's attempts to dissuade him, fearing 'some evil will befall him'.[46] As well as the actual initiations carried out in the course of the expedition, the journey itself was a test of individual resolve and determination, and a remarkable rite of passage.

For a period of several weeks the home camps of the ochre collectors were emptied of all young men. During that time Gason witnessed the preparations which the women and older men made for the return of the expedition. The men made special ceremonial head-gear and huts for the ochre-collectors, while women collected supplies of grass seed and other plant foods to sustain the large ceremonial gathering expected on their return. Remarkably, Gason's transcription of the song which the old men sang while making woven head-gear for the returning ochre-collectors was precisely duplicated nearly a century later, in 1976, by the Wangkangurru man, Jimmy Russell Wangamirri:[47]

Ceremonial head-ornament, *bukatu-billi*, worn by returning ochre collectors during ceremonies associated with the ancestral Emu, Warugati. Collected by J.G. Reuther at Killalpaninna, ca 1904. A2710, South Australian Museum.

Mulka-a-a-a – wora-a-a,
Yoong-arra-a-a Oondoo-o-o,
Ya Pillie-e-e-e Mulka-a-a-a angienie
Kooriekirra-a-a-ya-a-a-ya

[Translation]
Put colours in the bags,
Close it all round,
And make the netted bag,
All the colours of the rainbow[48]

The varying routes to the Pukardu mine linked the territories of neighbouring groups. The common interest in the mindari ceremony and the shared routes for pituri and red ochre trade mean that expeditions generally met with friendly receptions as they travelled, rather than fighting their way, as Howitt suggests. During the 1960s a Yandruwantha man, Murtee Johnny, recalled the privations of these journeys, but did not mention the 'hostile tribes' described by Gason and Howitt.[49] Fighting did occur along the route, but for particular reasons. These were temporary imbalances in relations requiring specific forms of redress, rather than any notion of general 'trespass' or invasion. As the anthropologist A.P. Elkin put it, 'travellers following the path of their totemic hero or heroes are free and safe, at least as far as the other members and local groups of their own totem are concerned'.[50] Writing at the Lutheran mission at Killalpaninna, Reuther was even more specific:

> In honour of their individual mura-muras, people often travel the way once traversed by their mura-mura, even into neighbouring tribal territories. They sing their sacred chants near the ceremonial stones and trees, just like their primeval ancestor did ... No harm befalls the wayfarers in [these] strange tribal countries.[51]

In fact, an ochre expedition gathered more members as it marched through new country at a steady pace of twenty miles (30 kilometres) a day. This solidarity in diversity gave added protection. Reuther even recorded a phrase describing the practice of combining with other tribal groups for protection on these expeditions, 'when crossing the boundaries of people not to be trusted'.[52] Mountford wrote of men from Charleville joining with the Wangkangurru, meeting the Yandruwantha at Innamincka, the Yawarrawarrka at Coongie, and the Piladapa, Diyari and Arabana at Mount Lyndhurst before the final leg of the journey to Parachilna. By then the party might have grown from 30 to 300 men.[53] Howitt and Siebert spoke of ochre expeditions being organised by the 'Blanchewater division of the Dieri' although the latter stressed that this had probably more to do with the relative proximity of this group to the mine than with any particular totemic affiliation.[54]

The expeditions were not unexpected by groups to the south. There seems to have been an obligation to send messages and even gifts before the parties set out from the north. In his descriptions of the ochre protocols Reuther did not suggest that these emissaries could be women, but this possibility (discussed below) adds a further dimension to the ochre trade.[55] George Aiston referred to the practice of sending message-sticks and 'presents' to the mine's custodians so as to obtain permission.[56] It appears that all participating groups had a similar 'division' responsible for organising the expeditions, affiliated through totem or kin links, just as specific 'clans' have been noted for the trade in pituri. George Aiston, who had an assigned totemic status among the Wangkangurru, claimed in 1928 that he was the sole remaining representative of the red ochre *mura* or ancestor, and that the responsibility for organising these expeditions now fell to him.[57]

According to Reuther these representatives also had power to 'bewitch' the ochre mine, preventing its misuse or wrongful access. They could do this by creating collapses and landslides. Oral records of a major collapse at the mine site, perhaps the very event to which Shanahan referred, persisted among Aboriginal and European residents of the Flinders Ranges until the 1980s.[58] For those participants in an adventure which was part epic, part Dreaming, these mishaps were interpreted as sorcery or retribution, a result of human agency. They could not be accidental. In most cases these events were linked to breaches of trading etiquette, such as the requirement to send messengers southwards to ask the local custodians of the mine to 'open the way'.

Woven fibre bag containing the drug pituri, obtained in 1899 from a red ochre expedition passing through Beltana, by the pastoralist Nathaniel Phillipson. A1810, South Australian Museum.

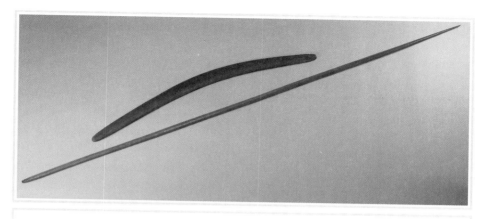

Wooden javelin and incised boomerang obtained by W.B. Sanders at Wooltana station in the Flinders Ranges from an ochre expedition coming 'from Queensland by way of Tilcha Creek to collect red ochre'. A39396, A39397, South Australian Museum.

During the mid-1980s the Adnjamanthanha elders John McKenzie and Rufus Wilton told me of such an incident which occurred in their grandfathers' time, during the 1870s. They recalled that the required messengers, two women, were not sent ahead before the main party set out. Deprived of their 'happy times', as Rufus Wilton put it, the older men of the local group closed the trade boundary. When the expedition arrived notwithstanding, in breach of apparent principles of sexual exchange, the local men led by the notorious 'Larrikin Tom' ambushed the party in the mine, clubbing all of them to death but one who escaped and lived to tell the tale.[59] Again, this incident may relate to that described by Shanahan.

The Diyari and related groups were people of wide plains, gentle sandhills and open horizons. They regarded the mountain and gorge-dwelling people of the Flinders Ranges with suspicion and dread. Reuther's Diyari informants told him that Flinders Ranges people were known to lure unsuspecting northerners into the Ranges. There they 'mentally confused' their captives so that they lost all sense of their homeward direction.[60] But this fear of capture was reciprocated. Reuther asserted that members of ochre expeditions often obtained wives by force in the Ranges. George Aiston was more forthright, describing the expeditions as part of 'a big exogamous raid to get wives'.[61] In 1986 the Adnyamathanha elder Pearl McKenzie recalled her people's apprehension of the northerners; even in the early twentieth century their impending arrival provoked a shift to camping places away from the ochre mine.[62]

Despite that, evidence shows that the northern visitors were usually treated well by the Pukardu mine's custodians. At Nepabunna in 1937 Mountford recorded several Diyari ceremonial songs known by local Flinders Ranges people – an indication of the reciprocal exchange prevailing in normal circumstances. At the least, etiquette demanded that visitors leave gifts for the mine's local custodians. The South Australian Museum has examples of pituri bags, spears and incised boomerangs brought south for this purpose by ochre expeditions. In an interview with the linguist Luise Hercus in 1976, Jimmy Russell Wangamirri recalled the different objects given in exchange for ochre: 'in exchange they give black [manganese], boomerangs, sticks suitable for rubbing to make fire, they give down-feathers, and sometimes even grass-seed flour in a bag, a bag meshed in the same way as when they make a net. And they take nets too'.[63] This was not a wholesale exchange of goods for ochre but conforms to what we know of Aboriginal trade elsewhere: a series of transactions defining and reflecting relationships between individuals already linked by kinship or shared mythologies.

As for mining the ochre, neither Gason nor Howitt describe the actual method used at Pukardu. Shanahan's letter is our only direct source of information. His explicit description distinguishes the mining of pukardu ochre from ochre-mining elsewhere in Australia, where wooden levers were used to dislodge and extract the substance. According to Shanahan, pukardu ochre was obtained only in powdered form. It was literally brushed from the walls or collected from the floor of the mine, actions suggesting a gentle reverence for the ancestral Emu. This method of mining the ochre was also stressed by Shanahan in a subsequent letter to Stirling:

> The raw ochre taken by the natives for ceremonial purposes is the pulverized material or powdered particles found in the cave. I am sending you a small pebble under separate cover which is not allowed to be taken and then pulverized though the same could easily be accomplished even in the palm of the hand.[64]

Once mined, the ochre was mixed with water (or urine) to form large cakes, or packed in bags made of animal skin or woven fibres. According to Gason, these cakes or 'loaves' weighed twenty pounds (about nine kilograms) and each man carried several, amounting to a load of 70 pounds (32 kilograms).[65] The men carried these cakes on their heads, cushioned by rings of grass wrapped in human hair-string. As mentioned above, Harry Bailes supplied details of the way in which the ochre was kneaded and then fitted to the shape of each bearer's head. Robert Bruce wrote of combined loads of ochre and grindstones from nearby quarries being carried in this way and Howitt also described grindstones being taken north from Parachilna.[66] In about 1890 the store-keeper at Wirrealpa head station, E.G. Waterhouse (himself an amateur ethnographer, whose father had been the South Australian Museum's curator during the 1860s and 1870s), weighed the loads carried by a returning expedition in exchange for a ration handout. He arrived at an average of 30 kilograms – close to Gason's estimate.[67] This accords with the observations of the Strangways Springs station-manager, J. Oastler, who weighed the loads carried by 'each member of those parties returning from Parachilna Creek, a distance of some 213 miles, and they weighed from 60 to 80 pounds'.[68] Shanahan's ochre is a scale model of these larger cakes.

The ochre parties themselves seem to have been all-male in composition. This had less to do with the privations of the journey than with the nature of the enterprise. It was men's business from start to finish, usually involving initiation of youths at specific sites along the southward routes – at Tooncatchyn and Caroowinnie for example – as well as at Pukardu itself.[69] Women were not allowed in the vicinity of the mine, nor were they permitted to see the initiated youths before their return to their home country, a restriction confirmed by elderly Aboriginal informants during the 1970s. This return took place under cover of night and signalled the beginning of the mindari, or Emu ceremonies. The possible role of women as emissaries or messengers preceding the expeditions does not conflict with these constraints, but several sources also assert that ochre parties returned to the north with women. Given that the participants in ochre parties had each achieved varying status, it may be that the strictures against involvement with women applied only to the newly initiated and younger men, rather than to the grey-bearded elders whose role as leaders may have entitled them to such rewards. As late as 1910, five years after his initiative had led to the Pukardu mine's protection, Harry Bailes expressed anger that he had not been recompensed with two young women, as promised by the leader of a subsequent ochre expedition comprising 'Oodnadatta, Innamincka and Birdsville blacks'. According to a journalist visiting Nilpena station, Bailes proposed that the government 'allow his people to fight the blacks who live out from the head of the line' (north of Marree and Oodnadatta), in order to right this injustice.[70]

The red ochre expeditions can be regarded as archetypal religious pilgrimages. Apart from being long and arduous (up to 500 kilometres), the journey was directed to a religious goal of fulfilment involving catharsis and renewal, and pukardu ochre was prized for its own sacramental, transformative qualities. For several weeks, while the expedition lasted, its members also shared a spirit of camaraderie and adventure common to all religious pilgrimages. The journey was embedded within the religious calendar of every adult male across a wide area of eastern Central Australia and had probably been so for hundreds of years. During the mid-nineteenth century all that was to change.

CONFRONTATION

Pastoral activity north of the Flinders Ranges began in earnest after 1855 and immediately affected the ochre expeditions. There are no extant accounts of first contacts between the pastoralists and expeditions, but a pattern soon emerged. At first this conformed to frontier situations elsewhere in Australia, but subsequently developed an entirely different character.

While local groups in the Flinders Ranges were quick to appreciate the attractions of sheep and cattle as a new and convenient food source, there were additional reasons for killing or attacking stock. Reminiscing about the late 1850s in the Blanchewater area, the former stockman Frank James wrote:

> To break a branch of a quandong tree was a grave offence amongst them, and they disliked cattle coming on their country because they broke down and ate the branches of these trees, besides eating and destroying many other edible plants. The stock making large rainwater holes muddy and thus killing the fish was another well founded grievance.[71]

Livestock began to disappear singly or en masse, and reprisals by shepherds, pastoralists and police followed. If counter-reprisals by Aborigines sometimes led to the murder of a white shepherd this was widely reported in the southern press as a 'Native Outrage'. Larger numbers of Aborigines were slain in retaliation but these killings were rarely reported in the press. It is difficult to measure their scale or incidence.

This process of 'dispersal' and 'pacification' has been documented elsewhere in Australia. Its duration varied according to local factors, but generally an accommodation of sorts was reached in less than ten years. The phrase 'letting the myalls in', found throughout the literature of the period, aptly describes the terms of the new accommodation. Writing of the Flinders Ranges, the pastoralist J.F. Hayward observed that 'each petty tribe on all sides of Pekina, and these were a number, had to be terrified before their depredations ceased, and that pretty well lasted all my sojourn, say three and a half years'.[72]

The ochre expeditions introduced a new element. In most other parts of Australia the tide of European settlement passed over established and relatively static Aboriginal territories. In north-eastern South Australia this situation was reversed. White settlements were sparse, never more than outposts, and each year they were confronted by large roving expeditions of armed Aboriginal men travelling well beyond their own territories. These 'saltwater blacks', as they became known by the pastoralists of the Flinders Ranges (a reference to the inland salt lakes Blanche and Gregory), were travelling to a defined objective along established, sacred paths. Setting out from country still largely beyond European influence, the intrepid young men had not yet been 'pacified'; they were prepared to raid stock and to take other risks which had become too great for local Aboriginal groups.

During the early 1860s the ochre expeditions increased in size and frequency, with inducements offered by unfenced mobs of sheep and cattle, unoccupied shepherds' huts and the good seasons preceding the great drought of 1864–1865. In the opinion of Corporal Wauhop, writing from Mount Serle in January 1864, 'the real object of the Lake Hope and Coopers Creek natives when they first came down through the sheep runs was to procure red ochre but having at first got easy access to unprotected huts on sheep runs made them come down in large numbers for the purpose of plunder as well as to get a supply of the red ochre'.[73] Other police reports supported this view. Writing 40 years later, Robert Bruce observed that during this period 'a solitary shepherd would have been about as safe as an unpopular land-agent in Tipperary during the good old toimes'.[74]

Matters came to a head in 1863, when a group of embattled settlers called upon the Police Commissioner for protection. Julius Jeffreys, a pastoralist on the Strangways Springs run, wrote in June 1863: 'it is with much regret that I have the honour to inform you that the Aborigines have now become really dangerous and unless immediate steps are taken by the government some frightful calamity will take place'.[75]

When these 'calamities' did occur they happened to Aborigines, rather than to Europeans. Aboriginal people of the Flinders Ranges still retain oral records of a massacre near Beltana involving members of an ochre expedition during November 1863. The police account of the episode, which was not reported until three days after it occurred, established that the trouble began when Aboriginal men refused to allow shepherds to water their sheep at waterholes on the Warioota Creek, 'saying that [the] water was theirs'.[76] Estimates of the number killed on this occasion vary. Years later, the Blinman mine director

T.A. Masey stated that '11 blacks were killed on the spot, and it is said that 40 or 50 others died of their wounds before they reached their own territory'. The event was significant enough for the local police corporal to claim that 'the late affray at Beltana will be a check to their visits for a time to the sheep districts for the sake of plunder'.[77]

The settlers themselves were not as confident of a respite. In July 1864, a concerned individual wrote to the *Observer* that 'it is not difficult for a person to conceive a frightful amount of outrage on lonely shepherds or their unprotected wives and families as likely to result from a hundred and fifty revengeful aborigines roaming about over the country, and with the disastrous results of their last year's campaign still fresh in their memories'.[78]

The events of 1863 and 1864 contain the clearest evidence for Aboriginal parties coming south for adventure and spoil rather than for ochre itself. A particular group of 'salt-water blacks' led by the infamous Pompey made several forays within this period, operating outside the normal period for collecting red ochre, during the winter months.[79] In January 1864, after robbing several huts, killing an uncooperative local Aboriginal man and bailing up a shepherd's wife on Umberatana station, Pompey was shot dead by Samuel Stuckey, the station-manager. Stuckey was charged with Pompey's murder – a measure of the attention generated by the affair – and was taken to Adelaide for trial. He was released from the charge by a motion brought in the South Australian legislature. Despite efforts to elevate Pompey to guerrilla status, he was more accurately described by the press of the time as an 'Aboriginal celebrity, the only regular South Australian bushranger'.[80]

The unusual character of this conflict, in which a small and scattered white population was exposed to frighteningly large parties of hostile and well organised 'salt-water blacks', persisted beyond the great drought of 1864–1865, into the 1870s. In the meantime the crisis of confidence among the new settlers and bewilderment within the police force soon provoked government action. In 1864 the Minister approved a consignment of rifles to the Angepena police station in response to Corporal Wauhop's assertion that 'breech-loading rifles are the only weapons that would intimidate such a determined lot of natives, for they appear to take no notice of pistols'.[81] Police Commissioner Warburton did not support 'such warlike preparations'. He toured the area and reported to the government on the nature and purpose of the ochre expeditions, noting the inevitability of conflict while shepherd's huts and stock remained unprotected along the route:

Red ochre is universally required by the blacks and they prudently continue to procure it – if while travelling south for this purpose they fall in with a hut which is unprotected no doubt they will take what they want out of it … if the owner does not like to take this precaution he ought to be prepared to part with a few head … If a hut properly guarded be attacked let the consequences fall upon the heads of the aggressors – they get shot; but when goods are taken from an unprotected hut and nobody knows who actually took them, the case is altogether different and so with the cattle – when the natives are on the move in a large body two or three active stockmen hanging on their flanks could clear the cattle off their line of march or at any rate prevent the beasts from being surrounded and mobbed to death.[82]

Warburton recommended that the Aboriginal parties be advised not to venture near shepherds' huts but to go instead to the head stations where they would be given rations. Local police and pastoralists were to use violence in repelling attacks only as a last resort. 'I am unable to follow the reasoning', wrote Warburton, 'which states that if a sufficient force to protect the Settlers be not supplied by Govt, the natives must be shot down like dogs – supposing more Police to be there are they to be sent there to relieve the settlers from the necessity of taking care of their lives & property?'[83] It is clear that both the Attorney General and the Chief Secretary in Adelaide approved of Police Commissioner Warburton's response to this issue. George Goyder's cautious response towards the spearing of J.W.O. Bennett in the Northern Territory during 1869 (discussed in chapter three), reflected a similar concern – in Adelaide's official circles at least – for rigorous application of the rule of law to all parties on the South Australian frontier, black and white.

During 1864 Corporal Wauhop implemented Warburton's moderate policy with a considered mix of military strategy and restraint. In July of that year he reported that an expedition of a hundred Aborigines had asked for rations at Parachilna Station, had been refused but had fortunately returned peacefully to their camp:

This forbearance was repaid when the party started on their homeward trek via Mt Deception. On going up the plain Captain McKay shot a bullock for them that he purchased from Mr Burnett and from the manner that they commenced to eat it I think they were very hungry. On arriving at Mt Deception head station Captain McKay gave them five sheep and nearly two bags of flour and allowed them to spell a day, impressing them that if they called at the head stations they would get flour etc. and to keep away from the shepherds' huts which they seemed to understand ... Police Trooper O'Reilly and I accompanied them as far as Leigh's Creek where Mr Smith, overseer at that station, gave them more flour ... The natives were from Lake Hope, Cooper Creek and Mulligan [River] and a good many of them could speak English. I believe that by seeing them through the sheep runs a few trips [this] will tend greatly to prevent them robbing huts as they formerly did.[84]

During this period the Strangways Springs station-manager J. Oastler, who served as a justice of the peace, developed his own approach to the problem. Expecting an ochre party, he camped one night at an outlying shepherd's hut on the line of march, yarding the sheep nearby. Looking out in the early morning he saw a 'painted and armed Aborigine', who demanded food in pidgin English:

At a glance I could see he was a stranger and meant mischief, besides I could see a lot of black heads and spears topping a sandhill some 200 yards away. By this time the man left in charge of the hut and stores was by my side, with his Colt revolver in hand, and knowing the time for prompt action had come. I told the man who I knew was a good shot to plant a bulllet in the mulga stump near the Aborigine, which he did, and it at once caused a stampede of the whole party, about sixty armed men, as near as I could make out, though they did not give me time for anything like a correct count. I then left Jones to stand by the hut and stores and took the flock of sheep down to the water myself. Then, leaving them there with Camp-oven Winkie, the black shepherd, I followed on the tracks of the aborigines to make sure they did not interfere with the Head station, and after seeing them well past their return, stayed the night to comfort my old cook, Thomas Maddock, with the assurance that danger was over for the present and that the party was well on their way to Parachilna.[85]

Trouble continued, despite the best efforts of men such as Oastler, Warburton and Wauhop. Although the great drought broke in 1866, the country did not recover for several years and the expeditions posed a continuing threat to the expanding herds of sheep and cattle. In 1869 the northern Sub-Protector of Aborigines, Buttfield, attempted to pre-empt these attacks by offering a wagon-load of provisions to an ochre party, but he was unable to intercept it in time. Huts were robbed and sheep killed in the following year also, despite Buttfield's ration distribution to a party of 150 Aboriginal men at Beltana.

Police station and cells at Blinman, 1868. The station also served as a ration depot, visited by ochre expeditions. GRG 5/2/1868/649, State Records, Adelaide.

By 1874 Police Commissioner Hamilton was ready to implement a remarkable strategy, which Warburton had first proposed soon after the Beltana massacre. In correspondence with Hamilton, who was also Chief Protector of Aborigines, Warburton had written: 'it would appear that the large mobs of Natives coming down from Lake Hope and Cooper Creek districts undertake the long journey if not solely – yet chiefly, for the purpose of procuring the red pigment – if this be the real state of the case, I should like the opinion of Corporal Wauhop as to whether it would not be a good plan to supply them with the required article nearer their homes?'[86]

Warburton's innovative suggestion was to locate an accessible source of the ochre in the north and to send a quantity of it to the Lake Hope region, removing the need for ochre parties to set off into the 'settled districts'. The Pukardu site had probably still not been visited by Europeans. Warburton had two other localities in mind, a site at Mount Flint, south of Lake Gregory, and another at Mundowianie Springs.[87] This well-intentioned but naïve plan was received sceptically by Corporal Wauhop who, even by 1874, must have gleaned something of the Pukardu mine's significance. His reply to Hamilton confirms this: 'I am not aware where this article can be procured further north than Parychannala [Parachilna] having made enquiry of the Natives in this neighbourhood and they all say that they get their supply of paint from the above place'.[88] An Adelaide journalist was less circumspect, but endorsed the scheme nevertheless:

> There is something grotesque in the thought of the Government of a British colony supplying red ochre to the savages to adorn their bodies on great occasions! But that is better than allowing them to pass into the settled districts, where their presence is always followed by mischief.[89]

In any event, the government could not find teamsters willing to cart the ochre from the Pukardu mine and the plan was dropped for ten years. In 1874 the South Australian government paid for four tons of red ochre to be extracted from the traditional mine of Kaurna Aborigines at Red Ochre Cove, south of Adelaide. A bullock team transported the load at a cost of £39 per ton to the Killalpaninna mission east of Lake Eyre for distribution by the Lutheran missionaries.[90] Not surprisingly, this experiment was a failure. According to the director of the Blinman copper mines, T.A. Masey, 'the natives would not use it. It did not give them that much-coveted shiny appearance that filled them with delight and admiration when contemplating their noble selves, and that also made them the pride of their lubras, and the envy of rival tribes'.[91]

ACCOMMODATION

Reprisals and 'pacification' techniques by white settlers and police inevitably affected the ochre parties and modified their behaviour. A loosely observed code of conduct emerged during the 1870s and 1880s, involving accommodation on both sides. The settlers generally allowed access to waterholes and passage through their properties, while the ochre parties kept away from stock and visited the head stations instead for rations and handouts, particularly in drought years.

Reuther recorded a poignant example of this code of conduct, from an Aboriginal viewpoint. He described an occasion (probably in the 1880s) when an ochre party comprising Diyari and Yawarrawarrka men reached the Flinders Ranges:

> After they had brought their *bukatu* down from the ranges they withdrew to a local waterhole to rest and relax. Here a shepherd was watering his sheep. The Jauraworka [men] suggested catching some sheep and killing them. The

Dieri men tried to restrain them from doing so, for they knew what sort of consequences would follow.

Not allowing themselves to be convinced the former carried out their intentions in spite of it. The result was that they were soundly whipped for their theft and turned loose. Still undaunted, the Jauraworkas attempted once more to invade the herds. As frequently happened in other instances, so also here: the innocent had to suffer with the guilty. Two Dieri men were shot.[92]

When the two groups returned north in separate parties, the Yawarrawarrka men, rather than the whites, were held responsible for the deaths. Reprisals and counter-reprisals between the Diyari and the Yawarrawarrka followed.

This graphic example of Aboriginal adjustment to new conditions imposed by the European presence helps account for the continuance of ochre expeditions beyond the turn of the century. After the early years of open conflict both sides knew what to expect of each other. Although the expeditions were probably never without the risk of white harassment, the period after 1880 was characterised by accommodation. On the Aboriginal side this meant restraint in the face of obvious temptation; on the European side the occasional philanthropy and goodwill displayed by police and pastoralists was now supplemented by a new factor – the operation of government-sponsored ration depots.

Although a few depots had been established in the Flinders Ranges during the 1860s, they did not play a significant part in the story of the ochre expeditions until some years later, when overstocking by pastoralists began to devastate the traditional food sources. There is evidence that some pastoralists even hastened this process so that local Aboriginal groups would move from their properties. One northern pastoralist was reputed to have issued his station-managers with deer-hounds so that the smaller marsupials which had been a mainstay of Aboriginal existence could be hunted out.[93]

The strain on ration depots at places such as Blinman and Beltana was greatly increased when ochre parties of up to 200 men arrived, particularly in drought years when local Aboriginal people required more rations. In the worst years, when important waterholes along the ochre routes had dried completely, ochre parties did not set out at all. Writing from Mount Serle in 1864, Corporal Wauhop considered that 'the Natives will not visit the Mt Deception neighbourhood again until the Gum and St A'Beckett waterholes are filled as they are now quite dry and therefore the natives will not be able to go their usual route for want of water on the plain'.[94]

Paradoxically, it was that symbol of European civilisation and dominance, the railway, which made it considerably easier for the smaller expeditions to reach their destination after the 1880s. Begun in 1878, the railway link from Port Augusta was extended first to Farina, and then to Marree in 1884. Free travel on South Australia's railways was officially available to Aborigines only by application to the Protector of Aborigines. This regulation did nothing to dampen the ochre parties' enthusiasm for the novelty and convenience of a train ride which saved a fortnight's hard trek and brought them within an afternoon's walk of the mine. It seems that the railway journey occasionally became an end in itself during the period before the First World War. Reminiscing in the 1980s, E.J. Finn recounted that Aboriginal men who had inveigled a free ride from the Marree station-manager by pleading the necessity for more red ochre sometimes alighted at Commodore siding and then waited for the next train to take them north again, without even venturing into the Ranges.[95] If 'jumping the rattler' sometimes became an end in itself, there is also no doubt that the railway played a crucial role in prolonging the red ochre expeditions, for at least a generation. Not only did the 300 kilometre stretch of railway from Marree to Leigh Creek eliminate an arduous section of the journey; it removed the ochre parties' dangerous exposure to armed pastoralists defending their runs.

The linguist Luise Hercus has recorded a song composed by the father of her Wangkangurru informant, Mick McLean Irinjili, describing the experience of seeing a steam train at Farina while on an ochre expedition. Jimmy Russell Wangamirri gave her an account of the journey home from the ochre mine:

> They go to the Commodore [railway cottages] and then they go by train. The guard gives them a free ride ... They'd jump off at the Mundowdna siding [just south of Marree]. They'd get off and go on by foot.[96]

In his 90s, Ben Murray Parlu-nguyu-thangkayiwarna, a Thirrari-Arabana man whose Afghan father, Bejah Dervish, accompanied the Calvert expedition in 1896 as cameleer, recalled that the Marree station-manager allowed the parties to travel in an empty truck concealed under a tarpaulin. On one occasion the returning party attempted to board the train through the passenger carriage, semi-naked and covered in red ochre.[97] Reuther's own description of Aboriginal men 'painted up' with red ochre conveys the impact: 'when men have painted themselves with *bukatu*, one can already recognize them from afar, like Frenchmen in red trousers'.[98] It is easy to imagine the consternation among a compartment full of white passengers attuned to the civilising effects of the railway in these remote areas. Both Ben Murray and Leslie Russell confirmed

Jimmy Russell's statement that ochre parties alighted from the train on the return journey at Mundowdna, south of Marree, to avoid the attention they would have attracted at the town's station. A more important reason undoubtedly applied: Gason and Reuther stressed that ochre parties returned to their home camps in secrecy and under cover of darkness, prior to the start of the mindari ceremonies.[99]

This photograph of two men dressed and armed in the manner of Aboriginal men of the Diamantina region near Birdsville, was taken by J.H. Nixon on an 1874 photographic excursion to the vicinity of Hergott Springs (Marree). These men may have been members of an ochre expedition en route to the Flinders Ranges. Photograph and provenance courtesy of Howard Speed.

The railway line from Marree to Parachilna followed the route taken by ochre parties on the western side of the Flinders Ranges. Aboriginal people on the Nullarbor Plain later made similar use of the Transcontinental Railway, conveying ceremonial objects between sites and camps in the region.[100] Instances of this incorporation and exploitation of changed circumstance and technology can be found throughout Australia. The ochre trade example is particularly striking, for it appears that the network of European communication through the region was used by Aborigines to maintain their trading practices. Ben Murray recalled that the Marree–Birdsville mail coach sometimes carried an anonymous parcel of pukardu ochre, which had already been brought north to Marree by train. The northern parties returned to the Birdsville country from Marree by foot, entrusting the load to Billy James's mail coach, either at Marree or along the track as he passed by.[101]

'AS THE BIBLE IS TO CHRISTIANS'

The grid of European settlement and communication was superimposed upon a complex Aboriginal network of tracks and trajectories. That the routes and the sites used by both cultures were often the same should not obscure the violent conflict which had often occurred before accommodation was reached. By the 1870s a balance had been reached in most areas of north-eastern South Australia. Access to land and water sources was now in European hands. As a result, with the waning of ceremonial life, ochre expeditions contracted in size and frequency. This is despite the availability of rations along the routes – scant compensation for the fouled waterholes and the diminution of native plants and animals through overgrazing.

During this period the Pukardu mine site had remained untouched by Europeans. It was first visited by a European in about 1875.[102] While travelling 'in the Far North' this individual met an Aboriginal man decorated with a 'peculiar shiny red ochre'. Being made aware of the mine's sacred nature, the traveller convinced the Aboriginal man to accompany him to it. Excited by the find, the traveller brought a geologist, Dr Ulrich, from Melbourne to examine the site. Ulrich analysed an ochre sample and confirmed the presence of pure red haematite, 'one of the richest of iron ores'. He mistakenly found that the ochre collected by Aborigines consisted of 'iron froth, a nearly pure oxide of iron', associated with globules of quicksilver or native mercury. Ulrich considered this occurrence of native mercury to be 'quite extraordinary, yet indirectly confirmed by the rumour that the natives who use the stuff for painting their bodies become more or less salivated'.[103]

Further investigation of the site by Europeans took place in 1883 when the Blinman mines director, T. Masey, convinced two local Aboriginal men to take him there. Like Ulrich, Masey was interested in the possibility of locating a source of mercury for commercial use, noting that 'whatever the result may be the deposit is very remarkable, and should be explored and followed a few fathoms into the mountain'. The reaction of his two guides to this interest can be judged from Masey's own words:

> Since my return the two blacks have, no doubt, suffered from guiltiness of conscience at what they have done, and have earnestly begged that I will make no use of the discovery. 'White man take away all copper, but not red ochre – that special property of black man'.[104]

Whether Masey heeded this plea or not, the mine remained safe from European interference for another twenty years. During this period it continued to exert its attraction as a religious focus for many Aboriginal groups throughout the north-east of the state. In 1904 the inevitable occurred, when Mr A.A. Raeck (a cooper of Waymouth Street, Adelaide) proposed to prospect on the site for iron ore. Raeck understood something of the site's significance; he had no qualms about naming his claim 'Sacred Land'.[105] He apparently also intended to use necessary force to prevent further Aboriginal access. It was this situation which precipitated the Aboriginal decision to enlist Shanahan's assistance later that year.

The alienation of the Pukardu site brought an immediate reaction, illuminating the nature of Aboriginal politics in the region in a way not previously documented. The local guardian of the mine, the King Hal or Harry Bailes of Shanahan's letter, was sufficiently familiar with English and with local authority to exert direct pressure on Shanahan and R.J. Matheson, owner of Nilpena Station to the north-west of the mine. But Harry Bailes was prepared to go much further than this. As Shanahan wrote in a letter to Mr Hamilton, the official Protector of Aborigines:

> I have spoken to the recognised King of the local tribes (a local who speaks excellent English) and he considers if the rights of the tribe be denied them by the Government issuing a mineral lease to whites there will be a native feud waged, which will possibly extend to a reprisal on the white population in our far Northern centres.[106]

Shanahan wrote that 'yabber sticks' (message-sticks) had been circulated in September 1904 to summon all interested Aboriginal groups from hundreds of miles around to a meeting in Brachina Gorge to discuss the crisis: 'The event seems centred in the possession of an ochre hill, the contents of which appear to be (to the aborigines) of as much import as the Bible is to Christians'. Moreover, Shanahan went on:

> the aforementioned King has informed me that he intends discussing at the projected conference the desirability of abolishing throughout the tribes the rite of circumcision and subincision in order that they may increase in numbers. To Ethnologists their fiat on such a question would be most interesting though it is almost futile to expect that they would be willing to jettison the main plank in their ceremonial rites.[107]

Shanahan's account of a planned Aboriginal council of war, followed by a guerrilla campaign with a defined objective, organised throughout Central Australia by numerous groups, is rare in Australian Aboriginal contact history. The episode is even more remarkable considering the likelihood that many of those attending King Harry's conference may have arrived from the north by rail.

But the 'projected conference' did not eventuate. Instead, as a result of King Harry's initiative, Shanahan and Matheson, joined by Stirling, influenced the government to take an interest in the matter. Matheson had already written to the Protector of Aborigines in August 1904:

> Lately the king of the tribe came to me saying he had heard that the whites were going to work these claims, and asking me to try and get the locality reserved for them. I think that this would be but just and right as the black man will be gone before long and the white man will have full opportunity. I should like to mention that during the course of the next three or four months there will be a great muster of blacks in Brachina Gorge and should you care to visit them there and hear what they have to say I shall be happy to drive you out to the spot. The king then can plead the natives' cause and act as interpreter.[108]

Edward Stirling had collected samples of red ochre from Aboriginal people during his own expeditions. He had written about its use among the Arrernte people in his report on anthropology for the Horn expedition of 1894, and had incorporated a display of ochre samples within the South Australian Museum's exhibition. On 29 September 1904 he wrote to the South Australian Premier, J.G. Jenkins:

> To deprive the natives of this would in my opinion be a real act of unkindness towards them and I am therefore induced to ask you if you will kindly look into the matter and see whether this place cannot be preserved for them. I know something about the natives and the value placed upon this article and this leads me to mention it to you.[109]

As a result of Stirling's intervention the government geologist, F.R. George, was sent to investigate the matter, and accompanied Shanahan and Matheson to the mine. His report, and the information sent by Shanahan to Stirling, reached the government in late 1904. In January 1905, apparently before any European mining had commenced and with extraordinary rapidity, the site was removed from the operation of the Mining Act and was gazetted as an Aboriginal reserve.[110]

REPRISE

Ochre expeditions continued to visit Pukardu with some regularity until the First World War. The 1919 Spanish Influenza epidemic dealt a blow to local Aboriginal populations in the region, but ceremonial life continued and with it, the imperative to retrace the ancestral Emu's path. As late as 1937,

T.P. Bellchambers captioned this photograph '"Larrikin Tom", and his turnout on our return from the ochre mine, after a night's exposure without food, water or blankets'. *Observer*, 31 December 1927.

C.P. Mountford observed that Aboriginal men at Charleville in south-west Queensland were contemplating a trip to the mine.[111]

During the 1920s, custodianship of the mine and its Emu mythology rested with a Parnkarla man known to Europeans as Larrikin Tom. He may have received this status as custodian directly from his predecessor, Harry Bailes, but he had also earned his credentials as a participant in the ambush of Diyari men at the mine during the 1870s. One of Larrikin Tom's last visits to Pukardu occurred during 1927 or 1928, in company with a naturalist and pioneer conservationist, Tom Paine Bellchambers. Hearing of the mine's significance, Bellchambers engaged Larrikin Tom to take him there. The pair travelled by Tom's own horse and cart from the Aboriginal camp on Parachilna Creek to the foot of the range, then made the long trek up the steep gullies and slopes. Bellchambers gave this account:

> It was 4 p.m. when we reached our destination – a slight depression just below the topmost peak ... The workings consisted of about a half a dozen shallow pits. The older of these were partly filled with boulders thrown out from the more recent. Two pits were just as they had been left by the native miners who last visited the place. While I was fixing the camera, Tom disappeared into one of the holes, and presently re-appeared with about five pounds of ochre in a small bag.
>
> 'What do you want with that, Tom?' I said.
>
> 'Mary [his wife] want 'em,' he replied.
>
> 'What she do with it?'
>
> 'Oh, she put 'em on herself.'
>
> So it would appear that even to this day early customs linger among the old folk.[112]

Larrikin Tom, Parnkarla custodian of the Pukardu mine, at one of the mine's pits. Photographer: T.P. Bellchambers. *Observer*, 31 December 1927.

Larrikin Tom confirmed that for him the ochre represented the blood of two Emus, 'hunted by the Cooper Creek natives across many leagues of hills and plains that lay between'.

Larrikin Tom died at the Nepabunna

mission in 1936, a year before Charles Mountford began his anthropological investigations there. Spending his last days at Nepabunna among survivors of the Wailpi, Parnkarla, Yadliyawarra and other peoples of the Ranges and adjacent plains, the old Parnkarla man must have encountered the dissonance between the two Pukardu Dreamings. Perhaps this contradiction was resolved through forms of syncretism or accommodation, similar to those applied in dealing with the recently arrived Christian missionaries at Nepabunna. By the time of Tom's death the missionaries were calling for an end to ceremony, and a close to the idolatrous regard of the Emu, Dingo and Lizard ancestors. Observing the missionaries' Christmas celebrations (a decorated tree and Santa Claus) at Nepabunna during 1937, Mountford was struck by the dilemma facing the old men. According to his later notes, red ochre for the last initiations in the region, in 1948, was taken from a site closer to the Nepabunna settlement. The Pukardu site seemed forgotten.

This was not the case. Local knowledge about the site and the story of the epic battle between the Lizard and the Dingo was retained and treasured. As the Adnyamathanha people consolidated a new identity, forged from the chaos

Looking across the red-stained mine site, over the range to the Lake Torrens plain.
Photographer: P. Jones, 1983.

of the colonial period, it was the Emu Dreaming of the Kuyani and the north-erners which gradually slipped from memory. Larrikin Tom's death in 1936 marked the end of the ancient tradition of expeditions to the mine from the 'far north', founded on that legend. But occasional visits by local people continued. During the 1920s local custodianship of the mine and its Dingo Dreaming had passed to a northern Parnkarla man, Percy Richards.

The perceived threat of renewed European mining in the region impelled Percy Richards' son Andrew and his relatives to peg out a miner's claim over the area during the 1960s, despite its apparent protected status as a gazetted Aboriginal reserve. During a visit to the mine in the 1980s I happened upon one of the handmade signs marking this claim. The irony of this resort to the very mechanism of exploitation which had threatened the mine in the first place was not lost on Andrew's two sons, who had assisted him in that exercise. More than 30 years later, in the early summer of 2000, they returned to the mine in company with this author, for what they saw as their last visit.[113]

It was a long, meandering climb into the ancient range, on a clear and sunny day. There was plenty of time to consider the view, to note the gradual staining tinge of pinkish-red over the earth and rocks as we approached the mine. Arriving, looking down across the hazy plain to the distant mirage of Lake Torrens, the profound calm of this scene seems to deny history, the fabric torn since those first encounters between ochre parties and Europeans, almost 150 years ago. The Aboriginal memories of Pukardu stretch back further than that, past Shanahan's time, and into the deep history of many generations.

Abbreviations used in endnotes and bibliography:

BA   –   Battarbee Archive, c/ Gayle Quarmby, Reedy Creek, Kingston, South Australia
BSL   –   Special Collections, Barr Smith Library, University of Adelaide
ML   –   Mitchell Library, Sydney
SAMA   –   South Australian Museum Archives
SLSA   –   State Library of South Australia
SRC   –   Strehlow Research Centre, Alice Springs
SRSA   –   State Records, South Australia
SAPP   –   South Australian Parliamentary Paper

INTRODUCTION

1   Attenbrow 2002, pp. 86–87.
2   I am grateful to Peter Lane, numismatist, for alerting me to the existence of the Killora medal, and for allowing me to photograph it. Only about 20 of the original 2000 medals have been found: eleven in New Zealand, three or four in Tahiti, two in New Caledonia, and one each in the New Hebrides, Canada and Australia (Lane 1992, p. 19; see also Lane 1995).
3   Evans-Pritchard 1940, p. 89.
4   Sobin 1999.

CHAPTER ONE
Master Blackburn's whip

1   Extract from Stirling Gallery exhibition label (displayed 1914–1982) at the South Australian Museum. AA298, SAMA.
2   Bennett 1995, p. 77.
3   For a discussion of this shift in attitude towards Aboriginal art by Europeans, and Mountford's role in engineering that shift, see Jones 1988.

4   Observations made by the author during fieldwork during the 1980s and, in the case of
    Mount Poole, during January 2004. The walls of a police station in South Australia's
    mid-north are said to incorporate slabs bearing Aboriginal rock-engravings.
5   See Jones 1996.
6   Similar clubs are described and figured in Attenbrow 2002, fig. 8.6, pp. 94–95.
7   Rodger 1986, p. 212.
8   Dening 1992, pp. 117, 119–120; Rodger 1986, p. 219.
9   *Ibid*, pp. 215, 219.
10 Flannery (1999, p. 25) states that the wooden spear-point extracted from Governor
    Phillip's shoulder in September 1790 (described later in this chapter) is 'a treasured item in
    the National Museum of Australia'. The National Museum considered bidding at a 1998
    auction for a metal spearhead claimed to be that object, but did not do so.
11 Collins 1971, vol. 1, pp. 487–488.
12 Tench 1996, p. 255.
13 Megaw 1993; Attenbrow 2002, p. 86.
14 Letter from David Blackburn to his sister, Margaret Blackburn, 12 July 1788,
    Mss 6937/1/12, ML.
15 Blackburn describes the event in letters to his sister Margaret (*ibid*), and to his friend
    Richard Knight (microfilm CY 1301, ML), both written on 12 July 1788. Blackburn was
    on board the *Supply* while the naming ceremony was taking place. He maintained that
    if he had been ashore the island 'should have been call'd Knight Isle'.
16 Neville 1975, p. 14.
17 The whip's sale price at Christie's was £2800; it was eventually purchased by the South
    Australian Museum in 2002, with the assistance of the National Australia Bank and the
    National Cultural Heritage Account, for AU$250,000.
18 Letter from David Blackburn to his sister, Margaret Blackburn, 2 September 1787,
    Mss 6937/10, ML.
19 These voyages are documented in varying detail in Neville 1975.
20 See Dawes mss. 1790, 1791, microfilm copy, ML.
21 Prior to Christie's sale of Blackburn's effects, the Mitchell Library had already
    received some of his papers, including the vocabulary of the Eora language mistakenly
    attributed wholly to him (see Berzins 1988, p. 37). That vocabulary is certainly in
    Blackburn's hand, but it is an annotated copy of a vocabulary first recorded by his
    fellow officer, Lieutenant William Dawes. It appears to be an abridged copy, but may
    also represent an early form of Dawes's own vocabulary, dating to late 1790 or early
    1791, when Blackburn's vocabulary was posted to England. Blackburn's vocabulary is
    written in two columns, headed 'Native of N.S. Wales' and 'English Explanation', on
    a large folded sheet enclosed with his letter to Richard Knight of 19 March 1791,
    written aboard the *Supply* (microfilm CY 1301, ML). Blackburn completed the letter
    to his friend with the request: 'The Inclosed is a kind of Vocabulary, which I will thank
    you to let my sister see'. The vocabulary contains some notable variations from
    Dawes's original list. Dawes's diacritics are not always completely transcribed,
    Blackburn's additional words and phrases are in darker ink and added between lines
    (suggesting that they were made after the initial transcription), and Blackburn
    occasionally makes an additional comment. Blackburn did not include the bracketed
    letters which appear on Dawes's list after certain letters, e.g. (W), (W.T.), (J), (C.C.),
    nor did Blackburn transcribe those phrases in which Dawes used numbers denoting
    word order.
22 See Smith 2001 for a biography of Bennelong. Following the usage established and
    commented on by Smith 2001, Troy 1994 and Attenbrow 2002, I use the term 'Eora' not
    as a tribal or language name, but as the term used by speakers of the unnamed 'Sydney
    language' to refer to themselves, as 'people'.
23 See Troy 1994 for a word list in the Sydney language.

24 Letter from David Blackburn to his mother, 4 April 1787, Mss 6937/1/2, ML. Note that Blackburn wrote according to the conventions of the time, often omitting the final 'e' of verbs in the past tense.

25 This reconstruction of the events leading up to his embarkation is drawn from letters from David Blackburn to his sister, Margaret Blackburn, 12 March 1787; 6 April 1787; 10 April 1787, Mss 6937/1/1–3, ML.

26 Letter from David Blackburn to his sister, Margaret Blackburn, 6 April 1787, Mss 6937/1/1, ML.

27 Letters from David Blackburn to his sister, Margaret Blackburn, 10 April, 6 May 1787, Mss 6937/1/1,3, ML.

28 Letter from David Blackburn to his sister, Margaret Blackburn, 6 May 1787, *ibid*.

29 Perhaps his family felt justified in bestowing this title, as Blackburn was, in fact, second in command on the *Supply*, as his letter of 6 May makes plain (*ibid*): 'the Armd Tender is a Brig – not Commanded by a Captn but a Lieut therefore no Lieut under him – the Master next – then Surgeon – Boatswain – Gunner – Carpenter – therefore I am second in command on Board & as tis known that my Commander Lieut Ball is to be made a Capt the first opportunity I think I stand an Equal Chance of Preferment'.

30 Letter from David Blackburn to his sister, Margaret Blackburn, 2 September 1787, Mss 6937/1/10, ML.

31 *Ibid*.

32 Letter from David Blackburn to his sister, Margaret Blackburn, 9 November 1787, Mss 6937/1/11, ML.

33 Extract of a letter from Governor Phillip to Mr Stephens, dated 13 November 1791. Blackburn Papers, ML.

34 By the 1799 campaign against Napoleon in Egypt, Ball had attained the rank of captain, commanding HMS *Daedalus*.

35 Letter from David Blackburn to his sister, Margaret Blackburn, 12 August 1790, Mss 6937/1/14, ML.

36 Blackburn to Richard Knight, 12 July 1788. ZSafe 1/120 (formerly Ab163): issue microfilm CY 1301. This letter was a more expansive version of one written to his sister on the same day.

37 King, quoted in Egan 1999, p. 2.

38 Bradley 1969, p. 63.

39 Phillip 1982, p. 80.

40 Worgan 1978, p. 14.

41 Blackburn to Richard Knight, 12 July 1788. ZSafe 1/120 (formerly Ab163): issue microfilm CY 1301, ML.

42 Collins, quoted in Egan 1999, p. 8; Tench 1996, p. 42.

43 Bradley 1969, p. 62.

44 *Ibid*, p. 60.

45 Smith 2001, p. 25.

46 Nagle, quoted in Egan 1999, p. 4.

47 Tench 1996, p. 43. Tench ascribes this action to an unnamed officer. Other sources suggest that it was Surgeon White. See Clendinnen 2003, p. 292.

48 The seaman George Thompson observed that the Aborigines of Port Jackson 'keep constantly singing while they paddle along' in their canoes: 'They have the French tune of "Malbrook" very perfect; I have heard a dozen or twenty singing it together' (quoted in Egan 1999, p. 303).

49 Blackburn to Richard Knight, 12 July 1788. ZSafe 1/120 (formerly Ab163): issue microfilm CY 1301, ML.

50 For an explanation of the 'Eora dilemma', see Attenbrow 2002, pp. 35–36.

51 Collins, quoted in Egan 1999, p. 8; Bowes Smyth, quoted in Smith 2001, p. 17. For a discusson of the estimated Aboriginal populations, see Attenbrow 2002, p. 17.

52   Nagle, quoted in Egan 1999, p. 51
53   Letter from David Blackburn to his sister, Margaret Blackburn, 15 November 1788,
      Mss 6937/1/13, ML.
54   See Attenbrow 2002, p. 87 for a discussion of Eora fishing technology. Attenbrow confirms
      that small hoop nets were also used for fishing.
55   White, quoted in Egan 1999, p. 10.
56   Worgan 1978, p. 29.
57   *Ibid*, p. 19.
58   Admiralty Account Book, quoted in Smith 2001, p. 150.
59   Hunter 1968, p. 56.
60   Clendinnen 2003, p. 32. This topic is discussed in more detail in chapter three.
61   White, quoted in Egan 1999, p. 64.
62   Colllins 1910, p. 30.
63   *Ibid*, p. 29.
64   Bradley 1969, p. 141.
65   Collins 1910, pp. 33–34.
66   Southwell, quoted in R. Neville 1997, p. 17.
67   Collins, quoted in Smith 2001, pp. 19–20.
68   Tench 1996, p. 146.
69   Tench 1996, p. 91.
70   Collins 1910, p. 19.
71   Letter from Henry Waterhouse to his father, 11 July 1788, Waterhouse Family Papers,
      1782–1819 ZML MSS 6544, ML.
72   Letter from David Blackburn to his sister, Margaret Blackburn, 12 July 1788,
      ML Mss 6937/1/12, ML.
73   Letter from David Blackburn to his sister, Margaret Blackburn, 15 November 1788,
      Mss 6937/1/13, ML.
74   Letter from David Blackburn to Richard Knight, 19 March 1791. ZSafe 1/120, ML.
75   Letter from David Blackburn to his sister, Margaret Blackburn, 12 July 1788, ML
      Mss 6937/1/12, ML.
76   Letter from Henry Waterhouse to his father, 11 July 1788, Waterhouse Family Papers,
      1782–1819 ZML MSS 6544, ML.
77   Letter from David Blackburn to his sister, Margaret Blackburn, 12 July 1788,
      ML Mss 6937/1/12, ML.
78   Letter from David Blackburn to his sister, Margaret Blackburn, 15 November 1788,
      ML Mss 6937/1/13, ML.
79   Letter from David Blackburn to his sister Margaret Blackburn, 17 March 1791.
      ML Mss 6937/1/12, ML.
80   Letter from Henry Waterhouse to his father, 11 July 1788. Waterhouse Family Papers,
      1782–1819 ZML MSS 6544, ML.
81   Letter from Henry Waterhouse to his father, 20 February 1789. Waterhouse Family
      Papers, 1782–1819 ZML MSS 6544, ML.
82   Bradley 1969, p. 128.
83   *Ibid*, p. 121.
84   *Ibid*, pp. 85–86.
85   Tench 1996, p. 59.
86   Letter from David Blackburn to his sister, Margaret Blackburn, 12 August 1790.
      ML Mss 6937/1/14, ML.
87   Tench 1996, p. 97.
88   Letter from David Blackburn to his sister, Margaret Blackburn, 12 August 1790, *ibid*. This
      rather pessimistic analysis was not shared by Tench, who maintained that linguistic terms
      and 'much information relating to the customs and manners of his country was also gained
      from him' (Tench 1996, p. 100).

89 Tench 1996, p. 108.
90 *Ibid*, p. 102.
91 These objects have not been traced. See Smith 2001 for a discussion of Boorong and her role as an intermediary.
92 See Smith 2001 for a detailed description of Bennelong's relations with the British.
93 Letter from David Blackburn to his sister, Margaret Blackburn, 12 August 1790 (the date of departure of the mail – most of the letter was probably written several months earlier), *ibid*.
94 Tench 1996, p. 108.
95 Inga Clendinnen (2003, p. 110) has aptly described it as an 'iconic moment in Australian history'. The following interpretation was written independently of either Clendinnen's or Smith's (2001) accounts of the same events, but comments upon them below.
96 Tench 1996, p. 135.
97 Bradley 1969, p. 226.
98 Tench 1996, p. 138.
99 *Ibid*, p. 228.
100 Collins 1910, p. 98; Tench 1996, pp. 138–139.
101 Tench 1996, p. 139.
102 Egan 1999, p. 193.
103 Smith 2001, p. 57.
104 Clendinnen 2003, p. 124.
105 Tench 1996, p. 138.
106 This phrase is used by the linguist-historian Mary Louise Pratt, in her insightful survey of South American colonial travel writing (Pratt 1992, p. 7).
107 Phillip, quoted in Egan 1999, p. 195.
108 Egan 1999, p. 191; Smith 2001, p. 70. The Christie's auction catalogue entry presents a case for the spearhead's authenticity, but makes it plain that it could not be the Governor Phillip spearhead. The unbarbed metal spearhead is photographed against Waterhouse's manuscript account of his assistance to Phillip, which reads in part: 'I was in the act of doing it when I recollected I should only haul the barb into his flesh again'. The presence of this detail did not deter a Waterhouse descendant from paying more than AU$170,000 (greatly exceeding the estimate of AU$20–30,000) to acquire the relic. *Christie's Exploration and Travel Catalogue*, 8 April 1998, lot 132, p. 117–119, Christie's, London.
109 Tench 1996, p. 150.
110 Egan 1999, p. 262.
111 Hunter 1968, p. 472.
112 Collins 1971, vol. 1, p. 498.
113 Dégerando 1969, p. 97.
114 Quoted in Smith 2001, p. 152.
115 Anon 1790–1791. See Troy 1994 for these terms in a modern orthography.
116 *Ibid*.
117 David Collins, quoted in Smith 2001, p. 139.
118 Letter from David Blackburn to his sister, Margaret Blackburn, 12 October 1790, Mss 6937/14, ML.
119 Smith 2001, pp. 117–118.
120 Blackburn's uncle had investigated the matter: 'the reason for his not writing he can by no means account for, he (Lieut King) says it is particularly strange as most likely it will be six months before you can hear again'. Peter Martineau to Mrs Blackburn, 19 February 1791, Mss 6937/11, ML.
121 J. Briggs to Margaret Blackburn, 20 February 1795, *ibid*.
122 This account is constructed from papers relating to Blackburn's death in Mss 6937/11/5, ML.

123 Letter from Mrs Blackburn to Mr Robertson, n.d. (probably 3 February 1795), Mss 6937/11/5, ML.
124 Unknown correspondent to Mrs Blackburn, 1 March 1795, Mss 6937/11, ML.

CHAPTER TWO
Broken shields

1 Letter from G.F. Edmunds to South Australian Museum, 29 June 1887, p. 202, 'Donations Book, 1882–1887', AA298, SAMA.
2 In the dialect recorded by the Milang policeman, C.O. Trounson, the Point Malcolm lighthouse (or probably the prominence on which it stands) was known as 'Rooidurng' (List of place-names submitted by C.O. Trounson, 1901, Docket 888/1901, Chief Secretary's Office, GRG 24, SRSA). The place-name record documented for this region by R.M. and C.H. Berndt (1993, p. 324) defines Point Malcolm as 'Katang', but that appears to be a coastal feature close to the locality of the cave in the cliff beneath the lighthouse.
3 See chapters on these events in Foster, Hosking and Nettlebeck (eds) 2001.
4 Mr C.B. Young's Report, *29th Annual Report*, Aborigines' Friends' Association, Adelaide, 1887.
5 See Taplin 1874; Taplin 1879.
6 Entry for 22 September 1860, Journal of George Taplin, PRG 186, SLSA.
7 That story, and Taplin's complex role in protecting Ngarrindjeri interests while assiduously transforming their culture and beliefs, is well told in Jenkin 1979.
8 Taplin 1879, p. 71–72. See also the corresponding entry in Taplin's journal, 9 November 1859.
9 Taplin journal, 8 May 1861.
10 Taplin 1879, p. 101.
11 Taplin journal, 13 August 1861. Much later, realising Pullami's role as the *rupulle* (*mungkumbuli*), Taplin wrote of him: 'Peter, who is the Rupulle of the Point Malcolm tribe, was not, I believe, the eldest son of his father, nor yet the most warlike or athletic, but was chosen by his tribe for his wisdom, moderation and good temper'. Taplin 1879, p. 32.
12 Taplin journal, 13 August 1861.
13 *Ibid*, 1, 2 November 1864.
14 *Ibid*, 10 November 1859.
15 *Ibid*, 1 December 1859; 4 March, 21 August 1860; 11 May 1861.
16 *Ibid*, p. 139. See also Taplin journal, 19 December 1862.
17 See the Berndts' discussion of this institution, which Taplin termed the *tandi* or *tendi* (Berndt and Berndt 1993, pp. 64–73).
18 See for example, Jenkin 1979, pp. 194–198.
19 Taplin journal, 1 January 1862. Nipper may have been introduced to literacy by the missionary James Reid, who had taught James Unaipon to read and write. Taplin's journal (8 May 1861) records that Nipper accompanied Reid on an evangelical voyage to the Coorong.
20 Taplin journal, 9 December 1863.
21 Berndt and Berndt 1993, pp. 254–255.
22 Taplin journal, 8 January 1867.
23 *Ibid*, 10 October 1864.
24 *Ibid*, 15 and 16 October 1864.
25 *Ibid*, 3, 4, 12, 18 November 1864.
26 *Ibid*, 5 January 1867.
27 *Ibid*, 12 January 1867.

28 *Ibid*, 17 February 1867.
29 Jenkin 1979, p. 150.
30 Berndt and Berndt 1993, p. 61.
31 Taplin journal, 27 September 1867.
32 *Ibid*, 13 November 1867.
33 'The first whites who came to Point Malcolm tried to kidnap women'. Taplin journal, 5 March 1867.
34 Taplin 1879, p. 113.
35 Entry for 'Peter (Aboriginal)', 10th admission for 1868, 'Register of patients, Adelaide Asylum, 1856–1880', GRG 34/140 SRSA.
36 70th admission for 1869, *ibid*; Taplin journal, 16 January 1872.
37 Taplin journal, 18 March 1870.
38 *Ibid*, 30 March 1870.
39 *Ibid*, 25 April 1870.
40 *Ibid*, 9–10 June 1870. On 19 July 1872, Taplin wrote: 'I always make their drying of dead bodies as inconvenient as possible to them. All the sensible men of the tribe are against it'.
41 *Ibid*, 9 April 1871.
42 *Ibid*, 21 July 1874.
43 *Ibid*, 20 January 1875.
44 *Ibid*, 21 July 1874.
45 *27th Annual Report*, Aborigines' Friends' Association, Adelaide, 1885, p. 12.
46 Berndt and Berndt 1993, p. 167. For Karloan's baptism, see entry for 7 May 1882, 'Church Book of the Church of our Lord & Saviour Jesus Christ at Reid Town, Point McLeay, South Australia', SRG 139/5, SRO.
47 Mr C.B. Young's Report, *29th Annual Report*, Aborigines' Friends' Association, Adelaide, 1887.
48 See Jones 1990.
49 *Observer*, 13 August 1887, p. 41.
50 *Observer*, 15 September 1887, p. 30.
51 Cawthorne, W. *Literarium Diarium*, 16 December 1842; 18 December 1842; 30 September 1844, A103–105, ML.
52 *Ibid*, 26 April 1844.
53 *Ibid*, 30 September 1844.
54 *Ibid*, 22 February 1844.
55 *Ibid*, 12 July 1843.
56 See for example, W. Finlayson ms., pp. 3, 23 and Finlayson 1903, p. 45.
57 Cawthorne, *Literarium Diarium*, 21 December 1842.
58 Stephens 1890, pp. 486–490.
59 Cawthorne, *Literarium Diarium*, 27 June 1843.
60 For biographical details of George Fife Angas, George French Angas, and Eyre, see Morgan 1966, pp. 15–19; and Dutton 1966, pp. 362–364. George French Angas's career as a painter is well covered in Tregenza 1982.
61 Cawthorne, *Literarium Diarium*, 22 August 1843.
62 Cawthorne 1844, 'Sketch of the Aborigines of South Australia'. A103–105, ML.
63 Moorhouse 1846.
64 Cawthorne, *Literarium Diarium*, 25 September 1843.
65 *Ibid*, 18 November 1843.
66 *Ibid*, n.d., vol. 27, p. 40, 'Begun August 29th [1844]'.
67 *Ibid*, 9 February 1844.
68 *Ibid*.
69 *Ibid*, 2 February 1844.
70 *Ibid*.

71 In fact, this form of shield served as the official emblem of the South Australian Museum for most of the twentieth century.
72 Cawthorne, *op. cit.*, 20 April 1844.
73 Cawthorne, *op. cit.*, 22 April 1844.
74 *Register*, 24 April 1844, p. 3.
75 *Observer*, 13 August 1887, p. 41.

CHAPTER THREE
Turning to metal

1 Hill 1905, p. 43. Tim Bonyhady's history of the Burke and Wills expedition (Bonyhady 1991), and his curation of the subsequent exhibition (National Library of Australia, 2002) highlighted the enduring mnemonic role of the expedition's artefacts, photographs and documents.
2 See Phillips 1993, pp. 235–236.
3 Letter from the Council of the South Australian Branch of the Royal Geographical Society of Australasia to Albert Calvert, probably February 1896, quoted in Hill 1905, p. 5.
4 See Birman 1979; Calvert 1892; 1893; 1895–1896 (containing his list of publications). It is clear that Baron Ferdinand von Mueller, that remarkable patron of Australian exploration, had little idea of Calvert's background, but thoroughly approved of his initiative. Von Mueller wrote to A.T. Magarey:

> Is this high-minded man possibly a relative of Mr Calvert, the companion of
> Dr Leichhardt on his first glorious expedition [?] Was he already before connected with
> South Australian interests or was he merely aroused to this noble action by the
> geografic [sic] Congress in London. It is particular [sic] gratifying to me that the
> forthcoming researches will comprise also inquiries amongst the nomadic tribes after
> the long lost expedition. In reality I had almost given up hopes that the mystery would
> be cleared up in my lifetime, and that I should not see the day when all the main
> portions of Australia had at least become preliminarily mapped.
> (Letter dictated by von Mueller to A.T. Magarey, 2 May 1896, Agent's Letter
> Book, Calvert Scientific Exploring Expedition (4 February 1896 to 25 January
> 1897), p. 2, SRG 507/1, SLSA.)

5 For Carnegie's biographical entry see Morison 1979, and see Carnegie's *Spinifex and Sand* (1898).
6 A.F. Calvert to Secretary, Royal Geographical Society, Adelaide, 29 April 1896, SRG 507/5, SLSA. For the Elder expedition instructions, see Council of the Royal Geographical Society of Australasia 1891.
7 See for example Jones 1996, p. 27.
8 A.T. Magarey to A.F. Calvert, 4 February 1896, Agent's Letter Book, Calvert Scientific Exploring Expedition (4 February 1896 to 25 January 1897), p. 2, SRG 507/1, SLSA.
9 See 'Memorandum of Agreement between L.A. Wells and George Lindsay Jones' signed by Jones as 'Scientist representing Anthropology, Mineralogy & Photography'. Each expedition member signed these detailed agreements governing their obligations and conditions, presumably to avert misunderstandings of the kind affecting the Elder expedition. Jones's father, J.W. Jones, had also been Honorary Secretary of the Royal Geographical Society in Adelaide. See 1345/11, SRG 507, SLSA. For J.W. Jones's motion and biographical details, see Peake-Jones 1985, pp. 13, 25.
10 Calvert 1896, p. 385.
11 *Ibid*, p. 386.

12 Carnegie was no better at obtaining Aboriginal place-names, despite having the services of Joseph Breaden's 'boy', Warri, a young Aboriginal man 'from the MacDonnell Ranges'. Before Warri's arrival Carnegie had contemplated enlisting a discharged Aboriginal prisoner from the Rottnest Island gaol. 'They make excellent boys very often', he wrote, 'though prison-life is apt to develop all their native cunning and treachery' (Carnegie 1898, p. 149).

13 See Calvert 1892.

14 A.T. Magarey to G.L. Jones, 30 May 1896, Agent's Letter Book, Calvert Scientific Exploring Expedition (4 February 1896 to 25 January 1897), p. 69, SRG 507/1, SLSA. Jones's diary entry for 11 August 1896, for example, reads: 'Observed two smokes one about 12 o'clock, the other just after camping, the first was a thin smoke lasting for 5 min, the second was a big black one, probably hunting smoke' (G.L. Jones diary, PRG 1011/11, SLSA). Jones's attempts to obtain water from tree roots, following Magarey's observations, are described below.

15 A.F. Calvert to Treasurer, South Australian Branch, Royal Geographical Society, Adelaide, 29 April 1896, no. 1345, SRG 507/1, SLSA.

16 A.T. Magarey to A.F. Calvert, 4 February 1896, Agent's Letter Book, Calvert Scientific Exploring Expedition (4 February 1896 to 25 January 1897), p. 2, SRG 507/1, SLSA.

17 Wells 1902, p. 7.

18 The site has subsequently been recognised as one of the most significant of its kind, and was integral to the success of the Martu people's native title claim during 2002. See Veth, Smith and Haley 2001.

19 Wells 1902, p. 21. Jones barely mentions this event in his diary.

20 Wells 1902, p. 25; entry for 17 September 1896, G.L. Jones diary, *ibid*.

21 Wells 1902, p. 13.

22 Magarey 1899.

23 Wells 1902, p. 26.

24 Entry for 23 September 1896, G.L. Jones diary, *ibid*. About 250 kilometres to the south-east, while tracking an Aboriginal group, Carnegie's party came across 'little heaps of the roots of a tree (known to me only as pine-mulga [probably a hakea]) stacked together, which had been sucked for water'. (Carnegie 1898, p. 231)

25 It is worth reflecting on their chances of survival had the pair decided to wait for a relief party at Separation Well, where they had a cache of 50 lbs of tinned meat, two ration cases and permanent water. Such an option was apparently not considered at any stage, by either party.

26 Wells 1902, p. 32.

27 *Ibid*, pp. 32–33.

28 Warburton 1875, pp. 186, 199, 220. Warburton mistakenly referred to Augustus Gregory's brother, Francis, and dated the expedition (which included Ferdinand von Mueller) to about 1861.

29 Carnegie 1898, p. 258.

30 *Ibid*, p. 244.

31 *Ibid*, p. 246.

32 Entry for 15 October 1896, L.A. Wells 'Journal of Proceedings of Calvert Exploration Expedition Book No. 1', PRG 315/4, SLSA.

33 Entry for 21 October 1896, G.L. Jones diary, *ibid*.

34 The sand-ridge figures are taken from Calvert 1902, p. 35.

35 Note from G.L. Jones to G.W. and J.R. Jones, Edwin St, Gilberton, Adelaide. PRG 1011/2, SLSA.

36 Wells 1902, p. 35.

37 In 1996 a Royal Geographical Society expedition to mark the centenary of the Calvert expedition discovered this site, and retrieved a number of Jones's geological samples. The samples are listed in the back of his notebook (G.L. Jones, *ibid*).

38   Months later George Keartland even speculated that the two parties, travelling at night, had actually crossed each other's tracks to the south of Joanna Spring (Hill 1905, p. 16). This seems impossible, and Keartland may not have realised that Jones and Wells probably did not set off until 25 October.

39   See Hill 1905, pp. 29–32 for a summary of Rudall's contribution and these events.

40   Wells 1902, p. 52.

41   *Ibid*, p. 53.

42   *Ibid*, p. 59.

43   *Ibid*.

44   *Ibid*, p. 60.

45   *Ibid*.

46   *Ibid*. The Burke and Wills statue originally stood in Collins Street, but was shifted to Spring Street when the tram system was installed. For a full discussion of the enduring effect of the Burke and Wills saga on the Australian popular imagination during the late nineteenth century, see Bonyhady 1991.

47   The full verse reads:

> Then out spake brave Horatius,
>
> The Captain of the Gate:
>
> To every man upon this earth
>
> Death cometh soon or late.
>
> And how can man die better
>
> Than facing fearful odds,
>
> For the ashes of his fathers
>
> And the temples of his gods?

48   A.T. Magarey to G.L. Jones, 30 May 1896, Agent's Letter Book, Calvert Scientific Exploring Expedition, p. 69, SRG 507/1, SLSA.

49   Wells 1902, p. 60.

50   Wells 1902, p. 62.

51   Bonyhady 1991, p. 236.

52   *Observer*, 24 July 1897, p. 14.

53   Quoted in Peake-Jones 1985, p. 21.

54   Many of these objects were documented as originating on the Fitzroy River, where Wells and his men were based as the search expeditions proceeded. This provenance fits several of the objects, but certainly not the metal axe or other metal objects, nor the sandals. They are described as having been collected '100 miles south of Joanna Spring', but it is clear that Wells encountered this category of artefact for the first time on 9 April 1897 (Wells 1902, p. 52). A small collection of sacred wooden boards which Wells collected from a cache at Joanna Spring on 16 April, during the final search expedition, has recently been repatriated to descendants of the desert people.

55   Tindale 1974, p. 104.

56   Letter from Gillen to Spencer, 13 March 1896. Mulvaney, Morphy and Petch (eds) 1997, p. 105.

57   F.J. Gillen, 'Camp Jottings' 28 June 1901, PRG 54/1/2, SLSA.

58   Bundock 1978, p. 263.

59   Hawdon 1952, p. 24.

60   Loose note in N.B. Tindale papers, Murray River Notes, AA338, SAMA.

61   Hawdon 1952, p. 29.

62   *Ibid*, p. 41.

63   Sharp 1952, p. 22.

64   Sharp 1952, p. 19.

65   Colliver 1971, p. 25.

66   Beaglehole (ed.) 1967, vol. 1, p. 302.

67 King 1827, vol. 1, pp. 111; see also pp. 118, 240.
68 Spillett 1972, p. 73.
69 Ninnis's interest in Aboriginal material culture was documented by the *Beatrice's* tide watcher, Alfred Webling (Webling 1864–1865).
70 Napier 1876, p. 38.
71 Thomson 1949, p. 90.
72 See Baker's excellent study of Mitchell's encounters with Aboriginal people of south-eastern Australia (Baker 1997).
73 Finniss (ed.) 1966, p. 36. Brock 1975, p. 38–39. Brock made further mention of an adapted iron implement on 6 October, 1844 (*ibid*, p. 42).
74 *Ibid*, p. 96. During his 1838 expedition along the Murray River, Joseph Hawdon also met Aboriginal people who had received news of tomahawks ahead of his arrival (Hawdon 1952, p. 31).
75 Brock, *ibid*, p. 113.
76 Mitchell 1838 vol. 1, pp. 304–305.
77 Andrews 1875.
78 N.B. Tindale, 'UCLA Expedition 1953 Field Notes', vol. 2, pp. 698; 972. AA338/1/19/2, SAMA.
79 Entry for 28 March 1872, diary of William A. Crowder, 1871–1872, D8065, SLSA.
80 Museum label for A3941, South Australian Museum.
81 Todd 1884.
82 One of the few anthropologists to comment on this congruence has been Charles Mountford (1955).
83 Alfred Giles to Edward Stirling, 12 July 1890. AA298, SAMA.
84 Bastian 1881, p. 63.

CHAPTER FOUR
Spearing Bennett

1 The label, found in a string bag registered as A68380 in the South Australian Museum's anthropology collection, also reads 'Lent by Mr W.I. Page, High St, Wimbledon'. The connection between Page and W.W. Hoare has not been traced. For a description of Hoare's life and career, see Callaway 1992.
2 Woods (ed.) 1879. The vocabulary was first published as a limited edition pamplet during 1869, shortly after Bennett's death (see Bennett 1869).
3 The notebook is catalogued as 'Note Book No. 36. Woolner Dialect. Adelaide R. Northern Territory. By G.W. Goyder, Surveyor General, 1869', GRG 35/256/11, SRSA. As an advocate of the linguistic and ethnographic work of another South Australian surveyor, R.H. Mathews, perhaps Tindale saw Goyder as a worthy precursor (see Tindale 1986, p. 239). For his attribution of the notebook to Goyder, see Tindale 1974, p. 366.
4 Neither the first nor second copies carry Bennett's name, reflecting the convention that a native vocabulary was an abstraction, rather than an authored work. The second copy contains only the 'English to Native' section of the vocabulary, in contrast to Bennett's original and Hoare's first copy. It lacks any of the diacritics which Hoare reproduced in the first copy, and does not contain the introductory notes on pronunciation. This, together with the omission of several words, suggests that the second copy was not as carefully made. But it also contains a list of Aboriginal men implicated in Bennett's killing (discussed below), and other additional information. The first copy is among uncatalogued manuscripts in the SAMA. The second copy is catalogued as PRG 140/6 among W.P. Auld's papers in the SLSA; I cite it here as: W.W. Hoare [attrib.] Copy of J.W.O. Bennett [attrib.], 'Escape Cliffs Native Dialect', PRG 140/6, SLSA.

5   Mulvaney and Green 1993, p. 82.

6   *Ibid*, p. 87.

7   *Ibid*, p. 154.

8   *Ibid*, p. 175.

9   Entry for 30 January 1865, D3058(L), A.C. Webling 'Journals', D3058(L), SLSA. Bob White (identifiable as an Iwaidja man, Nullamaloo), later assisted Captain Howard of the *Beatrice* with his navigation of the northern coast, and with Howard's attempts to locate the missing explorer, McKinlay (see Howard papers, PRG 1198, SLSA). For further reference to Flash Poll, see Lewis 1922, pp. 137, 150; Searcy 1907, pp. 57–58.

10   Entry for 6 June 1864, A.C. Webling 'Journals', D3058(L), SLSA.

11   *Ibid*.

12   Entry for 16 March 1865, *ibid*.

13   Entries for 17, 18 May 1865, *ibid*. Very few of Guy's photographs have been identified. See B31111, SLSA, reproduced in Macknight (ed.) 1969, facing p. 154, for an example.

14   Entry for 25 May 1865, *ibid*.

15   'Mr J.W.O. Bennett', *Observer*, 20 November 1869, p. 9. For Bennett's correspondence with W.M.C. Finniss during 1864 and 1865, see D7425(L), SLSA. W.M.C. Finniss later showed an interest in Aboriginal linguistics by transcribing a Nyulnyul vocabulary from an Aboriginal boy of the Broome region (see Parkhouse papers, AA247, SAMA).

16   Diary of B.T. Finniss, 1864–1866, PRG S27/2/2, SLSA.

17   J.P. Stow 1894.

18   Appendix 51, Finniss enquiry, *SAPP* 17, 1866.

19   Robert Henry Edmunds, 'Diary of the N.T. Survey Expedition, 1864–66', entry for 8 May 1865, D8043(L), SLSA.

20   Appendix 51, Finniss enquiry, *SAPP* 17, 1866.

21   Clune 1955, p. 155. For his Escape Cliffs meteorological readings see 'Analysis of Meteorological Tables, kept by John William Ogilvie Bennett, from the 25th of September, 1864, to the end of February, 1865, with other information'. Appendix no. 35, *SAPP* 17, 1866.

22   *Ibid*, Appendix, no. 53.

23   Letter from J.W.O. Bennett to William Finniss, 13 August 1864, D7425(L), SLSA.

24   Letter from J.W.O. Bennett to William Finniss, 11 April 1865, *ibid*.

25   Letter from J.W.O. Bennett to William Finniss, 12 June 1864, *ibid*.

26   Edmunds, 'Diary', entry for 7 March 1865, *ibid*. See also William McMinn's evidence to the Royal Commission into Finniss's leadership, *SAPP* 17, 1866, pp. 37–38.

27   Entries for November 19 and 25 December 1864. Diary of B.T. Finniss, D527/2/2, SLSA.

28   Entry for 9 August 1865, A.C. Webling 'Journals', D3058(L), SLSA.

29   After returning to Adelaide, Goldsmith deposited a spear and a spearhead, two 'womerahs', a paddle and '2 specimens of native ore used by the natives for making pigments' with the South Australian Museum. If subsequently registered, these objects have lost their documented association with Goldsmith and have not been traced. See Jones 1997, pp. 81–82.

30   Letter from Finniss to Henry Ayers, 10 August 1864. Appendix no. 81, in *SAPP* 17, 1866; Hill 1951, p. 83.

31   Edmunds, 'Diary', entry for 14 March 1865. Even then, the unfortunate individual did not expire and it was Chandler who, 'to put him out of his misery . . . placed the butt of his rifle on his throat and leant his weight on it'. Given that this individual was carrying a digging stick and a basket containing roots or tubers, and given the clear gender-based division of Aboriginal labour, it is very likely, as Ernestine Hill (1951, p. 84) has suggested, that this defenceless victim was not a man, but an elderly woman.

32   The enquiry at Escape Cliffs is recorded in Edmunds 'Diary'. The Adelaide Royal Commission proceedings are in *SAPP* 17, 1866.

33   Quoted in Reid, 1990, p. 33.

34   Letter from J.W.O. Bennett to T. Bennett, 13 August 1864, D7425, SLSA. Extracts from Bennett's letters were quoted in the official enquiry into this incident and it could be assumed that Bennett's father censored the letter (which may have compromised the reputations of B.T. and F. Finniss) before allowing the authorities to see it.

35   For these and other measures, including a system devised by Finniss for defending the smaller survey camps, and a directive that men were not to visit the nearby 'native encampment' after 7 pm, see 'Northern Territory Correspondence', *SAPP* 79, 1868.

36   Edmunds 'Diary', 7 March 1865; 5 June 1865; 22 June 1865.

37   *Ibid*, 29 August 1865.

38   *Ibid*, 29 August, 19 September 1865.

39   B.T. Finniss, reply to Rymill, *SAPP* 17, 1866, p. xxiii.

40   Edmunds 'Diary', 20 September 1865.

41   *Ibid*, 25 September 1865.

42   Letter from J.W.O. Bennett to T.D. Bennett, 22 April 1865, D7425(L), SLSA.

43   These land orders, nos 74 and 143, are listed in 'Northern Territory Land Order Holders', *SAPP* 129, 1869–1870.

44   Letter from J.W.O. Bennett to T.D. Bennett, 22 April 1865, D7425(L), SLSA.

45   *Ibid*. Bennett's letter to his father is paraphrased in Kerr 1971, p. 138.

46   Barley 2002.

47   See Earl 1846; 1849–1850.

48   Letter from B.T. Finniss to Henry Ayers, Escape Cliffs, 20 June 1865. *SAPP* 83, 1866.

49   W.W. Hoare, letter to his 'parents and sisters', 7 February 1869; diary entry for 6 February 1869. '1869 Adventures, Port Darwin, My Diary', PRG 294/1 SLSA.

50   *Observer*, 20 November 1869, p. 10.

51   Napier 1876, pp. 78–79. For an account of the Cadell expedition, see Nicholson 2004.

52   The weapon was described by Schultze as a 'kundillo', probably a wooden sword club. 'List of Specimens collected by Fr. Schultze, Naturalist', GRG 19/399/15, SRSA.

53   'Letter from Frederick Schultze concerning the extent of his collection, 1870', GRG 19/399/22, SRSA; *Observer*, 20 November 1869, p. 10. Unfortunately, none of the Aboriginal artefacts collected by the Schultzes can be identified in collections today. Goyder observed of his naturalist: 'Mr Schultze is merely a collector and preserver of plants and animals, perhaps this is better as he cannot be carried away by enthusiasm'. Entry for 29 January 1869 in G. Goyder 1868–1869. 'Northern Territory Survey Expedition 1868–1870. Journal kept by the Surveyor General, G.R. Goyder, Jan. 1 to Sept 28, 1869'. GRG 35/655, SRSA (hereafter referred to as 'G. Goyder, 'Journal').

54   Dated entries in W.W. Hoare, '1869 Adventures' *op. cit.* Hoare prepared a series of watercolour illustrations of natural history specimens, which were sent south with Schultze's collections. They were apparently presented to the South Australian Governor, but have not been traced.

55   Diary entry for 3 May 1869. W.W. Hoare, '1869 Adventures'.

56   'George Woodroofe Goyder', *Australian Dictionary of Biography*, vol. 4, pp. 278–280 (no author listed).

57   'Surveyor-General's Estimate of Northern Territory Survey', *SAPP* 101, 1868.

58   Edwin Smith 'Reminiscences', p. 71.

59   Entry for 29 April, 1869, G. Goyder 'Journal'.

60   *Ibid*. The canoe and paddles, together with spears, a spearthrower and 'a few trifling curiosities' were among specimens consigned to Adelaide on 3 May 1869. See 'Northern Territory Survey Progress Reports', *SAPP* 31, 1869, p. 3.

61   Entries for 'Billiamook and Umballa' in Carment, Maynard and Powell (eds) 1990, pp. 19–20. Hoare's journal contains the studio photograph of the trio (see page 161). It is captioned 'Lillawer, Billimuck, Lungaba, Port Darwin, Larrakia Tribe' ('Lungaba' could be another rendering of 'Umballa'). Hoare provides a variation on those names in his second copy of Bennett's vocabulary: 'Natives who visited Adelaide, brought down [by] McKinlay

& Davis [:]. Billimuc Lirawa Ungaba'. See W.W. Hoare, '1869 Adventures'; W.W. Hoare [attrib.] Copy of J.W.O. Bennett [attrib.], 'Escape Cliffs Native Dialect', PRG 140/6, SLSA.

62 See for example, A2728 (1878), A3525 (1879), 'Incoming correspondence received by Government Resident, Northern Territory', GRS11, N.T. Archives. Biliamuk's work is illustrated and discussed in Sayers 1994, pp. 80–82, 115. See also Venbrux and Jones 2002, p. 125, Jones 2005.

63 Entry for 15 April 1869, G. Goyder 'Journal', and see Northern Territory Survey Progress Reports', *SAPP* 31, 1869, p. 3, in which Goyder supplied more detail. The sole artefact in the South Australian Museum associated with Goyder is a marlin-spike (A40679) from a Malay prau. Perhaps it was obtained on this occasion.

64 Entry for 15 April 1869, W.W. Hoare, '1869 Adventures'.

65 Entries for 8–10 May 1869, G. Goyder 'Journal'.

66 *Observer*, 20 November 1869, p. 10.

67 Entry for 14 April 1869, W.W. Hoare, '1869 Adventures'.

68 *Observer*, 20 November 1869, p. 10.

69 Hoare's copy of Bennett's vocabulary, which I located and identified among N.B. Tindale's papers in 1998, is precisely as published in Bennett 1879.

70 Letter from J.W.O. Bennett to T.D. Bennett, 22 April 1865, D7425(L), SLSA.

71 For a plan of this township (unsigned, but probably Bennett's), see *SAPP* 204, 1869–1870.

72 Diary of B.T. Finniss, D527/2/2, SLSA.

73 The term was mistranscribed by Hoare, and subsequently published as 'Gua-kee' (Bennett 1879, p. 315).

74 Confalonieri's map is reproduced in Spillett 1972, p. 163. For Tindale's equivalent tribal names see Tindale 1974.

75 13 of Bennett's 15 place-names were in Woolna territory. The other two were Melville Island, or Yer.mal.ner (not marked on the map), and Win.din.din, south of Auld's Lagoon. The map also shows 'Port Darwin', confirming that it post-dates the Escape Cliffs expedition. The map is glued to the inside cover of the notebook containing Bennett's original vocabulary, GRG 35/256/11, SRSA.

76 Entry for 10 May 1869, W.W. Hoare, '1869 Adventures'. The term 'galah' does not appear either in Bennett's original surviving vocabulary or in the published version, suggesting that Bennett continued to collect words at Auld's Lagoon, after Hoare had transcribed his vocabulary during early April.

77 *Observer*, 20 November 1869, p. 9.

78 *Ibid*.

79 *Ibid*.

80 This and following quotations are drawn from Hoare's journal entries, *ibid*. An album containing 23 of Hoare's watercolour drawings of plants, crabs and fish was purchased by the State Library of South Australia during 2003 (PRG 294/4). It is likely that further drawings (featuring birds and artefacts for example) were given to the South Australian Governor of the period, Sir James Fergusson.

81 Entry for 8 May, 1869, W.W. Hoare, '1869 Adventures'.

82 For another account of the festivities, 'terminated by drinking the health of Her Majesty, and hearty cheers … for Mr Goyder and Dr Peel', see the *Observer*, 20 November 1869, p. 10.

83 This account is drawn from Guy's original report to Goyder on the spearing, produced in response to Goyder's request of 30 June 1869. For a copy of this report see NT 58/1869, N.T. Archives, Darwin. Goyder's 'Journal' contains extracts from this report, which is also partly reproduced in Goyder's published account (*Observer*, 20 November 1869, p. 9).

84 According to Edwin Smith (Goyder's nephew), Guy had 'been instructed to have his revolver on him but he was too lazy to do so'. Smith, 'Reminiscences', p. 91.

85 The accounts seem to vary at this point. Guy stated to Goyder that Knuckey and the other two men did not return until 'sundown', and that Knuckey then went to the main

camp at Manton Creek, six miles away, where Mitchell and Woods were camped, before sending a man to Fort Darwin. Goyder's official account in the *Observer* states that Knuckey discovered the wounded men on his return to Fred's Pass between 1 pm and 2 pm.

86 'Extract from Dr Peel's journal'; entry for 26 May 1869, G. Goyder 'Journal'.
87 Guy described the man who stood near the waterhole as 'about 25 or 30 years of age about 5ft 10 inches, small hands, round flat head and open pleasant countenance. I would recognise him again' (Guy's report to Goyder, N.T. 58/1869, N.T. Archives, Darwin). Hoare's second copy of the Bennett manuscript contains a list of 'Natives concerned with Bennet's [sic] Murder – Mundab, Lialoon-me, Adulma, Me-nin-dab, Me-pin-gee, Lume-qual'. This includes the four named by Guy in his report, but the last two are additions. It is possible that Bennett confided their names to Hoare before his death (W.W. Hoare [attrib.] Copy of J.W.O. Bennett [attrib.], 'Escape Cliffs Native Dialect', P. Auld papers, PRG 140/6, SLSA).
88 *Observer*, 20 November 1869, p. 10.
89 'Extract from Dr Peel's journal', NT 58/1869, N.T. Archives.
90 Entry for 28 May 1869, W.W. Hoare, '1869 Adventures'.
91 *Observer*, 20 November 1869, p. 9.
92 Entry for 28 May 1869, W.W. Hoare, '1869 Adventures'.
93 Entries for 30–31 May, *ibid*.
94 Entry for 1 June, *ibid*.
95 Entry for 12 June, *ibid*. According to Goyder's own rough journal (but unmentioned in his official journal), he did in fact fire into the mangroves, 'in direction of sound. All quiet after'. Entry for 12 June 1869, 'NoteBook no. 38, Northern Territory by G.W. Goyder, Surveyor General, 1869. GRG 35/256/12, SRSA. Goyder's account of the trip to Fort Darwin is contained in G. Goyder, letter dated 27 September 1869, published in the *Observer*, 20 November 1869, p. 10.
96 Entries for 17 and 20 June 1869, G. Goyder 'Journal'.
97 Entry for 1 August, *ibid*.
98 G. Goyder, letter dated 27 September 1869, *Observer*, 20 November 1869, p. 10.
99 *Ibid*.
100 Entry for 10 September 1869, Goyder 'Journal'.
101 Unsourced clipping pasted into Hoare's '1869 Adventures'.
102 *Observer*, 20 November 1869, p. 9.
103 *Ibid*. The memorial tablet was transferred to the Northern Territory Museum following the church's deconsecration in 1982.
104 *Ibid*.
105 *Ibid*.
106 *Observer*, 20 November 1869, p. 9.
107 Entries from October to December, W.W. Hoare '1869 Adventures'.
108 Entries for 11 and 27 December 1869, W.W. Hoare '1869 Adventures'.
109 Letter from P. Foelsche to W.W. Hoare, 5 October 1904, pasted into W.W. Hoare, 'Adventures'.
110 *Ibid*.

CHAPTER FIVE
Drilling for fire

1 The fire-sticks are registered as A12919 in the South Australian Museum's anthropology collection. Since 2003 these fire-sticks have been on loan to the Nyinkka Nyunyu Art and Culture Centre, Tennant Creek.

2   H.W. Marshall, General Secretary, Public Library, Museum and Art Gallery of South Australia, to Museum Director, 18 November 1924, specimen documentation file, A12919, South Australian Museum.

3   Meyer 1879, pp. 202–204.

4   Spencer and Gillen 1899, pp. 228; 446–447.

5   Brassey 1889, pp. 276–277. Annie Brassey died a few weeks later, shortly after the *Sunbeam* embarked from Darwin. Her husband, Earl Brassey, later became Governor of Victoria. See Penny 1979.

6   G.S. Lindsay 1927; G.S. Lindsay, writing as 'Larrapinta' (n.d.) 'More about Aboriginal fire-making', published in the *Bulletin*, probably during the late 1920s, H.A. Lindsay Scrapbooks, vol. 1, p. 77, 828a/L748a, BSL.

7   For David Lindsay's biography, see Edgar 1986.

8   D. Lindsay 1889; Lindsay's summary accounts of the expedition are contained in Lindsay 1887 and D. Lindsay 'Report of an exploring expedition across Australia, 1885–1886. ms. D7442, SLSA. For Lindsay's full journal of the Simpson Desert reconnaissance, titled 'Field notes of a journey from Dalhousie Station to Latitude 25°30' on the Queensland border', see GRS 1/162 of 1886, SRSA.

9   Lindsay 1887, p. 7. Harold Lindsay noted that these discoveries were made on David Lindsay's wedding anniversary, and that Mt Coghlan was named after the minister performing the ceremony (H.A. Lindsay 1953, p. 40).

10   This led ultimately not only to the discovery of gold but to the foundation of the township of Stuart (Alice Springs). The Lindsays later returned to Glen Annie with Cubadgee after the Adelaide and Melbourne exhibitions, still hoping to discover real rubies and gold among the garnets.

11   The four-page manuscript is held in the Royal Geographical Society library, Adelaide (Ms. 10d). The weapons have not been traced, although these may have become incorporated among Lindsay's Adelaide Jubilee Exhibition display, eventually finding their way to the Australian Museum in Sydney. The plants and seeds were sent on to von Mueller. For more on Dittrich, see 'Mr Lindsay's trip through the continent', *Observer*, 24 October 1885, p. 29.

12   David Lindsay's nephew Harold later claimed that the entire botanical collection was ruined in this way (H.A. Lindsay 1953, p. 35), but Lindsay's own 'Report' (*ibid*, p. 1) states:

> *From Dalhousie a collection of plants were sent to the Hon the Minister of Education to be forwarded to Baron von Mueller for classification; in this collection as well as in all others subsequently sent, were as far as possible three specimens of each plant so that one complete set could be kept by the Baron, one ditto by the Geographical Society and the other for Lieutenant Dittrich and myself to dispose of as we think fit.*

13   Entry for 22 March 1886, Lindsay 'Report', *ibid*.

14   Letter from D. Lindsay to Baron F. von Mueller, 21 October 1885, p. 399, Letterbook 1, ML Mss 5200/1, ML.

15   H.A. Lindsay 1953, p. 35.

16   Letter from D. Lindsay to Hon. Secretary, South Australian Branch, Royal Geographical Society, Adelaide, 12 February 1887, Ms 62c, RGS, Adelaide.

17   Selected photographs were republished in Elliott 2002. Several albums of original prints were produced after the expedition. These differ in content, as can be seen from albums in the South Australian Museum Archives, the National Library in Canberra and the Royal Geographical Society Archives in Adelaide.

18   Entry for 15 March 1886, Lindsay 'Report', *ibid*. Harold Lindsay (George Lindsay's son) wrote that while when his father was prospecting in the Eastern MacDonnell Ranges many years later, 'the local natives were very truculent until a young woman among them recognized my father as one of the party whom she had guided as a child' (Lindsay, H.A. 1953, p. 40).

19 Entry for 20 March 1886, *ibid*.
20 Entry for 22 March 1886, *ibid*.
21 *Ibid*.
22 G.S. Lindsay 1935.
23 *Ibid*. This account of the first meeting is corroborated by G.S. Lindsay 1927 and H.A. Lindsay 1968.
24 H.A. Lindsay 1968.
25 Roberts 2005, pp. 210–211; 217–222; 248–252.
26 See undated (1930s) *Bulletin* article by George Lindsay, titled 'Primitive Justice', published under the *nom de plume* 'Larrapinta'. H.A. Lindsay Scrapbooks, vol. 1, p. 97, 828a/L748a, BSL.
27 Traine, ca 1920, quoted in Roberts 2005, p. 102.
28 *Ibid*, p. 216.
29 G.S. Lindsay 1935.
30 Letter from H. Dittrich to A. Magarey, 9 June 1886, from Gregory Downs Station, Folder 6, ML Mss 200/3, ML.
31 Curr 1886–1887.
32 Letter from Lindsay to Honorary Secretary, South Australian Branch, Royal Geographical Society, 12 February 1887, Ms 62c, RGS.
33 Gillen's unpublished parallel vocabulary of Central Australian languages, including Warumungu, is in vol. 5 of Gillen's notebooks, BSL.
34 D. Lindsay's inscription accompanying Dick Cubadgee photograph, PXE724/24, ML.
35 Lindsay 1887, p. 10.
36 Spencer and Gillen 1899, pp. 90–91.
37 G.S. Lindsay 1935. In one of his *Bulletin* pieces written under the *nom de plume* 'Larrapinta', Lindsay related the story of shooting a large rock python, requiring Cubadgee's assistance to wrestle the writhing snake. In view of his totemic affiliation, Cubadgee must have done so with mixed feelings. H.A. Lindsay Scrapbooks, vol. 1, p. 64, 828a/L748a, BSL.
38 G.S. Lindsay 1935.
39 Letter from D. Lindsay to G. MacDonald, 9 May 1887. D. Lindsay Letterbook 2, Ms. 5200/2, ML.
40 Spencer and Gillen 1899, pp. 80,90.
41 David Lindsay papers, ML Mss. 200/4, ML. Although this note was headed 'Lake Nash', it clearly related to the Warumungu. This is made plain in Lindsay's published account (Lindsay 1887, p. 10).
42 See 'Lindsay's Statement of his previous operations from Feby 1878 to 1888', Ms. 112c, GRG 67/12, SRSA. David Lindsay's journals contain very little detail on the survey itself. George Lindsay's journal of this expedition consists only of brief entries up to 22 November 1885, on the Hale River (despite its listed title as 'Notebook kept by G. Lindsay describing a survey expedition to the Barkly Tableland, Northern Territory', D4120(L), SLSA).
43 D. Lindsay to Honorary Secretary, South Australian Branch of the Royal Geographical Society, Adelaide, 12 February 1887, MS 62c, RGS.
44 Letter from D. Lindsay to G. MacDonald, 9 May 1887. D. Lindsay Letterbook 2, Ms. 5200/2, ML.
45 Eight camels died during the course of the expedition. Joorak and Cubadgee brought the remaining four camels and a calf safely to Hergott ('The Lindsay Expedition', *Observer*, 22 January 1887, p. 29). Lindsay made a notable journey south across the continent in the following year, riding 1400 miles in five weeks, but I can find no evidence for Edgar's suggestion (Edgar 1986, p. 106) that Lindsay was accompanied by an Aboriginal man on that expedition.
46 'The Lindsay Expedition', *Observer*, 22 January 1887, p. 29.

47 George Lindsay was living at this time in the Cecil Mansions apartments in Rundle Street, Kent Town, Adelaide (pers. comm. from G. Lindsay's grand-daughter, Mrs J.M. Cockburn, 2003).

48 D. Lindsay papers, PXE 724/28,29, ML. Cubadgee also appears in an Adelaide studio photograph (see page 219), wearing the same clothes and carrying the same cane as in the 'coach-house' photographs (Nora Lindsay collection, AP 4929, SAMA).

49 *Ibid*.

50 Lewis 1922, p. 155.

51 G.S. Lindsay 1935.

52 G.S. Lindsay 1927.

53 H.A. Lindsay 1968.

54 Magarey 1899, p. 124.

55 H.A. Lindsay 1968.

56 Lindsay 1887, p. 1.

57 'Royal Geographical Society', *Observer*, 2 July 1887, p. 36. The full text of Lindsay's paper is reproduced in Lindsay 1887.

58 Royal Geographical Society', *ibid*.

59 Letter from D. Lindsay to G. MacDonald, 9 May 1887, p. 33, D. Lindsay Letterbook 2, Ms. 200/2, ML.

60 'Cubadgee, a tall Central Australian black', *Australasian Sketcher*, 14 June 1887, pp. 83b, 92.

61 Letter from D. Lindsay to G. MacDonald, June 1987, p. 64, D. Lindsay Letterbook 2, Ms. 200/2, ML.

62 See Poignant 1993, p. 44. Lindsay may have been in Darwin when Cunningham put in there, during 1883. The full and remarkable story of Cunningham's 'professional savages' is told in Poignant 2004.

63 Letter from D. Lindsay to Mr Renault, 29 August 1887, G. Champion ms., p. 74, La Trobe Library, Melbourne.

64 'Aboriginal Entertainment', *Observer*, 10 September 1887, p. 30.

65 Letter from D. Lindsay to G. MacDonald, 9 May 1887. D. Lindsay Letterbook 2, Ms. 200/2, ML.

66 Invoice of goods to be exhibited at the Centennial International Exhibition, Melbourne, 1889, by David Lindsay FRGS, Surveyor and Explorer, 11 June 1887, 'Letter Book 2', p. 91, ML Ms 5200/1, MLS. See also Lindsay 1889; Lindsay 1893. Some of Lindsay's collection was passed to the School of Mines, before reaching the South Australian Museum. The Australian Museum in Sydney also holds a large collection of Lindsay artefacts. Some artefacts remain with the Lindsay family.

67 G.S. Lindsay 1935.

68 See Elmslie and Nance 1990, for Watson's biography.

69 H.A. Lindsay 1968.

70 These details were confirmed by J. Stewart Rattray, pers. comm., 1991.

71 Published as an obituary for Cubadgee in the *Observer*, 21 September 1889, p. 30b; republished (for no apparent reason) in *Report of the Protector of Aborigines* 1906 (SA Government Printer, Adelaide), facing p. 8.

72 This plaster cast, painted black, was registered in the South Australian Museum collection as A48573 in about 1950, with the following information: 'Death mask. Dick Kubidji. Protegé of Sir E. Stirling, died of T.B. in Adelaide. Skeleton in Gallery'.

73 Article by George Lindsay writing as 'Larrapinta', 3 September 1925, *Bulletin*, p. 22. According to Clive Lindsay (pers. comm. 21 July 1991), the skeleton was intercepted in Cape Town, South Africa.

74 Pers. comm. Clive Lindsay, 21 July 1991.

75 'After 100 years, Dick Cubadgee comes back to his own country', *Land Rights News*, July 1991, p. 14.

CHAPTER SIX
Unearthing the toas

1   J.G. Reuther, writing in *Kirchen und Mssionsblatt Zeitung*, 11 July 1906, quoted in Stevens 1994, p. 163. For a discussion of the extraordinary population loss in the Lake Eyre region following European contact, see Jones 1991.

2   This manuscript was purchased from Reuther's widow by the South Australian Museum and was eventually fully translated during the 1970s (Reuther 1981). The volume of toa descriptions initially received by the Museum corresponds to volume 13 of that manuscript. Volume 12 was retained by Reuther until his death, and comprises another, slightly variant, set of toa descriptions, together with a listing of the remainder of Reuther's ethnographic collection.

3   Reuther 1981, vol. 13, pp. 1–2.

4   See for example, Sayers 1994; Hardy, Megaw and Megaw (eds) 1992.

5   See for example, the debate on the standing of the toas as 'art or artefact' in Brook 1986a; 1986b; Sutton 1986; 1987; 1991. A measure of this desire to enfold the toas within a corpus of 'traditional' Aboriginal practice is their recent inclusion as 'representations of country' in the *Macquarie Atlas of Indigenous Australia*, together with a map suggesting that they were made and used in an area greater than the size of Tasmania (Arthur and Morphy, eds, pp. 21–22).

6   See Jones 1988.

7   These descriptions are based upon those used in Jones and Sutton (1986), edited by this author from the translations of J.G. Reuther's original descriptions contained in both volumes 12 and 13 of his manuscript (Reuther 1981). These manuscript accounts vary in interesting ways, discussed below. The photograph was included as fig. 238 in Sutton (ed.) 1988.

8   An x-ray of one of these toas, the 'Lake Gregory' toa, is reproduced in Jones and Sutton (1986, p. 65).

9   Kaparlgo was established in 1899 as a 'native industrial mission' by Adelaide's St Luke's Mission and the self-appointed missionary and bush cyclist A.H. Lennox. It developed an ambitious programme of self-sufficiency and several hundred artefacts (in sets of 62 documented objects) were consigned to southern collectors. By 1903 the enterprise had failed and the mission was abandoned (see chapter eight; Jones 1997 ms.).

10 Howitt 1904, pp. 722–723.

11 N.B. Tindale slide no. 29, folder 22, AA338, and N.B. Tindale 1963 ms, pp. 93–94, SAMA.

12 Dixon 1991, pp. 23–24.

13 Letter from Mr James to R.H. Mathews, 31 May 1898, R.H. Mathews Papers, Ms. 1606, AIATSIS, quoted in Eagle 2004, p. 49.

14 See Mountford notebook no. 30, p. 19, Mountford-Sheard Collection, SLSA.

15 Referred to by Mountford, *ibid*.

16 Roth 1897, p. 133.

17 Reuther, vol. 7, p. 576. The Tudnapiti site (no. 1993), was associated with the ancestor Warlatana, and represented the quarry where he burnt gypsum to make ceremonial paint. Most outcrops of reflective sheet gypsum were associated with rain-making mythology.

18 Letter from G. Aiston to W.H. Gill, 4 December 1938. Mss. A2535–2537, ML.

19 Howitt 1904, pp. 678–679. See also Howitt 1889.

20 The transcription and the newspaper interview are discussed below.

21 Stirling first published an account of the toas in a Museum board report in 1908. His major publication on the toas was completed shortly after his death by Edgar Waite (Stirling 1908; Stirling and Waite 1919).

22 McCarthy 1947.

23   Howard Morphy's 1977 publication (based on Morphy 1972) took Reuther's characterisation of the toas at face value, analysing their designs in relation to their mythological categories. Jones and Sutton (1986) discussed the toas' historical background but elevated their artistic qualities, an aspect strengthened considerably through their inclusion in the influential 'Dreamings' exhibition of 1988 (Sutton (ed.) 1988).

24   Sutton (ed.) 1988; Luthi (comp.) 1993.

25   See for example, Morphy 1998, pp. 84–88.

26   For a useful discussion of these issues, see Bouquet 2002.

27   Reece 1974, p. 17. See also Reynolds 1982; Reynolds 1987; Loos 1982.

28   Jennings 1975; 1982.

29   Swain 1993, p. 143.

30   Fabian's *Time and the Other* (1983) remains one of the best formulations of this critique.

31   Beckett 1988, p. 205.

32   See Karp 1991, p. 16.

33   Gason, 1879, p. 290. Gason subsequently relayed his data on gesture language to Howitt in February 1881 (see Ms 69, AIATSIS). For Howitt's data on gesture language, incorporating Gason's material, see Howitt 1904, pp. 727–735.

34   Quoted in W. Bucknell 1902, p. 170–171.

35   See Stevens 1994, pp. 223–224, for an account of Siebert's rivalry with Reuther. Siebert published articles on Diyari mythology under his own name in 1910, but his greatest contribution was to Howitt's *Native Tribes* (1904), to which he contributed the substantial appendix of mythology.

36   The wooden object and its data card survive in the collection of the Frankfurt Museum fur Völkerkunde (AG no. 193). For Siebert's application of his analysis of carved symbols and motifs to F.C.A. Sarg's survey of boomerangs, see Sarg 1911. I am grateful to Chris Nobbs for alerting me to this object and its documentation.

37   See Kendon 1988, pp. 17–21 for discussion of this phenomenon. In Aboriginal terms of course, Ancient Egypt was relatively close to the modern era.

38   Letter from Gason to Howitt, 12 February 1881, Box 1052/1, Ms 9356, La Trobe Library, Melbourne. Copy in Rod Wilson papers, AA843, SAMA.

39   Letter from Gillen to Spencer, Letter 20, 25 April 1896. Mulvaney, Morphy and Petch 1997, p. 111.

40   *Observer*, n.d. 1906. Reuther papers, AA266, SAMA. Interestingly, there is a toa shaped in just this way, one of a small collection acquired by the Hermannsburg missionary Oskar Liebler. It is now in the Staatliches Museum für Völkerkunde, Stuttgart, registered as no. 85735 (Jones and Sutton 1986, p. 135).

41   Myers 1991, p. 88.

42   Reuther 1981, vol. 2, no. 326(44).

43   See for example, Reuther 1981: vol. 2, nos 129, 140, 326; vol. 6, nos 883, 888, 1288; vol. 7, no. 2459.

44   *Ibid*, no. 320(24); vol. 2, no. 1441. Here the word *milki* (eye) was combined with *wondrani* (show), to produce the expression, 'to show the eye'.

45   See Stevens 1994, p. 218. Reuther's fellow-missionary, Otto Siebert, gave much fuller descriptions of his own ethnographic method, but also referred to Reuther's 'poaching' of his informants: 'every time after the old men had been at my place he got them immediately to come over to his place and made them tell him everything that I had obtained from them at great trouble previously' (Siebert, quoted in Jones and Sutton 1986, p. 51; see also p. 52 for a further description by Reuther's son, R.B. Reuther).

46   An exhaustive search of these volumes, and of the map, was made possible through Bill Watt, of the S.A. Geographical Names Board, whose research has revealed that the map contains more than 2700 names, some 300 more than described in volume 7 of the Reuther manuscripts. Of these additional names, a much higher proportion (but still only 30 to 40 examples) are possibly toa names.

47 Reuther inserted marginal dates throughout his dictionary entries, and in several other volumes.

48 Reuther, vol. 4, no. 3348. Reuther's first-line reference to accompanying illustrations indicates his original intention to include Hillier's sketches of the toas as an element of his manuscript. This did not occur. His closing reference to 'another book' is to one of the two 'toa volumes', volume 12 or 13.

49 Reuther, *ibid*, vol. 13, p. 2.

50 Austin 1981, p. 51. Reuther also (*ibid*) explained that the toas had the suffix *-ri* appended as a dative (another error, according to Austin), but there are no examples of this suffix in use in Reuther's toa descriptions.

51 Reuther, *ibid*, vol. 7, no. 1890.

52 There is an error in the translation for this entry, which reads 'her dead brother', while it is clear from surrounding entries, and from the original German, that it was her son. *Ibid*, no. 1974. During June 2003 I participated in a field-trip to locate the Toari (Thuwari) site and related places, in the vicinity of Mount Termination in the northern Flinders Ranges. A site was located which conforms to the position of Toari on the Hillier map. There a large boulder rests in the centre of a spring, possibly representing the body of the dead ancestor, Kakalbuna. See Hercus 2003 ms.

53 I am grateful to Dr Luise Hercus for her confirmation of this reasoning, and the following details relating to Wangkangurru and Yarluyandi terms.

54 In modern orthography the verb *todina* would probably be rendered as *thuwarrinha* (Peter Sutton, pers. comm.).

55 An indication that this shift in meaning may have occurred in stages comes in Reuther's volume 6, in a rough summary list of 'cultural concepts'. There he scribbled the entry: '*toas* are *wondrani-malkas*'. Reuther, vol. 6, no. 1288(24).

56 *Ibid*, vol. 3, no. 2274(24). Reuther's entry no. 2274(25) provides another illustration of this verb form: *tali ngujamana* = 'to know the tongue, or language'.

57 Eylmann 1908; C.W. Nobbs, pers. comm. For a biography of Eylmann, see Schröder 2002.

58 Gregory 1906, pp. 191–192.

59 Letter from Reuther to Kaibel, 26 November 1901, Folder 5, Reuther correspondence, Lutheran Archives, Adelaide. I am grateful to Harriet Volker for alerting me to this letter.

60 Yashchenko 2001, pp. 100–101.

61 I examined this collection during a visit to St Petersburg in 1999, but was unable to ascertain whether Yashchenko's photographs survive, or whether Yashchenko had been successful in obtaining Ruediger's small zoological collection for the sum of ten pounds, which Reuther had offered to broker for him (*ibid*, p. 122).

62 This interpretation is confirmed by Harriet Volker's careful analysis of Reuther's correspondence and reports, which indicates quite clearly that Reuther's orientation had shifted away from mission matters and towards ethnography by late 1903 (Volker 1999).

63 One set of the Hillier illustrations was eventually acquired by the South Australian Museum. The other was retained by Hillier who gave it to his godson, T.G.H. Strehlow. It is now in the Strehlow Research Centre, Alice Springs. For a discussion of Hillier's role at the mission, see Jones and Sutton 1986; Strehlow 2005.

64 See Stevens 1994, pp. 160–163.

65 See Cooper 1989 for a listing of Carl Strehlow collections in European museums.

66 See Kenny 2005.

67 Letter from J.G. Reuther to L. Kaibel, 24 March 1904, Lutheran Archives, Adelaide.

68 Kaibel's letters to Reuther, December 1905 and early 1906, quoted in Stevens 1994, p. 160.

69 In December 1899 Reuther had informed Gustav Rechner, President of the Mission Committee, that Siebert was practically working full-time for the ethnographer Alfred Howitt, 'nothing else'. Letter from Reuther to Rechner, 5 December 1899, Lutheran Archives, Adelaide. Reuther's letter of 13 November 1899 concerns the same subject.

70 J.G. Reuther to A.W. Howitt, 6 April 1904, no. 291, Howitt Papers, Museum Victoria. Reuther was referring to the total number of his ethnographic artefacts. At no. 386, Mapajiri [not a toa], Reuther had reached no. 870 in his collection. From this I deduce that his toa collection constituted the original 382, and therefore ran from nos 483–865. After the toa entries he began cataloguing ordinary material culture items once more.

71 Memorandum written on reverse of cyclostyle copy of Howitt's March 20 1882 circular requesting information on message-sticks (Howitt papers, Box 6, paper 6, folder 2, Ms. 69, AIATSIS). This particular copy was addressed to a 'W^m G ... E^{sq}, Blanchewate[r]'. Eagle (2004, p. 49) has mistakenly attributed this as 'Gara [Samuel Gason]'. During 1866–1871 Samuel Gason had used Blanchewater as a base for police-work but in 1882 he was the licensee of the Beltana Hotel, 200 kilometres to the south. In any event, it is most unlikely that this particular copy was ever sent to (or from) Blanchewater. The memorandum on the reverse appears to be in Howitt's own handwriting, suggesting that it remained in his papers and was used for his transcription of a communication on the toas, received much later from another source. This communication was obviously written by someone with less command of the language. Howitt did not use the term 'nigger', and nor did Reuther (or Gason). The description, which refers only to a topographical, not mythological, link to place, conforms closely with other descriptions of toas given by Reuther's collaborator, H.J. Hillier, as later communicated, for example, to Hamlyn-Harris (1919, p. 18). Like Reuther, Hillier seemed not to perceive the logical absurdity of embellishing toas with elements deriving from the indicated destination. In this example, the idea that a few teaspoons of 'stinking water' might last long enough to provide a vital clue to the 'Napa-tunka' waterhole (on the Birdsville Track, a few kilometres north of Killalpaninna mission), is an additional tax on credulity.

72 For Gason's replies to Howitt's 1882 circular, see his initial response of 3 April 1882, and his full response, dated 9 October 1882 (Gason correspondence in Howitt papers, Box 1052/1 and 2, Ms. 9356, La Trobe Library, copies in R. Wilson papers, AA843, SAMA). See also Gason 1894, p. 173.

73 See Jones and Sutton 1986, pp. 136–137.

74 Von Leonhardi 1908.

75 Von Leonhardi 1909, p. 1065.

76 Letter from E.C. Stirling to J.G. Reuther, 14 October 1908, GRG 19, SRSA.

77 Stirling 1908.

78 Stirling and Waite 1919.

79 Ray 1920, p. 644.

80 For an account of Spencer's final years see Mulvaney and Calaby 1985.

81 Horn and Aiston 1924, p. 26.

82 Letter from G. Aiston to W.H. Gill, 18 May 1930. Mss.A2535–2537, ML.

83 Letter from G. Aiston to W.H. Gill, 4 December 1938, *ibid*.

84 Letter from G. Aiston to W.H. Gill, 26 September 1926, *ibid*.

85 Letter from A.S. Kenyon to E.R. Waite, 3 May 1920. GRG 19, SRSA.

86 Letter from A.S. Kenyon to General Secretary, Public Library, Museum and Art Gallery, Adelaide, 9 June 1920, GRG 19, SRSA.

87 See for example, Hercus 1987a; 1987b; Hercus and Potezny 1991.

88 See Jones and Sutton 1986, pp. 133–135 for an earlier, incomplete analysis of this collection. Liebler's complete ethnographic collections are summarised and discussed in Schlatter 1985.

89 I am grateful to Chris Nobbs for his documentation of these toas, supplementing information which I obtained during a 1985 trip to Germany.

90 Note accompanying A1336 (Liebler no. 255), South Australian Museum, Liebler collection, SAMA.

91 Reference supplied from Hermannsburg archival records by John Strehlow, 2003.

92 Jones and Sutton 1986, p. 133.

93 See for example, Morphy 1972; 1977; Jones and Sutton 1986; Morphy 1998; Eagle 2004.
94 Even ceremonial performers decorated in this fashion required their audience to understand the context of their performance. The meanings implicit in their body decorations could not be independently deduced.
95 Reuther, J.G. 1900, article in *Kirchen und Missions Zeitung* (Church and Mission Newspaper), vol. 4, 1900, p 28, quoted in Volker 1999, p. 46.
96 Quoted in Jones and Sutton 1986, p. 129.
97 See *ibid*, pp.51–53.
98 Note in frontispiece of vol. 1 of P.S. Hossfeld's translation of the Reuther dictionary, AA266, South Australian Museum Archives. Chris Nobbs (pers. comm.) has confirmed that these individuals figured among Otto Siebert's main informants at Killalpaninna, as recorded in his personal journal.

CHAPTER SEVEN
The magic garb of Daisy Bates

1 Hill 1973, p. 2.
2 Bates 1944, p. 198. She failed to mention the cotton or kid gloves always worn on her visits to the Aboriginal camps.
3 For biographical details on Bates, see Wright 1979, White's introduction to Bates 1985, White 1993, Bates 2004 and Reece 2007. Note that Daisy Bates's birthdate has recently been revised from 1863 to 1859 (see 'biographical note', Daisy Bates Papers, National Library of Australia, Canberra).
4 Bates 1944, p. 154.
5 *Ibid*, p. 191.
6 Daisy Bates to Allan and Mary McKinnon, 30 December 1940, Salter Papers, NLA Ms 6481, Box 2, 2/4.
7 Bates 1944, p. 172.
8 *Ibid*, p. 242
9 Letter from Bates to Herbert Hale, 7 July 1932. AA23, Bates Papers, SAMA.
10 Daisy Bates interview with Russell Henderson, 1941, OH543, SLSA.
11 Letter from Daisy Bates to an unknown correspondent, PRG 878/10, SLSA.
12 Bates ms. 1939, AA23, SAMA.
13 See Salter 1971, pp. 62–71.
14 *Ibid*, p. 75.
15 Hill 1973, p. 115.
16 *Ibid*, pp. 112–115.
17 Pers. comm. Tom Gara (who alerted me to the relevant Bates correspondence in the La Trobe Library, Melbourne), 2004.
18 Salter 1971, p. 131. Cleland maintained his good standing with Bates despite some scepticism of her claims about Aboriginal cannibalism. He was largely responsible for organising support for Bates from the Adelaide linguistics expert Professor Fitzherbert, who also directed the early linguistic work of T.G.H. Strehlow (*ibid*, p. 216).
19 Letter from Daisy Bates to Edward Stirling, 7 January 1919, AA23/1/1, Bates Papers, SAMA.
20 These manuscripts are held in the Australian National Library, the Special Collections of the Barr Smith Library, University of Adelaide, and in the SAMA (AA23).
21 Quoted in Salter 1971, p. 113. Lang's target here was Baldwin Spencer, as is evident from several references in Bates's correspondence. Bates's relationship with Lang, Mathews, Fraser and A.R. Brown is discussed by Salter (1971, pp. 127–148) and by Isobel White (Bates 1985, pp. 7–35). See also Reece 2005.

22   Hill 1973, p. 52.
23   Bates ms. 1939.
24   Letter from Bates to Hale, 7 June 1932. Bates Papers, AA23, SAMA.
25   Bates 1944, p. 108. This method, with distances calculated by querying 'how many sleeps?', was later adopted by Norman Tindale at the South Australian Museum, and subsequently by Charles Mountford and Ronald Berndt.
26   Bates 1944, pp. 111–112.
27   *Ibid*, p. 114. For another journalistic account of this experience, see Bates 1922.
28   Salter 1971, p. 185. In reference to the Eucla ceremonies, Salter wrote: 'Daisy's rations of tea, sugar, flour and jam made feasting possible in spite of the game shortage. In gratitude the groups bestowed upon her the "Freedom of the Totems"'.
29   Bates 1944, p. 130; Bates 1927, p. 9. Bates later informed Herbert Hale at the South Australian Museum of the attempted theft of sacred boards from this storehouse near Eucla. See letter from Bates to Hale, 7 February 1932, AA23, SAMA.
30   Letter from Bates to Hale, 20 March 1932, AA23, SAMA.
31   Letter from Bates to Hale, 7 February 1932, AA23, SAMA.
32   Letter from Bates to J.B. Cleland, 20 March 1932. Bates Papers, AA23, SAMA.
33   *Ibid*. Bates wrote at least two newspaper pieces about this group (Bates 1932; Bates 1933).
34   *Ibid*; Bates 1944, p. 216. Both objects were donated to the South Australian Museum by Bates in 1932.
35   Letter from Bates to Hale, 7 February 1932, AA23, Bates Papers, SAMA
36   *Ibid*. In a letter to Herbert Hale dated 10 March 1932, Bates recorded that the male Snake was 'made by Marn'gue; Guin-murda; Barraju'guna, Wom'baji (who only looked on I think) and Yalla Yalla – the two last named speak English – the others are only a year or so in civilization' (AA23, Bates Papers, SAMA).
37   *Ibid*. Bates elaborated in a later letter: 'the circumcised hordes … landed in the Nor West & zigzagged down through the ages, towards the Great Plain's northern edge, & along its western edge to Eucla, Israelite bay etc. All of those groups practised these Magic Snake ceremonies (Bates to Hale, 8 May 1932, AA23, Bates Papers, SAMA).
38   Bates 1944, p. 192.
39   Letter from Bates to Hale, 7 June 1932, AA23, Bates Papers, SAMA.
40   Bolam noted that the enthusiasm for boomerang throwing by inexperienced passengers at Ooldea meant that 'it had been found necessary to request that the throwing of boomerangs be conducted a little distance from the train whilst it is standing at Ooldea' (Bolam 1927, p. 82).
41   Bates 1944, p. 241.

CHAPTER EIGHT
Namatjira and the Jesus plaque

1   An earlier version of this chapter was published as Jones 1992.
2   See Sharp 1952, and further discussion in chapter three.
3   An exception to the marginalisation of these objects was their inclusion in the Namatjira retrospective curated by Alison French in 2002 (French 2002, pp. 4–7).
4   Albrecht, 1977, p. 70.
5   This vision, which was repeatedly witnessed by the children (even in front of hundreds of onlookers, once the word had spread), was officially recognised as a miracle by the Belgian church in 1949. See Sharkey and Deburgh, 1958.
6   Albrecht 1959. The trip is also described in Albrecht 1977, p. 51.
7   This plaque is registered as A72418 in the South Australian Museum collection.
8   See figs 6.6, 8.6 in Hardy, Megaw and Megaw (eds) 1992.

9   *Ibid*, fig. 2.14.

10   *Ibid*, fig. 3.22.

11   For an introduction to Namatjira's totemic affiliations, see Morton 1992, pp. 38–39.

12   F.W. Albrecht n.d. 'Tjurunga Stories', ms., Lutheran Archives, North Adelaide.

13   Henson 1992, p. 82.

14   *Ibid*, p. 33.

15   F.W. Albrecht 1934 Annual Report, SAMA.

16   *Ibid*.

17   Batty 1963, p. 27. The second plaque is illustrated in French 2002, p. 6.

18   Batty 1963, p. 108

19   Mountford 1944, pp. 74, 79; p. xxii. Namatjira was affiliated to the Yelka totem through his mother's connection to Palm Valley. It was not his primary totem (see Morton 1992, p. 38).

20   As an expression of this idea see for example, Burn and Stephen 1992.

21   F.W. Albrecht n.d. Typescript page with annotations. Burns-Albrecht Collection, SAMA.

22   Pers. comm. R. Kimber (per S. Klienert 1991).

23   This painting, held in the Northern Territory Art Gallery and Museum collection, was destroyed during Cyclone Tracy in December 1974.

24   For a further discussion of this aspect see Morton 1992, p. 53–54 and French 2002, p. 24.

25   Rex Battarbee diary, 26 August 1939, BA.

26   *Ibid*, and description of ceremony at back of diary.

27   An elderly Arrernte man's reaction in 1991 to being shown a reproduction of Namatjira's Pitjantjatjara Malu watercolour was to suggest that the artist's death could be explained by his action in depicting such subjects (pers. comm. J. Green 1991).

28   In 1949 Mountford's documentary film on Namatjira was shown at Hermannsburg to Haasts Bluff people. Strehlow recorded the fact that chaos broke out among the audience when a segment documenting sacred rock art was shown. Women and children ran from the room and trouble was expected from Haasts Bluff men as a result. This was later resolved, but it can be assumed that Namatjira himself received some blame for this transgression. T.G.H. Strehlow journal entry, 2 October 1949, Book 14.

29   See figs 1.16, 3.1, 3.23 in Hardy, Megaw and Megaw (eds) 1992.

30   See for example, Myers 1986.

31   Albrecht 1950, p. 23.

32   *Ibid*.

33   Batty 1963, p. 27.

34   Diane Austin-Broos, University of Sydney, pers. comm. 1990.

35   It is worth noting though, that during the early 1990s Arrernte women at Santa Teresa Mission, south of Alice Springs, expressed concern at the depiction of sacred motifs such as concentric circles in acrylic paintings (pers. comm., J. Green and D. Austin-Broos).

36   C. Duguid, 'The first ten years', as quoted in Hilliard 1968, p. 181.

37   Albrecht 1977.

38   See Albrecht 1977; Strehlow Journals, Book 14, p. 30, SRC.

39   Kubler 1971, p. 213.

40   Strehlow 1964, p. 50.

41   Elkin 1938, p. 268.

42   Berger 1980, p. 82.

43   Not even contemporary Arrernte watercolourists, who maintain that their site-depictions are interchangeable with Western Desert acrylic art, claim that their landscape paintings are sacred or that they are subject to viewing restrictions. The point seems obvious, but it is a way of marking a fundamental difference between a sacred object which encodes landscape and Dreaming, and an artwork which refers to that subject.

44   Rex Battarbee diary, entries for 6 and 7 June 1938; 2 October 1939, BA: 'Albert wanted some photo developer, so I gave him some, he says he can do it himself'.

45   Lohe 1977, p. 36.

46   Undocumented newspaper clipping, ca 1930, titled 'Aruntas give up their Churingas. Swayed by black Evangelist', Anthropology Newspaper Clippings, 1913–1961, vol. 5, SAMA.
47   'Mystery Stones of the Aruntas Cast Aside for Revivalist', *Observer*, 1 March 1930, p. 13.
48   Henson 1992, p. 54.
49   Strehlow Journals, Book 1, 17 April 1932, p. 9, SRC. A generation later, in 1955, the cave's taboo had been reinstated. On the occasion of Strehlow's second visit to the site, he concluded that he was the sole *rapata* man able to chant verses for the site. *Ibid*, 12 July 1955.
50   Strehlow Journals, Book 32, May 1964, p. 129, SRC.
51   Strehlow Journals, Book 1, 28 May 1932, p. 23, SRC.
52   Strehlow Journals, Book 32, May 1964, p. 128, SRC.
53   Strehlow Journals, Book 1, 24 May 1932, p. 22. Strehlow's embitterment is well documented in Hill 2002.
54   Roheim 1974, p. 55.
55   Teague papers, SAMA.
56   Henson 1992, p. 88.

CHAPTER NINE
That special property

1   Shanahan's cake of ochre is registered as A1863 in the anthropology collection of the South Australian Museum, Adelaide.
2   Letter from P.F. Shanahan to E.C. Stirling, 26 December 1904, AA298, SAMA.
3   The identity of the participants, together with other crucial information on the expedition and mythological and historical background to the ochre mine, is contained in J.W. Lindo's ms., 'Legend of the Ochre Pit near Parachilna', typescript, N.B. Tindale papers, AA338, SAMA.
4   See Mincham 1976.
5   Apart from the newspaper articles quoted below, Harry Bailes has left little trace in the archival record. A daughter Tilly was employed as a housemaid on Ediacara station in 1915. See Mattingley and Hampton 1988, p. 121.
6   Shanahan was wrong about the presence of mercury. In fact, it was the tiny flakes of mica, aligned by rubbing to reflect the light, which gave the appearance of a sheen. For a scientific analysis of the ochre see Jercher, Pring, Jones and Raven 1998.
7   These photographs have not been traced. As noted, the party also included J.W. Lindo and Percy Stone.
8   The word *kintalawoola* is a rendering of the Diyari word *kinthala-wurlu* 'two dogs'. According to the linguist Peter Austin, this is a distinctively Diyari phrase.
9   The word 'Warragurta' is identifiable as 'warrhukati', a widespread term for 'emu' in the Lake Eyre languages. Shanahan confuses 'kuringii' (a term for blood) with this word. 'Murragurta' is likely to be 'marrakata', a Diyari term for red ochre. 'Yerkinna' is likely to be the Diyari word 'yarrki-rna', the participial form of the Diyari verb 'yarrki' 'to burn', meaning 'burnt', etymologically linked to the site by the fact that red ochre was commonly produced by heating or burning yellow ochre to oxidise it. Writing in January 1905, Shanahan was again explicit about the application of the 'Yerkinna' name to the site.
10   According to J.W. Lindo's account, supplied to Norman B. Tindale at the South Australian Museum, a native pine tree standing at this first 'stopping place' had been 'lopped to represent an emu'. J.W. Lindo ms., uncatalogued Tindale papers, South Australian Museum. Native pines still stand in this locality today.

11   J.W. Lindo's account makes it clear that the initiates were obliged to take the steeper route up the gully:

> The leader follows the wallaby tracks up these hills, and has a relatively easy path. The initiates' track is more strenuous as they must scramble over all obstructions without deviating from the ordained line of travel, and if any of the initiates break down under the test he is sent back by the leader and all his previous labour is in vain. (J.W. Lindo ms.)

12   This description contains all the elements of the initiation performance for the north-eastern region of South Australia. Lindo's account corroborates Shanahan here: 'they all go to the pit; cut off their hair and beards and leave them in the pit. The hair represents the feathers of the emu' (J.W. Lindo ms.).

13   Mythology associated with the replacement of fire-stick initiation by circumcision in ancient times applies throughout north-eastern South Australia.

14   Sagona 1994 (ed.), pp. 33, 36.

15   Hovers, *et al.*, 2003.

16   Wreschner 1980, p. 633.

17   Reuther 1981, vol. 6.

18   *Ibid*, vol. 6, nos 223 (13); 1522 (18).

19   *Ibid*, vol. 10, no. 68; vol. 6, nos 1122 (17); 1319 (2); 3688.

20   *Ibid*, vol. 6, nos 556 (30); 1266 (18); 1419; 991; 1456 (10); 1456 (15).

21   *Ibid*, nos 525 (8); 1621 (4).

22   *Ibid*. no. 250 (6). For ochre defined as 'life' and 'joy' see Reuther 1981, vol. 1, nos 164(29); 199(9). Wreschner has observed the same associations in other cultures (Wreschner 1980, p. 631).

23   *Observer*, 16 July 1910, p. 35. At the time of Logic's capture, in December 1885, the two trackers involved were known only as 'Munniah' and 'Dick' (see Foster 1998, p. 177).

24   'The Far North', *Register*, 28 July 1910, p. 8. Unfortunately, no photograph of Harry Bailes has yet been traced.

25   'Red Ochre. Curious Request to the Government', *Register*, 16 December 1904, p. 6.

26   *Ibid*.

27   For a comprehensive report on the mine's significance to Parnkala people, prepared by the grandson of traditional custodian Percy Richards, see Richards and Richards 2002.

28   Elkin 1934, p. 188.

29   Reuther 1981, vol. 11, no. 8.

30   C.P. Mountford, notebook no. 30, pp. 117–118. Mountford-Sheard Collection, SLSA.

31   Tindale 1937.

32   C.P. Mountford, notebook no. 24. This legend was apparently known as far south as the Murray River. The policeman-ethnographer George Aiston also recorded a version of it at Mungeranie, well to the north of the Ranges, possibly from a Flinders Ranges traveller (Horne and Aiston 1924, pp. 128–129).

33   Richards and Richards 2002.

34   Howitt 1904, pp. 711–713; Elkin 1934, pp. 184–189; Fry 1937, pp. 196, 198; Gason 1879: 280–282; Horne and Aiston 1924, pp. 128–131; Siebert 1910; Reuther, ibid.

35   See Elkin 1934, p. 189.

36   See for example, McBryde 1978.

37   Watson 1983; Johnston and Cleland 1934.

38   Fred Teague (founder of Hawker Motors), pers. comm. 1983, from the Adnyamathanha man Fred Johnson ca 1935; C.P. Mountford, notebook no. 24; Hardy 1976, p. 5.

39   McBryde 2000, p. 160.

40   Author's interview with Ben Murray, 3 November 1983. Police correspondence of the 1860s describes ochre expeditions passing through the Strangways Springs and Mount Margaret regions (see GRG 5/2/479/1864, SRSA).

41   Teichelmann and Schürmann 1840, pp. 9, 61.
42   Howitt 1904, pp. 711–713; Gason 1879, pp. 280–282.
43   Reuther, vol. 1, no. 216 (15).
44   GRG 5/2/479/1864; GRG 5/2/1251/1863, SRSA.
45   Gason 1879, p. 281.
46   Reuther 1981, vol. 6, no. 872(4).
47   L. Hercus, n.d. 'Singing and talking about red ochre', ms., the author. Through her decades of dedicated linguistic research undertaken with knowledgeable Aboriginal men and women in the Lake Eyre region, Dr Luise Hercus has supplied this author with important insights into the history and cultural practices relating to the red ochre trade.
48   Gason 1879, p. 282.
49   Luise Hercus, n.d. 'Singing and talking about red ochre', ms., the author.
50   Elkin 1934, p. 174.
51   Reuther 1981, vol. 6, no. 1288 (36).
52   *Ibid*, no. 153(2).
53   C.P. Mountford, notebook no. 24, p. 17.
54   Howitt 1904, p. 711; Siebert 1910, p. 22.
55   Reuther 1981, vol. 6, nos 345 (37); 619 (10); vol. 11 no. 8.
56   See for example, Horne and Aiston 1924, p. 22.
57   Aiston 1929, p. 131. Aiston treated this status and its responsibilities rather more matter-of-factly than T.G.H. Strehlow in his relations with the Arrernte.
58   Reuther vol. 11, no. 8; Horne and Aiston 1924, p. 129. During the 1980s two Adnyamathanha men (John McKenzie and Rufus Wilton), and three European residents of the area (Fred Teague, Bert Pumpa, Michael Kenneth) related accounts to me of the mine collapse.
59   The author's interview with Rufus Wilton, 3 November 1983; Brock 1985, p. 28.
60   Reuther 1981, vol. 1, nos 124; 125.
61   Letter from George Aiston to W.H. Gill, 16 February, 1935, Ms. A2535–2537, ML.
62   Dorothy Tunbridge, pers. comm., 1986.
63   Luise Hercus, Pukardu ms.
64   Letter from P.F. Shanahan to E.C. Stirling, 1 February 1905. AA309, SAMA.
65   Gason 1879, p. 281.
66   Bruce 1902, p. 84; Howitt 1904, p. 713.
67   C.P. Mountford, notebook no. 19. A former policeman at Blinman, Michael Kenneth, retrieved a moulded cake of ochre from one of the collapsed pits at the Pukardu site in the 1960s. This cake was apparently shaped to fit the head of one of the expedition members – an interesting analogue to the weighty gypsum caps worn by Aboriginal widows throughout the region.
68   Oastler 1908a, p. 207; see also Oastler 1908b.
69   Shanahan's letter suggested that an initiation ceremony occurred immediately before the expedition approached the mine site. Reuther provides this corroboration (vol. 6, no. 880(2)): 'except for scalp hair the entire body is cleared of hair by means of fire before the men go up into the hills at Beltana to collect ochre … A man may appear at a sacred ceremony only when he is beardless and his body rubbed in with fat'. Reuther also described two sites on the 'Strzelecki route' as initiation sites (Carowinnie, on the Strzelecki itself, and Tooncatchyn, north of Blanchewater). An 1863 police report documented an initiation performed at Tooncatchyn by a 200-strong ochre party, travelling south from Lake Hope (GRG 5/2/1588/1863, SRSA).
70   'The Far North', the *Register*, 28 July 1910, p. 8. Reuther confirms that young marriagable women were deployed in settling disputes between northern visitors and the Kuyani owners of the mine. He cited the example of the Kuyani woman, Dirini:

As compensation for the number of men [the Diyari] had killed and the girls they had stolen, they sent the above Dirini down to them, so that the way for their bukatu should remain open (Reuther 1981, vol. 8, no. 28).

71 Letter from Frank James to Alfred Howitt, 20 October 1881, Box 1052/3, Ms. 9356, La Trobe Library, Melbourne, copy in Rod Wilson papers, AA843, SAMA.
72 Hayward 1928, p. 89.
73 Letter from Wauhop to Hamilton (Chief Inspector of Police) 4 January 1864, GRG 52/2/73/1864, SRSA.
74 Bruce 1902, p. 53.
75 Letter from Jeffreys to Chief Commissioner of Police, 6 June 1863, GRG 5/2/166/1863, SRSA.
76 Corporal Wauhop's report, Mount Serle Station, 3 December 1863. GRG 5/2/1863/1886, SRSA.
77 Masey 1882, p. 3; Wauhop to Hamilton, *ibid*. This was probably the same reprisal which followed the 'Native Outrage' described in *SAPP* 124 of 1865. See Ellis 1978, p. 94. Guarded accounts of similar incidents are given in Hayward 1928 and Bull 1902.
78 *Observer*, 9 July 1864, p. 4e.
79 An earlier raid involving Pompey is documented in GRG 5/2/662/1858, SRSA. This man was probably the same individual whom A.W. Howitt recorded as Jinabuthina, a renegade from the Flinders Ranges (see Howitt 1904, p. 47; Brock 1985, p. 30).
80 See Brock 1985, pp. 30–31; Letter from Frank James to Alfred Howitt, 20 October 1881, *ibid*; *Observer*, 16 July 1864, p. 4h. Pompey's status as an 'Aboriginal bushranger' was eclipsed during the 1880s by the Innamincka Aboriginal man, 'Logic' (Foster 1998).
81 Letter from Wauhop to Hamilton, 29 July 1863, GRG 5/2/1251/1863, SRSA.
82 Letter from Warburton to Chief Secretary, 16 October 1863, GRG, 5/1/1590/1863, SRSA.
83 P.E. Warburton, note on report regarding Beltana shootings, 11 November 1863, GRG 5/2/1863/1886.
84 Letter from Wauhop to Hamilton, 12 July 1864, GRG 5/2/1299/1864, SRSA.
85 Oastler 1908a, p. 207; Oastler 1908b.
86 Letter from Warburton to Hamilton 21 December 1863, GRG 52/2/1947/1863, SRSA.
87 GRG 52/2/1947/1863; GRG 52/2/73/1864; GRG 5/3/479/1863, SRSA.
88 Letter from Wauhop to Hamilton, 4 January 1864, GRG 52/2/73/1864, SRSA.
89 'Suggestion Government supply ochre for Far North Aborigines', *Advertiser*, 10 September 1874, p. 4.
90 'Thirty nine pounds per ton for not less than four tons': letter from J. Buttfield, Blinman. GRG 52/1/291/1874, SRSA.
91 Masey 1882.
92 Reuther 1981, vol. 8, no. 82.
93 E.J. Finn, pers. comm., 1983.
94 Letter from Wauhop to Hamilton, GRG 5/2/73/1864, SRSA.
95 E.J. Finn, pers. comm., 1983.
96 Hercus 1985, p. 32; L. Hercus, Pukardu ms.
97 Author's interview with Ben Murray, 3 November, 1983. A similar incident during a trip from Marree to Parachilna was recalled by Jimmy and Leslie Russell (Wangkangurru men), Luise Hercus, pers. comm.
98 Reuther 1981, vol. 8, no. 83.
99 Reuther 1981, vol. 6, no. 209 (59); no. 1288 (25); no. 1371 (27); Gason 1874, p. 72.
100 See for example Brady 1987, pp. 37–38.
101 Author's interview with Ben Murray, 30 June 1985. It is probable that Afghan cameleers also took ochre north at the request of Aborigines. For the role of Afghans in the pituri trade see Harney 1950, p. 42.
102 The following account is taken from Masey 1882.

103   *Ibid.* Despite the claim of the presence of native mercury made by Masey, more recent
       analyses confirm that the ochre's sheen is caused by the presence of mica flakes. Mercury
       does not occur naturally in Australia. See Jercher *et al.* 1998.
104   Masey 1882.
105   Documentation of Raeck's claim is provided under GRG 35/2/7318/1904;
       GRG 52/1/265/1904, SRSA. Raeck is listed in the *South Australian Directory* of 1904.
106   GRG 52/1/315/1904, SRSA.
107   *Ibid.* The role of subincision in Aboriginal society was much debated during the late
       nineteenth and early twentieth centuries. One explanation, mostly advanced by European
       commentators, was that this operation resulted in fewer fertilities; Shanahan's letter may
       provide evidence that this view originated with Aboriginal people.
108   GRG 52/1/265/1904, SRSA.
109   GRG 24/6/880/1904, SRSA.
110   GRG 52/1/40/1905 and see the *South Australian Government Gazette*, 26 January 1905.
111   Mountford C.P., notebook 19, p. 69.
112   Bellchambers 1931, p. 179.
113   Within three years of this visit in late 2000, both men, Leroy and Randolph Richards, had
       passed away. I owe them both and their family, who accompanied me to the mine, a great
       deal for their insights, particularly those contained in the subsequent report prepared by
       Leroy and Rosalie Richards (Richards and Richards ms. 2002) which contains an account
       of that trip.

LIST OF ILLUSTRATIONS AND MAPS

INTRODUCTION

Page 2: Engraving, hand-coloured by Felix Danvin, after Louis Auguste de Sainson's '*Premiere entrevue avec les sauvages*' ('first interview with the natives'), apparently documenting the 1826 encounter between J.S.C. Dumont d'Urville's expedition and the Aboriginal people of King George Sound in 1826, but actually based on a drawing by Jacques-Efienne Victor Arago, who portrayed an encounter (with a different background) at Shark Bay on 12 September 1818, as part of Louis-Claude de Freycinet's expedition. Published in D'Urville's *Voyage de la corvette l'Astrolabe, 1826–1829*. Tastu, Paris, 1833.

Page 4: John Webber's pen and wash drawing, *Cook meeting inhabitants of Van Dieman's Land*, 1777 (26 x 38³/8 in.). Naval Historical Branch, Ministry of Defence, London.

Page 5: Both faces of the *Resolution* and *Adventure* medal, found in 1914 at Killora, North Bruny Island, by Janet Cadell. The bronze medal has a small hole drilled into the rim, above the King's head, where a suspension ring had been fitted to enable ribbon to be threaded through. Diameter: 42 mm; thickness: 3 mm. Private collection.

CHAPTER ONE
Master Blackburn's whip

Page 8: Master Blackburn's whip, comprising an Aboriginal club from the Sydney region and four knotted lashes. A72553, South Australian Museum.

Page 10: The vicinity of Port Jackson, showing places mentioned in this chapter, and names of Aboriginal language groups.

Page 15: Silhouette of 'Lieutenant David Blackburn', retained in Blackburn's family from 1787 until 1999. Mss 6937, Mitchell Library, Sydney.

Page 18: Detail from David Blackburn's annotated transcription of William Dawes's Port Jackson vocabulary, sent to Richard Knight in March 1791. Microfilm CY 1301, Mitchell Library, Sydney.

Page 20: 'His Majesty's Brig *Supply* 1790, off Lord Howe Island'. George Raper, 1792. The Natural History Museum, London.

Page 29: 'The hunted rush-cutter', probably painted by George Raper, ca 1790. The Natural History Museum, London.

Page 31: 'Implements of Port Jackson'. George Raper's 1792 painting of artefacts obtained from Sydney Aborigines. A club similar to Blackburn's is shown, beneath a spearthrower. The Natural History Museum, London.

Page 41: 'The Governor making the best of his way to the Boat after being wounded with the spear sticking in his shoulder'. Unknown artist. Natural History Museum, London.

Page 43: 'Ban nel lang meeting the Governor by appointment after he was wounded by Wal le maring in September 1790'. Unknown artist. Natural History Museum, London.

Page 44: Vignette portrait of Bennelong, as dressed during his voyage to England, embellished with Aboriginal artefacts. Engraving, ca 1798. U4073, Rex Nan Kivell Collection, National Library of Australia.

Page 47: The surgeon, Mr White, visiting Colebee at Botany Bay after he was wounded in a tribal fight. Watling Collection, Natural History Museum, London.

CHAPTER TWO
Broken shields

Page 50: Bark shield found in a cave at Point Malcolm, South Australia, by the lighthouse-keeper G.F. Edmunds. A2210, South Australian Museum.

Page 52: The Lower Murray and Adelaide Plains, showing places mentioned in this chapter, and names of Aboriginal language groups.

Page 54: The Point Malcolm lighthouse, ca 1885. Photographer: Samuel Sweet. B9803, State Library of South Australia.

Page 56: Camp of King Peter, Pullami (seated at left) at Point McLeay mission, ca 1885. Photographer: Samuel Sweet. South Australian Museum Archives.

Page 57: The missionary George Taplin during the early 1860s, with a son of Pullami (probably David Laelinyeri, who died in 1865). Photographer unknown. M. Angas Collection, South Australian Museum Archives.

Page 68: Pullami in about 1870, perhaps at the time of his incarceration in the Adelaide Lunatic Asylum. Photographer unknown. M. Angas Collection, South Australian Museum Archives.

Page 71: Pullami with other Ngarrindjeri elders at Taplin's graveside, 2 November 1880. Photographer: Samuel Sweet. M. Angas Collection, South Australian Museum Archives.

Page 71: Detail of Samuel Sweet's photograph of Taplin's grave, showing Pullami, aged in his early 70s. South Australian Museum Archives.

Page 73: Adelaide Plains man warding off spears. Original watercolour painted by William Cawthorne, ca 1843. Mitchell Library, Sydney.

Page 77: Adelaide Plains warrior decorated for battle, late 1843. Original watercolour painted by William Cawthorne. Mitchell Library, Sydney.

Page 85: Kadlitpinna, Captain Jack. Original watercolour painted by George French Angas in Adelaide, 5 February 1844. South Australian Museum Archives.

Page 87: Confiscated shields lying on the field of battle, south of Adelaide, 22 April 1844. Original watercolour by William Cawthorne. Mitchell Library, Sydney.

CHAPTER THREE
Turning to metal

Page 90: Hafted axe fashioned from metal abandoned by doomed members of the Calvert Exploring Expedition, 1896. A31043, South Australian Museum.

Page 92: The Calvert expedition's route of 1896–1897 across the Great Sandy Desert, showing places mentioned in this chapter and Aboriginal language groups.

Page 95: The last blank spaces – the Royal Geographical Society's map of the 'unexplored portions of Australia, prepared as a justification for the Calvert expedition, ca 1895 (Hill 1905).

Page 97: Members of the Calvert expedition photographed in Adelaide in early 1896. Seated: C.F. Wells, L.A. Wells, G.A. Keartland. Standing: G.L. Jones, Bejah Dervish, A.T. Magarey (expedition organiser, did not accompany the expedition). Not included: Said Ameer, James Trainor. B9758, State Library of South Australia.

Page 101: Detail of the northern route of the Calvert expedition across the Great Sandy Desert, showing Jones and C. Wells' western traverse from Separation Well, the routes of rescue parties south from the Fitzroy River to the vicinity of Joanna Spring, together with portions of Warburton's 1873 route and Carnegie's 1896 route (Wells 1902).

Page 108: Sergeant Ord's photograph of Yallameri and Pallari, chained to a tree at Joanna Spring on 26 June 1897, one day before leading the party to the explorers' remains. B61249, State Library of South Australia.

Page 109: Ord's photograph at the scene of Wells' and Jones' demise, 27 June 1897, showing Said Ameer packing the camels. The camel at left is bearing the body of one of the dead explorers. B61225, State Library of South Australia.

Page 113: Detail of one of the memorial windows dedicated to Charles Wells and George Jones in the Brougham Place Uniting Church, North Adelaide, showing the expedition camel team traversing the desert. Photographer: P. Jones.

Page 114: Localities mentioned in chapter three.

Page 121: Iron axe-head collected at the Adelaide River, Northern Territory, by Belgrave Ninnis, surgeon aboard the South Australian survey vessel, *Beatrice*, 1865. A31044, South Australian Museum.

Page 127: A hafted axe made from the iron footplate of a telegraph pole, once owned by Sir Charles Todd. A3941, South Australian Museum.

CHAPTER FOUR
Spearing Bennett

Page 130: Knotted string bag collected by W.W. Hoare at Port Darwin, 1869. A68380, South Australian Museum.

Page 132: Localities and Aboriginal group names relating to the British and South Australian settlements in northern Australia, 1820s to 1870.

Page 133: W.W. Hoare's copy of J.W.O. Bennett's 1869 vocabulary of the 'Woolner District' (Djerimanga) language, marked for publication. South Australian Museum Archives.

Page 134: J.W.O. Bennett's original manuscript of the 'Woolner Dialect, Adelaide River'. Goyder Papers, GRG 35/256/11, State Records, Adelaide.

Page 135: Portraits of W.W. Hoare (left) and J.W.O. Bennett (right), before George Goyder's survey party sailed from Adelaide, late 1868. Photographers: H. Anson and W. Francis, Adelaide. W.W. Hoare album, PRG 294/1, State Library of South Australia.

Page 142: J.W.O. Bennett's September 1865 map of proposed survey regions to the south of Adam Bay (original map 82.5 x 97 cm). C25/2, State Library of South Australia.

Page 143: Four-metre long sewn-bark canoe obtained by Boyle Travers Finnis in 1864–1865 at Escape Cliffs. A6446, South Australian Museum.

Page 143: Bennett's plan of the proposed settlement of 'Palmerston North' at Escape Cliffs, 1865. Detail from larger map. C20, State Library of South Australia.

Page 146: Detail of a barbed spear removed from the leg of a horse at Escape Cliffs, 1864. A4699, South Australian Museum.

Page 153: Portrait of George Goyder, Surveyor-General, before his expedition's departure in late 1868. Photographers: H. Anson and W. Francis, Adelaide. W.W. Hoare album, PRG 294/1, State Library of South Australia.

Page 156: William Hoare's watercolour painting of a crab collected by the expedition naturalist, Friedrich Schultze. PRG 294/4, State Library of South Australia.

Page 157: William Hoare's watercolour painting of a blue-spotted fantail ray (*Taeniura lymma*) collected by the expedition naturalist, Friedrich Schultze. PRG 294/4, State Library of South Australia.

Page 158: Detail of a page from William Hoare's scrapbook, recording his acquisition of artefacts including a string bag, in exchange for a knife and a pocket handkerchief, April 1869. W.W. Hoare album, PRG 294/1, State Library of South Australia.

Page 159: The Port Darwin camp in 1869, from the top of Fort Hill, before the stockade was erected. The tent on the opposite slope was probably used by the naturalist, Friedrich Schultze. Photographer: Joseph Brooks. W.W. Hoare album, PRG 294/1, State Library of South Australia.

Page 161: Studio photograph of 'Lillawer, Billimuck [centre] and Lungaba', after their arrival in Adelaide, late 1870. From W.W. Hoare album, PRG 294/1, State Library of South Australia.

Page 162: Biliamuk Gapal, aged about 38 years, at Palmerston in 1890. Photographer: Paul Foelsche. Foelsche Collection, South Australian Museum Archives.

Page 167: Detail of Bennett's map, showing numbered sites along the Adelaide River, 1864, local boundaries and three tribal names. J.W.O. Bennett notebook, Goyder Papers, GRG 35/256/11, State Records, Adelaide.

Page 168: Detail of a photograph of one of Goyder's survey camps, south of Palmerston, 1869, taken by an unknown photographer. Goyder is the bearded figure seated at centre. The tents and drafting tables were probably very similar to those used by Bennett. State Library of South Australia.

Page 174: The Woolna (Djerimanga) man Lialoon-me, aged 40 in May 1879, ten years after Bennett's spearing. Photographer: Paul Foelsche. Foelsche Collection, South Australian Museum Archives.

Page 177: William Hoare's black-bordered journal entry describing Bennett's demise on 28 May 1869. PRG 294/1, State Library of South Australia.

Page 181: Marble memorial tablet commemorating J.W.O. Bennett, sculpted by Samuel Peters. Erected by subscription in St Paul's Anglican church, Pulteney Street, Adelaide, 1869. Photograph: Anglican Diocesan Archives, Adelaide.

Page 182: Photograph of Bennett's grave on Fort Hill, sent to W.W. Hoare in 1905 by his old friend, Paul Foelsche. W.W. Hoare album, PRG 294/1, State Library of South Australia.

Page 184: William Hoare (left) dressed as an 'Assouan Arab' on a donkey at the St Alban's fête, 1904. W.W. Hoare album, PRG 294/1, State Library of South Australia.

CHAPTER FIVE
Drilling for fire

Page 186: Dick Cubadgee's fire-sticks, donated to the South Australian Museum in 1924 by David Lindsay's widow. A12919, South Australian Museum.

Page 187: Detail of Dick Cubadgee's fire-sticks, showing spliced, 'billiard cue' mend in the fire-drill.

Page 188: Localities mentioned in chapter five, with relevant Aboriginal group names.

Page 190: Dick Cubadgee at the Adelaide Jubilee Exhibition in 1887, posed in front of artefacts collected by David Lindsay. Cubadgee's fire-sticks are displayed cross-wise, at his left shoulder. AA108, South Australian Museum Archives.

Page 191: Dick Cubadgee making fire at the Adelaide Jubilee Exhibition of 1887. PXE 724/26, Mitchell Library, Sydney.

Page 194: 'David Lindsay, Explorer, FRGS', photographed in 1894 astride his camel 'Devil' in Coolgardie, Western Australia. PXE 724/41, Mitchell Library, Sydney.

Page 207: Cubadgee in his coachman's attire, Adelaide, 1887. Photographer: Samuel Sweet. PXE 724/29, Mitchell Library, Sydney.

Page 216: Cubadgee as 'King of the Warramunga tribe', photographed at the Adelaide Jubilee Exhibition in 1887. South Australian Museum Archives.

Page 219: Two studio portraits of Dick Cubadgee, Adelaide, ca 1888. Photographers: W. Lingwood Smith and Tuttle & Co. South Australian Museum Archives.

Page 221: Portrait study of Cubadgee, from the collection of Nora Lindsay, daughter of David Lindsay. South Australian Museum Archives.

Page 223: Glass goblet with engraved inscription, 'Dick Cubagee 1887'; height 13 cm. It was probably presented to Cubadgee at the time of the Adelaide Jubilee Exhibition. Owned by Margaret Stuart, great-granddaughter of David Lindsay. Photographed by Lindsay's great-great-granddaughter, Kylie Gillespie, 2008.

CHAPTER SIX
Unearthing the toas

Page 224: One of Reuther's toas, directing travellers to the place where the mythological ancestors Mitjimanamana and Likimadlentji saw the spirits of the dead arriving from all around and climbing upwards to the stars. A6168, South Australian Museum.

Page 226: The eastern Lake Eyre region, with relevant Aboriginal group names.

Page 231: Group of 15 toas from Reuther's collection, showing the main forms and designs. South Australian Museum Archives.

Page 233: Head of a toa depicting two peninsulas jutting into Lake Gregory, where the two female Ancestors, Watapijiri and Nardutjelpani, gathered swan eggs. The x-ray image confirms that the gypsum head conceals a 'mortice and tenon' carpentry construction, unknown in the region's Aboriginal material culture; the wooden prongs are neatly pegged into the central shaft. A6169, South Australian Museum.

Page 235: Photograph included as fig. 48 in A.W. Howitt's *Native Tribes of South-Eastern Australia*, showing an unconvincing 'obal' hovering in mid-air, within a museum diorama of an Aboriginal camp-site (Howitt 1904).

Page 236: Charlie Witjawarakuru interpreting a direction marker in the Great Victoria Desert, 1963. Photograph: N.B. Tindale. AA338, South Australian Museum.

Page 238: Killalpaninna mission buildings, ca 1890. A pile of mud bricks, made by Aboriginal people at the mission, is visible at right. Tom Reuther Collection, South Australian Museum Archives.

Page 239: Toa referring to the mythological site where the children of the ancestor Narimalpari split mussel shells open. A mussel shell is embedded in the toa's gypsum head. A6269, South Australian Museum.

Page 239: Toa referring to the mythological site where the ancestor Pitipikapana watched a lizard climb to the top of a sandhill. Three lizard claws are fixed to the toa. A6300, South Australian Museum.

Page 240: Toa referring to the two sandhills where the ancestor Karuwontirina saw two animals crouching behind a bush. A6225, South Australian Museum.

Page 240: Toa referring to the part of Cooper Creek where Jelkabalubaluna was asked by another ancestor if he was tired. He replied that he was not, shaking his leg as proof. A6229, South Australian Museum.

Page 247: Johann and Pauline Reuther in Reuther's study at Killalpaninna, ca 1905. Lutheran Archives, Adelaide.

Page 254: Detail of H.J. Hillier's 1904 map of place-names, showing the concentration of names around Killalpaninna mission, on the Cooper Creek. South Australian Museum Archives.

Page 260: View of Killalpaninna mission from the north side of Lake Killalpaninna, full of water after a Cooper Creek flood, early 1890s. South Australian Museum Archives.

Page 262: H.J. (Harry) Hillier, school teacher and artist, ca 1940. Lutheran Archives, Adelaide.

Page 263: Hillier's watercolour minatures of shields and boomerangs in Reuther's ethnographic collection, ca 1904. South Australian Museum Archives.

Page 263: A sheet of Hillier's watercolour minatures of Reuther's toas, ca 1904. South Australian Museum Archives.

Page 264: Johann Reuther with his wife Pauline, seven children and Aboriginal maid at Killalpaninna, ca 1900. South Australian Museum Archives.

Page 268: Two dogs modelled in spinifex resin, painted with pipeclay and red ochre, representing Pajamiljakirina ('bird-like', 'small-eater') and Dundukurananani ('big-eater'), a female dog belonging to the ancestor Darana (at front). A68461, A68458, South Australian Museum.

Page 271: George Aiston, policeman, ethnographer and later, bush store-keeper, relaxing at Mungeranie Police Station, ca 1915. Aiston Collection, South Australian Museum Archives.

Page 273: Oskar Liebler and his wife leaving Hermannsburg for Germany, 1913. Lutheran Archives, Adelaide.

Page 274: The seven Oskar Liebler toas in the Linden Museum, Stuttgart, sketched by Theo Koch-Grünberg in 1921, eight years after their acquisition (Schlatter 1985, p. 150).

Page 278: Aboriginal camp within five kilometres of Killalpaninna, photographed in about 1895. South Australian Museum Archives.

Page 279: Pastor Johann Reuther (at right) with his Aboriginal congregation at the Killalpaninna mission church, ca 1895. South Australian Museum Archives.

CHAPTER SEVEN
The magic garb of Daisy Bates

Page 282: Gaberdine suit purchased by Daisy Bates in about 1904 and worn by her until her death in 1951. South Australian Museum Archives.

Page 284: Localities mentioned in chapter seven, with relevant Aboriginal group names.

Page 285: Daisy Bates among Aboriginal men at Ooldea, South Australia, ca 1922. Photographer: A.G. Bolam. South Australian Museum Archives.

Page 286: Daisy Bates in Adelaide in 1950, attired in her clothing of 50 years earlier. *People* magazine, 19 July 1950.

Page 287: 'Clothing a native for his entry into civilization' – this photograph was included in Daisy Bates's *Passing of the Aborigines* (1941). Photographer: probably A.G. Bolam, 1930, South Australan Museum Archives.

Page 288: Pair of carefully darned woollen gloves worn by Daisy Bates during her work with the Aboriginal people of Ooldea, preserved among her effects. South Australian Museum Archives.

Page 288: Repair kit used by Daisy Bates for maintaining her wardrobe during her time with Aboriginal people on the Nullarbor Plain. South Australian Museum Archives.

Page 290: 'Farewell to my natives' – Daisy Bates bidding adieu to Aboriginal men at Ooldea siding, 1934. South Australian Museum Archives.

Page 297: Daisy Bates and a group of women and childern who had recently arrived at Ooldea from the north, early 1920s. They are wearing clothing supplied by her. Photographer: A.G. Bolam. South Australian Museum Archives.

Page 298: The male and female Snake effigies presented to Daisy Bates at Ooldea, 1930. Photographed on arrival in Adelaide, 1931. A17228, A17229, South Australan Museum.

Page 299: The 'ganba' Snake, carved by Mujamujana, one of the 1930s arrivals, and decorated by women with hot wire for the railway tourist trade. A17131, South Australian Museum.

Page 301: X-ray image of the male snake, showing the wooden 'jaw' held in place with nails, and the snake's spine, consisting of a flexible rubber hose, reinforced with metal casing. Artlab Australia.

CHAPTER EIGHT
Namatjira and the Jesus plaque

Page 304: Engraved mulga plaque made by Albert Namatjira, early 1930s. A72418, South Australian Museum.

Page 305: Albert Namatjira painting in the MacDonnell Ranges during the mid-1950s. Photograph: *Herald Sun* newspapers.

Page 306: Localities mentioned in chapter eight, with relevant Aboriginal group names.

Page 307: 'Amulda, James Range', painted by Albert Namatjira in 1941, and acquired by the South Australian Museum in that year. A41747, South Australian Museum.

Page 308: Undated watercolour painting attributed to Richard Moketarinja, a pupil of Namatjira. Sacred objects hover above a Centralian landscape. This image is a reminder of the thin veil separating Arrernte landscape painting from the art of their ancestors. Moketarinja died in 1983, and if this was one of his late works, it reveals the influence of the rising Western Desert painting movement in its depiction of sacred motifs. A65295, South Australian Museum.

Page 311: Painted wooden plaque depicting the 1932 apparition of the Virgin Mary at Beauraing, Belgium. Photographer: P. Jones.

Page 312: Group of Warlpiri men and boys at Central Mount Stuart, 1927. Photographer: Ernest Kramer. South Australian Museum Archives.

Page 312: A native evangelist among a desert group, north of Hermannsburg, ca 1930. Photographer: Ernest Kramer. South Australian Museum Archives.

Page 313: Evangelical poster used by Hermannsburg missionaries, 1930s. Burns-Albrecht Collection, South Australian Museum Archives.

Page 314: Mulga plaque depicting two emus and palms at Palm Valley, near Hermannsburg, ca 1932. A68997, South Australian Museum.

Page 314: 'Other refuge have I none'. Mulga plaque made by Albert Namatjira, ca 1930–1934. Flinders University Art Museum.

Page 318: Albert Namatjira sketching his totemic motifs of the Carpet Snake for Charles Mountford, ca 1940 (Mountford 1944, p. xxii).

Page 320: Catalogue cover drawn by Namatjira for his 1938 Melbourne exhibition (Hardy, Megaw & Megaw (eds) 1992, fig. 8.5).

Page 322: Pintubi men absorbed in an exhibition of paintings by Namatjira's art mentor Rex Battarbee, at Haast Bluff, west of the MacDonnell Ranges, during the early 1940s. Photographer: Rex Battarbee. South Australian Museum Archives.

Page 325: Albert Namatjira with mulga wood plaques, early 1930s, Hermannsburg Lutheran Mission. South Australian Museum Archives.

CHAPTER NINE
That special property

Page 336: Cake of red ochre collected by Dr Patrick Shanahan, 1904, 18 cm in diameter. A1863, South Australian Museum.

Page 338: Localities in the Flinders Ranges and eastern Lake Eyre, with relevant Aboriginal group names.

Page 340: The first page of Patrick Shanahan's letter to Dr Edward Stirling at the South Australian Museum, December 1904. South Australian Museum Archives.

Page 341: Dr Patrick Shanahan, ca 1903. Photograph courtesy of Dr Michael Shanahan.

Page 356: Ceremonial head-ornament, *bukatu-billi*, worn by returning ochre collectors during ceremonies associated with the ancestral Emu, Warugati. Collected by J.G. Reuther at Killalpaninna, ca 1904. A2710, South Australian Museum.

Page 358: Woven fibre bag containing the drug pituri, obtained in 1899 from a red ochre expedition passing through Beltana, by the pastoralist Nathaniel Phillipson. A1810, South Australian Museum.

Page 359: Wooden javelin and incised boomerang obtained by W.B. Sanders at Wooltana station in the Flinders Ranges from an ochre expedition coming 'from Queensland by way of Tilcha Creek to collect red ochre'. A39396, A39397, South Australian Museum.

Page 367: Police station and cells at Blinman, 1868. The station also served as a ration depot, visited by ochre expeditions. GRG 5/2/1868/649, State Records, Adelaide.

Page 371: This photograph of two men dressed and armed in the manner of Aboriginal men of the Diamantina region near Birdsville, was taken by J.H. Nixon on an 1874 photographic excursion to the vicinity of Hergott Springs (Marree). These men may have been members of an ochre expedition en route to the Flinders Ranges. Photograph and provenance courtesy of Howard Speed.

Page 375: T.P. Bellchambers captioned this photograph '"Larrikin Tom", and his turnout on our return from the ochre mine, after a night's exposure without food, water or blankets'. *Observer*, 31 December 1927.

Page 376: Larrikin Tom, Parnkarla custodian of the Pukardu mine, at one of the mine's pits. Photographer: T.P. Bellchambers. *Observer*, 31 December 1927.

Page 377: Looking across the red-stained mine site, over the range to the Lake Torrens plain. Photographer: P. Jones, 1983.

PUBLISHED SOURCES

Aiston, G. 1929. 'Chipped stone tools of the Aboriginal tribes east and north-east of Lake Eyre, South Australia', *Proceedings of the Royal Society of Tasmania*, March 1929, pp. 123–131.

Albrecht, F.W. 1950. 'Albert Namatjira', *Aborigines' Friends' Association Annual Report*, Adelaide, pp. 22–28.

Albrecht, F.W. 1977. 'Hermannsburg from 1926 to 1962', pp. 42–90 *in* E. Leske (ed.) *Hermannsburg: A Vision and Mission*, Lutheran Publishing House, Adelaide.

Andrews, F.W. 1875. 'Notes on the Aborigines met with on the trip of the exploring party to Lake Eyre, in command of J.W. Lewis', *South Australian Register*, 20 July 1875, p. 7.

Attenbrow, V. 2002. *Sydney's Aboriginal past. Investigating the archaeological and historical records*, UNSW Press, Sydney.

Austin, P. 1981. *A Grammar of Diyari, South Australia*, Cambridge University Press, Cambridge.

Baker, D.W.A. 1997. *The civilised surveyor. Thomas Mitchell and the Australian Aborigines*, Melbourne University Press, Melbourne.

Barley, N. 2002. *White Rajah*, Little, Brown Books, London.

Barratt, G. 1981. *The Russians at Port Jackson 1814–22*, Australian Institute of Aboriginal Studies, Canberra.

Basedow, H. 1925. *The Australian Aboriginal*, Preece, Adelaide.

Bastian, A. 1881. *Die Vorgeschichte der Ethnologie*, Dummler, Berlin.

Bates, D. 1922. 'My Initiation: The Freedom of the Totem', *Sydney Morning Herald*, 26 December 1922, p. 5.

Bates, D. 1927. 'Totem Boards and Stones', *South Australian Register*, 9 November 1927, p. 9.

Bates, D. 1932. 'Along the East-West Line. 150 at Ooldea to Drink of the Waters. Derelicts and Orphans from Far Away, Observing Century-Old Customs of Their Ancestors', *Sydney Mail*, 17 September 1932.

Bates, D. 1933. 'Wild Tribes of the Inland. Aboriginal Degenerates Without a Country', *Melbourne Herald*, 19 January 1933.

Bates, D. 1944. *The Passing of the Aborigines*, John Murray, London.

Bates, D. 1985. *The Native Tribes of Western Australia* (edited by Isobel White), National Library of Australia, Canberra.

Bates, D. 2004. *My natives and I*, Hesperian Press, Carlisle.

Batty, J. 1963. *Namatjira. Wanderer between two worlds*, Hodder & Stoughton, Melbourne.

Beaglehole, J.C. (ed.) 1967. *The Voyage of the* Resolution *and* Discovery *1776–1780*, 2 vols, Hakluyt Society, Cambridge.

Beckett, J. 1988. 'The past in the present: constructing a national Aboriginality', pp. 191–217 *in* J. Beckett (ed.) *Past and present: the construction of Aboriginality*, Aboriginal Studies Press, Canberra.

Bellchambers, T.P. 1931. *A nature-lover's notebook*, Nature Lovers' League, Adelaide.

Bennett, J.W.O. 1869. *Vocabulary of the Woolner District Dialect, Adelaide River, Northern Territory*, W.C. Cox, Adelaide.

Bennett, J.W.O. 1879. 'Vocabulary of Woolner District (Northern Territory)', pp. 311–315 *in* J.D. Woods (ed.) *Native Tribes of South Australia*, E.S. Wigg, Adelaide.

Bennett, T. 1995. *The birth of the museum. History, theory, politics*, Routledge, New York.

Berger, J. 1980. *About looking*, Pantheon Books, New York.

Berndt, R.M. and C.H. 1985. *The world of the first Australians*, Rigby, Adelaide.

Berndt, R.M. and C.H. (with J. Stanton). 1993. *The world that was. The Yaraldi of the Murray River and the Lakes, South Australia*, Melbourne University Press, Melbourne.

Berzins, B. 1988. *The Coming of the Strangers. Life in Australia 1788–1822*, Collins Australia and The State Library of New South Wales, Sydney.

Birman, W. 1979. 'Albert Frederick Calvert (1872–1946)', pp. 528–529 *in* B. Nairn and G. Serle (eds) *Australian Dictionary of Biography*, vol. 7, Melbourne University Press, Melbourne.

Bolam, A.G. 1927. *The Trans–Australian Wonderland*, McCubbin James, Melbourne.

Bonyhady, T. 1991. *Burke and Wills. From Melbourne to Myth*, David Ell Press, Sydney.

Bouquet, M. (ed.). 2002. *Academic Anthropology and the Museum. Back to the Future*, Bergahn Books, New York.

Bradley, W. 1969. *A Voyage to New South Wales. The Journal of Lieutenant William Bradley RN of HMS Sirius 1786–1792*, Ure Smith, Sydney.

Brady, M. 1987. 'Leaving the spinifex: the impact of rations, missions and the atomic tests on the southern Pitjantjatjara', *Records of the South Australian Museum*, vol. 20, pp. 35–46.

Brassey, A. 1889. *The Last Voyage: to India and Australia in the Sunbeam*, Longmans Green, London.

Brock, D.G. 1975. *To the Desert with Sturt. A Diary of the 1844 Expedition*, Royal Geographical Society, Adelaide.

Brock, P. 1985. *Yura and Udnyu. A history of the Adnyamathanha of the North Flinders Ranges*, Wakefield Press, Adelaide.

Brook, D. 1986a. 'Without wishing to tread on anyone's toas', *Artlink*, vol. 6, pp. 4–5.

Brook, D. 1986b. 'Touching one's toas', *Adelaide Review*, vol. 33, p. 38.

Bruce, R. 1902. *Reminiscences of an Old Squatter*, W.K. Thomas, Adelaide.

Bucknell, W.W. 1902. 'Message sticks, or Aboriginal letters', *Science of Man*, vol. 10, pp. 170–171; vol. 11, pp. 187–188.

Bundock, M. 1978. 'Notes on the Richmond Blacks', pp. 261–266 *in* I. McBryde (ed.) *Records of Times Past: ethnohistorical essays on the culture and ecology of the New England tribes*, AIAS, Canberra.

Burn, I. and Stephen, A. 1992. 'Namatjira's white mask: a partial interpretation', pp. 249–283 *in* J. Hardy, J.V.S. Megaw and R. Megaw (eds), *The heritage of Namatjira. The watercolourists of Central Australia*, William Heinemann, Melbourne.

Callaway, A. 1992. 'William Webster Hoare (1841–1927)', pp. 366–367 *in* J. Kerr (ed.) *The dictionary of Australian artists: painters, sketchers, photographers and engravers to 1870*, Oxford University Press, Melbourne.

Calvert, A.F. 1892. *The Aborigines of Western Australia*, W. Miligan, London.

Calvert, A.F. 1893. *The discovery of Australia*, George Philip & Son, London.

Calvert, A.F. 1895–1896. *The exploration of Australia*, 2 vols, George Philip & Son, London.

Carment, D., Maynard, R. and Powell, A. (eds) 1990. *Northern Territory Dictionary of Biography. Vol. 1: to 1945*, NTU Press, Casuarina.

Carnegie, D. 1898. *Spinifex and sand. A narrative of five years' pioneering and exploration in Western Australia*, C. Arthur Pearson, London.

Cawthorne, W. 1926. 'Rough Notes on the Manners and Customs of the Natives', *Proceedings of the Royal Geographical Society of Australasia, South Australian Branch*, vol. 27, pp. 44–77.

Clendinnen, I. 2003. *Dancing with strangers*, Text Publishing, Melbourne.

Clune, F. 1955. *Overland Telegraph*, Angus and Robertson, Sydney.

Collins, D. 1971 [1798]. *An account of the English colony in New South Wales*, 2 vols (facsim.), Libraries Board of South Australia, Adelaide.

Collins, D. 1910. *An account of the English colony in New South Wales*, Whitcombe & Tombs, Christchurch.

Colliver, F.S. 1971. 'The "Endeavour" and Aboriginal Australian contacts', *Queensland Naturalist*, vol. 20, pp. 25–34.

Cooper, C. 1989. *Aboriginal and Torres Strait Islander collections in overseas museums*, Aboriginal Studies Press, Canberra.

Council of the Royal Geographical Society of Australasia, South Australian Branch. 1891. *Handbook of Instructions for the Guidance of Officers of the Elder Scientific Exploration Expedition to the Unknown Portions of Australia*, Adelaide.

Cunningham, R.A. 1884. *A History of R.A. Cunningham's Australian Aborigines, Tatooed Cannibals, Black Trackers and Boomerang Throwers*, Elliot, London.

Curr, E.M. 1886–1887. *The Australian Race. Its Origin, Languages, Customs, Place of Landing in Australia, and the Routes by which it Spread Itself Over that Continent*, 4 vols, John Ferres, Melbourne.

Dégerando, J-M. 1969 [1800]. *The observation of savage peoples*, Routledge and Kegan Paul, London.

Dening, G. 1992. *Mr Bligh's bad language. Passion, power and theatre on the Bounty*, Cambridge University Press, Cambridge.

Dixon, R.M.W. 1991. *Words of our country. Stories, place names and vocabulary in Yidiny, the Aboriginal language of the Cairns-Yarrabah region*, University of Queensland Press, Brisbane.

Dutton, G. 1966. 'Edward John Eyre (1815–1901)', pp. 362–364 *in* D. Pike (ed.) *Australian Dictionary of Biography*, vol. 1, Melbourne University Press, Melbourne.

Eagle, M. 2004. 'Holy, holy, holy', pp. 46–53 *in* Flinders University Art Museum (ed.) *Holy, Holy Holy*, Exhibition catalogue, Flinders University, Adelaide.

Earl, G.W. 1846. 'On the Aboriginal Tribes of the Northern Coast of Australia', *Journal of the London Geographical Society*, vol. 16, pp. 239–251.

Earl, G.W. 1849–1850. 'On the Leading Characteristics of the Papuan, Australian, and Malayan-Polynesian Nations', *Journal of the Indian Archipelago and Eastern Asia*, vol. 3, pp. 682–689; vol. 4, pp. 66, 172.

Edgar, S. 1986. 'David Lindsay (1856–1922)', pp. 105–106 *in* B. Nairn and G. Serle (eds) *Australian Dictionary of Biography*, vol. 10, Melbourne University Press, Melbourne.

Egan, J. 1999. *Buried Alive. Sydney 1788–1792. Eyewitness accounts of the founding of a nation*, Allen and Unwin, Sydney.

Elkin, A.P. 1934. 'Cult-totemism and mythology in northern South Australia', *Oceania*, vol. 5, pp. 171–192.

Elkin, A.P. 1938. *The Australian Aborigines: how to understand them*, Angus and Robertson, Sydney.

Elliott, F. 2002. *The Elder Scientific Exploration Expedition, 1891–2. Photographs*, Corkwood Press, North Adelaide.

Ellis, R.W. 1978. 'Beltana, South Australia', *International Council on Monuments and Sites (ICMOS) Proceedings: The Tide of European Settlement – Conservation of the Physical Evidence*, Beechworth, 4–16 April 1978.

Elmslie, R. and Nance, S. 1990. 'Archibald Watson (1849–1940)', pp. 394–396 *in* J. Ritchie (ed.) *Australian Dictionary of Biography*, vol. 12, Melbourne University Press, Melbourne.

Evans-Pritchard, E.E. 1940. *The Nuer*, Oxford University Press, Oxford.

Eylmann, E. 1908. *Die Eingeborenen der Kolonie Südaustralien*, Dietrich Reimer, Berlin.

Fabian, J. 1983. *Time and the other: How anthropology makes its object*, Columbia University Press, New York.

Finlayson, W. 1903. 'Reminiscences by Pastor Finlayson', *Proceedings of the Royal Geographical Society of Australasia, South Australian Branch*, vol. 6, pp. 39–55.

Finniss, H.J. (ed.). 1966. 'Dr John Harris Browne's Journal of the Sturt Expedition, 1844–1845', *South Australiana*, vol. 5, pp. 23–59.

Flannery, T.F. (ed.). 1999. *The Birth of Sydney*, Text Publishing, Melbourne.

Foster, R. 1998. 'Logic's unexpected celebrity', pp. 158–190 *in* J. Simpson and L. Hercus (eds) *History in Portraits. Biographies of nineteenth century South Australian Aboriginal people*, Southwood Press, Sydney.

Foster, R., Hosking, R. and Nettelbeck, A. (eds). 2001. *Fatal Collisions. The South Australian frontier and the violence of memory*, Wakefield Press, Adelaide.

French, A. 2002. *Seeing the Centre. The art of Albert Namatjira 1902–1959*, National Gallery of Australia, Canberra.

Fry, H.K. 1937. 'Dieri Legends', *Folklore*, vol. 48, pp. 187–206; pp. 269–287.

Gason, S. 1874. *The Dieyerie tribe of Australian Aborigines*, W.C. Cox, Adelaide.

Gason, S. 1879. 'The Manners and Customs of the Dieyerie Tribe of Australian Aborigines', pp. 253–307 *in* J.D. Woods (ed.) *The Native Tribes of South Australia*, E.S. Wigg & Son, Adelaide.

Gregory, J.W. 1906. *The Dead Heart of Australia*, John Murray, London.

Hamlyn-Harris, R. 1918. 'On messages and message sticks', *Memoirs Queensland Museum*, vol. 6, pp. 13–36.

Hardy, B. 1976. *Lament for the Barkindji. The vanished tribes of the Darling River region*, Rigby, Adelaide.

Hardy, J., Megaw, J.V.S. and Megaw, M.R. (eds). 1992. *The Heritage of Namatjira. The Watercolourists of Central Australia*, William Heinemann, Melbourne.

Harney, W.E. 1950. 'Roads and trade', *Walkabout*, May 1950, pp. 42–45.

Hawdon, J. 1952. *The Journal of a Journey from New South Wales to Adelaide, performed in 1838 by Mr Joseph Hawdon*, Georgian House, Melbourne.

Hayward, J.F. 1928. 'Reminiscences', *Proceedings of the Royal Geographical Society of Australasia, South Australian Branch*, vol. 29, pp. 79–170.

Henson, B. 1992. *A Straight-out Man. F.W. Albrecht and Central Australian Aborigines*, Melbourne University Press, Melbourne.

Hercus, L. 1985. 'Leaving the Simpson Desert', *Aboriginal History*, vol. 9, pp. 22–43.

Hercus, L. 1987a. 'Just one toa', *Records of the South Australian Museum*, vol. 20, pp. 59–69.

Hercus, L. 1987b. 'Looking for Ditji-minka', *Records of the South Australian Museum*, vol. 21, pp. 149–156.

Hercus, L. and Potezny, V. 1991. 'Locating Aboriginal sites: a note on J.G. Reuther and the Hillier map of 1904', *Records of the South Australian Museum*, vol. 24, pp. 139–151.

Hill, B. 2002. *Broken song: T.G.H. Strehlow and Aboriginal possession*, Knopf, Sydney.

Hill, E. 1951. *The Territory*, Angus and Robertson, Sydney.

Hill, E. 1973. *Kabbarli. A Personal Memoir of Daisy Bates*, Angus and Robertson, Sydney.

Hill, J.G. (comp.). 1905. *The Calvert Scientific Exploring Expedition*, George Philip & Son, London.

Hilliard, W. 1968. *The people in between. The Pitjantjatjara people of Ernabella*, Hodder & Stoughton, London.

Horne, G. and Aiston, G. 1924. *Savage Life in Central Australia*, Macmillan, London.

Hovers, E., Ilani, S., Bar-yosef, O. and Vandermeersch, B. 2003. 'An early case of color symbolism. Ochre use by modern humans in Qafzeh Cave', *Current Anthropology*, vol. 44, pp. 491–522.

Howitt, A.W. 1889. 'Notes on Australian message sticks and messengers', *Journal of the Royal Anthropological Institute*, vol. 18, pp. 317–332.

Howitt, A.W. 1904. *The Native Tribes of South-east Australia*, Macmillan, London.

Hughes, R. 1987. *The Fatal Shore*, Knopf, New York.

Hunter, J. 1968 [1793]. *An Historical Journal of the Transactions at Port Jackson and Norfolk Island ... including the journals of Governors Phillip and King, and Lieut. Ball, and the voyages from the first sailing of the Sirius in 1787 to the return of that Ship's company to England in 1792*, John Stockdale, Piccadilly, London (Australiana Facsimile Editions no. 148, Libraries Board of South Australia, Adelaide).

Jenkin, G. 1979. *Conquest of the Ngarrindjeri*, Rigby, Adelaide.

Jennings, F. 1975. *The invasion of America: Indians, colonialism and the cant of conquest*, University of North Carolina Press, Chapel Hill.

Jercher, M., Pring, A., Jones, P.G. and Raven, M.D. 1998. 'Rietveld x-ray diffraction and x-ray fluorescence analysis of Australian Aboriginal ochres', *Archaeometry*, vol. 40, pp. 383–401.

Johnston, T.H. and Cleland, J.B. 1933–1934. 'The history of the Aboriginal narcotic, pituri', *Oceania*, vol. 4(2), pp. 201–233; vol. 4(3), pp. 268–289.

Jones, P.G. 1988. 'Perceptions of Aboriginal art: a history', pp. 143–179 *in* P. Sutton (ed.) *Dreamings. The Art of Aboriginal Australia*, Viking, New York.

Jones, P.G. 1990. 'David Unaipon (1872–1967)', pp. 303–305 *in* J. Ritchie (ed.) *Australian Dictionary of Biography*, vol. 12, Melbourne University Press, Melbourne.

Jones, P.G. 1991. 'Ngapamanha: A case study in the population history of north-eastern South Australia', pp. 157–173 *in* P. Austin *et al.* (eds) *Language and History: Essays in Honour of Luise A. Hercus*, Pacific Linguistics, Canberra.

Jones, P.G. 1992. 'Namatjira: Traveller between two worlds', pp. 97–136 *in* J. Hardy, J.V.S. Megaw and M.R. Megaw (eds) *The heritage of Namatjira. The watercolourists of Central Australia*, Heinemann, Melbourne.

Jones, P.G. 1996. *Boomerang: behind an Australian icon*, Wakefield Press, Adelaide.

Jones, P.G. 1996. 'The Horn expedition's place among nineteenth-century inland Expeditions', pp. 19–28 *in* S.R. Morton and D.J. Mulvaney (eds) *Exploring Central Australia: Society, the environment and the 1894 Horn expedition*, Surrey, Beatty & Sons, Chipping Norton.

Jones, P.G. 2003. 'Naming the Dead Heart: Hillier's map and Reuther's gazetteer of 2468 place-names in north-eastern South Australia', pp. 187–200 *in* L. Hercus, F. Hodges and J. Simpson (eds) *The Land is a Map. Placenames of indigenous origin in Australia*, Pacific Linguistics, Canberra.

Jones, P.G. 2005. *The Policeman's Eye. The frontier photography of Paul Foelsche*, South Australian Museum, Adelaide.

Jones, P.G. and Sutton, P. 1986. *Art and Land. Aboriginal sculptures of the Lake Eyre region*, Wakefield Press, Adelaide.

Karp, I. 1991. 'Culture and representation', pp. 11–24 *in* I. Karp and S.D. Lavine (eds) *Exhibiting cultures. The poetics and politics of museum display*, Smithsonian Institution Press, Washington.

Kendon, A. 1988. *Sign languages of Aboriginal Australia*, Cambridge University Press, Cambridge.

Kenny, A. 2005. 'A sketch portrait: Carl Strehlow's German editor Baron Moritz von Leonhardi', pp.54–70 *in* A. Kenny and S. Mitchell (eds) *Collaboration and Language. Occasional Paper no.4*, Strehlow Research Centre, Alice Springs.

Kerr, M.G. 1971. *The surveyors. The story of the founding of Darwin*, Rigby, Adelaide.

King, P.P. 1827. *Narrative of a survey of intertropical and western coasts of Australia performed between the years 1818 and 1822, with an appendix containing various subjects relating to hydrography and natural history*, 2 vols, J. Murray, London.

Knight, G.H. 1880. 'A Study of the Savage Weapons at the Centennial Exhibition, Philadelphia, 1876', pp. 213–297 *in* Smithsonian Institution (ed.) *Annual Report of the Smithsonian Institution for 1879*, Washington, D.C.

Kubler, G. 1971. 'On the colonial extinction of the motifs of pre-Columbian art', pp. 212–226 *in* C.M. Otten (ed.) *Anthropology and Art*, The Natural History Press, American Museum of Natural History, New York.

von Leonhardi, M. 1908. 'Über einige Hundefiguren des Dieristammes in Zentralaustralien', *Globus*, vol. 94, pp. 378–380.

von Leonhardi, M. 1909. 'Der Mura und die Mura-Mura der Dieri', *Anthropos*, vol. 4, pp. 1065–1068.

Leske, E. (ed.). 1977. *Hermannsburg: A Vision and Mission*, Lutheran Publishing House, Adelaide.

Lewis, J. 1922. *Fought and Won*, W.K. Thomas, Adelaide.

Lindsay, D. 1887. 'Explorations in the Northern Territory of South Australia', *Proceedings of the Royal Geographical Society of Australasia, South Australian Branch*, vol. 2, pp. 1–16.

Lindsay, D. 1889. 'An expedition across Australia from South to North, between the Telegraph Line and the Queensland Boundary, in 1885–1886', *Proceedings of the Royal Geographical Society of Australasia, South Australasia Branch*, vol. 1, pp. 650–671.

Lindsay, G.S. 1927. 'Aboriginal Gentleman. Cubagee of Warramung Tribe', *The Mail*, 2 July 1927, p. 22.

Lindsay, G.S. ca 1935. [Article on Cubagee], *Australasian Post* (no citation), photocopy from H.A. Lindsay scrapbook, supplied to author by J. Stewart-Rattray, 1991.

Lindsay, H.A. 1953. 'Across Australia in 1886', *Proceedings of the Royal Geographical Society of Australasia, South Australian Branch*, vol. 54, pp. 35–41.

Lindsay, H.A. 1968. 'The dreamer. The amazing story of a 19th century Aboriginal who had a vision of his people as pastoral landowners', *Aboriginal Quarterly*, October–December, 1968.

Lohe, M. 1977. 'A Mission is established', pp. 6–40 *in* E. Leske (ed.) *Hermannsburg: A Vision and Mission*, Lutheran Publishing House, Adelaide.

Loos, N. 1982. *Invasion and resistance. Aboriginal-European relations on the north Queensland frontier, 1861–1897*, Australian National University Press, Canberra.

Luthi, B. (comp.). 1993. *Aratjara. Art of the First Australians*, Kunstammlung Nordhein-Westfalen, Dusseldorf.

McBryde, I. 1978. 'Wil-im-ee Moor-ring: or, where do axes come from?', pp. 354–382 *in* J. Specht and J.P. White (eds) 'Trade and exchange in Oceania and Australia', *Mankind*, vol. 11(3).

McBryde, I. (ed.). 1978. *Records of Times Past: ethnohistorical essays on the culture and ecology of the New England tribes*, AIAS, Canberra.

McBryde, I. 2000. 'Travellers in storied landscapes: a case study in exchanges and heritage', *Aboriginal History*, vol. 24, pp. 152–174.

McCarthy, F.D. 1957. *Australia's Aborigines. Their Life and Culture*, Colorgravure Publications, Melbourne.

Magarey, A.T. 1899. 'Australian Aborigines' Water Quest', *Proceedings of the Royal Geographical Society of Australasia, South Australian Branch*, vol. 3, pp. 67–82.

Magarey, A.T. 1899. 'Tracking by the Australian Aborigine', *Proceedings of the Royal Geographical Society of Australasia, South Australian Branch*, vol. 3, pp. 119–126.

Masey, T.A. 1882. 'The Red Ochre Caves of the Blacks', *The Port Augusta Dispatch and Flinders Advertiser*, 9 June 1882, p. 3.

Mattingley, C. and Hampton, K. (eds). 1988. *Survival in our own land*, Wakefield Press, Adelaide.

Megaw, J.V.S. 1993. 'Something old, something new: further notes on the Aborigines of the Sydney district as represented by their surviving artefacts, and as depicted in some early European representations', *Records of the Australian Museum*, Supplement 17, pp. 25–44.

Meyer, H.A.E. 1879. 'Manners and Customs of the Aborigines of the Encounter Bay Tribe, South Australia', pp. 185–206 *in* J.D. Woods (ed.) *The Native Tribes of South Australia*, E.S. Wigg & Son, Adelaide.

Mincham, H. 1976. 'Sir Edward Charles Stirling (1848–1919)', pp. 200–201 *in* B. Nairn (ed.) *Australian Dictionary of Biography*, vol. 6, Melbourne University Press, Melbourne.

Mitchell, T.L. 1838. *Journal of Three Expeditions into the Interior of Eastern Australia*, 2 vols, T. & W. Boone, London.

Moorhouse, M. 1846. *A Vocabulary and Outline of the Grammatical Structure of the Murray River Language*, Andrew Murray, Adelaide. Reprinted in *Journal of the Proceedings of the Royal Society of New South Wales*, vol. 20 (1886), pp. 64–68.

Morgan, E.J.R. 1966. 'George Fife Angas (1789–1879), George French Angas (1822–1886)', pp. 15–19 *in* D. Pike (ed.) *Australian Dictionary of Biography*, vol. 1, Melbourne University Press, Melbourne.

Morison, P. 1979. 'David Wynford Carnegie (1871–1900)', pp. 566–567 *in* B. Nairn and G. Serle (eds) *Australian Dictionary of Biography*, vol. 7, Melbourne University Press, Melbourne.

Morphy, H. 1977. 'Schematisation, meaning and communication in toas', pp. 77–89 *in* P.J. Ucko (ed.) *Form in indigenous art. Schematisation in the art of Aboriginal Australia and prehistoric Europe*, AIAS, Canberra.

Morphy, H. 1998. *Aboriginal Art*, Phaidon, London.

Morton, J. 1992. 'Country, people, art', pp. 23–62 *in* J. Hardy, J.V.S. Megaw and M.R. Megaw (eds) *The heritage of Namatjira. The watercolourists of Central Australia*, Heinemann, Melbourne.

Mountford, C.P. 1944. *The Art of Albert Namatjira*, Bread and Cheese Club, Melbourne.

Mountford, C.P. 1955. 'The Lightning Man in Australian mythology', *Man*, vol. 55, pp. 128–130.

Moyal, A. 1984. *Clear across Australia. A history of telecommunications*, Thomas Nelson, Melbourne.

Mulvaney, D.J. and Calaby, J.H. 1985. *'So much that is new'. Baldwin Spencer 1860–1929*, Melbourne University Press, Melbourne.

Mulvaney, D.J. and Green, N. (eds). 1993. *Commandant of solitude. The journals of Captain Collet Barker 1828–1831*, Melbourne University Press, Melbourne.

Mulvaney, D.J., Morphy, H. and Petch, A. (eds). 1997. *My dear Spencer. The letters of F.J. Gillen to Baldwin Spencer*, Hyland House, Melbourne.

Myers, F.P. 1986. *Pintupi country, Pintupi self. Sentiment, place and politics among Western Desert Aborigines*, University of California Press, Los Angeles.

Napier, F. 1876. *Notes of a Voyage from New South Wales to the North Coast of Australia from the Journal of the Late Francis Napier*, James Napier, Glasgow.

Neville, D. 1975. *Blackburn's Isle*, Terence Dalton, Lavenham.

Neville, R. 1997. *A rage for curiosity: visualising Australia 1788–1830*, State Library of New South Wales, Sydney.

Nicholson, J. 2004. *The incomparable Captain Cadell*, Allen and Unwin, Sydney.

Oastler, J. 1908a. 'Administration of justice in the back blocks', *The Honorary Magistrate*, vol. 16, July 1908, pp. 205–209.

Oastler, J. 1908b. 'Life in the Bush', *South Australian Register*, 9 May 1908, p. 11.

Peake-Jones, K. 1985. *The branch without a tree. The centenary history of the Royal Geographical Society of Australasia, South Australian Branch Incorporated, 1885 to 1985*, Royal Geographical Society of Australasia (South Australian Branch), Adelaide.

Penny, B.R. 1979. 'Thomas Brassey (1836–1918)', pp. 391–392 *in* B. Nairn and G. Serle (eds) *Australian Dictionary of Biography*, vol. 7, Melbourne University Press, Melbourne.

Phillip, A., Stockdale, J. (comp.). 1982 [1789]. *The Voyage of Governor Phillip to Botany Bay, with an Account of the Establishment of the Colonies of Port Jackson and Norfolk Island*, facsimile reprint 1982, Hutchinson Group, Melbourne.

Phillips, W. 1993. *James Jefferis: prophet of Federation*, Australian Scholarly Publishing, Melbourne.

Poignant, R. 1993. 'Captive Aboriginal lives: Billy, Jenny, Little Toby and their companions', pp. 35–57 *in* K. Darian-Smith (ed.) *Captured lives. Australian captivity narratives*, working papers in Australian Studies, nos. 85, 86 and 87, Sir Robert Menzies Centre for Australian Studies, University of London.

Poignant, R. 2004. *Professional savages. Captive lives and western spectacle*, University of New South Wales Press, Sydney.

Pratt, M.L. 1992. *Imperial eyes. Travel writing and transculturation*, Routledge, London and New York.

Ray, S.H. 1920. 'Australian signposts', *Nature*, vol. 104, pp. 643–644.

Reece, R.H.W. 1974. *Aborigines and colonists. Aborigines and colonial society in New South Wales in the 1830s and 1840s*, Sydney University Press, Sydney.

Reece, R.H.W. 2007. *Daisy Bates. Grand dame of the desert*, National Library of Australia, Canberra.

Reid, G. 1990. *A picnic with the natives. Aboriginal-European relations in the Northern Territory to 1910*, Melbourne University Press, Melbourne.

Reynolds, H. 1982. *The other side of the frontier: Aboriginal resistance to the European invasion of Australia*, Penguin, Ringwood.

Reynolds, H. 1987. *Frontier: Aborigines, settlers and land*, Allen and Unwin, Sydney.

Roberts, T. 2005. *Frontier justice. A history of the Gulf Country to 1900*, University of Queensland Press, St. Lucia.

Rodger, N.A.M. 1986. *The wooden world: an anatomy of the Georgian navy*, Collins, London.

Roth, W. 1897. *Ethnological studies among the north-west-central Queensland Aborigines*, Government Printer, Brisbane.

Roheim, G. 1974. *Children of the desert. The western tribes of Central Australia* (edited and with an introduction by Werner Muensterberger), Basic Books, New York.

Sagona, A. (ed.) 1994. *Bruising the red earth. Ochre mining and ritual in Aboriginal Tasmania*, Melbourne University Press, Melbourne.

Salter, E. 1971. *Daisy Bates. 'The Great White Queen of the Never Never'*, Angus and Robertson, Sydney.

Schröder, W. 2002. *Ich reiste wie ein Buschmann (Life and scientific work of the pioneer of Australian culture, Erhard Eylmann)*, W.P. Druck & Verlag, Darmstadt.

Sayers, A. 1994. *Aboriginal artists of the nineteenth century*, Oxford University Press, Melbourne.

Schlatter, G. 1985. *Bumerang und schwirrholz. Eine Einführung in die traditionelle Kultur australischer Aborigines*, Dietrich Reimer Verlag, Berlin.

Schröder, W. 2002. *Ich reiste wie ein Buschmann. Zum Leben und Wirken des Australienforschers Erhard Eylmann*, W.P. Druck & Verlag, Darmstadt.

Searcy, A. 1907. *In Australian Tropics*, Kegan, Paul, Trench, Trübner & Co., London.

Sharkey, D. and Deburgh, J. 1958. *Our Lady of Beauraing*, Hanover House, New York.

Sharp, R.L. 1952. 'Steel axes for stone age Australians', *Human Organization*, vol. 11(2), pp. 17–22.

Siebert, O. 1910. 'Legends and customs of the Dieri and neighbouring tribes in Central Australia', *Globus*, vol. 97, pp. 43–50; pp. 50–59.

Smith, K. 2001. *Bennelong*, Kangaroo Press, Sydney.

Sobin, G. 1999. *Luminous debris. Reflecting on vestige in Provence and Languedoc*, University of California Press, Berkeley.

Spencer, W.B. and Gillen, F.J. 1899. *The Native Tribes of Central Australia*, Macmillan, London.

Spillett, P.G. 1972. *Forsaken settlement. An illustrated history of the settlement of Victoria, Port Essington, North Australia 1838–1849*, Lansdowne Press, Melbourne.

Stephens, E. 1890. 'The Aborigines of Australia. Being personal recollections of those tribes which once inhabited the Adelaide Plains of South Australia', *Journal of Proceedings of the Royal Society of New South Wales*, vol. 23, pp. 476–503.

Stevens, C. 1994. *White man's dreaming. Killalpaninna mission 1866–1915*, Oxford University Press, Melbourne.

Stirling, E.C. 1908. 'Toas', pp. 21–23 *in* South Australian Museum (ed.) *Report of the Board of Governors of the Public Library, Museum and Art Gallery of South Australia for 1907–1908*, Government Printer, Adelaide.

Stirling, E.C. and Waite, E.R. 1919. 'Description of toas', *Records of the South Australian Museum*, vol. 1, pp. 105–155.

Stow, J.P. 1894. *The Voyage of the Forlorn Hope 1865*, Robertson, Melbourne.

Strehlow, T.G.H. 1964. 'The art of circle, line and square', pp. 44–59 *in* R.M. Berndt (ed.) *Australian Aboriginal Art*, Ure Smith, Sydney.

Sutton, P. 1986. 'The sculpted word: a reply to Donald Brook on toas', *Adelaide Review*, vol. 32, pp. 8–9; pp. 36–37.

Sutton, P. 1987. '"The really interesting suggestion" ... yet another reply to Donald Brook on toas', *Adelaide Review*, vol. 34, p. 5.

Sutton, P. (ed.). 1988. *Dreamings. The art of Aboriginal Australia*, Viking, New York.

Sutton, P. 1991. 'Unintended consequences', *The Interior*, vol. 1, pp. 24–29.

Swain, T. 1993. *A place for strangers. Towards a history of Australian Aboriginal being*, Cambridge University Press, Cambridge.

Taplin, G. 1874. *The Narrinyeri: an account of the tribes of South Australian Aborigines*, J.T. Shawyer, Adelaide.

Taplin, G. 1879. 'The Narrinyeri: An account of the tribes of South Australian Aborigines', pp. 1–181 *in* J.D. Woods (ed.) *The Native Tribes of South Australia*, E.S. Wigg & Son, Adelaide.

Teichelmann, C.G. and Schürmann, C.W. 1840. *Outlines of a Grammar, Vocabulary and Phraseology, of the Aboriginal Language of South Australia, Spoken by the Natives in and for some distance around Adelaide*, published by the authors, Adelaide.

Tench, W. 1996 [1788]. *Comprising a Narrative of the Expedition to Botany Bay and A Complete Account of the Settlement at Port Jackson* (edited and introduced by T. Flannery), Text Publishing, Melbourne.

Thomson, D. 1949. *Economic Structure and the Ceremonial Exchange Cycle in Arnhem Land*, Macmillan, Melbourne.

Tindale, N.B. 1937. 'Two legends of the Ngadjuri tribe from the middle north of South Australia', *Transactions Royal Society of South Australia*, vol. 61, pp. 149–153.

Tindale, N.B. 1974. *Aboriginal tribes of Australia. Their terrain, environmental controls, distribution, limits and proper names*, University of California Press, Berkeley.

Tindale, N.B. 1986. 'Anthropology', pp. 235–249 *in* C.R. Twidale, M.J. Tyler and M. Davies (eds) *Ideas and endeavours – the natural sciences in South Australia*, Royal Society of South Australia, Adelaide.

Todd, C. 1884. 'Report on the Post Office, Telegraph and Observatory Departments of South Australia. October 1884', *SAPP*, vol. 4, no. 191.

Tregenza, J. 1982. *George French Angas. Artist, traveller and naturalist 1822–1886*, Art Gallery of South Australia, Adelaide.

Troy, J. 1994. 'The Sydney language', pp. 61–78 *in* N. Thieberger and W. McGregor (eds) *Macquarie Aboriginal Words*, Macquarie Dictionary, Macquarie University, Sydney.

Venbrux, E. and Jones, P.G. 2002. '"Prachtaufnahmen" of Aborigines from Northern Australia, 1879', pp. 116–127 *in* Linda Roodenburg (ed.) *Anceaux's Glasses. Anthropological photography since 1860*, Rijksmuseum voor Volkenkunde, Leiden.

Veth, P., Smith, M. and Haley, M. 2001. 'Kaalpi: the archaeology of a sandstone outlier in the Western Desert', *Australian Archaeology*, vol. 52, pp. 9–17.

Warburton, P.E. 1875. *Journey across the western interior of Australia*, Sampson Low, London.

Watson, P. 1983. '"This Precious Foliage". A study of the Aboriginal psycho-active drug Pituri', *Oceania Monograph*, no. 26, University of Sydney, Sydney.

Wells, L.A. 1902. 'Journal of the Calvert Scientific Exploring Expedition, 1896–7', *Western Australia Parliamentary Paper* no. 46, Government Printer, Perth.

White, I. 1993. 'Daisy Bates: legend and reality', pp. 47–65 *in* J. Marcus (ed.) *First in their field. Women and Australian anthropology*, Melbourne University Press, Melbourne.

Willey, K. 1979. *When the sky fell down: the destruction of the tribes of the Sydney region 1788–1850s*, Collins, Sydney.

Woods, J.D. (ed.). 1879. *The Native Tribes of South Australia*, E.S. Wigg & Son, Adelaide.

Worgan, G. B. 1978. *Journal of a First Fleet surgeon*, Library Council of New South Wales, Sydney.

Wreschner, E. 1980. 'Red ochre and human evolution: a case for discussion', *Current Anthropology*, vol. 21, pp. 631–644.

Wright, R.V.S. 1979. 'Daisy May Bates (1863 [probably 1859]–1951)', pp. 208–209 *in* B. Nairn and G. Serle (eds) *Australian Dictionary of Biography*, vol. 7, Melbourne University Press, Melbourne.

Yashchenko, A.L. 2001 [1903]. *Australian journey 1903. The travel diary of Aleksandr Leonidovich Yashchenko* (translated from Russian, with an introduction and notes by Peter Tilley), University of Melbourne, Melbourne.

UNPUBLISHED SOURCES

Aiston, G. to W.H. Gill. 1920s–1940s. Correspondence, Ms A2535–2537, ML.

Albrecht, F.W. n.d. 'Tjurunga Stories', Lutheran Archives, Adelaide.

Albrecht, F.W. 1959. 'An address at the funeral of Albert Namatjira, 9.2.59', typescript, Burns-Albrecht collection, SAMA.

Anon. 1790. 'Grammatical forms of the language of N.S. Wales, in the neighbourhood of Sydney (Native and English), by Dawes'. Ms 41645(a), Marsden Collection Library of the School of Oriental & African Studies, London; microfilm copy, FM4/3431, reel 5, frames 771–794, ML.

Bates, D. 1939. 'My natives and I', typescript, together with other correspondence, AA23, SAMA.

Battarbee, R. 1930s. Diaries, Battarbee Archive, c/ Gayle Quarmby, Reedy Creek, Kingston, South Australia.

Bennett, J.W.O. 1864–1865. Letters written by John Bennett during the Northern Territory Survey Expedition, D7425(L), SLSA.

Bennett, J.W.O. 1864–1865, 1869. Maps of the Northern Territory, in the vicinity of Adam Bay, SLSA.

Blackburn D. 1780s–1790s. Papers, correspondence, Ms 6937, Microfilm Cy1301, ML.

Bull, J. 1902. 'Reminiscences: life of John Bull, Australian bushman and explorer', PRG 507, SLSA

Cawthorne, W. 1842–1846. 'Literarium Diarium', A103–105, ML.

Champion, G. 1993. 'Australia's forgotten explorer: David Lindsay FRGS', Ms 13041, La Trobe Library, Melbourne.

Crowder, W. A. 1871–1872. Diary, D8065, SLSA.

Dawes, W. 1790–1791. 'Vocabulary of the language of N.S. Wales, in the neighbourhood of Sydney, Native and English by Dawes', Ms 41645(b), Marsden Collection Library of the School of Oriental & African Studies, London; microfilm copy, FM4/3431, reel 5, frames 795–817, ML.

Edmunds, R.H. 1864–1866. 'Diary of the N.T. Survey Expedition, 1864–66', D8043(L), SLSA.

Finlayson, W. 1830s–40s. 'Extracts, jottings and memoranda of William Finlayson, Helenholme Mitcham, S.A', typescript copy of original Ms 16685, LaTrobe Library, Melbourne.

Finniss, B.T. 1864–1866. 'Diary of B.T. Finniss', D527/2/2, SLSA.

Foster, R. (ed.). 1991. 'Sketches of the Aborigines of South Australia', References in the Cawthorne Papers, Aboriginal Heritage Branch, S.A., Department of Environment and Planning, Adelaide.

Fry, H.K. n.d. 'Two more Aboriginal legends by Mark Wilson', Fry Papers, AA105, SAMA.

Gillen, F.J. 1901–1902. 'Camp Jottings', PRG 54/1/2, SLSA.

Goyder, G.R. 1868–1869. 'Northern Territory Survey Expedition 1868–1870. Journal kept by the Surveyor General, G.R. Goyder, Jan. 1 to Sept 28, 1869', GRG 35/655, SRSA.

Herbert, S.W. 1870–1872. 'Reminiscences by Sidney Wellington Herbert of life in the Northern Territory during the construction of the Overland Telegraph, August 1870 to November 1872', D6995(L), SLSA.

Hercus, L. n.d. 'Pukardu ms', Luise Hercus papers, SAMA.

Hercus, L. n.d. 'Singing and talking about red ochre', Luise Hercus papers, SAMA.

Hercus, L. 2003. 'Report on fieldwork in the Lakes area of South Australia, June 2003', Luise Hercus papers, SAMA.

Hoare, W.W. 1869–1870. '1869 Adventures, Port Darwin, My Diary', PRG 294/1, SLSA.

Hoare, W.W. 1869. Copy of J.W.O. Bennett's 'Escape Cliffs Native Dialect', PRG 140/6, SLSA.

Howard, F. 1864–1866. 'Papers of Frederick Howard RN, naval officer, relating to the Admiralty's hydrographic survey of the South Australian coast; logs of HM Surveying Schooner "Beatrice"', PRG 1198, SLSA.

Jones, G.L. 1896. 'Diary kept during Calvert Scientific Exploration Expedition', PRG 1011/11, SLSA.

Jones, P.G. 1997. '"A box of native things". Ethnographic collectors and the South Australian Museum, 1830s–1930s', Ph.D. thesis, Department of History, University of Adelaide.

Kenyon, A.S. 1920a. Letter to director, South Australian Museum, 3 May 1920, GRG 19, SRSA.

Kenyon, A.S. 1920b. Letter to General Secretary, Public Library, Museum and Art Gallery, 9 June 1920, GRG 19, SRSA.

Lindo, J.W. n.d. 'Legend of the Ochre Pit near Parachilna', typescript, N.B. Tindale papers, AA338, SAMA.

Lindsay, D. 1880s. Papers, Ms 200; PXE 724/28,29, ML.

Morphy, H. 1972. 'A reanalysis of the toas of the Lake Eyre tribes of Central Australia, a consideration of their form and function', M. Phil. thesis, University of London, London.

Mountford, C.P. 1937–1947. Flinders Ranges notebooks, 1937, 1939, 1947, Mountford-Sheard Collection, SLSA.

Reece, R.H.W. 2005. '"You would have loved her for her lore": the letters of Daisy Bates', paper delivered by Professor Bob Reece, Harold White Fellow, 3 November 2005, National Library of Australia, Canberra.

Reuther, J.G. 1981. 'The Diari, vols 1–13', translated by Rev. Philipp A. Scherer; vol. 5 trans. T. Schwarzchild and L.A. Hercus, AIAS microfiche no. 2, Australian Institute of Aboriginal Studies, Canberra.

Richards, L. and Richards, R. 2002. 'Pukatu ochre mine (Parachilna ochre mine). Stage 2 draft report', a National Estate project, the author.

Shanahan, P.F. 1904. Letter to Dr E.C. Stirling, South Australian Museum, 26 December 1904, AA298, SAMA.

Smith, E.M. n.d. 'Reminiscences', PRG 809, SLSA.

Stirling, E.C. 1908. Letter to J.G. Reuther, 14 October 1908, GRG19, SRSA.

Strehlow, T.G.H. 1930s–1960s. Journals, Strehlow Research Centre, Alice Springs.

Taplin, G. 1859–1879. Journal, PRG 186, SLSA.

Tindale, N.B. 1920s–1990s. Ms AA338, SAMA.

Tindale, N.B. 1963. Journal of a visit to the Rawlinson Range area in the Great Western Desert, Ms, carbon copy, AA338/4/44, SAMA.

Traine, T. ca 1920. 'Across the Barkly Tableland to the Kimberleys: Memories and Experiences of a Pioneer', Northern Territory Library, Darwin.

Völker, H. 1999. 'Projektion des Fremden. Beitrag deutscher lutherischer Missionare zur Darstellung der australischen Ürbevolkerung um 1900: Johan Georg Reuther, Carl Strehlow, Otto Siebert (Images of the other. Contribution of German Lutheran missionaries to the portrayal of the Australian Aboriginal people around 1900)', Magisterarbeit zur Erlangung der Würde des Magister Artium der Philosophischen Fakultäten der Albert-Ludwigs-Universitat zu Freiburg i. Br., Germany.

Webling, A.C. 1864–1865. 'The Journals of Alfred Charles Webling, aboard H.M. Schooner, "Beatrice"', D3058(L), SLSA.

LOCALITIES INDEX

LOCALITIES OUTSIDE AUSTRALIA

Batavia, 33
Belgium
    Beauraing, 310–11
    Brussels, 310
Britain (*see also* museums, European), 21
    Crystal Palace, London, 184
    Norfolk, 16
    Norwich, 14–15, 23, 35
    Portsmouth, 14, 19–21, 48
    Spithead, 19
    St Alban's, England, 184
Cape of Good Hope, 23
Germany, 273
    Neuendettelsau seminary, 225, 248
Livorno, Italy, 49
Malay archipelago, 122
Qafzeh cave, Middle East, 348
South America, 21, 23
    Rio de Janeiro, 17, 21
Sulawesi, 136
West Indies, 14, 19, 48

LOCALITIES WITHIN AUSTRALIA

New South Wales, 3, 22
    Abercrombie, 92, 118
    Bennelong Point, 44
    Blackburn's Isle, 15, 22, 380
    Blackbourne's Point, 15
    Botany Bay, 3, 12, 14, 19, 20, 23, 24, 25, 26,
        45, 47
    Collins Cove, 39, 42
    Depot Glen, 12
    Lake Mungo, 347
    Lord Howe Island, 15, 16, 20, 33
    Manly Cove, 38, 39
    Mt Poole, 12, 380

New South Wales, cont'd
    Murray River, 123
    Murrumbidgee River, 123
    Norfolk Island 15–17, 22, 33, 38, 44, 48
    Observatory Hill, 46
    Port Jackson, 12–15, 17–18, 21–2, 26, 31–3,
        36, 38, 40, 43, 48, 125, 342, 381
    Rabbit Island, *see* Blackburn's Isle
    Richmond River, 117
    River Darling, 353
    Sydney, 117, 327
    Sydney Cove, 26, 27, 33, 41, 43
    Sydney Harbour Bridge, 17
    Sydney Opera House, 44
    Tibooburra, 353
Northern Territory, 204, 205
    Adam Bay, 122, 141–2, 143
    Adelaide River, 121–2, 136, 139, 140, 141,
        143, 147, 148, 149, 152, 153, 163, 166,
        167, 179
    Alice Springs, 116, 202, 203, 296, 305, 309,
        333, 340, 342, 394
    Anthony Lagoon, 199, 201, 205
    Arnhem Land, 120, 122, 123, 135, 196, 234,
        309, 347
    Auld's Lagoon, 166, 167, 169, 172
    Barkly Tableland, 195, 201
    Bathurst Island, 122
    Borroloola, 205
    Brunette Downs, 201
    Central Mount Stuart, 312
    Chambers Bay, 144, 148–9, 165–7
    Cobourg Peninsula, 137–8, 167
    Corella Downs, 201
    Cresswell Downs, 201
    Daly Range, 165
    Daly River, 143

Northern Territory, cont'd
  Darwin, 161, 163, 165, 178–9, 205, 212, 342
  Elizabeth River, 175
  Ellery Creek, 319
  Escape Cliffs, 133, 135, 138, 141–3, 146–9,
    151, 154, 159, 163, 166–7, 170, 175,
    178–9, 181, 392
  Eva Downs, 199, 201
  Finke River, 196
  Finniss River, 143, 170
  Fort Darwin, 125–6, 131, 165, 170–1, 175–6,
    178, 181–4, 393
  Fort Hill, 176–7, 181, 183, 185
  Fort Point, 163–5, 168, 175, 178
  Fort Wellington, 136–7
  Fred's Pass, 165–7, 169, 172–3, 175,
    178–80, 393
  Glen Annie, 196, 215, 217, 394
  Glen Helen, 315
  Gulf of Carpentaria, 204
  Hale River, 395
  Haast Bluff, 322
  Harts Range, 196, 217
  Hermannsburg (see also missions), 250, 273,
    312, 314
  Howard River, 152
  James Range, 307
  Karrku ochre mine, 348
  Katherine, 128
  Liverpool River, 122
  MacDonnell Ranges, 116, 192, 196–7, 204,
    217, 264, 305, 322, 388–9, 394
  Malakunanja, 347
  Malangangerr, 115
  Manangananga Cave, 331–2
  Manton Creek, 173, 393
  Marshall River, 198–200
  Melville Island, 120, 122, 136, 392
  Minto Head, 122
  Mount Coghlan, 196, 394
  Mount Daly, 165
  Narrows, 143, 149, 166–7
  Palm Valley, 305, 314, 317–18, 403
  Palmerston, 143, 159
  Palmerston North, Palmerston South, 143
  Papunya, 317, 321, 328
  Plenty River, 197
  Point Ayers, 147
  Port Darwin, 125, 130–1, 135–6, 143, 151,
    153–5, 159, 163, 168, 186, 392
  Port Essington, 120, 136, 138–9, 141,
    167, 207
  Raffles Bay, 120, 136, 137, 141
  Roper River, 126, 217
  South Alligator River, 234
  Springvale, 128

Northern Territory, cont'd
  Stuart Highway, 309
  Tennant Creek, 200, 202–3, 208, 223
  Todd River, 196–7
  Victoria, 138
  Yuendumu, 348
Queensland
  Barkly Tableland, 195
  Birdsville, 12, 303, 353–4, 361, 371–2
  Burketown, 202
  Cape York, 115, 119, 122, 191, 293
  Charleville, 353, 357, 376
  Cloncurry, 353
  Cooktown, 212
  Diamantina River, 353, 371
  Georgina River, 353
  Gregory River, 202
  Gregory Downs, 395
  Lake Nash, 195–6, 199, 202, 204
  Mulligan River, 366
  Simpson Desert, 118
South Australia
  Adelaide, 6, 16, 53–5, 58, 66–7, 72–7, 79–83,
    85–8, 95–7, 110–2, 117, 128, 131, 133,
    140–1, 144–5, 147–8, 152–6, 161, 163,
    169–70, 181, 183–5, 189, 193, 195–6,
    202, 204–15, 217–20, 222–3, 243–4, 262,
    265, 270, 286, 288, 291, 294, 297–8, 331,
    342–3, 349–50, 353, 364–5, 368, 373, 396
  Adelaide Exhibition Building, 111
  Adelaide Lunatic Asylum, 67
  Adelaide Plains, 55, 74
  Congregational Church, North Adelaide,
    110, 112
  North Road cemetery, 111
  North Terrace, 193
  Appatoonganie (Napatunka), 267
  Beltana, 350, 355, 358, 363–4, 366–7, 369,
    400, 407
  Birdsville Track, 12, 303, 354, 400
  Blanchetown, 54
  Blanchewater, 357, 362, 400, 406
  Blinman, 363, 367–9, 373, 406
  Brachina Gorge, 339, 374
  Callabonna Creek, 353
  Commodore, 339, 341, 370
  Coongie, 357
  Cooper Creek, 225, 231–3, 240, 260, 344,
    348, 351, 353, 363, 366–7, 376
  Coorong, 54–5, 64, 66, 69, 87
  Copley, 237, 354
  Cowandilla, 77
  Cowarie, 354
  Dalhousie, 195–7
  Encounter Bay, 55, 79, 86, 88, 119, 191
  Ernabella, 325, 334

South Australia, cont'd
  Eucla, 285–6, 296, 402
  Eyre Peninsula, 353
  Farina, 370
  Finke River, 195
  Flinders Ranges, 7, 236, 339, 344–5, 348,
    351–4, 358–60, 362–3, 368–9, 371–2,
    399, 407
  Fowlers Bay, 301
  Glenelg, 86, 208
  Goolwa, 53, 55, 61, 66
  Hawker, 343
  Hergott Springs, 195, 205–6
  Hindmarsh Island, 58
  Innamincka, 344, 354, 357, 361, 407
  Kangaroo Island (*Karta*), 66
  Kanowana, 353–4
  Killalpaninna, *see* missions
  Lake Albert, 53
  Lake Alexandrina, 53–4, 72
  Lake Blanche, 363
  Lake Eyre, 124, 225, 227, 234, 237, 238,
    251, 253, 262, 270, 273, 348, 351–2,
    368, 397, 406
  Lake Gregory, 233, 354, 363, 367, 397
  Lake Hope, 280, 354–5, 363, 366–7
  Lake Howitt, 353–4
  Lake Killalpaninna, 260
  Lake Torrens, 339, 344, 377–8
  Leigh Creek, 340, 370
  Light Pass, 265
  Lyndhurst, 348, 357
  Mann Ranges, 299, 302
  Marree, 112, 195, 340, 361, 370, 371–2, 407
  Meningie, 66
  Milang, 53, 55, 66–7
  Moorunde, 54, 88
  Mt Barker, 55, 67, 79–81
  Mt Flint, 354, 367
  Mt Serle, 363, 369
  Mt Deception, 365, 369
  Mulka, 272
  Mundoo Island, 58–9, 69
  Mundowdna, 354, 370–1
  Mungeranie, 271
  Mungeranie Gap, 348
  Murray Mouth, 54, 58, 124
  Murray River, 53–4, 69, 80, 83, 86–7, 117,
    123, 217, 236, 405
  Nepabunna, 360, 376–7
  Ngakun, 59
  Ngapamana, 353
  Ngoingho, 65
  Nilpena, 339, 344, 349–50, 361, 373
  Nullarbor Plain, 96, 285–6, 288–9, 295–6,
    298, 372

South Australia, cont'd
  Oodnadatta, 218, 340, 351, 353, 361
  Ooldea, 285–93, 297–9, 301–03, 309, 402
  Parachilna, 339, 341, 344, 351, 357, 361,
    365–6, 368, 371–2, 407
  Parachilna Creek, 345, 376
  Point Malcolm, 50–4, 58–61, 65–6, 69–72,
    74, 384
  Point McLeay, 53, 55–7, 59, 62, 66–7,
    72–3, 214
  Port Augusta, 115, 126, 289, 340, 349, 370
  Red Ochre Cove, 368
  River Torrens, 75, 81
  Rufus River, 54, 117
  Simpson Desert, 196, 351, 353, 394
  South Moolooloo, 339
  St A'Beckett's Pool, 369
  St Mary's Peak, 345
  Strangways Springs, 361, 363, 366, 405
  Strzelecki Creek, 354, 406
  Strzelecki Track, 354
  Tilcha Creek, 359
  Tooncatchyn, 354, 361, 406
  Umberatana, 364
  Walkerville, 82
  Warburton River, 351
  Warioota Creek, 363
  Wellington, 55, 65
  Wirrealpa, 361
  Wooltana, 359
  Yandama Creek, 353
Tasmania, 337
  Adventure Bay, 3
  Killora, 4–5, 379
  North Bruny Island, 3–5
Victoria
  Dandenongs, 327
  Loddon River, 117
  Melbourne, 110–11, 117, 195, 202, 204, 206,
    209, 215, 217, 243, 272, 307, 319–20,
    334, 372
  Mt William, 119
  Murray River, 118
  Swan Hill, 118
Western Australia
  Anna Plains, 125
  Beagle Bay, 285, 293, 295
  Broome, 390
  Calvert Range, 99
  Coolgardie, 95, 194
  Cossack, 293
  Cue, 97
  Discovery Well, 107
  Fitzroy River, 93–4, 100–1, 106–7, 388
  Geraldton, 97
  Great Sandy Desert, 6, 94, 98, 101, 103

Western Australia, cont'd
  Great Victoria Desert, 235
  Joanna Spring (Pikarrangu), 100–1, 105, 106, 107, 108, 388
  Kimberley, 115, 300
  King George Sound, 2
  Lake Way, 98
  Meekatharra, 294, 296
  Mullewa, 97
  Murchison River, 94, 294

Western Australia, cont'd
  Nannine, 294
  Opthalmia Ranges, 106
  Perth, 97, 288, 294
  Pilbara, 348
  Roebourne, 293–4
  Rottnest Island, 387
  Sahara Well, 102–3
  Separation Well, 100–2, 104–5, 387
  Weld Range, 294, 296

GENERAL INDEX

A

Aboriginal groups
Adnyamathanha, 236–7, 351–2, 359, 377, 406
Anangu (*see also* Pitjantjatjara), 298
Arabana, 351, 354, 357, 370
Arrernte, 7, 192, 250, 264–5, 268, 274–5, 307, 309–10, 313–16, 319–35, 342, 353, 374
Bilatapa, 256–7
Cam-mer-ray, 14
Diyari (Dieri), 225, 237, 243, 246, 248–53, 255–60, 266–9, 274–5, 346, 351, 354–5, 357, 359–60, 368–9, 376, 398, 404, 407
Djerimanga, *see* Woolna (Wulna)
Dyirbal, 236
Eora, 17–18, 26–7, 32, 37, 46–7, 125, 380–1
Iwaidja, 120, 136–8, 207, 390
Karatindjeri clan (Ngarrindjeri), 53
Kaurna, 55, 73, 76–7, 83, 86, 353, 368
Kaytej, 205
Kokatha, 287
Kukatja, 326
Kurnai, 235
Kuyani, 339, 346, 349, 351, 378, 406
Larrakia, 125, 131, 136, 138, 153, 155–6, 160–1, 163–4, 167, 171, 178, 182, 342, 391
Loritja, 265, 315–16
Mangala, 98, 102, 106, 125
Martu, 98
Mirning, 287
Nakako, 235, 252
Nauo, 353

Ngadjuri, 352, 353
Ngameni, 351, 354
Ngarrindjeri, Narrinyeri (*see also* Yaraldi, Tangani), 6, 53, 55, 58–9, 61, 63–4, 68–72, 384
Nyangumarta, 125
Nyulnyul, 390
Parnkarla, 351–3, 376–8
Piladapa, 357
Piltindjeri clan (Ngarrindjeri), 56
Pintupi, 251, 322
Pitjantjatjara, 287, 298, 319, 321, 403
Ramindjeri, 119
Tangani (Ngarrindjeri), 55
Tasmanians, 3–4
Thirrari, 370
Tiwi, 120, 122
Wailpi, 351–2, 377
Walmadjeri, 125
Wambaya, 199–201, 203–4
Wangkangurru, 195, 257, 270, 351, 353–5, 357–8, 370, 399, 407
Warlpiri, 203, 222–3, 312
Warumungu, 193, 199–205, 208–210, 212, 217–18, 220, 222–3, 395
Wirangu, 287
Woolna (Wulna, Djerimanga), 131, 136, 138–42, 145–51, 153–6, 161, 163–72, 175, 178, 182, 185, 392
Yadliyawarra, 377
Yandruwantha, 351, 354, 357
Yankantjatjara, 319
Yaraldi (Ngarrindjeri), 53–7, 60, 64, 66, 71, 75
Yarluyandi, 257, 353, 399
Yawarrawarrka, 351, 357, 368–9
Yir Yiront, 119–20

Aboriginal languages, 1, 17–18, 22, 34–5, 40, 46, 48, 55, 57, 61, 64, 70, 82, 131, 133–5, 137, 141–2, 148, 153, 164–8, 170, 172–3, 185, 196, 202, 236, 242, 248, 252, 254–7, 273, 277, 286, 295, 331, 342–3, 353, 360, 370, 380, 389, 392, 398–9, 404

Aboriginal material culture, artefacts
  general, 1, 5, 9, 13–14, 18, 21–2, 30–3, 35, 44, 46, 51, 62–3, 76, 81–2, 86, 91, 99, 112, 115, 119, 125, 128–9, 131, 133, 148, 158, 170, 184, 189, 207, 211, 214–15, 217, 225, 227, 229, 234, 238, 242, 244–5, 252–3, 255–6, 259, 261–2, 264, 269, 272, 274, 276–80, 293–5, 298, 302–3, 308–9, 316, 334, 390–1, 397
  acculturation, innovation, hybrid objects (see also toas), 7, 9, 11, 18, 119, 229–30, 242, 244–5, 310
  emergence of sculptural forms, 9, 122, 230, 237, 260, 267–8, 299
  axes, metal, 6, 9, 39, 90–1, 93, 102–3, 107, 112, 116–29, 388
  axes, stone, 29, 32, 35, 44, 91, 112, 115, 117–20, 122–3, 128, 137, 316, 353
  bags, baskets, receptacles, 6, 9, 11, 74, 102, 123, 126, 130–1, 133, 135, 137–8, 141, 148, 155–6, 158, 170–1, 185, 213, 215, 231, 234, 293, 298, 346, 349–50, 353, 356, 358, 360, 376, 389–90
  bark paintings, 230, 231, 244, 309
  basketry mats, 11, 74, 213
  boomerangs, 6, 12, 74, 91, 105, 112, 117, 123, 189, 211–3, 217, 234, 248, 263, 294, 302, 359–60, 398, 402
  canoes, 18, 23, 26 , 29 , 34, 35, 37, 122–3, 138, 142–3, 161, 179, 381, 391
  clubs, 6, 8–9, 11–13, 16–18, 22, 25, 29, 31, 35, 36, 44, 46, 75–77, 86, 178, 189, 215, 234, 380, 391
  digging sticks, 148, 344, 390
  engraved mulga plaques, 304, 307, 309–17, 319, 322–5, 335
  fire-making equipment, 6, 186–7, 189, 191–2, 194, 210, 215, 360, 393
  fishing lines, hooks, 22, 28, 31–2, 35, 38
  fishing nets, 26, 118, 234, 360, 382
  gypsum, 9, 225, 233, 236, 238, 241, 274, 280, 397, 406
  marker pegs, 103, 252, 256–9, 281
  message-sticks, 98, 237, 242–3, 246–51, 259, 266–7, 270, 276, 357, 374, 400
  ochre (see also ochre mines), 1, 7, 51, 82, 119, 139, 233, 296, 336–7, 339, 341–70, 372–4, 376–8, 390, 404–8
  red ochre expeditions, 341, 352–64, 366, 369–75, 378, 404–8

mythology of Pukardu mine, 344–5, 351, 406–7
ornament, decoration, 9, 63, 76, 82, 86, 155–6, 170, 257, 277, 298, 315–6, 356, 360
pokerwork, pyrography, 7, 229, 299, 301, 307–10, 314, 324, 335
resin, spinifex, 35, 91, 103, 238, 241
resin dog models, 267–8
rock art, 98, 99, 123
shields, 6, 29, 31, 35, 45–7, 50–3, 55, 58–63, 71–2, 74–5, 77–80, 82, 84, 86–7, 191–2, 214–5, 234, 244, 260, 263, 294, 312, 316, 349
snake effigies, 298, 301
spears, 3, 11, 14, 22–5, 28–9, 31–2, 34–6, 39–47, 51, 58, 60, 62–5, 72–6, 78–80, 82, 86–89, 102, 117, 122–3, 126, 136–8, 140–1, 146–8, 150, 155–6, 163, 170–3, 175–8, 181, 189, 192, 198, 211, 213–5, 234, 244–5, 292–3, 316, 359–60, 366, 380, 383, 390–1
spearthrowers, 12, 14, 22, 29, 31, 62–3, 72, 77, 112, 123, 137–8, 141, 164, 170, 172–3, 189, 191–2, 215, 293–4, 298, 390–1
tjurunga, 230, 276, 296, 298, 308, 313–19, 322, 327–30, 332–4, 388
toas, 7, 9, 224–5, 227–8, 230–1, 233–5, 237–45, 248, 250–62, 265–7, 269–80, 351, 397–400
tourist artefacts, 302, 308–9
way-markers, 227–8, 235–7, 244, 259, 269
Western Desert painting, 229, 231, 244, 305, 308–9, 318, 321, 323, 328–9, 403
widows' caps, 406

Aborigines' Friends' Association, 55, 72
Adelaide Jubilee Exhibition, 53, 72, 74, 190, 191, 193, 210, 211, 214, 215, 216, 394
Adelaide Lunatic Asylum, 68
Afghan cameleers, 96–7, 107, 195, 205, 370, 407
Aiston, George, 242, 270–3, 277, 280, 303, 352, 357–9, 405
Albrecht, F.W., 310–11, 313, 315–16, 319, 323–4, 326, 330–5
Ameer, Said, 96–7, 109
Andrews, F.W., 124
Angas, George Fife, 82
Angas, George French, 81, 83–5, 214, 385
Anson and Francis (photographers), 135, 153
Arabanoo, 37–8
artists, Aboriginal, 161, 229, 305, 307, 308, 309, 310, 311, 316, 317, 318, 319, 320, 321, 322, 323, 326, 327, 328, 329, 330, 403

artists, European, 2–4, 20, 29, 31, 41, 43,
  73, 76, 77, 81, 83, 85, 86, 87, 131, 156,
  211, 214, 262, 263, 316, 317, 322, 327,
  330, 334
l'Astrolabe, 2
Auld, W.P., 133, 143, 146, 148, 165, 167
Austin, Peter, 255, 273, 399, 404
authenticity, 11, 217, 229, 242, 278, 327,
  346, 383
Ayers, Henry, 147, 152, 153

B

Bagot, Charles, 195
Bailes, Harry ('King Hal'), 339, 341, 343, 346,
  349–51, 355, 360–1, 373, 376, 404
Ball, Lieut. H.L., 15, 19, 21–2, 25, 47–8, 381
Bangai, 44
Banks, Joseph, 3
Barak, Willliam, 229
Barker, Captain Collet, 79, 137–8, 146, 161
Bastian, Adolf, 129
Bates, Daisy, 7, 282–3, 285–303, 401
Battarbee, Rex, 307, 316–17, 319–20, 322,
  330–31
Batty, Joyce, 317, 324
Baudin, Nicolas, 45
Beatrice survey vessel, 121–2, 138–41, 147,
  166, 390
Beckett, Jeremy, 246
Bellchambers, Tom Paine, 376
Benjamin, Walter, 69, 246
Bennelong, 17–18, 38–47, 119, 380, 383
Bennett, J.W.O., 4, 6, 125, 131, 133–5, 140–1,
  143–6, 148, 151–56, 159, 161, 163–83, 182,
  185, 342, 365, 389–93
Berger, John, 329
Berndt, Catherine, 61
Berndt, Ronald M., 58, 61, 72, 273, 384
Biliamuk, 156, 160–2, 170, 391–2
Blackburn, David, 6, 9, 12–27, 29, 33–5, 37–8,
  45–9, 380–4
  Blackburn family, 13, 15–16, 19, 21, 26, 33–4,
    48–9, 381, 383
  Blackburn's cosh, 13, 14, 16
  Blackburn's whip, 8–9, 12–18, 22, 36, 42,
    44–5, 48–9, 380
Board for Anthropological Research, 331
Bogner, Johannes, 259
Bolam, A.G., 287, 297, 302, 402
Bondel, 48
Bonyhady, Tim, 111
Boorong, 38, 43, 383
Bradley, Lieut. W., 24–5, 29, 35–6
Brassey, Lady Anne, 193, 394
Breaden, J., 387
Breaker Morant, 292

Breen, Gavan, 273
Broca, Paul, 218
Brooke, James (the 'White Rajah'), 152
Brooks, Joseph, 159
Browne, John Harris, 123
Bruce, Robert, 363
Burke and Wills, *see* exploring expeditions
Buttfield, J., 366

C

Cadell, Francis, 122, 154
Cadell, Janet, 4–5
Calvert expedition, *see* exploring expeditions
Calvert, Albert, 94–8, 388–9
camels, 6, 95–7, 99–101, 105, 107, 109, 112–3,
  194–6, 199–200, 205–6, 317, 333, 395
Camp-oven Winkie, 366
cannibalism, Daisy Bates belief in, 291, 343, 401
Captain Jack, *see* *Tooreetparne*
Carnegie, David, 94, 101, 103, 387
Carradah, 47
Catlin, George, 214
Cawthorne, William, 73, 75–84, 86–89, 342
ceremony, ritual, 1, 36, 55, 60, 65, 73, 75, 77, 79,
  99, 116, 119, 123, 155, 168, 191, 200, 203,
  223, 237–8, 245, 252, 276–7, 286–7, 292–3,
  295–301, 303, 315, 318–21, 325–8, 330–4,
  344–5, 348, 352–3, 355–7, 360–1, 371–2,
  374–5, 377, 402–3, 405–6
Christie's auction house, 12, 16, 43, 380, 383
Cleland, J.B., 294, 303, 401
Clendinnen, Inga, 28, 42, 383
Colebee, 38–40, 47
collecting natural history, 7, 30–2, 35, 106, 131,
  155–8, 160, 164, 168, 170–1, 178, 183,
  195–6, 261, 391–2, 394, 399
collectors of ethnographica, natural history,
  1, 5–6, 14, 32–3, 156, 207, 227, 234, 245–6,
  294, 296, 316, 327–8, 335, 355, 394, 399
Collins, David, 14, 22, 25, 29–32, 39–40, 42,
  45, 110
commodities, European, 3–4, 6–7, 9, 11, 18,
  22–5, 28, 30, 32, 40, 44, 57, 79, 87, 93, 116,
  120, 126–8, 137, 140, 147, 154, 158, 198,
  200, 202, 229, 245, 286–9, 293, 296–7,
  302–3, 335, 337
  metal, 3, 6, 9, 11, 28–30, 39–40, 42–5, 91,
    93–4, 99, 102–3, 107, 111–12, 115–20,
    122–6, 128–9, 136, 140, 149, 154, 158,
    202, 229, 234, 245, 286, 301, 308–9, 380,
    383, 388–9
Confalonieri, Angelo, 167, 392
conflict between Aboriginal groups, 35, 36, 47,
  53–5, 58–60, 62–3, 66, 73–80, 82, 86–8, 150,
  155, 171, 204, 214, 228, 354, 357–9, 361,
  369, 406–7

conflict between Aborigines and Europeans,
2–3, 22, 29–32, 36, 38, 65, 117, 126, 146–51,
154, 160, 163, 166, 169–70, 173, 178–82,
185, 201, 355, 362–6, 368–9, 373–4, 390–1,
393–4, 407
convicts, 15–17, 20–1, 26–8, 30–4, 38
Cook, Captain James, 3–4, 23, 26, 120
Cooper, Dr Lillian, 294
Croll, R.H., 316
Cubadgee, Dick, 6, 186–7, 189–91, 193–5, 197,
199–212, 214–23, 349, 395–6
Cunningham, R.A., 212, 214
Curr, E.M., 202

D

Danvin, Felix, 2
Davies, Harold, 331
Davis, Jack, 207–8
Dawes, Lieut. William, 17–18, 21–3, 35, 46–8,
342, 380
Degenhardt, G., 349
Dégerando, Joseph-Marie, 45
Dening, G., 12
Dervish, Bejah, 96–7, 107, 112, 370
Dibana, Andreas, 280
Dintibana, Sam, 270
Dittrich, Lieut. Hermann, 196–7, 202,
204–5, 394
Dixon, R.M.W., 236
drawings, illustrations
of Aboriginal people, artefacts, encounters, 2,
4, 31, 34, 41, 43–4, 73, 76–8, 81–7, 99,
131, 133, 164, 207, 211, 214, 255, 262–3,
275, 307–8, 318, 320–2, 327, 399
of natural history, 131, 156–7, 161, 317, 391
Dreamings, origin myths, 119, 123, 127–8, 187,
191–2, 204, 222, 224, 227, 229–31, 234, 237,
239, 241–2, 244, 249, 253, 255–6, 258,
266–7, 269, 272–4, 277–8, 281, 289, 292–3,
301, 308, 313, 315, 318, 321, 329–30, 337,
341, 344–5, 347–54, 356, 358, 360, 376–8,
397–8, 403, 405
Duguid, Charles, 334
Duke of Edinburgh, 60
Duryea, Townsend, 169
Dutton, George, 353

E

Eagle, Mary, 267, 400
Earl, G.S.W., 152
Ebsworth, Cecil, 353
Edinburgh, Duke of, 60, 65, 66
Edmunds, G.F., 50–1, 53, 61, 72, 74, 89
Edmunds, Robert, 144, 146–7, 149–51
Elder Scientific Exploring Expedition, *see*
exploring expeditions

Elkin, A.P., 328, 351–2, 357
Elliott, Dr Frederick, 197
encounters between Aborigines and Europeans,
1–6, 9, 13, 22–8, 30, 36–7, 39–40, 42, 46–7,
58, 79–80, 84, 86–7, 98, 117, 119–20, 122,
124–6, 135–42, 150, 163, 198, 202, 208, 225,
230, 242, 292, 301–2, 378
evangelism, 57, 64, 309, 311–13, 319, 326,
330–32, 384, 404
Evans, Arthur, 247
Evans-Pritchard, E., 5
exchange, barter, 1, 6, 14, 18, 22, 25, 27–30, 32,
34, 39, 43–5, 47, 79, 99, 116–20, 123, 125,
128, 137, 140, 142, 154, 156, 158, 161,
169–71, 178, 182, 199, 246, 287, 289, 296,
302–3, 334, 337, 353, 359–61
exploring expeditions
Burke and Wills expedition (1860–1861),
93–4, 110–11, 386, 388
Cadell's coastal exploration (1867),
122, 154–5
Calvert expedition (1896–1897), 6, 90, 93–8,
100–13, 125, 370, 386–8
Calvert rescue expeditions (1897),
106–11, 388
Carnegie expedition (1896–1897), 94–5, 101,
103, 387
Cook's first voyage (1768–1771), 3, 120
Cook's second voyage (1772–1775), 3
Cook's third voyage (1776–1777), 3, 4, 120
Dumont d'Urville's voyage (1826–1829), 2
Elder Scientific Exploring Expedition
(1891–1892), 95, 98–9, 111, 194,
197, 386
Finniss's Escape Cliffs expedition
(1864–1866), 133, 135–6, 138, 142, 144,
146, 149–51, 166, 170, 180, 390–1
Gregory's North Australian Exploring
Expedition (1855–1856), 4, 102–3
Grey's south-east of South Australia
expedition (1844), 86
Goyder's North Australian surveying
expedition (1869–1870), 4, 111, 125, 131,
133, 153–5, 160, 163, 172, 178–80, 182,
184–5, 342, 391–3
Horn expedition (1894), 96, 374
Howitt's Burke and Wills Relief Expedition
(1861), 246
Leichhardt's last expedition (1848), 94, 103,
195, 210
Lindsay's Central Australian expedition
(1885–1886), 195–8, 200, 202, 204, 206,
251, 394–5
Lewis's Lake Eyre expedition (1874), 124
Mitchell's Murray River expedition (1836),
123–4

Sturt's Murray River expedition (1830–1831), 123–4

Sturt's Central Australian expedition (1844–1845), 12, 86, 111, 123, 234, 251

Warburton's expedition (1873), 100–2

Eylmann, Erhard, 259–60, 399

Eyre, Edward John, 54, 94, 195

F

Finke River Mission Board, 325

Finn, E.J., 370

Finniss, B.T., 133, 135–6, 138, 141–51, 153–4, 160, 163–6, 179–80, 391

    enquiry into conduct at Escape Cliffs, 144, 148–9, 151, 160

Finniss, F., 148

Finniss, W., 142, 145, 390

First Fleet, 6, 12–14, 16–17, 19–20, 22, 26, 28, 36, 45, 117, 342

Fisherman Jack, 64

Flinders, Matthew, 136

Foelsche, Paul, 162–3, 174–5, 182, 184–5, 212

Forrest, John, 98, 293

Forster, Anthony, 82–3

Foulkes, Mr, 86

Free Church of Scotland, 57

French, Alison, 402

frontier, 1, 3–7, 9, 12, 18, 23, 28, 38–9, 42, 45, 49, 75, 77, 81, 91, 93, 112, 115–17, 119–20, 123, 125, 128–9, 135–7, 150–51, 154, 163, 175, 183, 189, 193, 195, 198, 200, 206, 211, 217, 220, 225, 227, 229–30, 234, 242, 244–6, 278, 280, 283, 291–2, 302, 308–9, 337, 342, 350, 362, 365

    frontier, protocols of encounter, 1, 24, 27, 116, 123, 124

Fry, H.K. (Kenneth), 352

Furneaux, Captain Tobias, 3

G

Ganba, mythical snake, 289, 292, 301

Gardner, John, 317, 330

Gason, Samuel, 246, 248–9, 251, 267, 352, 354–5, 357, 360–1, 371, 400

George, F.R., 339, 344, 375

Ghan railway (*see also* railways), 340

Gibney, Bishop, 293, 295

Giles, Alfred, 126, 128, 129

Giles, Ernest, 98

Gill, W.H., 270–2

Gillen, Francis J., 116, 128, 192, 202–04, 250, 266, 270, 296, 342, 395

Goldsmith, Dr, 147–48, 390

Goorongnabeer, 78

Gordon, Adam Lindsay, 103, 105, 110, 112

Goyder, David George, 159

Goyder, George Woodroffe, 4, 125–6, 131, 133, 135–6, 141, 153–6, 159–61, 163–5, 168–72, 175–80, 182–5, 365, 392, 391–3

Gregory, Augustus, 102, 249, 387

Gregory, J.W., 260–1

Grey, Governor George, 81, 83, 86, 88

Guy, Lieut. M.S., 141, 390

Guy, William, 172–3, 179, 181, 392–3

H

Hale, Herbert, 296–8, 303

Hamilton, George, 367

Hawdon, Joseph, 117–8

Hayward, J.F., 362

Heinrich, H.A., 334–5

Hercus, Luise, 257, 273, 353, 360, 370, 399, 406

Hewitson, T., 349

Hill, Ernestine, 147, 283, 293, 295, 390

Hillier, H.J., 253–4, 262–3, 274, 399

Hoare, William Webster, 130–1, 133, 135, 154–9, 161, 163–4, 168, 170–1, 176–8, 180, 182–5, 389, 391–2

Howard, Capt. Frederick, 138, 140

Howitt, Alfred, 235, 242–3, 246, 248–51, 266–7, 270, 277, 352, 354, 357, 360–1, 398–400

I

Ivo, 222

J

Jacky-Jacky, 195

James, Billy, 372

James, Frank, 362

Jefferis, Rev. James, 93, 111

Jeffreys, Julius, 363

Jenkins, J.G., 375

Jesus, 7, 60, 68, 74, 305, 309, 313, 321, 327

Johnson, Fred, 405

Johnson, Rev. Richard and Mary, 38, 43

Jones, G.L., 96–101, 104–6, 109–12, 387

Jones, George, 113

Joorak, 195, 199, 205–6, 395

Jurnkurakurr, 203, 222

K

Kadlitpinna (Captain Jack), 59–60, 77, 83–6

Kaibel, Pastor, 259, 261, 265–7

Karloan, Albert, 58, 62, 71, 385

Karrku ochre mine, 348

Katang, *see* Point Malcolm

Keartland, George, 96–7, 100, 105, 388

Kennedy, Edward, 195

Kenneth, Michael, 406

Kenyon, A.S., 272–3, 280

King George III, 3

King, Lieut. P.G., 23
King, P.P., 120
Kintalakadi, Emil, 280
Knight, Richard, 18, 23, 35
Knuckey, J., 165, 169, 172–3, 392–3
Koch-Grünberg, Theo, 274
Kondole, legend of, 191–2
Kramer, Ernest, 311–13
Kubler, George, 328

L

La Perouse, 26
Laelinyeri, David, 57
Laelinyeri, John (Nipper), 65, 67–8
Lambrick, Lieut., 139
Lang, Andrew, 295, 401
Larrapinta, *see* Lindsay, George
Larrikin Tom, 359, 375–76, 378
Leichhardt, Ludwig, 94, 103, 195, 210, 386
Levi-Strauss, Claude, 45
Lewis, John, 124, 207
Lialoon-me, 174–5, 185, 393
Liebler, Oskar, 273–6, 334, 398, 400
Light, Colonel William, 79
Lindo, J.W., 339, 341, 404–5
Lindsay, Annie, 189
Lindsay, Arthur, 206, 208, 218
Lindsay, David, 96, 98, 111, 186, 189–91,
      193–206, 209–15, 217–22, 223, 251,
      394–6
Lindsay, George ('Larrapinta'), 195, 199–201,
      203–6, 208–9, 217–18, 222, 396
Lindsay, Harold, 200
Lindsay, Nora, 221
'Linear B' script, 247
von Leonhardi, Baron Moritz, 265, 267–9,
      273, 277
Lirawa (Lillawer), 161, 391
Lirmi, 106–7
Litchfield, Frederick, 143, 148
Ljonga, Tom, 333–4
Lock, Annie, 301
Logic, 349, 405, 407
Luga, 137

M

Macassan fishermen ('Malays'), 116, 120, 122–3,
      136, 138, 158, 163, 392
Macaulay, T.B., 110
Magarey, A.T., 96–8, 100, 110, 209, 386
Maigena, 138
'Malbrooke', 25
Manton, J.T., 147, 151, 169, 173
maps, mapping, 94–5, 101, 107, 115, 141–4,
      148, 153, 164, 166–7, 196–7, 199, 203, 210,
      215, 249, 253, 296, 392, 397, 402

Maria shipwreck massacre (*see also* conflict
      between Aborigines and Europeans), 54, 66
Martineau, P., 15, 383
Masey, T.A., 364, 368, 373, 408
Matheson, R.J., 339, 341, 344, 349, 373–5
Mathews, R.H., 295, 389
Matthews, W.H., 349
Maugoran, 43
McCarthy, Frederick, 243
McConnel, Ursula, 293
McKay, Captain, 365
McKenzie, John, 359, 406
McKenzie, Pearl, 359
McKinnon, Constable W., 317
McLean, Mick (Irinjili), 370
Melbourne Exhibition 1888, 217
memorials
      marble tablet in St Paul's Anglican Church,
            Adelaide (J.W.O. Bennett), 181
      stained glass windows, Brougham Place
            Uniting Church, Adelaide (Calvert
            expedition), 113
Minkulutty, 64
Mira, 154–5, 161, 163, 167, 171, 178, 182–3, 185
Miranda, King of 'Burra Burra', 118
missionaries, *see* Albrecht, F.W., Bogner, J.,
      Confalonieri, A., Kramer, E., Lennox, A.H.,
      Liebler, O., Lock, A., Reid, J., Reuther, J.G.,
      Siebert, O., Strehlow, C., Taplin, G., Trappist
      missionaries
missions
      Cummeragunja, 236
      Ernabella, 325
      Hermannsburg, 250, 264, 268, 271, 274–5,
            305, 307, 310–11, 313–14, 316–17, 319,
            321, 323–7, 330–5, 403
      Kaparlgo, 234, 397
      Killalpaninna, 225, 227, 230, 233–4, 238,
            241–3, 247–8, 250, 253–4, 256, 259–62,
            264–5, 267–8, 270–2, 274–80, 346, 348,
            356–7, 368, 398, 401
      Point McLeay, 55, 56
      Santa Teresa, 403
      Mitchell, A.J., 169
Mitchell, Thomas, 123–4, 195
Moketarinja, Richard, 308
Moondoor, 301
Moonta, 154
Moorhouse, Matthew, 82
Morphy, Howard, 244, 276, 398
Moses, 332
Mountford, C.P., 11, 236–7, 318, 351–2, 357,
      360, 376–7, 379, 389, 403
von Mueller, Baron Ferdinand, 94, 196, 197,
      386, 394
Mullawirraburka (King John), 77, 83, 88

Murray, Ben (Parlu-nguyu-thangkayiwarna), 370
Murtee Johnny, 357
museums, general, 1, 5–7, 9, 11, 14, 91, 129, 131, 163, 187, 189, 191, 223, 227–8, 230, 235, 245–6, 254, 262, 264, 267, 277, 296–7, 309, 328, 330, 335
   Australian museums
      Australian Museum, Sydney, 394, 396
      Museum and Art Gallery of the Northern Territory, 393, 403
      National Museum of Australia, 380
      National Museum of Victoria, 235, 270
      South Australian Museum, 7, 16, 51, 53, 72, 74, 89, 91, 93, 112, 118, 128, 135, 142, 155, 186–7, 189, 193, 206, 218–20, 222–3, 225, 227–9, 243–4, 250, 262, 269–70, 272, 274–6, 280, 289, 294–7, 300, 303, 319, 335, 339–40, 343, 351, 360–61, 375, 379–80, 386, 390, 392–4, 396–7, 399, 402, 404
   European museums, 3, 14, 155, 218, 248, 262, 264, 267, 269, 273–4, 335, 398
      British Museum, London, 155, 262
      Cambridge University Museum of Anthropology and Archaeology, 3, 222, 262
      Horniman Museum, London, 262
      Linden Museum, Stuttgart, 274, 402
      Museum für Völkerkunde, Basel, 335
      Museum für Völkerkunde, Berlin, 267, 269, 273
      Museum für Völkerkunde, Frankfurt, 398
      Museum für Völkerkunde, Hamburg, 274
      Museum für Völkerkunde, Munich, 274
      Neprazi Museum, Budapest, 335
      Royal Scottish Museum, Edinburgh, 262
      St Petersburg Museum of Anthropology and Ethnography, 261
   museum exhibitions, 9, 16, 72, 161, 225, 244, 270, 276, 315, 319, 330, 375, 379, 386, 398
Myers, Fred, 251

N
Nagary, 138
Nagle, Jacob, 25, 26
Namatjira, Albert, 7, 229, 304, 305, 307, 308, 309, 310, 311, 312, 313, 314, 315, 316, 317, 318, 319, 320, 321, 322, 323, 324, 325, 326, 327, 328, 329, 330, 331, 335, 403
Namatjira, Rubina, 326
Nanyena, 207
Native Americans, 214
navy, British, 12–13, 19, 21, 23, 25–7, 34, 136
   Adventure, 3, 5
   Lady Penrhyn, 25

Pelorus, 120
Resolution, 3, 5
Sirius, 24, 27, 31–3, 36–7
Supply, 12, 15–23, 26–7, 33–4, 37–8, 47–8, 380–1
Neaylon brothers, 267
Nepean, Captain, 39
Neville, D., 15
Neville, D., 15, 16, 381
Newland, Simpson, 112
Ngurunderi, 68
Ninnis, Belgrave, 121, 122
Ninnis, Dr, 151
Nipper, 62, 64, 384
Nixon, J.H., 371
Nullamaloo, *see* White, Bob

O
O'Halloran, Major, 66, 87
O'Reilly, police-trooper, 366
Oastler, J., 361, 366
Observer newspaper, 72, 74, 111, 170, 181, 206, 332, 364
ochre, *see* artefacts, material culture
ochre mines, *see* Karrku ochre mine, Pukardu ochre mine, Red Ochre Cove ochre mine, Wilga Mia ochre mines
Ord, Sub-Inspector, 107–9, 111
Overland Telegraph Line, 116, 124–7, 200–1

P
Paddy ('of Murraburt'), 195
Palkalinna, Elias, 280
Pallarri, 107–8, 111
Parsons, J.L., 210–11
Patyegerang, 46, 342
Pearson, Edward, 144, 147–8, 150, 166
Peel, Dr Robert, 164, 170–1, 175–6, 178
Petrus, 275, 280
Phillip, Governor Arthur (*see also* First Fleet), 17, 20–9, 32–3, 36–47, 342, 380, 383
Phillipson, N.E., 358
photography, photographers, 70, 96, 98–9, 108–9, 135, 153, 159, 161–3, 174, 184–5, 189, 191, 193, 197, 206, 211, 215, 219, 235, 290, 310, 312, 331, 344, 371, 375–6, 386, 390–1, 395, 399
phrenology, 159
pictographic writing, 242–4, 251, 259, 266, 269, 279
Pingilina, Johannes, 280
Pinnaru, Peter, 270, 280
Piper, 195
pituri (*Duboisia hopwoodii*), 353, 356, 358, 360, 407
Poignant, R., 396

police, 54, 58, 61, 64, 67, 80–1, 87–9, 93, 103, 107, 128, 161, 163, 175, 184–5, 212, 246, 267, 271, 303, 317, 342, 349, 352, 354–5, 362–9, 380, 384, 400, 405

policies relating to Aboriginal people, 11, 125, 160, 325, 326, 365

Poll, Flash, 139, 390

Pompey, 364, 407

Port Jackson Painter, 43

Porteus, Stanley, 331

Pratt, Mary Louise, 383

Preston, Margaret, 327

Pukardu ochre mine, 352–4, 356, 360–1, 367–8, 372–3, 375–8, 404–8

Pullami (King Peter), 6, 16, 51–75, 89, 384

Pulleine, Dr R.H., 294

Q

Queen Victoria, 65, 72, 74, 108, 156, 171–2, 193, 285

R

Radcliffe Brown, A.R., 295

Raeck, A.A., 373, 412

railways, 206, 211, 218, 286, 288–90, 299, 302–3, 309, 333, 340–1, 370–2, 402

Raper, George, 20, 29, 31

rations, Aboriginal, 54, 57, 64, 286, 296, 361, 365–9, 372, 402

Ray, Sydney, 270

Reckitt's Blue, 11

Red Ochre Cove ochre mine, 368

Reece, Robert, 245

Register newspaper, 88, 350

Reid, James, 57, 384

Renault, Mr, 212

Resolution and *Adventure* medal, 3, 5, 339

Reuther, Johann Georg, 7, 224–5, 227–8, 231, 233–4, 238, 241–4, 247–8, 250–70, 273–81, 348–9, 351–2, 354–9, 368, 370–71, 397–400

Reuther manuscript, 225, 227, 231, 243, 251–4, 256, 259, 270, 279–80, 348, 397–9

Reuther's museum, 260–1, 266

Reuther, Pauline, 247, 264

Richards, Andrew, 378

Richards, Leroy and Randolph, 352, 378, 408

Richards, Percy, 378

Rickaby, police-trooper, 61

Ricketts, Willliam, 327

Roberts, T., 200

Rodger, N.A., 13

Roheim, Géza, 316, 331, 334, 335

Roth, Walter, 237, 266, 343

Royal Geographical Society (South Australian Branch), 94–6, 202, 206, 210, 390

'ruby rush', 196, 215, 217

Rudall, W., 106, 388

Ruediger, Jack, 261, 399

Rufus River massacre (*see also* conflict between Aborigines and Europeans), 54, 117

Russell, Jimmy (Wangamirri), 355, 360, 370–1, 407

Russell, Lester, 223

S

de Sainson, Felix Auguste, 2

Sanders, W.B., 359

Schultze, Friedrich, 155–61, 164, 178, 391

Schürmann, C., 354

Science of Man, 247

Scott, Edward Bates, 54

Shanahan, Dr Patrick, 7, 336, 339–43, 347, 349–51, 353–5, 358–61, 373–5, 378, 404–6

Sharp, Lauriston, 119, 120

Siebert, Otto, 243, 248, 250–1, 259, 261, 264–6, 268, 279–80, 352, 357, 398–9

sign language, 228, 246, 258, 259

smallpox, 38, 166

Smith, Keith, 42

Smith, W. Lingwood, 219

smoke-signals, 98–100, 106, 237, 246–7, 249–50, 266

Smyth, Surgeon Arthur Bowes, 32

Sobin, Gustaf, 7

Southwell, Daniel, 31

Spanish Influenza epidemic (1919), 333, 375

Spencer, Walter Baldwin, 116, 250, 266, 270, 400

spinifex (*Triodia irritans*), ode to, by L.A. Wells, 104

Stephens, Edward, 80, 81

Stirling, Edward, 128, 206, 218, 220, 228, 243–4, 250–1, 269–70, 272, 277, 339, 340, 342–3, 360, 374–5, 397

Stolz, J., 331

Stone, Percy, 339

Strehlow, Carl, 250, 259, 268, 273, 316, 326, 328, 399

Strehlow, T.G.H., 273, 292, 303, 319, 327–8, 332–4, 399

Strehlow Research Centre, 399

Stuart, John McDouall, 217

Stuckey, Samuel, 364

Sturt, Charles (*see also* exploring expeditions), 12, 54, 86, 94, 123, 251

Supply, *see* navy, British

Supreme Being (High God) controversy, 250

Sutton, Peter, 397

Swain, Tony, 245
Swedenborgianism, 159
Sweet, Samuel, 54, 56, 71

T
Taplin, Frederick, 58, 70
Taplin, George, 55–71, 384–5
Teague, Fred, 405
Teague, Una, 316–17, 334
Teague, Violet, 317
Teichelmann, C., 354
telegraph stations, 116, 127, 128, 200, 202, 203, 342
Tench, Lieut. Watkin, 14, 22, 25–6, 30, 32, 35–8, 41–2
tendi or *yanarumi* (Ngarrindjeri tribal council), 68–9
Thomson, Donald, 123
Tindale, Norman B., 115, 117, 125, 131, 133, 164, 167, 203, 235, 236, 252, 297, 300, 316, 352, 389, 392, 402
Tippo, Benjamin, 69
Titus, 280, 311, 326
Tjerkalina, Elias, 280
Todd, Charles, 126, 127
Tooreetparne (Captain Jack), 59
tourist art, souvenirs, 129, 299, 301–2, 307–11, 313–16, 328, 333, 335
trackers, Aboriginal, 107, 161, 195, 200, 317, 349, 405
trade, Aboriginal, 28, 31, 53, 103, 115, 119–20, 122, 123, 125, 136, 289, 292–3, 301, 353, 356–60, 372, 407
Trappist missionaries, 285
Traine, Frank and Tom, 201
Trainor, James, 96–7
trepang (*see also* Macassan fishermen), 116, 122, 136, 163
Trigona bees, 115
Trounson, C.O., 384
Tuttle & Co., 219

U
Ulrich, Dr, 372–3
Uluru (Ayers Rock), 319
Umballa (Tom Powell), 161, 391
Unaipon, David, 72
Unaipon, James, 56–7, 64, 68, 70, 72, 384
Unaipon, Nymbulda, 64
d'Urville, J.S.C. Dumont, 2

V
Virgin Mary, 311
Vogelsang, Ted, 280

W
Waite, Edgar, 272, 397
Waite, Peter, 349
Walker, Peter, 16
Wapiti, 326
Warburton, P.E., 100–2, 364–7, 387
Ward, Alaric, 144, 147–9
Warri, 387
Waterhouse, E.G., 361
Waterhouse, Henry, 32–6, 40–1, 43, 383
Waterloo (Yacana), 137–8
Watson, Archibald, 218, 220
Wauhop, Corporal James, 355, 363–7, 369
Way, Samuel, 194, 206, 209, 217
Webber, John, 3–4
Webling, Alfred, 138–41, 147
Wellington (Meriak), 137
Wells, Charles, 96–7, 100–1, 106, 109–10, 112–13
Wells, L.A. (Larry), 96–100, 102–3, 105–7, 111–12, 388
White, Bob, 138–9
White, Surgeon John, 47
Wileemarin, 40–3
Wilga Mia ochre mines, 294, 296, 348
Willawilla, 77, 83
Willshire, W.H., 342
Wilton, Rufus, 359, 406
Winnecke, Charles, 195–7, 199
Witjawarakuru, Charlie, 235
Witurindjina (Charlotte Jackson), 64
Worgan, George, 24, 27
Wreschner, Ernst, 348
Wylie, 195

X
x-ray images, 233, 301

Y
Yallamerri, 107–8, 111–12
Yashchenko, Aleksandr, 261, 265, 399
Yerkinna cave, *see* Pukardu ochre mine
Young, C.B., 55, 72
Yuranigh, 195

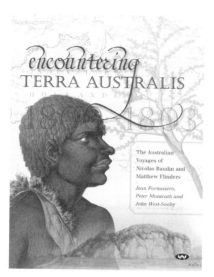

Encountering Terra Australis
The Australian Voyages of Nicolas Baudin and
Matthew Flinders
Jean Fornasiero, Peter Monteath and
John West-Sooby
ISBN 9781862546257

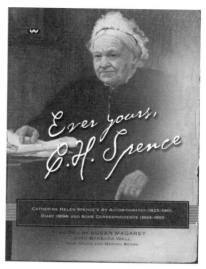

Ever Yours, C.H. Spence
Catherine Helen Spence's An Autobiography
(1825–1910), Diary (1894) and Some
Correspondence (1894–1910)
Edited by Susan Magarey with Barbara Wall,
Mary Lyons and Maryan Beams
ISBN 9781862546561

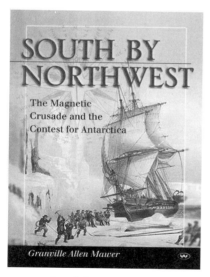

South by Northwest
The Magnetic Crusade and the Contest
for Antarctica
Granville Allen Mawer
ISBN 9781862546509

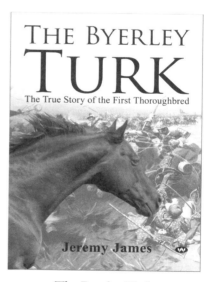

The Byerley Turk
The True Story of the First Thoroughbred
Jeremy James
ISBN 9781862546875

Wakefield Press is an independent publishing and
distribution company based in Adelaide, South Australia.
We love good stories and publish beautiful books.
To see our full range of titles, please visit our website at
www.wakefieldpress.com.au.